Persuasive Acts

Composition, Literacy, and Culture

David Bartholomae and Jean Ferguson Carr, Editors

Persuasive Acts

Women's Rhetorics *in the* Twenty-First Century

Shari J. Stenberg and Charlotte Hogg

University of Pittsburgh Press

Published by the University of Pittsburgh Press, Pittsburgh, Pa., 15260
Copyright © 2020, University of Pittsburgh Press
All rights reserved
Manufactured in the United States of America
Printed on acid-free paper
10 9 8 7 6 5 4 3 2 1

Library of Congress Cataloging-in-Publication Data

Names: Stenberg, Shari J., editor. | Hogg, Charlotte, 1970- editor.
Title: Persuasive acts : women's rhetorics in the twenty-first century /
    Shari J. Stenberg and Charlotte Hogg.
Description: Pittsburgh, Pa. : University of Pittsburgh Press, 2020. |
    Series: Pittsburgh series in composition, literacy, and culture |
    Includes bibliographical references and index.
Identifiers: LCCN 2019052163 | ISBN 9780822966135 (paperback) | ISBN
    9780822987512 (ebook)
Subjects: LCSH: American essays--Women authors--21st century. | Speeches,
    addresses, etc.--Women authors--21st century. | Persuasion (Rhetoric) |
    Women--Language. | Feminist theory. | Rhetoric--Political aspects. |
    Women--Social conditions--21st century.
Classification: LCC PS683.W65 P47 2020 | DDC 815/.60809287--dc23
LC record available at https://lccn.loc.gov/2019052163

ISBN 13: 978-0-8229-6613-5
ISBN 10: 0-8229-6613-1

Cover art and design by Melissa Dias-Mandoly

We dedicate this volume to Joy Ritchie and Kate Ronald, whose collection, *Available Means: An Anthology of Women's Rhetoric(s)*, inspired a whole field.

Contents

Acknowledgments   xiii

Note on Editorial Changes   xv

Introduction

  Gathering Women's Rhetorics for the Twenty-First Century   3

I. Rhetorics of Civic Engagement   23

Hillary Rodham Clinton

  Remarks at the Democratic National Convention   25

Shirin Ebadi

  "The Women Who Dared to Rise Up": Excerpt from *Until We Are Free*   38

Jeannette Urquilla

  "El Salvador's Shameful Treatment of Women Who Miscarry"   45

Nancy Pelosi

  Pelosi Floor Speech on Republican Amendments Defunding the Affordable
    Care Act   48

Sonia Sotomayor

  Excerpt from *Utah v. Strieff* Dissent   53

Maxine Waters

  Speech at Los Angeles Immigration Rally   58

Michelle Obama

  Remarks by the First Lady at Hillary for America Campaign Event in
    Manchester, New Hampshire   62

Jennifer Bailey

  "Strange Fruit of a Different Name"   71

Emma González

  Excerpt from *Glimmer of Hope: How Tragedy Sparked a Movement*   75

Sharon Brous

    "Israel in Trying Times: Unity Not Uniformity"   80

Lezley McSpadden

    "Michael Brown's Mom, on Alton Sterling and Philando Castile"   85

Cathy de la Cruz, Caroline Madden, and Keegan Osinski

    Mansplaining Tweets   89

Nadia Bolz-Weber

    "We're in the Midst of an Apocalypse: And That's a Good Thing"   93

Lindy West

    "Ask Not for Whom the Bell Trolls; It Trolls for Thee": Excerpt from *This American Life* Podcast   98

II. Rhetorics of Feminisms   107

Kimberlé Crenshaw

    "Why Intersectionality Can't Wait"   109

Robin M. Boylorn

    "Mama's Feminism": Excerpt from *The Crunk Feminist Collection*   113

Barbara Sostaita

    "This Women's History Month, I Refuse to Celebrate Your Feminism"   116

Patricia Valoy

    "Transnational Feminism: Why Feminist Activism Needs to Think Globally"   119

Amy Alexander

    "Today's Feminism: Too Much Marketing, Not Enough Reality"   125

Emi Koyama

    Excerpts from "The Transfeminist Manifesto"   129

Chimamanda Ngozi Adichie

    Wellesley College 2015 Commencement Address   134

Erica Thurman

    "Bell, Black Girls Are Healing, and It Is Glorious"   141

Claire Swinarski

"Why I'm a Pro-life Feminist"   145

Shannon Downey

The Future is Female, Badass Cross Stitch   151

Sara Ahmed

"A Killjoy Survival Kit," Excerpt from *Living a Feminist Life*   154

III. Rhetorics of Protest and Resistance   165

Alicia Garza

"A Herstory of the #BlackLivesMatter Movement"   169

Women's March on Washington Organizers

Guiding Vision and Definition of Principles   175

Women's March Signs   184

Riverbend

Excerpts from *Baghdad Burning: Girl Blog from Iraq*   188

Paola Bacchetta, Tina Campt, Inderpal Grewal, Caren Kaplan, Minoo
Moallem, and Jennifer Terry

"Transnational Feminist Practices against War"   194

Edwidge Danticat

"We Must Not Forget Detained Migrant Children"   202

Vandana Shiva

"Principles of Earth Democracy": Excerpt from *Earth Democracy: Justice, Sustainability, and Peace*   208

Tara Houska

"On the Struggle for Native American Rights"   216

Gina Adams

Treaty of Fort Laramie 1851, Broken Treaty Quilt Series, 2017   219

Sasha Weiss

"The Power of #YesAllWomen"   222

Suzanne Samin

"I'm a Female Gamer, and This is What It's Really Like"   227

Bree Newsome

    Civil Disobedience: Bree Newsome Removes Confederate Flag   232

Emily Doe (Chanel Miller)

    Victim Impact Statement from *People v. Turner* (Stanford Rape Case)   235

IV. Rhetorics of Education   251

Malala Yousafzai

    Speech to the United Nations, July 12, 2013   255

Jemelleh Coes

    "To the Educators Who Will Teach My Black Daughter"   260

Angy Rivera

    "DREAMer: Coming out as Undocumented"   264

Jennine Capó Crucet

    "How to Leave Hialeah": Excerpt from *How to Leave Hialeah* and

        Epilogue   268

Adrienne Keene

    "Dear Native College Student: You Are Loved"   276

Janet Tsai

    "An Engineering Approach to Feminism": Excerpt from *Click: When We Knew*

        We Were Feminists   281

Katharine Hayhoe

    Climate Change Evangelist   287

Wagatwe Wanjuki

    "Dear Tufts Administrators Who Expelled Me after My Sexual

        Assaults"   290

Kimberly Shappley

    "Texas Conservative Christian Mom Speaks out against SB6 'Bathroom

        Bill'"   295

Ananya Roy

    "We Are All Students of Color Now"   299

Marjane Satrapi

"The Veil": Excerpt from *Persepolis*   305

Jessica Valenti

Excerpt from *Full Frontal Feminism*   314

V. Rhetorics of Work and Labor   323

Linda Tirado

"This Is Why Poor People's Bad Decisions Make Perfect Sense"   325

Sheryl Sandberg

"Introduction: Internalizing the Revolution": Excerpt from *Lean In*   330

Jennifer Pozner

"Missing in Action: Whatever Happened to the Gender Gap?"   340

Brenda Berkman

"Remembering the 9/11 Women"   348

Tammy Duckworth

"What I Learned at War"   352

Gretchen Carlson

"Sexual Harassment Reckoning Has Been a Long Time Coming"   356

Thanu Yakupitiyage

"Why I March: Climate Change and Migration Have Everything to Do with
    Each Other"   361

Ai-jen Poo

"Lola Wasn't Alone"   366

National Domestic Workers Alliance Infographic   370

VI. Rhetorics of Identities and the Body   375

Melissa V. Harris-Perry

"Disaster": Excerpt from *Sister Citizen: Shame, Stereotypes, and Black Women
    in America*   379

Jennifer Baumgardner

"Introduction": Excerpt from *Abortion & Life*   388

Tarana Burke

"The Inception"   396

Eve Ensler

"My Cancer is Arbitrary: Congo's Atrocities Are Very Deliberate"   399

Kat Blaque

"Defecating While Trans"   404

Body-Positive Images: Hana Shafi, *The Scales*; Jessamyn Stanley, *Every Body Yoga*; Christine Yahya, *Natural Stains*   409

Julia Serano

"96 Percent"   414

Gabrielle Blair

Twitter Thread on Abortion   422

Karin Hitselberger

"Cheeky, Not Tragic: Defining Anti-Inspiration Porn"   434

Michelle Denise Jackson

"Reflections on Sandra Bland: My Black Body Was Not Meant to Bear All This Trauma"   439

Staceyann Chin

"On Rooms to Fight and Fuck and Crow"   443

Christina Cauterucci

"For Many Young Queer Women, *Lesbian* Offers a Fraught Inheritance"   448

Johanna Hedva

"Sick Woman Theory"   454

Permission Credits   467

Index   471

Acknowledgments

This project would not be possible without the foundational work of Joy Ritchie and Kate Ronald in *Available Means: An Anthology of Women's Rhetoric(s)*. We are deeply grateful to them for the path they forged and for their generous support as we sought to gather new rhetorics. We are better teachers, scholars, and feminists for knowing them. We are also thankful for the work of scholars in women's, gendered, and feminist rhetorics across our field who have fostered a vibrant, dynamic research area deeply needed in this historical moment.

We are indebted to the many research assistants at Texas Christian University and the University of Nebraska–Lincoln who spent time gathering sources, offering response and ideas, and meticulously attending to formatting details. At TCU: Angelica Hernandez, Jessica Menkin Kontelis, Callie Kostelich, James Chase Sanchez, Elissa Tatum, Sam Allen Wright, and Wilton Wright. At UNL: Luke Folk, Jade Kelly, Gina Keplinger, and Michael Reed. We are also grateful to Zach Beare and Joy Ritchie, colleagues who offered invaluable feedback and ideas. We thank the formidable LeAnn Messing for her support. Our editor Josh Shanholtzer has fielded many questions about this project, and we appreciate his patience and guidance. Our revision process was greatly aided by anonymous reviewers who offered advice during the review process that guided the text. Above all, we want to express deepest gratitude to the brilliant and inspiring rhetors who allowed us to reproduce their work in this collection.

We are most grateful to our home institutions for their generous support of this project. This work was supported by grants from the University of Nebraska–Lincoln Research Council, the TCU Research and Creative Activities Fund, and funds from the TCU English Department.

We each have additional thanks to offer.

Shari: I thank my amazing students in Rhetoric of Women Writers and Introduction to Women's and Gender Studies at UNL, who read selections, offered rich feedback, and introduced us to new voices, platforms, and perspectives. You were always at the forefront of my mind as we compiled this anthology. My fabulous writing group provided incisive feedback on introductions, enthusiasm for the project, and many, many laughs: Lexi Gardner, Lauren Gatti, Anne Johnson, and Jessica Masterson. The composition and rhetoric faculty at UNL sustain me with community and shared social vision. I am fortunate to also be part of the WGS core faculty, a fierce and funny powerhouse of women. Matt Wilson and John Munson, you are my favorite soundtrack. I am ever so grateful to dear colleagues and friends, near and far, who support me in scholarly projects and in life: Debbie Minter, Zach Beare, Chris Gallagher, Rose Holz, Katie Hupp, and James Crews. Steve North, I am deeply thankful for so many years of wisdom, mentorship, and friendship. My parents gave me a solid foundation and continue to fuel my growth; I am ever appreciative. I thank my husband, Jason Keese, who is my centering force and a wonderful cook, to boot. And my daughters, Zoe and Anika: You are my light. Your voices and visions give me hope for the future.

Charlotte: I'm so thankful to the undergraduate and graduate students at TCU who showed the need for this volume, weighed in and made smart suggestions, and modeled activism on diversity, equity, and inclusion on our campus. Thanks to Callie Kostelich for her feedback and processing far longer than she was a research assistant for the project. Thanks to Laurie Heidemann for her patience and care with permissions; to Rich Enos for his rhetorical guidance; and to Dean Andy Schoolmaster for his financial and moral support of boot camp that has sustained my work greatly. I'm so grateful for Karen Steele, who demonstrates feminist leadership and coaching. To those whose perspectives, levity, and counsel are priceless: Ann George, Theresa Gaul, and Betsy Flowers give me consistently brilliant advice on writing and all else; meetups with Rachel Brown Daugherty in Wichita keep me (more) balanced; and Erin Flanagan constantly buoys me with accountability checks, getaways, phone calls, and the best text GIFs. My parents have always supported me professionally and personally, and that means everything. I am most grateful to Chris Garland for listening, loving, and getting me even when I'm at my surliest. And I'm especially grateful for time spent with my son, Dean; nothing gives me better perspective or greater joy.

Note on Editorial Changes

Hyperlinks were removed for publication throughout this volume. Formatting for primary works was preserved when possible with the exception of spacing and formatting for consistency and clarity. Ellipses in brackets [. . .] within primary works indicates an abbreviation of the original source. Titles of works have been consistently formatted according to type of work for consistency and clarity. The capitalization of certain words and phrases (such as black/Black and white/White) follows University of Pittsburgh Press guidelines except when the original was retained to convey the author's intent.

Persuasive Acts

Gathering Women's Rhetorics for the Twenty-First Century

In June 2015 Bree Newsome scaled the flagpole in front of South Carolina's state capitol and removed the Confederate flag, ten days after the Charleston church massacre by a white supremacist and ahead of a pro-flag rally. The next month, the Confederate flag was permanently removed from the state capitol, having flown there since 1961—some say to commemorate the start of the Civil War; others say to oppose to the civil rights movement. You can find the photo of her taking down the flag in this collection—a powerful, persuasive act viewed as central to the permanent removal of the flag.

Newsome is a compelling example of a twenty-first-century women rhetor—along with bloggers, writers, politicians, activists, artists, and everyday social media users—who give new meaning to Aristotle's ubiquitous definition of rhetoric as the discovery of the "available means of persuasion." While persuasion may at first invoke classical or combative modes historically assigned to men, women's rhetorical practices encompass expansive means of persuasion, such as invitational, irenic (peacemaking), collaborative, humorous, and more. Women's persuasive acts from the first two decades of the twenty-first century include new technologies and repurposed old ones, engaged not only to persuade but to tell their stories, sponsor change, and challenge cultural forces that repress and oppress. In so doing, they insist on the presence of women's voices in the public sphere, which history has long denied. How far we have come from Quintilian's two-thousand-year-old definition of the rhetorical orator as a "good man speaking well." *Persuasive Acts: Women's Rhetorics in the Twenty-First Century* gathers an expansive array of voices and texts, so that you may converse with them, extend them, and build rhetorics of your own.

It is an exciting time to assemble and engage women's rhetorics, as we are hearing the voices of more women, and in more ways, than ever before. Women are represented in proliferating numbers in traditional sites of public oratory—politics, courtrooms, churches—that once excluded them as well as in new rhetorical spheres online. The following pages feature the Supreme Court justice Sandra Sotomayor, the Iranian lawyer and judge Shirin Ebadi, the first female major US party presidential nominee Hillary Rodham Clinton, the Reverend Jennifer Bailey, and Malala Yousafzai, to name just a few. These women are changing the shape and tenor of traditionally masculine public arenas, bringing their unique gendered (among other) identities to bear on interpreting law, sharing sacred texts, or delivering a stump speech.

The contents also reflect the rhetorical revolution that has occurred online. This century, social media platforms have opened a space for women and other marginalized groups to self-publish and amplify their voices in ways previously unimaginable. Through the blog of a young Iraqi woman, we have access to her daily accounts of life in Baghdad during the US occupation of Iraq. Thanks to the ease and speed of information sharing online, a rape survivor's victim impact statement, read aloud in court to her assailant, reached an international audience. The employment of social media platforms has now become an essential tool in organizing and sustaining social movements. We see this demonstrated in the Black Lives Matter movement, launched in 2013 by three black women in response to the acquittal of George Zimmerman for murdering the unarmed black teen Trayvon Martin. We also witness it in the Women's March, a grassroots movement begun in 2016 as a protest march to newly elected President Trump, and #YesAllWomen, the hashtag and social media campaign initiated in response to misogyny and violence spurred by the 2014 Isla Vista killings. We capture examples of these rhetorical acts as demonstrations of the powerful escalation of women's voices online.

Yet even in the face of so much progress, the mechanisms that silence women are far from absent in our culture. While these structures may not be as explicit as they once were—say, written in law or even publicly spoken—they remain insidious, sometimes more so because they are less visible. Mechanisms to silence women also appear in new forms, as in online harassment and doxxing (broadcasting one's private identifying information online). In fact, the impetus for some of the strongest surges of women's voices in the last two decades often comes back to the denial of women's voices, personhood, and agency. Many of the writers in this collection forcefully challenge systems and structures that silence women so the next generation of women may speak even more freely.

As we gathered rhetorics with an eye on the present and the future, we also attended closely to history—on what and who has made way for this groundswell of voices. As we witnessed in the #MeToo movement, a viral hashtag spurred by the sexual misconduct allegations against the movie mogul Harvey Weinstein in 2017, women's rhetorical acts enable one another. One woman breaking a silence creates a space for another to share her story, and another, and another. That's how we think of this anthology. Twenty-first-century women rhetors have benefited from the risk-taking, persistence, and conviction of rhetors across centuries—like Sor Juana Inés de la Cruz, Mary Wollstonecraft, Sojourner Truth, Ida B. Wells, Audre Lorde, Ruth Bader Ginsberg, and Gloria Anzaldúa—as well as the many women whose speech, writing, and art will never appear in print and whose names we may never know.

This collection is also possible because in the late twentieth century, feminist scholars of rhetoric undertook trailblazing work to recover and reclaim women's rhetoric as part of the rhetorical tradition, breaking open a male-only canon. Thirty years ago, anthologies of rhetoric included two or three women wedged among an ensemble of male voices. Joy Ritchie and Kate Ronald tell us that when they began teaching rhetoric in the 1980s, they learned to expect the persistent question from their female students: "Where are the women?" They answered this question by compiling the first, and still most expansive, collection of women's rhetorics: *Available Means: An Anthology of Women's Rhetoric(s)*. The seventy pieces in their collection span 5 BCE–CE 1999 and represent an emergent tradition of women's rhetorics. *Available Means* includes writers and speakers who fiercely advocated for women's public participation and civil rights alongside women who wrote in "unprivileged or devalued forms such as letters, journals, and speeches to other women" (xx). Often denied education and a public voice, these women borrowed and appropriated conventions of the male tradition to use to their own ends, and they invented their own "available means" when conventional forms did not suit their purposes. In *Persuasive Acts*, we continue this gathering of women's rhetorics into the twenty-first century, which extends, responds to, and critiques the voices, strategies, and forms that preceded them.

An Anthology of Women's Rhetorics for a New Millennium

Thanks to *Available Means*, alongside the work of scholars including—but certainly not limited to—Karlyn Kohrs Campbell, Cheryl Glenn, Gesa Kirsch, Jacqueline Jones Royster, Shirley Wilson Logan, Andrea Lunsford, and Krista Ratcliffe, students don't have to ask, "Where are the women?" Today, our syllabi and reading lists make clear that women are a cornerstone of rhetorical theory and practice. However, women's rhetorics in the twenty-first century are expanding faster than editors can anthologize them. *Available Means* is older than most college students, who have lived in a very different rhetorical era, where the vehicles for public participation, and the voices doing so, exceed what could have been predicted then.

In 2001 there was no Facebook, Twitter, Instagram, or Snapchat. We couldn't predict that high schoolers in Parkland, Florida, after suffering a devastating school shooting on Valentine's Day 2018, would demand gun control through tweets challenging politicians' statements. Or that millions of women would tweet #MeToo as a rallying cry against sexual assault and sponsor new social movements to transform a toxic culture for women. The democratization of the public sphere through social media—which, we hasten to add, also brings with it exclusionary and pernicious dynamics—has radically altered how we practice and theorize rhetoric. We knew it was time for a new collection to document these changing rhetorical practices and ever-widening group of participants.

The expansiveness suggested by the title *Persuasive Acts* aims to capture the myriad shapes of women's rhetorics in contemporary culture. While writing and speaking are traditional rhetorical forms, writing is now more likely to occur online than in print, and speeches are more often streamed on a device than delivered at a podium. Therefore, works in this anthology are gathered both from more traditional sites, like the *New York Times* and the Democratic National Convention, as well as newer rhetorical platforms like Twitter and podcasts.

In addition to speaking and writing, women in this collection also engage in making, which has long been part of women's rhetorical work. Women have participated in rhetorical making through quilting, crafts, recipes, and activist art. We use the term *making* even more expansively in this volume, referencing both digital and material creations, from Instagram posts to videos to feminist cross-stitch. We find the term apt because it emphasizes women's prolific *production*, both of rhetorical texts and of new knowledge and theory.

Along with dramatic changes in where and how women practice rhetoric, we also address significant cultural shifts pertinent to women, gender, and feminism. These are defined by more capacious conceptions of identity, which disrupt views of categories such as gender, race, ability, or sexuality as isolated or fixed. Within—and beyond—feminist rhetorics, the concept of intersectionality has taken on enormous importance as a way to understand ourselves, one another, and the interplay of identities, culture, and power. Intersectionality highlights the interconnectedness of categories like gender, race, religion, ability, geographic location, sexual identity, and class to show how they result in different experiences of systemic oppression and discrimination. The term *intersectionality* was coined by the legal scholar Kimberlé Crenshaw in 1986 in order to describe the marginalization of black women by both feminism and antiracist groups because their concerns were not fully addressed by either. Of course, as Crenshaw acknowledges in "Why Intersectionality Can't Wait," included in this collection, "[Intersectionality] was a lived reality before it became a term." As is true of so much feminist work, Crenshaw's theory gave conceptual language to the material realities of women. And while it was articulated on behalf of black women, Crenshaw argues that its power comes in bringing to light "the invisibility of many constituents within groups that claim them as members, but often fail to represent them . . . People of color within LGBTQ movements; girls of color in the fight against the school-to-prison pipeline; women within immigration movements; trans women within feminist movements; and people with disabilities fighting police abuse—all face vulnerabilities that reflect the intersections of racism, sexism, class oppression, transphobia, able-ism and more. Intersectionality has given many advocates a way to frame their circumstances and to fight for their visibility and inclusion."

The women featured in this collection repeatedly make explicit ways their gendered identity interlocks with other social locations. Karin Hitselberger discusses her "rebellious" use of selfies to showcase her experience as a disabled, plus-size woman. Amy Alexander offers a critique of the women's march from the perspective of a "black woman of a certain age, a divorced mom of two teenagers who has no choice but to focus daily on the challenges of keeping a home, my family, and myself on track." Jennine Capó Crucet describes her experience of leaving home as a Latina, first-generation, female college student. In the twenty-first century, the *woman* in women's rhetorics is not viewed as an isolated category or one that assumes whiteness. Instead, gender is always in interplay with other identities.

The last two decades have also seen an increase in public conversation, as well as within feminist rhetoric, that expands how *woman* is conceived. While contesting and rewriting cultural articulations of womanhood has always been integral to women's rhetorics, this century's transgender activists further challenge us to refuse rigid, biologically determined binaries of gender. In so doing, they point to problematic exclusions within the feminist movement. In her 2001 "Transfeminist Manifesto," Emi Koyama reframes this omission as an opportunity for growth: "Every time a group of women previously silenced begins to speak out, other feminists are challenged to rethink their idea of whom they represent and what they stand for. While this process sometimes leads to a painful realization of our own biases and internalized oppressions as feminists, it eventually benefits the movement by widening our perspectives and constituency."

You will find examples of transwomen taking part in this revolution in the pages ahead. The trans writer and performance artist Julia Serano, for instance, describes the important rhetorical shift from once making audiences comfortable with her "bodily incongruity" by delivering a one-liner penis joke to now turning the tables back on audiences to ask: "Why do so many people—even those who are otherwise well-meaning, open-minded, progressive, pro-trans and anti-sexist—continue to get so hung up over the status of our genitals?" Staceyann Chin adds to this dialogue, observing that we don't have a language large enough to capture our gendered identities, leaving us with only two pronoun choices, "with each of us forced to choose between one of the two ways of saying *I am here*." Increasingly, however, as the contributors to this text demonstrate, women are finding available means to articulate and embrace their gendered identities as complex, fluid, and contradictory. For example, Johanna Hedva prefers gender-neutral pronouns to name their identities. In fact, the increasing fluidity of the concept of womanhood led us to consider whether we should retain the category of "women's rhetoric" for this project. Ultimately, we decided that *woman*, while it should be interrogated, still needs both representation and celebration, especially in an era when women's rights are under siege. As Charlotte has argued elsewhere, "While the term 'woman' [can] be narrow and problematic, to lose it risks making invisible the particular challenges women have faced" (Hogg 189). We use the term *woman*, then, expansively and fluidly, with the aim of achieving greater inclusivity.

Such elasticity is also evident in the concept of feminism itself, particularly as more people grapple with the term *feminism* as it reverberates through social media. Beyoncé, arguably the most influential female icon in this century, ended her 2014 MTV Video Music Awards performance with the word FEMINIST blazing in lights behind her, a powerful celebrity endorsement that went viral. Public figures, from politicians to celebrities, are now often asked if they define themselves as feminist, and answers reflect a shift from second- to third-wave feminism and beyond, to the ire of some and the delight of others. Feminism in the twenty-first century, influenced by millennials, seeks a malleability that reflects a range of voices and positions. As the journalists Dave Sheinin, Krissah Thompson, and Soraya Nadia McDonald explain: "This New Wave feminism is shaped less by a shared struggle against oppression than by a collective embrace of individual freedoms, concerned less with targeting narrowly defined enemies than with broadening feminism's reach through inclusiveness, and held together not by a handful of national organizations and charismatic leaders but by the invisible bonds of the Internet and social media." This question of how the term *feminism*—and those who embrace or resist it—is taken up or taken on propels many rhetorical declarations, acts, and discussions in the following pages.

In addition to reflecting changing conceptions of gender, identity, and feminism, this collection showcases powerful responses to twenty-first-century events, economic developments, and cultural shifts. One of the most notable is the 9/11 attack on American soil. On September 11, 2001, two US passenger planes, hijacked by members of the terrorist group Al Qaeda, flew into the two World Trade Center towers in lower Manhattan, destroying the 110-story symbols of American economic power and prosperity. In a coordinated effort, terrorists also hijacked another plane to strike the Pentagon—a symbol of US military power—and a fourth plane crashed in rural Pennsylvania when passengers onboard thwarted the hijackers. These terrorist acts heightened Islamophobia in the United States and led to the US invasions of Afghanistan and Iraq. *Persuasive Acts* includes voices from the Iraq veteran and US senator Tammy Duckworth; Captain Brenda Berkman, a firefighter who was a first responder at Ground Zero after the 9/11 attack; and the anonymous Iraqi blogger known as Riverbend, who describes the effects of the US invasion on her life in Baghdad. In the tradition of feminist rhetorics, these writers challenge dominant narratives of war, patriotism, and heroism as well as reveal untold stories that center women's experiences.

Women rhetors have also both challenged and leveraged increased global-ization—a process that integrates national economies, societies, and cultures through a global network of trade, technology, media, transportation and immi-gration. While globalization is not unique to the twenty-first century, the anthro-pologist Arjun Appadurai argues that the *current* moment of globalization is "new in the sense that it combines high connectivity with new levels, forms, and types of circulation" (qtd. in Gries, 12). This heightened speed and connectivity impact the global spread of capitalism, the interdependence among national economies, the transmission of cultural and social norms and values, and the governance and political processes of and among nation-states. To be sure, the spread of global-ization is imbued with power and, most often, the wealthiest and most dominant nations exert the greatest influence. As the feminist scholar Virginia Vargas ob-serves, "Globalization—highly unequal in reach and impact—divides at the same time as it integrates. As such, it is a threat, but it is also a possibility and a promise" (906).

Our contributors wield the rhetorical affordances and challenge the conse-quences of globalization, particularly as they are experienced by women and mar-ginalized people. For instance, as globalization heightens the disparity between rich and poor, human migration increases: those from impoverished countries seek work in wealthy industrialized nations. And with increased migration comes increased risk of human trafficking, as Ai-jen Poo illustrates in "Lola Wasn't Alone." Here she narrates the devastating, and all too common, stories of wom-en trafficked into domestic slavery in the United States. The environmental orga-nizer Thanu Yakupitiyage furthers this conversation by showing the intersection of globalization, climate change, and migration, pointing to the hypocrisy of the Trump administration's expansion of the fossil fuel industry—which causes cli-mate disaster that leads to migration—alongside a crackdown on US immigration policy.

The growth of transnational feminism represents another development in twenty-first-century rhetorics, offering powerful critiques of the gendered conse-quences of globalization. Rooted in postcolonialist and antiracist feminist theo-ry, transnational feminism illuminates how women's lives are shaped by national boundaries and histories of colonialism. The renowned feminist scholar Chandra Talpade Mohanty places decolonization, anticapitalist critique, and solidarity at the center of transnational feminist work, with the goal of working toward "justice, participation, redistribution of wealth and resources, commitment to individual and collective human rights and to public welfare and services, and accountability to and responsibility for the collective" (9). This vision is evident in the environ-mental activist Vandana Shiva's call for "Earth Democracy," which rejects capital-ist ownership culture to promote a just sharing of the earth's resources.

Transnational feminists also critique the tendency of Western feminism to assume their values, methods of advocacy, and goals can be neatly applied to women in other countries. Instead, as contributor Patricia Valoy argues, "[Transnational feminists] see liberation as something that must come from within our own communities and nations—not something that is bestowed on us by people in power." From Shirin Ebadi's story of Iranian feminists' courageous activism in the face of a repressive political regime to Jeanette Urquilla's work to end the criminalization of abortion in El Salvador, we witness examples of context-sensitive feminist activism around the globe. In this collection, you'll see women's rhetorical acts spurred by these complex and momentous exigencies.

Bridging Theory and Practice in Twenty-First-Century Women's Rhetorics

As we shared early drafts of this anthology with students, one of Shari's undergraduates, KaDeja Songoyele, emphasized that a collection of women's rhetorics should bridge the gap between women in and outside of the university as well as between theory and practice. Her suggestion is an apt description of the lineage of women's rhetorics, which refuses a neat divide between theories about rhetoric and rhetorical acts themselves. As Ritchie and Ronald observe, "Women have purposefully sought to keep the context, the immediacy of experience, attached to theorizing rather than creating an abstract set of prescriptions disconnected from the context or stripped of the exigencies of everyday life" (xxvii). In short, they emphasize that we "read women's rhetorics as theory" (xxvii). The twenty-first-century texts gathered here follow in this tradition. They are often borne of deep urgency to respond to a problem of lived experience, whether in the community, a profession, or one's body. In the persuasive acts that follow, through various forms and approaches, they both provide new rhetorical theories and expand and resist existing ones. Such forms also reflect the flexibility of genre that can—and as Songoyele urges, *should*—reach multiple audiences. As a result, here you'll see pieces that look and sound less like traditional, academic genres of rhetorical theory and more like story, narrative, and testimony. According to Katherine Mack and Jonathan Alexander, this blend of personal and political in writing, which hearkens to the popular form of memoir, "Participates in distinctive and rhetorically powerful ways in twenty-first century culture," no doubt a responsiveness to more intimacy revealed on social media and the reach for broader audiences (67).

The texts in this anthology also work in close connection with the growing body of feminist rhetorical theory that has emerged alongside the recovery and reclamation of women's rhetorics. While we can't—and wouldn't want to—restrict categories of women's rhetorical acts, feminist rhetoricians trace key theoretical threads and sets of tactics that are often woven through, and result from, women's speaking, writing, and making. Cheryl Glenn, for instance, locates in women's rhetorics what she calls *rhetorical feminism*: "A tactic (actually a set of tactics)—a theoretical stance—that is responsive to the ideology that is feminism and to the key strategy that is feminist rhetoric" ("Introduction" 4). Many contributors' pieces reflect and extend Glenn's rhetorical feminism, whose key features include:

> (1) Disidentification with mainstream (hegemonic) rhetoric; (2) goals that are dialogic and *trans*actional rather than monologic and *reac*tional; (3) attention to marginalized audiences who may or may not have the power to address or resolve the problem at hand; (4) use of vernacular and experiences shared with marginalized audiences; (5) redesign of rhetorical appeals, to include *logos* based on dialogue and understanding, *ethos* rooted in experience, and *pathos* aligned with emotion; (6) use of and respect for alternative delivery systems, especially those long considered passive or feminine, such as emotion, silence, and listening; and perhaps most important; (7) a deep commitment to possibility and hope. ("A Feminist Tactic" 3–4)

You'll see features of rhetorical feminism as delineated by Glenn throughout this anthology, as contributors to *Persuasive Acts* use their voices to make connections with others, to foster understanding across differences, and to highlight the stories of women who have been forgotten or hidden. Employing conversational speech and stories, Jessica Valenti addresses young women with frankness about sex positivity not often heard in sex education, and Angy Rivera candidly shares her experiences of being undocumented. Through delivery systems such as photography and drawings, rhetors convey emotion with little to no text, as in Jessamyn Stanley's *Every Body Yoga* image or Hana Shafi's drawing of a woman on a scale. They show that pain, anger, joy, shame, and frustration are part of rhetorical acts, and in so doing they disrupt the ancient divide between reason and emotion, where pathos is a device employed to evoke to the audience's emotion, but the rhetor is expected to be "rational." Emma Gonzalez, after surviving a school shooting in Parkland, Florida, delivered a pivotal, powerful speech that marked the beginning of the #NeverAgain movement. In her piece, she tells the story behind that moment, an exemplar of rhetorical feminism, conveyed through tears, rife with righteous anger and stubborn hope, and grounded in evidence designed to change a national dialogue.

Indeed, one of the most powerful rhetorical vehicles employed by rhetors in this collection is testimony. The feminist scholar Leigh Gilmore forwards the concept of *testimonial agency*, which involves the movement, or the circulation, of a testimony in search of a listener, an adequate witness (66). While women's testimonies have historically been disbelieved or disregarded, Gilmore argues for their potential to "force repressed histories and contexts into view" and, therefore, to carve a path toward justice (158). We see adept engagement of testimony in individual rhetorical acts, like in Emily Doe's (Chanel Miller's) victim impact statement, delivered at the sentencing of the man who raped her. While her rapist, whom the media repeatedly described as a "Stanford swimmer," was required to serve a mere six months in jail, Doe's powerful testimony circulated to millions of readers, finding a supportive audience who provided a "feminist form of witness" to her story (165). We also see the commanding effect of testimonial collectives, as in #BlackLivesMatter, which teaches us "how to bear witness to histories of the present, and how to look at images of death, grief, and protest as a form of ethical engagement" (163). In the twenty-first century, testimonial networks increasingly develop online and across social media, circulating to diverse audiences and creating space for connection and affirmation—spaces where women are heard and believed.

Rhetors across the collection also participate in the making of feminist counterpublics; that is, they create spheres that welcome arguments, testimonies, and conversations that are devalued or disallowed in the larger public sphere. Nancy Fraser popularized the term *counterpublic* in 1990, arguing that the public sphere has never been a truly democratic forum in which all can freely participate. Nevertheless, women and other marginalized subjects have long created their own spheres for dialogue and action, through acts like consciousness-raising groups, civil rights sit-ins, and SlutWalks. This collection features examples of contemporary counterpublics, now increasingly occurring in digital spaces, which afford rhetors greater reach and circulation potential. Feminist counterpublics—like #MeToo, #YesAllWomen, body-positive Instagram feeds, and Black Lives Matter—serve as spaces for education, empowerment, and an exchange of ideas and stories that allow both withdrawal from and reentry into the wider public sphere, providing a space apart in order to eventually make change in the collective public (Fraser).

As we think about how movements form and messages spread online, new articulations of rhetorical circulation aid our examination of how and where rhetoric moves, which messages become viral and which dissipate without much attention, and what is the relationship between digital circulation and material change. As many of the digital pieces in this collection show, online rhetoric, especially, circulates in ways that are unanticipated and unplanned by the rhetor, taking on a life of its own (Gries 8). Sasha Weiss's essay on #YesAllWomen is one such example, where the hashtag circulated to spur demonstrations and gatherings, appeared on clothing, bumper stickers, and iPhone cases, was co-opted by some who opposed the movement, and was critiqued and revised into hashtags like #YesAllWhiteWomen, which highlighted the disproportionate impact of violence and discrimination on women of color (Edwards and Lang). As Dustin Edwards and Heather Lang observe of #YesAllWomen's circulation, its "broader makeup—from the material infrastructure of the Internet, to the politics of social media platforms, to human actors divergently using the tag—is messy, entangled, and always becoming" (131). We hope readers will trace how the rhetorics in this collection have circulated in ways that shape gendered narratives and social action.

Even as this collection forwards the import and relevance of feminist frameworks, and as Ritchie and Ronald note in *Available Means*, the trajectory of women's rhetorics may seem to "conflate women's rhetoric with feminism," it is critical to note that feminism and women's rhetorics are not synonymous or monolithic (xxiii). It is true that the struggle for rights has been and remains a primary and urgent exigence for women's rhetorical acts, but we are mindful that feminists do not solely represent women's rhetorics, even as they garner greatest representation here. As is the case with selections in *Available Means*, "It is difficult to separate the history of women's rhetorics from the history of the struggle for women's rights because the desire/demand for rights often becomes the impetus for writing" (xxii).

And yet, you will find in the pages ahead that arguments for women's rights, the rights of the marginalized, and social change emerge from rhetors who occupy multiple, and sometimes seemingly contradictory, social locations. Katharine Hayhoe, a climate scientist and evangelical Christian, insists not only that she can claim both locations, but that they do not negate one another. Kimberly Shappley relays the struggles she faced in reconciling the values she internalized as a conservative, evangelical Christian and as the mother of a transgender child. And rhetors in this collection often make the case that feminism is strengthened by flexibility that allows for contradictions, as in Erica Thurman's call for "a black womanhood that makes room for scholarly publications, a code-switching blog and twerking. Sometimes all at the same damn time." Across the pieces in *Persuasive Acts*, women remake and redefine their own identities, providing new tactics for and theories of rhetorical agency.

Gathering Twenty-First-Century Women's Rhetorics: Rhetorical Sway

Not surprisingly, making choices for inclusion was by far the most vexing element of amassing this anthology, given the abundance of riches of women's persuasive acts since the turn of the century. While we knew we couldn't be exhaustive in terms of coverage, we selected criteria for inclusion that worked from the exigencies we describe earlier: the proliferation of means of persuasion due to online platforms and the emergence of political and cultural shifts. In particular, we selected texts with these criteria in mind: (1) anticipation of endurance or rhetorical impact; (2) the blend, unique to these times, of voices that are well-known with those that are lesser-known or even "unknown"; (3) representation of rhetors from multiple social locations employing varied moves and forms; and (4) opportunities for pieces to speak with and against each other within and across sections of the book. As we worked through texts, we found ourselves increasingly adopting what we came to call *rhetorical sway*: rhetorical impact demonstrated through creating or connecting to cultural flashpoints that forward or respond to gendered issues. For us, rhetorical sway is determined in part by traditional rhetorical theories and features, but it is more profoundly influenced by women's rhetorical theories that value inclusion and representation and that encompass expansive forms of argument, evidence, and ethos.

We began by considering what constitutes rhetorical endurance or lasting impact—it quickly became clear that anthologizing a contemporary, rather than historical, collection does not allow us to measure a text's endurance using traditional measures, like historical weight or canonization. Instead, we saw this as an opportunity to resist traditional gauges of value determination, which in the past have served to delegitimize or overlook other voices—we did not want to narrow the rich rhetorical landscape before us. At the same time, we sought to acknowledge voices and pieces that *did* take hold in these times because of what they might signal rhetorically about a cultural or political moment. Ultimately, we assessed a piece's rhetorical impact and potential for endurance through both older and newer criteria. In the case of the former, we considered history-making events or rhetorics with profound cultural or political visibility, such as the acceptance speech of the first female major party presidential nominee or a notable dissent from a Supreme Court justice. We also located rhetorical sway through newer measures like going viral, trending, or reaching audiences through new media platforms. For us, this signaled not just fleeting popularity but a cultural contribution that held public attention during these fragmented, divisive times—often in ways that created dialogue or furthered a stalled conversation. We see this in, for instance, in Gabrielle Blair's tweet thread on abortion rights, which was retweeted sixty-five thousand times in two days. She seized a *kairotic* opportunity, posting the thread during the controversial confirmation process of the Supreme Court nominee (now justice) Brett Kavanaugh, and sparked an important conversation about abortion rights at a time when the Supreme Court could overturn *Roe v. Wade*.

We see potential in texts that are temporarily all-consuming to create further, long-term reverberations that forward new ways to understand rhetorical significance. For instance, as Feminista Jones observes, black women are at the forefront of deftly employed online platforms to shape cultural conversations; she notes that "among two dozen hashtags referred to in a 2016 article as influential in shaping the discussion around feminism, ten were created by Black women" (41). The Black Lives Matter movement began with a hashtag that was used about twelve million times from 2013 to 2016 to create an international movement (Anderson and Hitlin). Similarly, the high school students who inundated social media after the Parkland shooting not only captured national attention but leveraged the connectivity it fostered to build a more sustained movement, March for Our Lives, the largest youth protests in the United States since the Vietnam War (Lyons).

We also see evidence of rhetorical sway in rhetorics that intervene in a collective emotion or cultural narrative—like #YesAllWomen's disruption of the shame women often experience when they are harassed or assaulted—or that invite connection, which is important on its own but might also lead to further coalition building or activism. And in the best case, going viral or trending spurs further reverberations and possibilities for shifting understanding of an issue.

Even within women's rhetorics, however, rhetorical sway has often been associated with well-established (meaning well-accomplished but also socially and financially secure; read: usually white) women. For us, a rhetor with sway is sometimes well-known, but just as often is one we have deemed powerful because she represents a perspective and position not often heard. In this way, we challenge traditional, Aristotelian concepts of ethos that focus on men speaking in public venues—Kathleen J. Ryan, Nancy Myers, and Rebecca Jones explain that this classical definition was "used, primarily, in a homogenous community among male orators in positions of power" (5). Deemed unfit for public participation, women had to invent ways to establish credibility, working both within and against the criteria for good character, goodwill, and intellect valued by dominant publics (7). In this collection, women's rhetorical acts continue to extend the concept of ethos to better account for difference and collectivity. Deliberately, then, we put well-known voices alongside those who may not be familiar to further disrupt the connection between ethos, power, and privilege. To us, these disruptions constitute rhetorical sway.

Whereas traditional rhetoric tends to focus on canonical individual contributions, we also locate rhetorical sway in the powerful acts of women's collectives, which we can trace to the suffragists who composed the 1848 Declaration of Sentiments or the 1970s Combahee River Collective, a black feminist lesbian organization. As Feminista Jones argues of the latter, "What made their work incredibly important is the consideration they took to be more inclusive of intersectional identities and the experiences of Black women throughout the African diaspora" (9). The sensibility of working together continues to sustain black women in online spaces, where Jones says, "We truly feel that we are all we have" (9). In this anthology, you'll see women enacting collaboration as rhetorical sway to support themselves and each other, even among differences. The 2017 Women's March *Guiding Vision and Definition of Principles* is one example, in which (not without controversy) organizers created a document meant to inspire inclusion and acknowledge difference while building a coalition. Paola Bacchetta, Tina Campt,

Inderpal Grewal, Caren Kaplan, Minoo Moallem and Jennifer Terry co-authored "Transnational Feminist Practices against War" just after 9/11 to disavow the US military responses to terror. Other voices emerge from a collective via hashtags or as a part of the National Domestic Workers Alliance to promote and sustain action by and for women. These pieces reinforce that women's actions, shaped by cooperation and collaboration, often result in more powerful effects than could be accomplished by a lone rhetor as *the* source of knowledge.

Along with contributions from new and established voices whose acts demonstrate rhetorical sway, we sought voices that represent authors' intersectional experiences and identities. The primary moves within and across these women's persuasive acts create opportunities to better understand that rhetoric by white women has been the most visible but not the most viable. The impassioned rhetorics written from intersectional experience show that positionalities aren't simply identities to list but converge materially, emotionally, and structurally in everyday lived realities.

From these many locations, rhetors in this collection achieve sway through a plethora of rhetorical strategies and moves. One is the appeal of humor, traditionally deemed men's domain. Writers and makers in our collection such as Chimamanda Ngozi Adichie, the creators of mansplaining tweets, and Lindy West prove otherwise, showing that a little irreverence in the face of patriarchal systems can sustain us with wit while offering a biting cultural critique. Rhetors also engage in language play and subversion, challenging notions of decorum or "proper speech" commonly associated with rhetoric. For instance, Robin M. Boylorn demonstrates the rhythmic mix of vernaculars and sounds in her piece that originally appeared on the Crunk Feminist Collective website. As the Crunk Feminist mission statement describes, "Our relationship to feminism and our world is bound up with a proclivity for the percussive, as we divorce ourselves from 'correct' or hegemonic ways of being in favor of following the rhythm of our own heartbeats. In other words, what others may call audacious and crazy, we call CRUNK." Boylorn's piece is alive with sounds of hip-hop, code-switching, story, and razor-sharp critique.

Forms such as a feminist cross-stitch pattern that circulates on BuzzFeed and other sites, a tweet thread with thousands of retweets, a comic, a podcast, or a YouTube video invite women rhetors to broaden the scope and reach of their appeals. These forms allow art and sound to reach a range of audiences online, in order to persuade and cajole or to share and identify, as they encourage collective endorsement and response. Texts that demonstrate rhetorical sway, then, work within and against traditional rhetorical means to invent rhetorics that engage wide audiences, change conversations, and create openings for new rhetors to enter.

Constructing Women's Rhetorical Acts:
A Word about Structure and Constraints

This collection is divided into sections centered on key themes that represent women's rich rhetorical contributions to critical contemporary issues and arenas: Civic Engagement, Feminisms, Protest and Resistance, Education, Work and Labor, and Identities and the Body. Each section merges traditional and new themes, forms, and genres and encompasses perspectives located as close as the body and as broad as national and global politics. Some of these rhetorical arenas have long excluded women, like traditional sites of civic engagement (the courtroom, the political sphere, and places of worship), and some represent areas in which women have long engaged but now do so in new ways or from a wider range of perspectives. Whether these rhetors are breaking new ground with their sheer presence or expanding boundaries in existing conversations, each of these arenas is changed by their work.

While the anthology focuses primarily on US texts, each section includes pieces by transnational writers—and often, as Valoy reminds us, the personal is the transnational (for global anthologies, see *Decolonizing Feminism: Transnational Feminism and Globalization*, edited by Margaret A. McLaren, or *Women across Cultures: A Global Perspective*, edited by Shawn Meghan Burn). As we organized the collection, it was important to us not to group more recently emerging voices (like transnational or transgender rhetors) in their own categories—which risks cordoning them off—and instead to show how topics like feminism or education are changed when we attend closely to new perspectives. While we aimed for broad coverage of the first two decades of this century, the proliferation of media and assault on women's issues following the 2016 presidential election led to more entries from the 2010s.

Even as we have divided texts into themes, we intend for pieces to dialogue within and across them. In section 2, "Rhetorics of Feminisms," for example, Sheryl Sandberg's *Lean In*, which was on the *New York Times* best-seller list for over a year and had sold over four million copies by 2018, was also criticized for its blinders in terms of class and race. Two contributors in that same section, Barbara Sostaita and Amy Alexander, each take to task Sandberg's "third-wave corporatis[m]," (Alexander) disputing, expanding, and nuancing Sandberg's uses of feminism. We see dialogue across sections as well, as with Lindy West's piece on online harassment in section 1, "Rhetorics of Civic Engagement," and Suzanne Samin's discussion of the exclusion of female gamers in section 3, "Rhetorics of Protest and Resistance."

In finalizing our selections, we faced an overabundance, not only from the sources we searched and found but also from the generosity of colleagues, some we sought out and others who offered suggestions as we shared drafts at conferences, and undergraduate and graduate students, who led us to a wealth of voices, sites, and activities. So while the most challenging part of compiling this anthology was making difficult choices about selections, we were heartened both by the surplus of rhetorics and the sharing of voices.

But of course some constraints exist. At the most basic level, for every selection there are at least a dozen that we reluctantly didn't include due to the space limits for publication (which connects to the affordability of the book for students), challenges with permissions in terms of cost, and authors who declined inclusion or did not respond to our queries. We had to come to terms with the fact that, just as in choosing texts for syllabi, our choices must be representational rather than exhaustive. We were also limited to a print book, which means that we aren't able to capture the vividness of new media in its original form. Finally, the limits of our own positionalities—as two cisgender, Generation X, white tenured professors raised on the Plains—required us to do careful rhetorical listening (Ratcliffe) in order to better understand which voices are most audible to us, which voices we have not heard (and why), and how we can listen more closely across difference. In so doing, we read widely and deeply, and we benefited greatly from the recommendations of generous peers and students across disciplines, institutions, and social locations, whose suggestions we actively sought across our three years of work on this project.

Our hope is that as you engage the anthology, in or out of the classrooms, you'll bring—and compose—your own rhetorics that speak to, with, and against the pieces included in ways that further circulation, rebuttals, and continued conversation. We invite you to consider how definitions of womanhood and feminism take shape across the pieces, how they complicate and enrich one another, as well as how you would define and distinguish women's versus feminist rhetoric. Above all, we hope you will do your own theoretical work with these texts, noting recurrences and intersections across contributions and sections. How do these rhetorical acts allow us to discover new ways of enacting and understanding rhetorical work? What do they teach us about the power of writing, speaking, and making that we haven't before addressed, or valued, or sanctioned? How do they change how we might learn to practice rhetoric, or teach rhetoric to others?

A Coda: On Resilience and Hope

In the throes of compiling this anthology, we hoped it would feature an inaugural speech by the first US female president. We would be able to declare that a woman had finally broken the highest glass ceiling. Instead, with Hillary Clinton's loss in the 2016 presidential election, we faced a very different cultural and rhetorical climate—one in which women had to come to terms with the election of a man who boasted about his ability to grab women and whose proposed policies demeaned Muslims, immigrants, and people of color. It was yet another silencing.

And yet, even in the face of disappointment, fury, and grief, women began to act, to organize, to speak, to write, and to make. We found ourselves exchanging daily texts and emails with new discoveries of women's rhetorical force and resilience, imagining them as part of this anthology. Even more, our colleagues, students, and friends supplied us with a steady stream of women's rhetorics they wanted to share. Women, it became clear, would not be silenced.

In the process of creating this anthology, we were sustained by the voices that appear in the following pages, as well as the many we were not able to include, and the legacy of the voices from history that led the charge. We were buoyed by our undergraduate and graduate students teaching us about a new voice, collective, or venue. We were motivated by rhetorical moves of connection essential to rhetorical feminisms as seen by Adrienne Keene, who chooses the intimate form of a letter to remind Native college students that despite the pressures endured by colonialism and isolation, they are loved and they matter.

All around us, and reflected in this collection, we see examples of "feminist rhetorical resilience," a concept formulated by Elizabeth Flynn, Patricia Sotirin, and Ann Brady. Resilience is a response to adversity, and contributors write from experiences of trauma, natural disaster, war, disability, poverty, and other forms of pain. Their pieces make clear that the very requirement of resilience is disproportionately experienced by women of color, poor women, women with disabilities, and queer and trans women. Feminist resilience, though, is not the "pull yourself up by the bootstraps" variety, nor does it overlook the social conditions that make resilience more necessary for some than for others. Instead, it relies on support through relationships and involves "ongoing responsiveness" to challenging conditions (7). It is a transformative process, and while it may not change "bleak or oppressive" conditions, it "changes the way a life is lived" (7). Resilient living—and, we would add, rhetorical making—involves "determination, perseverance, hope and imagination" (7).

We see resilience beautifully displayed in Shirin Ebadi's essay, "The Women Who Dared to Rise Up," describing her work with a group of Iranian women's rights activists to regroup after an attempt to protest was halted by police brutality. As Ebadi writes, "It was the fateful crackdown . . . that actually gave the women their new direction. As I have experienced so often myself, being crushed simply gives you greater exercise in collecting the shards of yourself, putting them back together, and figuring out what to do next." Lezley McSpadden—the mother of Michael Brown, an unarmed black teenager killed by police officers in Ferguson, Missouri, in 2014—also powerfully articulates resilience through relationship building among mothers of victims, even as she expresses dismay and helplessness at the seemingly endless loss of black lives. In these examples, resilience involves both coping with and confronting oppressive cultural systems; it serves to build connections among women and offer strength through word and deed.

As we reluctantly had to stop amassing texts as we moved to publication—already exceeding our word count more than we care to confess—we were heartened by the 2018 midterm elections, which showed record gains for women in the House of Representatives—102 women, the most in US history—as well as the first two Muslim American representatives, the first two Native American congresswomen, and the youngest woman ever elected to Congress, Alexandria Ocasio-Cortez (Lu and Collins).

We see these acts of feminist resilience as intimately related to hope. Of course, as Glenn explains: "I may be hopeful, but I am not naïve. I believe that critical thinking without hope is cynicism, but hope without critical thinking is naïveté. I am a rhetorical feminist" ("A Feminist Tactic"). Contributors Michelle Obama, Jennifer Bailey, Nadia Bolz-Weber, Adrienne Keene, Thanu Yakupitiyage, Julia Serano, and Johanna Hedva each engage and richly inflect the concept of hope, even as they tackle painful issues and experiences. "Hope," clarifies Bailey, "is not the same as optimism." For her, hope is borne from bearing witness to pain and suffering and from collectivizing to change a broken world. Indeed, there is much work to be done, as women know all too well from the realities of their lives. But we need not go about this work alone. The women's rhetorical acts assembled here build upon the legacy of women who came before, and they offer community, strategies, and tactics for the women who live now. We hope that as you engage these voices, you feel a sense of community and support that buoys you to create your own rhetorics, to continue to listen to unheard voices, and to make space for future women rhetors.

Works Cited

Anderson, Monica, and Paul Hitlin. "Social Media Conversations About Race." *Pew Research Center: Internet and Technology*, 15 Aug. 2016.

Bradley, Kate. "The Effects of Globalization in the Twenty-First Century." *Classrooms*, n.d., classroom.synonym.com/effects-globalization-21st-century-13074.html.

Burn, Shawn Meghan, editor. *Women across Cultures: A Global Perspective*. McGraw-Hill Education, 2019.

Edwards, Dustin, and Heather Lang. "Entanglements That Matter: A New Materialist Trace of #YesAllWomen." *Circulation, Writing, and Rhetoric*, edited by Laurie E. Gries and Collin Gifford Brooke, Utah State UP, 2018, pp. 118–34.

Flynn, Elizabeth, Patricia Sotirin, and Ann Brady, editors. *Feminist Rhetorical Resilience*. Utah State UP, 2012.

Fraser, Nancy. "Rethinking the Public Sphere: A Contribution to the Critique of Actually Existing Democracy." *Social Text*, no. 25/26, 1990, pp. 56–80.

Gilmore, Leigh. *Tainted Witness: Why We Doubt What Women Say About Their Lives*. Columbia UP, 2018.

Glenn, Cheryl. "A Feminist Tactic of Hope." Conference on College Composition and Communication. Kansas City, MO, March 2018.

Glenn, Cheryl. Introduction. *Rhetorical Feminism and This Thing Called Hope*. Southern Illinois UP, 2018, pp. 1–4.

Gries, Laurie. Introduction. *Circulation, Writing, and Rhetoric*, edited by Laurie E. Gries and Collin Gifford Brooke, Utah State UP, 2018, pp. 3–26.

Hogg, Charlotte. "What's (Not) in a Name: Considerations and Consequences of a Field's Nomenclature." *Peitho: Journal of the Coalition of Women Scholars in the History of Rhetoric and Composition*, vol. 19, no. 2, 2017, pp. 181–209.

Jones, Feminista. *Reclaiming Our Space: How Black Feminists Are Changing the World from the Tweets to the Streets*. Beacon Press, 2019.

Lu, Denise, and Keith Collins. "'Year of the Woman' Indeed: Record Gains in the House." *The New York Times*, 16 Nov. 2018, https://www.nytimes.com/interactive/2018/11/09/us/women-elect ed-midterm-elections.html.

Lyons, Joseph D. "How Many People Attended March for Our Lives? It's Officially the Biggest in the Last 40 Years." *Bustle*, 4 Apr. 2018, https://www.bustle.com/p/how-many-people-attended -march-for-our-lives-its-officially-the-biggest-in-the-last-40-years-8605361.

Mack, Katherine, and Jonathan Alexander. "The Ethics of Memoir: Ethos in Uptake." *Rhetoric Society Quarterly*, vol. 49, no. 1, Jan. 2019, pp. 49–70.

McLaren, Margaret A., editor. *Decolonizing Feminism: Transnational Feminism and Globalization*. Rowman & Littlefield, 2017.

"Mission Statement." *Crunk Feminist Collective*, 8 Aug. 2016, www.crunkfeministcollective.com/ about/.

Mohanty, Chandra Talpade. *Feminism without Borders: Decolonizing Theory, Practicing Solidarity*. Point Par Point, 2007.

Ratcliffe, Krista. "Rhetorical Listening: A Trope for Interpretive Invention and a 'Code of Cross-Cultural Conduct.'" *College Composition and Communication*, vol. 51, no. 2, Dec. 1999, pp. 195–224.

Ritchie, Joy S., and Kate Ronald. "A Gathering of Rhetorics." *Available Means: An Anthology of Women's Rhetoric(s)*, U of Pittsburgh P, 2001, pp. xv–xxxi.

Sheinin, Dave, Krissah Thompson, and Soraya Nadia McDonald. "Betty Friedan to Beyoncé: Today's Generation Embraces Feminism on Its Own Terms." *The Washington Post*, 27 Jan. 2016, https://www.washingtonpost.com/national/feminism/betty-friedan-to-beyonce-todays-gen eration-embraces-feminism-on-its-own-terms/2016/01/27/ab480e74-8e19-11e5-ae1f-af46 b7df8483_story.html?noredirect=on.

Vargas, Virginia. "Feminism, Globalization and the Global Justice and Solidarity Movement." *Cultural Studies*, vol. 17, no. 6, Nov. 2003, pp. 905–20.

I

Rhetorics of Civic Engagement

The classical tradition of oratory located rhetoric in three primary branches: the legislature, the courtroom, and houses of worship. In these spheres, great (read: privileged) men held forth to persuade, defend or accuse, and praise (or blame) other men. Women were most often relegated to the private sphere, deemed unworthy of the high pursuits of civic engagement and denied a public voice.

In the twenty-first century, no laws (in the United States) prevent women from holding public office, but the residue of these ancient beliefs remains. Yet this has not stopped the women whose work appears in the pages ahead. Many, in fact, are "firsts" in their respective judicial or political roles. And while the ordination of women remains controversial even in the twenty-first century, this section features powerful contributions by female religious leaders. Of course, sites of civic engagement now extend far beyond the legislature, courtroom, and places of worship, so these texts also include women's rhetoric on sites ranging from newspaper opinion pages to Twitter. While the rhetorical contexts and professions of the rhetors in this section vary, each finds available means to work both within and against the contexts of civic engagement that once excluded them.

Opening this section is the speech that Hillary Clinton, the first female major party nominee for president, made at the 2016 Democratic National Convention. She challenges rhetoric and policy that valorizes individualism, instead articulating a collective vision for governing that insists we are "stronger together." Shirin Ebadi, the first female judge in Iran, works from a similar collective-oriented ethos, wielding her rhetorical acumen and knowledge of Islamic law to support a women's rights group in Iran. Jeannette Urquilla, the executive director of a human rights organization in El Salvador, uses her platform to illuminate how women experience the devastating effects of her country's total ban on abortion. Speaking on the floor of Congress, Nancy Pelosi, the first female Speaker of the House of Representatives, takes on her Republican colleagues to argue for maintaining the Affordable Health Care Act, passed during the Obama administration. She articulates the stakes in privileging profits for insurance companies over collective responsibility to the American people. ·

The civic leaders in this section also refuse a division between logic and emotion, delivering arguments that seamlessly synthesize reason and passion. Justice Sonia Sotomayor, the first Latinx appointed to the Supreme Court, writes a vehement dissenting opinion that insists unlawful police stops are anything but "isolated" incidents. Enacting Audre Lorde's famous claim that anger "focused with precision" can fuel change, Representative Maxine Waters minces no words or fury in taking the Trump administration to task for separating parents from their children at the US-Mexico border.

Rhetors in this section also use testimony and witness to intervene in civic conversations. In a campaign speech for Hillary Clinton, First Lady Michelle Obama describes being "shaken to her core" by Donald Trump's glib statement about grabbing women. Jennifer Bailey, a Christian minister, calls us to bear witness to the violence and pain inflicted on the black community. Emma Gonzalez, a founder of the gun control movement Never Again, testifies to the grief and pain she and her classmates endured as survivors of a school shooting. Rabbi Sharon Brous extends this trope, insisting that the conflict between Jerusalem and Palestine will be resolved only through a mutual witnessing of one another's humanity. Lezley McSpadden, the mother of Michael Brown, an unarmed black teenager shot by a police officer, testifies to the unending grief a mother endures in losing her child. For each of these rhetors, compassionate recognition of human suffering is a vital step toward its rectification.

Unfortunately, women's entry into public spheres is still often met with resistance. Consequently, women's rhetorical work often involves challenging the forces that deny them voice and agency. To this end, Cathy de la Cruz, Keegan Osinski, and Caroline Madden use humorous memes on Twitter to call out mansplaining as a form of silencing or dismissing women. In the wake of the #MeToo movement, the Lutheran minister Bolz-Weber argues that it is heresy to use the Bible to support the dominance of one group over another. The writer and comedian Lindy West addresses the relentless harassment women face in online forums in a podcast, where she confronts a man who trolled her.

In the twenty-first century, advocates for fuller—and more accurate—representation of women in the public sphere remind us, "You can't be what you can't see." Our hope is that the rhetorical acts in this section will invite more women forward, changing and challenging the public discourse in law, politics, and religion. The quality of civic life depends on the contribution and representation of all members of the public, particularly those whose presence and perspectives have, for too long, been overlooked.

Hillary Rodham Clinton

As Hillary Rodham Clinton stepped to the podium to accept the Democratic Party's nomination for president, she faced a daunting rhetorical task: to audition as the first female president of the United States. Clinton had to convince Americans not only that she was the right person for the job but that the right person for the job was a woman.

For Clinton, who had by 2016 held public roles for twenty-five years—as First Lady to President Bill Clinton, then senator of New York, then secretary of state during the Obama administration—this task involved cutting through decades of cultural narratives spun about her, which were sometimes positive, but more often harshly critical. Writes the *New York Times* correspondent Mark Leibovich, the phrase *polarizing figure* is never far from her name. But as Leibovich further explains, Clinton has also been *polarized* by a culture that hasn't known what to do with her as a feminist First Lady, who played an active political role in her husband's administration; as a wife who remained with her husband after his much-publicized affair with a twenty-two-year-old White House intern; or as woman, with her own ambitions to run for senate and then president.

Public discussion of her marriage, her feminism, and even her hair and pantsuits often overshadowed her many achievements as a public servant. As First Lady, Clinton collaborated with both parties to establish the Children's Health Insurance Program. She saw New York through 9/11 as a twice-elected senator and established a reputation among her fellow legislators as a hard worker, an attuned listener, and a bridge-builder across the political aisle (Davis). After losing the 2008 Democratic presidential nomination to Barack Obama, she accepted a cabinet position as secretary of state, serving as an ambassador for women's rights around the globe and improving the United States' international reputation. As Obama put it in his 2016 DNC address, "I can say with confidence there has never been a man or a woman—not me, not Bill [Clinton], nobody—more qualified than Hillary Clinton to serve as president of the United States of America."

Her qualifications, though, did not guarantee an easy path to the 2016 nomination. Vermont senator Bernie Sanders proved a fierce rival. Running on a progressive platform, he framed Clinton as an "establishment candidate" (Bordo). But as the feminist scholar Susan Bordo observes, Clinton's caution must be read in the context of decades of harsh schooling from the media, who chastised her for being too "shrill" on one hand, or unemotional and cold on the other. Citing the powerful role of gender in politics, CNN's Frida Ghitis writes, "Women candidates . . . face the daunting challenge of being strong without losing their ability to be liked."

Even with the nomination secure, Clinton had to use her DNC speech to make an appeal for acceptance from Sanders's supporters. "I've heard you. Your cause is our cause," she promises. She then moves to reintroduce herself, acknowledging that her relationship with the public has not been an easy one.

The speech gives those in the room, and the international audience listening, a new chance to meet Hillary Rodham Clinton—to decide what they will make of the first female major party nominee for president of the United States. In her characteristic deliberate, methodical manner, she tells her story; it is not a story, however, of individual accomplishments. Instead, it features the feminist values of coalition building, collaboration, and recognition of all who play a role in political change. "Our founders fought a revolution and wrote a Constitution so America would never be a nation where one person had all the power," Clinton forwards, showing that her message of collaboration is as deep and abiding as our history. Even the white suit she donned that evening was a nod to the US suffragists who came before her.

As for serving as the woman to receive a major party presidential nomination, she reminds the audience that this success benefits all: "When any barrier falls in America, for anyone, it clears the way for everyone. When there are no ceilings, the sky's the limit." While the election results would show that the ceiling had not yet broken, Clinton nevertheless carved an indelible pathway for the future first female president of the United States.

Remarks at the Democratic National Convention

Philadelphia, Pennsylvania, 2016

Thank you. Thank you so much. Thank you. Thank you all so much. Thank you. Thank you. Thank you all very, very much. Thank you for that amazing welcome. Thank you all for the great convention that we've had.

And, Chelsea, thank you. I am so proud to be your mother and so proud of the woman you've become. Thank you for bringing Marc into our family and Charlotte and Aidan into the world. And, Bill, that conversation we started in the law library forty-five years ago, it is still going strong.

That conversation has lasted through good times that filled us with joy and hard times that tested us. And I've even gotten a few words in along the way. On Tuesday night, I was so happy to see that my explainer-in-chief is still on the job. (Applause.) I'm also grateful to the rest of my family and to the friends of a lifetime.

For all of you whose hard work brought us here tonight and to those of you who joined this campaign this week, thank you. What a remarkable week it's been. We heard the man from Hope [Hope, Arkansas], Bill Clinton; and the man of hope, Barack Obama. America is stronger because of President Obama's leadership, and I am better because of his friendship.

We heard from our terrific vice president, the one and only Joe Biden. He spoke from his big heart about our party's commitment to working people as only he can do.

And First Lady Michelle Obama reminded us that our children are watching and the president we elect is going to be their president, too.

And for those of you out there who are just getting to know Tim Kaine, you— you will soon understand why the people of Virginia keep promoting him from city council and mayor, to governor, and now senator. And he will make our whole country proud as our vice president. And I want to thank Bernie Sanders. Bernie. Bernie, your campaign inspired millions of Americans, particularly the young people who threw their hearts and souls into our primary. You put economic and social justice issues front and center, where they belong.

And to all of your supporters here and around the country, I want you to know I have heard you. Your cause is our cause. Our country needs your ideas, energy, and passion. That is the only way we can turn our progressive platform into real change for America. We wrote it together. Now let's go out and make it happen together.

My friends, we've come to Philadelphia, the birthplace of our nation, because what happened in this city 240 years ago still has something to teach us today. We all know the story, but we usually focus on how it turned out, and not enough on how close that story came to never being written at all. When representatives from thirteen unruly colonies met just down the road from here, some wanted to stick with the king, and some wanted to stick it to the king.

The revolution hung in the balance. Then somehow they began listening to each other, compromising, finding common purpose. And by the time they left Philadelphia, they had begun to see themselves as one nation. That's what made it possible to stand up to a king. That took courage. They had courage. Our founders embraced the enduring truth that we are stronger together.

Now America is once again at a moment of reckoning. Powerful forces are threatening to pull us apart. Bonds of trust and respect are fraying. And just as with our founders, there are no guarantees. It truly is up to us. We have to decide whether we will all work together so we can all rise together. Our country's motto is *e pluribus unum*: out of many, we are one. Will we stay true to that motto?

Well, we heard Donald Trump's answer last week at his convention. He wants to divide us from the rest of the world and from each other. He's betting that the perils of today's world will blind us to its unlimited promise. He's taken the Republican Party a long way from "Morning in America" to "Midnight in America." He wants us to fear the future and fear each other.

Well, a great Democratic president, Franklin Delano Roosevelt, came up with the perfect rebuke to Trump more than eighty years ago, during a much more perilous time: "The only thing we have to fear is fear itself."

Now we are clear-eyed about what our country is up against, but we are not afraid. We will rise to the challenge, just as we always have. We will not build a wall. Instead, we will build an economy where everyone who wants a good job can get one. And we'll build a path to citizenship for millions of immigrants who are already contributing to our economy. We will not ban a religion. We will work with all Americans and our allies to fight and defeat terrorism.

Yet, we know there is a lot to do. Too many people haven't had a pay raise since the crash. There's too much inequality, too little social mobility, too much paralysis in Washington, too many threats at home and abroad.

But just look for a minute at the strengths we bring as Americans to meet these challenges. We have the most dynamic and diverse people in the world. We have the most tolerant and generous young people we've ever had. We have the most powerful military, the most innovative entrepreneurs, the most enduring values— freedom and equality, justice and opportunity. We should be so proud that those words are associated with us. I have to tell you, as your secretary of state, I went to 112 countries. When people hear those words, they hear America.

So don't let anyone tell you that our country is weak. We're not. Don't let anyone tell you we don't have what it takes. We do. And most of all, don't believe anyone who says, "I alone can fix it." Yes. Those were actually Donald Trump's words in Cleveland. And they should set off alarm bells for all of us. Really? "I alone can fix it?" Isn't he forgetting troops on the front lines, police officers and firefighters who run toward danger, doctors and nurses who care for us? Teachers who change lives, entrepreneurs who see possibilities in every problem, mothers who lost children to violence and are building a movement to keep other kids safe? He's forgetting every last one of us. Americans don't say, "I alone fix can it." We say, "We'll fix it together."

And remember. Remember. Our founders fought a revolution and wrote a Constitution so America would never be a nation where one person had all the power. Two hundred and forty years later, we still put our faith in each other. Look at what happened in Dallas. After the assassinations of five brave police officers,

Police Chief David Brown asked the community to support his force, maybe even join them. And do you know how the community responded? Nearly five hundred people applied in just twelve days.

That's how Americans answer when the call for help goes out. Twenty years ago, I wrote a book called *It Takes a Village*. And a lot of people looked at the title and asked, "What the heck do you mean by that?" This is what I mean. None of us can raise a family, build a business, heal a community, or lift a country totally alone. America needs every one of us to lend our energy, our talents, our ambition to making our nation better and stronger. I believe that with all my heart. That's why "Stronger Together" is not just a lesson from our history, it's not just a slogan for our campaign, it's a guiding principle for the country we've always been, and the future we're going to build.

A country where the economy works for everyone, not just those at the top. Where you can get a good job and send your kids to a good school no matter what ZIP code you live in. A country where all our children can dream, and those dreams are within reach. Where families are strong, communities are safe, and, yes, where love trumps hate. That's the country we're fighting for. That's the future we're working toward. And so, my friends, it is with humility, determination, and boundless confidence in America's promise that I accept your nomination for president of the United States.

Now, sometimes the people at this podium are new to the national stage. As you know, I'm not one of those people. I've been your First Lady, served eight years as a senator from the great state of New York. Then I represented all of you as secretary of state. But my job titles only tell you what I've done. They don't tell you why. The truth is, through all these years of public service, the service part has always come easier to me than the public part. I get it that some people just don't know what to make of me. So let me tell you.

The family I'm from, well, no one had their name on big buildings. My families were builders of a different kind, builders in the way most American families are. They used whatever tools they had, whatever God gave them, and whatever life in America provided, and built better lives and better futures for their kids.

My grandfather worked in the same Scranton lace mill for fifty years because he believed that if he gave everything he had, his children would have a better life than he did. And he was right. My dad, Hugh, made it to college. He played football at Penn State and enlisted in the navy after Pearl Harbor. When the war was over he started his own small business, printing fabric for draperies. I remember watching him stand for hours over silkscreens. He wanted to give my brothers and me opportunities he never had, and he did.

My mother, Dorothy, was abandoned by her parents as a young girl. She ended up on her own at fourteen, working as a housemaid. She was saved by the kindness of others. Her first grade teacher saw she had nothing to eat at lunch, and brought extra food to share the entire year. The lesson she passed on to me years later stuck with me: No one gets through life alone. We have to look out for each other and lift each other up. And she made sure I learned the words from our Methodist faith: "Do all the good you can, for all the people you can, in all the ways you can, as long as ever you can."

So I went to work for the Children's Defense Fund, going door-to-door in New Bedford, Massachusetts, on behalf of children with disabilities who were denied the chance to go to school. I remember meeting a young girl in a wheelchair on the small back porch of her house. She told me how badly she wanted to go to school. It just didn't seem possible in those days. And I couldn't stop thinking of my mother and what she'd gone through as a child. It became clear to me that simply caring is not enough. To drive real progress, you have to change both hearts and laws. You need both understanding and action.

So we gathered facts. We built a coalition. And our work helped convince Congress to ensure access to education for all students with disabilities. It's a big idea, isn't it? Every kid with a disability has the right to go to school. But how do you make an idea like that real? You do it step-by-step, year-by-year, sometimes even door-by-door. My heart just swelled when I saw Anastasia Somoza representing millions of young people on this stage because we changed our law to make sure she got an education.

So it's true. I sweat the details of policy, whether we're talking about the exact level of lead in the drinking water in Flint, Michigan; the number of mental health facilities in Iowa; or the cost of your prescription drugs. Because it's not just a detail if it's your kid, if it's your family. It's a big deal. And it should be a big deal to your president, too.

After the four days of this convention, you've seen some of the people who've inspired me, people who let me into their lives and became a part of mine, people like Ryan Moore and Lauren Manning. They told their stories Tuesday night. I first met Ryan as a seven-year-old. He was wearing a full body brace that must have weighed forty pounds because I leaned over to lift him up. Children like Ryan kept me going when our plan for universal health care failed, and kept me working with leaders of both parties to help create the Children's Health Insurance Program that covers eight million kids in our country. Lauren Manning, who stood here with such grace and power, was gravely injured on 9/11.

It was the thought of her, and Debbie Stage. John who you saw in the movie, and John Dolan and Joe Sweeney and all the victims and survivors, that kept me working as hard as I could in the senate on behalf of 9/11 families and our first responders who got sick from their time at Ground Zero. I was thinking of Lauren, Debbie, and all the others ten years later in the White House Situation Room, when President Obama made the courageous decision that finally brought Osama bin Laden to justice.

And in this campaign I've met many more people who motivate me to keep fighting for change, and with your help, I will carry all of your voices and stories with me to the White House. And you heard from Republicans and Independents who are supporting our campaign. Well, I will be a president for Democrats, Republicans, Independents; for the struggling, the striving, the successful; for all those who vote for me and for those who don't. For all Americans together.

Tonight, we've reached a milestone in our nation's march toward a more perfect union: the first time that a major party has nominated a woman for president. Standing here as my mother's daughter, and my daughter's mother, I'm so happy this day has come. I'm happy for grandmothers and little girls and everyone in between. I'm happy for boys and men—because when any barrier falls in America, it clears the way for everyone. After all, when there are no ceilings, the sky's the limit. So let's keep going until every one of the 161 million women and girls across America has the opportunity she deserves to have. But even more important than the history we make tonight is the history we will write together in the years ahead. Let's begin with what we're going to do to help working people in our country get ahead and stay ahead.

Now, I don't think President Obama and Vice President Biden get the credit they deserve for saving us from the worst economic crisis of our lifetimes. Our economy is so much stronger than when they took office. Nearly fifteen million new private-sector jobs. Twenty million more Americans with health insurance. And an auto industry that just had its best year ever.

Now, that's real progress. But none of us can be satisfied with the status quo. Not by a long shot. We're still facing deep-seated problems that developed long before the recession and have stayed with us through the recovery. I've gone around the country talking to working families. And I've heard from many who feel like the economy sure isn't working for them. Some of you are frustrated—even furious. And you know what? You're right. It's not yet working the way it should.

Americans are willing to work—and work hard. But right now, an awful lot of people feel there is less and less respect for the work they do. And less respect for them, period. Democrats, we are the party of working people. But we haven't done a good enough job showing we get what you're going through, and we're going to do something to help.

So tonight I want to tell you how we will empower Americans to live better lives. My primary mission as president will be to create more opportunity and more good jobs with rising wages right here in the United States. From my first day in office to my last. Especially in places that for too long have been left out and left behind. From our inner cities to our small towns, from Indian country to coal country. From communities ravaged by addiction to regions hollowed out by plant closures.

And here's what I believe. I believe America thrives when the middle class thrives. I believe our economy isn't working the way it should because our democracy isn't working the way it should. That's why we need to appoint Supreme Court justices who will get money out of politics and expand voting rights, not restrict them. And if necessary, we will pass a constitutional amendment to overturn Citizens United.

I believe American corporations that have gotten so much from our country should be just as patriotic in return. Many of them are, but too many aren't. It's wrong to take tax breaks with one hand and give out pink slips with the other. And I believe Wall Street can never, ever be allowed to wreck Main Street again.

And I believe in science. I believe that climate change is real and that we can save our planet while creating millions of good-paying clean-energy jobs.

I believe that when we have millions of hardworking immigrants contributing to our economy, it would be self-defeating and inhumane to try to kick them out. Comprehensive immigration reform will grow our economy and keep families together—and it's the right thing to do. So whatever party you belong to, or if you belong to no party at all, if you share these beliefs, this is your campaign.

If you believe that companies should share profits, not pad executive bonuses, join us. If you believe the minimum wage should be a living wage, and no one working full time should have to raise their children in poverty, join us.

If you believe that every man, woman, and child in America has the right to affordable health care, join us! If you believe that we should say no to unfair trade deals; that we should stand up to China; that we should support our steelworkers and autoworkers and homegrown manufacturers, then join us.

If you believe we should expand Social Security and protect a woman's right to make her own heath care decisions, then join us. And yes, yes, if you believe that your working mother, wife, sister, or daughter deserves equal pay, join us. That's how we're going to make sure this economy works for everyone, not just those at the top.

Now, you didn't hear any of this, did you, from Donald Trump at his convention. He spoke for seventy-odd minutes—and I do mean odd. And he offered zero solutions. But we already know he doesn't believe these things. No wonder he doesn't like talking about his plans. You might have noticed, I love talking about mine.

In my first one hundred days, we will work with both parties to pass the biggest investment in new, good-paying jobs since World War II. Jobs in manufacturing, clean energy, technology and innovation, small business, and infrastructure. If we invest in infrastructure now, we'll not only create jobs today, but lay the foundation for the jobs of the future.

And we will also transform the way we prepare our young people for those jobs. Bernie Sanders and I will work together to make college tuition-free for the middle class and debt-free for all. We will also—we will also liberate millions of people who already have student debt. It's just not right that Donald Trump can ignore his debts, and students and families can't refinance their debts.

And something we don't say often enough: Sure, college is crucial, but a four-year degree should not be the only path to a good job. We will help more people learn a skill or practice a trade and make a good living doing it. We will give small businesses, like my dad's, a boost; make it easier to get credit. Way too many dreams die in the parking lots of banks. In America, if you can dream it, you should be able to build it.

And we will help you balance family and work. And you know what, if fighting for affordable child care and paid family leave is playing the "woman card," then deal me in.

Now—now, here's the other thing. Now, we're not only going to make all of these investments. We're going to pay for every single one of them. And here's how. Wall Street, corporations, and the super-rich are going to start paying their fair share of taxes. This is—this is not because we resent success, but when more than 90 percent of the gains have gone to the top 1 percent, that's where the money is. And we are going to follow the money. And if companies take tax breaks and then ship jobs overseas, we'll make them pay us back. And we'll put that money to work where it belongs: creating jobs here at home.

Now, I imagine that some of you are sitting at home thinking, *Well, that all sounds pretty good, but how are you going to get it done? How are you going to break through the gridlock in Washington?* Well, look at my record. I've worked across the aisle to pass laws and treaties and to launch new programs that help millions of people. And if you give me the chance, that's exactly what I'll do as president.

But then—but then I also imagine people are thinking out there, but Trump, he's a businessman. He must know something about the economy. Well, let's take a closer look, shall we? In Atlantic City, sixty miles from here, you will find contractors and small businesses who lost everything because Donald Trump refused to pay his bills. Now, remember what the president said last night. Don't boo. Vote.

But think of this. People who did the work and needed the money, not because he couldn't pay them, but because he wouldn't pay them, he just stiffed them. And you know that sales pitch he's making to be president: put your faith in him, and you'll win big? That's the same sales pitch he made to all those small businesses. Then Trump walked away and left working people holding the bag.

He also talks a big game about putting America first. Well, please explain what part of America First leads him to make Trump ties in China, not Colorado; Trump suits in Mexico, not Michigan; Trump furniture in Turkey, not Ohio;

Trump picture frames in India, not Wisconsin. Donald Trump says he wants to make America great again. Well, he could start by actually making things in America again.

Now, the choice we face in this election is just as stark when it comes to our national security. Anyone—anyone reading the news can see the threats and turbulence we face. From Baghdad and Kabul, to Nice and Paris and Brussels, from San Bernardino to Orlando, we're dealing with determined enemies that must be defeated. So it's no wonder that people are anxious and looking for reassurance, looking for steady leadership, wanting a leader who understands we are stronger when we work with our allies around the world and care for our veterans here at home. Keeping our nation safe and honoring the people who do that work will be my highest priority.

I'm proud that we put a lid on Iran's nuclear program without firing a single shot. Now we have to enforce it, and we must keep supporting Israel's security. I'm proud that we shaped a global climate agreement. Now we have to hold every country accountable to their commitments, including ourselves. And I'm proud to stand by our allies in NATO against any threat they face, including from Russia.

I've laid out my strategy for defeating ISIS. We will strike their sanctuaries from the air and support local forces taking them out on the ground. We will surge our intelligence so we detect and prevent attacks before they happen. We will disrupt their efforts online to reach and radicalize young people in our country. It won't be easy or quick, but make no mistake we will prevail.

Now Donald Trump—Donald Trump says, and this is a quote, "I know more about ISIS than the generals do." No, Donald, you don't.

He thinks—he thinks he knows more than our military because he claimed our armed forces are "a disaster." Well, I've had the privilege to work closely with our troops and our veterans for many years, including as a senator on the Armed Services Committee. And I know how wrong he is. Our military is a national treasure. We entrust our commander-in-chief to make the hardest decisions our nation faces: decisions about war and peace, life and death. A president should respect the men and women who risk their lives to serve our country, including—including Captain Khan and the sons of Tim Kaine and Mike Pence, both Marines.

So just ask yourself: Do you really think Donald Trump has the temperament to be commander in chief? Donald Trump can't even handle the rough-and-tumble of a presidential campaign. He loses his cool at the slightest provocation—when he's gotten a tough question from a reporter, when he's challenged in a debate, when he sees a protestor at a rally. Imagine, if you dare imagine, imagine him in the Oval Office facing a real crisis. A man you can bait with a tweet is not a man we can trust with nuclear weapons.

I can't put it any better than Jackie Kennedy did after the Cuban Missile Crisis. She said that what worried President Kennedy during that very dangerous time was that a war might be started—not by big men with self-control and restraint, but by little men, the ones moved by fear and pride.

America's strength doesn't come from lashing out. It relies on smarts, judgment, cool resolve, and the precise and strategic application of power. And that's the kind of commander-in-chief I pledge to be.

And if we're serious about keeping our country safe, we also can't afford to have a president who's in the pocket of the gun lobby. I'm not here to repeal the Second Amendment. I'm not here to take away your guns. I just don't want you to be shot by someone who shouldn't have a gun in the first place.

We will work tirelessly with responsible gun owners to pass common-sense reforms and keep guns out of the hands of criminals, terrorists, and all others who would do us harm. For decades, people have said this issue was too hard to solve and the politics too hot to touch. But I ask you: How can we just stand by and do nothing? You heard, you saw, family members of people killed by gun violence on this stage. You heard, you saw family members of police officers killed in the line of duty because they were outgunned by criminals. I refuse to believe we can't find common ground here. We have to heal the divides in our country, not just on guns but on race, immigration, and more.

And that starts with listening, listening to each other, trying as best we can to walk in each other's shoes. So let's put ourselves in the shoes of young black and Latino men and women who face the effects of systemic racism and are made to feel like their lives are disposable. Let's put ourselves in the shoes of police officers, kissing their kids and spouses good-bye every day and heading off to do a dangerous and necessary job. We will reform our criminal justice system from end to end, and rebuild trust between law enforcement and the communities they serve. And we will defend—we will defend all our rights: civil rights, human rights, and voting rights; women's rights and workers' rights; LGBT rights and the rights of people with disabilities. And we will stand up against mean and divisive rhetoric wherever it comes from.

For the past year, many people made the mistake of laughing off Donald Trump's comments, excusing him as an entertainer just putting on a show. They thought he couldn't possibly mean all the horrible things he says, like when he called women "pigs" or said that an American judge couldn't be fair because of his Mexican heritage, or when he mocks and mimics a reporter with a disability, or insults prisoners of war—like John McCain, a hero and a patriot who deserves our respect.

Now, at first, I admit, I couldn't believe he meant it, either. It was just too hard to fathom, that someone who wants to lead our nation could say those things, could be like that. But here's the sad truth: There is no other Donald Trump. This is it. And in the end, it comes down to what Donald Trump doesn't get: America is great because America is good.

So enough with the bigotry and the bombast. Donald Trump's not offering real change. He's offering empty promises. And what are we offering? A bold agenda to improve the lives of people across our country—to keep you safe, to get you good jobs, to give your kids the opportunities they deserve.

The choice is clear, my friends. Every generation of Americans has come together to make our country freer, fairer, and stronger. None of us ever have or can do it alone. I know that at a time when so much seems to be pulling us apart, it can be hard to imagine how we'll ever pull together. But I'm here to tell you tonight— progress is possible. I know. I know because I've seen it in the lives of people across America who get knocked down and get right back up.

And I know it from my own life. More than a few times, I've had to pick myself up and get back in the game. Like so much else in my life, I got this from my mother too. She never let me back down from any challenge. When I tried to hide from a neighborhood bully, she literally blocked the door. "Go back out there," she said. And she was right. You have to stand up to bullies. You have to keep working to make things better, even when the odds are long and the opposition is fierce.

We lost our mother a few years ago, but I miss her every day. And I still hear her voice urging me to keep working, keep fighting for right, no matter what. That's what we need to do together as a nation. And though "we may not live to see the glory," as the song from the musical *Hamilton* goes, "Let us gladly join the fight." Let our legacy be about "planting seeds in a garden you never get to see."

That's why we're here, not just in this hall, but on this earth. The founders showed us that, and so have many others since. They were drawn together by love of country, and the selfless passion to build something better for all who follow. That is the story of America. And we begin a new chapter tonight.

Yes, the world is watching what we do. Yes, America's destiny is ours to choose. So let's be stronger together, my fellow Americans. Let's look to the future with courage and confidence. Let's build a better tomorrow for our beloved children and our beloved country. And when we do, America will be greater than ever.

Thank you and may God bless you and the United States of America.

FOR FURTHER READING

Bordo, Susan. *The Destruction of Hillary Clinton: Untangling the Political Forces, Media Culture, and Assault on Fact That Decided the 2016 Election*. Melville House, 2018.

Clinton, Hillary Rodham. *What Happened*. Simon & Schuster, 2017.

Davis, Susan. "Hillary Clinton's Senate Years Provide Insight into How She Might Govern." *NPR*, 28 Apr. 2016, www.npr.org/2016/04/28/476060514/hillary-clintons-senate-years-provide-insight-into-how-she-might-govern.

Ghitis, Frida. "The 'Shrill' Smear against Hillary Clinton." *CNN*, 8 Feb. 2016, www.cnn.com/2016/02/08/opinions/hillary-clinton-sexism-ghitis/index.html.

Leibovich, Mark. "What It Really Means to Call Hillary Clinton 'Polarizing.'" *The New York Times*, 7 Apr. 2015, www.nytimes.com/2015/04/12/magazine/what-it-really-means-to-call-hillary-clinton-polarizing.html.

"President Obama's Address at Democratic National Convention." Democratic National Convention, 27 July 2016, Philadelphia, PA.

Shirin Ebadi

Shirin Ebadi was the first Muslim woman and the first Iranian to receive the Nobel Peace Prize, awarded to her in 2003 for her tireless efforts to promote civil rights and democracy for women and children in Iran. Yet as she chronicles in her moving memoir, *Until We Are Free*, from which "The Women Who Dared to Rise Up" is excerpted, this achievement only served to escalate the Iranian regime's efforts to silence her.

Ebadi, who spent much of her life in Tehran, was born in 1947 to educated parents and a family atmosphere she describes as "filled with kindness and affection" (Ebadi, "Biographical"). She was the first woman to serve as a judge in Iran, but following the 1979 Islamic Revolution, she, along with all other female judges, was forced to resign. Ebadi's application to practice law was refused until 1992. As she awaited the renewal of her license, she taught at the University of Tehran. Once Ebadi's practice resumed, she become an advocate for civil rights, focusing on women and children. After Mahmoud Ahmadinejad was elected president of Iran in 2005, the regime elevated its efforts to intimidate Ebadi—bugging her law firm, stopping her lectures, and detaining her daughter. Ebadi left for a conference in 2009 and did not return, knowing she could no longer live safely in Iran.

Until We Are Free chronicles the escalation of threats Ebadi received following her receipt of the Nobel Peace Prize, providing an unflinching portrait of the struggle for human rights at both the personal and professional levels against a strict regime. The following section homes in on the practicalities, successes, and challenges faced by women working as a collective to affect change. Relying on the mentorship and advice of Ebadi, the organizers Noushin and Parvin formed the One Million Signatures Campaign, designed to end discriminatory laws against women in the Islamic Republic. Ebadi describes their tactical planning over tea, where she advises the leaders to include traditional religious people as well as secularists, demonstrating the importance of forming an inclusive collective. Ebadi also uses her legal savvy to ensure that the movement's handbook does not violate any tenet of Islam, which would result in their arrest. As they work within and against a stifling political system, securing gains and suffering losses, Ebadi enacts powerful feminist mentorship, advocates for reaching across boundary lines of religion and class, and advises deep knowledge of the system they seek to challenge.

Above all, she demonstrates that even within an oppressive regime, Iranian women have built a vibrant, agile movement.

"The Women Who Dared to Rise Up": Excerpt from *Until We Are Free*

2016

On June 12, 2006, a cloudless, summery afternoon, a group of women's rights activists began arriving at the Seventh of Tir Square, one of the capital's major public spaces. It is a sprawling, wide square, lined with manteau shops, office buildings, and florists, always busy with traffic, as the motorway that leads north to the city intersects the square to its north. The afternoon was warm, and some of the women wore sandals and light, modest manteaus. Although thick brown smog usually hangs over Seventh of Tir, that day the air was bright, the green patches of grass around the traffic islands looked lush and healthy, and the square bustled with the honking of taxis and the slow rumbling of buses.

Earlier, the activists had crossed the streets of Tehran passing out a pamphlet titled *Why We Don't Consider the Present Laws Just*. The tone of the pamphlet was simple and disarming; in natural language, it used anecdotal examples to illustrate why the country's laws—"which we often don't think about until we fall into a fix"—were so deeply problematic for women. The women had a few banners rolled up in their handbags, but they had not yet removed them, not wishing to attract attention before the crowd properly formed. Around seventy people had arrived and were milling about the central south side of the square, chatting and waiting for others to join. I passed through the square that afternoon, but I didn't stay for the protest itself. That night, the organizers recounted for me what had come to pass.

Just a few minutes before four o'clock, the key organizers, who had arrived early, noticed a small convoy of green-and-white police cars heading down from the north side of the square. As though the moves were coordinated, some motorbikes bearing policemen in riot-gear helmets poured in from a narrow side street to the east of the square. Out of several police vans flooded policewomen in severe, head-to-toe black chadors. They began running through the square, waving batons, the fabric of their chadors billowing around them. The protesters tried to melt into traffic, to scamper toward the sidewalks and into the crowd. But suddenly there were police officers everywhere, shouting for everyone to disperse but not letting anyone get away. The policewomen roughly grabbed women protesters by the arm and dragged them toward the waiting vans. Male police officers attacked the men in the crowd. Great plumes of tear gas shot out, and people screamed, "My eyes, my eyes!" Some women stumbled and doubled over, clutching at their faces.

One particular policewoman, with a heavy build and a brown *maghnaeh*, a cloaklike head covering, was the most violent. She looked almost like an execution-er, the activists recounted later, storming about and shouting and digging her nails into the arms of the protesters. Her face, they said, contorted in rage as she strode from assault to assault. When women collapsed from the tear gas, the policewoman grabbed them by their head scarves and dragged them along the pavement toward the police vans.

The authorities put down the protest before it even got started, crushing it with a violence no one had anticipated. They injured a number of the protesters and arrest-ed a number of the key organizers, even Ali Akbar Moussavi Khoeini, a reformist former member of parliament who had come out in solidarity with the women. In the days after the crushed protest, the Tehran public prosecutor declared that the arrested protesters were accused of disturbing public order, fostering tension and unrest, and spreading lies. The police had, of course, known about the protest in advance; the organizers had posted the date and time on their website, for they felt they had nothing to hide. But it was clear that the regime would not tolerate such public gatherings, even if they were peaceful. This directly violated the constitution, which upholds people's right to free assembly and public demonstration, on the con-dition that no weapons are carried and the principles and tenets of Islam are not undermined. But for the purposes of the organizers, with whom I was in touch, the crackdown and arrests made bruisingly clear that they would need to change tactics.

The activists met shortly afterward to discuss what had happened and to devise a new strategy that the state would tolerate. To be effective meant not crossing cer-tain red lines. A feminist movement that was locked up, imprisoned, and not permit-ted to organize, they knew, would be of little benefit to anyone. Their experience in the women's movement to that moment pointed to the need for legal reform, but it was the fateful crackdown at Seventh of Tir that actually gave the women their new direction. As I have experienced so often myself, being crushed simply gives you greater exercise in collecting the shards of yourself, putting them back together, and figuring out what to do next.

About a month later, two of the country's most prominent women's rights activ-ists came to my office. The trees outside the building were thick with green leaves, and the sun was shining so brightly that I flicked off the office lights. As Noushin Ahmadi Khorasani and Parvin Ardalan took off their manteaus and head scarves, I poured tea, waiting for the bubbles to settle across the amber liquid. Parvin had a commanding presence, with her mop of curly black hair, huge dark eyes, and winged eyebrows. Noushin was slighter and more unassuming. They were both in their early thirties and had worked for years as journalists and community ac-tivists. They seemed more energized than usual that day, and when we sat down around the dark oak table to talk, they explained that they were about to launch an important new campaign.

"It will be called the One Million Signatures campaign," said Noushin. "It will, of course, protest against legal discriminations against women, but it will get us out door-to-door across the country, moving forward the conversation about women's rights." Both of them looked at me expectantly.

"So, Khanoum Ebadi, do you agree with our idea?" Noushin finally asked. "Can you help us?"

I had been silent because I was so moved. It felt like all the efforts that women like me had made in the early years of the revolution, pushing back against all that discrimination and state bullying, were finally—nearly three decades later—bear-ing some fruit. Iran's feminist movement was one of the country's most striking features. Despite the state's fierce repressiveness—everything from laws that per-mitted stoning and polygamy to morality police sweeps that harassed women on the street for not dressing conservatively enough—Iran had a burgeoning, vibrant women's movement. Most important, it had grassroots support among women of all backgrounds. This wasn't a clique of upper-class women who had studied in Europe and were supported by their husbands but a real movement, with centers and seminars and training sessions with titles like "How to Cope with Interroga-tion." Though it was not something that I particularly wished to take credit for, it did seem that my receipt of the Nobel in 2003 had propelled the women's activists. To have a woman just like them, a woman they knew, whom they had seen going in and out of court for years under the Islamic Republic, be recognized in this way showed them that the world watched and appreciated their efforts. Most of the time they were struggling alone, but history was also watching them.

Because my position allowed me to travel around the region, I saw how special this was. No other Middle Eastern country had anything quite like it. Much of the region was still enamored with political Islam, and in countries like Saudi Arabia, many women were simply not interested in mounting an open challenge to the state's patriarchy. So in this, Iran was very special and ahead of its neighbors, and the movement had managed to flourish, despite Ahmadinejad's emergence.

"Your idea is tremendous," I said. "It is impressive and bold, and well-conceived. I just think you have to be careful to direct it in a way so that it has max-imum appeal. It needs to be an initiative that traditional and religious people also find themselves drawn to, not just the secularists."

The two nodded in agreement, but they said they had to discuss this aspect of their outreach with the committee charged with launching the campaign. Ev-eryone had to support the group's key ideas before they could be adapted. I was pleased to see how naturally democratic the activists were in organizing and planning their initiatives, and that they were not prepared to accept something without consulting with their colleagues. I wished them the best of luck, and I said I looked forward to their launch.

The following week, Parvin and Noushin returned and showed me a draft of their One Million Signatures campaign handbook and introduction, which the group's legal committee had drafted. I made a few minor changes to ensure that all the content was consistently defensible in any court of law. After that, a date was set for the launch of the campaign: August 27.

What discriminatory laws, Parvin asked, should they start with? Divorce law and polygamy? Inheritance and child custody? I said their campaign should have only one objective—namely, the reform of all discriminatory laws. They asked if such an objective could be achieved under the Islamic Republic system.

I told them, "This must be the aspiration, the ideal. An ideal is like the sun in the sky. Perhaps no one can ever reach the sun, but you shouldn't forget that it's there. As to which set of laws you should start with, I think this is something you'd best ask the signatories."

When it came to launching the campaign, the authorities refused the women a legal permit to hold their meeting in a public place or assembly hall. So they had no choice but to start the campaign from the office of one of the group's supporters. The plan was to hold a brief ceremony and announce the campaign's objectives. But two hours before the start of the meeting, security officials warned the owner of the office building that such a meeting should not go ahead.

There was no time to inform all the participants. Everyone gradually began to arrive, and they faced a locked door. Noushin and Parvin were standing there, arms crossed over their chests, absolutely furious. Others looked anxiously at the security forces, who were now standing at the entrance to the street. Gradually those who had been invited to the meeting began to arrive, forming a large crowd in the street. I spotted a few journalists, as well, in the crowd.

Suddenly, a young girl shouted from among the crowd: "You can't stop us! The campaign will begin here . . . right in the middle of this street!" The crowd broke into applause at her suggestion, and the organizers began distributing sheets of paper for everyone to sign. An hour later, the crowd dispersed, and the security forces left as well, probably thinking that they had successfully prevented the meeting.

The following month, while on a visit to the United States to attend a seminar along with Desmond Tutu, the Dalai Lama, and all the women winners of the Nobel Peace Prize, I passed out the campaign's petition paper and asked everyone to sign it. Soon the media announced that all these prominent figures had come out in support of this action by Iranian women.

Though the organizers called their effort the One Million Signatures campaign, the key goal was never to simply collect signatures. The main objective was to raise awareness across Iran about discriminatory laws and to propel a wider debate around how those laws could be updated or changed. The campaign, which had both men and women in its ranks, used the meeting point of a signature collection as an occasion to speak to people and to emphasize the peacefulness of their work. Campaigners visited government offices and organizations, and they asked people for signatures at metro and bus stations. They organized street-theater events, visited women in their homes, and fanned out across the country. They found support and expanded quickly from Tehran to a number of other cities. There, activists from Tehran held "train the trainer" sessions, and these local activists began doing in all these cities what the key founders had started in Tehran.

What this proved was something deeply distressing to the authorities: that the demand for legal reform extended to women across the country, across class, geography, and social background. The campaign's great success was to develop and build women's awareness around key legal issues like equitable inheritance rights and inflation adjustment for dowries—these were areas that had the support of traditional and more secularminded women alike, and the mounting pressure, plus the many thousands of accumulating signatures, made the state deeply nervous.

It was at around that time that the arrests began. Across the country, the authorities began going after activists, from senior leaders to even occasional participants. The chief prosecutor accused them of "conspiracy against national security" and the "dissemination of lies" in society. This was because after the officials had carefully scrutinized the handbook, the introduction, and all the material published and distributed by the campaign, they could not find even a single sentence that contravened an accepted tenet of Islam. This meant it would be impossible for the state to level charges of antagonism against Islam; there was not even enough to get a cleric who was on the state's payroll to declare that the activists were apostates. I had been watching out for this from the beginning. From that day at my office when Noushin and Parvin had brought over the campaign's draft documents, I had read them with an eye to what I suspected would someday happen.

When the activists went to court, I represented a number of them as their defense lawyer. In one of the trials, I openly challenged the state's claim that the women's work had somehow undermined national security.

"So a woman says she does not want her husband to have a second wife, and she refused to share her marital bed with another woman. Can you please explain to me how this will lead to Israel attacking Iran?" I asked the judge. He was not a cleric, but he had the required stubble and continuously played with a string of amber prayer beads.

The accusations were completely irrelevant and laughable. But with a justice system that had long ago lost its independence, that now walked in step with the whims of a higher, repressive authority, the fact that there was a court process meant very little. The judiciary sentenced both Noushin and Parvin to three years in prison, and a number of others also received convictions. Many who avoided prison found themselves later so harassed and vulnerable that they ended up leaving the country.

Despite this, I consider their work a success. New organizers continued to carry on their work, and kept on collecting signatures. The campaign transformed legal discrimination into a national social debate. The social aspect is key here, because the feminist activists managed to disentangle the women's question from the high politics of East versus West, Iran versus the world, and the Islamic Republic versus democracy. Topics like equal access to education for women, blood money, and polygamy became issues that ordinary women were engaged with, and as a result, in the elections to come they figured as a central part of candidates' campaign pledges.

There were some small legal victories as well. In 2008 the campaign pressured the parliament into amending the country's inheritance laws, ensuring that women could inherit their deceased husband's properties. That same year, the parliament also granted women the right to equal blood money in accidents covered by insurance companies. Members of parliament managed to block Articles 23 and 25 of the "Family Protection" bill the Ahmadinejad government had proposed in 2007, which would have enabled men to take additional wives without their first wife's consent and would have mandated that women pay a tax on their fiancé's *mehrieh* (dowry gift). None of this meant that Iran's lawmakers were suddenly liberal and concerned with women standing equally before the law, but they were sensitive enough to public opinion to see that society itself was growing more progressive. And, as is often the case in Iran, Iranians managed to either nudge the regime ahead or pull it along with them—I'm not sure which.

FOR FURTHER READING

Ebadi, Shirin. "Shirin Ebadi—Biographical." *Nobel Prize*, 2003, www.nobelprize.org/nobel_prizes/
     peace/laureates/2003/ebadi-bio.html.
Ebadi, Shirin. *The Golden Cage: Three Brothers, Three Choices, One Destiny.* Kales Press, 2011.
Ebadi, Shirin. *Until We Are Free: My Fight for Human Rights in Iran.* Random House, 2016.
Ebadi, Shirin, with Azadeh Moaveni. *Iran Awakening: A Memoir of Revolution and Hope.* Random
     House, 2006.
Encyclopedia Britannica. "Shirin Ebadi." *Encyclopedia Britannica*, 2 Jan. 2017, www.britannica.com/
     biography/Shirin-Ebadi.

Jeannette Urquilla

In El Salvador, where abortion is a crime, a woman who does not carry a pregnancy to term becomes a target of suspicion. This extends to women who miscarry—as was the case for Mayra Veronica Figueroa Marroquin—or birth a stillborn infant—as did Teodora del Carmen Vásquez—both of whom served jail time for "aggravated homicide." As the El Salvadoran social worker turned activist Jeannette Urquilla explains, poor women, who experience problems with their pregnancies and can't afford medical care or legal representation, are most at risk of being accused of the crime of *abortion*, a term that is used interchangeably with *homicide* by media and legal officials (Malkin). In Latin America, six small countries maintain a total restriction on abortion, including when the life of the woman is in danger—of these countries, El Salvador's punishments are the most severe (Malkin).

In the following op-ed, first published on Inter Press Service, a Global South news outlet, Urquilla enacts the transnational feminist practice of centering the perspective of the marginalized. Weaving women's stories with sobering statistics, Urquilla, executive director of Organización de Mujeres Salvadoreñas por la Paz (ORMUSA), underscores the ramifications that El Salvador's total abortion ban has on women, especially for women living in poverty. She further connects the abortion ban to the absence of full human rights for women in El Salvador, where femicide rates are the highest in the world. As Urquilla writes in a *Los Angeles Times* column, "El Salvador is one of the most dangerous countries in the world for women . . . A woman is murdered every 15 hours."

With ORMUSA, Urquilla strives to eradicate gender violence in El Salvador and to promote the equality and economic empowerment of women. She has been a vocal advocate of the necessity to decriminalize abortion and in this op-ed she advocates for passing legislation that would remove the ban in the case of rape, trafficking, incest, or when the health of the mother or fetus is at risk. While this legislation she describes did not pass, Urquilla continues to be a leading voice in an international campaign to lift an abortion ban that violates women's human rights and endangers their lives.

"El Salvador's Shameful Treatment of Women Who Miscarry"

Inter Press Service, 2016

Mayra Veronica Figueroa Marroquin (34) was released from prison earlier this month after serving time for what she argued was a miscarriage. Her sentence was reduced from 30 years to the 15 years she had already spent behind bars.

At age 19, she had been working as a housekeeper in 2003 when she was raped and subsequently suffered a miscarriage. She was convicted under El Salvador's abortion ban—one of the most extreme in the world.

Figueroa Marroquin is the second woman this year to have been freed from jail under such circumstances. Last month Teodora del Carmen Vasquez was also released 11 years into her 30 year sentence for what she stated was a stillbirth. Del Carmen Vasquez was waiting at the gates to meet the other woman this week.

Since 1998 under Article 133 of our penal code abortion has been completely illegal in El Salvador in all circumstances. Women have been sentenced to up to eight years in more typical cases, but if a judge decides that the abortion was in fact an "aggravated homicide" then a much higher sentence—up to 50 years—is passed down. And when a miscarriage takes place a woman is often at severe risk of being charged with this.

Pregnant women are often abandoned by the country's public hospitals and are often at severe risk of being arrested following a miscarriage. More often than not these women are also from economically disadvantaged backgrounds, which makes it difficult for them to pay for private medical care.

This means that instead of getting proper treatment if anything goes wrong during pregnancy they either do nothing at all and hope for the best—or they turn to unofficial covert channels, thereby putting themselves in serious physical danger.

The Alliance for Women's Health and Life previously reported that, between 2000 and 2014, 147 women from El Salvador were charged with abortion-related crimes. This year the Citizens' Association for the Decriminalisation of Abortion, of which my organization ORMUSA is a member, found that there are still 24 women in prison for what have been categorized as "homicidal" abortions. These women were all convicted in similar scenarios to the two that were released this year and many have already sent many years behind bars.

Not only do we need to ensure that these women are all released but also that the law on abortion is urgently changed. The Ministry of Health estimates that almost 20,000 abortions took place from 2005 to 2008. Regardless of whether abortion is legal or illegal it still takes place.

The only difference is the level of women's safety who undergo the procedure. The WHO confirms that 68,000 women die every year because of illegal and unsafe abortions. It is likely that a significant number of these deaths can be prevented.

El Salvador is one of only four countries in Latin America which bans abortion in all instances—including after rape and when a mother's health is at risk. It is also one of the most dangerous countries in the world to be a woman.

We have the highest rate of femicide globally—15.9 homicides for every 100,000 women. Between 2010 and 2017 we found that 3,138 women were murdered. This is not a country where the basic human rights of women are held in high regard.

We are hopeful though that things may be starting to change. The Supreme Court's decision to free these two women is encouraging. Last year the United Nations also urged El Salvador to review the discriminatory and harmful abortion law—at least in instances of any risk to the life and health of the pregnant woman, after rape, incest, or where there is severe fetal impairment.

We are still waiting to see if a 2016 parliamentary bill on reproductive rights will be debated and passed—a proposed reform of Article 133. In this bill abortion would be decriminalized in the following instances: after rape, statutory rape, or when the woman has been trafficked; where the fetus is likely to die, or when the pregnant woman's life is put at risk.

Despite having many allies such as the Ministry of Health as well as parliamentarians, resistance by many religious groups and politicians means that we still have a long way to go.

FOR FURTHER READING

"Abortion in Latin America and the Caribbean." *Guttmacher Institute*, 22 June 2018, www.guttmach er.org/fact-sheet/abortion-latin-america-and-caribbean.

Malkin, Elisabeth. "They Were Jailed for Miscarriages. Now, Campaign Aims to End Abortion Ban." *The New York Times*, 9 Apr. 2018, www.nytimes.com/2018/04/09/world/americas/el-salvador -abortion.html.

Organización de Mujeres Salvadoreñas por la Paz. ormusa.org/.

Urquilla, Jeannette. "What Happens When Abortion Is Illegal in All Circumstances." *Los Angeles Times*, 30 May 2017, www.latimes.com/opinion/op-ed/la-oe-urquilla-el-salvador-abortion-2017 0530-story.html.

Nancy Pelosi

Congresswoman Nancy Pelosi is formidable, regarded by many as the mightiest woman in US politics in the twenty-first century. She was elected the first female—and Italian American—Speaker of the House of Representatives in 2007, having served California's 12th District (San Francisco) since 1987, when a friend in Congress fell ill and encouraged Pelosi to run for her seat. Before then, Pelosi was a stay-at-home mom with five children born within six years, though still highly politically active. Pelosi consistently employs her ethos as a mother to both identify with voters and justify policy decisions and political tactics.

While Pelosi's role as a mother may appear to soften her image or to perhaps make her more "likeable," she complicates the nurturer trope by insisting that it was the organization, efficiency, and problem-solving earned by raising five children that contributed to her skills as a negotiator and dealmaker (McCarthy). Under her leadership, the 111th Congress passed Wall Street reforms, the Lilly Ledbetter Fair Pay Act, hate crimes legislation, and repealed Don't Ask, Don't Tell, the provision that prevented LGBTQ military from serving openly ("Full Biography").

In her role as Speaker, which began during George W. Bush's presidency, Pelosi became the focus of intense Republican ire. They often made Pelosi the target of sexist attacks, depicting her as a shrill, angry woman and positioning her as "the embodiment of the ideals that Republicans knew were anathema to much of middle America—a liberal, coastal elite whom they could paint as wanting to raise taxes and inflate the deficit" (Taylor).

This criticism only increased during the Obama administration, when Pelosi became a key figure in passing the Affordable Care Act (Obamacare) in 2010, which made health insurance more available and affordable to over forty-six million Americans (16 percent) previously uninsured ("Key Facts"). The battle for its passage was fierce, and the Affordable Care Act was immediately threatened when Democrats lost their majority in Congress in the 2010 election. Pelosi, then the Democratic leader but no longer Speaker, continued to fight for the ACA, and her speech here, delivered on the floor of Congress, responds to one of many attempts by Republicans to defund the Affordable Care Act. Pelosi's speech openly rebukes her Republican colleagues and extends empathy toward Americans who cannot afford to pay for their medical needs. She insists there is no gray area: legislators can either support the needs of Americans or they can align with the corporate greed of insurance companies. Invoking Representative Jack Kingston, Pelosi reminds lawmakers of their own privilege, urging them to provide health care for all Americans. She underscores her message with specific stories of Americans whose lives depend on the ACA, appealing to empathy in her audience. Ultimately, Pelosi's message is a populist refrain, insisting that it is Democrats who are truly in touch with the needs of the people.

Despite challenges from within her own party, Pelosi was reelected as Speaker of the House after Democrats regained the majority of the House of Representatives in the 2018 midterm elections. She continued to display her rhetorical prowess by repeatedly refusing President Trump's attempts to build a US-Mexico border wall. Analysts—and her own daughter—note that Pelosi would regard him as she did her children when having a tantrum, keeping calm and moving forward, reminding Americans that decisive political leadership and motherhood are not mutually exclusive (Taylor).

Pelosi Floor Speech on Republican Amendments Defunding Affordable Care Act

Congressional House Floor, 2011

Washington, DC, Democratic Leader Nancy Pelosi spoke on the House floor today on one of several amendments to the Republican Continuing Resolution that would defund the implementation of the Affordable Care Act. Below are the Leader's remarks:

Thank you, Mr. Chairman. I thank the gentlelady for yielding. I commend her for her leadership on the very important issue—the health and well-being of the American people.

I rise in opposition to the amendment that is on the floor today and also the underlying bill of which it is a part. The American people are desperate for jobs. They have sent us here to work together to create jobs. In the sixth week of this new majority, not one piece of legislation has come forward to create one job. Showing the lack of ideas to do so, the Republican majority has chosen instead to change the subject, to take up a bill of such consequence without hearings, without really an open process, to make amendments to it with the allusion of open debate.

And now, they come before us, again without hearings, in amendment form to this bill and say they want to repeal, have no funds go to enact provision of the health care bill, which was passed before. Let's talk about the consequences of your actions here today. What would it mean to people in our country if this amendment were to prevail? It may prevail on this floor, which is driving itself into irrelevance with the amendment process that is here, but that is another subject.

Let's talk about the subject of this amendment. Let's talk about what this means to America's families. Let's talk about a family that came before a hearing that we had earlier in January. We heard from Stacie Ritter. She has twelve-year-old twins. When those adorable little girls were four years old, they were both diagnosed with cancer. Imagine if that happened in your family. They faced years of treatment and recovery. Their mother said they were lucky they did have health insurance. But the additional cost of the care for these children drove their family into bankruptcy.

The children got well, thank God. But they had a preexisting medical condition for the rest of their lives—until this bill came along. And now, their mother was pleased to testify they are not to be the objects of discrimination because they have a preexisting medical condition. They will not face annual or lifetime caps on the benefits they receive. These healthy young girls now will be able to proceed in a healthy way, not discriminated against.

Or let's talk about Vernal Branch, a woman diagnosed with breast cancer fifteen years ago. Ever since, she has struggled to find health insurance because—even though she had cancer, and for the moment is free of cancer, and God willing forever free of cancer—she had a preexisting medical condition, which meant that she would be discriminated against in terms of getting health insurance—until this came along. Vernal Branch told us that the Affordable Care Act represented protection from the uncertainty and fear that came from being diagnosed and being denied health insurance coverage because of a past disease.

Passing this amendment would stop the reform and mean that 129 million Americans, like Vernal, 129 million Americans would lose coverage because of a preexisting medical condition. Do you understand what that means in the lives of these people?

And to our seniors—the subject has been brought up over and over again about our seniors. Claudette Therriault and her husband Richard are seniors on Medicare. Richard is a diabetic, and his insulin alone costs nearly $1,000 a month. When they fell into the donut hole, they were forced to choose between defaulting on the loan on their home or paying for Richard's health. As Claudette put it: "Well, we chose my husband's health." But changes that we made in this bill are starting to change the donut hole so families aren't forced to choose between paying their mortgage or paying for their medicine. Passing this amendment would mean that over 2.7 million Medicare beneficiaries would again fall into the donut hole, and Medicare would no longer be able to pay for the annual check-up for forty-four million seniors in our country.

Mr. Kingston says that his children are old enough, and they should be able to take care of themselves even though they are under twenty-six years old. Bravo for you. But that's not the way it is for many young people across the country even if they do have a job. You say they don't have insurance because they don't have a job. It may be news to you, but there are many, many, many working Americans who do not have health insurance—but they will under the Affordable Care Act. If this amendment were to pass, immediately, if it were to become law, immediately, all of those children who can now be on their parents' policy, if their parents are willing, would lose their health insurance.

With a job or without a job, these young people coming out of school are idealistic, ambitious. They want to follow their passions, their pursuits. That's what our founders told them they could do: life, liberty, pursuit of happiness. These young people want a healthier life to pursue their happiness, to choose a job not based on the health benefits it may or may not provide, but to choose an occupation which address their aspirations—not ours, theirs.

And so, I just want to repeat back to our colleagues something I heard them say over and over again. They said, "We didn't read the bill." Well, we did, but clearly, you did not. And I urge you to read the bill because, if you did, you would see that the bill puts medical decisions in the hands of patients and doctors, not your favorite insurance companies. You would see that it brings down the cost of prescription drugs for seniors. You would see that it ends the days of discrimination based on preexisting conditions and lifetime caps on care of children and families. You would see that no longer, under this bill, no longer would being a woman be a preexisting medical condition as it is now, as women are discriminated against in terms of price and access to insurance. You would see that it offers tax credits to millions of small businesses who choose to do right by their employees and offer insurance benefits.

It was for all of these Americans that we acted. It is for them that we stand here today to oppose this amendment. And if you read the bill, you will see contrary, contrary to misrepresentations that were set forth by those who do the bidding of the health insurance industry in our country, you would see what the bill does. You would see that it is about innovation. It's about prevention. It's about care, a healthier America, not just health care in America. It's about using the technologies of the future. It's about bringing health care closer to people where they live, to lower the cost, to improve the quality, to expand the access. You would see that it is a bill about the future. Instead of the misrepresentations about this, that, and the other thing, which I don't even want to repeat here, you would see that this is transformative for our country because it gives people—it gives people the liberty, again, to pursue their lives.

And so, I would like to know how many of you read the bill. We read it over and over again to each other, drilling down on different parts of it. So we know of what we speak when we come to this floor. And maybe if you knew more about it, you wouldn't be so quick to say: "We do not want to allow children to stay on their parents' policies. We do not want to end discrimination on the basis of preexisting condition for our children. We do not want to begin to close the donut hole. We do not want to have preventive medicines without cost and co-pay for our seniors." The list goes on and on. So that is what is happening here today.

This is, yet again, another example of our friends standing up for the insurance companies at the expense of the American people, standing up for the insurance company at the expense of the health and well-being of our country. It is, again, an example of Washington, DC, holding on to the special interests, status quo. It is again, this Congress saying to the American people: "We are here for the special interests. We are not here for the people's interests. To Stacie, we are not here for your two daughters. For Vernal, we are not here for women [or to end] being a woman [as] a preexisting condition." To Claudette and Richard, to say to them: "Too bad about your mortgage. If you can't pay your mortgage because you have to pay your medical bills, so be it."

I urge my colleagues to vote against this amendment which is another manifestation of the "so be it" attitude of some in Congress at the expense of many in our country.

For Further Reading

"Affordable Care Act." *Health Care*, n.d., https://www.healthcare.gov/glossary/affordable-care-act/.

"Full Biography." *Congresswoman Nancy Pelosi*, n.d., https://pelosi.house.gov/biography-0.

"Key Facts about the Uninsured Population." *Kaiser Family Foundation*, 18 Dec. 2018, https://www.kff.org/uninsured/fact-sheet/key-facts-about-the-uninsured-population/.

McCarthy, Ellen. "'Makes Going to Work Look Easy': Decades Before She Was House Speaker, Nancy Pelosi Had an Even Harder Job." *The Washington Post*, 12 Feb. 2019, https://www.washingtonpost.com/lifestyle/style/makes-going-to-work-look-easy-how-being-a-full-time-mom-prepared-nancy-pelosi-for-this-moment/2019/02/12/416cd85e-28bc-11e9-984d-9b8fba003e81_story.html?utm_term=.9ecf84599aa2.

Taylor, Jessica. "If Pelosi Returns as Speaker, so Would the GOP Playbook against Her." *NPR*, 12 Nov. 2018, https://www.npr.org/2018/11/28/671276005/if-pelosi-returns-as-speaker-so-would-the-gop-playbook-against-her.

Sonia Sotomayor

Justice Sonia Sotomayor was the third woman and first Latinx judge confirmed to the Supreme Court in 2009 after being nominated by President Barack Obama. She has been called fearless and tough—or, by critics, "abrupt and impatient"— descriptors that would likely not be used for white men (Stolberg). Before serving on the Supreme Court, in 1991 Justice Sotomayor was nominated by President George H. W. Bush to the United States District Court for the Southern District of New York, where she received accolades for a court decision that ended a Major League Baseball strike. She was later nominated by President Bill Clinton to the United States Court of Appeals for the Second Circuit.

Justice Sotomayor was born in 1954 in the housing projects of the Bronx to Puerto Rican native parents. Her mother was a nurse; her father a manual laborer ("Sotomayor"). Despite various childhood challenges, such as a diabetes diagnoses at age eight and the death of her father at age nine, Sotomayor's trajectory illustrates her vast accomplishments. She graduated valedictorian of her private Catholic high school and attended Princeton University, where she majored in history. Sotomayor attended Yale Law School, where she served as an editor for the *Yale Law Journal* and co-chaired the Latin American and Native American Students Association ("Sotomayor"). Upon graduating from Yale in 1979, she worked as an assistant district attorney in Manhattan before moving to private practice. Although Sotomayor confesses to feeling "not completely a part of the worlds I inhabit," she has established herself as a trailblazer in a profession historically unwelcoming to women and people of color (Stolberg). As Sotomayor said in a 2001 interview, "Each day on the bench I learn something new about the judicial process and about being a professional Latina woman in a world that sometimes looks at me with suspicion" (Stolberg).

As a Supreme Court justice, Sotomayor is best known for her responses to affirmative action cases. For instance, she wrote a fifty-eight-page dissent to the *Schuette v. Coalition to Defend Affirmative Action* decision, which held that it was constitutional to prohibit state universities from considering race in the admissions process. She sided with the "liberal majority" on key cases such as *Obergefell v. Hodges*, which legalized same-sex marriage.

Sotomayor's legal writing has been described as "technical" with "prosaic approachability," but her dissent in *Utah v. Strieff* is far from technical or distant ("Sonia"; Collins). In a 5–3 vote the Supreme Court narrowed the exclusionary rule of the Fourth Amendment, which prohibits unreasonable searches and seizures, allowing evidence obtained through unlawful means to be used against a defendant. Justice Sotomayor clearly and fervently expresses her dissent, providing a detailed narrative of how a police officer's illegal stop of white defendant Edward Strieff led to a search of his body and seizure of drugs.

In section IV, representing only her opinion, Sotomayor describes the indignity of being stopped without just cause, citing previous cases as evidence. She states explicitly that people of color endure such scrutiny more often than whites, connecting the issue to mass incarceration and systemic racism; she also links her statement to voices of black public intellectuals and invokes the Black Lives Matter movement. The urgency of her tone in a formal legal dissent in the highest court, as well as her directness on issues of race and the law, illustrate how intersectionality can impact even the most traditional forms of discourse.

Excerpt from *Utah v. Strieff* Dissent

2016

Cite as: 579 U. S. _____ (2016) 1 SOTOMAYOR, J., dissenting SUPREME COURT OF THE UNITED STATES No. 14–1373 UTAH, PETITIONER v. EDWARD JOSEPH STRIEFF JR. ON WRIT OF CERTIORARI TO THE SUPREME COURT OF UTAH [June 20, 2016] JUSTICE SOTOMAYOR, with whom JUSTICE GINSBURG joins as to Parts I, II, and III, dissenting.

The Court today holds that the discovery of a warrant for an unpaid parking ticket will forgive a police officer's violation of your Fourth Amendment rights. Do not be soothed by the opinion's technical language: This case allows the police to stop you on the street, demand your identification, and check it for outstanding traffic warrants—even if you are doing nothing wrong. If the officer discovers a warrant for a fine you forgot to pay, courts will now excuse his illegal stop and will admit into evidence anything he happens to find by searching you after arresting you on the warrant. Because the Fourth Amendment should prohibit, not permit, such misconduct, I dissent.

Minutes after Edward Strieff walked out of a South Salt Lake City home, an officer stopped him, questioned him, and took his identification to run it through a police database. The officer did not suspect that Strieff had done anything wrong. Strieff just happened to be the first person to leave a house that the officer thought might contain "drug activity." App. 16–19.

As the State of Utah concedes, this stop was illegal. App. 24. The Fourth Amendment protects people from "unreasonable searches and seizures." An officer breaches that protection when he detains a pedestrian to check his license without any evidence that the person is engaged in a crime. *Delaware v. Prouse*, 440 U. S. 648, 663 (1979); *Terry v. Ohio*, 392 U. S. 1, 21 (1968). The officer deepens the breach when he prolongs the detention just to fish further for evidence of wrongdoing. *Rodriguez v. United States*, 575 U. S. ___, ___–___ (2015) (slip op., at 6–7). In his search for lawbreaking, the officer in this case himself broke the law.

The officer learned that Strieff had a "small traffic warrant." App. 19. Pursuant to that warrant, he arrested Strieff and, conducting a search incident to the arrest, discovered methamphetamine in Strieff's pockets.

Utah charged Strieff with illegal drug possession. Before trial, Strieff argued that admitting the drugs into evidence would condone the officer's misbehavior. The methamphetamine, he reasoned, was the product of the officer's illegal stop. Admitting it would tell officers that unlawfully discovering even a "small traffic warrant" would give them license to search for evidence of unrelated offenses. The Utah Supreme Court unanimously agreed with Strieff. A majority of this Court now reverses. [...]

IV

Writing only for myself, and drawing on my professional dissenting experiences, I would add that unlawful "stops" have severe consequences much greater than the inconvenience suggested by the name. This Court has given officers an array of instruments to probe and examine you. When we condone officers' use of these devices without adequate cause, we give them reason to target pedestrians in an arbitrary manner. We also risk treating members of our communities as second-class citizens.

Although many Americans have been stopped for speeding or jaywalking, few may realize how degrading a stop can be when the officer is looking for more. This Court has allowed an officer to stop you for whatever reason he wants—so long as he can point to a pretextual justification after the fact. *Whren v. United States*, 517 U. S. 806, 813 (1996). That justification must provide specific reasons why the officer suspected you were breaking the law, *Terry*, 392 U. S., at 21, but it may factor in your ethnicity, *United States v. Brignoni-Ponce*, 422 U. S. 873, 886–887 (1975), where you live, *Adams v. Williams*, 407 U. S. 143, 147 (1972), what you were wearing, *United States v. Sokolow*, 490 U. S. 1, 4–5 (1989), and how you behaved, *Illinois v. Wardlow*, 528 U. S. 119, 124–125 (2000). The officer does not even need to know which law you might have broken so long as he can later point to any possible infraction—even one that is minor, unrelated, or ambiguous. *Devenpeck v. Alford*, 543 U. S. 146, 154–155 (2004); *Heien v. North Carolina*, 574 U. S. ___ (2014).

The indignity of the stop is not limited to an officer telling you that you look like a criminal. See [Charles E.] Epp, *Pulled Over*, at 5. The officer may next ask for your "consent" to inspect your bag or purse without telling you that you can decline. See *Florida v. Bostick*, 501 U. S. 429, 438 (1991). Regardless of your answer, he may order you to stand "helpless, perhaps facing a wall with [your] hands raised." *Terry*, 392 U. S., at 17. If the officer thinks you might be dangerous, he may then "frisk" you for weapons. This involves more than just a pat down. As onlookers pass by, the officer may "feel with sensitive fingers every portion of [your] body. A thorough search [may] be made of [your] arms and armpits, waistline and back, the groin and area about the testicles, and entire surface of the legs down to the feet." Id., at 17n13.

The officer's control over you does not end with the stop. If the officer chooses, he may handcuff you and take you to jail for doing nothing more than speeding, jaywalking, or "driving [your] pickup truck . . . with [your] 3-year-old son and 5-year-old daughter . . . without [your] seatbelt fastened." *Atwater v. Lago Vista*, 532 U. S. 318, 323–324 (2001). At the jail, he can fingerprint you, swab DNA from the inside of your mouth, and force you to "shower with a delousing agent" while you "lift [your] tongue, hold out [your] arms, turn around, and lift [your] genitals." *Florence v. Board of Chosen Freeholders of County of Burlington*, 566 U. S. ___, ___–___ (2012) (slip op., at 2–3); *Maryland v. King*, 569 U. S. ___, ___ (2013) (slip op., at 28). Even if you are innocent, you will now join the 65 million Americans with an arrest record and experience the "civil death" of discrimination by employers, landlords, and whoever else conducts a background check. [Gabriel J.] Chin, "The New Civil Death," 160 U. Pa. L. Rev. [*University of Pennsylvania Law Review*] 1789, 1805 (2012); see J. Jacobs, *The Eternal Criminal Record*, 33–51 (2015); [Katheryne M.] Young and [Joan] Petersilia, "Keeping Track," 129, Harv. L. Rev. [*Harvard Law Review*] 1318, 1341–1357 (2016). And, of course, if you fail to pay bail or appear for court, a judge will issue a warrant to render you "arrestable on sight" in the future. A. Goffman, *On the Run*, 196 (2014).

This case involves a *suspicionless* stop, one in which the officer initiated this chain of events without justification. As the Justice Department notes, *supra*, at 8, many innocent people are subjected to the humiliations of these unconstitutional searches. The white defendant in this case shows that anyone's dignity can be violated in this dissenting manner. See M. Gottschalk, *Caught*, 119–138 (2015). But it is no secret that people of color are disproportionate victims of this type of scrutiny. See M. Alexander, *The New Jim Crow*, 95–136 (2010). For generations, black and brown parents have given their children "the talk"—instructing them never to run down the street; always keep your hands where they can be seen; do not even think of talking back to a stranger—all out of fear of how an officer with a gun will react to them. See, e.g., W. E. B. Du Bois, *The Souls of Black Folk* (1903); J. Baldwin, *The Fire Next Time* (1963); T. Coates, *Between the World and Me* (2015). By legitimizing the conduct that produces this double consciousness, this case tells everyone, white and black, guilty and innocent, that an officer can verify your legal status at any time. It says that your body is subject to invasion while courts excuse the violation of your rights. It implies that you are not a citizen of a democracy but the subject of a carceral state, just waiting to be cataloged. We must not pretend that the countless people who are routinely targeted by police are "isolated." They are the canaries in the coal mine whose deaths, civil and literal, warn us that no one can breathe in this atmosphere. See L. Guinier and G. Torres, *The Miner's Canary*, 274–283 (2002). They are the ones who recognize that unlawful police stops corrode all our civil liberties and threaten all our lives. Until their voices matter too, our justice system will continue to be anything but.

I dissent.

For Further Reading

Collins, Laura. "Number Nine." *The New Yorker*, 11 Jan. 2010, www.newyorker.com/magazine/2010/01/11/number-nine.

Daum, Meghan. "My White Privilege Meets Sonia Sotomayor's Scathing Attack on Police Power." *Los Angeles Times*, 23 June 2016, www.latimes.com/opinion/op-ed/la-oe-daum-sotomayor-dissent-20160623-snap-story.html.

Ford, Matt. "Justice Sotomayor's Ringing Dissent." *The Atlantic*, 20 June 2016, www.theatlantic.com/politics/archive/2016/06/utah-streiff-sotomayor/487922/.

Gutgold, Nichola. *The Rhetoric of Supreme Court Women: From Obstacles to Options*. Lexington Books, 2012.

"Sonia Sotomayor." Oyez, 7 Sept. 2018, www.oyez.org/justices/sonia_sotomayor.

Stolberg, Sheryl Gay. "Sotomayor: A Trailblazer and a Dreamer." *The New York Times*, 12 May 2009, www.nytimes.com/2009/05/27/us/politics/27websotomayor.html.

"Utah v. Strieff." Oyez, 7 Sept. 2018, www.oyez.org/cases/2015/14-1373.

Maxine Waters

The longest-serving black woman in Congress, Los Angeles representative Maxine Waters—dubbed Auntie Maxine by millennials—is famous for breaking decorum and speaking her truth. Her sharp rhetoric and incisive wit have garnered her icon status, with her image and words appearing on memes, T-shirts, and protest signs. The activist Rashad Robinson observes, "People are shaking their heads when she talks, and they are saying, 'Thank God someone said that.' I think for many young black folks, they have that sort of auntie or matriarch in their family that sort of says it like it is" (Wire).

Waters is the child of a strong matriarch, number five of thirteen children raised by a single mother in St. Louis. At age thirteen, she began working in factories and restaurants, seeding her lifetime commitment to women, children, people of color, and the poor. After Waters's family moved to California, she attended college and became a public school teacher. Waters won her first seat in Congress in 1990. She has been elected for fifteen consecutive terms, consistently earning more than 70 percent of the vote. In 2019 she became the first African American and woman to chair the influential House Financial Services Committee. She has provided legislative leadership on various issues, including US divestment in South African apartheid, affirmative action, childhood abuse prevention training, and support of women veterans.

Waters is also a fierce critic of the Trump administration. In the following speech, which condemns the administration's "unconscionable" separation of immigrant parents from their children (see Edwidge Danticat's contribution to this volume), she directs her audience to put pressure on the Trump administration: "Create a crowd and you push back on them and you tell them they're not welcome anymore, anywhere." In response, Trump tweeted that Waters is "an extraordinarily low IQ person," and claimed she called for harm to his supporters. Waters clarified that she believes in "peaceful protests" and did not "call for the harm of anybody," but a firestorm ensued, leading to death threats, hate mail, and cancellation of her public appearances (Brown).

Even Democratic colleagues, including Representatives Nancy Pelosi and Chuck Schumer, rebuked Waters, reminding her of the need for civility. Calls for "civility" have long been deployed to silence people of color, requiring them to be polite and respectful in the face of gross mistreatment (Newkirk). Furthermore, black women who speak out are often summarily disregarded as "angry," "unhinged," or "crazy," terms all regularly attached to Waters (Traister). A collective of black female leaders and allies made just this point to Pelosi and Schumer in a letter expressing "profound indignation and deep disappointment" over their failure to defend Waters. "That failure was further compounded by your decision to unfairly deride her as being 'uncivil' and 'un-American'" (Morin).

A group of white women also posted an open letter to Pelosi, requesting she apologize to Waters: "When you attack a Black woman for speaking out about injustice, and when you call for 'civility' in the face of blatant racism, you invoke a long history of white supremacist power . . . To our great discredit, white women continue to act far too often in ways that support white supremacy" (Jacobson). Within a week, the letter circulated widely, gathering more than six thousand signatures (Traister). Pelosi later released a statement condemning threats to Waters's safety (Morin).

As for Waters's response to the backlash, it was true to form: "I know that there are those who are talking about censuring me, talking about kicking me out of Congress, talking about shooting me, talking about hanging me. All I have to say is this, if you shoot me you better shoot straight, there's nothing like a wounded animal" (Gstalter). Her audience responded with cheers.

Speech at Los Angeles Immigration Rally

2018

How dare you separate children from their parents? How dare you pull children out of the arms of their mothers? How dare you lie and say you couldn't do anything about it? You're the one who caused it and you're the one that we're going to make to turn it back because what you are doing now is lying, lying, lying. The American people have put up with this president long enough. What more do we need to see? What more lies do we need to hear? It is time for us to say, even though there are those that don't want us to say it, Mr. President, you need to be impeached.

He has done more than is needed to be impeached, but putting this on top of all that he has done—his alignment with Russia and Putin, his love of the dictators of the world, how he has not said one word about the fact that they tapped into our DNC [Democratic National Convention], undermined our democratic process. He has not said one thing about it, but he can wrap his arms around another dictator, Kim Jong Un, and tell us we ought to swallow it. We are through with you, Mr. President. We are not going to swallow it.

We are not going to swallow it. You have disrespected all of us. You have violated all of us. And now, you have sacrificed our children for your aims and your goals just because you want to build a wall. Mr. President, there will be no wall built on the back of this [inaudible]. You lied. You lied and you said you were going to make Mexico pay for it. They're not going to pay for it. We are not going to pay for it. You're going to find these children, you're going to reconnect them with their parents and we are going to get you out of office.

Ladies and gentleman, I thank you so much for coming out here because history is not going to be kind to this administration. But we want history to recall that we stood up. That we pushed back. That we fought. That we did not consider ourselves victims of this president. History will recall that while he tried to step on all of us, we kicked him in his rear and we stepped on him.

And so the president, who lies all the time, who would change on the drop of a dime. The president is watching what is going on. The only reason he came up with this fake initiative of his is to try and say to the people that he's seen come out in huge numbers, "Okay, okay, okay. I'm sorry. I'm scared. I'm going to back it up." But he didn't back it up enough. He didn't back it up enough because that initiative that he's put out has not defined how they're going to connect these children with their parents. They don't know where our children are. They don't have numbers or identifications where they can connect parents, and some parents have been deported and their children are still here somewhere. That's unconscionable. And between this president and that racist attorney general Jeff Sessions and John Kelly, they all said that they were going to do this. They said publicly that they were going to separate these children from their parents in an issue that they have tried to use to get that wall built so they can intimidate all of us. But again, the message has to be: Mr. President, we are not afraid of you, we are not afraid of Jeff Sessions, we are not afraid of John Kelly, we are not afraid of your administration, and while you think you have gotten away with everything that you've done, we are going to show you that you haven't gotten away with anything. We want the children back. We want them connected to their parents. We want it done now. We are going to insist on it. If you think we're rallying out here, you ain't seen nothing yet.

Already, you have members of your cabinet that have been booed out of restaurants, who have protesters taking up at their house who sang, "No peace, no sleep. No peace, no sleep." And guess what, we're going to win this battle because while you try and quote the Bible, Jeff Sessions and others, you really don't know the Bible. God is on our side. On the side of the children, on the side of what's right, on the side of what's honorable, on the side of understanding that if we can't protect the children, we can't protect anybody. And so let's stay the course. Let's make sure we show up wherever we have to show up. And if you see anybody from that cabinet in a restaurant, in a department store, at a gasoline station, you get out and you create a crowd and you push back on them and you tell them they're not welcome anymore, anywhere. We've got to get the children connected to their parents. The children are suffering. We don't know if the shock that they are going through can ever be overcome. We don't know what damage has been done to these children. All that we know is they're in cages, they're in prisons, I don't care what they call it, that's where they are. And Mr. President, we will see you every day, every hour of the day, everywhere that we are to let you know you cannot get away with this. Thank you so very much.

FOR FURTHER READING

"Biography." *Congresswoman Maxine Waters*, n.d., waters.house.gov/about-maxine/biography.

Gstalter, Morgan. "Maxine Waters Responds to Death Threats: 'You Better Shoot Straight.'" *The Hill*, 1 July 2018, thehill.com/homenews/house/395016-maxine-waters-responds-to-serious-death -threats-you-better-shoot-straight.

Morin, Rebecca. "Black Female Leaders Criticize Pelosi, Schumer for 'Failure to Protect' Waters." *Politico*, 5 July 2018, www.politico.com/story/2018/07/04/black-female-leaders-waters-pelosi -schumer-trump-693967.

Newkirk, Vann R. "Sometimes There Are More Important Goals Than Civility." *The Atlantic*, 5 Dec. 2016, www.theatlantic.com/politics/archive/2016/12/discussing-racism-white-voters /509528/.

Traister, Rebecca. *Good and Mad: The Revolutionary Power of Women's Anger*. Simon & Schuster, 2019.

Wire, Sarah D. "How Maxine Waters Became 'Auntie Maxine' in the Age of Trump." *Los Angeles Times*, 30 Apr. 2017, www.latimes.com/politics/la-pol-ca-maxine-waters-20170430-htmlstory .html.

Michelle Obama

The *New York Times* called Michelle Obama the breakout voice of the 2016 presidential election, and the *Nation* lauded her for delivering "the most powerful speech of the 2016 campaign" (Nichols). That speech was delivered in New Hampshire on October 11, 2016, in a campaign event for the presidential nominee Hillary Clinton.

It was a moment of cultural paradox for women. In many ways, the outlook appeared bright. Obama had just participated in White House celebrations of International Women's Day and of her Let Girls Learn initiative. National pollsters agreed that we were on the cusp of electing our first female president. At the same time, Americans had just heard an eleven-year-old recording—soon after dubbed the "Trump Tape"—of the presidential candidate Donald Trump bragging to *Access Hollywood*'s Billy Bush that "when you're a star," women let you do anything: "Grab 'em by the pussy. You can do anything."

For a First Lady who rallied behind women's causes and mothered two daughters, the exigence for her speech was clear. "I have to tell you that I can't stop thinking about this. It has shaken me to my core in a way that I couldn't have predicted," Obama shared. So she revised her "normal campaign speech" to address a political moment that was anything but normal. "This is disgraceful. It is intolerable. And it doesn't matter what party you belong to . . . no woman deserves to be treated this way. None of us deserves this kind of abuse."

Obama is a graduate of Princeton University and Harvard Law School and left corporate law after four years for community outreach in the public sector. During her eight years as First Lady, she advocated for childhood nutrition and exercise, military families, and girls' education. She nicknamed herself "Mom in Chief." But this mom was also a "potent weapon" (Davis) on the campaign trail. Barack Obama dubbed her "the closer" on his 2008 march to Washington; she had a unique ability to convince people to register to vote, to go the polls, and to volunteer (Davis). When Obama stepped up to the podium in Manchester, New Hampshire, however, it was to accomplish more than to support her candidate. It was to reach the women for whom words like Trump's were all too familiar.

In an unusual move for a stump speech, Obama offers a testimony, an emotion-filled account, of how it feels to be a woman and to hear yourself disparaged or objectified. Using direct address, she forms a collective with the women in the crowd, pointing to a shared experience of "that sick sinking feeling" when vulgar words are addressed to you, or a man stands too close or stares too long. As Chris Cillizza of the *Washington Post* wrote, "She expressed . . . emotions in ways you rarely see any politician (or private citizen do)—particularly one as well-known as Obama."

But Obama doesn't stop there. As she famously proclaimed in her speech at the 2016 National Democratic Convention: "When they go low, we go high!" She encourages this collective to "do what women have always done in this country"—to get to work, to use their anger to act, to take advantage of rights—to vote, to speak out—that women haven't always held. Finally, Obama calls her listeners to something higher than politics: to decency and morality. America's children are watching, and the world is watching, she asserts. "If we have a president who routinely degrades women, who brags about sexually assaulting women, then how can we maintain our moral authority in the world? How can we continue to be a beacon of freedom and justice and human dignity?" Her questions continue to reverberate.

Remarks by the First Lady at Hillary for America Campaign Event in Manchester, New Hampshire

2016

MRS. OBAMA: My goodness! (Applause.) You guys are fired up! (Applause.) Well, let me just say hello, everyone. (Applause.) I am so thrilled to be here with you all today in New Hampshire. This is like home to me, and this day—thank you for a beautiful fall day. You just ordered this day up for me, didn't you? (Applause.) It's great to be here. Let me start by thanking your fabulous governor, your next US senator, Maggie Hassan. (Applause.)

I want to thank her for that lovely introduction. I also want to recognize your congresswoman, Annie McKlane Kuster, who's a dear, dear friend. (Applause.) Your soon-to-be congresswoman once again, Carol Shea Porter (applause), all of whom have been just terrific friends to us. And your executive council and candidate for governor, Colin Van Ostern. (Applause.) And, of course, thanks to all of you for taking the time to be here today. (Applause.)

AUDIENCE MEMBER: We love you! (Applause.)

MRS. OBAMA: Thanks so much. That's very sweet of you. I love you guys too. I can't believe it's just a few weeks before Election Day, as we come together to support the next president and vice president of the United States, Hillary Clinton and Tim Kaine! (Applause.) And New Hampshire is going to be important, as always.

So I'm going to get a little serious here, because I think we can all agree that this has been a rough week in an already rough election. This week has been particularly interesting for me personally because it has been a week of profound contrast.

See, on Tuesday, at the White House, we celebrated the International Day of the Girl and Let Girls Learn. (Applause.) And it was a wonderful celebration. It was the last event that I'm going to be doing as First Lady for Let Girls Learn. And I had the pleasure of spending hours talking to some of the most amazing young women you will ever meet, young girls here in the US and all around the world. And we talked about their hopes and their dreams. We talked about their aspirations. See, because many of these girls have faced unthinkable obstacles just to attend school, jeopardizing their personal safety, their freedom, risking the rejection of their families and communities.

So I thought it would be important to remind these young women how valuable and precious they are. I wanted them to understand that the measure of any society is how it treats its women and girls. (Applause.) And I told them that they deserve to be treated with dignity and respect, and I told them that they should disregard anyone who demeans or devalues them, and that they should make their voices heard in the world. And I walked away feeling so inspired, just like I'm inspired by all the young people here (applause) and I was so uplifted by these girls. That was Tuesday.

And now, here I am, out on the campaign trail in an election where we have consistently been hearing hurtful, hateful language about women—language that has been painful for so many of us, not just as women, but as parents trying to protect our children and raise them to be caring, respectful adults, and as citizens who think that our nation's leaders should meet basic standards of human decency. (Applause.)

The fact is that in this election, we have a candidate for president of the United States who, over the course of his lifetime and the course of this campaign, has said things about women that are so shocking, so demeaning that I simply will not repeat anything here today. And last week, we saw this candidate actually bragging about sexually assaulting women. And I can't believe that I'm saying that a candidate for president of the United States has bragged about sexually assaulting women.

And I have to tell you that I can't stop thinking about this. It has shaken me to my core in a way that I couldn't have predicted. So while I'd love nothing more than to pretend like this isn't happening, and to come out here and do my normal campaign speech, it would be dishonest and disingenuous to me to just move on to the next thing like this was all just a bad dream.

This is not something that we can ignore. It's not something we can just sweep under the rug as just another disturbing footnote in a sad election season. Because this was not just a "lewd conversation." This wasn't just locker-room banter. This was a powerful individual speaking freely and openly about sexually predatory behavior, and actually bragging about kissing and groping women, using language so obscene that many of us were worried about our children hearing it when we turn on the TV.

And to make matters worse, it now seems very clear that this isn't an isolated incident. It's one of countless examples of how he has treated women his whole life. And I have to tell you that I listen to all of this and I feel it so personally, and I'm sure that many of you do too, particularly the women. The shameful comments about our bodies. The disrespect of our ambitions and intellect. The belief that you can do anything you want to a woman.

It is cruel. It's frightening. And the truth is, it hurts. It hurts. It's like that sick, sinking feeling you get when you're walking down the street minding your own business and some guy yells out vulgar words about your body. Or when you see that guy at work that stands just a little too close, stares a little too long, and makes you feel uncomfortable in your own skin.

It's that feeling of terror and violation that too many women have felt when someone has grabbed them, or forced himself on them and they've said no but he didn't listen—something that we know happens on college campuses and countless other places every single day. It reminds us of stories we heard from our mothers and grandmothers about how, back in their day, the boss could say and do whatever he pleased to the women in the office, and even though they worked so hard, jumped over every hurdle to prove themselves, it was never enough.

We thought all of that was ancient history, didn't we? And so many have worked for so many years to end this kind of violence and abuse and disrespect, but here we are, in 2016, and we're hearing these exact same things every day on the campaign trail. We are drowning in it. And all of us are doing what women have always done: We're trying to keep our heads above water, just trying to get through it, trying to pretend like this doesn't really bother us maybe because we think that admitting how much it hurts makes us as women look weak. Maybe we're afraid to be that vulnerable. Maybe we've grown accustomed to swallowing these emotions and staying quiet, because we've seen that people often won't take our word over his. Or maybe we don't want to believe that there are still people out there who think so little of us as women. Too many are treating this as just another day's headline, as if our outrage is overblown or unwarranted, as if this is normal, just politics as usual.

But, New Hampshire, be clear: This is not normal. This is not politics as usual. (Applause.) This is disgraceful. It is intolerable. And it doesn't matter what party you belong to—Democrat, Republican, Independent—no woman deserves to be treated this way. None of us deserves this kind of abuse. (Applause.)

And I know it's a campaign, but this isn't about politics. It's about basic human decency. It's about right and wrong. (Applause.) And we simply cannot endure this, or expose our children to this any longer—not for another minute, and let alone for four years. (Applause.) Now is the time for all of us to stand up and say enough is enough. (Applause.) This has got to stop right now. (Applause.)

Because consider this: If all of this is painful to us as grown women, what do you think this is doing to our children? What message are our little girls hearing about who they should look like, how they should act? What lessons are they learning about their value as professionals, as human beings, about their dreams and aspirations? And how is this affecting men and boys in this country? Because I can tell you that the men in my life do not talk about women like this. And I know that my family is not unusual. (Applause.) And to dismiss this as everyday locker-room talk is an insult to decent men everywhere. (Applause.)

The men that you and I know don't treat women this way. They are loving fathers who are sickened by the thought of their daughters being exposed to this kind of vicious language about women. They are husbands and brothers and sons who don't tolerate women being treated and demeaned and disrespected. (Applause.) And like us, these men are worried about the impact this election is having on our boys who are looking for role models of what it means to be a man. (Applause.)

In fact, someone recently told me a story about their six-year-old son who one day was watching the news—they were watching the news together. And the little boy, out of the blue, said, "I think Hillary Clinton will be president." And his mom said, "Well, why do you say that?" And this little six-year-old said, "Because the other guy called someone a piggy, and," he said, "you cannot be president if you call someone a piggy." (Applause.)

So even a six-year-old knows better. A six-year-old knows that this is not how adults behave. This is not how decent human beings behave. And this is certainly not how someone who wants to be president of the United States behaves. (Applause.)

Because let's be very clear: Strong men—men who are truly role models—don't need to put down women to make themselves feel powerful. (Applause.) People who are truly strong lift others up. People who are truly powerful bring others together. And that is what we need in our next president. We need someone who is a uniting force in this country. We need someone who will heal the wounds that divide us, someone who truly cares about us and our children, someone with strength and compassion to lead this country forward. (Applause.)

And let me tell you, I'm here today because I believe with all of my heart that Hillary Clinton will be that president. (Applause.)

See, we know that Hillary is the right person for the job because we've seen her character and commitment not just in this campaign, but over the course of her entire life. The fact is that Hillary embodies so many of the values that we try so hard to teach our young people. We tell our young people, "Work hard in school, get a good education." We encourage them to use that education to help others—which is exactly what Hillary did with her college and law degrees, advocating for kids with disabilities, fighting for children's health care as First Lady, affordable child care in the Senate. (Applause.)

We teach our kids the value of being a team player, which is what Hillary exemplified when she lost the 2008 election and actually agreed to work for her opponent as our secretary of state (applause) earning sky-high approval ratings serving her country once again. (Applause.)

We also teach our kids that you don't take shortcuts in life, and you strive for meaningful success in whatever job you do. Well, Hillary has been a lawyer, a law professor, First Lady of Arkansas, First Lady of the United States, a US senator, secretary of state. And she has been successful in every role, gaining more experience and exposure to the presidency than any candidate in our lifetime—more than Barack, more than Bill. (Applause.) And, yes, she happens to be a woman. (Applause.)

And finally, we teach our kids that when you hit challenges in life, you don't give up, you stick with it. Well, during her four years as secretary of state alone, Hillary has faced her share of challenges. She's traveled to 112 countries, negotiated a ceasefire, a peace agreement, a release of dissidents. She spent eleven hours testifying before a congressional committee. We know that when things get tough, Hillary doesn't complain. She doesn't blame others. She doesn't abandon ship for something easier. No, Hillary Clinton has never quit on anything in her life. (Applause.)

So in Hillary, we have a candidate who has dedicated her life to public service, someone who has waited her turn and helped out while waiting. (Applause.) She is an outstanding mother. She has raised a phenomenal young woman. She is a loving, loyal wife. She's a devoted daughter who cared for her mother until her final days. And if any of us had raised a daughter like Hillary Clinton, we would be so proud. We would be proud. (Applause.)

And regardless of who her opponent might be, no one could be more qualified for this job than Hillary—no one. And in this election, if we turn away from her, if we just stand by and allow her opponent to be elected, then what are we teaching our children about the values they should hold, about the kind of life they should lead? What are we saying?

In our hearts, we all know that if we let Hillary's opponent win this election, then we are sending a clear message to our kids that everything they're seeing and hearing is perfectly okay. We are validating it. We are endorsing it. We're telling our sons that it's okay to humiliate women. We're telling our daughters that this is how they deserve to be treated. We're telling all our kids that bigotry and bullying are perfectly acceptable in the leader of their country. Is that what we want for our children?

AUDIENCE: No!

MRS. OBAMA: And remember, we won't just be setting a bad example for our kids, but for our entire world. Because for so long, America has been a model for countries across the globe, pushing them to educate their girls, insisting that they give more rights to their women. But if we have a president who routinely degrades women, who brags about sexually assaulting women, then how can we maintain our moral authority in the world? How can we continue to be a beacon of freedom and justice and human dignity? (Applause.)

Well, fortunately, New Hampshire, here's the beauty: We have everything we need to stop this madness. You see, while our mothers and grandmothers were often powerless to change their circumstances, today, we as women have all the power we need to determine the outcome of this election. (Applause.)

We have knowledge. We have a voice. We have a vote. And on November the 8th, we as women, we as Americans, we as decent human beings can come together and declare that enough is enough, and we do not tolerate this kind of behavior in this country. (Applause.)

Remember this: In 2012 women's votes were the difference between Barack winning and losing in key swing states, including right here in New Hampshire. (Applause.) So for anyone who might be thinking that your one vote doesn't really matter, or that one person can't really make a difference, consider this: Back in 2012 Barack won New Hampshire by about forty thousand votes, which sounds like a lot. But when you break that number down, the difference between winning and losing this state was only sixty-six votes per precinct. Just take that in. If sixty-six people each precinct had gone the other way, Barack would have lost.

So each of you right here today could help swing an entire precinct and win this election for Hillary just by getting yourselves, your families, and your friends and neighbors out to vote. You can do it right here. (Applause.) But you could also help swing an entire precinct for Hillary's opponent with a protest vote or by staying home out of frustration.

Because here's the truth: Either Hillary Clinton or her opponent will be elected president this year. And if you vote for someone other than Hillary, or if you don't vote at all, then you are helping to elect her opponent. And just think about how you will feel if that happens. Imagine waking up on November the 9th and looking into the eyes of your daughter or son, or looking into your own eyes as you stare into the mirror. Imagine how you'll feel if you stayed home, or if you didn't do everything possible to elect Hillary.

We simply cannot let that happen. We cannot allow ourselves to be so disgusted that we just shut off the TV and walk away. And we can't just sit around wringing our hands. Now, we need to recover from our shock and depression and do what women have always done in this country. We need you to roll up your sleeves. We need to get to work. (Applause.) Because remember this: When they go low, we go—

AUDIENCE: High!

MRS. OBAMA: Yes, we do. (Applause.) And voting ourselves is a great start, but we also have to step up and start organizing. So we need you to make calls, and knock on doors, and get folks to the polls on Election Day, and sign up to volunteer with one of the Hillary campaign folks who are here today just waiting for you to step up. (Applause.)

And, young people and not-so-young people, get on social media. (Applause.) Share your own story of why this election matters, why it should matter for all people of conscience in this country. There is so much at stake in this election.

See, the choice you make November 8th could determine whether we have a president who treats people with respect—or not. A president who will fight for kids, for good schools, for good jobs for our families—or not. A president who thinks that women deserve the right to make our own choices about our bodies and our health—or not. (Applause.) That's just a little bit of what's at stake.

So we cannot afford to be tired or turned off. And we cannot afford to stay home on Election Day. Because on November the 8th, we have the power to show our children that America's greatness comes from recognizing the innate dignity and worth of all our people. On November the 8th, we can show our children that this country is big enough to have a place for us all—men and women, folks of every background and walk of life—and that each of us is a precious part of this great American story, and we are always stronger together. (Applause.)

On November 8th, we can show our children that here in America, we reject hatred and fear—(applause)—and in difficult times, we don't discard our highest ideals. No, we rise up to meet them. We rise up to perfect our union. We rise up to defend our blessings of liberty. We rise up to embody the values of equality and opportunity and sacrifice that have always made this country the greatest nation on earth. (Applause.)

That is who we are. (Applause.) And don't ever let anyone tell you differently. (Applause.) Hope is important. Hope is important for our young people. And we deserve a president who can see those truths in us—a president who can bring us together and bring out the very best in us. Hillary Clinton will be that president. (Applause.)

So for the next twenty-six days, we need to do everything we can to help her and Tim Kaine win this election. I know I'm going to be doing it. Are you with me? (Applause.) Are you all with me? (Applause.) You ready to roll up your sleeves? Get to work knocking on doors? All right, let's get to work. Thank you all. God bless. (Applause.)

For Further Reading

Cillizza, Chris. "Michelle Obama's Speech on Donald Trump Was Remarkable." *The Washington Post*, 13 Oct. 2016, www.washingtonpost.com/news/the-fix/wp/2016/10/13/michelle-obama-just -put-a-huge-and-emotional-exclamation-point-on-trumps-hot-mic-tape/.

Davis, Julie Hirschfeld. "The Closer: Michelle Obama." *The New York Times*, 5 Nov. 2016, www .nytimes.com/2016/11/06/us/politics/michelle-obama-2016-presidential-election-first-lady .html.

Nichols, John. "Michelle Obama Just Delivered the Most Powerful Speech of the 2016 Campaign." *The Nation*, 14 Oct. 2016, www.thenation.com/article/michelle-obama-just-delivered-the-most -powerful-speech-of-the-2016-campaign/.

Obama, Michelle. *Becoming*. Crown, 2018.

Obama, Michelle. "Transcript: Michelle Obama's Convention Speech." *NPR*, 4 Sept. 2012, www.npr .org/2012/09/04/160578836/transcript-michelle-obamas-convention-speech.

Rogak, Lisa, and Michelle Obama. *Michelle Obama: In Her Own Words*. PublicAffairs, 2009.

Jennifer Bailey

"May we bear witness to the pain and not turn from it," wrote Reverend Jennifer Bailey in a 2018 Holy Week reflection ("May We"). This prayer speaks to the center of Bailey's Christian message: to turn toward those who are oppressed and marginalized and to serve on their behalf. Bailey is a millennial minister, who was educated at Tufts and Vanderbilt and then ordained by the African Methodist Episcopal Church. The founder of the Faith Matters Network, Bailey was named one of "Fifteen Leaders to Watch" by the Center for American Progress. The Faith Matters Network unites faith leaders marginalized in their religious traditions in order to amplify their voices, issue a unified call for justice, and train future leaders.

Bailey opens her *Huffington Post* column with the lyrics of the 1939 Billie Holiday song "Strange Fruit," whose lyrics about white brutalization of black bodies continue to resound more than seventy-five years later. Bailey bears witness to this historical and contemporary pain by naming the black lives lost to police brutality in the recent past. While the Christian minister is often expected to issue messages of hope and reconciliation, she contends that there must be room to acknowledge pain and sorrow. Shared lament, Bailey argues, is a needed offering to those who suffer. Too often, however, the Christian church has remained silent about the pain and suffering experienced by the black community. For this reason, Bailey implores readers to bear witness to the pain caused by US Christianity—namely, to Christianity's complicit relationship to white supremacy. "For centuries," she writes, "the name of Christ was used as a tool to inflict physical, psychological, economic, and social violence on black people." While this racism is often viewed as a shameful relic of our past, Bailey challenges Christians to consider their present response to the devaluing of black lives in the face of police brutality and institutionalized racism.

Given the complicated relationship between Christianity and racism, Bailey recognizes that it would be easy for people of color to abandon Christianity altogether. But she won't turn away from it. Instead, Bailey remains a "prisoner of hope," one who believes that it is only by facing suffering, by dwelling with and caring for those who suffer, as Jesus does, that the resurrection comes.

"Strange Fruit of a Different Name"

Huffington Post, 2015

Southern trees bear a strange fruit
Blood on the leaves and blood at the root
Black body swinging in the Southern breeze
Strange fruit hanging from the poplar trees
              —**Billie Holiday, "Strange Fruit" (1939)**

Before it was a sample for a hit Kanye West song, Billie Holliday's "Strange Fruit" was a cornerstone of the American songbook. Named the Song of the Century by *Time Magazine* in 1999 because of its historical significance, the piece reflected an era in which black bodies were summarily brutalized and discarded at the whim of white mobs at epidemic levels. A recent report from the Equal Justice Initiative in Montgomery, Alabama, names 3,959 victims of "racial terror lynchings" in 12 Southern states from 1877 to 1950. Many victims were murdered without being accused of any crime, for minor social transgressions, or for demanding basic rights.

Blood on the trees and blood at the root. Over 75 years after Billie Holiday first performed the song, the question of whether #blacklivesmatter is still up for debate. What remains consistent is the branding of black bodies as innately criminal and suspect. Today, ashes in Baltimore still smolder in the wake of riots resulting from the death of yet another black man in police custody. I know it is not a coincidence that these lyrics haunt my mind. Like Tanisha Anderson, Michael Brown, Renisha McBride, Eric Garner, Yvette Smith, Trayvon Martin, Miriam Carey, Eric Garner, and Tamir Rice before him, Freddie Gray is strange fruit of a different name. His body hangs from a tree whose twisted branches of urban blight, mass incarceration, and intergenerational poverty are attached to a trunk of white supremacy. The roots of the tree predate the founding of the American republic.

Freddie Gray's story is personal for me. It hits to the core of my identity as a young Christian minister who is the direct descendant of African slaves, Southern sharecroppers, and civil rights activists. As a clergywoman, part of my job is to accompany those who mourn. In these bleak times, faith leaders are often quick to jump to messages of hope and reconciliation without giving space for despair, frustration, and rage. Yet I must confess that in these moments, I find little comfort in lyrical biblical poetry about the promises waiting for us in heaven. I find no salvation in an image of a God removed from the depths of human suffering. Wading in the darkness, I am more prone to lean into the laments of Jeremiah (Lamentations

2:11), the moan of Rachel (Matthew 2:18), and the tears of Christ (John 11:35). I find myself humming the melodies of spirituals, hymns, and freedom songs that fortified the ancestors and elders of my community. It is then that I remember that in the circular nature of time, I am never alone in my lament.

This sense of shared lament is part of what faith traditions can offer those in suffering. And yet, one of the more painful parts of this year of violence has been the aloneness I have felt in the relative silence on this issue from some of my Christian brothers and sisters. I have been reminded that American Christianity has often been complicit in the complex web of white supremacy. The emergence of a theology of white supremacy during the colonial era of our nation's history tilled the soil that allowed strange fruit to become such a profitable crop. Central to the tenets of this theology was the construction of black people not as humans but as cursed objects who were to be conquered and ruled over. For centuries, the name of Christ was used as a tool to inflict physical, psychological, economic, and social violence on black people. Slavery was justified through theological means. Terrorists groups like the Ku Klux Klan were founded as "Christian" organizations. The social issue that prompted the rise of the Christian Right was not abortion, but the racial integration of public schools.

The legacy of this perversion of the gospel continues today in the dehumanization of black people both in Christian spaces and in the use of self-proclaimed Christian rhetoric in the public square. I would argue that the theology that allows some white Christians to "opt-out" of the national conversation on race and violence because it is uncomfortable or inconvenient is at its core the same that allows George Zimmerman to rationalize his killing of Trayvon Martin as "God's plan." Both use deflection to deny an undeniable fact: American Christianity is implicated in the white supremacy and institutional racism that allows some of its members to prosper while others are denied their basic humanity.

The current state of affairs is bleak indeed. I can certainly understand why some might break with religion altogether. But part of my mission as a minister and founder of the Faith Matters Network is to recover religious traditions as sources of positive social change even as they have been co-opted and twisted in the past for oppressive ends. One of my organization's central aims is to put the power of interfaith organizing into action, but from my own location as a minister of the gospel of Jesus Christ I can share with disillusioned Christians that I remain a prisoner of hope. Hope is not the same as optimism. My hope is a resurrection hope. A hope born out of the suffering of Maundy Thursday, the pain and uncertainty of Good Friday, and the silence of Holy Saturday. My hope remembers that in order for the promise of a reconciled world to manifest we must, like the women in Luke 24, go to the tomb—a site of death. We must go to sites of death like Baltimore, Ferguson, North Charleston, Cleveland, and Staten Island, where black blood was sacrificed on altars of pavement and playgrounds to appease the gods of white supremacy.

When my fellow Christians and I go to the tomb, I suspect that we will find, like the women, that Jesus is no longer there. Jesus is in the world. Jesus is weeping alongside mothers who will never again know the warmth of their child's embrace because their lives were cut tragically short. Jesus is marching in the streets lovingly calling systems of power to accountability. May we be brave enough to join him.

For Further Reading

Bailey, Jennifer. "May We Bear Witness To the Pain and Not Turn From It." *Auburn Seminary*, 9 June 2018, auburnseminary.org/rev-jennifer-bailey-may-we-bear-witness-to-the-pain-and-not-turn-from-it/.

Cone, James H. *The Cross and the Lynching Tree*. Orbis Books, 2016.

Markham, Claire, and Lauren Kokum. "15 Faith Leaders to Watch in 2015." *Center for American Progress*, 26 June 2015, www.americanprogress.org/issues/religion/news/2015/01/22/105158/15-faith-leaders-to-watch-in-2015/.

"Our Vision." *Faith Matters Network*, 2017, https://www.faithmattersnetwork.org/our-vision.

Emma González

The students attending Marjory Stoneman Douglas High School in Parkland, Florida, in 2018 never knew a world without school shootings. Born in the first years of the twenty-first century, just following the 1999 shooting massacre at Columbine High School in Colorado, they are sometimes dubbed "Generation Columbine." As of 2019 more than 229 schools have seen gun violence since the Columbine shooting (Woodrow Cox et al.). On February 14, 2018, Stoneman Douglas High School lost seventeen lives at the hands of a student armed with a semiautomatic weapon, a brutal act that turned the survivors into activists.

Within hours of the trauma, the school's students began tweeting about gun control and sharing images of the attack they'd captured on their phones. Within just four days, a group of students formed an activist movement called Never Again, established a policy goal for stricter background checks for gun purchases, and set a date for their national protest, March for Our Lives (Witt). Emma González is one of the leaders of Never Again, a senior at Stoneman Douglas at the time of the shooting, who delivered a speech credited with launching the movement. Through tears and fury, González pledged that Stoneman Douglas would be the last mass shooting in the United States. "Because if all our government and president can do is send thoughts and prayers," she said, "then it's time for victims to be the change that we need to see."

This speech was delivered at an anti-gun rally in Fort Lauderdale just two days after the shooting. Her pain was palpable, but passion drove her forward, as she built to a refrain that became a rallying cry of the movement: "We call B.S.!" González used the phrase to indict politicians, the NRA, and a generation of voters who created a problem left for kids to solve. "The people in the government who are voted into power are lying to us," she charged. "And us kids seem to be the only ones who notice and are prepared to call B.S." (CNN).

González's speech went viral and thrust her into the international spotlight. Images of the young activist, who drew attention for her shaved head, became the face of the movement, and her intersectional identity as a queer, Cuban American youth sent its own message about the country's future. As the NYU professor Ana María Dopico explains: "Queerness connects her both to a US politics of social

justice and to Cuban and Cuban American struggles for queer rights. She is part
of a generation that feels freer about claiming identities and loyalties" (Morales).
González's message, and her identity, clearly resonated; shortly after the shooting
González created a Twitter account and quickly garnered more followers than the
NRA. Not surprisingly, she also drew online trolls and hateful attacks.

The following piece, an excerpt of González's chapter in *Glimmer of Hope: How
Tragedy Sparked a Movement* adapted for publication in the *New York Times*, tells
the story of the moments leading to her powerful Fort Lauderdale speech and to
her life as an activist. The grief of the estimated 220,000 students who have been
exposed to gun violence in their schools is largely hidden from the public (Woodrow Cox et al.). In the tradition of feminist rhetoric, however, González uncovers
what is commonly rendered invisible and uses emotion as a resource for knowing,
showing how tears, anguish, and pain were part of—not distinct from—the students' political action and rhetorical effectiveness.

While the primary audience for González's piece is fellow teens seeking to
spark a movement of their own, adults are an important secondary audience—after all, it is the adults whose inaction forced students to intercede on their own be-
halves. And their actions are remarkable: from a national march to meetings with
politicians to a voter registration campaign, the Parkland students have kept the
national spotlight on gun control and, in so doing, provided a nation traumatized
by mass shootings a glimmer of hope for the future.

Excerpt from *Glimmer of Hope: How Tragedy Sparked a Movement*

2018

I don't remember exactly when I found out Carmen Schentrup was dead. Carmen
and I became friends in middle school. We had science together. I got my period
one day and didn't have a pad, and Carmen gave me one—what a queen. We rode
the bus together every day after school. She would vent about her a cappella club,
and we would compare the TV shows we were watching. At her birthday parties
everyone would eat pizza and watch a movie in the Schentrups' living room, and
then after the movie we would all just talk—about school, politics, life. I still have
one of her party invitations taped up on my mirror.

I found out she was dead on Feb. 15. I think it was the 15th—that's when the
Miami Herald released the names of those who had been killed the day before in
the shooting at my high school, Marjory Stoneman Douglas, in Parkland, Fla. I'd

thought she'd only been injured. I remember thinking that very clearly; she has only been injured, don't worry about her.

On the 16th, I was asked to speak at a gun control rally by a woman on the school board. For what seemed like the first time, adults were treating me and my peers as though they cared about what we had to say. I started writing my speech and didn't stop until I got up to the lectern. I gave it my all. All of my words, my thoughts, my energy, every political fact I knew. My mom had [The] Rachel Maddow [Show] on the TV and was saying: "Pay attention to this! It's about Chuck Grassley! You should consider putting it in your speech!" and I did. The speech followed a pattern: I had a thought, I wrote a new paragraph, I filled in the gaps, I ranted, and then deleted the rants. I had waves where all I wrote was a kind of scream of consciousness: "How could this have happened? So many people died, so many people died. I can't do this. How do I do this? How do we do this?"

My friend Cameron Kasky called after I gave my speech and asked if I wanted to join the movement. He was getting a group of students together to organize what we ended up calling the March for Our Lives—a march on Washington to call for better gun laws.

We worked out of Cameron's house in the early days. A lot of my friends outside the movement were having trouble sleeping. Even those who weren't on campus the day of the shooting had nightmares. But for those of us in the movement, there wasn't time to sleep. You can see very clearly in those early interviews that all of us had deep dark circles under our eyes. No one had an appetite. No one wanted to leave Cameron's house, not even to take a shower. None of us wanted to stop working. To stop working was to start thinking. And thinking about anything other than the march and the solutions to gun violence was to have a breakdown.

One day all of us seemed to have a breakdown around 4:00 p.m. Cameron ran off, and I ran after him, because I was worried. Once I saw that he was O.K., I realized that I was having a breakdown, too.

I lay in the grass. The sky was spotted with clouds, so when they passed over the sun, it felt too cool, and when the sun was out, it felt too warm. There were trees all around, and I was fully realizing, once more, how miserable we all were. How miserable I felt. How much I wished I could just be a tree so that I didn't have to know people who had been murdered in a mass shooting in a life I thought would be forever safe from this kind of mourning.

Suddenly I couldn't stand being alive. I didn't want to kill myself—let me make that very clear. I just didn't want to have a human consciousness. Trees face many difficulties, what with deforestation and pollution, but that didn't stop me from wanting to be one—to just stop feeling and live.

I wanted to go back to when blood hadn't stained the walls of our campus. Back to when I would hang out with Carmen on the bus. Back to before people would stop me to say, "Aren't you one of those kids from Parkland?"

But we couldn't go back. All of us know what it feels like to be Harry Potter now. Even when people come up to us quietly to say thank you, you never know if they're just trying to shoot you at close range.

Going up against the country's largest gun lobby organization was obviously something that needed to be done, but it means that the people we're arguing against are the ones with the guns. I am personally deathly afraid of them, and I know, from traveling the country during the summer for the Road to Change tour, that many of the people who disagree with us mean it when they say that they only want to talk if we're standing on the other end of their AR-15s.

In the midst of all this, I try to take good care of myself. I shaved my head a week or two before senior year. People used to ask me why, and the main reason is that having hair felt terrible. It was heavy, it made me overheated, and every time I put it up in a ponytail (and I looked terrible in a ponytail) it gave me a headache. And, it sounds stupid, but it made me insecure; I was always worried that it looked frizzy or tangled. What's the best thing to do with an insecurity? Get rid of it. It's liberating to shave my head every week.

I also cry a lot. But crying is healthy and it feels good—I really don't know why people are so against it. Maybe because it's loud. Crying is a kind of communication, and communication is awesome. The lack of communication is what keeps us in this situation.

People say, "I don't play the politics game, I don't pay attention to politics"— well, the environment is getting poisoned, families are getting pulled apart and deported, prisons are privatized, real-life Nazis live happily among us, Native Americans are so disenfranchised our country is basically still colonizing them, Puerto Rico has been abandoned, the American education system has been turned into a business, and every day 96 people get shot and killed.

You might not be a big fan of politics, but you can still participate. All you need to do is vote for people you believe will work on these issues, and if they don't work the way they should, then it is your responsibility to call them, organize a town hall and demand that they show up—hold them accountable. It's their job to make our world better.

It has been months since the shooting. But whenever one of my friends finds an old picture of someone who died that day, or another shooting happens, or I hear helicopters or one too many loud bangs in one day, it all starts to slip. It feels like I'm back at the vigil, in the hot Florida sun, with volunteers handing out water bottles to replenish what the sun and sadness had taken away. Looking for friends and finding them, hugging them, saying, "I love you." Looking for friends and not finding them.

Everything we've done and everything we will do is for them. It's for ourselves. It's for every person who has gone through anything similar to this, for every person who hasn't yet, for every person who never will. This isn't something we are ever going to forget about. This isn't something we are ever going to give up on.

FOR FURTHER READING

"Florida Student Emma Gonzalez to Lawmakers and Gun Advocates: 'We Call BS.'" *CNN*, 18 Feb. 2018, www.cnn.com/2018/02/17/us/florida-student-emma-gonzalez-speech/index.html.

Founders of March for Our Lives, *Glimmer of Hope: How Tragedy Sparked a Movement.* Razorbill, 2018.

Morales, Ed. "Emma González: La Nueva Cara of Florida Latinx." *The Washington Post*, 1 Mar. 2018, www.washingtonpost.com/news/post-nation/wp/2018/03/01/emma-gonzalez-la-nueva -cara-of-florida-latinx/?noredirect=on&utm_term=.12faec0a46f9.

Turkewitz, Julie, et al. "Emma González Leads a Student Outcry on Guns: 'This Is the Way I Have to Grieve.'" *The New York Times*, 18 Feb. 2018, www.nytimes.com/2018/02/18/us/emma-gonza lez-florida-shooting.html.

Witt, Emily. "How the Survivors of Parkland Began the Never Again Movement." *The New Yorker*, 17 Apr. 2018, www.newyorker.com/news/news-desk/how-the-survivors-of-parkland-began-the -never-again-movement.

Woodrow Cox, John, et al. "Database: More than 228,000 Students Have Experienced Gun Violence at School since Columbine." *The Washington Post*, 8 May 2018, https://www.washingtonpost .com/graphics/2018/local/school-shootings-database/.

Sharon Brous

For more than seventy years, Israel and Palestine have been ensnared in political and military conflict over control of the Gaza Strip, the West Bank, and Jerusalem—land that is steeped in cultural and religious history for both groups. Israel is the world's only Jewish state, formed when Jews fled persecution in Europe in the mid-twentieth century to reclaim their ancestral and spiritual homeland. In the Hebrew Bible, King David named Jerusalem the capital of Israel, which became the site of his son Solomon's temple. Arabs, however, already populated this territory and regarded it as rightfully their own. Jerusalem is also holy land for Muslims, as the Quran describes Jerusalem as the last place Mohammad visited before he ascended into heaven.

This struggle over territory has led to decades-long violent conflict between the two states. While the United Nations, as well as the US government, has entered the strife at different moments, dividing the land between the two groups and negotiating peace talks, Israel and Palestine remain bitterly divided. As Rabbi Sharon Brous demonstrates in the column included here, this political unrest makes violence and terror part of the daily landscape for both Israelis and Palestinians.

To render the personal implications of the conflict, Brous describes her connection to two women, each on the cusp of her wedding day—one in Jerusalem and the other in Ramallah—both hoping for a peaceful marriage celebration, a day without violence. Whether Jewish or Muslim, her friend explains, "We really all want the same thing." While feminist thought has long touted the personal as political, Brous shows that the political is also personal; she provides a window into the lives of the people who must endure this bitter war, reminding us that no matter which side one identifies with, we must remember the full humanity of the other.

Brous is the founding rabbi of IKAR, a congregation in Los Angeles that has become an exemplar for Jewish revitalization in and beyond the United States (IKAR). A national spiritual figure, Brous blessed President Obama and Vice President Joe Biden at the 2017 Inaugural National Prayer Service, and her TED Talk, "Reclaiming Religion," has been translated into twenty languages and viewed over a million times. In 2013 the *Daily Beast* placed Brous at the top of their list of America's most influential rabbis.

In this column, first published in the *Huffington Post*, Brous uses her ethos to argue that peace in the Middle East will never be achieved through military ends; instead, she delivers a countercultural message, insisting that peace is built from diplomacy centered upon empathy, sympathy, and self-reflection. While one might expect a rabbi to make a pro-Israel argument, Brous refuses the "us" and "them" binary, reminding readers that embracing the humanity of the other is "the deepest manifestation of Jewish values."

"Israel in Trying Times: Unity Not Uniformity"

Huffington Post, 2014

My friend Candice, a Talmud professor, recently posted her hope that the fighting ends soon in Israel and Gaza, with a note of concern for her sister in Jerusalem who plans to get married later this month. Her colleague at UCLA, Awad, a Palestinian American, responded that his sister, too, was planning an August wedding, hers in Ramallah. It turns out that both celebrations are planned for the same day, so these two friends shared blessings that they might both dance at their sisters' weddings and meet for coffee afterward. "It turns out," Candice told me, "we really all want the same thing."

Look at this story as a conflict Rorschach test. Many will read it and say, "This is precisely the problem. We do not all want the same thing. We want quiet, they want our destruction. We build schools, they build terror tunnels (alternatively: we want freedom, they ignore our suffering until rockets start to fall). We protect civilians, they target them. This is not a battle between two rights: it is an epic battle between life and death, good and evil."

But some will read it and say, "This is the heart of the matter. At the end of the day, human beings—Jews and Muslims, Israelis and Palestinians—yearn for the chance to live and love in freedom and with dignity. Recognizing our shared humanity is the only way we'll ever have a chance at peace."

This latest round of warfare has revealed unprecedented polarization. Decent and reasonable people are stunned to discover how hard it is to find common ground with other decent and reasonable people; everyone seems to feel that the rest of the world has gone mad. This matters now more than ever because many have argued that there is no military solution to this conflict, that when the fighting finally ends the only thing that will have been made clear is the necessity of a diplomatic solution. This means that grueling conversations about a shared future, including talk of borders, water rights and refugees, will have to emerge from a context of exacerbated contention and distrust, rooted in radically conflicting narratives. The morning after the fighting ceases, Israelis and Palestinians, Jews and Muslims, will have to contend with the devastating aftershocks of grief, pain and fear, which have made it so hard for us to even see one another.

That's why all the talk about sympathy and empathy and self-reflection, even during wartime, is not only spiritually essential, but also strategically critical.

I cannot speak with authority for the Palestinian community, but here's how things look in much of the Jewish community: over the past month in Israel and abroad, many have been holding our collective breath, obsessively checking in with family and friends, anxiously waiting to be reassured they and their children are safe. We worry about the toll the sirens will take on the Israeli children who take shelter from Hamas rockets multiple times each day, rockets intended to kill, maim and wreak havoc. Another generation of children raised with fear embedded in their hearts. Last week we learned of families in the south whose children for months heard strange voices in their home at night but could never tell where they were coming from. Now they know: there was a terror tunnel being built just beneath their home.

And we see the dreaded notifications about young Israeli soldiers killed trying to upset Hamas' military stockpile. Greenberg, a father of three, salt of the earth. Bar Rahav, who played water polo. Bar-Or, with his pregnant wife and one-year-old daughter. Shamash, married only five months ago, who went to Haiti to help rebuild after the earthquake of 2010. Steinberg, the Lone Soldier from Woodland Hills. The always optimistic Biton. Because it's a small nation and serving in the IDF [Israel Defense Forces] is obligatory, every family in Israel is touched.

Add to that the perilous resurfacing of anti-Semitism sweeping Europe.

This is a lot to hold, it's true. Which is precisely why some are pained by the suggestion that the Jewish heart must nevertheless make space to hold Palestinian suffering as well. We do not want to see the twisted images of the four Bakr boys on the beach, all between nine and eleven years old: sweet boys, from a family of fisherman. We do not want to hear about the twenty-five members of the Abu Jama'e family or the shelling of a UN school in Gaza. The death toll keeps climbing: thousands of families shattered, lives and homes and dreams uprooted. It's not easy to talk or think about it, especially when we're worried for our own kids.

But seeing the humanity in the other is not an act of disloyalty or an abdication of Jewish values. It is the deepest manifestation of Jewish values. A false dichotomy has been set up between particularism and universalism. Do you care about your tribe or do you care about the world? But I am a Jew AND a human being. It is precisely because my people knows terror and recognizes the world's silent complicity that my heart is awake to human suffering. So many Jews expressed shock and disgust at the murder of Palestinian teen Muhammed Abu Khdeir last month. But know this: the road from callousness to brutality is short and direct. If we abide the growing apathy toward Palestinians, Israeli society will find itself overcome not by individual incidents, but by waves of racist violence.

We are now in the beginning of the month of Av, the time in the Jewish calendar dedicated to holding the memory of the destruction of the temple, when nearly one million Jews were killed or died of starvation and most of the rest sent into exile. Our rabbis grappled for centuries with how a loving God could have allowed innocents to suffer so profoundly. The answer they came to: we weren't so innocent. They draw a direct line from *sinat hinam*, senseless hatred among Jews, to catastrophe. Rabbi Asher Lopatin teaches in the name of Rabbi Naftali Zvi Yehuda Berlin (the Netziv): the problem is not having strong ideas, but dismissing other people's ideas as heresy. This is so dangerous, he argues, that it led to the destruction of the temple.

So the nine days before Tisha b'Av became days not only of national mourning but also of reflection. The mourning aligns perfectly with our people's collective emotional state these days as the number of fallen soldiers continues to rise, each one a national tragedy. But what about the self-reflection? There are some who insist on reminding us that we must remove the protective armor from the heart, look beyond our victimization and vulnerability, consider how we got here, what could have done differently and how we might find a way out. They reflect, knowing that for even intimating a need for compassion Israeli artists have been mocked, writers marginalized and academics castigated. Even former heads of the Shin Bet have been scorned. But their introspection is born not out of self-hatred, but out of love for their country and its people. I listen carefully to those animated by core Jewish values and the founding vision of the state, those willing to be mocked and derided, those who risk being blocked out of bunkers when the sirens sound (yes, this actually happened at a recent peace rally in Tel Aviv). It may feel like a nuisance to be reminded of the humanity of your enemy's neighbor's child. But it is precisely those unwilling to let us forget, I am certain, who will save us from the abyss.

As for me, I will not wave someone else's banner or shout slogans that don't honor all the sides of my heart. I will continue to strive to recognize the painful complexity of this situation. I will take solace in the fact that for Jews, unity does not mean uniformity. I love Israel. I care deeply about the lives of my brothers, sisters and friends there, some of whom are now serving in Gaza. I want Hamas' horror-show terror schemes to be thwarted. I also grieve the deaths of Israel's neighbors and their children. I yearn to hear acknowledgment that Hamas' vulgar fanaticism was able to root in part because the 47-year occupation seeded despair amongst Palestinians. I understand that the rapidly shifting realities of the Middle East make peace more challenging now than ever, but I want Israeli and Palestinian leaders to invest as much time, ingenuity, and resources in a diplomatic resolution to the conflict as they invest in the military option. I pray that all of us, left and right, Israeli and Palestinian, despite our grief, pain and fear, will be able to stretch our hearts to see one another.

I pray that shouts of joy and gladness will be heard on the streets of Jerusalem and Ramallah at the weddings of Candice and Awad's sisters. And I pray that these two friends can sit together afterward and dream great dreams about the future. Because, at the end of the day, they both really want the same thing.

For Further Reading

Beauchamp, Zack. "What Are Israel and Palestine? Why Are They Fighting?" *Vox*, 31 Mar. 2014, www
.vox.com/cards/israel-palestine/intro.

IKAR LA. ikar-la.org/.

Little, Becky. "Why Jews and Muslims Both Have Religious Claims on Jerusalem." *History*, 6 Dec.
2017, www.history.com/news/why-jews-and-muslims-both-have-religious-claims-on-jerusalem.

Lezley McSpadden

On August 9, 2014, Lezley McSpadden lost her eighteen-year-old son, whom she affectionately called Mike Mike. He had just graduated from high school and was learning to drive her Chevy. McSpadden's son, Michael Brown, was shot and killed in Ferguson, Missouri, by a white police officer. Brown's death quickly made national headlines as another high-profile case in a series of highly publicized incidents of police brutality against unarmed black men.

At the news of his shooting, protests erupted in Ferguson, marking a deep fissure between the black community and the largely white police force ("What Happened"). Among the protesters was a group of six hundred who traveled by bus to Ferguson from all over the United Stated as part of the Black Lives Matter Freedom Ride. The Freedom Ride was organized by Black Lives Matter cofounder Patrisse Cullors to support Brown's family and to peacefully protest state-sanctioned violence inflicted on the black community. The massive protests, however, were not without violence, and media images of unrest led the public to falsely equate violent protest and Black Lives Matter—a misconception that would continue to plague the movement. Even so, Ferguson was a turning point for the Black Lives Matter movement, where the group harnessed their pain to organize and launch chapters all over the country (see also Alicia Garza's contribution to this volume).

The fury over Brown's death was reignited in November 2014, when Darren Wilson, the police officer who shot Brown, was exonerated by a grand jury. This led to renewed protests and fresh agony for Brown's family, both of which were projected on screens around the country. As the *Washington Post* reporter Wesley Lowery writes, "Since her son's death, McSpadden has served as the prevailing image of pain at the center of the Black Lives Matter protest movement. The nation listened as [McSpadden] wailed on the night of her son's death and again three months later when a grand jury declined to indict his killer." But McSpadden's maternal grief was also a form of testimony, demanding to be heard. As she described after the grand jury announcement, "It was just like, like I had been shot. Like you shoot me now—just no respect, no sympathy, nothing. This could be your child. This could be anybody's child" (Ford and Levs). McSpadden's grief served as a public reminder that her son's life mattered in the world, as it mattered, profoundly, to her.

In the column included here, originally written for the *New York Times*, Mc-Spadden centers the ethos of motherhood; she explains what it means to be part of this sisterhood of women whose children were shot by the police, the impossibility of easing pain, and the requirement of working for peace when there is no peace to be found. Her primary offering to other mothers is one of connection. Yet she extends her message to a larger audience, demanding justice for those who "didn't pull the trigger."

McSpadden has served as a peaceful warrior for justice since her son's death. She began the Michael O. D. Brown Foundation to advance health, education, and economic empowerment in low-income communities as well as to sponsor better relations between the black community and the police. At the age of thirty-seven, McSpadden received her high school diploma to honor Michael, and she authored the book *Tell the Truth and Shame the Devil: The Life, Legacy, and Love of My Son Michael Brown* (2016). McSpadden's efforts to sponsor civic change continue as she engages in local politics in Ferguson.

"Michael Brown's Mom, on Alton Sterling and Philando Castile"

New York Times, 2016

I cried on Wednesday as I watched, like much of the country, the horrifying video images from Baton Rouge, La., showing a black man being shot to death, in the back and chest, after being wrestled into submission by two white police officers. On Thursday, I woke up to the news of a black man in Minnesota, shot by the police during a traffic stop. I am devastated and infuriated.

Alton Sterling is dead. Philando Castile is dead. My son, Michael Brown, has been dead for almost two years now.

Death isn't pretty for anyone, but what these families now face is the horror of seeing their loved one die over and over, in public, in such a violent way. They face the helplessness of having strangers judge their loved one not on who he was or what he meant to his family but on a few seconds of video. Mr. Sterling died in a very lonely way, surrounded by his killers. Can you imagine a lonelier death? Mr. Castile died with his girlfriend and her young daughter watching as he was gunned down.

Sometimes it seems like the only thing we can do in response to the police brutality that my son and so many other black boys and men have suffered is to pray for black lives. Yes, they matter, but is that changing anything? What is going to be different this time?

There is again an uproar, and people are going to once again do a lot of talking about black-on-black crime versus white-on-black crime. Truth is, black-on-black crime is perpetuated by systemic injustice and social ills. But, real talk, this debate is meaningless so long as we still live in a world where a black man can get killed for selling cigarettes on the street, where a black boy can get killed for waving a toy gun.

It's a problem when you look to the law as a protector and it comes into your community and shoots people dead with no remorse or consequences. It is a problem that you have some law officers trying to do the right thing, and then others who bring shame on the badge.

Someone asked me what I would say to Mr. Sterling's family, if I had the chance. To tell the truth, I wouldn't know what to say. When Michael was killed, people tried to talk to me, but I was in shock; I didn't know how to respond. I know enough now to advise well-meaning people to pause before offering kind words. So many told me, "I am so sorry for your loss." After a while, all the "sorrys" bled together, and at the end of it, nothing changed. Let Mr. Sterling's family members grieve with the people in their lives who knew him before everyone else saw these shocking images and felt they had to put their two cents in.

The mothers I've met along the way—Sybrina Fulton, Trayvon Martin's mother; Wanda Johnson, Oscar Grant III's mother—we've helped one another cope, and we'll try to do the same for Mr. Sterling and Mr. Castile's families. I'll never forget meeting Samaria Rice, the mother of Tamir Rice. I looked at this strong woman and was amazed to think that she was just starting a horrible journey, one that will never end, one that I am still on.

When their children are killed, mothers are expected to say something. To help keep the peace. To help make change. But what can I possibly say? I just know we need to do something. We are taught to be peaceful, but we aren't at peace. I have to wake up and go to sleep with this pain every day. Ain't no peace. If we mothers can't change where this is heading for these families—to public hearings, protests, un-asked-for martyrdom, or worse, to nothing at all—what can we do?

Since I lost my son to a police shooting, I've done a lot of thinking. I've gone to therapy, as have my other children. I've started a foundation in Michael's honor. I've campaigned in St. Louis to mandate body cameras on police officers at all times. We cannot assume that justice will be done. So I will never stop talking about my son or fighting for justice for him.

People will try to twist the words of Mr. Sterling and Mr. Castile's families and turn them into something ugly. These men will be called "thugs" and much, much worse. It's already happening. Click on the comments section of any article you read about their deaths, and you will be shocked by the racist comments of people who insist—*insist*—that they obviously deserved to die.

So what would I say to their families? When you're ready, and if you need me, I'll be there for you. But the people I would really like to say something to are the ones who claim that justice will prevail. Whose justice? When justice comes to the one who didn't pull the trigger, that's when I'll believe you.

For Further Reading

Brown, DeNeen L. "For the Family of Michael Brown, Grief, Sorrow and Anger Play out in Public Eye." *The Washington Post*, 1 Dec. 2014, https://www.washingtonpost.com/politics/for-the-fam ily-of-michael-brown-grief-sorrow-and-anger-play-out-in-public-eye/2014/12/01/4e919494 -7294-11e4-8808-afaa1e3a33ef_story.html.

Ford, Dana, and Josh Levs. "Michael Brown's Mother: 'This Could Be Your Child.'" *CNN*, 27 Nov. 2014, www.cnn.com/2014/11/26/justice/ferguson-grand-jury-reaction/index.html.

Garza, Alicia. "A Herstory of the #BlackLivesMatter Movement." *The Feminist Wire*, 12 July 2016, www.thefeministwire.com/2014/10/blacklivesmatter-2/.

McSpadden, Lezley, and Lyah Beth LeFlore. *Tell the Truth and Shame the Devil: The Life, Legacy, and Love of My Son Michael Brown*. Regan Arts, 2016.

"What Happened in Ferguson?" *The New York Times*, 13 Aug. 2014, www.nytimes.com/interact ive/2014/08/13/us/ferguson-missouri-town-under-siege-after-police-shooting.html.

Mansplaining Tweets

Twitter was founded in 2006 by Jack Dorsey, Noah Glass, Biz Stone, and Evan Williams, originally conceived as a way for groups to share status updates, "like texting, but not," and has since become "one of the biggest communications technologies of the last 100 years" (MacArthur). As of 2018, Twitter had 330 million monthly active users (Shearer and Gottfried). Twitter is popular for cultural commentary and political opinions via comments, humor, memes (typically visuals and pithy text created and spread quickly online), GIFs (static or animated images), and videos. Ideas are circulated via retweets and hashtags and, if popular, gain "trending" status; such circulation has powerful rhetorical impact in shaping public views and sponsoring civic engagement. The tweets included here are by Cathy de la Cruz, who works in publishing and holds art degrees from the University of California San Diego and the University of Arizona; Keegan Osinski, librarian at Vanderbilt University, specializing in sacramental and liturgical theology; and Dr. Caroline Madden, marriage therapist and author of books on healing from infidelity.

This trio of tweets appeared as part of a piece on BuzzFeed—a social news and entertainment website—that featured Twitter memes on mansplaining, a term that surfaced shortly after a piece by Rebecca Solnit called "Men Who Explain Things" appeared in the *Los Angeles Times*. While Solnit didn't coin the term *mansplaining*, it circulated first among feminist blogs and quickly became part of cultural consciousness. Solnit's piece describes how, during an exchange with a man at a party, he explained Solnit's own book to her even after learning she was the author. "Men explain things to me, and to other women, whether or not they know what they're talking about. Some men. Every woman knows what I mean" (Solnit).

While the term *mansplaining* is relatively new, the practice is not. Now, though, women have a precise term to label behavior that before could be read as "just the way things are." The term has in fact resonated globally with women: it has been translated into many languages and is canonized in the *Oxford English Dictionary*. In these examples, humor provides levity on this problematic phenomenon, which has serious consequences in the workplace, academia, and politics, and online. The following tweets play off of historical images and make a play on words to bitingly drive home the ways men can—and do—talk over or ignore what women have to say. In doing so, women insist that their words, insights, and knowledge do not need to be explained by men.

Cathy de la Cruz

 **Cathy de la Cruz**
@SadDiego

 Follow

A friend spotted this in Texas: #Mansplaining The Statue.

3:16 PM - 22 May 2015

1,720 Retweets   **2,502** Likes

💬 183   🔁 1.7K   ♡ 2.5K

1. "A friend spotted this in Texas: #Mansplaining the Statue." The statue portrays a woman sitting on a bench with an open book in her lap, and a man standing with one foot on the bench, speaking down to the seated woman. Photo Credit Ash Hernandez. @SadDiego (Cathy de la Cruz), Twitter, May 22, 2015, 3:16 p.m.

Caroline Madden

 Dr. Caroline Madden
@cmaddenmft

#Mansplain

4/17/17, 6:13 PM

193 Retweets **302** Likes

2. "#Mansplain." The image portrays a man and a woman in Regency dress, with superimposed text: "Women are so hard to read." "Well actually we just wan—" "Such complex creatures." "If you just liste—" "So mysterious." @cmaddenmft (Caroline Madden), Twitter, April 17, 2017, 6:13 p.m.

Keegan Osinski

Keegan Osinski
@keegzzz

(Follow) ⌄

Where do mansplainers get their water

From a well, actually

3:42 PM - 13 Apr 2016

7,575 Retweets **12,517** Likes

💬 110   ⟲ 7.6K   ♡ 13K

3. "Where do mansplainers get their water? From a well, actually." @keegzzz
(Keegan Osinski), Twitter, April 13, 2016, 3:42 p.m.

FOR FURTHER READING

Carlson, Nicholas. "The Real History of Twitter." *Business Insider*, 11 Apr. 2013, http://www.business
   insider.com/how-twitter-was-founded-2011-4.

Guillaume, Jenna. "23 Tweets About Mansplaining That Will Make Women Both Laugh And Sigh."
   BuzzFeed, 12 Oct. 2017, https://www.buzzfeed.com/jennaguillaume/well-actually?utm_
   term=.sxPAMqJM0m#.qbEAeM0eNV.

MacArther, Amanda. "The Real History of Twitter, in Brief." *Lifewire*, 27 Apr. 2018, https://www.life
   wire.com/history-of-twitter-3288854.Madden, Caroline. *Blindsided by His Betrayal: Surviving
   the Shock of Your Husband's Infidelity*. Train of Thought Press, 2016.

Newberry, Christina. "28 Twitter Statistics All Marketers Need to Know in 2019." *Hootsuite*, 17 Jan.
   2018, https://blog.hootsuite.com/twitter-statistics/.

Rothman, Lily. "A Cultural History of Mansplaining." *The Atlantic*, 1 Nov. 2012, https://www.theat
   lantic.com/sexes/archive/2012/11/a-cultural-history-of-mansplaining/264380/.

Shearer, Elisa, and Jeffrey Gottfried. "News Use across Social Media Platforms 2017." *Pew Research
   Center*, 7 Sept. 2017, http://www.journalism.org/2017/09/07/news-use-across-social-media
   -platforms-2017/.

Solnit, Rebecca. "Men Who Explain Things," *Los Angeles Times*, 13 Apr. 2018, http://articles.latimes
   .com/2008/apr/13/opinion/op-solnit13.

Nadia Bolz-Weber

Nadia Bolz-Weber is a Lutheran minister, public theologian, national speaker, and bestselling author of four books. But as her website biography explains: "Nobody really believes she's an ordained pastor in the Evangelical Lutheran Church in America (ELCA). Maybe it's the sleeve tattoos or the fact that she swears like a truck driver." Bolz-Weber doesn't give much credence to traditional church decorum. That's because, as she explains in an interview in the *Atlantic*, a lot of mainline Protestantism "has confused the gifts and the wrapping" (Green). The "wrapping" involves a surface-level focus on piety and polish, which often means rigid boundaries around who belongs. What people crave, Bolz-Weber believes, is a home, where the gifts of grace, forgiveness, and love abide: "A place where they can speak the actual truth about themselves in the world and they don't have to pretend" (Green).

So Bolz-Weber created a place: the House of All Saints and Sinners, a Denver ELCA Lutheran church that welcomes those who have been harmed by or excluded from Christianity, or who feel marked as outsiders. This includes Bolz-Weber herself, who characterizes her religious upbringing as "fundamentalist, legalistic, [and] sectarian" and is upfront about her own history of drug and alcohol abuse (Little). The House of All Saints and Sinners began as a small gathering place for people like Bolz-Weber—"underside dwellers" and "cynics, alcoholics and queers" (*Pastrix* 9); then, as her profile grew, it began to draw more suburban dwellers, eventually hosting an eclectic congregation, diverse in background and appearance, but seeking a common experience.

While Bolz-Weber, a weightlifter and former stand-up comic, may not look (or act) like a typical Lutheran minister, the House of All Saints and Sinners is built upon centuries of theological tradition. As she explains, "I really feel strongly that you have to be deeply rooted in tradition in order to innovate with integrity" (Tippett). For instance, members of the congregation actively participate in leading the church service, an inclusive innovation, but the liturgy that guides their worship is ancient. Because Bolz-Weber preaches that Christianity is the process of dying and renewal, confession and absolution are central to the service.

Dying and renewal is also a central theme of the following op-ed. Written at the height of the #MeToo movement (see Tarana Burke's contribution to this volume), Bolz-Weber, in a characteristically unabashed tone, describes the moment as an apocalypse, which in Greek means "to uncover, to peel away, to show what's underneath." Women's mass-scale revelation of men's abuse of power allows us to look closely at its cause, including, she argues, the way the Bible and Christianity have been used to protect the powerful, and to claim male domination as God's will. Like so many female rhetoricians before her, Bolz-Weber uses her theological knowledge to upend patriarchal renderings of Christianity, describing domination of the powerless by the powerful as "toxic heresy," directly contradicting the Christian tenet to love one's neighbor. Always one to examine her own implication in the problem she names, Bolz-Weber make the powerful rhetorical choice to reflect on how she—even as a minister—has internalized the sexism that has thwarted women's leadership in the Christian church. But there is hope, she shows, because by facing the sin of domination, Christians find their way to repentance and transformation, and only then can the mere appearance—the wrapping—of Christianity be exchanged for the gift of radical love at its core.

"We're in the Midst of an Apocalypse: And That's a Good Thing"

Washington Post, 2018

As a clergyperson, I'd like to welcome you all to the apocalypse. Pull up a chair and make yourself uncomfortable.

If, when you think of an apocalypse, you picture a scary, doom-filled, punishment-from-above type of thing, you are not alone. Originally, though, apocalyptic literature—the kind that was popular around the time of Jesus—existed not to scare the bejeezus out of children so they would be good boys and girls, but to proclaim a big, hope-filled idea: that dominant powers are not ultimate powers. Empires fall. Tyrants fade. Systems die. God is still around.

An apocalypse is a good thing, and I'm delighted to welcome you to this one.

In Greek, the word apocalypse means to uncover, to peel away, to show what's underneath. That's what this country has been experiencing in the past six months. There has not been a sudden uptick in sexual misconduct and assault in our country, the #MeToo and #TimesUp movements are simply exposing what was already there. The reality that some men comment on, threaten, masturbate in front of, intimidate, and assault female bodies is finally being brought out of the dark ubiquity of women's personal experience and into the light of public discourse. The male domination at the center of the sexual harassment issue—how those in positions of power (usually, but not always, men) have used that power to sexually gratify themselves at the expense of those who are subordinate to them (usually, but not always, women)—is being revealed apocalyptically in prime time.

The corner has peeled up, and now there is a little cat fur and dust on it, and we can't get it to stick back down.

Some people may think policy change and sensitivity training will take care of everything eventually, and that the #MeToo movement is already showing the success some women are having holding abusers accountable. But real, lasting change requires an understanding of why gender inequality is a reality in the first place. To do that, we must take that peeled-up corner and pull, even if it hurts.

If we look as deep as we can stomach, we will find heresy at the center. [The] nineteenth-century theologian Friedrich Schleiermacher defined heresy as "that which preserves the appearance of Christianity, and yet contradicts its essence."

The heresy is this: With all the trappings of Christianity behind us, those who seek to justify or maintain dominance over another group of people have historically used the Bible to prove that that domination was not actually an abuse of power at the expense of others, but indeed was part of "God's plan." And there you have the appearance of Christianity (Bible verses and God-talk) contradicting its essence (love God, and love your neighbor as yourself).

Sexual harassment and misconduct persist in the United States for a reason.

The venom of domination runs deeply in us as a country and a people. And it does so because the fangs that delivered it were given not the devil's name, but God's. When the subordination of women is established as God's will, when slavery is established as God's will, when discrimination against queer folks is established as God's will, when the CEO of the National Rifle Association claims the right to buy a semiautomatic assault rifle is "not bestowed by man, but granted by God," it delivers a poison that can infect the deepest parts of us. Because messages that are transmitted to us in God's name embed far beneath the surface, all the way down to our original place, our createdness, our source code.

In polite company, and even in our conscious thoughts, we may not "agree" with the subjugation of women, but the toxic heresy of God-ordained domination is a spiritual malady, not a cosmetic one. Wokeness and policy change are a start, but not enough to dig out the full infection.

I know this, because I, too, am infected.

The messages I received from my highly religious upbringing—one shared by millions in this country—was that it is God's will that women be subordinate to men. Every Tuesday night in 1981, I joined the other 12- to 13-year-old girls at church for Christian Charm Class. "Femininity," my workbook explained, was my "crowning glory: purity, sweetness, a quiet spirit, modesty, chastity, a demure manner." We were patiently directed on the skills needed to get ahead: prettiness, humility, and a modest amount of lip gloss. The boys in the Sunday school classroom next to us received instruction on how to become confident leaders.

I never heard a woman speak in church or pray aloud until I was in my late 20s.

I now have a graduate degree in theology, a decade of ordained ministry, and am unapologetic about being a woman who is also a Lutheran clergyperson. I have embraced my calling to be a preacher. I have written books about it. I have rebutted the criticism from conservative Christians that women have no spiritual authority. Every Sunday, I wear a black clergy shirt and stand before my congregation. And yet, on occasion, when I catch a glimpse of a female pastor, for a fraction of a second, before I can stop it, I recoil.

"Who does she think she is?"

The toxic "it is God's will that women remain silent" message I received from well-meaning church-folk runs too deeply in me to dig it out with my own hand.

This is why I welcome our moment of uncovering; we need to see how deep the heresy of domination runs, and then remind one another that dominant powers are not ultimate powers. We Christians need to repent of our original sins, and see where we have embraced the appearance of Christianity only to reject its essence. This is not a new idea. Black Bible scholars, feminist and liberation theologians have done this work well and for decades now. So if those who came before looked to the Bible to justify their dominance then let us look to it to justify our dignity. It's in there. Hebrew midwives who defy Pharaoh. Ethnic outsider women who insisted on their dignity. African eunuchs who knew where water was in a desert.

We must do this. The Bible, Christian theology, and liturgy are too potent to be left to those who would use them, even unwittingly, to justify and protect their own dominance. And sometimes the origin of the harm can be the most powerful source of healing.

That's how anti-venom works.

FOR FURTHER READING

Bolz-Weber, Nadia. *Accidental Saints: Finding God in All the Wrong People*. Convergent, 2016.
Bolz-Weber, Nadia. *Pastrix: The Cranky, Beautiful Faith of a Sinner & Saint*. Jericho Books, 2014.
Bolz-Weber, Nadia. *Shameless: A Sexual Reformation*. Convergent, 2019.
Boorstein, Michelle. "Bolz-Weber's Liberal, Foulmouthed Articulation of Christianity Speaks to Fed-up Believers." *The Washington Post*, 3 Nov. 2013, https://www.washingtonpost.com/local/bolz-webers-liberal-foulmouthed-articulation-of-christianity-speaks-to-fed-up-believers/2013/11/03/7139dc24-3cd3-11e3-a94f-b58017bfee6c_story.html?utm_term=.96733aeefb4al.
Green, Emma. "Why Every Church Needs a Drag Queen." *The Atlantic*, 3 Sept. 2015, www.theatlantic.com/politics/archive/2015/09/bringing-sin-back-into-church/402391/.

Little, Jane. "Nadia Bolz Weber: A Pastor for America's Outsiders." *BBC News*, 6 July 2015, www.bbc.com/news/33377925.

Nadia Bolz-Weber. www.nadiabolzweber.com/.

Tippett, Krista. "Seeing the Underside and Seeing God: Tattoos, Tradition, and Grace: Nadia Bolz-Weber." *On Being*, 23 Oct. 2014, https://onbeing.org/programs/nadia-bolz-weber-seeing-the-underside-and-seeing-god-tattoos-tradition-and-grace/.

Lindy West

Podcasts, a digital audio file for a computer or mobile device, have surged in the twenty-first century—as of 2019, ninety million Americans listened to this format monthly (Baer). Begun in 2004, developments in technology increased the ease of downloading and listening on personal devices. While podcasts would soon become ubiquitous, shows first popularized on the radio were foundational to the growing genre. Such is the case for the NPR program *This American Life*, considered journalistic nonfiction, or "journalism built around a plot" ("Overview"). The hour-long broadcast often features a few segments focused on a theme and is played on over five hundred radio stations with an additional 2.5 million people downloading weekly episodes. It is consistently one of the top five downloaded podcasts on iTunes and has helped launch the careers of writers such as David Sedaris and Sarah Vowell ("Overview").

A 2015 episode, "If You Don't Have Anything Nice to Say, SAY IT IN ALL CAPS," featured four acts on the problems of online anonymity, which included "Ask Not For Whom the Bell Trolls; It Trolls for Thee" by the writer Lindy West. West's work has appeared in the *Stranger* (an alternative biweekly newspaper in Seattle), on the popular website Jezebel, and she is a columnist for the *Guardian* and the *New York Times*, where she writes about feminism and pop culture. Her first book, *Shrill: Notes from a Loud Woman*, was lauded for its humor and honesty in addressing topics like fat acceptance, cyberbullying, and rape jokes; in 2019 *Shrill* was developed as a television series for Hulu starring Aidy Bryant.

West's piece on *This American Life*, adapted from an essay in *Shrill*, covers the intense threats she consistently receives from internet trolls—an insidious problem for women in the public sphere. West, like many other women on social media, even received death threats, which she alludes to in the following piece by invoking the 2015 shooting at the headquarters of the French satirical weekly magazine *Charlie Hebdo*. West deftly uses humor to cut straight to what is often unsaid. In "For Whom the Bell Trolls," she confronts an internet troll who bullied her by pretending to be her dead father. Through their two-hour conversation, West confirms what she has long suspected: the man lashing out was threatened by a woman unafraid of her power and, in particular, by West's acceptance of her own fat body. West describes the horrific realities of the abuse faced by women online. Female

authors such as West, Jessica Valenti, and Saachi Koul, to name just a few, have re-
layed stories of online abuse that threatened to or did silence them, leading them to
delete their social media accounts in order to protect not only their mental health
but sometimes their very lives.

Engaging in a civil, direct conversation with West's internet troll is groundbreaking on its own, but the dialogue further reveals linkages between bullying
and sexism, power and silencing. Through the podcast, the audience hears the
emotion in the voices of both West and the bully, as they move among anger, pain,
laughter, and kindness. The backdrop of music behind the exposition reinforces
pathos—in this case, music is absent during the intense conversation and provides
a driving accompaniment to West's reflections. Aurally, the story brings a compelling immediacy through emotive voices, reminding us that humanity that can still
be recognized through open dialogue.

"Ask Not for Whom the Bell Trolls: It Trolls for Thee": Excerpt from *This American Life* Podcast

2015

LINDY WEST: One midsummer afternoon in 2013, I got a message on Twitter from
my dead dad. I don't remember what it said exactly and I didn't keep a copy for my
scrapbook, but it was mean. And my dad was never mean, so it couldn't really be
from him. Also, he was dead.

Just eighteen months earlier, I'd watched him turn gray and drown in his own
lungs. So I was, like, 80 percent sure. And I don't believe in heaven. And even if
I did, I'd hope to God they don't have fucking Twitter there. It's heaven. Go play
chocolate badminton on a cloud with Jerry Orbach and your childhood cat.

But there was a message. Some context. In the summer of 2013, in certain circles
of the internet, comedians and feminists were at war over rape jokes. Being both
a comedy writer and a committed feminist killjoy, I weighed in with an article in
which I said that I think a lot of male comedians are careless with the subject of rape.

Here's just a sample of the responses I got on social media. A quick warning—
these are internet comments about rape, so it's going to suck. "I love how the bitch
complaining about rape is the exact kind of bitch that would never be raped."
"Holes like this make me want to commit rape out of anger." "I just want to rape her
with a traffic cone."

"No one would want to rape that fat, disgusting mess." "Kill yourself." "I want to put an apple into that mouth of yours and take a huge stick and slide it through your body and roast you." "That big bitch is bitter that no one wants to rape her."

It went on like that for weeks. It's something I'm used to. I have to be. Being insulted and threatened online is part of my job, which is not to say it doesn't hurt. It does. It feels, well, exactly like you'd imagine it would feel to have someone call you a fat cunt every day of your life.

When I got that message from my dad, it was well into rape joke summer. I was eating thirty rape threats for breakfast at that point. Or more accurately, "you're fatter than the girls I usually rape" threats. And I thought I was coping. But if you get a blade sharp enough, it'll cut through anything.

The account was called PawWestDonezo. Paw West because his name was Paul West. And Donezo because, I guess, he was done. He was done being alive, done doing crossword puzzles, done forcing me to sing duets at dinner parties. Done writing little poems on the back of every receipt. Done being my dad.

The little bio on Twitter read, "Embarrassed father of an idiot." Other two kids are fine, though. His location—dirt hole in Seattle. The profile photo was a familiar picture of him. He's sitting at his piano smiling in the living room of the house where I grew up.

The day they sold that house, when I was twenty-five, I sat on the stairs and sobbed harder than I ever had before. Because a place is kind of like a person, you know? It felt like death. I wouldn't cry that hard again until December 12, 2011, when I'd learn that a place is not like a person at all. Only a person is a person. Only a death is really a death.

My dad lost consciousness on a Saturday night. That afternoon, when we could feel his lucidity slipping, we called my brother in Boston. You were such a special little boy, he said. I love you very much. He didn't say very many things after that. I would give anything for one more sentence. I would give anything for 140 more characters.

The person who made the PawWestDonezo account clearly put some time into it. They'd researched my father and my family. They'd found out his name.

And then they figured out which Paul West he was among all the Paul Wests on the internet. They knew that I have a brother and a sister. And if they knew all that, they must have known how recently we'd lost my dad.

Conventional wisdom says never feed the trolls. Don't respond. It's what they want. I do that. It doesn't help.

I could just stop reading comments altogether, but sometimes I get threatening ones. Like the other day, someone said I should get Charlie Hebdoed. Colleagues of mine have had their addresses published online, had trolls actually show up in person at their public events. If I don't read comments, how will I know when they've crossed the line?

I could just stop writing altogether. I've thought about it. But it seems to me that our silence is what the trolls want.

Faced with PawWestDonezo, I was stuck with the question, what should I do? If I respond, I'm a sucker. But if I don't respond, I'm a punching bag.

So I did what you're not supposed to do. I fed the troll. I wrote about PawWest-Donezo in an article for Jezebel.com. I wrote sadly, candidly, angrily about how much it hurt. How much that troll had succeeded.

And then something amazing happened. The morning after that post went up, I got an email. "Hey, Lindy, I don't know why or even when I started trolling you. It wasn't because of your stance on rape jokes. I don't find them funny, either.

"I think my anger towards you stems from your happiness with your own being. It offended me because it served to highlight my unhappiness with my own self. I have emailed you through two other Gmail accounts just to send you idiotic insults. I apologize for that.

"I created the PawWestDonezo@gmail.com account and Twitter account. I have deleted both. I can't say sorry enough. It was the lowest thing I had ever done.

"When you included it in your latest Jezebel article, it finally hit me. There is a living, breathing human being who is reading this shit. I'm attacking someone who never harmed me in any way and for no reason whatsoever.

"I'm done being a troll. Again, I apologize. I made a donation in memory to your dad. I wish you the best."

They attached a receipt for a $50 donation to Seattle Cancer Care Alliance, where my dad was treated. I guess he found that out in his research, too. It was designated *Memorial Paul West*. I didn't know what to say. I wrote, "Is this real? If so, thank you."

The troll wrote back one more time, apologized again, and this time, he gave me his real name. I could have posted it online, which he knew. But I didn't and I'm not going to be saying it here, either.

That was almost eighteen months ago. But I still think about it all the time. Because I still get trolled every day. If I could get through to one troll—the meanest one I ever had—couldn't I feasibly get through to any of them? All of them? Was he special or did I do something right? I wonder how he would tell me to respond to the people trolling me today. I wish I could ask him. But then I realized, I could.

[...]

Lindy West: Hi, how are you?

MAN: I got to tell you, I'm really nervous at the moment.

WEST: I'm a little nervous also.

MAN: At least I'm not alone.

WEST: No. No, not at all.

I asked him why he chose me. He'd said in his email that it wasn't because of the rape joke thing. So what exactly did I do?

> MAN: Well, it revolved around one issue that you write about a lot, which was your being heavy.
> [...]
> MAN: The struggles you had regarding being a woman of size, or whatever the term may be.
> WEST: You can say fat. That's what I say.
> MAN: OK. Fat.

I write a lot about body image. About the stigma and discrimination that fat people face. About being a fat woman. He told me that, at the time, he was about seventy-five pounds heavier than he wanted to be. He hated his body. He was miserable. And reading about fat people—particularly fat women—accepting and loving themselves as they were infuriated him for reasons he couldn't articulate at the time.

> MAN : When you talked about being proud of who you are and where you are and where are you're going, that kind of stoked that anger that I had.
> WEST: OK. So you found my writing. [...]
> MAN: I found your writing.
> WEST: And you did not like it.
> MAN: Certain aspects of it.
> WEST: Yeah.
> MAN: You used a lot of all caps.
> [LAUGHTER]
> You're just a very—you almost have no fear when you write. You know? It's like you stand on the desk and you say, this is—"I'm Lindy West and this is what I believe." And you know, fuck you if you don't agree with me. And I—even though you don't say those words exactly, I'm like, who is this bitch who thinks she knows everything?

I asked him if he felt that way because I'm a woman.

> MAN: Oh, definitely. Definitely. Women are being more forthright in their writing. You know, they're not—there isn't a sense of timidity to when they speak or when they write. They're saying it loud. And I think that—and I think—for me, as well—it's threatening at first.
> WEST: Right. You must know that I—that's why I do that. Because people don't expect to hear from women like that. And I want other women to see me do that and I want women's voices to get louder.
> MAN: I understand. I understand. Here's the thing. I work with women all day. And I don't have an issue with anyone. I could have told you back then, if someone had said

to me, "Oh you're a misogynist. You hate women." And I could say, "Nah-ah. I love my mom, I love my sisters. You know, I've loved my girlfriends that I've had in my life." But you can't claim to be OK with women and then you go online and insult them. You know? Seek them out to harm them emotionally.

In my experience, if you call a troll a misogynist, he'll almost invariably say, "Oh, I don't hate women. I just hate what you're saying. And what that other woman is saying. And that woman. And that one. For totally unrelated reasons."

So it was satisfying, at least, to hear him admit that, yeah, he hated women. He says he doesn't troll anymore and that he's really changed. He tells me that period of time—when he was trolling me for being loud and fat—was a low point for him.

He hated his body. His girlfriend dumped him. He spent every day in front of a computer at an unfulfilling job. A passionless life, he called it.

And then gradually, he changed. He enrolled in graduate school. He found a new relationship. He started teaching little kids. He had a purpose. Slowly, his interest in trolling dried up.

We verified nearly everything that he told us about himself, except did he really stop trolling? I have no way of knowing, but I believe him. It felt true. And if this was all a con, it's one that cost him a $50 charity donation.

We talked for over two hours. And I spent a lot of time trying to get him to walk me through his transgressions in detail. The actual physical and mental steps and how he justified it all to himself. I felt like if I could just get the specifics—gather them up and hold them in my hands—then maybe I could start to understand all the people who are still trolling me.

WEST: How did you even find out that my dad died? How did you—
MAN: I went to my computer. I googled you, found out you had a father who had passed. I found out that he had—you had siblings. [...]
WEST: Did you read his obituary?
MAN: I believe I did. I knew he was a musician.
WEST: Yeah. I wrote that. I wrote his obituary.
MAN: What I did was this. I created a fake Gmail account using your father's name. Created a fake Twitter account using his name. The biography was something to the effect of, my name is—um, sorry, I forget the name—the first name.
WEST: His name was Paul West.
MAN: It said—I wrote, "My name is Paul West. I've got three kids. Two of them are great and one of them is an idiot."
WEST: Yeah, you said, "Embarrassed father of an idiot."
MAN: OK.
WEST: "Other two kids are fine, though." And then—

MAN: That's much more worse.

WEST: And you got a picture of him.

MAN: I did get a picture of him.

WEST: Did you—do you remember anything about him? Did he—did you get a sense of him as a human being?

MAN: I read the obit and I knew he was a dad that loved his kids?

WEST: How did that make you feel?

MAN: Not good. I mean, I felt horrible almost immediately afterwards. You tweeted something along the lines of, "Good job today, society." Or something along those lines.

WEST: Yeah.

MAN: It just wouldn't—for the first time, it wouldn't leave my mind. Usually, I would put out all this internet hate and oftentimes I would just forget about it. This one would not leave me. It would not leave me. I started thinking about you because I know you had read it. And I'm thinking, *How would she feel?* And the next day, I wrote you.

[. . .] And I truly am sorry about that.

WEST: Yeah, I mean—have you lost anyone? Can you imagine? Can you imagine?

MAN: I can't. I can't. I don't know what else to say except that I'm sorry.

WEST: Well, you know, I get abuse all day, every day. It's part of my job. And this was the meanest thing anyone's ever done to me.

MAN: Oh.

WEST: I mean, also—I mean, it was really fresh. He had just died. But you're also— you're the only troll who has ever apologized. Not just to me. I've never heard of this happening before. I mean, I don't know anyone who's ever—who's ever gotten an apology. And I just—I mean, you know, thank you. I—

MAN: I'm glad that you have some solace.

Honestly, I did have some solace. I forgave him. I felt sorry for him. It's so difficult to believe that anyone ever really changes. And he did it. I found immense comfort in that.

Toward the end of our conversation, I remembered that, in his email, he confessed that he'd harassed me from multiple troll accounts, not just PawWestDonezo.

Did I ever write back? Was there anything I didn't know? He said, "Yeah." One time, he'd sent something mean from his personal account and I retweeted it to all my forty thousand followers. He was mortified.

[. . .]

WEST: Well, you know, I mean it's such a normalized part of my life now. I mean, honestly—and it's kind of a relief to talk to someone who really knows what I'm talking about, even though he's coming at it from the other direction. You know, there's almost no one who understands—

MAN: Well, you know what? As a former troll, I never told a single living human being until now that I did this. So it's good, in a way, to get that off my chest. To get my secret life—my old life—I don't know. It just feels good to kind of exorcise these demons.

It felt really easy—comfortable, even—to talk to my troll. I liked him and I didn't know what to do with that. It's frightening to discover that he's so normal. He has female coworkers who enjoy his company. He has a real live girlfriend who loves him. They have no idea that he used to go online and traumatize women for fun.

Trolls live among us. I've gotten anonymous comments from people saying they met me at a movie theater and I was a bitch or they served me at a restaurant and my boobs aren't as big as they look in pictures. People say it doesn't matter what happens on the internet—that it's not real life. But thanks to internet trolls, I'm perpetually reminded that the boundary between the civilized world and our worst selves is just an illusion.

Trolls still waste my time and tax my mental health on a daily basis. But honestly, I don't wish them any pain. Their pain is what got us here in the first place. That's what I learned from my troll.

If what he said is true—that he just needed to find some meaning in his life—then what a heartbreaking diagnosis for all the people who are still at it. I can't give purpose and fulfillment to millions of anonymous strangers. But I can remember not to lose sight of their humanity the way that they lost sight of mine.

Humans can be reached. I have proof. Empathy, boldness, kindness—those are things I learned from my dad, though he never knew how much I'd need them. Or maybe he did. He was a jazz musician and when I was born he wrote a song about me. And listening to it now, it feels like he wrote it for just this moment. I'll give the last word to him [song plays].

IRA GLASS: Lindy West in Seattle. So since we first ran Lindy's story a year ago, something interesting happened. Her story spurred a discussion inside Twitter that led its CEO at the time, Dick Costolo, to write a memo to employees that was leaked to the public.

It said, quote, "We suck at dealing with abuse and trolls. And we've sucked at it for years. It's no secret. And the rest of the world talks about it every day. I'm frankly ashamed of how poorly we've dealt with this issue. It's absurd. There's no excuse for it." In the months since then, Twitter has introduced some new anti-bullying tools and policies. They've gotten decidedly mixed reviews, like "not far enough."

FOR FURTHER READING

Baer, Jay. "The 14 Critical Podcast Statistics of 2019." *Convince and Convert*, n.d., https://www.con vinceandconvert.com/podcast-research/2019-podcast-statistics/.

Goldberg, Michelle. "Feminist Writers Are so Besieged by Online Abuse That Some Have Begun to Retire." *The Washington Post*, 20 Feb. 2015, www.washingtonpost.com/opinions/online-femi nists-increasingly-ask-are-the-psychic-costs-too-much-to-bear/2015/02/19/3dc4ca6c-b7dd- 11e4-a200-c008a01a6692_story.html?utm_term=.24c7ad08bb66.

Gross, Terry. "Columnist Lindy West Sees 'Straight Line' From Trolls Who Targeted Her to Trump." *NPR*, 1 Nov. 2017, www.npr.org/2017/11/01/561350775/columnist-lindy-west-sees-straight -line-from-trolls-who-targeted-her-to-trump.

"Overview." *This American Life*, n.d., www.thisamericanlife.org/about.

West, Lindy. "Ask Not for Whom the Bell Trolls; It Trolls for Thee." "If You Don't Have Anything Nice to Say, SAY IT IN ALL CAPS." *This American Life*, NPR, 15 Jan. 2015.

West, Lindy. *Shrill: Notes from a Loud Woman*. Hachette, 2016.

II

Rhetorics of Feminisms

During the last decades of the twentieth century, the media declared a postfeminist era—feminism was irrelevant, headlines announced. But women rhetors in the twenty-first century tell a much different story, revitalizing feminism as more inclusive of a range of identities, expanding feminism's focus to encompass transnational views, and amplifying feminism's rhetorical reach through art, activism, and digital media.

Perhaps most notably, twenty-first-century feminist rhetors insist upon *intersectionality*, a term coined in 1986 by Kimberlé Crenshaw, whose piece "Why Intersectionality Can't Wait" opens this section. Intersectional feminism considers gender as necessarily interwoven with other identities, resulting in power differentials among how women across racial groups, socioeconomic status, and sexuality experience systemic oppression in their gendered lives. Robin Boylorn, Barbara Sostaita, Patricia Valoy, and Amy Alexander deepen and expand Crenshaw's argument, articulating the necessity of a feminism that is inseparable from their intersectional identities and histories as women of color and challenging feminism's long association with white women. To this end, Boylorn details a black feminism borne from the legacy of her female relatives, and Sostaita calls for a celebration of Women's Month that makes women of color "the heart and soul of the narrative." Valoy insists that twenty-first-century feminism must be transnational, attentive to how national borders, histories of colonialism, and global capitalism shape gender oppression around the world. Finally, Alexander argues that despite the intersectional claims of the Women's March movement, much work remains to foster truly intersectional and inclusive feminist activism.

Another defining trait of twenty-first-century feminists is their insistence on an expansive, inclusive feminism. Emi Koyama extends feminism's boundaries in a transfeminist manifesto, which challenges biological essentialism and welcomes all those, including trans men, women, and genderqueer people, who "view their liberation to be intrinsically linked to the liberation of all women and beyond." The author Chimamanda Adichie argues for a feminism that is welcoming, adaptable, and fun: "A big raucous inclusive party." Beyoncé has perhaps issued the century's most visible invitation to the party, encouraging legions to see feminism anew. Celebrity endorsements of feminism, however, have fueled criticism for watering down and corporatizing the movement. Erica Thurman's piece is a response to the feminist scholar bell hooks's critique of Beyoncé, arguing that while Beyoncé's vision may be different from hooks's, it is just as legitimate and necessary. In "Why I'm a Pro-Life Feminist," Claire Swinarski addresses yet another divisive issue among feminists and women more broadly: reproductive rights. While feminists are often expected to be staunchly pro-choice, she makes a different case and shows how the rhetorical tactics from both sides of the debate prevent women from finding common ground on this issue.

To be sure, the digital affordances of the twenty-first century have also changed the rhetorical landscape of feminist work, altering the way feminists organize, communicate, and circulate their messages. Many of the pieces in this section first appeared as blog posts or in online media outlets. But feminists also repurpose traditional mediums to new ends. Through her needlepoint craftivism piece, *The Future is Female*, Shannon Downey relies on a traditional form that she then circulates through social media—encouraging other women to participate in feminist making.

The section concludes with Sara Ahmed's "A Killjoy's Survival Kit," which offers advice for self-care and self-preservation to those who may be weary from the sometimes grueling work of feminist activism. Taken together, this set of feminist rhetorical acts articulates a twenty-first-century feminism that is expansive, inclusive, and adaptable to the changing problems and issues of our time.

Kimberlé Crenshaw

One of the most referenced terms with regard to feminism in the twenty-first century is *intersectionality*, coined by Kimberlé Crenshaw in 1986. While the term is ubiquitous, its beginnings and fullest meaning are less known, something Crenshaw seeks to correct in this piece, published on the heels of two race-related tragedies. The first was the June 2015 shooting by a white supremacist of nine African American parishioners at a South Carolina church. The second was Sandra Bland's death in a Texas jail cell following a disputed arrest in July 2015 (see Michelle Denise Jackson's contribution to this volume). These events served as a *kairotic* moment for the crucial reminder that "if women and girls of color continue to be left in the shadows, something vital to the understanding of intersectionality has been lost."

Crenshaw, born in 1959 and raised in Ohio, received her law degree from Harvard University and a Master of Laws degree from the University of Wisconsin. A leader in critical race theory, her distinguished career also includes writings on the law and civil rights, black feminist legal theory, and race and law. Her work has appeared in numerous law reviews, and she also serves as a public intellectual, contributing to publications like *Ms.* magazine, the *Nation*, and the *New York Times*. In 1996 Crenshaw co-founded the African American Policy Forum, a think tank focused on structural inequality, and in 2011 she spearheaded Columbia Law School's Center for Intersectionality and Social Policy Studies. Crenshaw's work has shaped national and international policy, including the equality clause in the South African constitution.

While intersectionality is now a central tenet in feminist conversations, Crenshaw reminds us that it is not a new concept, hearkening to the nineteenth-century rhetors Anna Julia Cooper and Maria Stewart: "In every generation and in every intellectual sphere and in every political moment, there have been African American women who have articulated the need to think and talk about race through a lens that looks at gender, or think and talk about feminism through a lens that looks at race" (Adewunmi). In this piece, Crenshaw historicizes her exigence for coining the term *intersectionality*: a 1976 General Motors case, in which the discrimination suit by Emma DeGraffenreid and other black women was dismissed because the court did not find it justifiable to combine gender and race discrimination.

With keen awareness of the mainstream audience of a national newspaper, Crenshaw explains that intersectionality is a theory for addressing identity and power as broad and systemic. It is not a synonym for "identity politics"—though it is often reduced to such—in which a particular identity group promotes only their interests. At every turn, she points out that the institutional and structural issues brought forth by intersectionality must be answered through action, which is evident in movements like #WhyWeCan'tWait—the campaign to include women and girls in President Obama's My Brother's Keeper initiative, which provides pathways to opportunity for boys and young men of color—and #SayHerName, which targets police violence against black women. Crenshaw's writing here is deliberate but urgent, explaining the concept with care and context, and insisting that there is no possibility for social justice without attention to intersectionality.

"Why Intersectionality Can't Wait"

Washington Post, 2015

Today, nearly three decades after I first put a name to the concept, the term seems to be everywhere. But if women and girls of color continue to be left in the shadows, something vital to the understanding of intersectionality has been lost.

In 1976 Emma DeGraffenreid and several other black women sued General Motors for discrimination, arguing that the company segregated its workforce by race and gender: Blacks did one set of jobs and whites did another. According to the plaintiffs' experiences, women were welcome to apply for some jobs, while only men were suitable for others. This was of course a problem in and of itself, but for black women the consequences were compounded. You see, the black jobs were men's jobs, and the women's jobs were only for whites. Thus, while a black applicant might get hired to work on the floor of the factory if he were male; if she were a black female she would not be considered. Similarly, a woman might be hired as a secretary if she were white, but wouldn't have a chance at that job if she were black. Neither the black jobs nor the women's jobs were appropriate for black women, since they were neither male nor white. Wasn't this clearly discrimination, even if some blacks and some women were hired?

Unfortunately for DeGraffenreid and millions of other black women, the court dismissed their claims. Why? Because the court believed that black women should not be permitted to combine their race and gender claims into one. Because they could not prove that what happened to them was just like what happened to white women or black men, the discrimination that happened to these black women fell through the cracks.

It was in thinking about why such a "big miss" could have happened within the complex structure of anti-discrimination law that the term "intersectionality" was born. As a young law professor, I wanted to define this profound invisibility in relation to the law. Racial and gender discrimination overlapped not only in the workplace but in other arenas of life; equally significant, these burdens were almost completely absent from feminist and anti-racist advocacy. Intersectionality, then, was my attempt to make feminism, anti-racist activism, and anti-discrimination law do what I thought they should—highlight the multiple avenues through which racial and gender oppression were experienced so that the problems would be easier to discuss and understand.

Intersectionality is an analytic sensibility, a way of thinking about identity and its relationship to power. Originally articulated on behalf of black women, the term brought to light the invisibility of many constituents within groups that claim them as members, but often fail to represent them. Intersectional erasures are not exclusive to black women. People of color within LGBTQ movements; girls of color in the fight against the school-to-prison pipeline; women within immigration movements; trans women within feminist movements; and people with disabilities fighting police abuse—all face vulnerabilities that reflect the intersections of racism, sexism, class oppression, transphobia, able-ism and more. Intersectionality has given many advocates a way to frame their circumstances and to fight for their visibility and inclusion.

Intersectionality has been the banner under which many demands for inclusion have been made, but a term can do no more than those who use it have the power to demand. And not surprisingly, intersectionality has generated its share of debate and controversy.

Conservatives have painted those who practice intersectionality as obsessed with "identity politics." Of course, as the DeGraffenreid case shows, intersectionality is not just about identities but about the institutions that use identity to exclude and privilege. The better we understand how identities and power work together from one context to another, the less likely our movements for change are to fracture.

Others accuse intersectionality of being too theoretical, of being "all talk and no action." To that I say we've been "talking" about racial equality since the era of slavery and we're still not even close to realizing it. Instead of blaming the voices that highlight problems, we need to examine the structures of power that so successfully resist change.

Some have argued that intersectional understanding creates an atmosphere of bullying and "privilege checking." Acknowledging privilege is hard—particularly for those who also experience discrimination and exclusion. While white women and men of color also experience discrimination, all too often their experiences are taken as the only point of departure for all conversations about discrimination.

Being front and center in conversations about racism or sexism is a complicated privilege that is often hard to see.

Although the president's recent call to support black women was commende able, undertaking intersectional work requires concrete action to address the barriers to equality facing women and girls of color in US society.

Intersectionality alone cannot bring invisible bodies into view. Mere words won't change the way that some people—the less-visible members of political constituencies—must continue to wait for leaders, decision-makers, and others to see their struggles. In the context of addressing the racial disparities that still plague our nation, activists and stakeholders must raise awareness about the intersectional dimensions of racial injustice that must be addressed to enhance the lives of all youths of color.

This is why we continue the work of the #WhyWeCantWait campaign, calling for holistic and inclusive approaches to racial justice. It is why Say Her Name continues to draw attention to the fact that women too are vulnerable to losing their lives at the hands of police. And it is why thousands have agreed that the tragedy in Charleston, SC, demonstrates our need to sustain a vision of social justice that recognizes the ways racism, sexism, and other inequalities work together to undermine us all. We simply do not have the luxury of building social movements that are not intersectional, nor can we believe we are doing intersectional work just by saying words.

FOR FURTHER READING

Adewunmi, Bim. "Kimberlé Crenshaw on Intersectionality: 'I Wanted to Come Up with an Everyday Metaphor that Anyone Could Use.'" *New Statesman*, 2 Apr. 2014, www.newstatesman.com/life style/2014/04/kimberl-crenshaw-intersectionality-i-wanted-come-everyday-metaphor-any one-could.

Crenshaw, Kimberlé. *On Intersectionality: Essential Writings.* New Press, 2019.

Crenshaw, Kimberlé, et al., editors. *Critical Race Theory: The Key Writings that Formed the Movement.* New Press, 1996.

"Faculty Profiles: Kimberlé W. Crenshaw." *Columbia Law School,* n.d., www.law.columbia.edu/fac ulty/kimberle-crenshaw.

"Faculty Profiles: Kimberlé W. Crenshaw." *UCLA Law,* n.d., https://law.ucla.edu/faculty/faculty -profiles/kimberle-w-crenshaw/.

"Intersectionality Primer." *African American Policy Forum,* 17 Jan. 2013, www.aapf.org/2013/2013/01/ intersectionality-primer?rq=A%20Primer%20on%20Intersectionality.

Robin M. Boylorn

In 1983 Alice Walker coined the term *womanist*, explaining that "womanist is to feminist as purple is to lavender." For Walker, womanism is a deeper shade of feminism, centered on the lives of black women and attentive to perspectives historically overlooked by white feminists. Indeed, women of color have long had to challenge and expand definitions of feminism to account for their lived realities. In her definitional essay here, Robin Boylorn—a scholar, activist, and writer—follows in this tradition, rewriting feminism as an unnamed inheritance she received from the women who raised her.

Though she is a professor at the University of Alabama, Boylorn's feminism is not rooted in academe—it grew from the lives of her mother, grandmother, and aunts—women who were powerful because they had to survive. Through their lived examples, she learned that feminism can be contradictory, questioning, and evolving. As a result, Boylorn learned to own her feminism like she owns herself.

In the following essay Boylorn advances the phrase *my feminism* as a percussive beat, rolling out a definition that is all her own, but that also makes room for other women—especially women of color. Ultimately, she defines her feminism as "crunk." Boylorn is part of the Crunk Feminist Collective, whose digital platform creates a supportive space for the "hip-hop generation of feminists of color, queer and straight, in the academy and without" (Mission Statement). In their mission, the Crunk Feminist Collective explains that while the term *crunk* originally combined *crazy* or *chronic* with *drunk*, meaning you were out of your mind, crunk feminism is a "mode of resistance [that] will help you *get your mind right.*" Just like the feminism Boylorn learned from her mama, crunk feminism promotes "following the rhythm of our own heartbeats."

Boylorn has followed this rhythm in her activist and scholarly work, writing for a range of publications, including *Slate*, *Ebony*, and the *Guardian*, in addition to scholarly journals. In her award-winning autoethnography, *Sweetwater: Black Women and the Narratives of Resilience*, Boylorn honors her familiar heritage, tracing the intergenerational experiences of black women in a rural North Carolina community. Her forthcoming book, *Blackgirl Blue(s)*, theorizes the experience of blackgirl (one word) identity—insisting, as does her feminism, that gender is inseparable from race and that the stories our culture has silenced must be amplified.

"Mama's Feminism":
Excerpt from *The Crunk Feminist Collection*

2017

I don't have a lot of friends who identify as feminist. My nonacademic, nonactivist friends don't see themselves as feminists, don't call themselves feminists, don't all the way understand what it means. They spend a lot of time trying to resist myths around being Black and a woman, and don't have the energy or motivation to also resist myths of feminism—of bra-burning White women who hate men and stand in picket lines, or bourgeois Black women who understand the theoretical nexus that connects their lives to "the cause" but become disconnected from movements close to home.

Feminism as a term was born in academe (in an environment that polices people's behaviors to dictate who can and cannot be feminist and what is and is not feminist). Feminism was conceived at my mama's house (in a space that made woman power and intentional equality a survival strategy and mechanism to make up for oppression, the absence of men, and lifestyles that were without the luxury of adhering to strict gender scripts).

I learned feminism from my mama and them, rural women who did not have the benefit of formal college education or fancy words for how they lived. They would, no doubt, by strict standards, in the vulnerable moments of their lives that were necessary for sanity and survival, have been called unfeminist while the world called them unfeminine. They would have had little investment in either label, learning from experience how dangerous it is to let outside people dictate your inside thoughts. They would have been resented by traditional feminists for the way they were conditioned to desire men and canonical lifestyles while being single parents to multiple children, fantasizing about whitewashed happily-ever-afters. Their lifestyles were feminist, but their dreams and desires, for being kept women with White women's problems, would have been read as problematic. They would have rebelled because they wouldn't let a label like *feminist* tell them what to do. They wouldn't give a damn what people thought about them.

I learned/realized I was a feminist from a teacher who described my mama without saying her name, gave her secrets away without giving her credit, and put struggling on a pedestal. Feminism became a metaphorical stepping stool, giving me access to the self-actualization I would have otherwise not known to reach for.

I got my feminism from my mama, even though she doesn't know it. And my grandmother. And my aunties. They had a feminism that would fight back and hide behind the mask of smiles or scorn. My mama's feminism was wrapped up in God and respectability politics she could never live up to. She taught me to have mustard-seed faith. My grandmama's feminism was housed in her meanness and caution. She carried it with her for emergencies and protection, like the cigarettes in her pocket and the gun in her bra. She taught me how and when to fight. My aunties held their feminism in their laughter and occasional anger. They used it to cover up pain. They taught me to get mad, but not stay mad. My mothers didn't know they were feminists. They didn't mean to pass it on to me but they couldn't help it.

My mama's feminism is inherited but unnamed. She taught me how to own my feminism like I own myself. She taught me how to be a feminist by being herself.

My feminism needs space to breathe and room to stretch out. My feminism never gets old. It is quiet sometimes. It listens to hip-hop and gospel music, watches soap operas, and likes to be listened to. My feminism shows up in the bedroom and the classroom. It asks for what it wants, doesn't apologize for what it needs, and isn't afraid of being alone. My feminism is androgynous. It loves football and basketball, and dances when no one is looking. My feminism is soulful and historic, sexual and conscientious. It is standoffish and suspicious. My feminism needs to drink more water.

My feminism has daddy issues. It talks back, snaps back, hits back, and doesn't take any shit. My feminism kicks ass and takes names. My feminism says no. My feminism cries and doesn't cover its eyes in shame. It gets mad and doesn't try to explain it away. My feminism is peaceful in practice but ready for war. My feminism is in conversation with other feminisms and makes room for difference. My feminism takes mental health days and moves on when people walk away. My feminism loves Jesus and critiques the church, wears black fingernail polish and red lipstick, and loves reality TV. My feminism is homegrown. Rebellious. Reckoning. Evolving. Unapologetic. And beautiful. My feminism is opinionated. It questions everything.

My feminism is not always right, but it's never wrong. My feminism has insomnia. My feminism gets tired. My feminism is antiracist, antisexist, and conscious of class issues. My feminism knows what misogyny means. It takes days off. It tells people off.

My feminism, like my mama, is braver than me, stronger than me, and keeps me grounded. My feminism, like me, is complicated and full of contradictions.

My feminism is crunk. My feminism has dreams.

FOR FURTHER READING

"BIO/GRAPHY." *Robin-Boylorn*, 2018, www.robinboylorn.com/blank-c161y.

Boylorn, Robin M. *Sweetwater: Black Women and Narratives of Resilience.* Peter Lang, 2017.

Cooper, Brittney C., et al. *The Crunk Feminist Collection.* Feminist Press, 2017.

"Mission Statement." *Crunk Feminist Collective*, 8 Aug. 2016, www.crunkfeministcollective.com/about/.

Walker, Alice. *In Search of Our Mother's Garden.* Women's Press, 2000.

Barbara Sostaita

In 1980 President Jimmy Carter declared March 2–8 National Women's History Week. He quoted Gerda Lerner, chair of the Women's History Institute, to describe its importance: "Women's history is women's right—an essential, indispensable heritage from which we can draw pride, comfort, courage, and long-range vision" (Zorthian). In 1987 Congress officially declared March National Women's History Month. Even as the month is designed to recognize women whose vital contributions to US history have been erased or ignored, Women's Month, Barbara Sostaita declares, has too long focused on the accomplishments of white women. Her polemical piece included here is designed to right that wrong.

Sostaita received her master's degree in religion from Yale Divinity School and is completing her doctorate at the University of North Carolina at Chapel Hill, where she researches issues of religion and migration. Like others in this volume, however, her rhetoric reaches a range of audiences. As a regular contributor to the popular websites Latina, Feministing, Vivala, and the *Huffington Post*, Sostaita writes about immigration issues, the US-Mexico border wall, Latinx culture, and feminism. Through her op-eds, she weaves her own stories with US political and cultural events. For example, in one piece Sostaita describes her move from Argentina to the United States when she was in the first grade, detailing the arduous process of learning to live in a new country, and revealing that at age twenty, she learned at the DMV of her undocumented status. In another article, Sostaita publicly rebuts the racist assumptions of an anonymous internet troll and corrects their misinformation about immigration. Sostaita's pieces are not meant to make white or US native readers comfortable—for instance, she doesn't translate Spanish phrases, and she unabashedly describes the loss of community and the tokenization that accompanies her identity as a "high-achieving" immigrant.

In the following piece, Sostaita potently confronts Women's History Month as an enterprise that lauds white feminism and tokenizes the accomplishments of women of color. With repetitive *I* statements, Sostaita foregrounds her agency as a feminist of color, forwarding her own vision of Women's History Month, which celebrates migrant women and honors women like Lezley McSpadden, whose unarmed black son, Michael Brown, was killed by a police officer (see Lezley McSpadden's contribution to this volume). Sostaita takes white feminism to task for heralding the Facebook executive Sheryl Sandberg, without accounting for her racial and economic privilege. Sostaita showcases the often invisible achievements by women of color—such triumphs should be front and center, she proclaims, since a history in which women see themselves reflected is, indeed, the right of *all* women. In this way, Sostaita offers us a revised Women's History Month that upends whitewashed, monolithic ideas of feminism.

"This Women's History Month, I Refuse to Celebrate Your Feminism"

Huffington Post, 2016

March 1st marks the beginning of Women's History Month; also known as 31 days during which I am subjected to the celebration of white women's accomplishments and victories, many of which have come at the expense of women and communities of color.

During this month, "exceptional" women and "important" milestones are celebrated. We hear about and honor the suffragettes, whose campaign for the right to vote was rooted in racist and exclusionary politics. We laud women such as Hillary Clinton, who said Central American refugee children "should be sent back" and whose support for her husband's policies "decimated black America." We call women like Sheryl Sandberg, whose formula for workplace success depends heavily on her worldview as a wealthy white woman, revolutionary.

But you see, revolutionary means something completely different to me. My Women's History Month celebrates the migrant women in detention centers who find ways to resist even in their captivity. My Women's History Month honors women like Lezley McSpadden, Michael Brown's mother, who marched to mark the 50th anniversary of Selma and denounced the systemic racism that killed her son and so many others who look like him. My Women's History Month recognizes women like my professor, Alicia Schmidt Camacho, who was arrested last week at a rally calling on President Obama to stop the deportations of Central American refugees. My Women's History Month uplifts and elevates women of color who struggle every day to make room for ourselves in hostile spaces and fight to break down structures that keep us down.

This Women's History Month, I refuse to celebrate a white feminism that keeps women of color on the margins. This Women's History Month, I refuse to celebrate a white feminism that alienates, subjugates, and oppresses women of color. I don't want to be hear about the first Latina (insert public office title) or the first Asian (insert professional sports title). I'm sick of women of color only being mentioned and deemed worthy when we are the "first," when we fit neatly into a box crafted by white women's version of history. We have been, are, and will always be "exceptional" and "important."

I don't want a whitewashed feminism that tokenizes, fetishizes, and abuses women of color. You can keep your Taylor Swift squad goals, Ready for Hillary, Ban Bossy feminism. I want Nicki Minaj's *"Miley what's good?"* feminism. Beyoncé's ****flawless* feminism. Sandra Cisneros's *"becoming a woman comfortable in her skin"* feminism. Toni Morrison's *thick love* feminism. Warsan Shire's *give your daughters difficult names* feminism. Maya Angelou's *still I rise* feminism. Gloria Anzaldúa's *mestiza consciousness* feminism. Ntozake Shange's *for colored girls* feminism.

I want a feminism and a women's history that puts women of color at the center. At the heart and soul of the narrative. Because if anyone knows about heart and soul, it's us. Because we've learned to turn pain into art. Because, as Gloria Anzaldúa reminds us, "even when our bodies have been battered by life . . . we make a home out of the cracks." Because we've made a way out of no way. Because as Delores Williams tells us, we are sisters in the wilderness. I refuse to celebrate your whitewashed feminism. I commit to celebrating *mis mujeres, en la lucha.*

FOR FURTHER READING

"Barbara Sostaita." *University of North Carolina at Chapel Hill Department of Religious Studies,* n.d.,
    religion.unc.edu/_people/graduate-students/barbara-sostaita/.
Sostaita, Barbara. "For Colored Girls in Academe." *Huffington Post,* 31 May 2016, www.huffington
    post.com/entry/for-colored-girls-in-acad_b_7480014.html.
Sostaita, Barbara. "I Annotated This Facebook Message from a Troll." *Feministing,* n.d., feministing
    .com/2017/03/17/facebook-message-from-a-troll-annotated/.
Sostaita, Barbara. "It Happened to Me: I Was an Undocumented Immigrant." *Huffington Post,* 13 Nov.
    2014,www.huffingtonpost.com/2014/11/13/it-happened-to-me-i-was-a_1_n_6151664.html.
Sostaita, Barbara. "Making Crosses, Crossing Borders: The Performance of Mourning, the Power of
    Ghosts, and the Politics of Countermemory in the U.S.-Mexico Borderlands." Mediation, *MAV-
    COR Journal,* 2016, https://mavcor.yale.edu/conversations/mediations/making-crosses-cross
    ing-borders-performance-mourning-power-ghosts-and.
Sostaita, Barbara. "No Quiero Salir Adelante." *Huffington Post,* 6 Dec. 2017, www.huffingtonpost
    .com/entry/no-quiero-salir-adelante_b_9662472.html.
Zorthian, Julia. "March Is Women's History Month: How It Started." *TIME,* 29 Feb. 2016, time
    .com/4238999/womens-history-month-history/.

Patricia Valoy

The transnational feminist Chandra Talpade Mohanty argues that in the twentieth century, we saw a flourishing and maturing of feminist ideas and movements; at the same time, we also witnessed a recolonizing of the world by global capitalism and an increase in ethnic, nationalist, and religious fundamentalist movements (2–3). For Mohanty, as for the feminist activist, blogger, and civil engineer Patricia Valoy, whose piece follows, a twenty-first-century transnational approach to feminism is a necessary answer to the deepening problems of colonization, imperialism, and oppression that impact women around the globe.

While transnational feminism may be more commonly known in the US academy than outside of it, Valoy employs accessible and engaging language to describe its tenets and establish its import to the wide online readership of the online magazine *Everyday Feminism*. Because transnational feminism eschews universal approaches to gender oppression, urging consideration of the contexts, locations, and particularities of women's lives, Valoy opens the following piece by locating her own multiplicities. As a foreign-born Latina feminist and STEM advocate living in the United States, "I am transnational," she writes, so her feminism must both account for and see beyond borders.

This transnational approach shifts feminism away from a US or Western-centric view, which overlooks crucial differences among women and too often assumes a one-size-fits-all Western model of liberation. As the transnational feminist scholars Inderpal Grewal and Caren Kaplan insist, "There is an imperative need to address the concerns of women around the world in the historicized particularity of their relationships to multiple patriarchies as well as to international economic hegemonies" (17). Valoy grounds this idea with the example of the SlutWalk, which might be an effective way to argue for sexual liberation in the United States, but may not be appropriate, or feel liberating, to women in locations where women are the victims of sex trafficking. While enactments of and issues addressed by feminist movements around the globe might be different, Valoy challenges the common assumption that women in third world countries lack agency, offering examples of transnational feminist movements in developing nations that aid women and resist political oppression.

Transnational feminism is an identifier and a way of life for Valoy, and this means attending to the plight of women in her current home, the United States; in her homeland, the Dominican Republic; and also to women beyond those national boundaries, asking "how my activism and writing translates to those that need it the most." In a world that is increasingly connected but rife with disparity and subjection, Valoy calls readers to a transnational feminist way of life that involves vigilant attention to the global impact of feminist issues—to a feminism that thinks across and beyond borders.

"Transnational Feminism: Why Feminist Activism Needs to Think Globally"

Everyday Feminism, 2015

My identity is multifaceted and intersectional, and I suspect that most of you reading this feel the same way. But as a foreign-born, woman of color feminist in the United States, it can be hard to find the group within feminism that feels just right for me.

I am a foreign-born Latina feminist who is all about STEM advocacy, so I fit into a lot of categories all at the same time. The terms intersectional, Latina, Afro-Indigenous, Black, STEM-inist, and women of color all make my heart race with excitement. I feel at home within all those circles—and, simultaneously, foreign.

For this reason, I adopted transnational feminism as an identifier and way of life. Rather than negate my other identities, it complements them.

So What Exactly Is Transnational Feminism?

Transnational feminists examine issues from a global perspective while considering how they intersect with our lived experiences in the United States.

We focus on intersections across nationality (including race and ethnicity), sex, gender, and class within the context of modern-day imperialism and colonialism.

Most people think imperialism and colonialism are terms of the past, of history, but we use these terms often in transnational feminist thought because we live with the effects of them.

As feminists, it's important to understand the various historical happenings that led to the way our modern world is shaped.

The violent acquisition of countries with Black and Brown populations by powerful empires—*which were mostly European*—led to the exploitation of our resources and subjugation of our people. For some of us, that means the loss of culture, language, and heritage.

To many, the beginning was the famous voyage by Christopher Columbus in 1492, but to legions of others, it started earlier and has continued for much longer (see Africa and the Middle East).

Western feminism, which is largely based on liberal thought, overemphasizes gender roles as the sole reason for women's oppression.

By working within the structures of mainstream society, liberal feminists aim to gain political and social gains by integrating women into powerful positions, thus assimilating into patriarchal and Eurocentric standards of leadership and equity.

It's understandable why this is a feminist thought that appeals to white women in developed nations (who don't have to deal with the intersecting oppressions of colonialism and imperialism), **but this sort of feminism does not consider the ways in which women of color are oppressed along racial and class lines.**

Furthermore, non-Western women are often painted as oppressed and lacking agency. This is evident in the way in which mainstream media shows veiled women to imply a lack of freedom, meanwhile ignoring that covering the face can be an act of defiance for political representations, such as in the case of the Zapatistas.

We are consolidated into a homogeneous group without any historical, political, or geographical context. Groups such as the Zapatistas, Women Living Under Muslim Laws, and AF3IRM paint a different story of so-called third world women. These organizations employ direct revolutionary action and raise consciousness to help women in their current lifestyle, while also fighting the political issues that oppress them.

This is unlike Western feminist campaigning.

While Western feminism overemphasizes commonalities with women across nations, transnational feminism recognizes inequalities across different groups of women, so that in essence, **it's a series of feminisms addressing particular issues and not one uniform movement.**

This is a crucial aspect of feminism for transnational women of color because although we all might identify as women, **the ways in which global issues affects us is not always the same.** And more importantly, our positions of privilege and/ or disenfranchisement can change depending on our geographical location.

These differences are crucial to forming solidarity within feminism that does not erase the lived experiences of marginalized groups. **For this reason, transnational feminists always consider the global impact of the issues for which they advocate.**

One way they do so is in the fight to end the hypermilitarization of our society.

In the United States, one way in which (primarily) men of color can achieve financial independence and economic advancement is by joining the military.

Yet supporting the military also means turning our backs on people (who are primarily women) in the Philippines, Afghanistan, Iraq, and many other countries, who live under American and/or European military violence.

One can't have solidarity with nations living under US military occupation while simultaneously promoting the power structures that allow this to happen.

For this reason, transnational feminists aim to end social constructs that pit people of color against their own for imperialist motives disguised as liberation. We see liberation as something that must come from within our own communities and nations—not something that is bestowed on us by people in power.

How Do We Promote the Success of People of Color in the US and Dismantle Oppressive Regimes Worldwide?

Transnational feminist organizations provide people of color with alternative resources so they don't feel that joining the military is the only choice for economic success.

Transnational feminists also question the types of advocacy that liberal, Western feminist practice to promote the sexual liberation of women.

This is not to suggest that transnational feminists do not believe in women's sexual autonomy, but rather that we consider the context in which our bodies are being asked to be displayed and for what purpose. Sexual liberation is a shared issue among all feminists. Whether we hold traditional values or otherwise, we all firmly believe that our bodies are primarily ours and we should be able to do with them as we desire.

But unlike common Western sexual liberation advocacy, **transnational women of color see sexual liberation as more than freely displaying our bodies**; it's also about practicing our respective religions, customs, and ideologies safely and without threat of harassment or discrimination.

Further, when the majority of victims of sexual trafficking are women of color living under vulnerable circumstances, one must question the bias and privilege one must have to organize movements that depict sexual liberation with casual sex, nudity, and the reclamation of words that continue to harm and marginalize us—such as "slut."

Transnational feminists feel that before we ask women of color to participate in campaigns such as SlutWalk and FEMEN's naked advocacy, we need to address the ways in which so many of them are sexually exploited. Women of color are criminalized for being "sluts" under racist laws that vilify sex workers, as in the case of New Orleans. **For women who are constantly reduced to sex objects, it's not always empowering to call ourselves sluts.**

And although organizations like FEMEN can help denounce such slut shaming, they spend considerable time asking women to uncover (rather than welcoming foreign-born women of color into leadership positions to help generate more inclusive strategies for the movement).

Sex tourism and militarized prostitution overwhelmingly occur in developing countries, especially those that have a history of colonialism.

If the inequalities that were set in place during American and European colonialist history of genocide and slavery are not dismantled, they will continue to affect individuals along ethnic and racial lines, which is then compounded by sexism.

Transnational feminists feel that in order to attain true sexual agency, we must first dismantle the systems that make sexual exploitation a daily experience for many women worldwide. For example, instead of telling women to unveil or wear miniskirts to show us how sexually liberated they are, we should be supporting them in all their choices—*regardless of whether that does or does not include sexualized clothing or behavior*—and fight to end social constructs that allow women to be labeled based on their attire.

Domestic worker's rights and immigration rights are also at the forefront of transnational feminist activism. Transnational women of color living in the United States represent the largest number of domestic workers: 46% of them are foreign-born, and 35% are noncitizens.

And while Western feminism has acknowledged that domestic worker protections are a feminist issue, many fail to make a connection between immigration reform, worker's rights, and gender violence throughout the world. **It's all about race and class inequalities, and one cannot be fixed without the other.**

Transnational feminist organizations ensure that the needs of those marginalized within minority groups are also being met. This is the case for the Sylvia Rivera Law Project, who provide legal services to trans immigrants.

It is important to support immigrant communities, but also fighting to stop the US capitalist endeavors in developing countries that make immigration a necessity and not a choice.

To be feminist is to be anti-capitalist, anti-imperialist, and anti-patriarchal because these systems function together to create inequality and maintain the status quo.

As an American, I care deeply about US policies and how they affect women in this country. But as a Dominican Latina, my mind is always on the plight of women in my homeland and other Latin American countries.

As a foreign-born woman, I consider the way that global issues affect marginalized women in other parts of the world. And as a foreign-language speaker, I wonder how my activism and writing translates to those that need it the most.

My feminism transcends borders because my identity does.

I am transnational. For my feminism to have an impact, I must fight the countries that put up the borders; otherwise, there will never be an end to systemic oppression.

FOR FURTHER READING

Fernandes, Leela. *Transnational Feminism in the United States: Knowledge, Ethics, and Power*. NYU P, 2013.

Grewal, Inderpal, and Caren Kaplan. *Scattered Hegemonies: Postmodernity and Transnational Feminist Practices*. U of Minnesota P, 2006.

McLaren, Margaret A. *Decolonizing Feminism: Transnational Feminism and Globalization*. Rowman & Littlefield, 2017.

Mohanty, Chandra Talpade. *Feminism without Borders: Decolonizing Theory, Practicing Solidarity*. Point Par Point, 2007.

Amy Alexander

The largest single-day demonstration in US history, the Women's March brought women together in cities worldwide to protest president-elect Donald Trump and his policy proposals that threatened devastating setbacks for women, people of color, immigrants, people with disabilities, and members of the LGBTQ community. Building upon the momentum of the march, the organizers formed Women's March Global to plan a series of actions designed to promote equality and diversity.

Largely celebrated as a unifying coalition for women, the journalist Amy Alexander highlights who is overlooked in this collective. As part of NPR's weekly podcast *Code Switch*, Alexander observes that even as the march was led by a diverse group of women who touted intersectionality, its manifestation seemed "tone-deaf, at best, to the daily, on-the-ground realities of nonfamous black women and Latinas" (see Women's March on Washington Organizers, *Guiding Vision and Definition of Principles*, this volume).

Alexander opens the following piece by locating herself as one of these forgotten woman: a divorced, African American, "precariously middle-class" mother of two teenagers, whose central task must be to keep her family "on track." Providing statistical evidence, she explains to her listeners that black and Latina women are not only more likely than white women to head their households but also to receive lower wages than their white counterparts. Using her journalistic acumen to meld individual stories and factual evidence, Alexander uncovers the stories buried by mainstream media coverage. Indeed, this is the driving force of her career, from covering the Los Angeles riots to authoring books, including *Uncovering Race: A Black Journalist's Story of Reporting* and *Fifty Black Women Who Changed America*.

In her commentary for *Code Switch*, Alexander exposes some issues that were buried in the largely celebrative accounts of Women's March Global—like how a "nonfamous" black or Latina women might experience a call to miss work, to participate in a Day Without a Woman protest. In so doing, Alexander pushes us to interrogate what it means to attend both to collectivity and intersectionality and to imagine a feminism that adopts and values core experiences of women of color.

"Today's Feminism: Too Much Marketing, Not Enough Reality"

NPR's *Code Switch*, 2017

I'm a black woman of a certain age, a divorced mom of two teenagers who has no choice but to focus daily on the challenges of keeping a home, my family, and myself on track. I'm college educated, work in media communications, am precariously middle class—and I am *tired* of what I witness of today's feminism.

I'd hoped that the Women's March might help me update my perception of feminism, at least as it is commonly portrayed and disseminated of late.

I'd followed the back and forth in the alternative and mainstream press during its hurried, urgent formation, and chalked up reports about internal squabbles over the race and class makeup of the group's leadership to the same kind of growing pains that beset every activist group that I've ever followed or covered during my years in newsrooms. But now, a month after the Women's March masterfully pulled off a massive protest in DC that also inspired similar ones in major American and global cities, my nascent investigation of the March 8 "general strike" and "Day Without Women" raised only more concerns, and a few questions, all located in what I see as a big void in today's marketing-driven expression of "feminism."

At this moment, whether expressed by the second-wave Gloria Steinem wing, or the third-wave corporatist Sheryl Sandberg arm, or the rowdy, genitalia-obsessed Lena Dunham arm, it seems that "feminism" in 2017 is more concerned with promoting superficial trappings of genuine equality than with doing the tough work required to address the hard, cold facts of gender and racial inequality.

For example, across all US occupations, women's median weekly earnings are $706 per week, compared with $860 for men, and the top 30 occupations for women cover a range of essential—but relatively low-paying—jobs such as elementary school teachers, administrative assistants, customer service representatives, and retail sales, according to the most recent data available (2013) from the United States Bureau of Labor Statistics Women's Bureau. And, while black and Latina women together make up nearly 18 million of the total number of America's 67 million working women, they are disproportionately more likely to be heads of households, yet also more likely to receive less pay than white women and white men.

Moreover, in addition to stubborn disparities in the workforce and incomes, women of color see huge gaps between themselves and white men and women in health outcomes and other key life-expectancy indicators.

The Women's March, while apparently "led" by a diverse collection of black, white, Latina, and Asian women from across age groups, is the latest entry in a recent bumper crop of "feminist movements," "collectives," [and] "initiatives" that claim inclusivity and egalitarian principles, but which somehow always seem tone-deaf, at best, to the daily, on-the-ground realities of nonfamous black women and Latinas.

How, then, will working-class black women and Latinas respond to the idea of missing a day of work in a general strike as part of political resistance? It is a case of high-minded ideology that, while well-meaning, doesn't take into account the fact that some women can't miss even a single day of work without fear of being fired or docked a full day's pay. Consider that the "Day Without Immigrants," on Feb. 16— organized by disparate workers' and immigrant rights organizations in response to President Trump's proposal to build a wall between the US and Mexico, and to impose a strict immigration ban on seven Middle Eastern nations—resulted in private companies in several cities firing dozens of workers who participated in the boycott.

While the symbolism of the "Day Without Immigrants" is certainly valuable, for the immigrant and women workers who got fired for participating, and who now must find new jobs, you have to wonder if they now genuinely believe they received appropriate return on their investment. I have similar concerns about the upcoming "Day Without Women." As Jessa Crispin noted in a recent essay, "The pro-woman power elite peers deeply into the savage inequalities of American life and asks, 'Where's my half of the profits?'"

Akin to the debate over white privilege, the debate over feminism is similar-ly stuck in a binary construct, largely defined in middle- or upper-middle-class white-lady contexts. Variations exist along generational lines: See the Lena Dun-ham crowd contrasted against the Steinem wing. But the marketing of modern feminism, and the oxygen-sucking place it holds in the public imagination, is large-ly occupied by white women.

The occasional invocation of Audre Lorde, Fannie Lou Hamer, or Angela Da-vis by some leaders within these status quo or emerging white feminist camps in 2017 is notable—if also to me superficial and insufficient. (Yes, I know Davis is among a group of women who are advocating for a general strike.)

Today's purveyors of hashtag feminism—exemplified by pink "pussy hats," safety pins, and cheeky-ballsy slogans on T-shirts—have forgotten that women of color have to learn how to navigate their own universes but also those of white women and men to literally be able to pay the rent and afford decent schools. We have to succeed in both spheres not only to achieve success, but to fundamentally *cope*. To ask us, then, to participate in a Lysistrata-like action makes me wonder if the gesture is designed more to give white ladies another opportunity for dis-playing unity, a kind of safari solidarity, than it is to provide women of color and working-class women tangible relief.

However out of fashion it is to say so in the wake of the 2016 presidential election, identity politics are inherently personal. Identity politics do, in fact, drive political outcomes, which in turn drive policy, economic, and social developments.

I don't now and never have viewed the conventional version of feminism as a defining part of my identity; rather, based on what I have experienced and learned from the black women I've known my entire life, I have absorbed a degree of resilience, appreciation for common sense, and unflashy problem-solving that many women of color demonstrate. It is no accident that Black Lives Matter [BLM] was co-founded by Alicia Garza, Opal Tometi, and Patrisse Cullors in the wake of the death of 18-year-old Michael Brown in Ferguson, Mo. Within the span of two years, BLM expanded into an effort to organize the energies and intellect of people of color and whites toward strategically resisting police brutality and other American institutions where systemic race and gender discrimination put us at risk. The energy and determination of BLM, its ability to spur dozens of protests nationwide since 2014, garnering condemnations from some police unions and elected politicians, seems to have inspired organizers of the Women's March without, apparently, deeply informing the group about the full range of potential negative consequences for participants.

Telling also is the group's tepid nod to intersectionality, the concept coined by Kimberlé Williams Crenshaw, a black legal scholar, which has informed the positions and actions of many emerging protest movements in recent years. Crenshaw's concept of intersectionality—the critical analysis of gender, ethnic, and class aspects that drive inequality in populations and social structure—was earlier identified as "interlocking" factors by Chicana playwright Cherríe Moraga. This intellectual trait, the ability to recognize the multidimensional layers of inequality, are bedrocks of effective leadership across disciplines—although when demonstrated by women of color they are rarely characterized as such by the dominant society.

Today's iteration of feminism might gain wider credibility by recognizing and adopting core aspects of women of color's experiences: resilience, self-love, and fundamental understanding that one's self-worth is not defined by the same markers of success that have defined white male status since the beginning of time in America.

For Further Reading

Alexander, Amy. *Fifty Black Women Who Changed America*. Dafina, 2003.

Alexander, Amy. *Uncovering Race: A Black Journalist's Story of Reporting and Reinvention*. Beacon Press, 2011.

Bates, Karen Grigsby. "Race and Feminism: Women's March Recalls the Touchy History." *NPR*, 21 Jan. 2017, www.npr.org/sections/codeswitch/2017/01/21/510859909/race-and-feminism-womens-march-recalls-the-touchy-history.

Emi Koyama

From Mary Wollstonecraft's *A Vindication of the Rights of Woman* (1792) to Donna Haraway's "Cyborg Manifesto: Science, Technology, and Socialist-Feminism in the Late Twentieth Century" (1985) to Chimamanda Adichie's *Dear Ijeawele, or A Feminist Manifesto in Fifteen Suggestions* (2017), feminist rhetors have employed the manifesto to challenge gender norms, expand conceptions of feminism, and imagine more inclusive futures. In the introduction to *Feminist Manifestos: A Global Documentary Reader*, Penny Weiss writes, "Manifestos differ dramatically in form, one resembling an indictment, another an oath; one an essay, another a letter; one a set of demands; another a set of principles" (2). This rhetorical suppleness, Weiss explains, allows the form to be adapted by a range of subjects, bending it to their particular needs in a given moment. Writing at the turn of the twenty-first century, a time when mainstream awareness of transgender identity was burgeoning, Emi Koyama did just this, crafting a manifesto to introduce transfeminism to the larger feminist movement.

Koyama first published "The Transfeminist Manifesto" on her blog *Eminism. org*. She is an active blogger, writer, and speaker on topics including feminism; sexual and domestic violence; sex work, trade, and trafficking; queer and trans liberation; and intersex and disability issues. Koyama, along with the activist Diana Kourvant, is often credited for coining the term *transfeminist* (Stryker and Bettcher). In the following excerpts, Koyama locates transfeminism as a necessary expansion of the feminist movement, in keeping with feminism's commitment to—though not always its practice of—viewing diversity as a strength. Using an inclusive *we* to speak with other transwomen, she declares that it is time for transwomen to openly take part in the feminist revolution.

In addition to calling for this inclusive new vision, Koyama also uses "The Transfeminist Manifesto" to define *trans* and *transfeminism* and to challenge imposed definitions that have limited conceptions of trans identity. The feminist manifesto, Weiss argues, often melds theory and practice, and as Koyama calls for a more inclusive feminist movement, she also calls for retheorizing biological sex. While second-wave feminists did well to establish gender as a social construct, it largely left biological sex untouched. Transfeminism, "The Transfeminist Manifesto" proclaims, holds that sex and gender are both socially constructed, such that one is free to assign their own sex.

In her own life, Koyama uses she/her pronouns but does not currently identify as a particular gender, explaining that this might be attributed to her Japanese background: "There is no native Japanese word for 'identity,' and gendered pronouns (he, she, etc.) did not exist in Japanese language until they were invented in order to translate Western documents."

In 2018 Koyama delivered a talk at the University of Oregon that revisited "The Transfeminist Manifesto" nearly twenty years later. She now regards the document as historical, and has written elsewhere about how she would revise it with more attention to female-to-male trans and genderqueer people as well as with more analysis of intersectionality (Koyama 258). While manifestos, like all acts of rhetoric, are inseparable from the contexts in which they arise, Koyama brought much-needed attention in the early twenty-first century to feminism's long exclusion of transgender women, making a strong case that transfeminism deepens and enriches the larger feminist movement.

Excerpts from "The Transfeminist Manifesto"

Eminism.org, **2001**

The latter half of the twentieth century witnessed an unprecedented broadening of American feminist movement as a result of the participation of diverse groups of women. When a group of women who had previously been marginalized within the mainstream of the feminist movement broke their silence, demanding their rightful place within it, they were first accused of fragmenting feminism with trivial matters, and then were eventually accepted and welcomed as a valuable part of the feminist thought. We have become increasingly aware that the diversity is our strength, not weakness. No temporary fragmentation or polarization is too severe to nullify the ultimate virtues of inclusive coalition politics.

Every time a group of women previously silenced begins to speak out, other feminists are challenged to rethink their idea of whom they represent and what they stand for. While this process sometimes leads to a painful realization of our own biases and internalized oppressions as feminists, it eventually benefits the movement by widening our perspectives and constituency. It is under this understanding that we declare that the time has come for transwomen to openly take part in the feminist revolution, further expanding the scope of the movement.

Trans is often used as an inclusive term encompassing a wide range of gender-norm violations that involve some discontinuity between one's sex assigned at birth to her or his gender identity and/or expression. For the purpose of this manifesto, however, the phrase *transwomen* is at times used to refer to those individuals who identify, present, or live more or less as women despite their birth sex assignment to the contrary. *Transmen*, likewise, is used to describe those who identify, present, or live as men despite the fact that they were perceived otherwise at birth. While this operational definition leaves out many trans people who do not conform to the male/female dichotomy or those who are transgendered in other ways, it is our hope that they will recognize enough similarities between issues that we all face and find our analysis somewhat useful in their own struggles as well.

Transfeminism is primarily a movement by and for transwomen who view their liberation to be intrinsically linked to the liberation of all women and beyond. It is also open to other queers, intersex people, transmen, non-transwomen, non-transmen, and others who are sympathetic toward needs of transwomen and consider their alliance with transwomen to be essential for their own liberation. Historically, transmen have made greater contribution to feminism than transwomen. We believe that it is imperative that more transwomen start participating in the feminist movement alongside others for our liberation.

Transfeminism is not about taking over existing feminist institutions. Instead, it extends and advances feminism as a whole through our own liberation and coalition work with all others. It stands up for trans and non-transwomen alike, and asks non-transwomen to stand up for transwomen in return. Transfeminism embodies feminist coalition politics in which women from different backgrounds stand up for each other, because if we do not stand for each other, nobody will.

[. . .]

While the second wave of feminism popularized the idea that one's gender is distinct from her or his physiological sex and is socially and culturally constructed, it largely left unquestioned the belief that there was such a thing as true physical sex. The separation of gender from sex was a powerful rhetoric used to break down compulsory gender roles, but allowed feminists to question only half of the problem, leaving the naturalness of essential female and male sexes until recently.

Transfeminism holds that sex and gender are both socially constructed; furthermore, the distinction between sex and gender is artificially drawn as a matter of convenience. While the concept of gender as a social construct has proven to be a powerful tool in dismantling traditional attitudes toward women's capabilities, it left room for one to justify certain discriminatory policies or structures as having a biological basis. It also failed to address the realities of trans experiences in which physical sex is felt more artificial and changeable than their inner sense of who they are.

Social construction of biological sex is more than an abstract observation: it is a physical reality that many intersex people go through. Because society makes no provision for the existence of people whose anatomical characteristics do not neatly fit into male or female, they are routinely mutilated by medical professionals and manipulated into living as their assigned sex. Intersex people are usually not given an opportunity to decide for themselves how they wish to live and whether or not they want surgical or hormonal "correction." Many intersex people find it appalling that they had no say in such a major life decision, whether or not their gender identity happen to match their assigned sex. We believe that genital mutilation of intersex children is inherently abusive because it unnecessarily violates the integrity of their bodies without proper consent. The issue is not even whether or not the sex one was assigned matches her or his gender identity; it is whether or not intersex people are given real choice over what happens to their bodies.

Trans people feel dissatisfied with the sex assigned to them without their consent according to the simplistic medical standard. Trans people are diverse: some identify and live as members of the sex different from what was assigned to them by medical authorities, either with or without medical intervention, while others identify with neither or both of male and female sexes. Trans liberation is about taking back the right to define ourselves from medical, religious, and political authorities. Transfeminism views any method of assigning sex to be socially and politically constructed, and advocates a social arrangement where one is free to assign her or his own sex (or non-sex, for that matter).

As trans people begin to organize politically, it is tempting to adopt the essentialist notion of gender identity. The cliché popularized by the mass media is that trans people are "women trapped in men's bodies" or vice versa. The attractiveness of such a strategy is clear, as the general population is more likely to become supportive of us if we could convince them that we are somehow born with a biological error over which we have no control over it. It is also often in tune with our own sense of who we are, which feels very deep and fundamental to us. However, as transfeminists, we resist such temptations because of their implications.

Trans people have often been described as those whose physical sex does not match the gender of their mind or soul. This explanation might make sense intuitively, but it is nonetheless problematic for transfeminism. To say that one has a female mind or soul would mean there are male and female minds that are different from each other in some identifiable way, which in turn may be used to justify discrimination against women. Essentializing our gender identity can be just as dangerous as resorting to biological essentialism.

Transfeminism believes that we construct our own gender identities based on what feels genuine, comfortable, and sincere to us as we live and relate to others within given social and cultural constraint. This holds true for those whose gender identity is in congruence with their birth sex, as well as for trans people. Our demand for recognition and respect shall in no way be weakened by this acknowledgement. Instead of justifying our existence through the reverse essentialism, transfeminism dismantles the essentialist assumption of the normativity of the sex/gender congruence.

FOR FURTHER READING

Eminism. http://eminism.org/.

Enke, Anne. *Transfeminist Perspectives in and beyond Transgender and Gender Studies.* Temple UP, 2012.

Koyama, Emi. "The Transfeminist Manifesto." *Catching a Wave: Reclaiming Feminism for the 21st Century,* edited by Rory Dicker and Alison Piepmeier, Northeastern UP, 2004, pp. 244–59.

Stryker, Susan, and Talia M. Bettcher. "Introduction: Trans/Feminisms." *TSQ: Transgender Studies Quarterly,* vol. 3, no. 1–2, May 2016, pp. 5–14.

Weiss, Penny A., and Megan Brueske. *Feminist Manifestos: A Global Documentary Reader.* NYU P, 2018.

Chimamanda Ngozi Adichie

The novelist Chimamanda Ngozi Adichie has been called a "global feminist icon," famous for popularizing feminism within mainstream cultural conversations (Brown). Her 2009 TED talk, "The Danger of a Single Story," is one of TED's twenty-five most viewed lectures; her 2012 TED talk, "We Should All Be Feminists," became a book, the tagline later sampled by Beyoncé and splashed across Dior T-shirts (Allardice).

Adichie was born in Nigeria in 1977 and moved to the United States at age nineteen, where she received degrees from Eastern Connecticut State University and Johns Hopkins University; she currently divides her time between the United States and Nigeria. She is the author of the novels *Purple Hibiscus, Half of a Yellow Sun, Americanah,* and the short-story collection *The Thing Around Your Neck.* Her book *Dear Ijeawele, or A Feminist Manifesto in Fifteen Suggestions* began as a letter to a friend. In 2008 Adichie received the prestigious MacArthur Foundation Fellowship.

Being a prominent voice on feminism has resulted in some controversy—in 2017 Adichie was criticized for comments she made about transwomen's experiences being different from those born biologically female—she later clarified that she was referring to differing but not hierarchical experiences. In her clarification, Adichie was characteristically straightforward. As Lisa Allardice comments, "Simplicity and accessibility are the point: Adichie is not preaching to the converted; she doesn't do 'jargon' and finds the classic feminist texts 'boring.'" Emma Brockes notes that Adichie also rejects what she thinks of as "professional feminism"—a term coined by Roxane Gay, where feminism is narrowly defined by those with the largest platform—because "it runs counter to her ideas as a writer: that people contain multitudes. She is a brilliant novelist and a serious thinker, and she is also someone who makes no apology for her own trivial interests."

This rhetorical approach is wonderfully exhibited in Adichie's 2015 Wellesley College commencement address. In an essayistic speech that refuses linearity but is guided by a controlling idea, Adichie combines powerful reminders of the blinders of privilege with playful anecdotes about her fondness for makeup. Her thoughts on feminism are grounded in her experience, yet she connects to her audience by calling attention to the Wellesley tradition of "big sisters" imparting advice. Above all, Adichie drives home the message she offers in her novels, nonfiction, TED talks, and thoughts as a public intellectual, that "Feminism should be an inclusive party. Feminism should be a party full of different feminisms."

Wellesley College 2015 Commencement Address

Hello, class of 2015. Congratulations! And thank you for that wonderful welcome. And thank you President Bottomly for that wonderful introduction. I have admired Wellesley—its mission, its story, its successes—for a long time and I thank you very much for inviting me.

You are ridiculously lucky to be graduating from this bastion of excellence and on these beautiful acres. And if the goddesses and gods of the universe do the right thing, then you will also very soon be the proud alumnae of the college that produced America's first female president! Go Hillary! I'm truly, truly happy to be here today—so happy, in fact, that when I found out your class color was yellow, I decided I would wear yellow eye shadow. But on second thoughts, I realized that as much as I admire Wellesley, even yellow eye shadow was a bit too much of a gesture. So I dug out this yellow—yellowish—head wrap instead.

Speaking of eye shadow, I wasn't very interested in makeup until I was in my twenties, which is when I began to wear makeup. Because of a man. A loud, unpleasant man. He was one of the guests at a friend's dinner party. I was also a guest. I was about twenty-three, but people often told me I looked twelve. The conversation at dinner was about traditional Igbo culture, about the custom that allows only men to break the kola nut, and the kola nut is a deeply symbolic part of Igbo cosmology. I argued that it would be better if that honor were based on achievement rather than gender, and he looked at me and said, dismissively, "You don't know what you are talking about, you're a small girl." I wanted him to disagree with the substance of my argument, but by looking at me, young and female, it was easy for him to dismiss what I said. So I decided to try to look older. So I thought lipstick might help. And eyeliner. And I am grateful to that man because I have since come to love makeup, and its wonderful possibilities for temporary transformation. So, I have not told you this anecdote as a way to illustrate my discovery of gender injustice. If anything, it's really just an ode to makeup. It's really just to say that this, your graduation, is a good time to buy some lipsticks—if makeup is your sort of thing—because a good shade of lipstick can always put you in a slightly better mood on dark days.

It's not about my discovering gender injustice, because of course I had discovered years before then. From childhood. From watching the world. I already knew that the world does not extend to women the many small courtesies that it extends to men.

I also knew that victimhood is not a virtue. That being discriminated against does not make you somehow morally better.

And I knew that men were not inherently bad or evil. They were merely privileged. And I knew that privilege blinds because it is the nature of privilege to blind.

I knew from this personal experience, from the class privilege I had of growing up in an educated family, that it sometimes blinded me, that I was not always as alert to the nuances of people who were different from me.

And you, because you now have your beautiful Wellesley degree, have become privileged, no matter what your background. That degree, and the experience of being here, is a privilege. Don't let it blind you too often. Sometimes you will need to push it aside in order to see clearly.

I bring greetings to you from my mother. She's a big admirer of Wellesley, and she wishes she could be here. She called me yesterday to ask how the speechwriting was going and to tell me to remember to use a lot of lotion on my legs today so they would not look ashy.

My mother is seventy-three and she retired as the first female registrar of the University of Nigeria—which was quite a big deal at the time.

My mother likes to tell a story of the first university meeting she chaired. It was in a large conference room, and at the head of the table was a sign that said CHAIRMAN. My mother was about to get seated there when a clerk came over and made to remove the sign. All the past meetings had of course been chaired by men, and somebody had forgotten to replace the CHAIRMAN with a new sign that said CHAIRPERSON. The clerk apologized and told her he would find the new sign, since she was not a chairman.

My mother said no. Actually, she said, she *was* a chairman. She wanted the sign left exactly where it was. The meeting was about to begin. She didn't want anybody to think that what she was doing in that meeting at that time on that day was in any way different from what a CHAIRMAN would have done.

I always liked this story, and admired what I thought of as my mother's fiercely feminist choice. I once told the story to a friend, a card-carrying feminist, and I expected her to say bravo to my mother, but she was troubled by it.

"Why would your mother want to be called a chairman, as though she needed the *man* part to validate her?" my friend asked.

In some ways, I saw my friend's point. Because if there were a standard handbook published annually by the Secret Society of Certified Feminists, then that handbook would certainly say that a woman should not be called, nor want to be called, a *chairman*.

But gender is always about context and circumstance. If there is a lesson in this anecdote, apart from just telling you a story about my mother to make her happy that I spoke about her at Wellesley, then it is this: Your standardized ideologies will not always fit your life. Because life is messy.

When I was growing up in Nigeria I was expected, as every student who did well was expected, to become a doctor. Deep down I knew that what I really wanted to do was to write stories. But I did what I was supposed to do and I went into medical school.

I told myself that I would tough it out and become a psychiatrist and that way I could use my patients' stories for my fiction. But after one year of medical school, I fled. I realized I would be a very unhappy doctor and I really did not want to be responsible for the inadvertent death of my patients. Leaving medical school was a very unusual decision, especially in Nigeria, where it is very difficult to get into medical school.

Later, people told me that it had been very courageous of me, but I did not feel courageous at all. What I felt then was not courage but a desire to make an effort. To try. I could either stay and study something that was not right for me or I could try and do something different. I decided to try. I took the American exams and got a scholarship to come to the US where I could study something else that was *not* related to medicine. Now it might not have worked out. I might not have been given an American scholarship. My writing might not have ended up being successful. But the point is that I tried.

We cannot always bend the world into the shapes we want but we can try, we can make a concerted and real and true effort. And you are privileged that, because of your education here, you have already been given many of the tools that you will need to try. Always just try. Because you never know. And so as you graduate, as you deal with your excitement and your doubts today, I urge you to try and create the world you want to live in.

Minister to the world in a way that can change it. Minister radically in a real, active, practical, get your hands dirty way. Wellesley will open doors for you. Walk through those doors and make your strides long and firm and sure.

Write television shows in which female strength is not depicted as remarkable but merely normal. Teach your students to see that vulnerability is a *human* rather than a *female* trait. Commission magazine articles that teach men "How to Keep a

Woman Happy." Because there are already too many articles that tell women how to keep a man happy. And in media interviews make sure fathers are asked how they balance family and work. In this age of "parenting as guilt," please spread the guilt equally. Make fathers feel as bad as mothers. Make fathers share in the glory of guilt.

Campaign and agitate for paid paternity leave everywhere in America. Hire more women where there are few. But remember that a woman you hire doesn't have to be exceptionally good. Like a majority of the men who get hired, she just needs to be good enough.

Recently, a feminist organization kindly nominated me for an important prize in a country that will remain unnamed. I was very pleased. I've been fortunate to have received a few prizes so far and I quite like them, especially when they come with shiny presents. To get this prize, I was required to talk about how important a particular European feminist woman writer had been to me. Now the truth was that I had never managed to finish this feminist writer's book. It did not speak to me. It would have been a lie to claim that she had any major influence on my thinking. The truth is that I learned so much more about feminism from watching the women traders in the market in Nsukka where I grew up, than from reading any seminal feminist text. I could have said that this woman was important to me, and I could have talked the talk, and I could have been given the prize and a shiny present.

But I didn't.

Because I had begun to ask myself what it really means to wear this *feminist* label so publicly. Just as I asked myself after excerpts of my feminism speech were used in a song by a talented musician whom I think some of you might know. I thought it was a very good thing that the word *feminist* would be introduced to a new generation. But I was startled by how many people, many of whom were academics, saw something troubling, even menacing, in this. It was as though feminism was supposed to be an elite little cult, with esoteric rites of membership. But it shouldn't. Feminism should be an inclusive party. Feminism should be a party full of different feminisms.

And so, class of 2015, please go out there and make feminism a big, raucous, inclusive party.

The past three weeks have been the most emotionally difficult of my life. My father is eighty-three years old, a retired professor of statistics—a lovely, kind man. I am an absolute daddy's girl. Three weeks ago, he was kidnapped near his home in Nigeria. And for a number of days, my family and I went through the kind of emotional pain that I have never known in my life. We were talking to threatening strangers on the phone, begging and negotiating for my father's safety, and we were not always sure if my father was alive. He was released after we paid a ransom. He is well, in fairly good shape and, in his usual lovely way, is very keen to reassure us all that he is fine.

I am still not sleeping well, I still wake up many times at night, in panic, worried that something else has gone wrong, I still cannot look at my father without fighting tears, without feeling this profound relief and gratitude that he is safe, but also rage that he had to undergo such an indignity to his body and to his spirit.

And the experience has made me rethink many things, what truly matters, and what doesn't. What I value, and what I don't.

And as you graduate today, I urge you to think about that a little more. Think about what really matters to you. Think about what you *want* to really matter to you.

I read about your rather lovely tradition of referring to older students as "big sisters" and younger ones as "little sisters." And I read about the rather strange thing about being thrown into the pond—and I didn't really get that—but I would very much like to be your honorary big sister today.

Which means that I would like to give you bits of advice as your big sister:

All over the world, girls are raised to be make themselves likeable, to twist themselves into shapes that suit other people. Please do not twist yourself into shapes to please. Don't do it. If someone likes that version of you, that version of you that is false and holds back, then they actually just like that twisted shape, and not you. And the world is such a gloriously multifaceted, diverse place that there are people in the world who will like you, the real you, as you are.

I am lucky that my writing has given me a platform that I choose to use to talk about things that I care about, and I have said a few things that have not been so popular with a number of people. I have been told to shut up about certain things—such as my position on the equal rights of gay people on the continent of Africa, such as my deeply held belief that men and women are completely equal. I don't speak to provoke. I speak because I think our time on earth is short and each moment that we are not our truest selves, each moment we pretend to be what we are not, each moment we say what we do not mean because we imagine that is what somebody wants us to say, then we are wasting our time on earth.

I don't mean to sound precious, but please don't waste your time on earth, but there is one exception. The only acceptable way of wasting your time on earth is online shopping.

Okay, one last thing about my mother. My mother and I do not agree on many things regarding gender. There are certain things my mother believes a person should do, for the simple reason that said person "is a woman." Such as nod occasionally and smile, even when smiling is the last thing one wants to do. Such as strategically give in to certain arguments, especially when arguing with a non-female. Such as get married and have children. I can think of fairly good reasons for doing any of these. But "because you are a woman" is not one of them.

And so, class of 2015, never ever accept "because you are a woman" as a reason for doing or not doing anything.

And, finally, I would like to end with a final note on the most important thing in the world: love.

Now girls are often raised to see love only as giving. Women are praised for their love when that love is an act of giving. But to love is to give *and* to take. Please love by giving and by taking. Give and be given. If you are only giving and not taking, you'll know. You'll know from that small and true voice inside you that we females are so often socialized to silence. Don't silence that voice. Dare to take.

Congratulations.

For Further Reading

Allardice, Lisa. "Chimamanda Ngozi Adichie: 'This Could Be the Beginning of a Revolution.'" *The Guardian*, 28 Apr. 2018, www.theguardian.com/books/2018/apr/28/chimamanda-ngozi-adichie-feminism-racism-sexism-gender-metoo.

"Biography." *The Chimamanda Ngozi Adichie Website*, n.d., www.cerep.ulg.ac.be/adichie/cnabio.html.

Brockes, Emma. "Chimamanda Ngozi Adichie: 'Can People Quit Telling Me That Feminism Is Hot?'" *The Guardian*, 4 Mar. 2017, www.theguardian.com/books/2017/mar/04/chimamanda-ngozi-adichie-stop-telling-me-feminism-hot.

Brown, Lauren Alix. "Chimamanda Ngozi Adichie: 'Sometimes It Feels like the Universe Is Conspiring against Me.'" *Quartzy*, 11 Dec. 2017, quartzy.qz.com/1133732/chimamanda-ngozi-adichie-talks-about-feminism-and-raising-her-daughter-in-a-gendered-world/.

Chimamanda Adichie. www.chimamanda.com/.

Crockett, Emily. "The Controversy over Chimamanda Ngozi Adichie and Trans Women, Explained." *Vox*, 15 Mar. 2017, www.vox.com/identities/2017/3/15/14910900/chimamanda-ngozi-adichie-transgender-women-comments-apology.

McKeon, Lucy. "Let's Be Real: Two New Books by Roxane Gay." *Boston Review*, 28 Aug. 2014, bostonreview.net/books-ideas/lucy-mckeon-roxane-gay-bad-feminist-untamed-state.

Erica Thurman

The singer and pop cultural phenomenon Beyoncé released her visual album *Lemonade* in 2016 to nearly universal acclaim by critics and mainstream audiences. The album, a complex blend of topics—including Beyoncé's marriage to Jay-Z, the Black Lives Matter movement, and black women's power, healing, and hope—cannot be easily summarized, though many, usually writers who aren't black women, have tried. It was the commentary of bell hooks, a well-known black feminist theorist and intellectual, however, that sparked public fury for critiquing *Lemonade* and Beyoncé herself. In her piece, hooks praises much about *Lemonade* but ultimately argues that its commodification of black women and glamorization of female violence is not a feminist endeavor.

The pushback against hooks surfaced generational differences within feminism, particularly since this wasn't the first time she publicly criticized Beyoncé. During a 2014 New School panel about black female bodies, which included the writer and transgender activist Janet Mock, hooks called Beyoncé a "cultural terrorist" because of her "impact on young girls," adding that "the major assault on feminism in our society has come from visual media and from television and videos" (Coker). Mock responded to hooks's critique of *Lemonade* on Twitter, decrying what she deemed hooks's "dismissal of feminists who present themselves in more traditionally feminine modes" (Pulliam-Moore).

Amid this swirl of controversy, Erica Thurman wrote a heartfelt response to hooks's critique of Beyoncé on her blog, *Life Behind the Veil*. The *Veil*'s mission is to "foster and facilitate the academic, employment, personal, physical, mental and social health of Black girls and women," a goal evident through her blog and other writings. An activist for black girls and women, Thurman has also served as a grant writer for women's advocacy organizations, such as the National Partnership for Women & Families.

In the following piece, Thurman both disputes hooks's points and writes from emotion—acknowledging she is disappointed and hurt by hooks, a black feminist icon to so many, wondering if the rejection of Beyoncé in black feminism is also a rejection of Thurman. Contained within Thurman's critique is a discussion about how women can better work as a collective, despite their differences. Given the intimacy of the blog form, Thurman's critique is conversational—she refers to hooks by her first name and to Beyoncé as Bey. In both her rhetorical style and in the content of her argument, Thurman calls for a more expansive feminism than hooks's view articulates. Thurman also responds to the comments on her blog, exchanging candid thoughts, reinforcing connections with her readership, and answering commenters directly with a meaningful response rather than defense. In short, Thurman models the kind of collective she insists hooks failed to support.

"Bell, Black Girls Are Healing, and It Is Glorious"

Life Behind the Veil, 2016

Yesterday bell hooks dropped her critique of *Lemonade*/all things Beyoncé. Spoiler alert—bell still feels the same about Beyoncé. And it still reads violently. And it still hurts to watch. Be not deceived, couched in a lengthy word count and what appear to be concessions that allude to bordering on positivity, bell publicly came at Bey's head. Also a Black woman. Again.

The easy stuff. Bell said Bey ain't saying nothing new or revolutionary. I addressed that in my last piece. I must say I'm surprised to hear that from bell whose own work built on what had been said by Black feminists before her. The point is that bell, like Bey, found her own way of saying it, a way that speaks to many. But in case you ain't convinced, bell drops a few works she does believe worthy of praise. And they are. I just would have expected bell to cite work by the first Black feminists to touch American soil since she's making the "but she ain't saying nothing new" argument. For the last time (today), say it with me . . . shared experiences mean few of us are saying anything new. Doesn't make it any less valid. Moving on.

Bell argues that *Lemonade* doesn't solve patriarchal domination. Did those fifty'leven books bell wrote solve it?? Ok. I legit might need a good talking to for that one. #ButWhereTheLie. My point is that none of this works alone to solve patriarchal domination. Why are we suddenly putting that burden on Bey alone? Collective. It's a collective. And so is the effort.

"Beyoncé wreaks violence." Memba when folks accused Black activists and protesters of being violent when property got damaged in Ferguson? The same folks who weren't mad that an actual person was killed? To accuse Bey of being violent when she in fact harms no one physically and visually plays out reconciliation without leaving Jay Z short a couple of limbs . . . That particular comment feels like people who tell Black folks that we should always respond to oppression with peace. Bey made it clear which side she stands on when it comes to the Martin/ Malcolm dichotomy. But I suppose after you've labeled a Black woman a terrorist, calling her violent is light work.

"The scantily-clothed dancing image of athlete Serena Williams also evokes sportswear." Where bell? Where? I swear fo'Lawd I ain't think about sports or sportswear once when I watched Serena dance. I'm pretty sure that was the point. Much like the *Sports Illustrated* cover Serena, which depicted a similarly scantily clothed Serena. A cover Serena dictated. All I thought about watching Serena was the wholeness of my Black womanhood. A Black womanhood that makes room for scholarly publications, a code-switching blog and twerking. Sometimes all at the same damn time.

Bell's issue with Black femmes. Janet Mock dropped the mic on that one so ain't no need to say what Janet said better.

"Can we really trust the caring images of Jay Z which conclude this narrative." So many layers to this particular point of bell's. First, because that trust ain't ours to give. It's Bey's. Second, on a larger scale it reads like the exclusionary nature of historical white feminism that had no room for Black women who insisted upon not leaving Black men behind. If we can't trust the caring image of Jay, are we to not trust the caring images of any of our brothers? What's the criteria? Who determines which brothers can be trusted? Must we depend on bell to tell us?

In accusing Beyoncé of falling into stereotypes, bell attempts to force Bey and Serena into quite a few of her own choosing. Serena, according to bell, is only [an] athlete. Not the powerful woman Serena herself puts forth herself in *Lemonade* and on the *SI* cover. In continuing to deny Bey and Serena agency time and time again, bell herself invokes the patriarchy. Bell reinforces the notion that Bey's agency is not hers to claim and must be validated by an outside source. This is problematic, even when that outside source is the legendary bell hooks who, in her own right been putting in that work.

Bell's critique lends to the idea that *Lemonade* is static in that it does not move beyond pain. As I stated in my first piece, the presence of so many young women speaks to the future, of moving beyond the pain. The presence of grieving mothers speaks to moving beyond pain. Those mothers are still here. They survived. That alone speaks to the ability to move (sometimes literally) beyond pain while still acknowledging it. Because that's necessary and because Black women are often deprived of the ability to express pain and to be justifiably angry about it. To rest in that anger if necessary. Yes bell, to celebrate the rage. Because the fact is that the sisters are healing. And that might not look familiar to many. Might not even look familiar to bell. The beauty of our healing is that it doesn't have to be recognized by anyone else.

I'm going to be transparent. Writing this piece has me feeling some type of way. My feelings are hurt. For a few reasons. I don't expect bell to agree with all things all Black woman. Or anything Beyoncé. I do expect that her love for Black women would include a respect that I don't see evident in her critiques of Beyoncé. Bell's continued public assaults tell me that her Black feminism has no room for Beyoncé. And I'm left to wonder, did bell ever have room for me?

FOR FURTHER READING

Adams, Joshua. "Let Black Women Write about Beyoncé's *Lemonade*." *Huffington Post*, 9 Apr. 2016, https://www.huffingtonpost.com/joshua-adams/let-black-women-write-abo_b_9790372.html.

Coker, Hillary Crosley. "What bell hooks Really Means When She Calls Beyoncé a 'Terrorist.'" *Jezebel*, 20 Feb. 2015, jezebel.com/what-bell-hooks-really-means-when-she-calls-beyonce-a-t-1573991834.

hooks, bell. *Black Looks: Race and Representation*. Routledge, 2014.

hooks, bell. *Feminism Is for Everybody: Passionate Politics*. South End Press, 2000.

hooks, bell. "Moving beyond Pain." *bell hooks Institute*, 9 May 2016, http://www.bellhooksinstitute.com/blog/2016/5/9/moving-beyond-pain.

Life Behind the Veil. https://kehindethurman.com/.

Logan, Erin. "Twitter Reacts to bell hooks' Critique of *Lemonade*." *Blavity*, 2016, https://blavity.com/twitter-reacts-bell-hooks-critique-lemonade.

Matti, Dominique. "Why *Lemonade* is for Black Women despite Centering a Man's Misdeeds." *Medium*, 25 Apr. 2016, https://medium.com/@DominiqueMatti/how-lemonade-is-for-black-women-2d45f2eb1b9.

Pulliam-Moore, Charles. "In Six Tweets, Janet Mock Takes down a Controversial Critique of Beyonce's *Lemonade*." *Splinter*, 10 May 2016, https://splinternews.com/in-6-tweets-janet-mock-takes-down-a-controversial-crit-1793856721.

Sieczkowski, Cavan. "Feminist Activist Says Beyoncé Is Partly 'Anti-Feminist' and 'Terrorist.'" *Huffington Post*, 6 Dec. 2017, https://www.huffingtonpost.com/2014/05/09/beyonce-anti-feminist_n_5295891.html.

Tinsley, Omise'eke Natasha. "Beyoncé's *Lemonade* Is Black Woman Magic." *Time*, 25 Apr. 2016, http://time.com/4306316/beyonce-lemonade-black-woman-magic/.

Claire Swinarski

The debate over abortion rights is perhaps one of the most divisive and vicious for American women in the twenty-first century, and since *Roe v. Wade* secured legal access to abortion in the United States in 1973, there has been no shortage of efforts to overturn it (see Jennifer Baumgardner's contribution to this volume). With changes in the makeup of Supreme Court under President Trump, *Roe v. Wade* has been further threatened, sparking greater intensity between the pro-life and pro-choice movements. For many, the issue is one without nuance, which author Claire Swinarski challenges in this piece.

Swinarski's background is emblematic of the nuance she seeks—she is both a proud feminist and a proud Catholic—two identities that most would not meld. She published a book on this theme and founded the *Catholic Feminist*, a popular spirituality podcast. Swinarski's writing has appeared in major publications and websites such as the *Washington Post*, Vox, *Seventeen*, and she is the author of a middle-grade novel.

In the following piece, Swinarski both calls for and enacts rhetorical moves that aim to refresh a deadlocked debate. She first identifies unequivocally as a feminist to gather readers who may dismiss or doubt her. Rather than focusing on the troubling and reductive choice of supporting an embryo or the mother, Swinarski consistently seeks common ground, starting where feminists likely agree: that many abortions occur due to a lack of financial and emotional support for women. Citing a study on the lack of childcare facilities at colleges and data showing that many women choose to have an abortion in order to avoid single motherhood or financial limitations, Swinarski underscores issues that have rendered motherhood challenging (Miller, Gault, and Thorman; Biggs, Gould, and Foster).

Using invitational gestures, Swinarski explains how she straddles feminism and her pro-life beliefs, directly appealing to the values aligned with feminism, such as social justice. She also admits that she finds pro-lifers' inflammatory tactics, like wielding graphic images of dead fetuses, off-putting. She concludes her piece by invoking feminist icons to argue that any woman has the potential to be a mother if properly supported in choosing to do so, while still maintaining her sense of self and purpose beyond motherhood.

"Why I'm a Pro-life Feminist"

Vox, 2016

As long as I can remember, I've called myself a feminist. I visited the Women's Rights National Historic Park long before I ever went to Disney World. In fifth grade, when we had biography book reports, I proudly put on a lab coat and taught my classmates about Elizabeth Blackwell, the first woman with a medical degree from an American university. I surprised my college professor by being the only one in our women's studies class to have heard of the Triangle Factory fire.

Women have a long, muddy history; our struggles both then and now are fascinating. Particularly of interest is the way we can climb and climb (voting rights in the US, access to higher-paying jobs) and still seem to never quite reach the top (like equal pay). I've seen these kinds of struggles up close: During a summer in Washington, DC, where I interned at a newspaper, I had a state senator look me in the face and tell me I shouldn't be working if I wanted kids one day.

I'm also pro-life.

I became involved in the pro-life movement in college, through my friends. They showed me that being pro-life doesn't necessarily mean you're backward, or hateful, or ignorant. It doesn't even have to mean you're religious—I met plenty of passionate pro-life students that weren't religious at all. I started to embrace the idea that being pro-life is pro-woman.

I joined the pro-life campus group at my liberal state school. We prayed outside of a Planned Parenthood (after hours), had discussions with fellow students, and tried to spread a different point of view than typically encountered on a college campus. It was incredibly hard—I once had someone tell me they wished I'd been aborted—but it was also empowering in the way it always is when you feel you're doing the right thing.

Still, I faced skepticism for calling myself pro-life and a feminist. Most of my pro-life friends shudder at the word "feminist." Most of my feminist friends think it's impossible to be "pro-life."

A 2013 Jezebel essay called "There's No Such Thing as a Pro-life Feminist" does a good job of articulating how a lot of people feel about my position. "Sure, you can be a feminist and make a personal decision to never get an abortion," the author writes. "But who the fuck are you to actively work at taking away other women's right to make their own personal decisions about their uteruses?"

First of all, no one's forcing anyone to do or not do anything: Humans have free will. The pro-life movement is trying to make legal abortion less available, sure, but we're also trying to make cultural changes so that women won't want to seek abortions in the first place, and we have no interest in legal punishment for women who've had abortions.

Second, society projects a moral code on people every day. We have laws to prevent harm. It could easily be said that police are "taking away the right to make their own personal decisions" from burglars or drunk driver—society has deemed that these things do harm and should not be done. We also hinder body autonomy (snorting cocaine, for example, is illegal).

We as a society agree that we cannot do whatever we want with our bodies. (If you don't agree, try dancing naked in the street and see what happens.)

So not only do I think that there's such thing as a pro-life feminist, I also believe that to be pro-life *is* to be feminist. To quote the slogan of Feminists for Life, "Women deserve better than abortion." Here is what I wish people understood about my position.

1. I think abortions should be made unnecessary in the first place

Women seek out abortions for a variety of complex reasons. But the often-cited pro-choice reason of life of the mother (ectopic pregnancies, typically) is extremely unusual. Instead, the most common reasons center on not having the support they need to raise the child: The top three reasons women choose to get an abortion, according to a 2013 study in peer-reviewed journal *BMC Women's Health*, are that it would dramatically change their life, they can't afford a baby, or they don't want to be a single mother.

I've heard this reasoning myself. I used to work as a Catholic missionary. While working on a private school campus, I once had a student tell me she had an abortion because she believed her education was the most important thing to her, and there was no way she could have a baby while studying and taking exams.

It doesn't need to be this way: Bad policies have led many women to believe they are unable to be mothers. The United States is one of the very, very few countries—essentially the only Western country—that does not require paid maternity leave. As a result, pregnant women are often stuck. They need to support themselves; they can't take unpaid leave for things like ultrasounds and breastfeeding classes and, eventually, a sick child.

It's not any easier for women in school: According to a 2011 report, child care facilities at universities are rare. Only 49 to 57 percent of two- and four-year public colleges and universities, and 7 to 9 percent of two- and four-year private colleges, offer child care facilities for their students. Another report found that "in most states, average child care center fees for an infant are higher than a year's tuition and fees at a public college."

Family leave and child care access are areas where the feminist and pro-life agendas perfectly intersect: Better policies are good for women, and could help reduce the perceived need for abortion.

2. Abortion disproportionately affects female fetuses and women of color

According to the Centers for Disease Control and Prevention, an African-American woman is five times more likely than a white woman to receive an abortion. This most likely has to do with complicated social structures and other disadvantages that minority women face throughout their lifetimes.

But instead of shrugging shoulders and letting abortion be the solution, society should instead look for ways to tackle these structures at their base and try to realize why exactly so many African-American women find themselves in a situation where they don't have the resources to make it through a pregnancy and potentially adoption or parenthood.

Internationally, fetuses are targeted by gender. In China and India, where baby boys are frequently considered more desirable due to financial gains for a family, sex-selective abortion is thriving. In China and parts of India, 120 boys are being born for every 100 girls.

If the goal of feminism is truly equality with men, this needs to start in the place where everything starts: the womb. Girls are killed before they have a chance to *become* girls.

The solution to this terrible trend shows yet again how feminism and opposition to abortion go hand in hand. The *Economist* writes that South Korea has managed to dramatically reduce sex-selective abortions not through legislation but through cultural change:

In the 1990s South Korea had a sex ratio almost as skewed as China's. Now, it is heading towards normality. It has achieved this not deliberately, but because the culture changed. Female education, anti-discrimination suits, and equal-rights rulings made son preference seem old-fashioned and unnecessary.

The larger social issue is that women are seen as less than men, and making a preference for a boy seem unnecessary was key in eliminating the problem. We can't fight one evil with another.

3. Pro-lifers bug me, too

Typical tactics of the pro-life movement simply don't work. I remember being on multiple college campuses during my time as a missionary and walking by graphic images of dead fetuses, being told to "repent," and hearing pro-life protesters call other women "pro-abortion Nazis." Even on a smaller scale, I frequently see Facebook posts in my circle of friends referring to women seeking abortion as needing to learn to "live with their choices" and "grow up."

These means of debate will bring us no closer to an agreement with pro-choice thinkers. They simply enforce the narrative that pro-life people have Donald Trump bumper stickers and an inability to form a complete sentence. And instead of demonstrating an authentic care for women, these tactics shame, embarrass, and anger women. They make no effort to understand or empathize, instead choosing to simply scream views with no care to the end outcome.

Pro-lifers who don't embrace the feminist movement are frequently the reason that pro-choice advocates choose not to engage in discussion. I wouldn't want to engage in discussion with someone waving a dead baby poster either. Until a greater piece of the pro-life movement supports a method that embraces feminism, it will be nearly impossible to have rational conversations with the pro-choice community, and even more impossible to convince anyone of anything.

And rational conversations are possible. While working at a private liberal college, I got a panicked text from a student asking me to show up at a campus pro-life protest before all hell broke loose. A pro-choice counter-protest had popped up, and what was taking place involved shouting matches, chanting, and unruly behavior from both sides.

After a quick pep talk and some deep breaths, we re-approached the situation with calm voices and a tactic more focused on asking questions. Getting to know the people we spoke with was essential to having a dialogue. I sat and talked with one student for more than 30 minutes, simply raising points she possibly hadn't considered and learning more of her story.

At the end, she looked me in the eyes and said, in a friendly tone, "Thanks for actually talking to me like a human. You raised some interesting thoughts, and I have a lot to think about."

When talking with people about abortion, the tactic I've found most helpful is empathy. You never know if the person you're talking to had an abortion (or if their sister did, or their best friend, or their mom). Compassion will always be key to explaining your point of view—and when that compassion is lacking, it sets back any progress the pro-life movement has made tenfold.

The annual March for Life is this week. On Friday, you might glimpse pictures of thousands of freezing people marching on Washington to protest abortion. They are not just conservative, mindless drones. They support women.

Gloria Steinem dedicated her recently published autobiography to the doctor who performed her illegal abortion at age 22. She writes:

"He said, 'You must promise me two things. First, you will not tell anyone my name. Second, you will do what you want to do with your life.'

"Dear Dr. Sharpe, I believe you, who knew the law was unjust, would not mind if I say this so long after your death: I've done the best I could with my life."

Ms. Steinem, a feminist icon who has fought for Title IX rights for rape victims and against the horrors of female genital mutilation, still could have done what she wanted to do with her life if she'd had her baby. Mothers do that, every day.

Hillary Clinton's a mother, and she's running for president. Adele's a mother, and she released the biggest no. 1 single in three years in 2015. Madeleine Albright, J. K. Rowling: Mothers—successful, thriving mothers—are everywhere. Having children should not rob you of your identity or your purpose. Pro-life feminists believe it doesn't have to.

FOR FURTHER READING

"About." *Claire Swinarski*, n.d., http://www.claireswinarski.com/about/.

Biggs, M. Antonia, Heather Gould, and Diana Greene Foster. "Understanding Why Women Seek Abortions in the US." *BMC Women's Health*, vol. 13, no. 29, 2013.

Feminists for Life. https://www.feministsforlife.org/.

Miller, Kevin, Barbara Gault, and Abby Thorman. "Improving Child Care Access to Promote Post-secondary Success among Low-Income Parents." Institute for Women's Policy Research Student Parent Success Initiative, 2011.

Morrissey, Tracie Egan. "There is No Such Thing as a 'Pro-Life Feminist.'" *Jezebel*, 4 Jan. 2013, https://jezebel.com/there-is-no-such-thing-as-a-pro-life-feminist-5972943.

Swinarski, Claire. *Girl, Arise!: A Catholic Feminist's Invitation to Live Boldly, Love Your Faith, and Change the World.* Ave Maria Press, 2019.

Shannon Downey

Creator of the website Badass Cross Stitch, Shannon Downey turned to crafting to restore herself from an overly digital environment—in her case, as head of a digital marketing company. She now has legions of followers and encourages others to craft to gain a better balance between their analog and digital lives. Her search for balance has shifted from a hobby to *craftivism*, the term coined by Becky Greer to mean "craft + activism = craftivism . . . each time you participate in crafting you are making a difference, whether it's fighting against useless materialism or making items for charity or something betwixt and between."

The seeds of Downey's craftivism were planted when she posted an embroidered image of a gun on Instagram. She asked others to make their own and send them her way, then sold them at a show in order to raise money for an organization that aids youth harmed by violence (Bahler). Downey's following grew when a post of her embroidered protest sign at the Chicago Women's March in 2017— "I'm so angry I stitched this just so I could stab something 3,000 times"—went viral (Bahler). One of her other designs, "Boys will be boys held accountable for their fucking actions," went viral, shared by millions when #MeToo stories broke (Taylor). (See also Tarana Burke's and Gretchen Carlson's contributions to this volume.) Unfortunately and ironically, Downey's work was often shared without attribution. As she noted, "This is exactly what's wrong, right? That we just erase women" (Taylor).

The legacy of women denied credit for activities such as crafting is not new, nor is the practice of craftivism (see Hermanson and Ward). Yet in the late twentieth century, crafting's relationship with feminism was often "contested . . . as both reclamation of feminine history and pride, and a symbol of historical and female subjugation" (Hermanson). This perception seems to be changing, with overt political displays in the form of pink pussy hats, the symbol of the Women's March in 2017, and in needlework like Downey's. Rhetorically, craftivism combines the medium and the message in order to persuade. As Downey notes, needlework is one of the more accessible kinds of crafting—not terribly challenging to learn and inexpensive to undertake (Bahler). In fact, Downey's website features three video blogs that teach beginners in less than thirty minutes. Additionally, the *act* of crafting is often collaborative, serving as a space for women to connect, sharing ideas about or over crafting while producing.

In the needlework example here, *The Future is Female*, one can see the overtly feminist message of the raised fist and the rallying cry for women through a medium that is historical and calls forth the long legacy of women's domestic labor in producing goods for utility, providing income, or raising funds for charity. The modern iconography against the textile and basic black thread makes a direct aesthetic point to reinforce the message. And in this digital era, the circulation of such visuals is immediate and free tutorials are ubiquitous, inviting women around the globe to participate in the rhetorical work of craftivism.

The Future is Female, Badass Cross Stitch

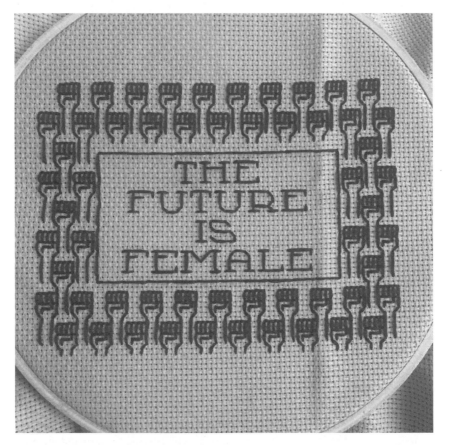

4. A cross-stitch designed and made by Shannon Downey consisting of burlap fabric with black thread. The pattern depicts multiple raised fists surrounding a text block with stitched text, THE FUTURE IS FEMALE.

For Further Reading

Badass Cross Stitch. www.badasscrossstitch.com/.

Bahler, Kristen. "Inside the World of 'Craftivism,' the DIY Protest Art Fueling Knitting Circles Everywhere." *Money*, 21 Feb. 2018, time.com/money/5160613/craftivism-protest/.

Goggin, Maureen Daly. "Joie de Fabriquer: The Rhetoricity of Yarn Bombing." *Peitho*, vol. 17, no. 2, 2015, pp. 145–71.

Greer, Betsy. *Craftivism: The Art and Craft of Activism*. Arsenal Pulp Press, 2014.

Hermanson, Tove. "Knitting as Dissent: Female Resistance in America since the Revolutionary War." *Textile Society of America, Symposium Proceedings*, Sept. 2012, digitalcommons.unl.edu/tsaconf/696.

Luther, Elaine. "Badass Cross Stitch: Activism through Stitching with Shannon Downey." *Moore Women Artists*, n.d., moorewomenartists.org/badass-cross-stitch-activism-stitching-shannon-downey/.

Matchar, Emily. *Homeward Bound: Why Women Are Embracing the New Domesticity*. Simon & Schuster, 2013.

Pristash, Heather Elizabeth. *A Sharper Point: A Feminist, Multimodal Heuristic for Analyzing Knitted Rhetoric*. 2014. Bowling Green State U, PhD dissertation.

Taylor, Elise. "How That 'Boys Will Be Boys' Embroidery Became the Internet's Response to Harvey Weinstein." *Vogue*, 16 Oct. 2017, www.vogue.com/article/boys-will-be-boys-badass-crossstitch-harvey-weinstein.

Ward, Beth. "How Women Are Using Knitting And Needlework as a Form of Protest." *Bust*, Jan. 19, 2018, https://bust.com/feminism/194090-craftivism-knitting-protest.html.

Sara Ahmed

Sara Ahmed introduces herself as a feminist killjoy: "It is what I do. It is how I think. It is my philosophy and my politics," she writes on her blog's home page. A feminist killjoy is provoked—wound up—by sexism, racism, or inequality. Often, the feminist killjoy is called oversensitive, or accused of overreacting, when she calls attention to problems others would rather overlook. And for killing the joy of denial, she becomes the problem.

Ahmed's life is laced with feminist killjoy moments, which she describes in her blog—*feministkilljoys*—and across her eight books. Until 2016, Ahmed was a professor at Goldsmiths, University of London, where she served as the inaugural director of the Centre for Feminist Research. When the university failed to address the problem of sexual harassment, Ahmed resigned in protest. As she explained on her blog, "Sometimes we have to leave a situation because we are feminists. Wherever I am, I will be a feminist. I will be doing feminism. I will be living a feminist life. I will be chipping away at the walls" (Resignation).

Ahmed's eighth book, *Living a Feminist Life*, from which the following excerpt is taken, addresses audiences beyond the academy. A queer woman of color, Ahmed moves adeptly between personal narratives and her own unique amalgamation of feminist and critical race theory, literary theory, disability studies, and philosophy. Her prose, likewise, disrupts confines of genre, fluctuating from reflective to analytical to poetic, multiple, and intersectional, reflecting her feminism.

In the following text, Ahmed takes a more direct approach, offering a Killjoy Survival Kit to her readers. The kit acknowledges that feminist work can feel grueling, painful, hopeless. But self-care does more than aid recovery, she reminds us—it claims one's life as vital. Ahmed's kit gives direction and specificity to Audre Lorde's famous proclamation that "caring for myself is not self-indulgence, it is self-preservation, and that is an act of political warfare."

Writing directly to her readers in the form of a list, Ahmed encourages us to listen to other killjoys, who will challenge us and help us to attend to our blind spots. Listen, too, to your body, she says, "If it screams, stop. If it moans, slow down" (247). Rather than denying emotions, Ahmed names them as a resource: "Your feelings can be the site of a rebellion" (246). These are the lessons of feminist survival, drawn from a collective of feminist wisdom, now offered to a new generation.

"A Killjoy Survival Kit":
Excerpt from *Living a Feminist Life*

2015

For those who have to insist they matter to matter, self-care is warfare. We could think here of #BlackLivesMatter, a movement with a hashtag; a hashtag can be snap; a movement begun by black feminist and queer activists Alicia Garza, Patrisse Cullors, and Opal Tometi to protest against how black lives do not matter, how black deaths are not mourned, how injustices against black people are not recognized. Mattering for some requires and involves collective agency: "Black Lives Matter affirms the lives of black queer and trans folks, disabled folks, black undocumented folks, folks with records, women and all black lives along the gender spectrum."[1] You have to affirm that some lives matter when a world is invested in saying they do not.

Protest can be a form of self-care as well as care for others: a refusal not to matter. Self-care can also be those ordinary ways we look out for each other because the costs of protesting are made so high, just as the costs that lead to protest remain so high. In directing our care toward ourselves, we are redirecting care away from its proper objects; we are not caring for those we are supposed to care for; we are not caring for the bodies deemed worth caring about. And that is why in queer, feminist, and antiracist work, self-care is about the creation of community, fragile communities as I explored in part III, assembled out of the experiences of being shattered. We reassemble ourselves through the ordinary, everyday, and often painstaking work of looking after ourselves; looking after each other.

We need a handle when we lose it. A killjoy survival kit is about finding a handle at the very moment one seems to lose it, when things seem to fly out of hand; a way of holding on when the possibility you were reaching for seems to be slipping away. Feminist killjoys: even when things fly out of hand, even when we fly out of hand, we need a handle on things.

ITEM 1: BOOKS

You need your favorite feminist books close to hand; your feminist books need to be handy. You need to take them with you; make them with you. Words can pick you up when you are down. And note: it is often books that name the problem that help us handle the problem. Kick-ass feminist books have a special agency, all of their own. I feel propelled by their kick.

Books in my tool kit include *Sister Outsider, A Burst of Light, Zami,* and *The Cancer Journals* by Audre Lorde; *Feminist Theory and Talking Back* by bell hooks; *The Politics of Reality* by Marilyn Frye; *Gender Trouble, Bodies That Matter* and *Precarious Lives* by Judith Butler; *Mrs. Dalloway* by Virginia Woolf; *The Mill on the Floss* by George Eliot; *Rubyfruit Jungle* by Rita Mae Brown. Yes I know this list includes a lot of books by Audre Lorde and Judith Butler. Their words reach me. Their words teach me.

Wherever I go, they go.

ITEM 2: THINGS

A feminist life too is surrounding by things. Living a feminist life creates feminist things. We all have tendencies; we might be a feminist hoarder, keep every little poster, button, scrap of paper from a meeting; or we might not. But think of how a convention is a thing maker (the wedding photographs, the signs of a reproductive life that can gather like weights on walls). We need to have things too; things that gather around, reminders of a feminist life, happy objects even, reminders of connections, shared struggles, shared lives. We might have more or fewer things, but a feminist needs her things.

Surround yourself with feminism. In a conversation with Gloria Steinem, bell hooks describes how she surrounded herself with her precious objects, feminist objects, so that they are the first things she sees when she wakes up.[2] Think of that: you create a feminist horizon around you, the warmth of memories; feminism as memory making. Feminism too leaves things behind. Things can also be how you handle what you come up against: you are reminded why you are doing what you are doing. Things are reminders.

Our feminist politics makes things as well as breaks things.

ITEM 3: TOOLS

A survival kit is also a feminist toolbox. What are your feminist tools? Mine include a pen and a keyboard, a table; the things around me that allow me to keep writing, to send my words out. Maybe a survival kit is also a toolbox. We need to have things to do things with; a killjoy needs more tools, the more she is up against. Maybe she uses her computer to write a blog. A tool: a means to a killjoy end. The blog itself becomes a tool; it is how she can extend her reach; how she can find a community of killjoys. A feminist end is often a new means. We need more means available the harder it is to achieve our ends. We need to diversify our tools, expand our range; we need to become more and more inventive, because so often when we do one thing, we find ourselves blocked. She has to keep going when she is blocked;

she can pick herself up again by picking something else up, maybe something she finds nearby. Of course, then, a feminist killjoy approaches things as potentially useful things, as means to her own ends. She has a use for things. She might not be using things the way she is supposed to. She might queer use or find a queer use for things. Her killjoy survival kit, to fulfill the purpose for which it is intended, will itself become another useful thing. But hand that survival kit to another, and it might not be quite so useful. In fact: a killjoy survival kit might even be deemed as compromising the health and safety of others. In fact: a killjoy survival kit might be deemed useless by others.

A feminist tool is sharp; we need to keep sharpening our tools. When we speak, we are often heard as sharp. Hear her: shrill, strident, the killjoy voice. A voice can be a tool. And yet somehow sharp can become blunt. One person once turned this bluntness into an insult, describing me "as not the sharpest tool in the house [of being]." I turn the insult into a willful aspiration: to make feminist points requires being willing to be blunt. My own citation policy in this book is a case in point.

In my previous chapter I described lesbian feminism as willful carpentry. So yes we need feminist carpenters, feminist builders; we need to make feminist buildings by not using the master's tools, as Audre Lorde notes, most willfully, by proclaiming unflinchingly that the master's tools will never dismantle the master's house. We might need feminist tools to make feminist tools. We can become tools; we can become bricks, feminist bricks.

Of course, sometimes a feminist has to go on strike. To strike is to put your tools down, to refuse to work by working with them. A feminist sometimes refuses to work, when the conditions of working are unjust. A tool can be what she puts down when she is striking.

ITEM 4: TIME

Did your heart quicken when you read that e-mail? Did your fingers quicken when you typed that response, as if driven by the force of your own rage? Do you have a sense that this is happening to you, and that you are caught by hap, and shudder because of what happens? Whatever you decide, whether to send something, or not, say something, or not, pause, breathe; take some time. Slow down. Frown. You might still send it, but you will be glad you have given yourself room to decide; you will be glad.

Time also means having time out. Even when you have willingly accepted the killjoy assignment, you are more than this assignment. Take breaks; do other things, with things. Time out might be required for time in.

Time out from being a killjoy is necessary for a killjoy if she is to persist in being a killjoy. Being a killjoy is not all that you are, and if you are too consumed by her, she can drain too much energy and will. Come back to her; she will come back to you: you will, she will.

ITEM 5: LIFE

There is so much in life, as we know, things that are ordinary or just there, beautiful things, to love; those things that come and go; things that are all the more valuable because they are fragile. Being a killjoy is too occupying, if it takes you away from the worlds you are in; the rise and fall of the sun, the way the trees are angled like that, the smile of a friend when you share a joke, the cold fresh water; the feel of the sea as immersion; the familiar smells of spices cooking.

Twice in my life an animal has come into my life and made life feel more possible, made life vibrate with possibility: when I was twelve, it was Mulka, a horse who was with me for almost thirty years (I mentioned him in chapter 2), always there even when we were living on separate continents. Mulka saved my life, of that I am sure, helped me to find another path when I was hurtling toward a miserable fate. He brought with him a world, a world of horsey people, in the Adelaide hills, a world apart from school and family. He brought with him Yvonne and Meredith Johnson, who in caring for him when I was away, cared for me. And then there was Poppy, our puppy, who came into my life while I was writing this book. It is the first time I have shared a life with a dog. She makes everything better. She brought with her so much, so intent on the task of being herself; a bounding presence who keeps me in the present. She wiggled her way into my affections. She also wiggled her way into this survival kit. She will wiggle right out again. Of that too, I am sure.

To survive as to be: to be with Mulka; to be with Poppy; to be in a present; to be out in the world; to be alive with a world.

Life matters; we are killjoys because life matters; and life can be what killjoys are fighting for; life requires we give time to living, to being alive, to being thrown into a world with others. We need to be thrown by how others are thrown. We need to be unsettled by what is unsettling. We need to let life in, in all of its contingencies. I think of this as being open to hap. And, as I suggested in chapter 8, to affirm hap is a kind of snap; we snap a bond that decides for us the kind of shape a life should have to count as a good life. But that does not mean breaking our bond to life. To snap a bond is for life. We believe in life all the more when we have to struggle for life, whether we have to snap, because we have to struggle to exist or struggle to transform an existence.

Being involved in a life project is affirmative. That is what those of us assigned killjoys know too well; yes we are assigned negative, but in being willing to receive that assignment we are affirming something. We might have different words, names, for this something.

ITEM 6: PERMISSION NOTES

There is only so much you can do. I have in my killjoy survival kit some permission notes to step back when it is too much. I noted in chapter 7 that you can learn to choose your battles wisely, but battles can also choose you. You don't always know when you can or will use your permission notes even when you have given them to yourself. But the mere fact of having them there, as a way you give yourself permission to exit a situation, can make the situation more bearable. You can leave; you can grieve.

I have already described how I left my academic post. I resigned because I gave myself permission to resign. That's not the only reason. But you need to be able to leave a situation, whether or not you do leave that situation. Being able to leave requires material resources, but it also requires an act of will, of not being willing to do something when it compromises your ability to be something.

I also have in my kit some sick notes. Do you anticipate that an event or meeting will be compromising? Do you feel you will be upset without being able to do anything? Well, put some sick notes in your kit. Use them sparingly, but given that we can be sick from the anticipation of being sick, the notes express a political as well as personal truth. Of course that is not to say that what we anticipate will happen will happen; of course not. But sometimes, just sometimes, we are not willing to take that risk. Be willful in your not willingness. Always.

ITEM 7: OTHER KILLJOYS

I think other killjoys are an essential part of my killjoy survival kit. I know it might sound odd to put other people in a place you have designated as your space (in a bag, I keep thinking of bags; how can we breathe in bags?). But I cannot think of being a killjoy without the company of other killjoys. This is not about identity; it is not about assuming a community of killjoys (I have discussed the problem with making this assumption). Rather, it is about the experience of having others who recognize the dynamics because they too have been there, in that place, that difficult place. This is not to say we cannot become killjoys to killjoys. We can and we do. And that is just one more reason that other killjoys need to be part of our survival kit. It helps us to recognize how we too can be the problem; we too can be involved in erasing the contributions or chances of others.

I learned this lesson recently when my own participation in a conversation on black British feminism was challenged by black women who saw me as participating in their erasure from public spaces and discussions. I responded too quickly and became defensive, hearing their voices as part of the same chorus of what I would call more questionable critiques that positioned brown women as gaining position by taking up places that did not belong to them, which used the familiar narrative that women of color use diversity as a career advancement. I heard as a killjoy. And that stopped me from hearing killjoys, those who were getting in the way of what I thought of as a lifeline: black British feminism as my intellectual community. Staying close to other killjoys is thus not about being on the same side. It is how we can ask more of ourselves; it is how we can be and stay vigilant.

Our crossness can and should be directed toward ourselves. We get things wrong. I did. And I do.

ITEM 8: HUMOR

A close kin of the figure of the feminist killjoy is the figure of the humorless feminist: the one who cannot or will not get the joke; the one who is miserable. Oh the proximity of kinship! Of course, we refuse to laugh at sexist jokes. We refuse to laugh when jokes are not funny. I consider this point to be so vital that it forms the fourth of the ten principles of my killjoy manifesto. But we do laugh; and feminist laughter can lighten our loads. In fact we laugh often in recognition of the shared absurdity of this world; or just in recognition of this world. Sometimes we make jokes out of the points left severed, the bleeding arteries of our institutional knowledge. Sometimes we laugh with each other because we recognize that we recognize the same power relations.

What I am implying here: lightening our loads becomes part of a killjoy survival strategy. When we are dealing with heavy histories, lightening becomes a shared activity. When we are dealing with norms that tighten the more we fail to inhabit them, making it difficult to breathe, loosening becomes a shared activity. Part of the work of lightening and loosening is sharing: because diversity work is costly, we have to share the costs of doing that work.

My interviews with diversity practitioners that I drew on in part II were thus full of laughter. Like the time a diversity practitioner talked about how she just had to open her mouth in meetings to witness eyes rolling as if to say, "Oh here she goes." How we laughed as killjoys recognizing that killjoy moment. Or like the time a diversity practitioner told me of how a friend asked, "Are they related?" about a photo of her (all white male) management team. How we laughed, at that moment, at that exposure of how institutions work as kinship structures. When we catch with words a logic that is often reproduced by not being put into words, it can be such a relief. We recognized that each other recognized the logic. Laughter, peals of it; our bodies catching that logic, too.

We don't always laugh, of course. Sometimes we have to let the full weight of a history bear down on us. Sometimes we need to let ourselves be down. But sometimes this sense of being down can convert into energy, because we can laugh at it;

because what we come up against gives us the resources to bear witness, to expose things, to bring things to the surface, so they can be laughed at.

To laugh at something can be to make something more real, to magnify it, and to reduce something's power or hold over you, simultaneously.

ITEM 9: FEELINGS

Our emotions can be a resource; we draw on them. To be a killjoy is often to be assigned as being emotional, too emotional; letting your feelings get in the way of your judgment; letting your feelings get in the way. Your feelings can be the site of a rebellion. A feminist heart beats the wrong way; feminism is hearty.

One male professor where I work kept telling me, telling others, that he did not get the feminist killjoy; that she made no sense to him. He kept saying it repeatedly. Explain it to me. Really he was saying: explain yourself. And he kept saying things like, she doesn't make sense because we have women who are senior managers. In other words, he thought the right feminist feeling would be joy, gratitude even, for the good fortune of our arrival and progression. We have to be willing to be experienced as ungrateful, to use this refusal of joy as an exposure of what we have been commanded not to express. There was an implication in his refusal to get the feminist killjoy that my organizing of my own intellectual and political project through her was an institutional disloyalty; one that would potentially damage the institution.

I think of Adrienne Rich's (1979) killjoy invitation to be "disloyal to civilization." Our emotions are opened up when we refuse the commandment to be loyal and joyful. We don't always know how we feel even when we feel something intensely. Put all those feelings into your kit. See what they do. Watch the mess they stir up. A survival kit is all about stirring things up and living in the stew.

ITEM 10: BODIES

It is true, it is wearing. We can be worn down as well as becoming down. Bodies need to be looked after. Bodies need to be nourished and fed. Feminism too can be thought of as a diet; a feminist diet is how we are nourished by feminism. In my killjoy survival kit I would have a bag of fresh chilies; I tend to add chilies to most things. I am not saying chilies are little feminists. But you would have in your kit whatever you tend to add to things; however you adapt dishes to your own requirements. If we have a diversity of bodies, we have a diversity of requirements.

And this item is related to all the others. Bodies are the mediating relation. When we do not survive, we become body; a body is what is left. A body is behind. A body is vulnerable; we are vulnerable. A body tells us the time; bodies carry traces of where we have been. Perhaps we are these traces. A killjoy has a body before she can receive her assignment.

Bodies speak to us. Your body might tell you it is not coping with what you are asking; and you need to listen. You need to listen to your body. If it screams, stop. If it moans, slow down. Listen. Feminist ears: they too are in my survival kit.

So much energy is involved in the struggle not to be compromised by an existence. But as I have noted throughout this book, claiming the figure of the killjoy, saying in this situation or that "I am her" can be energizing; there is something about her, a sense of vitality, perhaps, a sense of rebelliousness and mischief, perhaps, naughtiness, even, which might be why and how killjoys keep circulating, keep proliferating; she seems to be popping up everywhere. As I said in an earlier chapter, if we pick her up, she picks up.

And that too is why bodies must be in our survival kit. Bodies that prance; bodies that dance; "bodies that matter," to borrow Judith Butler's (1993) terms; bodies that have to wiggle about to create space.

Wiggling is in my survival kit.

Dancing, too.

Bodies that dance: how often feminists have claimed dance as essential to their liberation. One might think of Emma Goldman's famous statement, "I won't join your revolution if I cannot dance." Or I think of the film about the survival of Audre Lorde, *The Berlin Years*, and its final sequences that show Audre dancing, sequences that seem to capture so well the generosity of her black feminist spirit. I think of the dancing at Lesbian Lives conferences that I have enjoyed over the years (the talking too, but the dancing is what I recall most quickly). A dancing feminist body, a dancing lesbian body, dancing black and brown bodies; the affirming of how we inhabit bodies through how we are with others. We are here, still. Anyone can dance with anyone to form a collective. I am not saying killjoys have a specific genre or style of dancing. I am not saying that that there is a killjoy dance. (Though maybe, just maybe, there is a killjoy dance.) Perhaps in her stance is a certain kind of prance; perhaps in the energy that saturates her figure, she becomes an assembly.

Look at her move: what a movement.

And, in putting dance in my killjoy survival kit, I am saying something affirmative. Is there a contradiction here? When I am joyful, have I ceased to be a killjoy? Dance can be how we embrace the fragility of being thrown. And joy too is part of killjoy survival, without any question. We need joy to survive killing joy; we can even take joy from killing joy. And so too is the erotic part of my kit, the kind of erotic that Audre Lorde spoke of with such eloquence; a feminist killjoy in being charged up is warmed up; she is an erotic figure. She might come to be as or in negation, but that negation trembles with desire; a desire for more to life, more desire; a desire for more. Feminist killjoys tend to spill all over the place. What a spillage.

Feminist killjoys: a leaky container.

And so:

Be careful, we leak.

We can recall again Shulamith Firestone's (1970, 90) call for a "smile embargo" in her revolutionary manifesto, *Dialectic of Sex*. She wants us to stop smiling as a force of habit; something that has become involuntary; to stop smiling until we have something to smile about. A smile boycott would be a collective action; it would only work if we all stopped smiling. Not smiling becomes a feminist strike. I will return to this striking feminism in my killjoy manifesto. But note too how Firestone's call is also a call to open up the erotic, to release the erotic from the habit of happiness that directs life down a "narrow, difficult-to-find alleyway of human experience" (1970, 155).

I explored in my chapter "Feminism Is Sensational" how feminism can be a coming alive to a world that had been closed off by the requirement to live your life in a certain way. Things come to life when they are not overlooked. So it is important to say this: we need to allow ourselves to be sad and angry; when joy and happiness become ideals, sadness becomes too quickly an obstacle, a failure to achieve or approximate the right feelings. Sadness can require a permission note (item 6). But at the same time, joy can be part of a killjoy survival kit. I personally don't need a permission note for joy; in my own experience, joy is culturally mandated even if it can be the site of rebellion (the collective joy of dissent); but if you do need to give yourself permission to be joyful, write yourself one. I think joy can only be part of a killjoy survival kit when we refuse to give joy the status of an aspiration. When joy becomes aspiration, then joy becomes what a killjoy has to kill. But even if survival for killjoys requires refusing to make joy (or its heavier friend happiness) into an aspiration, it does not mean we have an obligation to be sad or unhappy either. A killjoy is not joyless.

To return to Emma Goldman, to her book *Living My Life*, she affirms the freedom to dance when she is told not to dance; she dances and is told that it is not the right time to dance, because of the "death of a dear comrade" ([1931] 2008, 56). As she relays the story, she says a young boy with a solemn face whispered to her, "It did not behoove an agitator to dance." Goldman affirms at this moment dance as an affective rebellion against the requirement to be mournful; against the requirement not to live in her body through joyful abandon. This is what I call an affect alien moment. A killjoy survival kit is also about allowing your body to be the site of a rebellion, including a rebellion against the demand to give your body over to a cause or to make your body a cause. Maybe not dancing, too, can be what a body does; refusing to dance when dancing becomes a requirement, standing back, to one side, stopping.

AND FINALLY: A KILLJOY SURVIVAL KIT

Putting together a killjoy survival kit can also be a survival strategy. My killjoy survival kit is in my killjoy survival kit. Writing a feminist manifesto too might be a survival strategy. My manifesto, up next, is in my kit. In writing a feminist manifesto, you must first read other feminist manifestos. What a joy! Manifestos are "companion species," to borrow a description from one of Donna Haraway's (2003) manifestos. Reading manifestos is also in my killjoy survival kit. A kit can be a container for activities that are ongoing; projects that are projects insofar as they have yet to be realized.

A killjoy: a project that comes from a critique of what is.
Speaking of projects:
We are our own survival kits.

NOTES

1. See Black Lives Matter, "About #BlackLivesMatter," http://www.blacklivesmatter.com (last accessed September 22, 2015).

2. The conversation is available here: New School, "bell hooks and Gloria Steinem at Eugene Lang College," YouTube, October 8, 2014, https://www.youtube.com/watch?v=tkzOFvfWRn4.

FOR FURTHER READING

"About." *Feministkilljoys*, n.d., feministkilljoys.com/about/.
Ahmed, Sara. *Living a Feminist Life*. Duke UP, 2017.
Lorde, Audre. *A Burst of Light: Essays*. Firebrand, 1988.

III

Rhetorics of Protest and Resistance

The myriad rhetorics of social protest and resistance on public display show that there are as many possible available means of persuasion as there are motivations to protest and resist. Women speaking out for their own and others' rights is an enduring motivation for their rhetorical acts, and this remains true in the twenty-first century. The rhetors in this section address critical issues such as a misogynistic and xenophobic presidential administration; a war in Iraq; trans-exclusionary legislation; climate change and globalization; and the cultural, economic, and environmental ramifications of racism. In so doing, they employ and repurpose more traditional forms, such as quilting, marches, and narrative, and they make use of newer forms like blogs and Twitter.

Indeed, contemporary protest and resistance are dramatically altered in the twenty-first century by the proliferation of social media platforms, which afford widespread connectivity, speed of delivery, and international circulation. For instance, the Black Lives Matter (BLM) movement originated from a Twitter hashtag and grew into an international movement that blends online and street activism. BLM co-founder Alicia Garza's "Herstory" opens this section with the origins and principles of BLM. And the 2017 Women's March on Washington, the largest single-day protest in US history, was built from nimble organizing through new and traditional means (Chenowith and Pressman).

The examples of protest and resistance collected here also exhibit rhetorical approaches employed by women across centuries to create coalitions and to forward movements: identification, where one emphasizes shared values or perspectives with an audience (Kenneth Burke); experience as evidence; and embodied rhetoric. Addressing allies of BLM, Garza explains why the movement must be centered on black lives, urging those who identify with the core values of BLM not to appropriate it for their own ends. The *Guiding Vision and Definition of Principles* for the 2017 Women's March on Washington, "an uprising against the systemic, interconnected oppressions crystallized in the form of Trump's election," seeks to create an inclusive space for all women through intersectional identification entrees (Tetreault). Photos from the march both support and complicate that identification: one protest sign uses disidentification with Republicans to connect with other protesters over reproductive rights; another photo depicts the realities of nonwhite protesters who experience a continued history of exclusion from white feminism; yet the aerial view of the march outside the US Capitol in Washington shows the breathtaking number of protestors collectively claiming their rights.

Rhetors in this section also render their experiences—and illuminate the experience of marginalized groups—to highlight the exigencies for their protests of international conflicts and crises. Riverbend blogs about the realities of the Iraq War as an Iraqi citizen caught in its crossfire, juxtaposing the ordinariness of everyday life with the face of warfare. Bacchetta et al. unite as an academic collective of transnational feminists to illuminate the broader, sociopolitical and economic ramifications of war, providing an argument that, when read alongside Riverbend's, adds further perspective through logos. Edwidge Danticat offers powerful testimony of her experience as an immigrant torn from her mother to condemn the Trump administration's separation of immigrant children from their parents. And Vandana Shiva centers the struggles of Indigenous peoples borne from globalization and "ownership society," instead forwarding a set of principles for "earth democracy."

In protest of the Dakota Access Pipeline, which skirts the Standing Rock Reservation, Tara Houska builds upon her experience was a member of the Couchiching First Nation to denounce the US government's ongoing disregard for Native lands. As a response to the pipeline standoff, Gina Adams employs quilting as rhetoric by remixing a medium known for utility with resistance to highlight the legacy of broken treaties with Natives.

Sasha Weiss and Suzanne Samin, who protest the assault and harassment of women in material and digital spaces, also employ experience as evidence. Weiss describes—and connects to—the powerful Twitter protest #YesAllWomen, which highlighted the cultural normalization of sexism and misogyny. Samin uses her experience as a female gamer to depict the damage of sexism in digital spaces, highlighting the ramifications, even in the twenty-first century, for women entering spheres traditionally dominated by men.

This section concludes with two pieces of great rhetorical sway that feature embodied rhetoric—both pieces went viral to become touchstones of unflinching protest. First, a photo of the activist Bree Newsome removing the Confederate flag from in front of South Carolina's state capitol building shows the physicality of her resistance. Her carefully executed act drew much-needed attention to this marker of hate that is still present in public spaces. Finally, Emily Doe's arresting statement, delivered at the sentencing of the perpetrator in her sexual assault case, shows the devastating psychological and physical realities experienced by rape survivors and challenges a system that punishes the victim for the crime.

Collectively, then, this section represents the many efforts women make daily, merging new and traditional means to protest and resist injustice and to connect with others through identification, shared experiences, and embodied action. This approach seems to be working, especially for younger people. Reflecting on a study that shows high levels of millennial social involvement through both old and new activist methods, Derrick Feldmann observes, "Millennials possess the ability to organize, drive awareness and influence the behavior of other generations through vast social media networks, with an ease and to a degree this country has never seen." The future, then, is ripe for resistance.

Works Cited

Burke, Kenneth. *A Rhetoric of Motives*. U of California P, 2013.

Chenoweth, Erica, and Jeremy Pressman. "This Is What We Learned by Counting the Women's Marches." *The Washington Post*, 7 Feb. 2017, www.washingtonpost.com/news/monkey-cage/wp/2017/02/07/this-is-what-we-learned-by-counting-the-womens-marches/.

Feldmann, Derrick. "Millennials Are Engaging in Political Action Now More Than Ever." *VICE*, 11 Oct. 2017, https://www.vice.com/en_us/article/gy57km/millennials-are-engaging-in-political-action-now-more-than-ever.

Tetreault, Laura. "'White Women Voted for Trump': The Women's March on Washington and Intersectional Feminist Futures." *Computers and Composition Online*, Mar. 2019, http://cconlinejournal.org/techfem_si/01_Tetreault/index.html.

Alicia Garza

The Black Lives Matter (BLM) international activist movement, called "the most significant manifestation of [its] kind since civil rights," was founded by three women: Alicia Garza, Opal Tometi, and Patrisse Cullors (Lebron). They were spurred into action by the 2013 acquittal of George Zimmerman for shooting Trayvon Martin, an unarmed seventeen-year-old black youth, as he walked home from a 7-Eleven store (Lebron). Through grassroots mobilization, social media deployment, and on-the-ground protest, BLM turned the country's attention to police brutality and racism by spotlighting the high-profile shootings of Trayvon Martin, Michael Brown (see Lezley McSpadden's contribution to this volume), Eric Garner, and Freddie Gray.

While its initial efforts centered on the treatment of black men, as Garza explains in the following herstory, BLM is designed to "affirm the lives of Black queer and trans folks, disabled folks, Black-undocumented folks, folks with records, women and all Black lives along the gender spectrum." In fact, in both design and aim, the movement's organizers are influenced by forty years of work by black feminist and LGBTQ scholars and activists (Ransby). As the history professor Barbara Ransby observes, the BLM founders' "writings and practice emphasize collective models of leadership instead of hierarchical ones, center on society's most marginalized people and focus on how multiple systems of oppression intersect and reinforce one another."

An award-winning activist, speaker, and writer, Alicia Garza, who identifies as a black queer woman, is dedicated to correcting the misconception that only cisgender black men endure police and state violence. She serves as the special projects director for the National Domestic Workers Alliance (see Ai-jen Poo's contribution to this volume), which advocates for dignity and fair labor practices for domestic workers in the United States. In 2018 Garza founded the Black Futures Lab, a collective that "transforms black communities into constituencies that change the way power operates—locally, statewide, and nationally" ("About"). She is also a prominent voice on issues of racial justice, contributing to publications such as *Time*, the *Guardian*, *Elle*, and the *New York Times*.

In the following piece Garza addresses an audience of other progressive leaders, urging them not to misappropriate #BlackLivesMatter for their own purposes—a practice she links to a history of cultural theft of black queer women's work. Using direct address, Garza reminds readers that #BlackLivesMatter is a social movement and counterculture that must remain centered on black lives. It is not a denial that all lives matter, as some charge. Rather, she explains, the movement requires precise focus on black history, black contributions, and black experiences because of the particular ways they have been erased, dehumanized, and criminalized by a white patriarchal culture. In this way, Garza employs identification not to emphasize a shared identity or history with her audience but to argue that a commitment to shared goals—a world where all lives matter—requires acknowledging the specific, disproportionate impact of state violence and racism on black lives. For allies, then, the movement is an invitation to stand with the black community in affirming black lives, because "when black people get free, we all get free."

"A Herstory of the #BlackLivesMatter Movement"

Feminist Wire, 2014

I created #BlackLivesMatter with Patrisse Cullors and Opal Tometi, two of my sisters, as a call to action for Black people after 17-year-old Trayvon Martin was posthumously placed on trial for his own murder and the killer, George Zimmerman, was not held accountable for the crime he committed. It was a response to the anti-Black racism that permeates our society and also, unfortunately, our movements.

Black Lives Matter is an ideological and political intervention in a world where Black lives are systematically and intentionally targeted for demise. It is an affirmation of Black folks' contributions to this society, our humanity, and our resilience in the face of deadly oppression.

We were humbled when cultural workers, artists, designers, and techies offered their labor and love to expand #BlackLivesMatter beyond a social media hashtag. Opal, Patrisse, and I created the infrastructure for this movement project—moving the hashtag from social media to the streets. Our team grew through a very successful Black Lives Matter ride, led and designed by Patrisse Cullors and Darnell L. Moore, organized to support the movement that is growing in St. Louis, MO, after 18-year-old Mike Brown was killed at the hands of Ferguson police officer Darren Wilson. We've hosted national conference calls focused on issues of critical importance to Black people working hard for the liberation of our people. We've connected people across the country working to end the various forms of injustice impacting our people. We've created space for the celebration and humanization of Black lives.

The Theft of Black Queer Women's Work

As people took the #BlackLivesMatter demand into the streets, mainstream media and corporations also took up the call, #BlackLivesMatter appeared in an episode of *Law & Order: SVU* in a mash-up containing the Paula Deen racism scandal and the tragedy of the murder of Trayvon Martin.

Suddenly, we began to come across varied adaptations of our work—all lives matter, brown lives matter, migrant lives matter, women's lives matter, and on and on. While imitation is said to be the highest form of flattery, I was surprised when an organization called to ask if they could use "Black Lives Matter" in one of their campaigns. We agreed to it, with the caveat that: (a) as a team, we preferred that we not use the meme to celebrate the imprisonment of any individual, and (b) that it was important to us they acknowledged the genesis of #BlackLivesMatter. I was surprised when they did exactly the opposite and then justified their actions by saying they hadn't used the "exact" slogan and, therefore, they deemed it okay to take our work, use it as their own, fail to credit where it came from, and then use it to applaud incarceration.

I was surprised when a community institution wrote asking us to provide materials and action steps for an art show they were curating, entitled "Our Lives Matter." When questioned about who was involved and why they felt the need to change the very specific call and demand around Black lives to "our lives," I was told the artists decided it needed to be more inclusive of all people of color. I was even more surprised when, in the promotion of their event, one of the artists conducted an interview that completely erased the origins of their work—rooted in the labor and love of queer Black women.

Pause.

When you design an event/campaign/et cetera based on the work of queer Black women, don't invite them to participate in shaping it, but ask them to provide materials and ideas for next steps for said event, that is racism in practice. It's also heteropatriarchal. Straight men, unintentionally or intentionally, have taken the work of queer Black women and erased our contributions. Perhaps if we were the charismatic Black men many are rallying around these days, it would have been a different story, but being Black queer women in this society (and apparently within these movements) tends to equal invisibility and nonrelevancy.

We completely expect those who benefit directly and improperly from White supremacy to try and erase our existence. We fight that every day. But when it happens amongst our allies, we are baffled, we are saddened, and we are enraged. And it's time to have the political conversation about why that's not okay.

We are grateful to our allies who have stepped up to the call that Black lives matter, and taken it as an opportunity to not just stand in solidarity with us, but to investigate the ways in which anti-Black racism is perpetuated in their own communities. We are also grateful to those allies who were willing to engage in critical dialogue with us about this unfortunate and problematic dynamic. And for those who we have not yet had the opportunity to engage with around the adaptations of the Black Lives Matter call, please consider the following points.

Broadening the Conversation to Include Black Life

Black Lives Matter is a unique contribution that goes beyond [the] extrajudicial killings of Black people by police and vigilantes. It goes beyond the narrow nationalism that can be prevalent within some Black communities, which merely call on Black people to love Black, live Black and buy Black, keeping straight cis Black men in the front of the movement while our sisters, queer and trans and disabled folk take up roles in the background or not at all. Black Lives Matter affirms the lives of Black queer and trans folks, disabled folks, Black undocumented folks, folks with records, women, and all Black lives along the gender spectrum. It centers those that have been marginalized within Black liberation movements. It is a tactic to (re)build the Black liberation movement.

When we say Black Lives Matter, we are talking about the ways in which Black people are deprived of our basic human rights and dignity. It is an acknowledgement that Black poverty and genocide is state violence. It is an acknowledgment that 1 million Black people are locked in cages in this country—one half of all people in prisons or jails—is an act of state violence. It is an acknowledgment that Black women continue to bear the burden of a relentless assault on our children and our families and that assault is an act of state violence. Black queer and trans folks bearing a unique burden in a heteropatriarchal society that disposes of us like garbage and simultaneously fetishizes us and profits off of us is state violence; the fact that 500,000 Black people in the US are undocumented immigrants and relegated to the shadows is state violence; the fact that Black girls are used as negotiating chips during times of conflict and war is state violence; Black folks living with disabilities and different abilities bear the burden of state-sponsored Darwinian experiments that attempt to squeeze us into boxes of normality defined by White supremacy is state violence. And the fact is that the lives of Black people—not ALL people—exist within these conditions is consequence of state violence.

When Black People Get Free, Everybody Gets Free

#BlackLivesMatter doesn't mean your life isn't important—it means that Black lives, which are seen as without value within White supremacy, are important to your liberation. Given the disproportionate impact state violence has on Black lives, we understand that when Black people in this country get free, the benefits will be wide reaching and transformative for society as a whole. When we are able to end [the] hypercriminalization and sexualization of Black people and end the poverty, control, and surveillance of Black people, every single person in this world has a better shot at getting and staying free. When Black people get free, everybody gets free. This is why we call on Black people and our allies to take up the call that Black lives matter. We're not saying Black lives are more important than other lives, or that other lives are not criminalized and oppressed in various ways. We remain in active solidarity with all oppressed people who are fighting for their liberation and we know that our destinies are intertwined.

And, to keep it real—it is appropriate and necessary to have strategy and action centered around Blackness without other non-Black communities of color, or White folks for that matter, needing to find a place and a way to center themselves within it. It is appropriate and necessary for us to acknowledge the critical role that Black lives and struggles for Black liberation have played in inspiring and anchoring, through practice and theory, social movements for the liberation of all people. The women's movement, the Chicano liberation movement, queer movements, and many more have adopted the strategies, tactics and theory of the Black liberation movement. And if we are committed to a world where all lives matter, we are called to support the very movement that inspired and activated so many more. That means supporting and acknowledging Black lives.

Progressive movements in the United States have made some unfortunate errors when they push for unity at the expense of really understanding the concrete differences in context, experience, and oppression. In other words, some want unity without struggle. As people who have our minds stayed on freedom, we can learn to fight anti-Black racism by examining the ways in which we participate in it, even unintentionally, instead of the worn out and sloppy practice of drawing lazy parallels of unity between peoples with vastly different experiences and histories.

When we deploy "All Lives Matter" as to correct an intervention specifically created to address anti-blackness, we lose the ways in which the state apparatus has built a program of genocide and repression mostly on the backs of Black people—beginning with the theft of millions of people for free labor—and then adapted it to control, murder, and profit off of other communities of color and immigrant communities. We perpetuate a level of White supremacist domination by reproducing a tired trope that we are all the same, rather than acknowledging that non-Black oppressed people in this country are both impacted by racism and domination, and simultaneously, BENEFIT from anti-Black racism.

When you drop "Black" from the equation of whose lives matter, and then fail to acknowledge it came from somewhere, you further a legacy of erasing Black lives and Black contributions from our movement legacy. And consider whether or not when dropping the Black you are, intentionally or unintentionally, erasing Black folks from the conversation or homogenizing very different experiences. The legacy and prevalence of anti-Black racism and heteropatriarchy is a lynchpin holding together this unsustainable economy. And that's not an accidental analogy.

In 2014 heteropatriarchy and anti-Black racism within our movement is real and felt. It's killing us and it's killing our potential to build power for transformative social change. When you adopt the work of queer women of color, don't name or recognize it, and promote it as if it has no history of its own such actions are problematic. When I use Assata's powerful demand in my organizing work, I always begin by sharing where it comes from, sharing about Assata's significance to the Black Liberation Movement, what its political purpose and message is, and why it's important in our context.

When you adopt Black Lives Matter and transform it into something else (if you feel you really need to do that—see above for the arguments not to), it's appropriate politically to credit the lineage from which your adapted work derived. It's important that we work together to build and acknowledge the legacy of Black contributions to the struggle for human rights. If you adapt Black Lives Matter, use the opportunity to talk about its inception and political framing. Lift up Black lives as an opportunity to connect struggles across race, class, gender, nationality, sexuality, and disability.

And, perhaps more importantly, when Black people cry out in defense of our lives, which are uniquely, systematically, and savagely targeted by the state, we are asking you, our family, to stand with us in affirming Black lives. Not just all lives. Black lives. Please do not change the conversation by talking about how your life matters, too. It does, but we need less watered-down unity and a more active solidarities with us, Black people, unwaveringly, in defense of our humanity. Our collective futures depend on it.

For Further Reading

"About." *Black Futures Lab*. blackfutureslab.org/about/.

Black Lives Matter. blacklivesmatter.com/.

Jones, Feminista. *Reclaiming Our Space: How Black Feminists Are Changing the World from the Tweets to the Streets*. Beacon Press, 2019.

Lebron, Chris. "Who First Showed Us That Black Lives Matter?" *The New York Times*, 5 Feb. 2018, www.nytimes.com/2018/02/05/opinion/black-lives-matter-philosophy.html.

Ransby, Barbara. "Black Lives Matter Is Democracy in Action." *The New York Times*, 21 Oct. 2017, www.nytimes.com/2017/10/21/opinion/sunday/black-lives-matter-leadership.html.

Women's March on Washington Organizers

Within days of Donald Trump's 2016 presidential victory, Theresa Shook, a retired attorney in Hawaii, and Bob Bland, a New York City fashion designer, each began planting seeds for a protest. On election night, discouraged and dumbfounded, Shook posted a call on Facebook for a post-inauguration march in Washington, DC. She woke up the next morning to ten thousand responses (Agrawal). In New York City, Bland, who had gained a following thanks to her "Nasty Woman" and "Bad Hombre" T-shirts—slurs Trump used in the debates to disparage Clinton and immigrants, respectively—rallied for a "Million Pussy March," reappropriating an infamous recording of Trump on *Access Hollywood* in which he boasted, "When you're a star, you can grab [women] by the pussy." Bland worked to unite various protest efforts, including Shook's, and joined with three New York–based activists to serve as march cochairs: Tamika Mallory, a gun control advocate; Carmen Perez, head of a criminal-justice reform group; and Linda Sarsour, an advocate for American Muslims (Agrawal).

From the inception of the Women's March, the co-organizers sought to foster an intersectional vision. A racially diverse group of women themselves—African American, Latina, Palestinian American Muslim, and white—their *Guiding Vision and Definition of Principles* insists that liberation must address interlocking forces of oppression, including racism, sexism, classism, ableism, homophobia, gender discrimination, and religious persecution. Their attention to intersectionality also acknowledges that the burden of oppression is experienced unevenly by women.

Their vision statement draws ethos from some of the country's most foundational rhetoric, including the Pledge of Allegiance, the Constitution, and "The New Colossus," the poem inscribed on the Statue of Liberty. In a political moment when Trump's supporters cheered his promise to build a US-Mexico border wall and to ban citizens from seven Muslim-majority counties entry into the United States, these activists weave Emma Lazarus's words into their mission: "Rooted in the promise of America's call for huddled masses yearning to breathe free, we believe in immigrant and refugee rights regardless of status or country of origin." They are clear that their vision of "liberty and justice for all"—including people with disabilities, women of color, transwomen, immigrants, Muslims—is not a departure from our foundational values as a country, but an affirmation of our deepest roots.

On January 21, 2017, their vision transpired into mighty action in the form of some 500,000 marching in Washington, 400,000 in New York City, 250,000 in Chicago, and more than two million in 673 sister marches in the United States and around the world. The Women's March is, in fact, the largest single-day protest in US history. Women, many donning pink pussy hats, filled the streets with signs (see Women's March Protest Signs, this volume) and chanting slogans like "Love Trumps Hate," "We Need a Leader, Not a Creepy Tweeter," and "Let Me Hear it Loud and Clear, Refugees Are Welcome Here."

While the march was a powerful, moving display of women's resilience and solidarity, it also uncovered the need for still deeper attention to intersectional issues and differences among women. The pink pussy hats, for instance, drew criticism from transwomen and women of color for their presumed assumption that all women have vaginas and that they are pink. Even earlier, during the planning, contentious discussion arose on the march's Facebook page, with women of color imploring white women to check their privilege—particularly since 53 percent of white women voted for Trump—and some white women taking offense and bowing out of the march (Stockman). As the *New York Times* writer Farah Stockman explains, however, some of the tension was by design: "Even as they are working to ensure a smooth and unified march next week, the national organizers said they made a deliberate decision to highlight the plight of minority and undocumented immigrant women and provoke uncomfortable discussions about race."

Further, disability rights activists criticized the lack of acknowledgement of disability as a social justice issue, since disabilities intersect with every identity. As Emily Ladau explains, up to 80 percent of women with disabilities have been victims of sexual assault; they also experience disproportionate levels of domestic violence and police violence. The Women's March, then, was not only an event designed to protest state-backed oppression—it was also an opportunity for women to face the ways they oppress one another, intentionally or not. (Following Ladau's article, the Women's March national team publicly recognized the exclusion of disability rights from their platform and took steps to change it).

Tension also surfaced over one of the march's unity principles—"open access to safe, legal, affordable abortion and birth control"—which led women who identify as both feminist and pro-life to feel excluded. Some of these women formed a counterdemonstration holding signs that read, "Real Feminists Reject Abortion" and "Life Empowers Women," which sparked back-and-forth exchanges between the two groups (Sheppard). While heated, this tension could also be regarded as productive, exhibiting the need for more conversation about whether abortion must remain a fault line in the feminist movement (see Claire Swinarski's contribution to this volume).

Indeed, the Women's March on Washington did not end with the January 21 protest—it grew into a movement, beginning with Ten Actions in the First 100

Days of Trump's presidency (see Amy Alexander's contribution to this volume). The organizers continue to collaborate with groups targeting racial justice, gun legislation, disability rights, LGBTQ rights, voter registration, and support for women running for office (North). In a historical moment when women's rights are especially precarious, the movement borne of the Women's March ensures that women remain central to the fight for liberty, every step of the way.

Guiding Vision and Definition of Principles

2017

Overview & Purpose

The Women's March on Washington is a women-led movement bringing together people of all genders, ages, races, cultures, political affiliations, disabilities, and backgrounds in our nation's capital on January 21, 2017, to affirm our shared humanity and pronounce our bold message of resistance and self-determination.

Recognizing that women have intersecting identities and are therefore impacted by a multitude of social justice and human rights issues, we have outlined a representative vision for a government that is based on the principles of liberty and justice for all. As Dr. King said, "We cannot walk alone. And as we walk, we must make the pledge that we shall always march ahead. We cannot turn back."

Our liberation is bound in each other's. The Women's March on Washington includes leaders of organizations and communities that have been building the foundation for social progress for generations. We welcome vibrant collaboration and honor the legacy of the movements before us—the suffragists and abolitionists, the civil rights movement, the feminist movement, the American Indian movement, Occupy Wall Street, marriage equality, Black Lives Matter, and more—by employing a decentralized, leader-full structure and focusing on an ambitious, fundamental and comprehensive agenda.

#WhyWeMarch

We are empowered by the legions of revolutionary leaders who paved the way for us to march, and acknowledge those around the globe who fight for our freedoms. We honor these women and so many more. They are #WHYWEMARCH.

Bella Abzug • Corazon Aquino • Ella Baker • Grace Lee Boggs Berta Cáceres • Rachel Carson • Shirley Chisholm • Angela Davis • Miss Major Griffin Gracy

• LaDonna Harris • Dorothy I. Height • bell hooks • Judith Heumann • Dolores Huerta • Marsha P. Johnson • Barbara Jordan • Yuri Kochiyama • Winona LaDuke • Audre Lorde • Wilma Mankiller • Diane Nash • Sylvia Rivera • Barbara Smith • Gloria Steinem • Hannah G. Solomon • Harriet Tubman • Edith Windsor • Malala Yousafzai.

Values and Principles

• We believe that women's rights are human rights and human rights are women's rights. This is the basic and original tenet for which we unite to march on Washington.

• We believe gender justice is racial justice is economic justice. We must create a society in which all women—including black women, Indigenous women, poor women, immigrant women, disabled women, Muslim women, lesbian, queer, and trans women—are free and able to care for and nurture themselves and their families, however they are formed, in safe and healthy environments free from structural impediments.

• Women have the right to live full and healthy lives, free of all forms of violence against our bodies. One in three women have been victims of some form of physical violence by an intimate partner within their lifetime, and one in five women have been raped. Further, each year, thousands of women and girls, particularly black, Indigenous, and transgender women and girls, are kidnapped, trafficked, or murdered. We honor the lives of those women who were taken before their time and we affirm that we work for a day when all forms of violence against women are eliminated.

• We believe in accountability and justice for police brutality and ending racial profiling and targeting of communities of color and Indigenous peoples. Women of color and Indigenous women are killed in police custody at greater rates, and are more likely to be sexually assaulted by police, and women with disabilities are disproportionately likely to experience use of force at the hands of police, and sexual assault in general. We also call for an immediate end to arming police with the military-grade weapons and military tactics that are wreaking havoc on communities of color and sovereign tribal lands. No woman or mother should have to fear that her loved ones will be harmed at the hands of those sworn to protect.

• We believe it is our moral imperative to dismantle the gender and racial inequities within the criminal justice system. The rate of imprisonment has grown faster for women than men, increasing by 700% since 1980, and the majority of women in prison have a child under the age of 18. Incarcerated women also face a high rate of violence and sexual assault. We are committed to ensuring access to gender-responsive programming and dedicated health care, including substance abuse treatment, [and] mental and maternal health services for women in prison. We believe in the promise of restorative justice and alternatives to incarceration. We are also committed to disrupting the school-to-prison pipeline that prioritizes incarceration over education by systematically funneling our children—particularly children of color, queer and trans youth, foster care children, and girls—into the justice system.

- We believe in reproductive freedom. We do not accept any federal, state, or local rollbacks, cuts, or restrictions on our ability to access quality reproductive health care services, birth control, HIV/AIDS care and prevention, or medically accurate sexuality education. This means open access to safe, legal, affordable abortion and birth control for all people, regardless of income, location, or education. We understand that we can only have reproductive justice when reproductive health care is accessible to all people regardless of income, location, or education.

- We believe in gender justice. We must have the power to control our bodies and be free from gender norms, expectations, and stereotypes. We must free ourselves and our society from the institution of awarding power, agency, and resources disproportionately to masculinity to the exclusion of others.

- We firmly declare that LGBTQIA rights are human rights and that it is our obligation to uplift, expand, and protect the rights of our gay, lesbian, bi, queer, trans, two-spirit, or gender nonconforming brothers, sisters, and siblings. This includes access to nonjudgmental, comprehensive healthcare with no exceptions or limitations; access to name and gender changes on identity documents; full anti-discrimination protections; access to education, employment, housing, and benefits; and an end to police and state violence.

- We believe in an economy powered by transparency, accountability, security, and equity. We believe that creating workforce opportunities that reduce discrimination against women and mothers allow economies to thrive. Nations and industries that support and invest in caregiving and basic workplace protections—including benefits like paid family leave, access to affordable childcare, sick days, health care, fair pay, vacation time, and healthy work environments—have shown growth and increased capacity.

• We believe in equal pay for equal work and the right of all women to be paid equitably. We must end the pay and hiring discrimination that women, particularly mothers, women of color, Indigenous women, lesbian, queer, and trans women still face each day in our nation, as well as discrimination against workers with disabilities, who can currently legally be paid less than federal minimum wage. Many mothers have always worked in our modern labor force, and women are now 50% of all family breadwinners. We stand for the 82% of women who become moms, particularly moms of color, being paid, judged, and treated fairly. Equal pay for equal work will lift families out of poverty and boost our nation's economy.

• We recognize that women of color and Indigenous women carry the heaviest burden in the global and domestic economic landscape, particularly in the care economy. We further affirm that all care work—caring for the elderly, caring for the chronically ill, caring for children and supporting independence for people with disabilities—is work, and that the burden of care falls disproportionately on the shoulders of women, particularly women of color. We stand for the rights, dignity, and fair treatment of all unpaid and paid caregivers. We must repair and replace the systemic disparities that permeate caregiving at every level of society.

• We believe that all workers—including domestic and farm workers—must have the right to organize and fight for a living minimum wage, and that unions and other labor associations are critical to a healthy and thriving economy for all. Undocumented and migrant workers must be included in our labor protections, and we stand in full solidarity with the sex workers' rights movement. We recognize that exploitation for sex and labor in all forms is a violation of human rights.

• We believe civil rights are our birthright. Our constitutional government establishes a framework to provide and expand rights and freedoms—not restrict them. To this end, we must protect and restore all the constitutionally mandated rights to all our citizens, including voting rights, freedom to worship without fear of intimidation or harassment, freedom of speech, and protections for all citizens regardless of race, gender, age, or disability. We honor and respect tribal laws and jurisdictions.

• We support Indigenous women's right to access, own, develop, and control land and its resources. We affirm that now is the time for the US implementation of the UN Declaration on the Rights of Indigenous Peoples and to honor existing treaty rights and fulfill promises made.

- We believe that all women's issues are issues faced by women with disabilities and deaf women. As mothers, sisters, daughters, and contributing members of this great nation, we seek to break barriers to access, inclusion, independence, and the full enjoyment of citizenship at home and around the world. We strive to be fully included in and contribute to all aspects of American life, economy, and culture.

- We believe it is time for an all-inclusive Equal Rights Amendment to the US Constitution. Most Americans believe the Constitution guarantees equal rights, but it does not. The 14th Amendment has been undermined by courts and cannot produce real equity on the basis of race and/or sex. And in a true democracy, each citizen's vote should count equally. All Americans deserve equality guarantees in the Constitution that cannot be taken away or disregarded, recognizing the reality that inequalities intersect, interconnect, and overlap.

- Rooted in the promise of America's call for huddled masses yearning to breathe free, we believe in immigrant and refugee rights regardless of status or country of origin. It is our moral duty to keep families together and empower all aspiring Americans to fully participate in, and contribute to, our economy and society. We reject mass deportation, family detention, violations of due process, and violence against queer and trans migrants. Immigration reform must establish a road map to citizenship, and provide equal opportunities and workplace protections for all. We recognize that the call to action to love our neighbor is not limited to the United States, because there is a global migration crisis. We believe migration is a human right and that no human being is illegal.

- We believe that every person, every community, and Indigenous peoples in our nation have the right to clean water, clean air, and access to and enjoyment of public lands. We believe that our environment and our climate must be protected, and that our land and natural resources cannot be exploited for corporate gain or greed—especially at the risk of public safety and health.

- We recognize that to achieve any of the goals outlined within this statement, we must work together to end war and live in peace with our sisters and brothers around the world. Ending war means a cessation to the direct and indirect aggression caused by the war economy and the concentration of power in the hands of a wealthy elite who use political, social, and economic systems to safeguard and expand their power

About This Document

The guiding vision and definition of principles were prepared by a broad and diverse group of leaders. The Women's March on Washington is grateful to all contributors, listed and unlisted, for their dedication in shaping this agenda.

J. Bob Alotta, executive director, Astraea Lesbian Foundation for Justice

Monifa Bandele, vice president, MomsRising

Zahra Billoo, Council on American Islamic Relations—San Francisco Bay Area

Gaylynn Burroughs, director of policy and research, Feminist Majority Foundation

Melanie L. Campbell, convener, Black Women's Roundtable, president and CEO, NCBCP

Sung Yeon Choimorrow, interim executive director, National Asian Pacific American Women's Forum

Alida Garcia, immigrant rights and diversity advocate

Alicia Garza, National Domestic Workers Alliance, Indigenous Women Rise Collective

Carol Jenkins, board of directors, ERA Coalition

Dr. Avis Jones-DeWeever, president, Incite Unlimited, LLC

Carol Joyner, director, Labor Project for Working Families, Family Values @ Work

Janet Mock, activist and author of *Redefining Realness and Surpassing Certainty*

Jessica Neuwirth, president, ERA Coalition

Terry O'Neill, president, National Organization for Women (NOW)

Carmen Perez, executive director, the Gathering for Justice

Jody Rabhan, director of Washington operations, National Council of Jewish Women

Kelley Robinson, deputy national organizing director, Planned Parenthood Federation of America

Kristin Rowe-Finkbeiner, executive director and co-founder, MomsRising

Linda Sarsour, founder, MPower Change

Heidi L. Sieck, co-founder and CEO, #VOTEPROCHOICE

Emily Tisch Sussman, campaign director, Center for American Progress

Jennifer Tucker, senior policy advisor, Black Women's Roundtable

Winnie Wong, activist, organizer and co-founder, People for Bernie

For Further Reading

"About Us." *Women's March*, n.d., http://womensmarch.com/mission-and-principles.

Agrawal, Nina. "How the Women's March Came into Being." *Chicago Tribune*, 22 Jan. 2017, https://www.chicagotribune.com/la-na-pol-womens-march-live-how-the-women-s-march-came-into-1484865755-htmlstory.html.

"Domestic Violence and Disabilities." *National Coalition against Domestic Violence*, n.d., hope-eci.org/_documents/disabilities.pdf.

Ladau, Emily. "Disability Rights Are Conspicuously Absent from the Women's March Platform." *Medium*, 16 Jan. 2017, https://medium.com/the-establishment/disability-rights-are-conspicuously-absent-from-the-womens-march-platform-1d61cee62593.

North, Anna. "How the Women's March Made Itself Indispensable." *Vox*, 19 Jan. 2018, http://www.vox.com/identities/2018/1/19/16905884/2018-womens-march-anniversary.

Plank, Liz. "Women's March Expected to be Largest Gathering of People with Disabilities in US History." *Vox*, 19 Jan. 2017, https://www.vox.com/2017/1/19/14327496/womens-march-largest-gathering-disability-community.

Sheppard, Kate. "Anti-Abortion Group Bumped from Women's March Stakes out a Place Anyway." *Huffington Post*, 21 Jan. 2017, www.huffingtonpost.com/entry/womens-march-abortion_us_5883d51be4b096b4a23245f8.

Stockman, Farah. "Women's March on Washington Opens Contentious Dialogues about Race." *The New York Times*, 9 Jan. 2017, www.nytimes.com/2017/01/09/us/womens-march-on-washington-opens-contentious-dialogues-about-race.html.

Women's March Organizers, and Condé Nast. *Together We Rise: Behind the Scenes at the Protest Heard Around the World*. Dey Street Books, 2018.

Women's March Signs

While the Women's March, which galvanized women around the world, was organized largely through social media, when women took to the streets, the protest sign was one of their most prominent rhetorical tools. In many ways, the images of women flooding the streets with signs held high—like the first one included here—hearken to the women's movement of the early twentieth century, when women carried placards demanding the right to vote. Contemporary marchers, however, added their own rhetorical flair; as members of the Twitter generation well-schooled in the art of a pithy phrase, their clever messages grabbed attention in the streets, captured by cameras phones, then circulated across the digital sphere.

Women's March signs ran the gamut—from advocating for key issues like reproductive rights and immigration protections, to appropriating words Donald Trump used against women—such as "Pussies Grab Back" and "Nasty Women Will Change the World." Others melded pop culture and politics, evoking figures like Princess Leia, Wonder Woman, Harry Potter, and Beyoncé in support of the feminist resistance. Still others used humor to mock Trump: "We Shall Overcomb" and "Hands Too Tiny to Build a Wall." More than any other message, however, was that of women's empowerment and refusal to back down: "Glass Ceilings Are Meant to Be Broken"; "Women's Rights Are Human Rights"; "We Are Stronger Than Fear."

As the nation faced a Republican president and a Republican–majority House of Representatives and Senate in 2017, many women's minds were on the soon-to-be-vacated Supreme Court seats and the potential consequences future justices would have for reproductive rights. The first sign included here, crafted by the college student Haley Talati at the Washington march, speaks to this issue, employing clever wordplay and design to challenge Republican intrusion on women's reproductive rights.

The signs also captured issues important to the feminist movement itself. This is evident in the second image included here, also taken in DC, which features an African American woman with a raised fist, a gesture commonly associated with black power. She stands next to several women of color, including a mother and daughter; the mother's sign says, "Why I March: My Rights, Her Future," which denounces racism and misogyny. This image headlined a BET.com article on DC march signs that called out white women for voting for Trump and insisted on the intersectional nature of gender and race. The article also included a viral image of a black woman holding a sign stating, "Don't forget, white women voted for Trump" as white women in pink pussy hats take selfies in the background. These signs collectively made a powerful argument that the women's movement must be intersectional to be successful—an issue the Women's March organizers have continued to foreground in their communications.

The third image, an aerial view of the Washington Mall, demonstrates the profound and indelible visual impact of the march, showing that despite differences, women formed a history-making collective prepared to resist any threats to their civil rights.

Indeed, the signs of the Women's March had shelf lives—and did rhetorical work—long past the event itself. In the days following both the 2017 and 2018 marches, nearly every mainstream media outlet compiled a listicle of the best signs spotted at the marches, extending their circulation and reach. Museum curators from institutions like the New-York Historical Society and the Smithsonian National Museum of American History also collected signs, preserving the artifacts of protest, and of women's rhetorics, for generations to come (Cascone).

Women's March Images

5. "We need to talk about the elephant in the womb." This Women's March on Washington, DC, protest sign by Haley Talati features a hand-drawn uterus with the GOP elephant symbol inside.

6. A racially diverse group of women gather at the Women's March on Washington, DC. One woman stands with her daughter and holds a sign that states: "#WhyIMarch: My Rights, Her Future. Reject Racism (and) Misogyny." Getty Images, photo by Mike Coppola.

7. An aerial view of the Women's March on Washington, DC, depicts the mass protest of Donald Trump's election with marchers filling a street as they move toward the US Capitol, pictured on the horizon. Photo by Mark Kauzlarich.

FOR FURTHER READING

Akin, Alexander. "Protest Signs: Barometers of Social Change." *The New Antiquarian*, 7 Apr. 2017, www.abaa.org/blog/post/protest-signs-barometers-of-social-change.

Cascone, Sarah. "Signs of the Times: Museums Are Collecting Protest Posters From the 2018 Women's March." *Artnet News*, 22 Jan. 2018, news.artnet.com/art-world/museums-already-enshrining-2018-womens-march-us-history-1204031.

Gibson, Caitlin. "Today's Protest Signs Are Sharper, Meaner, Funnier—and Live on Long after the Rallies." *The Washington Post*, 2 Feb. 2017, www.washingtonpost.com/news/arts-and-entertainment/wp/2017/02/02/todays-protest-signs-are-sharper-meaner-funnier-and-live-on-long-after-the-rallies/.

Herron, Rachel. "Look: These DC March Signs Saying More White Women Voted for Trump Ignited a National Debate over the Intersectionality of Feminism." *BET*, 23 Jan. 2017, www.bet.com/news/national/2017/01/23/women-of-color-blamed-for-dividing-women-s-march.html.

Riverbend

Riverbend is the pseudonym for the anonymous creator of the blog *Baghdad Burning: Girl Blog from Iraq*, credited for depicting an early, rare view of civilian life after the US invasion of Iraq in 2003. From her blog, we know that she is a young Iraqi woman who was a computer specialist before the invasion, and whose life, like so many in her country, was brought to turmoil afterward. Salam Pax, dubbed the father of Iraqi blogs, encouraged Riverbend to write her own after she guest posted on his. Riverbend's blog and the book that followed earned the 2005 Lettre Ulysses Prize for Reportage, a 2006 Bloggie award, and was a finalist for the Samuel Johnson Prize in nonfiction.

Feminist Press was the first publisher who reached out to Riverbend without asking her to discontinue her blog in real time; they published the first year of *Baghdad Burning*, which chronicles daily life in Iraq from August 2003 through September 2004. Riverbend continued posting until 2007, when her family relocated to Syria. She last posted in 2013, ten years after the invasion, with some lessons learned, such as: "No one is ashamed of the hypocrisy anymore. You can be against one country (like Iran), but empowering them somewhere else (like in Iraq). You can claim to be against religious extremism (like in Afghanistan), but promoting religious extremism somewhere else (like in Iraq and Egypt and Syria)." Riverbend shares that she has moved from Syria to another country to a third Arab country, asking how long it will take to live normally again.

This is part of the strong rhetorical appeal of Riverbend's posts, moving from personal, daily details of life to political protest—what she calls rants—and then back again. Her prose is intimate and conversational, often relying on ellipses, but never short of detail on the graphic toll of war. While sometimes depicting anger or resentment about the occupation, her entries, visible in two early ones that are featured here, are also sympathetic, seeking humanity for all without laying blame in only one place. As Riverbend is quick to note in her blog and in interviews, she is not anti-American, but she is anti-occupation.

Blogging invites meandering, personal musings, as early blogs were typically informal journals for an online audience. During the time of Riverbend's writing, blogs were taking the internet by storm (in 2004 *Merriam-Webster* declared *blog* the word of the year), allowing for anybody's voice—theoretically—to find an audience online. In this case, blogs allowed readers from all over the world first-hand access to the strife of daily life of occupation not covered by Western media. For Riverbend, *Baghdad Burning* became a forum to meld personal and protest rhetoric, as she challenged Western-centric coverage of the occupation. Blogs are less popular in the second decade of the twenty-first century, making way for microblogging or newer platforms, but the kind of direct outreach possible for global audiences served as an important precursor to the on-the-ground live tweeting. In both medium and message, then, Riverbend was on the vanguard of a cultural shift that changed how, and by whom, global events are reported and understood.

Excerpts from *Baghdad Burning: Girl Blog from Iraq*

2009

"My New Talent"

Thursday, August 21, 2003

Suffering from a bout of insomnia last night, I found myself in front of the television, channel-surfing. I was looking for the usual—an interesting interview with one of the council, some fresh news, a miracle . . . Promptly at 2 a.m., the electricity went off and I was plunged into the pitch black hell better known as "an August night with no electricity in Iraq." So I sat there, in the dark, trying to remember where I had left the candle and matches. After 5 minutes of chagrined meditation, I decided I would "feel" my way up the stairs and out onto the roof. Step by hesitant step, I stumbled out into the corridor and up the stairs, stubbing a toe on the last step (which wasn't supposed to be there).

(For those of you who don't know, people sleep up on the roof in some of the safer areas because when the electricity goes off, the houses get so hot, it feels like you are cooking gently inside of an oven. The roof isn't much better, but at least there's a semblance of wind.) Out on the roof, the heat was palpitating off of everything in waves. The strange thing is that if you stand in the center, you can feel it emanating from the walls and ground toward you from all directions. I stood there trying to determine whether it was only our area, or the whole city, that had sunk into darkness.

A few moments later, my younger brother (we'll call him E.) joined me—disheveled, disgruntled, and half-asleep. We stood leaning on the low wall enclosing

the roof watching the street below. I could see the tip of Abu Maan's cigarette glow-
ing in the yard next door. I pointed to it with the words,

"Abu Maan can't sleep either..."

E. grunted with the words, "It's probably Maan." I stood staring at him like he
was half-wild—or maybe talking in his sleep. Maan is only 13 . . . how is he smoking? How can he be smoking?

"He's only thirteen," I stated.

"Is there anyone only thirteen anymore?" he asked.

I mulled the reality of his remark over. No, no one is thirteen anymore. No one
is 24 anymore . . . everyone is 85 and I think I might be 105. I was too tired to speak
and, in spite of his open eyes, I suspected E. was asleep. The silence was shattered a
few moments later by the sound of bullets in the distance. It was just loud enough
to get your attention, but too far away to be the source of any real anxiety. I tried to
determine where they were coming from . . .

> E.: How far do you think that is?
> Me: I don't know . . . 'bout a kilometer?
> E: Yeah, about.
> Me: Not American bullets—
> E: No, it's probably from a . . .
> Me: Kalashnikov
> E: (impressed): You're getting good at this.

No—I'm getting great at it. I can tell you if it's "them" or "us."

I can tell you how far away it is. I can tell you if it's a pistol or machine gun,
tank or armored vehicle, Apache or Chinook . . . I can determine the distance and
maybe even the target. That's my new talent. It's something I've gotten so good at, I
frighten myself. What's worse is that almost everyone seems to have acquired this
new talent . . . young and old. And it's not something that anyone will appreciate
on a resume . . .

I keep wondering . . . will an airplane ever sound the same again?

Posted by River @ 3:15 p.m.

"Have You Forgotten"

Wednesday, September 3, 2003

September 11 was a tragedy. Not because 3,000 Americans died . . . but because
3,000 humans died. I was reading about the recorded telephone conversations of
victims and their families on September 11. I thought it was . . . awful, and perfectly
timed. Just when people are starting to question the results and incentives behind
this occupation, they are immediately bombarded with reminders of September
11. Never mind Iraq had nothing to do with it.

I get emails constantly reminding me of the tragedy of September 11 and telling me how the "Arabs" brought all of this upon themselves. Never mind it was originally blamed on Afghanistan (who, for your information, aren't Arabs).

I am constantly reminded of the 3,000 Americans who died that day . . . and asked to put behind me the 8,000 worthless Iraqis we lost to missiles, tanks, and guns.

People marvel that we're not out in the streets, decking the monstrous, khaki tanks with roses and jasmine. They wonder why we don't crown the hard, ugly helmets of the troops with wreaths of laurel. They question why we mourn our dead instead of gratefully offering them as sacrifices to the gods of democracy and liberty. They wonder why we're bitter.

But, I *haven't* forgotten . . .

I remember February 13, 1991. I remember the missiles dropped on Al-Amriyah shelter—a civilian bomb shelter in a populated, residential area in Baghdad. Bombs so sophisticated, that the first one drilled through to the heart of the shelter and the second one exploded inside. The shelter was full of women and children—boys over the age of 15 weren't allowed. I remember watching images of horrified people clinging to the fence circling the shelter, crying, screaming, begging to know what had happened to a daughter, a mother, a son, a family that had been seeking protection within the shelter's walls.

I remember watching them drag out bodies so charred, you couldn't tell they were human. I remember frantic people, running from corpse to corpse, trying to identify a loved one . . . I remember seeing Iraqi aid workers, cleaning out the shelter, fainting with the unbearable scenes inside. I remember the whole area reeked with the smell of burnt flesh for weeks and weeks after.

I remember visiting the shelter, years later, to pay my respects to the 400-plus people who died a horrible death during the small hours of the morning and seeing the ghostly outlines of humans plastered on the walls and ceilings.

I remember a family friend who lost his wife, his five-year-old daughter, his two-year-old son, and his mind on February 13.

I remember the day the Pentagon, after making various excuses, claimed it had been a "mistake."

I remember 13 years of sanctions, backed firmly by the US and UK, in the name of WMDs nobody ever found. Sanctions so rigid, we had basic necessities, like medicine, on waiting lists for months and months, before they were refused. I remember chemicals like chlorine, necessary for water purification, being scrutinized and delayed at the expense of millions of people.

I remember having to ask aid workers, and visiting activists, to "please bring a book" because publishing companies refused to sell scientific books and journals to Iraq. I remember having to "share" books with other students in college, in an attempt to make the most of the limited resources.

I remember wasted, little bodies in huge hospital beds—dying of hunger and of disease; diseases that could easily be treated with medications that were "forbidden." I remember parents with drawn faces peering anxiously into doctors' eyes, searching for a miracle.

I remember the depleted uranium [DU]. How many have heard of depleted uranium? Those are household words to Iraqi people. The depleted uranium weapons used in 1991 (and possibly this time too) have resulted in a damaged environment and an astronomical rise in the cancer rate in Iraq. I remember seeing babies born with a single eye, 3 legs, or no face—a result of DU poisoning.

I remember dozens of dead in the "no-fly zones," bombed by British and American planes claiming to "protect" the north and south of Iraq. I remember the mother, living on the outskirts of Mosul, who lost her husband and five kids when an American plane bombed the father and his sons in the middle of a field of peaceful, grazing sheep.

And we are to believe that this is all being done for the sake of the people.

> "Have you forgotten how it felt that day
> To see your homeland under fire
> And her people blown away?"

No . . . we haven't forgotten—the tanks are still here to remind us.

A friend of E.'s, who lives in Amiriyah, was telling us about an American soldier he had been talking to in the area. E.'s friend pointed to the shelter and told him of the atrocity committed in 1991. The soldier turned with the words, "Don't blame me—I was only 9!" And I was only 11.

American long-term memory is exclusive to American traumas. The rest of the world should simply "put the past behind," "move forward," "be pragmatic," and "get over it."

Someone asked me whether it was true that the "Iraqi people were dancing in the streets of Baghdad" when the World Trade Center fell. Of course it's not true. I was watching the TV screen in disbelief—looking at the reactions of the horrified people. I wasn't dancing because the terrified faces on the screen, could have been the same faces in front of the Amiriyah shelter on February 13 . . . it's strange how horror obliterates ethnic differences—all faces look the same when they are witnessing the death of loved ones.

Posted by River @ 6:08 p.m.

FOR FURTHER READING

Al-Atraqchi, Firas. "Interview: Iraqi Blogger Riverbend." *Al Jazeera*, 9 Apr. 2006, www.aljazeer
a.com/archive/2006/04/200849145721773400.html.

Chaudhry, Lakshimmi. "The Girl Blogger from Iraq." *AlterNet*, 19 Apr. 2005, www.alternet.org/sto
ry/21782/the_girl_blogger_from_iraq.

Grosfield, Lynsey. "For Freelancers: Are Blogs Still Important?" *The Freelancer*, 22 July 2016, content
ly.net/2016/07/22/resources/career-advice/blogging/freelancers-blogs-still-important/.

Riverbend. *Baghdad Burning: Girl Blog from Iraq*. Feminist Press, 2005.

Riverbend. "The Beginning." *Baghdad Burning*, 17 Aug. 2003, www.riverbendblog.blogspot
.com/2003_08_01_archive.html.

Ridgeway, James. Introduction. *Baghdad Burning: Girl Blog from Iraq*, by Riverbend, Feminist Press,
2005, pp. xi–xxiii.

Paola Bacchetta, Tina Campt, Inderpal Grewal, Caren Kaplan, Minoo Moallem, and Jennifer Terry

On October 7, 2001, a US-led coalition began massive airstrikes on Afghanistan as part of Operation Enduring Freedom. The Bush administration believed the Taliban, an Islamic terrorist group in Afghanistan, was harboring Osama bin Laden, who was blamed for the 9/11 terrorist attacks on the United States. When the Taliban refused to turn over bin Laden, the United States launched a war, which is still ongoing as of this writing.

The Bush administration justified the necessity of war through a rhetoric of patriotism and nationalism. In contrast, a collective of transnational feminist scholars united their voices to call for a nonviolent response to the 9/11 attacks. In the statement included here, these women trace the gendered and racialized implications of patriotism and nationalism and critique simplistic binaries of West vs. East, civilization vs. barbarism, and modernity vs. tradition. More specifically, they challenge depictions of women in developing regions as "abject, backward, oppressed by their men," calling attention to the poverty and violence Afghan women face as a product of both the Taliban regime and of a long legacy of Western colonialism (another kind of violence) and conflict in the area.

Demonstrating the power of a feminist collective, this group of transnational scholars melds its scholarly expertise to produce a statement of protest and resistance that is steeped in history and determined in its commitment to bring an end to violence. This collective comprises:

Paola Bacchetta, professor of gender and women's studies at the University of California, Berkeley;

Tina Campt, the Claire Tow and Ann Whitney Olin Professor of Africana and Women's Gender and Sexuality Studies and director of the Barnard Center for Research on Women;

Inderpal Grewal, professor and chair in the program in women's, gender, and sexuality studies at Yale University;

Caren Kaplan, professor of American studies at the University of California, Davis;

Minoo Moallem, professor of gender and women's studies at the University of California, Berkeley; and

Jennifer Terry, professor of women's studies/gender and sexuality studies at the
University of California, Irvine.

While written primarily for an academic audience in *Meridians*—a journal that features issues of feminism, race, and transnationalism—the authors organize their
critique in accessible list form and offer concrete examples to ground their protest.
The statement was later reprinted in *The W Effect: Bush's War on Women*, a collection of feminist responses to Bush-era policies. For many contemporary readers,
this 2001 piece may seem prescient, predicting the consequences of war that would
unfold in the decades that followed, including the racist scapegoating of Muslims in
the United States and the futility of war as a solution to terrorist acts.

Now the longest military engagement in US history, there is a generation of
Americans old enough to deploy who cannot remember the 9/11 terrorist attacks.
Spanning three presidential administrations, as of 2018 the war on terror as has
resulted in the deaths of more than 4,500 US soldiers and tens of thousands of
Afghans, and it costs US taxpayers $45 billion a year (Rafferty, Pennington). As
the *Atlantic* writer Krishnadev Calamur reasons, "The duration of the engagement
might be due to Afghanistan's place in the American imagination—the place from
which terrorists planned and carried out a dramatic attack on the U.S. homeland,
an attack that arguably has reshaped the U.S. worldview over the past 17 years." It
is this American imagination, and US–centered world view, that the transnational collective seeks to change, urging readers to consider a view that relies less on
borders and divisions among people and more on collective, peaceful strategies to
address violence and terror around the globe.

"Transnational Feminist Practices against War"

Meridians, 2001

As feminist theorists of transnational and postmodern cultural formations, we
believe that it is crucial to seek nonviolent solutions to conflicts at every level of
society, from the global, regional, and national arenas to the ordinary locales of everyday life. We offer the following response to the events of September 11 (9/11)
and its aftermath:

First and foremost, we need to analyze the thoroughly gendered and racialized
effects of nationalism, and to identify what kinds of inclusions and exclusions are
being enacted in the name of patriotism. Recalling the histories of various nationalisms helps us to identify tacit assumptions about gender, race, nation, and class

that once again play a central role in mobilization for war. We see that instead of a necessary historical, material, and geopolitical analysis of 9/11, the emerging nationalist discourses consist of misleading and highly sentimentalized narratives that, among other things, reinscribe compulsory heterosexuality and the rigidly dichotomized gender roles upon which it is based. A number of icons constitute the ideal types in the drama of nationalist domesticity that we see displayed in the mainstream media. These include the masculine citizen-soldier, the patriotic wife and mother, the breadwinning father who is head of household, and the properly reproductive family. We also observe how this drama is racialized. Most media representations in the US have focused exclusively on losses suffered by white, middle-class, heterosexual families even though those who died or were injured include many people of different races, classes, sexualities, and religions and of at least ninety different nationalities. Thus, an analysis that elucidates the repressive effects of nationalist discourses is necessary for building a world that fosters peace as well as social and economic justice.

Second, a transnational feminist response views the impact of war and internal repression in a larger context of global histories of displacement, forced migrations, and expulsions. We oppose the US and European sponsorship of regimes responsible for coerced displacements, and we note how patterns of immigration, exile, and forced flight are closely linked to gender oppression and to the legacies of colonialism and structured economic dependency. Indeed, history shows us that women, as primary caretakers of families, suffer enormously under circumstances of colonization, civil unrest, and coerced migration. Taking this history into account, we critique solutions to the contemporary crisis that rely on a colonial, Manichean model whereby "advanced capitalist freedom and liberty" is venerated over "backward extremist Islamic barbarism." Furthermore, we draw upon insights from postcolonial studies and critical political economy to trace the dynamics of European and US neocolonialism during the Cold War and post–Cold War periods. Thus questions about the gendered distribution of wealth and resources are key to our analytical approach. Neoliberal economic development schemes create problems that impact women in profound and devastating ways in both the "developing regions" as well as the "developed world." So while middle-class Euro-American women in the United States are held up as the most liberated on earth even while they are being encouraged to stand dutifully by their husbands, fathers, and children, women in developing regions of the world are depicted as abject, backward, and oppressed by their men. One of the important elements missing from this picture is the fact that many women in Afghanistan are starving and faced with violence and harm on a daily basis not only due to the Taliban regime but due also in large part to a long history of European colonialism and conflict in the region. The Bush administration's decision to drop bombs at one moment and, in the next, care packages of food that are in every way inadequate to the needs of the population offers a grim image of how pathetic this discourse of "civilization" and "rescue" is within the violence of war. We see here a token and uncaring response to a situation to which the US has contributed for at least twenty years, a situation that is about the strategic influence in the region and about the extraction of natural resources, not the least of which is oil.

Third, we want to comment on the extent to which domestic civil repression is intrinsically linked to the violence of war. Thus the effects of the current conflict will be played out in the US and its border zones through the augmentation of border patrolling and policing, as well as in the use of military and defense technologies and other practices that will further subordinate communities (especially nonwhite groups) in the US. Such state violence has many gendered implications. These include the emergence of patriarchal/masculinist cultural nationalisms whereby women's perspectives are degraded or wholly excluded to create new version of cultural "traditions." And, for many immigrant women, other devastating effects of state repression include increased incidents of unreported domestic violence, public hostility, and social isolation. In practical terms, policing authorities charged with guaranteeing national security are likely to have little sympathy for the undocumented immigrant woman who is fleeing a violent intimate relationship, unless her assailant fits the profile of an "Islamic fundamentalist." Thus we need an analysis and strategy against the "domestication" of the violence of war that has emerged in these last few weeks and whose effects will be felt in disparate and dispersed ways.

Fourth, we call for an analysis of the stereotypes and tropes that are being mobilized in the current crisis. These tropes support, sustain, and are enabled by a modernist logic of warfare that seeks to consolidate the sovereign (and often unilateral) power of the First World nation-state. When President Bush proclaims that "terrorist" networks must be destroyed, we ask what this term means to people and how it is being used to legitimate a large-scale military offensive. The term is being used to demonize practices that go against US national interests and it permits a kind of "dragnet" effect at home and abroad, which legitimates the suppression of dissent. We also want to inquire into constructions of "terrorism" that continue to target nonnative or "foreign" opposition movements while cloaking its own practices of terror in euphemisms such as "foreign aid." Deconstructing the trope of "terrorism" must include a sustained critique of the immense resources spent by the US in training "counter-terrorists" and "anti-Communist" forces who then, under other historical circumstances, become enemies rather than allies, as in the now famous case of Osama bin Laden. We are concerned about the ways in which the "war against terrorism" can be used to silence and repress insurgent movements across the globe. We also emphasize how racism operates in the naming of "terrorism." When the "terrorists" are people of color, all other people of color are vulnerable to a scapegoat backlash.

Yet when white supremacist Timothy McVeigh bombed the Murrah federal building in Oklahoma City, killing 168 men, women, and children, no one declared open season to hunt down white men, or even white militia members. The production of a new racial category, "anyone who looks like a Muslim," in which targets of racism include Muslims, Arabs, Sikhs, and any other people with olive or brown skin, exposes the arbitrary and politically constructed character of new and old racial categories in the US. It also reveals the inadequacy of US multiculturalism to resist the hegemonic relationship between being "white" and "American."

Finally, the short memory of the media suppresses any mention of the Euro-American anticapitalist and anti-imperialist "terrorist" groups of the 1970s and 1980s. A critical attention to the idioms of the present war mobilization compels us to deconstruct other politically loaded tropes, including security, liberty, freedom, truth, civil rights, Islamic fundamentalism, women under the Taliban, the flag, and "America."

Fifth, we recognize the gendered and ethnocentric history of sentimentality, grief, and melancholy that have been mobilized in the new war effort. We do not intend to disparage or dismiss the sadness and deep emotions raised by the events of 9/11 and its aftermath. But we do think it is important to point out that there has been a massive deployment of therapeutic discourses that ask people to understand the impact of the events of September 11 and their aftermath solely as "trauma." Such discourses leave other analytical, historical, and critical frameworks unexplored. Focusing only on the personal or narrowly defined psychological dimension of the attacks and the ensuing war obscures the complex nexus of history and geopolitics that has brought about these events. We are not suggesting that specific forms of therapy are not useful. But the culture industry of "trauma" leads to a mystification of history, politics, and cultural critique. Furthermore, therapeutic discourse tends to reinforce individualist interpretations of globally significant events and it does so in an ethnocentric manner. Seeking relief through a psychotherapeutic apparatus may be a common practice among Euro-American upper- and middle-class people in the United States, but it should not be assumed to be a universally appealing or effective way to counter experiences of civil repression and war among people of other classes, ethnicities, and cultural backgrounds. Signs of the current trauma discourse's ethnocentricity come through in media depictions staged within the therapeutic framework that tend to afford great meaning, significance, and sympathy to those who lost friends and family members in the attacks on the World Trade Center and the Pentagon. By contrast, people who have lost loved ones as a consequence of US foreign policy elsewhere are not depicted as sufferers of trauma or injustice. In fact, they are seldom seen on-camera at all. Similarly, makeshift centers in universities around the US were set up in the immediate wake of 9/11 to help college students cope with the psychological effects of the attacks. They tended to assume that 9/11 marked the first time Americans experienced vulnerability, overlooking not only the recent events of the Oklahoma City federal building bombing, but moreover erasing the personal experiences of many immigrants and US people of color for whom "America" has been a site of potential or realized violence for all of their lives.

Sixth, our transnational feminist response involves a detailed critical analysis of the role of the media, especially in depictions that include colonial tropes and binary oppositions in which the Islam/Muslim/non-West is represented as "uncivilized" or "barbaric." We note the absence or co-optation of Muslim women as "victims" of violence or of "Islamic barbarism." We note as well the use of those groups of women seen as "white" or "Western" both as "rescuers" of non-Western women but also as evidence of the so-called civilizing efforts of Europe and North America. We see these discursive formations as a result not only of colonialism's discursive and knowledge-producing legacies but also of the technologies and industrial practices that produce contemporary global media, and transnational financing of culture industries. We seek especially to analyze the participation of women in these industries as well as the co-optation of feminist approaches and interests in the attack on a broad range of Islamic cultural and religious institutions, not just "Islamicist/extremist" groups. Thus we point out as a caution that any counter or resistance media would need to have a firm grasp of these histories and repertoires of practice or risk reproducing them anew.

Seventh, we call for a deeper understanding of the nature of capitalism and globalization as it generates transnational movements of all kinds. Thus, we seek to counter oppressive transnational movements, from both the "West" as well as the "non-West," with alternative movements that counter war and the continued production of global inequalities. We note in particular that religious and ethnic fundamentalisms have emerged across the world within which the repression of women and establishment of rigidly dichotomized gender roles are used both as a form of power and to establish a collectivity. Such fundamentalisms have been a cause of concern for feminist groups not only in the Islamic world but also in the US. Feminist and other scholars have noted that these movements have become transnational, through the work of nation-state and nongovernmental organizations, with dire consequences for all those who question rigid gender dichotomies. Since these movements are transnational, we question the notion of isolated and autonomous nation-states in the face of numerous examples of transnational and global practices and formations. The recent displays of national coherence and international solidarity (based on nineteenth- and twentieth-century constructions of international relations) cannot mask the strains and contradictions that give rise to the current crisis. Thus, we need an analysis of the numerous ways in which transnational networks and entities both limit and at the same time enable resistance and oppression. That is, the complex political terrain traversed by transnational networks as diverse as al-Qaida and the Red Cross must be understood as productive of new identities and practices as well as of new kinds of political repression. Transnational media has roots in pernicious corporate practices yet it also enables diverse and contradictory modes of information, entertainment, and communication. Feminist analysis of these complex and often contradictory transnational phenomena is called for.

In closing, we want to make it very clear that we oppose the US and British military mobilization and bombing that is underway in Afghanistan and that may very well expand further into the West, Central, and South Asian regions. We are responding to a crisis in which war, as described by the George W. Bush administration, will be a covert, diversified, and protracted process. At this moment we call for a resistance to nationalist terms and we argue against the further intensification of US military intervention abroad. We refuse to utilize the binaries of civilization vs. barbarism, modernity vs. tradition, and West vs. East. We also call for an end to the racist scapegoating and "profiling" that accompanies the stepped up violations of civil liberties within the territorial boundaries of the US. We urge feminists to refuse the call to war in the name of vanquishing a so-called traditional patriarchal fundamentalism, since we understand that such fundamentalisms are supported by many nation-states. We are also aware of the failures of nation-states and the global economic powers such as the IMF and the World Bank to address the poverty and misery across the world and the role of such failures in the emergence of fundamentalisms everywhere. Nationalist and international mobilization for war cannot go forward in our name or under the sign of "concern for women." In fact, terror roams the world in many guises and is perpetrated under the sign of many different nations and agents. It is our contention that violence and terror are ubiquitous and need to be addressed through multiple strategies as much within the "domestic" politics of the US as elsewhere. It is only through developing new strategies and approaches based on some of these suggestions that we can bring an end to the violence of the current moment.

FOR FURTHER READING

Calamur, Krishnadev. "No End in Sight." *The Atlantic*, 11 Sept. 2018, www.theatlantic.com/interna
    tional/archive/2018/09/9-11-us-troops-afghanistan/569803/.
Emadi, Hafizullah. *Repression, Resistance, and Women in Afghanistan*. Praeger, 2002.
Flanders, Laura, editor. *The W Effect: Bush's War on Women*. Feminist Press, 2004.

Pennington, Matthew. "Pentagon Says War in Afghanistan Costs Taxpayers $45 Billion per Year."
    PBS NewsHour, 6 Feb. 2018, www.pbs.org/newshour/politics/pentagon-says-afghan-war-costs
    -taxpayers-45-billion-per-year.
Rafferty, Andrew. "The War in Afghanistan: By the Numbers." *NBC News*, 21 Aug. 2017, www.nbc
    news.com/politics/politics-news/war-afghanistan-numbers-n794626.

Edwidge Danticat

Edwidge Danticat's essay was spurred by the "zero-tolerance" immigration policy enacted by the Trump administration in April 2018, which gave federal authorities permission to separate children from adults who illegally crossed the border into the United States. As a result, thousands of infants and children were taken from parents and placed in the care of Health and Human Services. Media outlets circulated heartbreaking images of children crying in detention centers, and world leaders from across the political spectrum spoke out in protest. Three months later, an executive order walked back the policy in light of political and public condemnation, but chaos continued as the number of children separated remained unclear, and treatment of the children raised alarm. The American Academy of Pediatrics released a statement warning that "studies of detained immigrants have shown that children and parents may suffer negative physical and emotional symptoms from detention, including anxiety, depression and posttraumatic stress disorder." Further complicating matters was the US government's lack of a plan for the family reunification process.

For the esteemed author Danticat, the border crisis provided the *kairotic* moment to shed more light on immigrant children and parents. She understands the issue intimately; when Danticat was just four years old, her mother left Haiti to join her husband in the United States. Danticat eventually reunited with her parents when she was twelve years old. She later received her MFA at Brown University, and her first novel, *Breath, Eyes, Memory,* was selected for Oprah's Book Club. Her novel *Krik? Krak!* and memoir, *Brother, I'm Dying,* were both National Book Award finalists. Danticat's extensive body of literature—five works of fiction, four books of nonfiction, and six children's or young adult novels—often grapples with issues of identity and immigration.

The following piece from the *New Yorker* begins with the intimate and painful moment when Danticat's mother says good-bye before leaving her children in Haiti. In sharing memories of their separation, she dispels the myth that parents who immigrate don't love their children as fully as other parents love theirs. Rather, Danticat's poignant prose shows the deep pain that her parents endured while separated from their daughter and son for eight years. From her own evocative narrative, Danticat pans out to present wrenching information on the erasure of detainees, which can result not only in invisibility but abuse. She cites information from an ACLU report of abuse at detention centers, fleshing out the data with names and stories of immigrant children. Danticat also reminds readers three times of images of children housed in cages and sleeping under Mylar blankets following the 2018 "zero-tolerance" policy. Ultimately, Danticat implores readers to continue to pay attention and to protest the mistreatment of immigrant children, even after this crisis passes. Her plaintive testimony, woven with other children's stories of separation, insists that we remember and resist.

"We Must Not Forget Detained Migrant Children"

The *New Yorker*, 2018

One of my earliest childhood memories is of being torn away from my mother. I was four years old and she was leaving Haiti for the United States to join my father, who'd emigrated two years earlier, to escape both a dictatorship and poverty. My mother was entrusting my younger brother and me to the care of my uncle and his wife, who would look after us until our parents could establish permanent residency—they had both travelled on tourist visas—in the United States.

On the day my mother left, I wrapped my arms around her legs before she headed for the plane. She leaned down and tearfully unballed my fists so that my uncle could peel me off her. As my brother dropped to the floor, bawling, my mother hurried away, her tear-soaked face buried in her hands. She couldn't bear to look back. We would not see her again for three years.

Some may assume that certain immigrant parents, because they leave their children behind, or send them alone on possibly perilous journeys, don't love their children as much as, say, parents whose parental love is never tested in this way. When I was a teenager, I asked my parents about their immigration choices. If the lives of my brother and me had been in danger, or if they'd had no one to leave us with, they certainly would have taken us with them, they said. Though they would have never been granted visas if they hadn't left us behind to prove that they had a reason to return.

Even the type of carefully planned separation that my parents chose tore their hearts out. Whenever they were eating, my mother used to say, they wondered whether my brother and I were eating, too. When they went to bed at night, they wondered if my brother and I were sleeping. Even though we spoke to them on a scheduled call once a week, they never stopped worrying and longing for us.

It is perhaps that ache and longing that made my parents take me to visit Haitian refugees and asylum seekers who were being held at a detention center near the Brooklyn Navy Yard when our family was reunited in New York, in the early nineteen-eighties. Back then, Rudolph Giuliani was the associate attorney general of the United States and the most vocal opponent of parole for twenty-one hundred Haitian refugees being held at different detention facilities around the US. After travelling to Haiti and speaking to Jean-Claude (Baby Doc) Duvalier, the dictator whom these migrants had fled, Giuliani concluded that the Haitians had nothing to fear and should be deported.

I've continued to visit detention facilities over the years, including ones where children are held, either alone or with their parents. It is not easy to enter such places. At many facilities, one can get only a curated view, either alongside a group of journalists or by attaching oneself to a congressional delegation. At a children's facility in Cutler Bay, Florida, which I used to visit with a registered volunteer, most boys and girls were waiting to be reunited with a parent or relative already living in the United States. Many of these young people had experienced such horrible trauma during their long journey from Central America to the US border with Mexico that they could barely focus on the activities the volunteers prepared for them, which included gardening and crafts. Some had been detained for so long that they'd transitioned from childhood to adolescence behind those walls. Then there were the Miami hotels turned detention centers that immigration lawyers and advocate friends would allow me to accompany them to, places where women and children were being held for weeks or months at a time. Up to six women spent twenty-four hours a day in one room, often with crying babies and toddlers, while armed guards patrolled the halls.

One of the most distressing aspects of immigration detention, for both adults and children, is how invisible the detained can become, even when they're imprisoned in our proverbial back yards. Had the world not seen the images of children wrapped in Mylar blankets and sleeping inside cages, and heard babies and toddlers crying for their parents, both as a result of the Trump administration's "zero-tolerance" policy, some might not have believed that these children had been yanked from their parents' arms—one, reportedly, while being breast-fed. Even in the light of clear and horrifying evidence, many would rather hold fast to their willful denial, branding the cages sets, the detained children actors, and the detention facilities the equivalent of boarding schools and summer camps.

In May, an ACLU report produced from thirty thousand pages of official documents, dated between 2009 and 2014, detailed incidents of US Customs and Border Protection officers verbally, physically, and sexually abusing migrant children. The cases cited include accounts of children being Tased, punched, kicked in the head and ribs. Young migrants complained of being denied food and water and medical care, of being strip-searched and threatened with rape and murder while confined to freezing and unsanitary rooms. Teenagers detained at the Shenandoah Valley Juvenile Center, in Virginia, testified in court filings that they were hand-cuffed to chairs with bags over their heads and were left naked in cold concrete cells. Others, detained elsewhere, have reported being thrown on the ground in order to be force-fed or injected with psychotropic drugs. US Customs and Border Protection has either dismissed or denied these charges.

This is what may await many of the children who have already been separated from their parents under the current administration's "zero-tolerance" policy. (The Department of Homeland Security has said that, out of the twenty-three hundred separated children, five hundred and twenty-two have been reunited with their parents.) The executive order that Trump passed last week to end family separation makes no provisions for the children who are still separated from their parents.

Some of these children have already arrived in Florida, where I live. Last Saturday, a social-worker friend and I drove around the fenced perimeters of one of those facilities, the His House Children's Home, in Miami Gardens, which, according to the *Miami Herald*, is currently housing ten children ranging from "newborns to 5 year olds." Made up of a series of yellow and beige buildings, some of which are boarded up, His House Children's Home has been linked to the death of at least one child, who suffocated under a blanket, in 2007. His House has also been accused, by some of the US-born children who have been placed in foster care there, of treating them like prisoners. His House staff has denied that children are mistreated there. My friend works in the state foster system, and said that places like His House are a last resort for the children in her care. "Here we are trying to do all we can to keep children with their parents, and our country is separating other children from theirs," she said.

Jennifer Anzardo Valdes, the program director of the Children's Legal Program at the Florida–based Americans for Immigrant Justice, has represented unaccompanied minors in the foster-care system and also those in immigration detention. Her team is now representing some of the children who have been taken from their parents at the border. Valdes and her team were aware of families being separated months before the zero-tolerance policy was officially announced, by Attorney General Jeff Sessions, in April. One of their clients, Ana, a three-year-old girl from Guatemala, was separated from her father in July, 2017. Ana's father came to the US with her; her mother, who stayed behind, died shortly afterward. They were held together in a crowded facility for two days. Then Ana's father was told that she was going to be looked after elsewhere. Nobody told him where she was being taken. He was told that they would return her to him when he was released. Before he was deported, in early December, 2017, he asked if he could take her with him. He has not seen her since.

Ana was released into the custody of relatives in South Florida this past January. If not for Valdes and her team, and other immigration lawyers like them, many migrant children, like Ana, would have to find their ways through the immigration system alone. Valdes uses a coloring book, designed by her organization and illustrated by a local artist, to help small children like Ana make sense of the immigration process. One illustration in their "Conozca sus Derechos" ("Know Your Rights") brochure shows a smiling family of four holding hands. Another page shows a map of the United States, to help the children identify where they are. Another shows a Santa Claus–like judge with the words "La Corte" ("The Court") printed above his head. "I'm sure you can imagine the challenges we have trying to explain the court process to a three-year-old," Valdes said.

It's worth remembering that the Trump administration has been finding ways to divide families from the very beginning. The so-called Muslim ban kept US citizens and others from being reunited with their spouses and children from five Muslim-majority countries. The dismantling of the Obama–era executive order Deferred Action for Childhood Arrivals, or DACA, has left eight hundred thousand Dreamers, some of them heads of households, in personal and financial limbo. The revocation of temporary protected status for Haiti, Nicaragua, Honduras, and El Salvador—some of the very places from which the current waves of migrants at the border are fleeing—could lead to the deportation of more than three hundred thousand men and women, including some who have US-born children, whom they may have no choice but to leave behind.

When vulnerable populations are kept hidden, or are forced into hiding—which is the daily reality of so many of the undocumented in Trump's America—they not only live in the shadows; they become slowly erased. At the moment, everyone seems to be paying attention. But these families and children, and others who find themselves in the crosshairs of this administration's draconian immigration policies, will still need us to keep paying attention, even when the media coverage wanes and we are no longer seeing photographs of children in cages, or hearing recordings of their pleas and cries.

FOR FURTHER READING

"ACLU Obtains Documents Showing Widespread Abuse of Child Immigrants in U.S. Custody." *ACLU*, 22 May 2018, https://www.aclu.org/news/aclu-obtains-documents-showing-widespread-abuse-child-immigrants-us-custody.

"AAP Statement on Executive Order on Family Separation." *American Academy of Pediatrics*, 22 June 2018, https://www.aap.org/en-us/about-the-aap/aap-press-room/Pages/AAP-Statement -on-Executive-Order-on-Family-Separation.aspx.

Blitzer, Jonathon. "How the Trump Administration Got Comfortable Separating Immigrant Kids from Their Parents." *The New Yorker*, 30 May 2018, https://www.newyorker.com/news/news-desk/ how-the-trump-administration-got-comfortable-separating-immigrant-kids-from-their-par ents.

Danticat, Edwidge. *Brother, I'm Dying*. Alfred A. Knopf, 2007.

Danticat, Edwidge. *The Dew Breaker*. Vintage Books, 2005.

Domonoske, Camila, and Richard Gonzales. "What We Know: Family Separation And 'Zero Toler-ance' at the Border." *NPR*, 19 June 2018, www.npr.org/2018/06/19/621065383/what-we-know -family-separation-and-zero-tolerance-at-the-border.

EdwidgeDanticat.com. http://www.edwidgedanticat.com/.

Vandana Shiva

Vandana Shiva is known as a celebrity activist for environmental issues, most notably for her challenge to GMOs (genetically modified organism, or a living thing that has been genetically altered in a lab) and multinational corporations, which she argues impose "food totalitarianism" on the world (Specter). According to the journalist Michael Specter, "She describes the fight against agricultural biotechnology as a global war against a few giant seed companies on behalf of the billions of farmers who depend on what they themselves grow to survive. Shiva contends that nothing less than the future of humanity rides on the outcome."

An ecofeminist and transnational scholar, Shiva promotes Indigenous ways of living and knowing and advocates for the importance of biodiversity yielded by local, organic farming. Yet she is also a controversial figure, criticized by experts for fuzzy science, such as conflating causation and correlation or inciting fear that GMOs cause illness when there is no conclusive research on the subject (Specter). Shiva is also criticized for representing herself as a scientist, when her doctorate is in philosophy (though her dissertation focused on quantum theory).

Shiva, born in 1952 and raised near the Himalayas in Dehradun, India, has authored more than twenty books and has served as an environmental activist since the late 1970s. In 1982 she founded what is now called the Research Foundation for Science, Technology and Ecology (RFSTE). Within that organization, in 1991 she founded Navdanya, which creates seed banks to protect India's biodiversity and supports practices that sustain organic farming. Through these organizations, grassroots activism, publications, and speaking engagements, Shiva has garnered a large following; even her skeptics acknowledge her strength in reaching "green-inclined young people" on issues of biodiversity (Jonathon). She uses social media to circulate her message and spark conversations with over sixty thousand followers.

The following excerpt from Shiva's book *Earth Democracy* illustrates rhetorical features compelling to an audience concerned with environmental crises. She situates the globalized, free market economy, with its privatized control by large corporations, against her vision of the earth as a commons for all living beings. Centering Indigenous knowledge making, Shiva quotes Suquamish chief Seattle's mid-nineteenth-century speech on the connection among all living things. Shiva links contemporary "ownership society" to the colonial practice of a government enclosing, or seizing, land held as "commons" by Indigenous people. She argues that this practice of enclosure has displaced peoples and destroyed lands for centuries and led to other social ills, such as terrorism and ethnic cleansing. Shiva's Principles of Earth Democracy are the antidote. In a call to reverse the damage already done to the earth, she promotes a vision of a future that is attainable by focusing on what is possible at the local, everyday level. The principles are malleable concepts, sharpened by declarative language that seeks justice, sustainability, and the worth of all humans, offering a broad prescription for doing nothing short of saving the earth.

"Principles of Earth Democracy": Excerpt from *Earth Democracy: Justice, Sustainability, and Peace*

2006

Earth Democracy is both an ancient world view and an emergent political movement for peace, justice, and sustainability. Earth Democracy connects the particular to the universal, the diverse to the common, and the local to the global. It incorporates what in India we refer to as *vasudhaiva kutumbkam* (the earth family)—the community of all beings supported by the earth. Native American and Indigenous cultures worldwide have understood and experienced life as a continuum between human and nonhuman species and between present, past, and future generations. An 1848 speech attributed to Chief Seattle of the Suquamish tribe captures this continuum.

> How can you buy or sell the sky, the warmth of the land? The idea is strange to us.
> If we do not own the freshness of the air and the sparkle of the water, how can you buy them?
> Every part of this earth is sacred to my people. Every shining pine needle, every sandy shore, every mist in the dark woods, every clearing and humming insect is holy in the memory and experience of my people. The sap which courses through the trees carries the memories of the red man.
> This we know; the earth does not belong to man; man belongs to the earth. This we know. All things are connected like the blood which unites our family. All things are connected.

Earth Democracy is the awareness of these connections and of the rights and responsibilities that flow from them. Chief Seattle's protest that "the earth does not belong to man" finds echoes across the world: "Our world is not for sale," "Our water is not for sale," "Our seeds and biodiversity are not for sale." This response to privatization under the insane ideology known as corporate globalization builds Earth Democracy. Corporate globalization sees the world only as something to be owned and the market as only driven by profits. From Bangalore in 1993, when half a million Indian peasants pledged to resist the classification of seeds as private property required by the Trade Related Aspects of Intellectual Property Rights (TRIPS) agreement of the World Trade Organization (WTO) to Seattle in 1999 and Cancún in 2003 when protests stopped the WTO ministerial meetings, the corporate globalization agenda has been responded to creatively, imaginatively, and courageously by millions of people who see and experience the earth as a family and community consisting of all beings and humans of all colors, beliefs, classes, and countries.

In contrast to viewing the planet as private property, movements are defending, on a local and global level, the planet as a commons. In contrast to experiencing the world as a global supermarket, where goods and services are produced with high ecological, social, and economic costs and sold for abysmally low prices, cultures and communities everywhere are resisting the destruction of their biological and cultural diversity, their lives, and their livelihoods. As alternatives to the suicidal, globalized free market economy based on plundering and polluting the earth's viral resources, which displaces millions of farmers, craftspeople, and workers, communities are resolutely defending and evolving living economies that protect life on earth and promote creativity.

Corporate globalization is based on new enclosures of the commons; enclosures which imply exclusions and are based on violence. Instead of a culture of abundance, profit-driven globalization creates cultures of exclusion, dispossession, and scarcity. In fact, globalization's transformation of all beings and resources into commodities robs diverse species and people of their rightful share of ecological, cultural, economic, and political space. The "ownership" of the rich is based on the "dispossession" of the poor—it is the common, public resources of the poor which are privatized, and the poor who are disowned economically, politically, and culturally.

Patents on life and the rhetoric of the "ownership society" in which everything—water, biodiversity, cells, genes, animals, plants—is property express a worldview in which life forms have no intrinsic worth, no integrity, and no subjecthood. It is a world view in which the rights of farmers to seed, of patients to affordable medicine, of producers to a fair share of nature's resources can be freely violated. The rhetoric of the "ownership society" hides the anti-life philosophy of those who, while mouthing pro-life slogans, seek to own, control, and monopolize all of the earth's gifts and all of human creativity. The enclosures of the commons that started in England created millions of disposable people. While these first enclosures stole only land, today all aspects of life are being enclosed—knowledge, culture, water, biodiversity, and public services such as health and education. Commons are the highest expression of economic democracy.

The privatization of public goods and services and the commoditization of the life support systems of the poor is a double theft which robs people of both economic and cultural security. Millions, deprived of a secure living and identity, are driven toward extremist, terrorist, fundamentalist movements. These movements simultaneously identify the other as enemy and construct exclusivist identities to separate themselves from those with whom, in fact, they are ecologically, culturally, and economically connected. This false separation results in antagonistic and cannibalistic behavior. The rise of extremism and terrorism is a response to the enclosures and economic colonization of globalization. Just as cannibalism among factory-farmed animals stops when chicken and pigs are allowed to roam free, terrorism, extremism, ethnic cleansing, and religious intolerance are unnatural conditions caused by globalization and have no place in Earth Democracy.

Enclosures create exclusions, and these exclusions are the hidden cost of corporate globalization. Our movement against the biopiracy of neem, of basmati, of wheat have aimed at and succeeded in reclaiming our collective biological and intellectual heritage as a commons. Movements such as the victorious struggle started by the tribal women of a tiny hamlet called Plachimada in India's Kerala state against one of the world's largest corporations, Coca-Cola, are at the heart of the emerging Earth Democracy.

New intellectual property rights enclose the biological, intellectual, and digital commons. Privatization encloses the water commons. The enclosure of each common displaces and disenfranchises people, which creates scarcity for the many, while generating "growth" for the few. Displacement becomes disposability, and in its most severe form, the induced scarcity becomes a denial of the very right to live. As the use of genetically modified seed and sex-selective abortions spread, large groups of people—especially women and small farmers—are disappearing. The scale and rate of this disappearance is proportional to the "economic growth" driven by the forces of neoliberal corporate globalization. However, these brutal extinctions are not the only trend shaping human history.

On the streets of Seattle and Cancún, in homes and farms across the world, another human future is being born. A future based on inclusion, not exclusion; on nonviolence, not violence; on reclaiming the commons, not their enclosure; on freely sharing the earth's resources, not monopolizing and privatizing them. Instead of being shaped by closed minds behind closed doors, as the hawkish right-wing Project for the New American Century was, the people's project is unfolding in an atmosphere of dialogue and diversity, of pluralism and partnerships, and of sharing and solidarity. I have named this project Earth Democracy. Based on our self-organizing capacities, our earth identities, and out multiplicities and diversity, Earth Democracy's success concerns not just the fate and well-being of all humans, but all beings on the earth. Earth Democracy is not just about the next protest or the next World Social Forum; it is about what we do in between. It addresses the global in our everyday lives, our everyday realities, and creates change globally by making change locally. The changes may appear small, but they are far-reaching in impact—they are about nature's evolution and our human potential; they are about shifting from the vicious cycles of violence in which suicidal cultures, suicidal economies, and the politics of suicide feed on each other to virtuous cycles of creative nonviolence in which living cultures nourish living democracies and living economies.

Earth Democracy is not just a concept, it is shaped by the multiple and diverse practices of people reclaiming their commons, their resources, their livelihoods, their freedoms, their dignity, their identities, and their peace. While these practices, movements, and actions are multifaceted and multiple, I have tried to identify clusters that present the ideas and examples of living democracies, living cultures, and live economies which together build Earth Democracy. Economy, politics, culture are not isolated from each other. The economies through which we produce and exchange goods and services are shaped by cultural values and power arrangements in society. The emergency of living economies, living cultures, and living democracies is, therefore, a synergistic process.

Living economies are processes and spaces where the earth's resources are shared equitably to provide for our food and water needs and to create meaningful livelihoods. Earth Democracy evolves from the consciousness that while we are rooted locally we are also connected to the world as a whole, and, in fact, to the entire universe. We base our globalization on ecological processes and bonds of compassion and solidarity, not the movement of capital and finance or the unnecessary movement of goods and services. A global economy which takes ecological limits into account must necessarily localize production to reduce wasting both natural resources and people. And only economies built on ecological foundations can become living economies that ensure sustainability and prosperity for all. Our economies are not calculated in the short-term of corporate quarterly returns or the four-to-five-year perspective of politicians. We consider the evolutionary potential of all life one earth and re-embed human welfare in our home, our community, and the earth family. Ecological security is our most basic security; ecological identities are our most fundamental identity. We are the food we eat, the water we drink, the air we breathe. And reclaiming democratic control over our food and water and our ecological survival is the necessary project for our freedom.

Living democracy is the space for reclaiming our fundamental freedoms, defending our basic rights, and exercising our common responsibilities and duties to protect life on earth, defend peace, and promote justice. Corporate globalization promised that free markets would promote democracy. On the contrary, the free markets of global corporations have destroyed democracy at every level. At the most fundamental level, corporate globalization destroys grassroots democracy through the enclosure of the commons. The very rules of globalization, whether imposed by the World Bank and the International Monetary Fund (IMF) or by the WTO, have been written undemocratically, without the participation of the most affected countries and communities. Corporate globalization undermines and subverts national democratic processes by taking economic decisions outside the reach of parliaments and citizens. No matter which government is elected, it is locked into a series of neoliberal reform policies. Corporate globalization is in effect the death of economic democracy. It gives rise to corporate control and economic dictatorship.

When economic dictatorship is grafted onto representative, electoral democracy, a toxic growth of religious fundamentalism and right-wing extremism is the result. Thus, corporate globalization leads not just to the death of democracy, but to the democracy of death, in which exclusion, hate, and fear become the political means to mobilize votes and power.

Earth Democracy enables us to envision and create living democracies. Living democracy enables democratic participation in all matters of life and death—the food we eat or do not have access co; the water we drink or are denied due to privatization or pollution; the air we breathe or are poisoned by. Living democracies are based on the intrinsic worth of all species, all peoples, all cultures; a just and equal sharing of this earth's viral resources; and sharing the decisions about the use of the earth's resources. [...]

Principles of Earth Democracy

1. All Species, Peoples, and Cultures Have Intrinsic Worth

All beings are subjects who have integrity, intelligence, and identity, not objects of ownership, manipulation, exploitation, or disposability. No humans have the right to own other species, other people, or the knowledge of other cultures through patents and other intellectual property rights.

2. The Earth Community is a Democracy of All Life

We are all members of the earth family, interconnected through the planet's fragile web of life. We all have a duty to live in a manner that protects the earth's ecological processes, and the rights and welfare of all species and all people. No humans have the right to encroach on the ecological space of other species and other people, or to treat them with cruelty and violence.

3. Diversity in Nature and Culture Must Be Defended

Biological and cultural diversity is an end in itself. Biological diversity is a value and a source of richness, both materially and culturally, that creates conditions for sustainability. Cultural diversity creates the conditions for peace. Defending biological and cultural diversity is a duty of all people.

4. All Beings Have a Natural Right to Sustenance

All members of the earth community, including all humans, have the right to sustenance—to food and water, to a safe and clean habitat, to security of ecological space. Resources viral to sustenance must stay in the commons. The right to sustenance is a natural right because it is the right to life. These rights are not given by states or corporations, nor can they be extinguished by state or corporate action. No state or corporation has the right to erode or undermine these natural rights or enclose the commons that sustain life.

5. Earth Democracy is Based on Living Economies and Economic Democracy

Earth Democracy is based on economic democracy. Economic systems in Earth Democracy protect ecosystems and their integrity; they protect people's livelihoods and provide basic needs to all. In the earth economy there are no disposable people or dispensable species or cultures. The earth economy is a living economy. It is based on sustainable, diverse, pluralistic systems that protect nature and people, are chosen by people, and work for the common good.

6. Living Economies Are Built on Local Economies

Conservation of the earth's resources and creation of sustainable and satisfying livelihoods are most caringly, creatively, efficiently, and equitably achieved at the local level. Localization of economies is a social and ecological imperative. Only goods and services that cannot be produced locally—using local resources and local knowledge—should be produced nonlocally and traded long distance. Earth Democracy is based on vibrant local economies, which support national and global economies. In Earth Democracy, the global economy does not destroy and crush local economies, nor does it create disposable people. Living economies recognize the creativity of all humans and create spaces for diverse creativities to reach their full potential. Living economies are diverse and decentralized economies.

7. Earth Democracy Is a Living Democracy

Living democracy is based on the democracy of all life and the democracy of everyday life. In living democracies people can influence the decisions over the food we eat, the water we drink, and the health care and education we have. Living democracy grows like a tree, from the bottom up. Earth Democracy is based on local democracy, with local communities—organized on principles of inclusion, diversity, and ecological and social responsibility—having the highest authority on decisions related to the environment and natural resources and to the sustenance and livelihoods of people. Authority is delegated to more distant levels of governments on the principle of subsidiarity. Self-rule and self-governance is the foundation of Earth Democracy.

8. Earth Democracy Is Based on Living Cultures

Living cultures promote peace and create free spaces for the practice of different religious and the adoption of different faiths and identities. Living cultures allow cultural diversity to thrive from the ground of our common humanity and our common rights as members of an earth community.

9. Living Cultures Are Life Nourishing

Living cultures are based on the dignity of and respect for all life, human and nonhuman, people of all genders and cultures, present and future generations. Living cultures are, therefore, ecological cultures which do not promote life—destroying lifestyles or consumption and production patterns, or the overuse and exploitation of resources. Living cultures are diverse and based on reverence for life. Living cultures recognize the multiplicity of identities based on identity of place and local community—and a planetary consciousness that connects the individual to the earth and all life.

10. Earth Democracy Globalizes Peace, Care, and Compassion

Earth Democracy connects people in circles of care, cooperation, and compassion instead of dividing them through competition and conflict, fear, and hatred. In the face of a world of greed, inequality, and overconsumption, Earth Democracy globalizes compassion, justice, and sustainability.

FOR FURTHER READING

Jonathon, Nathanael. "Why Vandana Shiva is So Right and So Wrong." *Grist*, 20 Aug. 2014, https://grist.org/food/vandana-shiva-so-right-and-yet-so-wrong/.

Navdanya. http://www.navdanya.org/site/.

Shiva, Vandana. *Stolen Harvest: The Hijacking of the Global Food Supply.* South End Press, 2000.

Specter, Michal. "Seeds of Doubt." *The New Yorker*, 25 Aug. 2014, http://www.newyorker.com/magazine/2014/08/25/seeds-of-doubt.

Tara Houska

In the spring of 2016, protesters began to gather in North Dakota to fight the construction of the Dakota Access Pipeline (DAPL), the proposed 1,800-mile-long oil pipeline running from near the Standing Rock Indian Reservation to Illinois. Over the next few months, the dissent grew into the largest Native American protests since the 1800s, with at least 280 tribes rallying in support of the Lakota and Dakota tribes (Healy, "From 280 Tribes"). The protests led to over 750 arrests through the fall and winter of 2016, continuing through court orders and other measures designed to halt construction of the pipeline (Meyer). Climate change activists and over two thousand veterans from across the United States came to support those at Standing Rock. Shortly after taking office, President Trump issued an executive order allowing completion of the pipeline.

In addition to increasing global warming through continued dependence on fossil fuels, the DAPL will run through ancestral burial grounds and impact the Standing Rock Reservation's only water source. The protests also challenge the continuous invasion of tribal lands since Europeans arrived in North America, followed by the US government seizure of land promised to Native people in treaties.

Enter Tara Houska, an Ojibwe and member of the Couchiching First Nation. Born in Minnesota, Houska attended the University of Minnesota, where she also received her law degree. As a tribal attorney, Houska works for tribal nations on a range of advocacy issues. She served as Vermont senator Bernie Sanders's advisor for Native American issues during the 2016 presidential campaign and co-founded Not Your Mascots, a campaign committed to changing the stereotypes and racist depictions of Native Americans. Houska remained at Standing Rock for six months protesting the DAPL and became one of the most visible figures of the movement. In the speech transcript included here, she highlights the history of the US government dehumanizing Native Americans. As she argues in a 2017 TEDWomen talk, "87 percent of references in textbooks, children's textbooks, to Native Americans are pre-1900s . . . When you aren't viewed as real people, it's a lot easier to run over your rights."

Houska locates the Standing Rock protest in the context of the continued mistreatment of Indigenous people by deploying facts and a series of questions to illuminate the injustices. Speaking directly to Native people, she builds on the idea of a collective in two ways, celebrating the unprecedented coming together of various tribal members and calling on justice for all. She punctuates this with a call-and-response, where the audience joins in a unified voice to proclaim "Water is life!" For Houska, correcting history, challenging injustices, and coming together as a coalition are the paths toward true change.

"On the Struggle for Native American Rights"

Transcript of September 2016 Speech in Washington, DC
(Our Revolution, via Facebook)

I just want to say a little bit about why I'm here. I'm from Couchiching First Nation. I'm Ojibwe. And we've been fighting a pipeline in Minnesota for the past four and a half years, the Sandpiper project in line 3. And Enbridge, the company behind it, pulled the funding from Sandpiper and put it toward Dakota Access. They decided to contaminate our relatives, and when that call went out, I knew I had no choice but to go out there.

I think that we're standing in a moment in history in which we're seeing Indigenous people come together in a way that's unprecedented. You know, this has not happened in a very, very, very long time. It's an incredible moment, but it's also a moment in which we're saying, "Enough is enough." Enough is enough.

According to the history books, we died out after Manifest Destiny. According to the federal government, a project like this that would destroy sacred sites, that would contaminate the only drinking water for the Standing Rock Sioux Reservation and the seventeen million people that live along the Missouri River, is okay and needs a lowest level environmental assessment.

That's not okay.

According to Dakota Access, they can treat us like less than human beings. They can sic dogs and Mace on Native American women and children trying to protect their sacred sites. That's what we saw. But the world is watching. The world is now watching and they're seeing what's happening. If America is the great nation that we claim to be, how can we treat our Indigenous people the way that we are?

How is it that Native American people do not have the right to prosecute non-Native people that come onto our lands when we know that the among Native American women, one in three will be raped in her lifetime? When these projects come in, that means there's a man camp right next to it, thousands of workers that directly impacts that community, and we are without authority to protect our own people. We cannot prosecute like every other state in this nation.

Instead, it's a lessened version of justice.

That's not okay. It's supposed to be justice for all, not just for some.

Dakota Access is a project that should not happen. It should never have gotten this far. Never. But it did. But we're also saying, "Enough is enough." Right? We're all here because we heard this call from the Standing Rock Sioux Reservation, but we heard the call from Indigenous people from all over the world that are saying, "We know what this feels like. We've watched as these things have contaminated and destroyed our own communities." And it's not okay.

Our children's lives matter just like everyone else's. This is a people issue. Water is life. We hear that again and again. Water is life!

[Audience: "Water is life!"]

Water is life!

[Audience: "Water is life!"]

For Further Reading

Archambault II, David. "Taking a Stand at Standing Rock." *The New York Times*, 24 Aug. 2016, www
.nytimes.com/2016/08/25/opinion/taking-a-stand-at-standing-rock.html.

Healy, Jack. "From 280 Tribes: A Protest on the Plains." *The New York Times*, 11 Sept. 2016. https://
www.nytimes.com/interactive/2016/09/12/us/12tribes.html.

Healy, Jack. "North Dakota Oil Pipeline Battle: Who's Fighting and Why." *The New York Times*, 26
Aug. 2016, www.nytimes.com/2016/11/02/us/north-dakota-oil-pipeline-battle-whos-fighting
-and-why.html.

Houska, Tara. "The Standing Rock Resistance and Our Fight for Indigenous Rights." *TED*, Nov. 2017,
www.ted.com/talks/tara_houska_the_standing_rock_resistance_and_our_fight_for_indig
enous_rights.

McKibben, Bill. "A Pipeline Fight and America's Dark Past." *The New Yorker*, 16 Sept. 2016, www
.newyorker.com/news/daily-comment/a-pipeline-fight-and-americas-dark-past.

Meyer, Robinson. "Oil is Flowing through the Dakota Access Pipeline." *The Atlantic*, 9 June 2017,
www.theatlantic.com/science/archive/2017/06/oil-is-flowing-through-the-dakota-access
-pipeline/529707/.

"Standing Rock: The Biggest Story That No One's Covering." *Indian Country Today*, 6 Sept. 2016,
newsmaven.io/indiancountrytoday/archive/standing-rock-the-biggest-story-that-no-one-s
-covering-Ua8gKUqonU-3S2y2ecQFkQ/.

Gina Adams

Gina Adams is a contemporary, hybrid artist who works in sculpture, ceramics, painting, printmaking, and drawing. Her work is included in both private and public collections and is featured extensively in US exhibits. Growing up first in the San Francisco Bay area and later in Maine, she has a BFA from the Maine College of Art and an MFA from the University of Kansas. The image here, from her *Broken Treaty Quilt Series*, is a project inspired by stories and heritage learned from her Ojibwe-Lakota grandfather, particularly through his forced time at the Carlisle Indian Boarding School.

Adams's art, as she described in an interview with *Indian Country Today*, was always suggestive of her heritage, but her *Broken Treaty Quilts* moved her work more fully into the realm of protest rhetoric. Her quilts are also a response to the Dakota Access Pipeline standoff at Standing Rock (see Tara Houska's contribution to this volume), which are directly related to past water and land treaties, particularly the 1868 Treaty of Fort Laramie, which includes the Standing Rock land.

Adams chose the medium of quilts because of their use in both Native and US cultures and to juxtapose softness with trauma, emphasizing the pain Native people endure as a result of severed promises by the US government. The legacy of quilts in North America is complicated and vexed. As the art historian Jennifer McLerran explains, quilting was introduced to Native people in North America by European Americans, but the practice was quickly adapted for Native purposes (68). And for Natives who may have been taught the practice under colonialism—such as learning European domestic skills in boarding schools—quilting could be repurposed as a site of resistance, a tradition Adams follows here. According to McLerran, "This practice of double coding, or dual signification, is one of the most effective tools of the indigenous artist as it works to preserve Native imagery, histories, and stories that may not have otherwise survived colonization and assimilation, fostering a sense of shared identity among members of a group threatened with fragmentation and dissolution" (69).

In preparation for her quilt making, Adams analyzed over three hundred broken treaties, whose language seemed deliberately confusing and designed to mislead; in hand-cutting letters, she displays the duplicitousness and disjointedness of these words. The letters are made from colorful calico fabric, in Goudy Old Style font, reminiscent of newspapers during the Indian Wars. Calico was the first industrialized commodity made in the United States and sold in Europe, and as Adams observes, "This fabric made many white men very wealthy" ("Bio"). The calico words now become a way to hold white settlers accountable. Adams fuses and bastes the letters onto one-hundred-year-old quilts she finds at estate sales or flea markets, explaining that the "age in the quilt speaks to the language and implied weariness that still exists in the treaties" (Fallon). As the *Treaty of Fort Laramie 1851 Broken Treaty Quilt* shows, the stunning beauty of colors against the sorrow of broken promises makes a strong statement of protest and affirms the rhetorical richness of making.

Treaty of Fort Laramie 1851, Broken Treaty Quilt Series, 2017

8. This quilt features a variation of a Texas Lone Star block pattern with a border of half-square triangles in blue and red. Lines of text from the 1851 Treaty of Fort Laramie cross the entire quilt in rows in multicolored fabrics. Hand-cut calico letters, thread on antique quilt, 74″×72″. Courtesy of the artist and Accola Griefen Fine Art. Photography by Aaron Paden.

For Further Reading

"Bio." *Gina Adams*, n.d., www.ginaadamsartist.com/about-1/.

Carter, Sue. "'Using the Needle as the Sword': Needlework as Epideictic in the Women's Christian Temperance Union." *Rhetorical Agendas: Political, Ethical, and Spiritual*, edited by Patricia Bizzell, Lawrence Erlbaum Associates, 2006, pp. 325–34.

Fallon, Claire. "Artist Honors the History of Broken Promises That Preceded Standing Rock." *Huffington Post*, 3 Mar 2017, www.huffingtonpost.com/entry/artist-honors-the-history-of-broke -promises-that-preceded-standing-rock_us_58b75079e4b019d36d108903.

Jones, Rachel Elizabeth. "The Broken Promises of American Indian Treaties, Sewn onto Quilts." *Hyperallergic*, 2 Feb. 2017, hyperallergic.com/361418/the-broken-promises-of-american-indian -treaties-sewn-onto-quilts/.

Keyes, Bob. "A Stitch in Time: The 'Broken Treaties Quilts' of Gina Adams." *Indian Country Today*, 2 Sept. 2017, https://newsmaven.io/indiancountrytoday/archive/a-stitch-in-time-the-broken -treaties-quilts-of-gina-adams-HZdSQBPY6UukCCbabywZIg/.

McLerran, Jennifer. "Difficult Stories: A Native Feminist Ethics in the Work of Mohawk Artist Carla Hemlock." *Feminist Studies*, vol. 43, no. 1 2017, pp. 68–107.

"'Workt by Hand': Hidden Labor and Historical Quilts." *Brooklyn Museum*, n.d., https://www.brook lynmuseum.org/opencollection/exhibitions/3278

Sasha Weiss

On May 24, 2014, a young Muslim woman of color who goes by Kaye M. sat in a local mosque, reading the news on her laptop. The night before, in Isla Vista, California, a twenty-two-year-old man named Elliot Rodger shot and killed six people and injured fourteen more. He left videos and a manifesto that detailed his hatred for women and justified his rampage as retribution for the women who sexually rejected him. As Kaye M. scrolled her Twitter feed, she saw men responding in what she calls a "growing wave of male denial" in the form of #NotAllMen. Not all men, the tweets insisted, are part of the problem. "Not all men hurt women like Elliot." "Not all men go that far." But they also blamed women for their sexual frustration: "Not all men can be patient with your uptight rejection, though." "Not all men can sit tight and smile while you go for the beta males" (Kaye M).

"I was sick to my stomach," Kaye M. writes. "I was still angry. But I wasn't alone. I was never alone. I was not the only one who felt this way." So she tweeted three friends a hashtag of her own: #YesAllWomen. In two hours, the hashtag was trending nationally; in four days, #YesAllWomen had been tweeted 1.6 million times. Participants included prominent feminist activists, cultural critics, and celebrities, which amplified the hashtag and circulated it across multiple publics (Jackson and Banaszczyk). In this torrent of tweets, women created a counterculture that provided searing accounts of the everyday acts of sexism, harassment, and abuse they endure. The hashtag #YesAllWomen built the collective case that, while the shooting was extreme, there is nothing unusual about misogyny in US culture.

Sasha Weiss's *New Yorker* column included here is one example of the heavy media coverage captured by #YesAllWomen, demonstrating not only the force of the hashtag but also its personal resonance with women. Weiss's opening story of feeling threatened by a man in a subway station highlights this connection and links her to countless other women who have felt simultaneously afraid, angry, and choked by silence in the face of sexist violations. The gift of #YesAllWomen, Weiss argues, is that it allows women to speak about their ubiquitous experiences of misogyny to a counterpublic who will listen to and believe them.

Weiss, culture editor of the *New York Times Magazine*, declares #YesAllWomen a vehicle for action and place of liberation. But Twitter activism, sometimes called slacktivism, has faced its share of criticism for presumably failing to produce tangible results. And yet, #YesAllWomen spurred substantive media attention to myriad gender-related issues: the normalization of sexism, misogyny, and rape culture; the need for men to witness women's experiences and to participate in the solution; and the linkage between misogyny and mass shootings. Women of color also responded with their own hashtag, #YesAllWhiteWomen, calling for intersectional attentiveness to any universal claim about women, issuing the reminders that women of color are less likely to be believed in cases of assault and that violence against women of color often goes unreported by the media (Jackson and Banaszczyk).

In a retrospective about #YesAllWomen a year later, Kaye M. described the trolling, including death threats, she faced as the visibility of #YesAllWomen grew. Ironically, as more and more women added their voices to this platform, Kaye M. retreated from social media, experiencing trauma and fear as a result of harassment. While she regrets the pain she suffered for speaking out, her commitment to the issue remains steadfast: "I do not regret giving women a place to speak and be heard and acknowledged on a worldwide scale . . . I am here. This is my mouth. You cannot silence me." As #YesAllWomen proved to be a wave that built to the tsunami of #MeToo (see Tarana Burke's contribution to this volume), millions of women shared the sentiment that they too refuse to be silenced.

"The Power of #YesAllWomen"

The *New Yorker*, 2014

On Saturday night at around eight, I went into my local subway station with a friend. There was a man lingering behind the turnstile, swaying a little. My friend was wearing a miniskirt and a brightly colored lace bra that was visible underneath her shirt. I was in a short black dress. The man growled. I heard the words "beautiful ladies." My friend didn't notice. I kept an eye on him.

She reached into her purse. The man was reaching for something, too. He was loosening his belt buckle, and his hand was roving. I felt panic. Was he . . . no. But yes—he was about to touch himself. The atmosphere was airless, sour. I formulated indignant phrases in my head—"What the hell do you think you're doing?" "What you're doing is disgusting"—but the words stuck in my throat like a wad of gum. I worried for my safety: if I confronted him, perhaps I would anger him, and he'd come charging through the turnstile. But, more important, I worried that I was making something out of nothing—that I was imagining this, or that he was drunk or mentally ill, and that calling him out would be needlessly humiliating to him.

I ushered my friend down to the platform. I wondered if he would still be there when I returned alone, late at night, when the station would be desolate, and started charting another route home. The experience of feeling simultaneously threatened and unable to speak, of feeling as if I would be persecuting this man who was committing a sexual impropriety were I to pipe up and tell him to knock it off, was unsettlingly familiar.

This was still fresh in my mind as I scrolled through a series of tweets about sexual harassment, rape, and misogyny, categorized under the hashtag #YesAllWomen. It was started after Elliot Rodger, a twenty-two-year-old man, went on a shooting spree on Isla Vista, near the University of California, Santa Barbara, killing six people before committing suicide. In the weeks leading up to the killings, Rodger posted a series of angry, bathetic YouTube videos and a hundred-and-thirty-seven-page autobiographical "manifesto," declaring his hatred of all women for the rejection and disdain he claims they dealt him throughout his life. Rodger had a pointillist, obsessive memory, and he detailed everything from the food at his ninth birthday party to the names of the kids he played hacky-sack with. Even as a child, he was acutely attuned to power hierarchies and social slights, and he had a peculiar fixation on houses and real estate.

The first half of the manifesto is lucid and reflective—we see glimmers of a happy boyhood and an affectionate, curious personality—which makes his spewings of misogyny and hatred in the second half even more chilling. He wanted to abolish sex, thereby equalizing men and ridding society of women's manipulative and bestial natures, and to lock women in concentration camps so they would die out. ("I would have an enormous tower built just for myself, where I can oversee the entire concentration camp and gleefully watch them all die," he wrote. "If I can't have them, no one will, I imagine thinking to myself as I oversee this. Women represent everything that is unfair in this world, and in order to make this world a fair place, women must be eradicated.") His idea was to imprison a few select women in a lab, where they would be artificially inseminated to propagate the species.

Rodger's fantasies are so patently strange and so extreme that they're easy to dismiss as simply crazy. But, reading his manifesto, you can make out, through the distortions of his raging mind, the outlines of mainstream American cultural values: Beauty and strength are rewarded. Women are prizes to be won, reflections of a man's social capital. Wealth, a large house, and fame are the highest attainments. The lonely and the poor are invisible. Rodger was crazier and more violent than most people, but his beliefs are on a continuum with misogynistic, class-based ideas that are held by many.

And that is why #YesAllWomen is moving and needed. Elliot Rodger earned the fame and infamy he wished for through his act of violence, and now everyone can read about his grotesque ideas. #YesAllWomen offers a counter-testimony, demonstrating that Rodger's hate of women grew out of attitudes that are all around us. Perhaps more subtly, it suggests that he was influenced by a predominant cultural ethos that rewards sexual aggression, power, and wealth, and that reinforces traditional alpha masculinity and submissive femininity. (This line of thought is not intended in any way to make excuses for Rodger's murderousness, but to try to imagine him as part of the same social world we all live in and not as simply a monster.) The thread has produced over a million tweets, and they are by turns moving, enraging, astute, sorrowful, and terrifying. Even though most of the tweets do not directly mourn the people Rodger killed, the tweets accumulate into a kind of memorial, a stern demand for a more just society. Here are just a few examples:

YesAllWomen because "I have a boyfriend" is more effective than "I'm not interested"—men respect other men more than my right to say no.

Because I've already rehearsed "Take whatever you want, just don't hurt me." #YesAllWomen

YesAllWomen because every time I try to say that I want gender equality I have to explain that I don't hate men.

Men's greatest fear is that women will laugh at them, while women's greatest fear is that men will kill them. -Margaret Atwood #YesAllWomen

Because in about 30 states, rapists whose victims choose to keep the baby can get parental rights, like weekend visitation. WTF #YesAllWomen

YesAllWomen because apparently the clothes I wear is a more valid form of consent than the words I say

I repeat: the fact that there are male victims isn't proof it's not misogyny. It's evidence that misogyny hurts men too. #YesAllWomen

Last night, emboldened by the sense of safety created by a mass of voices speaking of their private fears in a public forum, I added my own:

Because if I know I will be out 'til after dark, I start planning my route home hours, even days, beforehand #YesAllWomen

There is something about the fact that Twitter is primarily designed for speech—for short, strong, declarative utterance—that makes it an especially powerful vehicle for activism, a place of liberation. Reading #YesAllWomen, and participating in it, is the opposite of warily watching a man masturbate and being unable to confront him with language. #YesAllWomen is the vibrant revenge of women who have been gagged and silenced.

FOR FURTHER READING

Jackson, Sarah J., and Sonia Banaszczyk. "Digital Standpoints: Debating Gendered Violence and Racial Exclusions in the Feminist Counterpublic." *Journal of Communication Inquiry*, vol. 40, no. 4, 2016, pp. 391–407.

Kaye M. "On #YesAllWomen, One Year Later." *The Toast*, 25 May 2015, the-toast.net/2015/05/26/yesallwomen-one-year-later/.

Solnit, Rebecca. "Why #YesAllWomen Matters." *Mother Jones*, 24 June 2017, www.motherjones.com/politics/2014/06/yesallwomen-shape-conversation-isla-vista-massacre-violence-against-women/.

Valenti, Jessica. "#YesAllWomen Reveals the Constant Barrage of Sexism That Women Face." *The Guardian*, 28 May 2014, www.theguardian.com/commentisfree/2014/may/28/yesallwomen-barage-sexism-elliot-rodger.

Williams, Sherri. "Digital Defense: Black Feminists Resist Violence with Hashtag Activism." *Feminist Media Studies*, vol. 15, no. 2, 2015, pp. 341–44.

Suzanne Samin

Gaming culture is often regarded as a boys' club, and Suzanne Samin seeks to transform that perception. Drawing upon stats and her own memories of growing up as a gamer, Samin resists the notion that gaming is the bastion of men. In fact, when mobile games are included, female players constitute just over half of the gaming community. She is quick to point out, however, that it can be difficult for girls and women to find joy in gaming, with many games' objectification of female characters, and because of the abuse faced by female game developers and critics.

Samin's piece in *Bustle*, an online magazine popular with younger women, was published shortly after Gamergate—an internet culture war involving abuse and death threats against female game developers and critics, including Anita Sarkeesian, who launched *Feminist Frequency*, a video blog series that critiques sexist video games (Parkin). Many see Gamergate, which received mainstream attention, as ultimately a clash among the changing demographics of gaming culture: women and progressives seeking inclusion in gaming and misogynists and traditionalists who don't want gaming to evolve (Dewey, Parkin). More broadly, Gamergate reflects the tension between voices in social media that invite more participants into public conversations in the twenty-first century and the loud and sometimes abusive voices seeking to reinforce the boundaries of exclusion. Like other pieces in this volume (see Linda Tirado's, Jessica Valenti's, and Lindy West's contributions to this volume), Samin's shows that harassment and abuse often follow women who break silences and participate in conversations from which they've been excluded.

But Samin, a social media professional and fantasy novel author, refuses to back down. Her piece for *Bustle* begins as a personal narrative that draws upon her experiences of gaming, which earns her credibility with readers, while also conveying her deep investment and joy in gaming. The piece then escalates into a manifesto, declaring her space in the gaming community as a woman and for women. Samin acknowledges that it is a challenge to not be intimidated amid the threats female gamers face, and in an effort to rally others to speak out, she provides strategies by way of "small steps" she takes to normalize women in gaming culture. Unlike Princess Peach, often portrayed as a damsel in distress in *Super Mario Bros.*, Samin and others are bravely fighting their own battles through rhetorical tactics used by women for centuries: establishing their presence and skills in domains that have shut out and silenced women.

"I'm a Female Gamer, and This is What It's Really Like"

Bustle, 2015

The first controller I ever held in my hand was that of the N64. It was 1997, I was 6 years old, and my parents had given me my very first console for Christmas along with two games, *Yoshi Story* and *Mario Kart.* They knew I'd have fun with it, but they didn't know it would be something I would cherish for over a decade to come.

Video games have been with me through everything. As an only child with parents who worked long hours, the bright, cheery cartoon characters I controlled with my thumbs got me through many a lonely summer. I had a seemingly unlimited world at my fingertips. I could race cars on the turnpike, save the princess, and learn about world history all in the matter of an afternoon. Every time I got close to getting bored, a new game or console would come out and make me fall in love all over again. I was a gamer girl, and I loved every single minute of it.

That little gamer girl turned into a gamer woman, and I am still holding a controller. It's not usually the N64 one anymore; I moved on to the PS2 and Game Boy Advanced, then the GameCube, and finally the XBOX 360. But it's there, and I'm still saving princesses in between running off to my full-time editorial job, writing on the side, walking my dog, working on my novel, and all the other things I've found to bring me joy.

And I'm not the only one. A staggering 52 percent of gamers are women, many of whom, like me, started as little girls and held onto it throughout adolescence and young adulthood. We've kicked our friends' asses in *Halo* and *Mario Party*; gotten lost in the incredible, immersive worlds of *Skyrim* and *Legend of Zelda*; and we've even teared up a little during emotionally intense games like *Heavy Rain* and *Final Fantasy VII.*

We love the gaming world, but the gaming world doesn't love us back. The industry has time and time again refused to include women in their marketing or tell women's stories in their games. There is one female character for every five male characters in video games, and 76 percent of solo video game protagonists are male. Male characters are also far more likely to appear on video game covers than women.

When women *do* show up in games, they're often depicted in sexually suggestive situations, and frequently serve as a romantic or sexual interest to a more prominent, male character. They've oversexualized us, demeaned us, and continue to do so for the entertainment of their only prioritized clientele: men.

Lara Croft's breasts are still unrealistically large. The women in the *Grand Theft Auto* series are vapid and treated like garbage. Female body shapes are unrealistic (I'm looking at you, *Dragon Age*), and/or overly sexualized. And consensual sexual encounters? Nice try—ahem, *Silent Hill.*

I've been blatantly and rudely butted out of conversations about video games amongst fellow gamers, at conventions, in college, at my own house. I've been asked by video game store employees if I "understand" what I'm buying, or told how cute it is that I'm buying my boyfriend a game more times than I can count. I've been interrogated by male gamers to make sure I'm "legit," while hanging out with friends—and then promptly been hit on, too.

And forget even trying to step foot into the online gaming community—after having a handful of guys creepily follow me around in *Ragnarok Online* a few years back, you won't be seeing me in an MMORPG (mass multiplayer online role-playing game) again. Because there's nothing like being actively followed by a swarm of faceless male gamers, being pelted with messages demanding me to show them my breasts or asking if I have a boyfriend for hours until I have to log off because the game just isn't fun anymore.

It's made me feel gross and unsafe amongst people who should, for all intents and purposes, be my friends—or, at least, my fellow party members on an orc-slaying mission.

Gamergate—the predominately male-led harassment campaign against female game developers and critics—has broken the hearts of female gamers and developers everywhere, showing us that a horrifyingly large and vocal portion of people who also enjoy video games don't want us anywhere near them. They don't want us playing them, making them, or writing about them, and they're willing to resort to any level of intimidation necessary to make sure we stay out of their territory.

Women have been pushed out of the clubhouse, which now bears a sign that reads: "Boyz only." We're not wanted, we're not welcome, and if we try to make a place for ourselves, we have everything to lose: our careers, our relationships, our homes, our money, and our own safety.

Just ask the brave women (Brianna Wu, Anita Sarkeesian, and Zoe Quinn—just to name a few) who have attempted to break down the clubhouse door or create a new space for women have been treated with a villainous, inhumane cruelty. They've been harassed, slandered, doxxed, and threatened with physical and sexual assault.

They have been forced out of their homes. They have been silenced by a group of radicalized, misinformed misogynists who lurk in the shadows of the internet looking for the next opportunity for an easy target under the guise of advocating for "ethics in game journalism." They are willing to do any and everything to knock the controllers out of our hands, to send the next generation of gamer girls back to their dollhouses cowering in fear.

I'll admit it: it's tempting to let them intimidate us. It's tempting to be afraid; to decide "nothing" is worth risking the kind of hell these people can turn your life into—certainly not video games.

But we can't—I can't. I can't do it, and I won't. I love video games, and I want them to be part of my writing career. I'm going to express my opinions, and I'm going to have them be heard. I'm going to keep talking, playing, and writing—even if it scares people or threatens their collective fractured masculinity. I stand with Anita Sarkeesian, Zoe Quinn, Brianna Wu, and all the other brave, wonderful women who have worked to pave a road for women in gaming. I won't put my controller down, or my keyboard away.

Every day, I am taking steps to stand up for women in gaming. They are small steps, but they give me the courage to take even bigger ones each time. I do not allow myself, or any of my fellow gamer girls, to get cut off in conversations about gaming. If a game is sexist, I speak about it, regardless of who it might annoy or offend. I do my best to support games created by or featuring women. I tweet, Facebook, and tumble about games I like and games I don't. I don't allow myself to be afraid of what the world will think of me for taking up space in the gaming community.

It's taken me a long while to build up the courage to write about games. But here I am, and I'm not planning on going anywhere.

Video games are for everyone. They're for me, they're for you, they're for our little sisters, and our daughters to create, to play, and to critique. We cannot allow cruel, sadistic people to take our joy away from us. We need to stand up to Gamergate and keep being ourselves. But it starts with you and me.

It starts with us refusing to shut up.

FOR FURTHER READING

Dames Making Games. dmg.to/.

Feminist Frequency. feministfrequency.com/.

Dewey, Caitlin. "The Only Guide to Gamergate You Will Ever Need to Read." *The Washington Post*, 14 Oct. 2014, www.washingtonpost.com/news/the-intersect/wp/2014/10/14/the-only-guide-to-gamergate-you-will-ever-need-to-read/?utm_term=.22806f3c43e5.

Jayanth, Meg. "52% of Gamers are Women, but the Industry Doesn't Know It." *The Guardian*, 18 Sept. 2014, www.theguardian.com/commentisfree/2014/sep/18/52-percent-people-playing-games-women-industry-doesnt-know.

Nakamura, Lisa. "Queer Female of Color: The Highest Difficulty Setting There Is? Gaming Rhetoric as Gender Capital." *Ada: A Journal of Gender, New Media, and Technology*, no. 1, n.d., adanewme dia.org/2012/11/issue1-nakamura/.

Parkin, Simon. "Gamergate: A Scandal Erupts in the Video-Game Community." *The New Yorker*, 17 Oct. 2014, www.newyorker.com/tech/elements/gamergate-scandal-erupts-video-game-com munity.

Tognotti, Chris. "What Is '#Gamer Gate'? It's Misogyny, under the Banner of 'Journalistic Integrity.'" *Bustle*, 5 Sept. 2014, www.bustle.com/articles/38742-what-is-gamer-gate-its-misogyny-un der-the-banner-of-journalistic-integrity.

Trembley, Kaitlin. "Intro to Gender Criticism for Gamers: From Princess Peach, to Claire Redfield, to FemSheps." *Gamasutra: The Art and Business of Making Games*, 1 June 2012, https://www .gamasutra.com/blogs/KaitlinTremblay/20120601/171613/Intro_to_Gender_Criticism _for_Gamers_From_Princess_Peach_to_Claire_Redfield_to_FemSheps.php.

Bree Newsome

On June 17, 2015, the white supremacist Dylann Roof killed nine African American parishioners at the Emanuel African Methodist Episcopal Church in Charleston, South Carolina, one of the oldest black churches in the United States. Ten days later, Bree Newsome—artist, writer, and activist—climbed the flagpole in front of South Carolina's capitol building in Charleston and removed the Confederate flag. She was arrested for civil disobedience as photos and video of her climb of the thirty-foot pole went viral.

Newsome was born in Charlotte, North Carolina, and raised largely in Maryland. She attended New York University's Tisch School of the Arts, where she studied film. Her great-great-great-grandparents were enslaved at the start of the Civil War. The daughter of a renowned scholar and educator of African American religious history, Newsome's love of the arts was fostered early, and by the age of eighteen she received a $40,000 scholarship for a short-film competition. Her earlier activist work includes Occupy Wall Street and protesting legislation (later overturned by the US Court of Appeals for the Fourth Circuit) that disenfranchised black voters in North Carolina. Newsome has won many awards, including a 2016 NAACP Image Award.

Following her arrest for removing the Confederate flag, Newsome released a statement to *Blue Nation Review* explaining her motives:

> For far too long, white supremacy has dominated the politics of America resulting in the creation of racist laws and cultural practices designed to subjugate non-whites. And the emblem of the confederacy, the stars and bars, in all its manifestations, has long been the most recognizable banner of this political ideology. It's the banner of racial intimidation and fear whose popularity experiences an uptick whenever black Americans appear to be making gains economically and politically in this country … I removed the flag not only in defiance of those who enslaved my ancestors in the southern United States, but also in defiance of the oppression that continues against black people globally in 2015, including the ongoing ethnic cleansing in the Dominican Republic. I did it in solidarity with the South African students who toppled a statue of the white supremacist, colonialist Cecil Rhodes. I did it for all the fierce black women on the front lines of the movement and for all the little black girls who are watching us. I did it because I am free.

Newsome also explains in her statement that removing the flag was a collective effort—it was a deliberate choice that a black woman would scale the pole, and a white man would assist her over the fence, to show gender and racial solidarity. Clad in black with proper climbing gear and wearing a focused expression, Newsome reinforces the purposefulness and import of her actions. Once she retrieved the flag, she shouted, "You come against me with hatred, oppression, and violence. I come against you in the name of God. This flag comes down today." In short: every move of the protest was rhetorical.

Incarnations of Newsome removing the Confederate flag have gone viral, including comic versions in which Newsome is clad as Wonder Woman or perched atop the flagpole. The circulation of these images visually illustrates resistance and empowerment through embodiment, a protest that centers a black female body whom the Confederacy would not have regarded as fully human.

Civil Disobedience: Bree Newsome Removes Confederate Flag

2016

9. Clad in climbing gear, Bree Newsome scales the flagpole at the South Carolina statehouse to remove the Confederate Flag. Photo by Bruce Smith/Associated Press. Bree Newsome.

For Further Reading

"About Bree." *Bree Newsome*, 2017, www.breenewsome.com/about.

Botelho, Greg, and Emanuella Grinberg. "Bree Newsome Hailed for Removing Confederate Flag." *CNN*, 27 June 2015, www.cnn.com/2015/06/27/politics/south-carolina-confederate-flag/in dex.html.

Contrera, Jessica. "Who is Bree Newsome? Why the Woman Who Took down the Confederate Flag Became an Activist." *The Washington Post*, 28 June 2015, www.washingtonpost.com/news/ arts-and-entertainment/wp/2015/06/28/who-is-bree-newsome-why-the-woman-who-took -down-the-confederate-flag-became-an-activist/.

Cox, John W. "Backlash over Confederate Flag Is, for Some, 'an Attack on . . . Our Heritage.'" *The Washington Post*, 27 June 2015, https://www.washingtonpost.com/local/backlash-over-confed erate-insignia-is-for-some-an-attack-on--our-heritage/2015/06/27/4b1821cc-1b75-11e5-93b7 -5eddc056ad8a_story.html?utm_term=.e9716555f288.

Locker, Melissa. "Activist Bree Newsome Arrested After Daring South Carolina Confederate Flag Removal." *Vanity Fair*, June 2015, www.vanityfair.com/news/2015/06/activist-bree-new some-arrested-after-daring-south-carolina-confederate-flag-removal.

Taylor, Goldie. "EXCLUSIVE: Bree Newsome Speaks for the First Time After Courageous Act of Civil Disobedience." *Blue Nation Review*, 29 June 2015, archives.bluenationreview.com/exclu sive-bree-newsome-speaks-for-the-first-time-after-courageous-act-of-civil-disobedience/.

"This Flag Comes Down Today": Bree Newsome Scales SC Capitol Flagpole, Takes Down Confed erate Flag." *Democracy Now*, 7 Mar. 2015, www.democracynow.org/2015/7/3/this_flag_comes _down_today_bree.

Emily Doe (Chanel Miller)

On January 18, 2015, two Stanford graduate students came upon a horrific scene: a woman lay unmoving near a dumpster outside a fraternity house while a man raped her. The students confronted the man, who fled, leaving his victim unconscious, partially unclothed, and physically and emotionally violated. The perpetrator, Brock Turner, was repeatedly described by the media as a white, blond, blue-eyed Stanford student and "all-American swimmer" (Koren).

Turner was convicted by a jury with charges of "assault with intent to commit rape of an intoxicated woman, sexually penetrating an intoxicated person with a foreign object, and sexually penetrating an unconscious person with a foreign object" (Koren). Prosecutors requested a six-year prison sentence for Turner; the judge assigned him six months, explaining, "A prison sentence would have a severe impact on him. I think he will not be a danger to others" (Fantz and Wills).

The trial made national headlines not only because of public outrage induced by the short prison sentence of a privileged white man but also because during the hearing, his victim read an impact statement directly addressed to the man who raped her. Within four days of its release on BuzzFeed, the letter was viewed eleven million times and was covered in media outlets ranging from CNN to *Cosmopolitan*. Eighteen members of Congress from across party lines read it aloud, in an effort to raise awareness about sexual assault and to protest rape culture. In a country where one in five women is the victim of an attempted or completed rape in her lifetime and 86 percent of assaults go unreported (Rape Response Services), with survivors fearing they won't be believed or nothing will be done, this letter made a powerful ripple in the still waters of silence.

As important as the message was for other survivors of assault, Emily Doe makes Turner her primary audience: "You don't know me, but you've been inside of me, and that's why we're here today." Most survivors don't have the opportunity to hold their assailants accountable; she uses this *kairotic* moment to its fullest potential.

In harrowing detail, Emily Doe demands that Turner listen to her story. She describes awakening to find her body violated, only to experience further layers of violation that occurred afterward, as she was examined in the hospital; as she read about herself in the media; as she was interrogated by the police. Then, she describes the reviolation that surfaced with Turner's testimony, providing a countertestimony to statements she knew were untrue. Survivors' stories are notoriously doubted in the public sphere. Emily Doe provides a gripping account of her violation, refusing to let Turner write the narrative.

In a follow-up statement she makes to *Glamour*, who named her a Woman of the Year, she (still using the pseudonym Emily Doe) shares that after hearing the judge's sentence of six months in prison for Turner, "I was struck silent." Her silence was answered with thunderous support, from online commenters to a letter praising her "spine of steel" from Vice President Joe Biden to emails from around the world.

In fact, she would not remain silent. In September 2019 Viking published *Know My Name*, in which Chanel Miller reclaims her identity, describes her trauma and courage since the assault, and challenges a criminal justice system that favors predators. Andrea Schultz, Viking's editor in chief, says *Know My Name* is "one of the most important books that I've ever published" with potential to "change the culture that we live in and the assumptions we make about what survivors should be expected to go through to get justice" (de León).

Whether as Chanel Miller or Emily Doe, Miller issues a resounding call for the justice system to do better. She argues that victims are survivors. When so much has been taken from her, she uses her testimony to reclaim agency and resilience and to make room for other women to do the same.

Victim Impact Statement from *People v. Turner* (Stanford Rape Case)

2016

Your Honor, if it is all right, for the majority of this statement I would like to address the defendant directly.

You don't know me, but you've been inside me, and that's why we're here today. On January 17, 2015, it was a quiet Saturday night at home. My dad made some dinner and I sat at the table with my younger sister, who was visiting for the weekend. I was working full time and it was approaching my bedtime. I planned to stay at home by myself, watch some TV and read, while she went to a party with her friends. Then, I decided it was my only night with her, I had nothing better to do, so why not, there's a dumb party ten minutes from my house, I would go, dance like a fool, and embarrass my younger sister. On the way there, I joked that undergrad guys would have braces. My sister teased me for wearing a beige cardigan to a frat party like a librarian. I called myself "Big Mama," because I knew I'd be the oldest one there. I made silly faces, let my guard down, and drank liquor too fast, not factoring in that my tolerance had significantly lowered since college.

The next thing I remember I was in a gurney in a hallway. I had dried blood and bandages on the backs of my hands and elbow. I thought maybe I had fallen and was in an admin office on campus. I was very calm and wondering where my sister was. A deputy explained I had been assaulted. I still remained calm, assured he was speaking to the wrong person. I knew no one at this party. When I was finally allowed to use the restroom, I pulled down the hospital pants they had given me, went to pull down my underwear, and felt nothing. I still remember the feeling of my hands touching my skin and grabbing nothing. I looked down and there was nothing. The thin piece of fabric, the only thing between my vagina and anything else, was missing and everything inside me was silenced. I still don't have words for that feeling. In order to keep breathing, I thought maybe the policemen used scissors to cut them off for evidence.

Then, I felt pine needles scratching the back of my neck and started pulling them out my hair. I thought maybe, the pine needles had fallen from a tree onto my head. My brain was talking my gut into not collapsing. Because my gut was saying, "Help me, help me."

I shuffled from room to room with a blanket wrapped around me, pine needles trailing behind me; I left a little pile in every room I sat in. I was asked to sign papers that said "Rape Victim" and I thought something has really happened. My clothes were confiscated and I stood naked while the nurses held a ruler to various abrasions on my body and photographed them. The three of us worked to comb the pine needles out of my hair, six hands to fill one paper bag. To calm me down, they said, "It's just the flora and fauna, flora and fauna." I had multiple swabs inserted into my vagina and anus, needles for shots, pills, had a Nikon pointed right into my spread legs. I had long, pointed beaks inside me and had my vagina smeared with cold, blue paint to check for abrasions.

After a few hours of this, they let me shower. I stood there examining my body beneath the stream of water and decided, I don't want my body anymore. I was terrified of it, I didn't know what had been in it, if it had been contaminated, who had touched it. I wanted to take off my body like a jacket and leave it at the hospital with everything else.

On that morning, all that I was told was that I had been found behind a dumpster, potentially penetrated by a stranger, and that I should get retested for HIV because results don't always show up immediately. But for now, I should go home and get back to my normal life. Imagine stepping back into the world with only that information. They gave me huge hugs and I walked out of the hospital into the parking lot wearing the new sweatshirt and sweatpants they provided me, as they had only allowed me to keep my necklace and shoes.

My sister picked me up, face wet from tears and contorted in anguish. Instinctively and immediately, I wanted to take away her pain. I smiled at her, I told her to look at me, I'm right here, I'm okay, everything's okay, I'm right here. My hair is washed and clean, they gave me the strangest shampoo, calm down, and look at me. Look at these funny new sweatpants and sweatshirt, I look like a PE teacher, let's go home, let's eat something. She did not know that beneath my sweat suit, I had scratches and bandages on my skin, my vagina was sore and had become a strange, dark color from all the prodding, my underwear was missing, and I felt too empty to continue to speak. That I was also afraid, that I was also devastated. That day we drove home and for hours in silence my younger sister held me.

My boyfriend did not know what happened, but called that day and said, "I was really worried about you last night, you scared me, did you make it home okay?" I was horrified. That's when I learned I had called him that night in my blackout, left an incomprehensible voicemail, that we had also spoken on the phone, but I was slurring so heavily he was scared for me, that he repeatedly told me to go find [my sister]. Again, he asked me, "What happened last night? Did you make it home okay?" I said, "Yes," and hung up to cry.

I was not ready to tell my boyfriend or parents that actually, I may have been raped behind a dumpster, but I don't know by who or when or how. If I told them, I would see the fear on their faces, and mine would multiply by tenfold, so instead I pretended the whole thing wasn't real.

I tried to push it out of my mind, but it was so heavy I didn't talk, I didn't eat, I didn't sleep, I didn't interact with anyone. After work, I would drive to a secluded place to scream. I didn't talk, I didn't eat, I didn't sleep, I didn't interact with anyone, and I became isolated from the ones I loved most. For over a week after the incident, I didn't get any calls or updates about that night or what happened to me. The only symbol that proved that it hadn't just been a bad dream was the sweatshirt from the hospital in my drawer.

One day, I was at work, scrolling through the news on my phone, and came across an article. In it, I read and learned for the first time about how I was found unconscious, with my hair disheveled, long necklace wrapped around my neck, bra pulled out of my dress, dress pulled off over my shoulders and pulled up above my waist, that I was butt naked all the way down to my boots, legs spread apart, and had been penetrated by a foreign object by someone I did not recognize. This was how I learned what happened to me, sitting at my desk reading the news at work. I learned what happened to me the same time everyone else in the world learned what happened to me. That's when the pine needles in my hair made sense; they didn't fall from a tree. He had taken off my underwear; his fingers had been inside of me. I don't even know this person. I still don't know this person. When I read about me like this I said, "This can't be me, this can't be me." I could not digest or accept any of this information. I could not imagine my family having to read about this online. I kept reading. In the next paragraph, I read something that I will never forgive—I read that according to him, I liked it. I liked it. Again, I do not have words for these feelings.

It's like if you were to read an article where a car was hit, and found dented, in a ditch. But maybe the car enjoyed being hit. Maybe the other car didn't mean to hit it, just bump it up a little bit. Cars get in accidents all the time, people aren't always paying attention, can we really say who's at fault.

And then, at the bottom of the article, after I learned about the graphic details of my own sexual assault, the article listed his swimming times. She was found breathing, unresponsive with her underwear six inches away from her bare stomach curled in fetal position. By the way, he's really good at swimming. Throw in my mile time if that's what we're doing. I'm good at cooking, put that in there, I think the end is where you list your extracurriculars to cancel out all the sickening things that've happened.

The night the news came out I sat my parents down and told them that I had been assaulted, to not look at the news because it's upsetting, just know that I'm okay, I'm right here, and I'm okay. But halfway through telling them, my mom had to hold me because I could no longer stand up.

The night after it happened, he said he didn't know my name, said he wouldn't be able to identify my face in a lineup, didn't mention any dialogue between us, no words, only dancing and kissing. *Dancing* is a cute term—was it snapping fingers and twirling dancing, or just bodies grinding up against each other in a crowded room? I wonder if kissing was just faces sloppily pressed up against each other? When the detective asked if he had planned on taking me back to his dorm, he said, "No." When the detective asked how we ended up behind the dumpster, he said he didn't know. He admitted to kissing other girls at that party, one of whom was my own sister, who pushed him away. He admitted to wanting to hook up with someone. I was the wounded antelope of the herd, completely alone and vulnerable, physically unable to fend for myself, and he chose me. Sometimes I think, if I hadn't gone, then this never would've happened. But then I realized, it would have happened, just to somebody else. You were about to enter four years of access to drunk girls and parties, and if this is the foot you started off on, then it is right you did not continue. The night after it happened, he said he thought I liked it because I rubbed his back. A back rub.

Never mentioned me voicing consent, never mentioned us even speaking, a back rub. One more time, in public news, I learned that my ass and vagina were completely exposed outside, my breasts had been groped, fingers had been jabbed

inside me along with pine needles and debris, my bare skin and head had been rub-
bing against the ground behind a dumpster, while an erect freshman was humping
my half-naked, unconscious body. But I don't remember, so how do I prove I didn't
like it.

I thought there's no way this is going to trial—there were witnesses, there was
dirt in my body, he ran but was caught. He's going to settle, formally apologize, and
we will both move on. Instead, I was told he hired a powerful attorney, expert witnesses, private investigators who were going to try and find details about my personal life to use against me, find loopholes in my story to invalidate me and my sister, in order to show that this sexual assault was in fact a misunderstanding. That he
was going to go to any length to convince the world he had simply been confused.

I was not only told that I was assaulted, I was told that because I couldn't remember, I technically could not prove it was unwanted. And that distorted me,
damaged me, almost broke me. It is the saddest type of confusion to be told I was
assaulted and nearly raped, blatantly out in the open, but we don't know if it counts
as assault yet. I had to fight for an entire year to make it clear that there was something wrong with this situation.

When I was told to be prepared in case we didn't win, I said, "I can't prepare for
that." He was guilty the minute I woke up. No one can talk me out of the hurt he
caused me. Worst of all, I was warned, because he now knows you don't remember,
he is going to get to write the script. He can say whatever he wants and no one can
contest it. I had no power, I had no voice; I was defenseless. My memory loss would
be used against me. My testimony was weak, was incomplete, and I was made to believe that perhaps I am not enough to win this. His attorney constantly reminded
the jury, the only one we can believe is Brock, because she doesn't remember. That
helplessness was traumatizing.

Instead of taking time to heal, I was taking time to recall the night in excruciating detail, in order to prepare for the attorney's questions that would be invasive,
aggressive, and designed to steer me off course, to contradict myself, my sister,
phrased in ways to manipulate my answers. Instead of his attorney saying, "Did
you notice any abrasions?" He said, "You didn't notice any abrasions, right?" This
was a game of strategy, as if I could be tricked out of my own worth. The sexual assault had been so clear, but instead, here I was at the trial, answering questions like:

*How old are you? How much do you weigh? What did you eat that day? Well what
did you have for dinner? Who made dinner? Did you drink with dinner? No, not even
water? When did you drink? How much did you drink? What container did you drink
out of? Who gave you the drink? How much do you usually drink? Who dropped you off
at this party? At what time? But where exactly? What were you wearing? Why were you
going to this party? What'd you do when you got there? Are you sure you did that? But
what time did you do that? What does this text mean? Who were you texting? When*

did you urinate? Where did you urinate? With whom did you urinate outside? Was your phone on silent when your sister called? Do you remember silencing it? Really because on page 53 I'd like to point out that you said it was set to ring. Did you drink in college? You said you were a party animal? How many times did you black out? Did you party at frats? Are you serious with your boyfriend? Are you sexually active with him? When did you start dating? Would you ever cheat? Do you have a history of cheating? What do you mean when you said you wanted to reward him? Do you remember what time you woke up? Were you wearing your cardigan? What color was your cardigan? Do you remember any more from that night? No? Okay, well, we'll let Brock fill it in.

I was pummeled with narrowed, pointed questions that dissected my personal life, love life, past life, family life—inane questions, accumulating trivial details to try and find an excuse for this guy who had me half-naked before even bothering to ask for my name. After a physical assault, I was assaulted with questions designed to attack me, to say, "See, her facts don't line up, she's out of her mind, she's practically an alcoholic, she probably wanted to hook up, he's like an athlete right, they were both drunk, whatever, the hospital stuff she remembers is after the fact, why take it into account, Brock has a lot at stake so he's having a really hard time right now."

And then it came time for him to testify and I learned what it meant to be revictimized. I want to remind you, the night after it happened he said he never planned to take me back to his dorm. He said he didn't know why we were behind a dumpster. He got up to leave because he wasn't feeling well when he was suddenly chased and attacked. Then he learned I could not remember.

So one year later, as predicted, a new dialogue emerged. Brock had a strange new story, almost sounded like a poorly written young adult novel with kissing and dancing and hand-holding and lovingly tumbling onto the ground, and most importantly in this new story, there was suddenly consent. One year after the incident, he remembered, "Oh yeah, by the way she actually said yes, to everything, so . . ."

He said he had asked if I wanted to dance. Apparently I said, "Yes." He'd asked if I wanted to go to his dorm, I said, "Yes." Then he asked if he could finger me and I said, "Yes." Most guys don't ask, "Can I finger you?" Usually there's a natural progression of things, unfolding consensually, not a Q and A. But apparently I granted full permission. He's in the clear. Even in his story, I only said a total of three words—"Yes, yes, yes"—before he had me half-naked on the ground. Future reference, if you are confused about whether a girl can consent, see if she can speak an entire sentence. You couldn't even do that. Just one coherent string of words. Where was the confusion? This is common sense, human decency.

According to him, the only reason we were on the ground was because I fell down. Note: if a girl falls down, help her get back up. If she is too drunk to even walk and falls down, do not mount her, hump her, take off her underwear, and insert your hand inside her vagina. If a girl falls down, help her up. If she is wearing a cardigan over her dress, don't take it off so that you can touch her breasts. Maybe she is cold, maybe that's why she wore the cardigan.

Next in the story, two Swedes on bicycles approached you and you ran. When they tackled you why didn't say, "Stop! Everything's okay, go ask her, she's right over there, she'll tell you." I mean you had just asked for my consent, right? I was awake, right? When the policeman arrived and interviewed the evil Swede who tackled you, he was crying so hard he couldn't speak because of what he'd seen.

Your attorney has repeatedly pointed out, "Well we don't know exactly when she became unconscious." And you're right—maybe I was still fluttering my eyes and wasn't completely limp yet. That was never the point. I was too drunk to speak English, too drunk to consent way before I was on the ground. I should have never been touched in the first place. Brock stated, "At no time did I see that she was not responding. If at any time I thought she was not responding, I would have stopped immediately." Here's the thing: if your plan was to stop only when I became unresponsive, then you still do not understand. You didn't even stop when I was unconscious anyway! Someone else stopped you. Two guys on bikes noticed I wasn't moving in the dark and had to tackle you. How did you not notice while on top of me?

You said, you would have stopped and gotten help. You say that, but I want you to explain how you would've helped me, step by step, walk me through this. I want to know, if those evil Swedes had not found me, how the night would have played out. I am asking you: Would you have pulled my underwear back on over my boots? Untangled the necklace wrapped around my neck? Closed my legs, covered me? Pick the pine needles from my hair? Asked if the abrasions on my neck and bottom hurt? Would you then go find a friend and say, "Will you help me get her somewhere warm and soft?" I don't sleep when I think about the way it could have gone if the two guys had never come. What would have happened to me? That's what you'll never have a good answer for, that's what you can't explain even after a year.

On top of all this, he claimed that I orgasmed after one minute of digital penetration. The nurse said there had been abrasions, lacerations, and dirt in my genitalia. Was that before or after I came?

To sit under oath and inform all of us, that yes I wanted it, yes I permitted it, and that you are the true victim attacked by Swedes for reasons unknown to you is appalling, is demented, is selfish, is damaging. It is enough to be suffering. It is another thing to have someone ruthlessly working to diminish the gravity of validity of this suffering.

My family had to see pictures of my head strapped to a gurney full of pine needles, of my body in the dirt with my eyes closed, hair messed up, limbs bent, and dress hiked up. And even after that, my family had to listen to your attorney say the pictures were after the fact, we can dismiss them. To say, "Yes her nurse confirmed there was redness and abrasions inside her, significant trauma to her genitalia, but that's what happens when you finger someone, and he's already admitted to that." To listen to your attorney attempt to paint a picture of me, the face of girls gone wild, as if somehow that would make it so that I had this coming for me. To listen to him say I sounded drunk on the phone because I'm silly and that's my goofy way of speaking. To point out that in the voicemail, I said I would reward my boyfriend and we all know what I was thinking. I assure you my rewards program is nontransferable, especially to any nameless man that approaches me.

He has done irreversible damage to me and my family during the trial and we have sat silently, listening to him shape the evening. But in the end, his unsupported statements and his attorney's twisted logic fooled no one. The truth won, the truth spoke for itself.

You are guilty. Twelve jurors convicted you guilty of three felony counts beyond reasonable doubt, that's twelve votes per count, thirty six yeses confirming guilt, that's one hundred percent, unanimous guilt. And I thought, *Finally it is over, finally he will own up to what he did, truly apologize, we will both move on and get better.* Then I read your statement.

If you are hoping that one of my organs will implode from anger and I will die, I'm almost there. You are very close. This is not a story of another drunk college hookup with poor decision making. Assault is not an accident. Somehow, you still don't get it. Somehow, you still sound confused. I will now read portions of the defendant's statement and respond to them.

You said, "Being drunk I just couldn't make the best decisions and neither could she."

Alcohol is not an excuse. Is it a factor? Yes. But alcohol was not the one who stripped me, fingered me, had my head dragging against the ground, with me almost fully naked. Having too much to drink was an amateur mistake that I admit to, but it is not criminal. Everyone in this room has had a night where they have regretted drinking too much, or knows someone close to them who has had a night where they have regretted drinking too much. Regretting drinking is not the same as regretting sexual assault. We were both drunk, the difference is I did not take off your pants and underwear, touch you inappropriately, and run away. That's the difference.

You said, "If I wanted to get to know her, I should have asked for her number, rather than asking her to go back to my room."

I'm not mad because you didn't ask for my number. Even if you did know me, I would not want to be in this situation. My own boyfriend knows me, but if he asked to finger me behind a dumpster, I would slap him. No girl wants to be in this situation. Nobody. I don't care if you know their phone number or not.

You said, "I stupidly thought it was okay for me to do what everyone around me was doing, which was drinking. I was wrong."

Again, you were not wrong for drinking. Everyone around you was not sexually assaulting me. You were wrong for doing what nobody else was doing, which was pushing your erect dick in your pants against my naked, defenseless body concealed in a dark area, where partygoers could no longer see or protect me, and my own sister could not find me. Sipping Fireball is not your crime. Peeling off and discarding my underwear like a candy wrapper to insert your finger into my body, is where you went wrong. Why am I still explaining this.

You said, "During the trial I didn't want to victimize her at all. That was just my attorney and his way of approaching the case."

Your attorney is not your scapegoat, he represents you. Did your attorney say some incredulously infuriating, degrading things? Absolutely. He said you had an erection, because it was cold.

You said you are in the process of establishing a program for high school and college students in which you speak about your experience to "speak out against the college campus drinking culture and the sexual promiscuity that goes along with that."

Campus drinking culture. That's what we're speaking out against? You think that's what I've spent the past year fighting for? Not awareness about campus sexual assault, or rape, or learning to recognize consent. Campus drinking culture. Down with Jack Daniels. Down with Skyy Vodka. If you want talk to people about drinking, go to an AA meeting. You realize, having a drinking problem is different than drinking and then forcefully trying to have sex with someone? Show men how to respect women, not how to drink less.

"Drinking culture and the sexual promiscuity that goes along with that." Goes along with that, like a side effect, like fries on the side of your order. Where does promiscuity even come into play? I don't see headlines that read, "Brock Turner, Guilty of Drinking Too Much and the Sexual Promiscuity That Goes along with That." Campus Sexual Assault: There's your first PowerPoint slide. Rest assured, if you fail to fix the topic of your talk, I will follow you to every school you go to and give a follow-up presentation.

Lastly you said, "I want to show people that one night of drinking can ruin a life."

A life, one life, yours, you forgot about mine. Let me rephrase for you, "I want to show people that one night of drinking can ruin two lives." You and me. You are the cause, I am the effect. You have dragged me through this hell with you, dipped me back into that night again and again. You knocked down both our towers, I collapsed at the same time you did. If you think I was spared, came out unscathed, that today I ride off into sunset, while you suffer the greatest blow, you are mistaken. Nobody wins. We have all been devastated; we have all been trying to find some meaning in all of this suffering. Your damage was concrete; stripped of titles, degrees, enrollment. My damage was internal, unseen, I carry it with me. You took away my worth, my privacy, my energy, my time, my safety, my intimacy, my confidence, my own voice, until today.

See, one thing we have in common is that we were both unable to get up in the morning. I am no stranger to suffering. You made me a victim. In newspapers my name was "unconscious intoxicated woman," ten syllables, and nothing more than that. For a while, I believed that that was all I was. I had to force myself to relearn my real name, my identity. To relearn that this is not all that I am. That I am not just a drunk victim at a frat party found behind a dumpster, while you are the all-American swimmer at a top university, innocent until proven guilty, with so much at stake. I am a human being who has been irreversibly hurt, my life was put on hold for over a year, waiting to figure out if I was worth something.

My independence, natural joy, gentleness, and steady lifestyle I had been enjoying became distorted beyond recognition. I became closed off, angry, self-deprecating, tired, irritable, empty. The isolation at times was unbearable. You cannot give me back the life I had before that night either. While you worry about your shattered reputation, I refrigerated spoons every night so when I woke up, and my eyes were puffy from crying, I would hold the spoons to my eyes to lessen the swelling so that I could see. I showed up an hour late to work every morning, excused myself to cry in the stairwells, I can tell you all the best places in that building to cry where no one can hear you. The pain became so bad that I had to explain the private details to my boss to let her know why I was leaving. I needed time because continuing day to day was not possible. I used my savings to go as far away as I could possibly be. I did not return to work full time as I knew I'd have to take weeks off in the future for the hearing and trial, that were constantly being rescheduled. My life was put on hold for over a year, my structure had collapsed.

I can't sleep alone at night without having a light on, like a five-year-old, because I have nightmares of being touched where I cannot wake up, I did this thing where I waited until the sun came up and I felt safe enough to sleep. For three months, I went to bed at six o'clock in the morning.

I used to pride myself on my independence, now I am afraid to go on walks in the evening, to attend social events with drinking among friends where I should be comfortable being. I have become a little barnacle always needing to be at someone's side, to have my boyfriend standing next to me, sleeping beside me, protecting me. It is embarrassing how feeble I feel, how timidly I move through life, always guarded, ready to defend myself, ready to be angry.

You have no idea how hard I have worked to rebuild parts of me that are still weak. It took me eight months to even talk about what happened. I could no longer connect with friends, with everyone around me. I would scream at my boyfriend, my own family, whenever they brought this up. You never let me forget what happened to me. At the end of the hearing, the trial, I was too tired to speak. I would leave drained, silent. I would go home turn off my phone and for days I would not speak. You bought me a ticket to a planet where I lived by myself. Every time a new article come out, I lived with the paranoia that my entire hometown would find out and know me as the girl who got assaulted. I didn't want anyone's pity and am still learning to accept victim as part of my identity. You made my own hometown an uncomfortable place to be.

You cannot give me back my sleepless nights. The way I have broken down sobbing uncontrollably if I'm watching a movie and a woman is harmed—to say it lightly, this experience has expanded my empathy for other victims. I have lost weight from stress; when people would comment I told them I've been running a lot lately. There are times I did not want to be touched. I have to relearn that I am not fragile, I am capable, I am wholesome, not just livid and weak.

When I see my younger sister hurting, when she is unable to keep up in school, when she is deprived of joy, when she is not sleeping, when she is crying so hard on the phone she is barely breathing, telling me over and over again she is sorry for leaving me alone that night, "Sorry, sorry, sorry," when she feels more guilt than you, then I do not forgive you. That night I had called her to try and find her, but you found me first. Your attorney's closing statement began, "[Her sister] said she was fine and who knows her better than her sister." You tried to use my own sister against me? Your points of attack were so weak, so low, it was almost embarrassing. You do not touch her.

You should have never done this to me. Secondly, you should have never made me fight so long to tell you, you should have never done this to me. But here we are. The damage is done, no one can undo it. And now we both have a choice. We can let this destroy us, I can remain angry and hurt and you can be in denial, or we can face it head on, I accept the pain, you accept the punishment, and we move on.

Your life is not over, you have decades of years ahead to rewrite your story. The world is huge, it is so much bigger than Palo Alto and Stanford, and you will make a space for yourself in it where you can be useful and happy. But right now, you do not get to shrug your shoulders and be confused anymore. You do not get to pretend that there were no red flags. You have been convicted of violating me, intentionally, forcibly, sexually, with malicious intent, and all you can admit to is consuming alcohol. Do not talk about the sad way your life was upturned because alcohol made you do bad things. Figure out how to take responsibility for your own conduct.

Now to address the sentencing. When I read the probation officer's report, I was in disbelief, consumed by anger which eventually quieted down to profound sadness. My statements have been slimmed down to distortion and taken out of context. I fought hard during this trial and will not have the outcome minimized by a probation officer who attempted to evaluate my current state and my wishes in a fifteen-minute conversation, the majority of which was spent answering questions I had about the legal system. The context is also important. Brock had yet to issue a statement, and I had not read his remarks.

My life has been on hold for over a year, a year of anger, anguish and uncertainty, until a jury of my peers rendered a judgment that validated the injustices I had endured. Had Brock admitted guilt and remorse and offered to settle early on, I would have considered a lighter sentence, respecting his honesty, grateful to be able to move our lives forward. Instead he took the risk of going to trial, added insult to injury, and forced me to relive the hurt as details about my personal life and sexual assault were brutally dissected before the public. He pushed me and my family through a year of inexplicable, unnecessary suffering, and should face the consequences of challenging his crime, of putting my pain into question, of making us wait so long for justice.

I told the probation officer I do not want Brock to rot away in prison. I did not say he does not deserve to be behind bars. The probation officer's recommendation of a year or less in county jail is a soft time-out, a mockery of the seriousness of his assaults, an insult to me and all women. It gives the message that a stranger can be inside you without proper consent and he will receive less than what has been defined as the minimum sentence. Probation should be denied. I also told the probation officer that what I truly wanted was for Brock to get it, to understand and admit to his wrongdoing.

Unfortunately, after reading the defendant's report, I am severely disappointed and feel that he has failed to exhibit sincere remorse or responsibility for his conduct. I fully respected his right to a trial, but even after twelve jurors unanimously convicted him guilty of three felonies, all he has admitted to doing is ingesting alcohol. Someone who cannot take full accountability for his actions does not deserve a mitigating sentence. It is deeply offensive that he would try and dilute rape with a suggestion of "promiscuity." By definition, rape is the absence of promiscuity, rape is the absence of consent, and it perturbs me deeply that he can't even see that distinction.

The probation officer factored in that the defendant is youthful and has no prior convictions. In my opinion, he is old enough to know what he did was wrong. When you are eighteen in this country, you can go to war. When you are nineteen, you are old enough to pay the consequences for attempting to rape someone. He is young, but he is old enough to know better.

As this is a first offense I can see where leniency would beckon. On the other hand, as a society, we cannot forgive everyone's first sexual assault or digital rape.

It doesn't make sense. The seriousness of rape has to be communicated clearly—we should not create a culture that suggests we learn that rape is wrong through trial and error. The consequences of sexual assault needs to be severe enough that people feel enough fear to exercise good judgment even if they are drunk, severe enough to be preventative.

The probation officer weighed the fact that he has surrendered a hard-earned swimming scholarship. How fast Brock swims does not lessen the severity of what happened to me, and should not lessen the severity of his punishment. If a first time offender from an underprivileged background was accused of three felonies and displayed no accountability for his actions other than drinking, what would his sentence be? The fact that Brock was an athlete at a private university should not be seen as an entitlement to leniency, but as an opportunity to send a message that sexual assault is against the law regardless of social class.

The probation officer has stated that this case, when compared to other crimes of similar nature, may be considered less serious due to the defendant's level of intoxication. It felt serious. That's all I'm going to say.

What has he done to demonstrate that he deserves a break? He has only apologized for drinking and has yet to define what he did to me as sexual assault; he has revictimized me continually, relentlessly. He has been found guilty of three serious felonies and it is time for him to accept the consequences of his actions. He will not be quietly excused.

He is a lifetime sex registrant. That doesn't expire. Just like what he did to me doesn't expire, doesn't just go away after a set number of years. It stays with me; it's part of my identity; it has forever changed the way I carry myself, the way I live the rest of my life.

To conclude, I want to say, "Thank you." To everyone from the intern who made me oatmeal when I woke up at the hospital that morning, to the deputy who waited beside me, to the nurses who calmed me, to the detective who listened to me and never judged me, to my advocates who stood unwaveringly beside me, to my therapist who taught me to find courage in vulnerability, to my boss for being kind and understanding, to my incredible parents who teach me how to turn pain into strength, to my grandma who snuck chocolate into the courtroom throughout this to give to me, my friends who remind me how to be happy, to my boyfriend who is patient and loving, to my unconquerable sister who is the other half of my heart, to Alaleh, my idol, who fought tirelessly and never doubted me. Thank you to everyone involved in the trial for their time and attention. Thank you to girls across the nation that wrote cards to my DA to give to me, so many strangers who cared for me.

Most importantly, thank you to the two men who saved me, who I have yet to meet. I sleep with two bicycles that I drew taped above my bed to remind myself there are heroes in this story. That we are looking out for one another. To have known all of these people, to have felt their protection and love, is something I will never forget.

And finally, to girls everywhere, I am with you. On nights when you feel alone, I am with you. When people doubt you or dismiss you, I am with you. I fought every day for you. So never stop fighting, I believe you. As the author Anne Lamott once wrote, "Lighthouses don't go running all over an island looking for boats to save; they just stand there shining." Although I can't save every boat, I hope that by speaking today, you absorbed a small amount of light, a small knowing that you can't be silenced, a small satisfaction that justice was served, a small assurance that we are getting somewhere, and a big, big knowing that you are important, unquestionably, you are untouchable, you are beautiful, you are to be valued, respected, undeniably, every minute of every day, you are powerful and nobody can take that away from you. To girls everywhere, I am with you. Thank you.

For Further Reading

Aguilera, Jasmine. "House Members Unite to Read Stanford Rape Victim's Letter." *The New York Times*, 16 June 2016, https://www.nytimes.com/2016/06/17/us/politics/congress-stanford-letter.html.

Anonymous. "Stanford Sexual Assault Case Survivor Emily Doe Speaks Out." *Glamour*, Nov. 2016, www.glamour.com/story/women-of-the-year-emily-doe.

Fantz, Ashley, and Amanda Wills. "Who Is the Judge Who Gave Brock Turner 6 Months?" *CNN*, 9 June 2016, www.cnn.com/2016/06/08/us/aaron-persky-brock-turner-stanford-rape/index.html.

Koren, Marina. "Telling the Story of the Stanford Rape Case." *The Atlantic*, 6 June 2016, www.theatlantic.com/news/archive/2016/06/stanford-sexual-assault-letters/485837/.

León, Concepción De. "You Know Emily Doe's Story. Now Learn Her Name." *The New York Times*, 4 Sept. 2019, www.nytimes.com/2019/09/04/books/chanel-miller-brock-turner-assault-stanford.html.

Miller, Chanel. *Know My Name: A Memoir*. Viking, 2019.

Rape Response Services. www.rrsonline.org/.

IV

Rhetorics of Education

According to the United Nations, education is not a privilege: it is a universal human right. And in the twenty-first century—in Latin America, Europe, East Asia, and the United States—girls, once denied education, are surpassing boys in secondary and postsecondary enrollment and graduation ("How Far"). While this is promising news, the fuller picture is more complicated, since access does not guarantee inclusion, safety, or equity. The rhetors in this section urge us to examine how our schools reinforce practices and values that obstruct girls' and women's educational opportunities, particularly for those of color.

Malala Yousafzai's speech to the United Nations serves as a sobering reminder of the 130 million girls around the globe who are denied safe and equitable education due to poverty, war, and gender discrimination. Known as the girl who was shot for going to school, Yousafzai issues a moving call to world leaders to ensure children access to education. Turning our attention to inequity in the United States, Jemelleh Coes offers a powerful challenge to the "pushout" culture of education experienced by black girls (Morris), which mischaracterizes and devalues them; as the mother of a black daughter, Coes addresses a letter to her daughter's teachers, imploring them to see the full humanity and potential of the black girls they teach.

Addressing intersectional issues at the postsecondary level, Angy Rivera, Jennine Capó Crucet, and Adrienne Keene each share their experiences to extend support to Native, undocumented, Latinx, and first-generation students on their educational journeys. In so doing, they point to hurdles that such students may encounter: depression and isolation, lack of representation in curricula, and loss of connection with those at home. In each case, these rhetors offer community and recognition to students of color, insisting that they are welcome and that they belong.

Women continue to be underrepresented in STEM (Science, Technology, Engineering, and Math) and, in fact, there has been no employment growth from women in STEM jobs since 2000 (Hedges). The problem begins as early as elementary school, when, studies show, girls are not adequately encouraged in math and science. And for those who do eventually choose to focus on STEM as college students, as Janet Tsai did, women often feel marginalized and fraudulent in male-dominated classrooms. As Tsai discovers, it is important for female scientists to be visible, something the scientist Katharine Hayhoe has mastered—drawing from her ethos as a climate change scientist and an evangelical Christian, she is not only a role model for female scientists but she agilely employs her intersectional ethos to educate wider Christian audiences, who often disbelieve climate science.

Another impediment to women's education is lack of safety: one in five college women experiences sexual assault (Office on Women's Health). Wagatwe Wanjuki's gripping letter to Tufts University describes the academic, psychological, and economic consequences experienced when survivors of sexual assault are not supported by their institutions. Protesting a bathroom bill that would endanger her transgender child, Kimberly Shappley, a Republican and evangelical Christian, describes the essential role self-education played in learning to understand and support her daughter. She urges fellow Christians to seek out education on transgender issues, so all children can feel safe and recognized in and beyond school. Ananya Roy, writing at the time of the 2008 economic recession, addresses yet another obstacle to educational access: the skyrocketing costs of postsecondary education and the subsequent debilitating debt students face upon graduation.

Marjane Satrapi provides a transnational perspective on girls' education, in the form of a graphic memoir frequently taught in middle and high schools across the United States. The included excerpt captures her experience as a young student who must navigate the tension between the Iranian government's edict that girls must wear a veil in public and her own desire for freedom and self-expression.

The section closes with an excerpt from Jessica Valenti's *Full Frontal Feminism*, which offers young readers a feminist, positive approach to sex education. In contrast to the three-quarters of high schools focused on abstinence-only sex education (Carroll), which conflates female sexuality activity with impurity, Valenti advocates for an approach to sex that is responsible, safe, and enjoyable. She, like all rhetors in this section, reminds us that access to education is a minimum requirement—the ultimate goal is to create systems that foster inclusive, safe, supportive atmospheres in which girls and women can thrive.

WORKS CITED

Carroll, Aaron E. "Sex Education Based on Abstinence? There's a Real Absence of Evidence." *The New York Times*, 22 Aug. 2017, www.nytimes.com/2017/08/22/upshot/sex-education-based-on-ab stinence-theres-a-real-absence-of-evidence.html.

Hedges, Kristi. "STEM Fields and the Gender Gap: Where Are the Women?" *Forbes*, 2 Aug. 2012, www.forbes.com/sites/work-in-progress/2012/06/20/stem-fields-and-the-gender-gap-where -are-the-women/.

"How Far Will Her Success Ripple Out to Others?" *ShareAmerica*, 24 Mar. 2016, share.america.gov/ women-have-right-education/.

Morris, Monique W. *Pushout: The Criminalization of Black Girls in Schools*. New Press, 2018.

Office on Women's Health, US Department of Health. "Sexual Assault on College Campuses Is Common." *Women's Health*, 13 Sept. 2018, www.womenshealth.gov/relationships-and-safety/sexual -assault-and-rape/college-sexual-assault.

Malala Yousafzai

Malala Yousafzai is a vivid example of the power—and perceived threat—of girls' activism in the twenty-first century. When Yousafzai was fifteen years old, a masked gunman boarded her school bus and fired two bullets in the young Pakistani girl's head. The shooter was a member of the Taliban, a terrorist organization, who deemed Yousafzai a threat to Islam because she advocated for girls' right to education.

Yousafzai was born in 1997 in Swat Valley, known as the "Switzerland of Pakistan." Her father, Ziaudden, marked her birth by entering her name on a family register, breaking the patriarchal tradition of only recognizing sons. A strong advocate for education and women's rights, Ziaudden founded the school Yousafzai and her brothers attended. Beginning in 2007, though, Yousafzai's education—and the Pakistani way of life—were deeply threatened when the Taliban gained control of the region. In 2008 the Taliban banned girls from attending school. When asked if he still allowed his children to attend, Yousafzai's father told CNN, "[Yousafzai] is insistent she continues going to school . . . It is her right to get an education, but in any case, I'm not sure even if I tried if I could stop her!" (Mohsin).

Yousafzai could not be stopped from attending school, nor could she be silenced. When she was eleven years old, Yousafzai's father took her to a press club to deliver a speech to national press titled "How Dare the Taliban Take Away My Basic Right to an Education?" Yousafzai also blogged for the BBC under the pen name Gul Makai, recording the realities of daily life under the terrorist regime, gaining her a worldwide following. In 2009 the Pakistan Army entered into combat with the Taliban in the Swat region, and the violence forced Yousafzai's family to flee the area. Once Pakistan regained control of Swat, her family returned home, and her father assumed it was safe to reveal Yousafzai as the author of the BCC blog. This revelation made Yousafzai both a celebrity—she was nominated by Desmond Tutu for the International Children's Peace Prize and won Pakistan's National Youth Peace Prize—and the Taliban's latest target.

Yousafzai's assassination attempt sparked international outrage. She underwent surgery in England, later crediting her astonishing recovery to prayers of support from around the world. Speaking after release from the hospital, she fearlessly recommitted to activism: "God has given me this new life. I want to serve the people. I want every girl, every child, to be educated." She would later go on to record her story in the bestselling memoir *I Am Malala* and to receive the Nobel Peace Prize, the youngest laureate in history.

The following speech, part of the United Nations Youth Takeover, marks Yousafzai's first formal public speaking event after the shooting. The speech was delivered on her sixteenth birthday, which the UN declared "Malala Day." Even as her striking individual contributions to girls' education are known around the world, Yousafzai uses this occasion to emphasize her connection and commitment to others. Cloaked in the shawl of Benazir Bhutto, the first female prime minister of Pakistan, who was assassinated in 2007, Yousafzai links her work to the peaceful and countercultural movements of Gandhi, Mother Teresa, and Jesus. In a violence-ridden world, Yousafzai argues for the power of knowledge and the shield of unity.

Speech to the United Nations, July 12, 2013

Bismillah al Rahman al Rahim. In the name of God, the most beneficent, the most merciful. Honorable UN secretary general Mr. Ban Ki-moon, respected president general assembly Vuk Jeremić, honorable UN envoy for global education Mr. Gordon Brown, respected elders and my dear brothers and sisters: *A salaam alaikum.*

Today, it is an honor for me to be speaking again after a long time. Being here with such honorable people is a great moment in my life. And it's an honor for me that today I am wearing a shawl of Benazir Bhutto Shaheed.

I don't know where to begin my speech. I don't know what people would be expecting me to say. But first of all, thank you to God for whom we all are equal, and thank you to every person who has prayed for my fast recovery and a new life. I cannot believe how much love people have shown me. I have received thousands of good-wish cards and gifts from all over the world. Thank you to all of them. Thank you to the children whose innocent words encouraged me. Thank you to my elders whose prayers strengthened me.

I would like to thank my nurses, doctors, and all of the staff of the hospitals in Pakistan and the UK. And the UAE [United Arab Emirates] government, who have helped me get better and recover my strength.

I fully support Mr. Ban Ki-moon, the secretary general, in his Global Education First Initiative, and the work of the UN special envoy Mr. Gordon Brown. And the respected president of the General Assembly, Vuk Jeremić. I thank all of them for their leadership, which they continue to give. They continue to inspire all of us to action.

But, dear brothers and sisters, do remember one thing. Malala Day is not my day. Today is the day of every woman, every boy, and every girl who have raised their voice for their rights. There are hundreds of human rights activists and social workers who are not only speaking for their rights but who are struggling to achieve their goals of peace, education, and equality. Thousands of people have been killed by the terrorists and millions have been injured. I am just one of them.

So here I stand . . . so here I stand, one girl among many.

I speak—not for myself, but so those without voice can be heard. Those who have fought for their rights.

Their right to live in peace.

Their right to be treated with dignity.

Their right to equality of opportunity.

Their right to be educated.

Dear Friends, on the 9th of October 2012, the Taliban shot me on the left side of my forehead. They shot my friends, too. They thought that the bullets would silence us. But they failed. And out of that silence came thousands of voices. The terrorists thought that they would change my aims and stop my ambitions, but nothing changed in my life except this: weakness, fear, and hopelessness died. Strength, power, and courage were born.

I am the same Malala. My ambitions are the same. My hopes are the same. My dreams are the same.

Dear sisters and brothers, I am not against anyone. Neither am I here to speak in terms of personal revenge against the Taliban or any other terrorist group. I am here to speak up for the right of education of every child. I want education for the sons and the daughters of the Taliban, and all the terrorists and extremists.

I do not even hate the Talib who shot me. Even if there is a gun in my hand and he stands in front of me, I would not shoot him. This is the compassion that I have learnt from Muhammad, the prophet of mercy, and Jesus Christ and Lord Buddha. This is the legacy of change that I have inherited from Martin Luther King [Jr], Nelson Mandela, and Muhammad Ali Jinnah. This is the philosophy of nonviolence that I have learnt from Gandhiji [Gandhi], Bacha Khan, and Mother Teresa. And this is the forgiveness that I have learnt from my mother and father. This is what my soul is telling me, be peaceful and love everyone.

Dear sisters and brothers, we realize the importance of light when we see darkness. We realize the importance of our voice when we are silenced. In the same way, when we were in Swat, the north of Pakistan, we realized the importance of pens and books when we saw the guns.

The wise saying "the pen is mightier than sword" was true. The extremists were and are afraid of books and pens. The power of education frightens them. They are afraid of women. The power of the voice of women frightens them. And that is why they killed fourteen innocent students in the recent attack in Quetta. And that is why they killed female teachers and polio workers in Khyber Pakhtunkhwa. That is why they are blasting schools every day. Because they were and they are afraid of change, afraid of the equality that we will bring into our society.

And I remember that there was a boy in our school who was asked by a journalist, "Why are the Taliban against education?" He answered very simply. By pointing to his book, he said, "A Talib doesn't know what is written inside this book." They think that God is a tiny little conservative being who would send girls to the hell just because of going to school. The terrorists are misusing the name of Islam and Pashtun society for their own personal benefits. Pakistan is a peace-loving, democratic country. Pashtuns want education for their daughters and sons. And Islam is a religion of peace, humanity, and brotherhood. Islam says it is not only each child's right to get education—rather, it is their duty and responsibility.

Honorable secretary general, peace is necessary for education. In many parts of the world, especially Pakistan and Afghanistan, terrorism, wars, and conflicts stop children to go to their schools. We are really tired of these wars.

Women and children are suffering in many ways, in many parts of the world. In India, innocent and poor children are victims of child labor. Many schools have been destroyed in Nigeria. People in Afghanistan have been affected by the hurdles of extremism for decades. Young girls have to do domestic child labor and are forced to get married at early age. Poverty, ignorance, injustice, racism, and the deprivation of basic rights are the main problems faced by both men and women.

So dear sisters and brothers, now it's time to speak up. So today, we call upon the world leaders to change their strategic policies in favor of peace and prosperity.

We call upon the world leaders that all the peace deals must protect women and children's rights. A deal that goes against the rights of women is unacceptable.

We call upon all governments to ensure free compulsory education all over the world for every child.

We call upon all governments to fight against terrorism and violence, to protect children from brutality and harm.

We call upon the developed nations to support the expansion of educational opportunities for girls in the developing world.

We call upon all the communities to be tolerant—to reject prejudice based on cast, creed, sect, religion, or gender. To ensure freedom and equality for women so that they can flourish. We cannot all succeed when half of us are held back.

We call upon our sisters around the world to be brave—to embrace the strength within themselves and realize their full potential.

Dear brothers and sisters, we want schools and education for every child's bright future. We will continue our journey to our destination of peace and education. No one can stop us. We will speak up for our rights and we will bring change through our voice. We believe in the power and the strength of our words. Our words can change the whole world.

Because we are all together, united for the cause of education. And if we want to achieve our goal, then let us empower ourselves with the weapon of knowledge and let us shield ourselves with unity and togetherness.

Dear brothers and sisters, we must not forget that millions of people are suffering from poverty, injustice, and ignorance. We must not forget that millions of children are out of their schools. We must not forget that our sisters and brothers are waiting for a bright, peaceful future.

So let us wage a global struggle against illiteracy, poverty, and terrorism. Let us pick up our books and pens. *They* are our most powerful weapons.

One child, one teacher, one book, and one pen can change the world.

Education is the only solution. Education first.

Thank you.

FOR FURTHER READING

"Interactive Timeline: Malala Yousafzai's Extraordinary Journey." *Time*, n.d., http://poy.time.com
    /2012/12/19/interactive-timeline-malala-yousafzai/.
Malala Fund. www.malala.org/.
"Malala Yousafzai." *Biography*, 29 Mar. 2018, www.biography.com/people/malala-yousafzai-2136
    2253.
Mohsin, Saima. "Malala's Father Brings Hope of a Brighter Future for Pakistan's Women." *CNN*, 11
    Oct. 2013, www.cnn.com/2013/10/11/world/asia/pakistan-malala-father-mohsin/index.html.
Yousafzai, Malala, with Christina Lamb. *I Am Malala: How One Girl Stood up for Education and
    Changed the World*. Little, Brown, 2013.

Jemelleh Coes

Jemelleh Coes is a mother, teacher, and education advocate who remembers well her experience of being a black girl in school. In her public letter shared here, she draws from the strength of this intersectional identity to argue that our US public education system too often overlooks, and works against, black girls. The daughter of immigrant parents and a first-generation college student, Coes acknowledges that while she "made it because of her education," she also made it in spite of her schooling.

Thanks to the work of Coes, the 2014 Georgia State Teacher of the Year, as well as to scholars like Monique Morris and Brittney Cooper, educators are gaining deeper insight into how schools work against black girls. For instance, black girls are often stereotyped as defiant or sassy and, therefore, disrespectful; they are punished at rates even more disproportionate than are black boys (Kamenetz). Black girls also experience "age compression." Hypersexualized in society's eyes, they don't have a chance to be girls—in others' eyes, and thus, in their own. This in turn leads to harassment, abuse, and sexual exploitation. Furthermore, African American girls are overrepresented in juvenile centers, where they describe schoolwork as "repetitive, uninspiring, and often below their skill level" (Chang).

Coes seeks to intervene in black girls' schooling long before they suffer these consequences. A middle-grade teacher pursuing a doctorate in education, Coes begins with the teachers. Through the epistolary form, she creates an intimacy with her recipients, while allowing a larger audience to listen in. While she, too, is an educator, Coes's strongest appeal comes from her location as a mother: see my daughter as I do, she implores, as an "inquisitive, funny, opinionated, loquacious, creative" girl. She reminds teachers that black girls are gifted students with potential for leadership—if that potential is nurtured. By repeating the phrases *black girls are* and *black girls need*, Coes works to both rewrite cultural images of black girls, and to emphasize how schooling must change in order to better see and serve them.

"To the Educators Who Will Teach
My Black Daughter"

Education Week, 2017

Every holiday season, I celebrate the year with my sorority sisters, a group of professional women of color. The conversation often turns to the topic of education, including our observations about how education can empower, and at the same time marginalize, oppress, and discriminate.

We find ourselves returning to this topic because my sisters and I were all Black girls raised in the American public school system. Because we have become educators, nurses, lawyers, business owners, and dedicated professionals, many acknowledge our successes, and say we've "made it because of our education." What they often do not see is that many of us have achieved our career goals *in spite of* our nation's public education systems rather than *because of* them. (Note: *Pushout* by Monique Morris does an excellent job of detailing the dangers of this phenomenon.)

My daughter's name is Gabby. She's three, a true threenager—inquisitive, funny, opinionated, loquacious, creative. I often wonder how attending public school will affect her self-esteem, her intellectual and emotional well-being, and her safety. She already has questions and well-formulated demands about her appearance, noting that girls should have long, straight and European-like hair. She is bombarded by messages about gender roles, and she attempts to actualize her own gender within those parameters. "Girls clean up the house, and boys go to work," she reminds me. I worry that as she enters public school, often away from my watchful parental surveillance, she will be exposed to even more specific parameters and possibly negative stereotypes of what Black girls are "supposed" to do and be.

My anxieties are deeply rooted in my experiences as a schoolteacher. I have intimate knowledge about how the education system may not act in her best interest. At three, she has yet to experience the wide range of road bumps and brick walls that she will have to navigate and negotiate. But, as an educator, I know the power of educators. I believe that if they are conscientious and intentional about their interaction, most will do right by Gabby and the other Black girls—girls who still trust teachers to care for and nurture them.

Here is what I need her educators to know:

Black girls are gifted. They are worthy, intelligent, and capable of greatness (like all students). However, sometimes their giftedness is overlooked until it is too late. Too often we educators miss critical opportunities to help them develop their talents.

Black girls are leaders. Their leadership abilities are often stifled because those abilities are falsely categorized as anger, aggression, rebellion, sassiness, and/or bossiness. Instead, educators should recognize their skills and help them channel their abilities in productive and beneficial ways.

Black girls need to see and study other Black women regularly. If a parent asks when you will provide instruction about Black women, and your first thought is *February* (Black History Month) or *March* (Women's History Month), you have missed the point! Black girls need to know that they are not regulated to two of the ten school months, and that Black women have made some of the most important contributions to our world throughout history. The recently released film *Hidden Figures* is a perfect example of this. Integrate Black women and girls throughout your curriculum.

Black girls need you to know their history. Educators need a thorough understanding of American history coupled with specific attention to Black history in order to help Black girls foster a critical understanding of their history, present, or future. Do not shy away from the ugliness; they'll know that you are being dishonest or short-sighted. Help them think through the truth so that they may become agents of change, develop compassion for others, and learn to advocate for themselves.

Black girls want to understand the world beyond the one that is in front of them. They are interested in exploring many different opportunities. Show them unforeseen possibilities, support them in creating new ones, and help them prepare a path to achieve their goals. Make sure they know that Black girls do science, technology, engineering, and math very well. Show them that Black women are scholars, world-changers, community builders, and leaders.

Black girls are resilient. NOTE: Resiliency is a last resort, not a starting place. Start with love, attention, and care, and if a given situation demands resiliency, they will exercise it. In fact, they are created from it. They do not need practice using it. Resiliency comes at a price, and constantly having to tap into it takes a toll physically, emotionally, and psychologically. Sometimes educators unintentionally ignore, forget, or dismiss the needs or concerns of Black girls by overlooking the fact that many Black girls are expected to thrive in spaces where they see few and/or negative representations of themselves; where they regularly combat "angry Black woman" stereotypes; where they embrace the responsibility of community care by postponing attention to self-care; where they persistently aspire to higher expectations than the ones others have placed on them; and where they are cast off into the margins when they should be front and center.

Dear Educator, please SEE MY DAUGHTER. Do not look past her. Do not look through her. Look at her. Teach her. Challenge her. Learn with her. Remind her that she is more than enough. Be honest with her. If you do, she will learn that you are a trusted part of her community, and she will know that you carry that lauded responsibility each time she enters your classroom.

FOR FURTHER READING

Chang, Clio. "How Black Girls Are Locked Out of America's Schools." *New Republic*, 14 Mar. 2016, www.newrepublic.com/article/131482/black-girls-locked-americas-schools.

Cooper, Brittney. "Black Girls' Zero-Sum Struggle: Why We Lose When Black Boys Dominate the Discourse." *Salon*, 6 Mar. 2014, www.salon.com/2014/03/06/black_girls_zero_sum_struggle _why_we_lose_when_black_men_dominate_the_discourse/.

Crenshaw, Kimberlé Williams, et al. *Black Girls Matter: Pushed Out, Overpoliced and Underprotected. African American Policy Forum*, 2015, https://www.atlanticphilanthropies.org/ wp-content/uploads/2015/09/BlackGirlsMatter_Report.pdf.

Kamenetz, Anya. "The Untold Stories of Black Girls." *NPR*, 23 Mar. 2016, www.npr.org/sections/ ed/2016/03/23/471267584/the-untold-stories-of-black-girls.

Morris, Monique W. *Pushout: The Criminalization of Black Girls in Schools.* New Press, 2016.

Angy Rivera

Colombian-born Angy Rivera grew up undocumented, raised by her single mother, who repeatedly warned Rivera of the great risks of revealing her status. But in 2010, when she was nineteen, Rivera discovered the New York State Youth Leadership Council, a youth-led organization for undocumented immigrants, and found the courage to come out. She began an advice blog, *Ask Angy*, for other undocumented people and soon found herself the subject of the 2015 documentary *Don't Tell Anyone (No Le Digas a Nadie)*. The film follows Rivera's escape from war-torn Columbia, her struggles with an inequitable immigration system, and her courageous turn to activism. It also addresses her experience of sexual abuse, an all too common experience for undocumented women.

In this piece Rivera candidly describes her decision to come out as undocumented. The *Progressive* reprinted the piece originally posted in 2012 after President Obama announced he would move forward with immigration reform, despite resistance from Republicans. Various versions of the DREAM Act—geared to provide a path toward US citizenship to those brought to the United States as children—have been proposed since 2001 but, as of this writing, none have passed. In the meantime, in 2012 Janet Napolitano, former secretary of the Department of Homeland Security, created Deferred Action for Childhood Arrivals (DACA) under the Obama administration to protect those eligible from deportation and to provide work authorization, renewable every two years. As Rivera explains, DACA students may attend college, but they are not eligible for federal aid. As of this writing, the Trump administration has vacillated on DACA, largely touting a strict anti-immigration stance.

While Rivera's narrative is shared in a straightforward, linear way, her decision was laden with psychological challenges, particularly as she defied her mother's advice, "Don't tell anyone," borne from worry for their safety and livelihood. As Rivera explains elsewhere, she chose the language of "coming out" deliberately, inspired by the many queer women who led immigration rights activism (Herwees). Rivera shares the great risks to her and her family, as well as the painful stigma of living undocumented amid the narrow, ill-informed, and often racist mainstream conversations on immigration. Along the way, she describes her mother's evolution in accepting Rivera's outing and tentatively sharing her own story. Rivera's narrative builds on the rich history of women coming out of the shadows in their refusal to be invisible or silenced. In doing so, Rivera has succeeded not only in reaching other undocumented people but in working to shift the cultural conversation about immigration in the United States.

"DREAMer: Coming out as Undocumented"

The *Progressive*, 2014

When I was younger, I knew I was undocumented. My mother would always tell me we didn't have papers. She would waitress and bartend to make ends meet, and she even took up construction work despite her small frame. But I didn't believe that my immigration status would make my life difficult. After all, I was being raised in America, the land of opportunities.

Instead of opportunities, I found fear. My mother's friends suggested we go into hiding and stay away from public places like hospitals, post offices, and airports. I was warned never to reveal our secret to anyone.

It wasn't until I became a high school student that my immigration status actually started to make an impact on my life. I accompanied my friends as they applied for working papers. I listened to them discuss their adventures at the DMV, as well as their tales about voting for the first time and traveling outside of the country. I sat and stared from the passenger's seat—never the driver's seat. I silently struggled with this exclusion, not knowing that I wasn't the only person in the state, or the country, in this situation.

When I was a senior, I attended a City Youth Conference at John Jay College of Criminal Justice that highlighted several issues faced by Latino youth. One of the workshops was about immigration. I first heard about the DREAM Act, and undocumented youth organizing in the state of New York, during this workshop that was facilitated by the New York State Youth Leadership Council. I listened carefully, took notes, collected handouts, and signed up for their newsletter, but I never revealed my immigration status.

I was accepted into several colleges, but the problem was financing my education. In June 2009 I found myself walking across a stage, receiving my high school diploma with my first semester of college covered with the help of the Leadership Council's fellowship program and my mother's savings. I felt guilty for having her spend her hard-earned money on me, and I swore that it would never happen again. I would attend college in the fall of August 2009 and would make it on my own.

I became more actively involved with the council during this time, and it was there that the wall I had built around myself to protect my secret—and my mother's—would be put to the test. In solidarity with the Immigrant Youth Justice League in Illinois, we decided to host our first Coming Out of the Shadows event in New York in March 2010. This would be the first time undocumented youth publicly declared their undocumented status. I would be one of them. I had been practicing my story for some months already with other members of the organization, and I couldn't get past the first sentence without my vision being clouded by tears. My throat would close up, and I couldn't get a word out after that. We started spray-painting T-shirts with the slogan "I am undocumented." I took mine home, preparing myself for what I would be telling my mom once she saw it.

I still have her tears from the night I told her I would be coming out—tears laced with fear, etched on my heart. My mom blankly stared at me, and then she accused me of wanting to put myself and our family at risk. I was going against all the warnings she had given me. The look in her eyes convinced me that this was something I needed to do, not just for myself but also for her.

I couldn't stand to see how government officials had power over my mother's freedom and over mine, as well.

I couldn't stand to see how each day we were living in fear pretending to be invisible. We were settling for anything that was handed to us instead of demanding to be treated as equals and to have our voices heard.

In her eyes, I saw that she believed the entire stigma attached to our undocumented status, and it angered me. This anger pushed me further into action as I laid my shirt out and got the rest of my clothes ready for the big day.

Coming out wasn't as bad as I thought it would be. Yes, there were immigration agents at the event listening to our stories. But none of them said anything or approached us in any way. They just stood there trying to intimidate us or maybe they were mocking us, but no one paid attention to them. There was a small group of us, full of love and support each time someone shared his or her story. We shed happy tears of freedom, and we gave hugs all around.

Coming out was an emotional experience that I will never regret. I was able to state something about myself that had remained hidden for so long. I didn't have to lie about not having a license, not receiving financial aid or not being able to travel back to my country of origin.

Coming out was like breaking invisible chains that tied me down. I crushed my chains and my mother's—all at once.

Two years later, my mother has not joined me at a coming out event, but she has completed her first interview, through the phone, with a reporter, and she even let an online magazine publish a photo of her. At her own pace, my mother has been able to let go of her fears, partly by watching me do it. She is still scared to wear the T-shirt; however, she has shared her story more openly with friends and has come to a realization that hiding won't change anything. My mother is a courageous woman who left everything behind to provide both of us with a better life. My mother's story goes untold in so many spaces. When her experience is actually shared, she is criminalized for wanting to raise her daughter in a safer living condition.

It is up to me to make sure she is elevated and acknowledged through my story. By coming out, I didn't only embrace my story and my struggle, but I embraced my mother, too.

For Further Reading

"About." *New York State Youth Leadership Council*, n.d., https://www.nysylc.org/what-we-do.

"Ask Angy." *New York State Youth Leadership Council*, n.d., www.nysylc.org/askangy/.

"Fact Sheet: The Dream Act, DACA, and Other Policies Designed to Protect Dreamers." *American Immigration Council*, 3 June 2019, www.americanimmigrationcouncil.org/research/dream-act -daca-and-other-policies-designed-protect-dreamers.

Herwees, Tasbeeh. "Angy Rivera's Journey to 'Coming Out' as an Undocumented Immigrant." *Vice*, 25 Sept. 2015, www.vice.com/en_us/article/jmad9p/what-its-like-to-come-out-as-an-undocument ed-immigrant-263.

Madrid, Isis. "Angy Rivera Hopes to Make 'Coming Out' as Undocumented Less Taboo." *PRI*, 15 Sept. 2015, https://www.pri.org/stories/2015-09-15/angy-rivera-hopes-make-coming-out-un documented-less-taboo.

Jennine Capó Crucet

Before Jennine Capó Crucet began her career as a university professor, she served as a college access counselor at One Voice, a nonprofit organization in Los Angeles that supports first-generation, low-income college students. Her 2015 debut novel—*Make Your Home among Strangers*, a *New York Times* Book Review Editor's Choice selection and the winner of the 2016 International Latino Book Award—is dedicated to three of those students. In an interview with the *Miami Herald*, Crucet explained, "They asked me for books to help them understand what they were about to do, coming from low-income backgrounds and going to a places where suddenly, they were going to be minorities. I thought, 'I have to write it! I'm the only one who can speak to these things the way these kids need to hear.' I let this book take over my life. I served it" (Ogle).

Crucet, a Cuban American first-generation student who left Miami to attend Cornell University, has firsthand experience with the loss, displacement, and discovery that accompanies departure from one's cultural home. So, too, does her narrator in the story included here, an excerpt from "How to Leave Hialeah," the last piece in Crucet's 2009 award-winning short-story collection by the same name. Crucet's incisive use of direct address and present tense infuses the prose with immediacy. Melding humor and deft cultural insight, her narrator offers instructions for navigating new cultural and social terrain, from losing one's virginity to trying out newly acquired academic language on one's working-class father.

The story is followed by a personal epilogue that describes Crucet's sometimes uneasy relationship with the piece because, despite being fiction, it feels close to her. Crucet comes to understand the powerful effect on readers who feel recognized in the story, seeing their experiences reflected and validated. Through the interplay of story and epilogue, we are given insight into the way a writer may re-experience her work, and its larger rhetorical purpose, through her readers. The combination of the story and epilogue first appeared in *Wise Latinas: Writers on Higher Education*, a collection of personal essays that documents the often untold experiences of Latina women across generations entering university life. While their stories narrate complex and sometimes alienating paths, the wisdom borne from these experiences provides support and community for the next generation of Latinas.

This attention to the next generation is a through line in Crucet's work, and her razor- sharp prose has resonated powerfully with audiences and critics alike. The acclaimed author Julia Alvarez declares Crucet "a young writer to watch for, sassy, smart, with an unerring ear for a community's voices, its losses, its over-the-top telenovela extravagances, and its poignant struggles to understand itself in a new land." *Make Your Home among Strangers* is being adapted into a TV drama and has been chosen as a "common read" (a book read by all first-year students) at more than twenty-five US colleges and universities, another way Crucet's writing supports students on their academic paths.

An associate professor of English and ethnic studies at the University of Nebraska–Lincoln and a contributing opinion writer for the *New York Times*, Crucet's recent work—an essay collection titled *My Time among the Whites*—examines race, gender, immigration, and the "American Dream" after the 2016 presidential election. In a politically divisive moment, Crucet once again speaks a truth in the way her readers need to hear.

"How to Leave Hialeah": Excerpt from *How to Leave Hialeah* and Epilogue

2009

It is impossible to leave without an excuse—something must push you out, at least at first. You won't go otherwise; you are happy, the weather is bright, and you have a car. It has a sunroof (which you call a moonroof—you're so quirky) and a thunderous muffler. After fifteen years of trial and error, you have finally arranged your bedroom furniture in a way that you and your father can agree on. You have a locker you can reach at Miami High. With so much going right, it is only when you're driven out like a fly waved through a window that you'll be outside long enough to realize that, barring the occasional hurricane, you won't die.

The most reliable (and admittedly the least empowering) way to excuse yourself from Hialeah is to date Michael Cardenas Junior. He lives two houses away from you and is very handsome and smart enough to feed himself and take you on dates. Your mother will love him because he plans to marry you in three years when you turn eighteen. He is nineteen. He also goes to Miami High, where he is very popular because he plays football and makes fun of reading. You are not so cool: you have a few friends, but all their last names start with the same letter as yours because, since first grade, your teachers have used the alphabet to assign your seats. Your friends have parents just like yours, and your moms are always hoping another mother comes along as a chaperone when you all go to the movies on Saturday nights because then they can compare their husbands' demands—*put my socks on for me before I get out of bed, I hate cold floors*, or *you have to make me my lunch because only your sandwiches taste good to me*—and laugh at how much they are like babies. Michael does not like your friends, but this is normal and to be expected since your friends occasionally use polysyllabic words. Michael will repeatedly try to have sex with you because you are a virgin and somewhat Catholic and he knows if you sleep together, you'll feel too guilty to ever leave him. Sex will be tempting because your best friend Carla is dating Michael's best friend Frankie, and Michael will swear on his father's grave that they're doing it. But you must hold out—you must push him off when he surprises you on your eight-month anniversary with a room at the Executive Inn by the airport and he has sprung for an entire five hours—because only then will he break up with you. This must happen, because even though you will get back together and break up two more times, it is during those broken-up weeks that you do things like research out-of-state colleges and sign up for community college classes at night to distract you from how pissed you are. This has the side effect of boosting your GPA.

During these same break-up weeks, Michael will use his fake ID to buy beer and hang out with Frankie, who, at the advice of an ex-girlfriend he slept with twice who's now living in Tallahassee, has applied to Florida State. They will talk about college girls, who they heard have sex with you without crying for two hours afterward. Michael, because he is not in your backyard playing catch with your little brother while your mother encourages you to swoon from the kitchen window, has time to fill out an application on a whim. And lo and behold, because it is October, and because FSU has rolling admissions and various guarantees of acceptance for Florida residents who can sign their names, he is suddenly college-bound.

When you get back together and he tells you he's leaving at the end of June (his admission being conditional, requiring a summer term before his freshman year), tell your mom about his impending departure, how you will miss him so much, how you wish you could make him stay just a year longer so you could go to college at the same time. A week later, sit through your mother's vague sex talk, which your father has forced her to give you. She may rent *The Miracle of Life*; she may not. Either way, do not let on that you know more than she does thanks to public school and health class.

I was a virgin until my wedding night, she says.

Believe her. Ask if your dad was a virgin, too. Know exactly what she means when she says, sort of. Try not to picture your father as a teenager, on top of some girl doing what you and Carla call a Temporary Penis Occupation. Assure yourself that TPOs are not sex, not really, because TPOs happen mostly by accident, without you wanting them to, and without any actual movement on your part. Do not ask about butt sex, even though Michael has presented this as an option to let you keep your semi-virginity. Your mother will mention it briefly on her own, saying, for that men have prostitutes. Her words are enough to convince you never to try it.

Allow Michael to end things after attempting a long-distance relationship for three months. The distance has not been hard: you inherited his friends from last year who were juniors with you, and he drives down to Hialeah every weekend to see you and his mother and Frankie. Still, you're stubborn about the sex thing, and still, you can't think of your butt as anything other than an out hole. Michael has no choice but to admit you're unreasonable and dump you.

Cry because you're genuinely hurt—you *love* him, you *do*—and because you did not apply early decision to any colleges because you hadn't yet decided if you should follow him to FSU. When the misery melts to fury, send off the already-completed applications you'd torn from the glossy brochures stashed under your mattress and begin formulating arguments that will convince your parents to let you move far away from the city where every relative you have that's not in Cuba has lived since flying or floating into Miami; you will sell your car, you will eat cat food to save money, you are their American Dream. Get their blessing to go to the one school that accepts you by promising to come back and live down the street from them forever. Be sure to cross your fingers behind your back while making this promise, otherwise you risk being struck by lightning.

Once away at school, refuse to admit you are homesick. Pretend you are happy in your tiny dorm room with your roommate from Long Island. She has a Jeep Cherokee and you need groceries, and you have never seen snow and are nervous about walking a mile to the grocery store and back. Ask the RA what time the dorm closes for the night and try to play it off as a joke when she starts laughing. Do not tell anyone your father never finished high school. Admit to no one that you left Hialeah in large part to piss off a boy whose last name you will not remember in ten years.

Enroll in English classes because you want to meet white guys who wear V-neck sweaters and have never played football for fear of concussions. Sit behind them in lecture but decide early on that they're too distracting. You must do very well in your classes; e-mails from the school's Office of Diversity have emphasized that you are special, that you may feel like you're not cut out for this, that you should take advantage of the free tutors offered to students like you. You are important to our university community, they say. You are part of our commitment to diversity. Call your mother crying and tell her you don't fit in, and feel surprisingly better when she says, just come home. Book a five hundred dollar flight to Miami for winter break.

Count down the days left until Noche Buena. Minutes after you walk off the plane, call all your old friends and tell them you're back and to get permission from

their moms to stay out later than usual. Go to the beach even though it's sixty degrees and the water is freezing and full of Canadians. Laugh as your friends don
their back-of-the-closet sweaters on New Year's while you're perfectly fine in a hal-
ter top. New England winters have made you tough, you think. You have earned
scores of ninety or higher on every final exam. You have had sex with one and a
half guys (counting TPOs), and yes, there'd been guilt, but God did not strike you
dead. Ignore Michael's calls on the first of the year and hide in your bedroom—
which has not at all changed—when you see him in his Seminoles hoodie, stomp-
ing toward your house. Listen as he demands to talk to you, and your mom lies like
you asked her to and says you're not home. Watch the conversation from between
the blinds of the window that faces the driveway. Swallow down the wave of nausea when you catch your mother winking at him and titling her head toward that
window. Pack immediately and live out of your suitcase for the one week left in
your visit.

Go play pool with Myra, one of your closest alphabetical friends and say, *Oh
man, that sucks* when she tells you she's still working as a truck dispatcher for El
Dorado Furniture. She will try to ignore you by making fun of your shoes, which
you bought near campus, and which you didn't like at first but now appreciate for
their comfort. Say, seriously chica, that's a high school job—you can't work there
forever.

Shut up with this chica crap like you know me, she says.

Then she slams her pool cue down on the green felt and throws the chunk of
chalk at you as she charges out. Avoid embarrassment by shaking your head no as
she leaves, like you regret sending her to her room with no dinner, but she left you
no choice. Say to the people at the table next to yours, what the fuck, huh? One guy
will look down at your hippie sandals and ask, how do you know Myra? Be confused, because you and Myra always had the same friends thanks to the alphabet,
but you've never in your life seen this guy before that night.

While you drive home in your mom's car, think about what happened at the
pool place. Replay the sound of the cue slapping the table in your head, the clinking
balls as they rolled out of its way but didn't hide in the pockets. Decide not to talk
to Myra for a while, that inviting her to come visit you up north is, for now, a bad
idea. Wipe your face on your sleeve before you go inside your house, and when your
mom asks you why you look so upset tell her the truth: you can't believe it—Myra
is jealous.

Become an RA yourself your next year so that your parents don't worry as much
about money. Attend all orientation workshops and decide, after a sexual harassment prevention role-playing where Russel, another new RA, asked if tit fucking
counted as rape, that you will only do this for one year. Around Rush Week, hang

up the anti–binge drinking posters the hall director put in your mailbox. On it is a group of eight grinning students; only one of them is white. You look at your residents and are confused: they are all white, except for the girl from Kenya and the girl from California. Do not worry when these two residents start spending hours hanging out in your room—letting them sit on your bed does not constitute sexual harassment. Laugh with them when they make fun of the poster. *Such Diversity in One University!* Recommend them to your hall director as potential RA candidates for next year.

When you call home to check in (you do this five times a week), ask how everyone is doing. Get used to your mom saying, fine, fine. Appreciate the lack of detail—you have limited minutes on your phone plan and besides, your family, like you, is young and indestructible. They have floated across oceans and sucker-punched sharks with their bare hands. Your father eats three pounds of beef a day and his cholesterol is fine. Each weeknight, just before crossing herself and pulling a thin sheet over her pipe-cleaner legs, your ninety-nine-year-old great-grandmother smokes a cigar while sipping a glass of whiskey and water. No one you love has ever died—just one benefit of the teenage parenthood you've magically avoided despite the family tradition. Death is far off for every Cuban—you use Castro as your example. You know everyone will still be in Hialeah when you decide to come back.

Join the Spanish Club, where you meet actual lisping Spaniards and have a hard time understanding what they say. Date the treasurer, a grad student in Spanish literature named Marco, until he mentions your preference for being on top during sex subconsciously functions as retribution for *his* people conquering *your* people. Quit the Spanish Club and check out several Latin American history books from the library to figure out what the hell he's talking about. Do not tell your mother you broke things off; she loves Spaniards, and you are twenty and not married and you refuse to settle down.

We are not sending you so far away to come back with nothing, she says.

At the end of that semester, look at a printout of your transcript and give yourself a high-five. (To anyone watching, you're just clapping.) Going home for the summer with this printout still constitutes coming back with nothing despite the good grades, so decide to spend those months working full-time at the campus movie theater, flirting with sunburned patrons. Come senior year, decide what you need is to get back to your roots. Date a brother in Iota Delta, the campus's Latino fraternity, because one, he has a car, and two, he gives you credibility in the collegiate minority community you forgot to join because you were hiding in the library for the past three years and never saw the flyers. Tell him you've always liked Puerto Ricans (even though every racist joke your father has ever told you involved Puerto Ricans in some way). Visit his house in Cherry Hill, New Jersey, and meet his third-generation American parents who cannot speak Spanish. Do not look confused when his mother serves meatloaf and mashed potatoes and your boyfriend calls it *real home cooking*. You have only ever had meatloaf in the school dining hall, and only once. Avoid staring at his mother's multiple chins. Hold your laughter even as she claims that Che Guevara is actually still alive and living in a castle off the coast of Vieques.

Scribble physical notes inside your copy of *Clarissa* (the subject of your senior thesis) detailing all the ridiculous things his mother says while you're there: taking a shower while it rains basically guarantees you'll be hit by lightning; paper cannot actually be recycled; Puerto Ricans invented the fort. Wait until you get back to campus to call your father.

After almost four years away from Hialeah, panic that you're panicking when you think about going back—you had to leave to realize you ever wanted to. You'd thank Michael for the push, but you don't know where he is. You have not spoken to Myra since the blowout by the pool table. You only know she still lives with her parents because her mom and your mom see each other every Thursday while buying groceries at Sedano's. At your Iota brother's suggestion, take a Latino studies class with him after reasoning that it will make you remember who you were in high school and get you excited about moving back home.

Start saying things like, what does it really mean to be a minority? How do we construct identity? How is the concept of race forced upon us? Say these phrases to your parents when they ask you when they should drive up to move your stuff back to your room. Dismiss your father as a lazy thinker when he answers, what the fuck are you talking about? Break up with the Iota brother after deciding he and his organization are posers buying into the Ghetto-Fabulous-Jennifer-Lopez-Loving Latino identity put forth by the media; you earned an A in the Latino studies course. After a fancy graduation dinner where your mom used your hotplate to cook arroz imperial—your favorite—tell your family you can't come home, because you need to know what home means before you can go there. Just keep eating when your father throws his fork on the floor and yells, what the fuck are you talking about? Cross your fingers under the table after you tell them you're going to grad school and your mom says, but *mamita*, you made a promise.

[...]

How to Leave "How to Leave Hialeah": A Real-Life Epilogue

For a long time, whenever I gave readings, I would immediately eliminate this story—or any part of this story—as a possibility. *It just feels too close*, I told myself. *I don't want people thinking this is me.* I reminded myself, of course, that this was fiction; I'd made this story up, and only the feelings inside it were true. Still, my initial resistance to reading it in public indicated something about what the story had become; yes, this was fiction, but it *felt* so true—the feelings and reactions of the narrator had been, at one point, my feelings—that reading it out loud made me feel exposed.

Despite my efforts to avoid this story, after the book came out, and when I gave readings, something odd kept happening: I would read from some other story, and when the time came for questions, there would always be a woman in the audience—sometimes she was Latina, sometimes she was from Miami, but all of them, I'd soon find out, were some of the first people in their families to go to college—and she would always ask the same question: is the book's last story about *you*?

While I was thrilled that someone—someone I wasn't even related to!—had bought my book and read it and had come out for a reading, I was scared of this question, of the reasons why the women asked it. *She knows*, I thought. *She knows because it's her in this story, too.* I could talk all I wanted about fiction and emotional truth versus factual truth, but these women saw themselves in the story, could recognize the slight differences between it and whatever they'd gone through. And that meant it had to be me—how else could I have written about it?

In one of the greatest compliments I've ever received, a professor who once introduced me at a reading, a fellow Latina in the humanities, said in her opening remarks that when she read that last story, she felt she was reading her own history. She said it felt like I'd read her journals, even read her mind. She said the story made her feel exposed. That's when I realized what I really did when I wrote this story. We've all felt so alone and guilty—about the choices (good ones, right?) that we've made and the consequences (good and bad, right?) we were now living out—that we were desperately searching for each other without even knowing it, and this story was, for many of these women, equivalent to me throwing open my arms for a hug and yelling, *I know! Come here, I know!*

This story came from a place of loneliness and anger and confusion, a place in which a lot of us have had to live because we decided, of all things, to go to college. And this story tells us we aren't alone, and we will be okay—we are strong enough to take this hit for our daughters' sakes, strong enough to have said to the families that made us, *We gotta go. There's some things we want to do.* We can tell them, our voices stronger thanks to the growing chorus of women who see through the fiction and find themselves in it.

FOR FURTHER READING

"About." *Jennine Capó Crucet*, n.d., www.jcapocrucet.com/about.

Crucet, Jennine Capó. *How to Leave Hialeah.* U of Iowa P, 2009.

Crucet, Jennine Capó. *Make Your Home among Strangers.* Picador, 2015.

Crucet, Jennine Capó. *My Time among the Whites.* Picador, 2019.

De Leon, Jennifer. *Wise Latinas: Writers on Higher Education.* U of Nebraska P, 2014.

Ogle, Connie. "Interview: Jennine Capó Crucet Talks Miami, Writing." *Miami Herald*, 31 July 2015, www.miamiherald.com/entertainment/books/article29630989.html.

Adrienne Keene

Adrienne Keene's poignant love letter to Native American students is borne from tragedy: a suicide committed by a Native student at her alma mater, Stanford University. While Keene didn't personally know the student, she knows all too well the isolation and marginalization that Native students encounter on college campuses. Research shows that students of color experience higher rates of emotional distress in their first year of college and are less likely to seek help than their white classmates (Primm). Even when students of color do seek support, white counselors are not always prepared to address the race-related stress and anxiety they suffer (Kingkade). Since Native students make up only 1 percent of college attendees nationally, feelings of isolation are compounded. Keene uses this letter to make an impassioned intervention, offering love, empathy, and community to her Native readers.

A member of the Cherokee Nation, and a scholar, activist, and blogger, Keene has dedicated her career to advocating for Native students. Keene holds a doctorate from Harvard and is an assistant professor of American studies and ethnic studies at Brown University, where she researches college access, transition, and persistence for Native students. Through the blog she founded, *Native Appropriations*, Keene reaches a wide audience, examining and disrupting pop cultural misrepresentations of Native people. *Native Appropriations* was nominated for the Women's Media Center Social Media Award and has received national and international attention for spotlighting contemporary Indigenous concerns.

Keene first posted her letter to Native students on *Native Appropriations*; it was later reprinted on the *Huffington Post*. Employing direct address, Keene makes an intimate connection with Native college students, reminding them through rhythmic repetition that they are loved, they are needed, and they are not alone. She offers her own experiences of pain and struggle, moving beyond the "it will get better" cliché to insist on an abiding hope that it will "get different"—that change is coming.

Just as Keene did not personally know the young man who killed himself, she does not personally know her readers; yet she regards them with familiarity and affection. After all, they share ancestors—ancestors who love them, as she does. Keene closes her letter with an invitation to write comments that share stories, advice, and community. In a moment when campuses are rife with racial conflict and hostility, Keene deploys her rhetorical platform to build a different reality for Native American students, one founded on a love that is as deep and long as her people's history.

"Dear Native College Student: You Are Loved"

Native Appropriations, 2015

Dear Native College Student,

You are loved. You are loved so deeply and immensely that there are not words to convey the power of that love. Before I say any more, I want you to know that. Your ancestors love you. Your family loves you. Your friends, roommates, classmates love you. Your professors love you. Your RA loves you. The student support staff and administrators love you. We love you. And we need you. We need you here, we need you to fight, and survive and thrive. But above all else, please, please know that you are loved.

Last week, a Native student at my alma mater took his own life. When I heard the news, I was standing on top of a cliff in Hawaii overlooking the Pacific Ocean, looking out into the endless shades of blue, breathing deep and full for the first time in a long time. When I looked at my phone, I felt the familiar weight come back. The elephant that sits on my chest of worry, of fear, of concern. I silently held my friend's arm and blinked back tears, saving them for later, when I was alone and didn't have to express the complexity of the feelings I was holding inside.

I didn't know this student personally. I didn't know his joy, his love, his pain, or his fear—but I know the campus community he was a part of and that he has left behind. I know how broken they feel, how devastated, and how empty. I know because we felt it, the exact same feelings, seven years ago when our classmate, friend, and little brother took his life. When I got that text message on the cliff, all of those emotions came rushing back, experiencing the loss all over again.

I know, for you as a Native student, things are not easy. I know that it may feel like there are very few people on campus who understand you, understand where you come from, and the pressures you face above and beyond other students of color. Sometimes your fellow non-Native students don't and can't understand what it means to be you.

These are the things that keep me up at night. I worry endlessly about the personal costs of pushing you to college. In my research I focus on college access and transition for Native students. I talk about reframing Western education from a tool of colonialism to a tool of self-determination and liberation. I talk about nation building, and your responsibilities as a tribal citizen. I share stories of goodness and success, to show you, your communities, and colleges that you can do it—because you can. But I worry constantly about the pressures, and the costs to you. I worry that we're selling you a false bill of goods.

The students in my dissertation talked to me about the sacrifices they make in order to "give back" with their college degrees. One of my premed students schedules her days so tightly she has to include her times to sleep and eat, or she won't. Another gets up every morning at 5 a.m. so he can greet the sun and pray, offering his corn pollen on the edge of his dorm next to a dumpster so he can face his sacred mountain. I think about my Native friends, and how many of us have struggled with depression, anxiety, and suicidal thoughts while in college.

Because we are not just in college for ourselves. We are there for our communities, and our people, and there is an expectation that we will use our degree to help make change. The academic research shows that this desire to give back for Native students can be a powerful motivator to get us through, and is a form of resistance to these oppressive college institutions formed on ideals of colonialism and white supremacy. But this is an enormous pressure. Especially when the paths to giving back aren't clear, and instead are paved with resistance from our own communities, accusations of "thinking we're better" than those back home, and tribal governments who won't even look at résumés from their young, educated citizens. Our classmates don't have to weigh these pressures daily.

I don't want to fall on the clichéd idea that "it gets better"—because there will always be challenges. But it gets different. Some days I wake up and can barely get out of bed because I feel like I'm not strong enough to make it in the academic world. I've struggled with my own darkness, though I don't think most would know, because the outside world thinks Dr. K has it all together. But other days I am so full of faith and hope and joy for the incredible things this life has brought, the vibrancy and stories I hear from our communities, the change I see coming, so close I can touch it. I think of my friends who have made it through college, the lives they are changing, the jobs and careers forever changed for the better simply because of their presence. Yes there is responsibility, but that responsibility brings such good for the world.

We lost our friend in his sophomore year. He had so much of his college career ahead of him. This student was a last-quarter senior. Ready to graduate. Times of transition are particularly hard, when the weight of responsibility can feel most acute.

But despite all this—we love you and we need you. We need your light, we need your story, we need your words, your love, and your strength. We need you here.

Asking for help is one of the hardest things to do. I know. But please know that there are always people who care, even when it feels like you are alone. We as Native people still only make up less than 1 percent of college students nationally, but that is still thousands of students. Thousands of alumni who made it, who want to support you and who love you.

And I want to take a moment to talk beyond you—to your family, your professors, your community, your school administrators. We have a responsibility as well. It is not enough to push Native students to enroll in college, and expect them to conform to the norms and expectations of spaces not meant for them, and then forge their own path home. We need to embody the Cherokee concept of *gadu-gi*—working together toward a common goal that benefits the entire community. College can't be the sole responsibility of our students. Colleges need to work to make environments supportive and degrees relevant to Indian Country. Families need to send unconditional love without expectation. Communities need, above all, to welcome our students back. We hold ceremonies, powwows, giveaways, and honor songs for our veterans—but what about our students? They have been fighting a battle as well, and need the recognition and support. We need to welcome them back.

But back to you, brave, beautiful Native college student. It's ok to be scared. It's ok to fuck up. It's ok to not know what the future holds. It's ok if you need to take time off and come back. But it's not ok to leave us here without you forever. The scars on our community were just beginning to heal seven years later—the innumerable lives changed forever with the loss of one. And now we must start again.

I also want you to take the time to tell your friends and fellow classmates that they matter and are important to you. We don't do that often enough. Tell your friends how much they mean to you—thank them for the late nights of easy mac and laughter, for the study sessions, for the evenings of smoky fry-bread kitchens, and for listening. The only way to counter the invisibility we often feel is to truly see others, and let them see us. Because college isn't just hard, it's also amazing and fun and bright. There is often more laughter than tears, and the relationships that form are so important to hold onto.

To my beloved Stanford community, I send you all of my love. Let this time bring you together and share in healing. Our loss those years ago brought me closer to my Native friends than I ever had been, and we got through it by leaning hard on one another, and by lifting each other up. Remember to eat, remember to breathe, and remember that it's ok to ask for help. The Stanford Native alums are here for you if you need us. I'm here if you need me. I'm so sorry that you're having to experience this pain, and I'm so sorry that your friend and classmate is no longer here with us. Through the outpouring of support on Facebook I can see that he was special and deeply loved—as are all of you.

I know these words aren't enough; I know that they're rambling and too full of commas and clauses, but I hope they let at least one of you know that you are not alone, and that you are constantly on my mind.

I am going to ask in the comments for readers and friends to share their stories, their advice, and their support to show you that you are not alone. To show you that you are loved. I pray for you, and I know countless others do too.

You are loved. You are loved so deeply and immensely that there are not words to convey the power of that love. Before I end, I want you to know this, again. Your ancestors love you. Your family loves you. Your friends, roommates, classmates love you. Your professors love you. Your RA loves you. The student support staff and administrators love you. We love you. And we need you. We need you here, we need you to fight, and survive and thrive. But above all else, please, please know that you are loved.

With all my heart,
Adrienne

For Further Reading

"Adrienne Keene." *SpeakOut*, n.d., www.speakoutnow.org/speaker/keene-adrienne.

Keene, Adrienne J. "College Pride, Native Pride: A Portrait of a Culturally Grounded Precollege Access Program for American Indian, Alaska Native, and Native Hawaiian Students." *Harvard Educational Review*, vol. 86, no. 1, 2016, pp. 72–97.

Kingkade, Tyler. "Students of Color Aren't Getting the Mental Health Help They Need in College." *The Huffington Post*, 2 Feb. 2017, www.huffingtonpost.com/entry/students-of-color-mental-health_us_5697caa6e4b0ce49642373b1.

Native Appropriations. nativeappropriations.com.

Primm, Annelle B. "College Students of Color: Confronting the Complexities of Diversity, Culture, and Mental Health." *Higher Education Today*, 2 Apr. 2018, www.higheredtoday.org/2018/04/02/college-students-color-confronting-complexities-diversity-culture-mental-health/.

Janet Tsai

Janet Tsai's piece is part of the anthology *Click: When We Knew We Were Feminists*, which explores the moment when contributors experienced a "lightbulb" recognition of gender inequalities that sparked their feminist consciousness. The collection features writers in their teens, twenties, and thirties, showcasing that feminism is alive and well in a younger generation.

Tsai's contribution depicts a lived example behind the statistics of women in STEM (Science, Technology, Engineering, and Math) professions. According to the US Department of Commerce, "Women in the United States hold nearly half of all jobs but hold less than 25 percent of STEM jobs" ("Women in STEM"). Research shows that socialization and gender bias contribute to the disparity, and here Tsai walks us through her emerging discovery of these realities. She begins her narrative with an experience of racism, where she faced stereotypes of being the "smart Asian kid." These assumptions, Tsai comes to see, in some ways cloaked other, sexist assumptions about being female with interests and proclivities in math and science. New to an engineering program in college, Tsai was soon met with overt sexism by other students, whose comments compounded her insecurities.

By embarking on research that validated her own experiences, Tsai was motivated to make a change. With a doctorate in mechanical engineering, she is now a professor at the University of Colorado, where she studies how society and culture impact engineers' technological choices. Her research encourages nontraditional demographic groups to study engineering, as do her contributions to Engineer Girl, a website that promotes engineering for girls and women. Tsai's story provides a compelling example of a "click" moment, where inquiry into a pivotal moment leads to deeper understanding of larger, systemic gender discrimination.

"An Engineering Approach to Feminism": Excerpt from *Click: When We Knew We Were Feminists*

2010

"Go stand next to your sister," a ten-year-old boy on the playground told me as we lined up to play basketball.

I answered, confused, "She's not my sister, duh. She's just my friend."

"Well, who cares? You look the same to me," he concluded, as if that were a fair explanation of his assumption that because we both had black hair and dark eyes, we must be related.

There were only a handful of non-Caucasians in the college mountain town where I grew up, and being mistaken for a sister to all other Asians within sight was a frequent occurrence during my childhood. While obviously annoying in some ways, growing up a minority was, in hindsight, also surprisingly beneficial—no one ever told me it was weird or inappropriate that, as a girl, I liked math and science, because I already fit easily into the stereotype of being a nerdy, smart Asian kid.

A shy and self-conscious girl, I didn't enjoy sharing my opinions out loud. Instead I preferred subjects like math and science because the answers rarely required class discussion and were simply right or wrong. I felt that my cultural differences stuck out less with numbers than with words; it was easy for me to hide out with logic, free of interpretation or personal expression that could lead to embarrassment. Since I was used to feeling different because of my ethnicity, it didn't occur to me that it was also different that I, as a girl, liked math and science. In this way, I let my race trump my gender throughout elementary, junior high, and high school.

I applied to a highly selective, innovative, start-up engineering college. During the admissions process they mentioned that one of the goals of the inaugural class was a fifty-fifty gender balance. After an on-campus interview weekend with many other potential students, I got in! I thought it was amazing that they chose me out of all those other qualified, smart, diverse people.

Yes, by miracles of miracles the little engineering college that could did accomplish a nearly equal gender balance for my pioneering class of seventy-five people, something unheard of in engineering. The beginning was cool, just meeting and greeting lots of friendly (mostly white) faces. The first month passed quickly with everyone in the class of only seventy-five making first impressions and getting to know each other. Notable characteristics among the students quickly emerged:

who raises their hands, who is really slow to understand stuff, who loves to hear themselves talk, who brought a rice cooker, who likes basketball, and of course, who is "smart."

During that first month, everyone was figuring out where they fit in and questioning how they got there in the first place. Students started talking/reasoning/ slippery sloping about the admissions process, asking out loud and publicly: "Exactly how did the college achieve this fifty-fifty gender balance when more men applied than women? . . . That must mean that it was easier for women to get in than men, that they were given preferential treatment . . . That must mean that some women were given their spots just because they were women . . . That must mean there are women here who aren't as qualified as some of the male applicants and, consequently, don't deserve it! . . . AND, that must mean that the women, on average, are stupider than the men and don't belong here—they shouldn't be here!"

Since I was initially very surprised that I had been admitted to this prestigious institution, this runaway train of bad conclusions ran me over, preying on my inexperience in being summarily judged as a female. Unlike high school, where my race helped me fit in as a stereotypical nerdy Asian doing math and science, it now seemed to make my situation even worse—as both a minority and a female, I counted doubly for the diversity of the college, a stated goal of the admissions process. So I had to wonder, was checking the boxes for "female" and "Asian/Pacific Islander" what got me in? Did I not deserve to be here by my own merit?

I had previously found solace in the unbiased, impartial nature of math and statistics but now had difficulty reassuring myself using the numbers. How could a heavily male applicant pool equal a gender-balanced incoming class? That equation did not have any purely logical solution. There had to be another factor at play, some variable I had not considered and did not understand.

To make matters worse, some of my classmates felt compelled to make a list of the ten smartest students in the class. Looking back, this insidious list was the result of awkward eighteen-year-olds who were formerly the smartest fish in their high school ponds, now swimming into a new school and trying to understand where they fit in. Not surprising, the list was dominated by men who volunteered their opinions all the time in class, naturally responded to questions with authority, and easily stated things in tones that really meant "I know the answer, and it is trivially obvious to someone with brainpower as superior as mine."

Missing from the list, of course, were the meek ones: students who knew all of the answers but didn't need to broadcast them and, like me, students who sometimes had correct answers but stated them with uncertainty instead of condescending self-assuredness. I had more respect for the people who didn't need to announce their intelligence to everyone else, yet "the list" seemed to indicate that to be considered smart, you had to be the type to let everyone know—a type that was overwhelmingly male.

I knew that the people making these lists and starting rumors about the admissions process were being completely baseless assholes. We all had different means of "belonging" in the small community of seventy-five people, but if this start-up college was to be a success, we had to be in it together, dammit! I wanted to be able to tell them to shut up with absolute factual (and not-too-emotional) certainty. I needed to understand, for myself, how the system actually worked—did I really get extra points for being an Asian woman? Were the men really more qualified and generally smarter than the women? Why did people seem to think so? The need to answer these questions marked the beginning of my journey into feminism.

I went to the dean of student life and the dean of admissions and asked each of them, point-blank, if the admitted women were less qualified than the men, if there was purposeful bias in the admissions procedure. They both told me the same story:

Female applicants tend to be more self-selecting than the males in several ways. Women who do not think they will get in do not apply, whereas men are more likely to apply regardless of their level of preparation/qualification. Moreover, women who are interested in engineering have already made a personal choice. Rarely pushed into math and science fields, the women who are interested in engineering already have legitimate self-engagement—whereas for males, some apply to engineering school because of recommendations from guidance counselors or parents. Consequently, the quality of the women applicants is, as a whole, higher than the quality of the male applicants. Despite the discrepancy in the sheer numbers of applications, those accepted are of equal quality and, of course, equally deserving of being enrolled at the college.

Was it really a satisfactory explanation? I was reassured by their soft reasoning but had to wonder if their argument really explained what was going on. There was a lot more to the story than just the numbers of male and female applicants; there were real differences in the treatment and approach to math, science, and engineering careers for men and women, and the consequences of those differences were evident in my very own class. I could no longer trust the numbers to tell the full story; I could no longer ignore that there were structural and institutional factors that encouraged and celebrated men in technical fields but simultaneously dissuaded and ignored women. The missing variable in the admissions equation was how each of us had been individually socialized: Every one of our personal experiences shaped the path to our current destination at school, and on the whole, these experiences were particularly different between men and women.

I started to consider—how deep did this go? Every equation or law we were learning in class had a man's name attached to it: Isaac Newton's laws, James Maxwell's equations, the calculus of Gottfried Leibniz, James Watson and Francis Crick's DNA helix . . . yes, the list of equations named after (white) male names felt endless. Growing up I had been reassured by the unbiased nature of math and science, yet in my college education, all I could see were male names getting all the glory. Was this also an indication that somehow men were naturally better at making scientific discoveries, or was it just like the smart list? Were these men just better at publicizing their knowledge? Would this ever get better? Beginning to feel truly discouraged for the first time, I realized that it was situations like these that reinforced society's prejudices and assumptions, feeding into the spiraling feedback loop discouraging women in science, math, and engineering.

During my junior year, I decided to do research with a physics professor who, in addition to studying physical phenomena in the lab, was also interested in engineering education. Her project looked at how teaching students with hands-on projects instead of lectures affected the way the students, particularly women, responded to the subjects of math, science, and engineering. It was my job to transcribe, read, and tag relevant sections of one-on-one interviews a neutral party had conducted with male and female engineering students about their experiences both inside and outside the classroom during their first semesters on our campus.

To my amazement, while listening and reading through multitudes of these interviews I found several people whose stories mirrored mine closely—others who had experienced the same self-doubts after classmates questioned the fairness of the admissions process, others who wondered if they really deserved to be at the school. Ridiculously enough, the interviewees even described the creation of a mostly male smart list during the first semester! The similarity of these stories to my own experiences was striking.

Hearing my worries and concerns repeated by other people convinced me that the questions I was facing were not rare. Now my logical and mathematical mind was thinking statistically: Anything that happened twice in these independent populations was likely to happen again and again unless significant changes were made to convince women that they really were equal, despite the smart lists and stupid rumors of preferential treatment. My desire to prevent these events from reoccurring drove me to be more vocal and outspoken, to make everyone feel welcome in studying engineering, math, and science.

I began to read and discuss more—first about gender differences in the sciences and gradually more about feminism. Previously, when I thought that adhering to the smart Asian stereotype protected me from being judged as a female, I had been covering my eyes and limiting what I could see. Now I understood that there was no hiding from the real world and the real prejudices that do exist, and I finally took the blinders off. With the full imperfect picture in sight I had a clear goal—to keep others from falling into the same holes I had in doubting my own abilities because I was a woman—and in accepting that goal I also accepted my role to create change as a feminist.

For Further Reading

Cummins, Denise. "Why the STEM Gender Gap Is Overblown." *PBS NewsHour*, 17 Apr. 2015, www
.pbs.org/newshour/nation/truth-women-stem-careers.

Khazan, Olga. "The More Gender Equality, the Fewer Women in STEM." *The Atlantic*, 18 Feb. 2018,
www.theatlantic.com/science/archive/2018/02/the-more-gender-equality-the-fewer-women
-in-stem/553592/.

Martin, Courtney E., and J. Courtney Sullivan, editors. Introduction. *Click: When We Knew We Were
Feminists*, Seal Press, 2010, pp. i–viii.

Tsai, Janet. *Engineering Plus*. U of Colorado Boulder, n.d.

"Women in STEM: 2017 Update." *United States Department of Commerce*, 13 Nov. 2017, www.com
merce.gov/news/fact-sheets/2017/11/women-stem-2017-update.

Katharine Hayhoe

An atmospheric scientist and evangelical Christian, Dr. Katharine Hayhoe is a leading voice—and rare female one—in the public conversation on climate change. She has been featured in the *New York Times* and *O, The Oprah Magazine* about her appeal to climate change skeptics, and research shows that because she is regarded as a "trusted source," her message persuades evangelical audiences that climate change is real (Nuccitelli). Hayhoe's work is instructive both about the power of rhetorical appeals and climate change education.

Hayhoe's rhetorical effectiveness stems largely from her use of identification, as she employs her faith-based knowledge to reach other evangelicals who may be skeptical about climate change. She employs identification not only by situating herself as evangelical but by striving for connection with her audience as she offers scientific evidence. As the *New York Times* writer John Schwartz describes, "She has found that she gets her science across more effectively if she can connect with people personally. In a nation seemingly addicted to argument as a blood sport, she conciliates. On a topic so contentious that most participants snarl, she smiles. She is an evangelical Christian, and she does not flinch from using the language of faith and stewardship to discuss the fate of the planet."

Hayhoe's appeal has not been successful with all audiences, however; climate-change deniers have attacked her viciously online, and former Speaker of the House Newt Gingrich pulled her chapter from a co-authored book upon receiving flack for including her perspective. Hayhoe contends that confronting intimidation is part of the fight climate scientists must endure, as discrediting the messenger is part of the strategy of climate-change deniers.

Hayhoe is a Toronto native and received her bachelor's in physics and astronomy from the University of Toronto and her master's and doctorate in atmospheric science from the University of Illinois at Urbana-Champaign. She has published over 125 papers, abstracts, publications, and reports, including national reports presented to Congress. Currently she is professor in the Department of Political Science at Texas Tech University, where she directs the Climate Science Center. Hayhoe is also the CEO of ATMOS Research, designed to connect scientists and stakeholders on strategies to deal with climate change.

Hayhoe's contribution is a transcription from the web series *The Secret Life of Scientists & Engineers* from the long-running PBS television series *NOVA*. In the video, Hayhoe stands in front of a black backdrop in jeans and a dark green tank top, adding to her approachable demeanor. She is expressive in tone and quick to laughter. While the video mainly features close-ups of Hayhoe, at times images appear beside her. At one point a white cross is shown above her left shoulder and an atom above her left, symbolizing two typically opposed identities. At other times, world maps show hot spots, photos of crops, people of color in arid climates, and pristine lakes and other natural landscapes, offering visual reminders of the stakes of climate change.

Hayhoe explains that conversation about climate change is fraught with fear, acknowledging the emotions entangled in the issue. Through a faith-based lens, she reiterates that God is love, not fear, and that acting through love—doing for our "global neighbors"—is in fact a Christian response.

Climate Change Evangelist

The Secret Life of Scientists & Engineers, 2014

One of the first times that we went to church in Texas, I met a couple and we were introducing ourselves. They asked, "What do you do?" I explained that I study global warming and they said, "Oh, that's wonderful! We *need* somebody like you to tell our children the right things. You would not *believe* the lies that they're being taught at school. They told us that the ice in the Arctic is melting, and it's threatening the polar bears."

And I said, "Well, I'm afraid that that's true."

There's often a perceived conflict between science and faith. It's a little bit like coming out of the closet, admitting to people that you are a Christian and you are a scientist.

My husband, he is the pastor of an evangelical church, and many people would approach *him* to ask him questions about climate change. If anything, there's even *more* questions in the Christian community because we are targeted by so much of the disinformation that's going on.

So that's why my husband and I decided to write a book together—a scientist and a pastor—on what a faith-based response to this problem looks like. With climate change, much of our response to this issue is emotional: the fear of how our lives would be irrevocably changed if we uprooted our entire economy, and how our right to enjoy the luxuries of energy and water might be ripped away from us.

Well, as a Christian, we're told that God is not the author of fear. God is love. When we're acting out of fear, we're thinking about ourselves. When we act about love, we are not thinking about ourselves, we are thinking about others—our global neighbors—the poor and the disadvantaged, the people who do not have the resources to adapt. And so I believe that we are called, first of all, to love each other, and second of all, to act.

Am I a climate change evangelist? The evangel means good news. Climate change is not really very good news right now, but at the same time, I think it is good news to know that we have choices. And by making wise and responsible choices *now*, we can ensure that we protect the things that we care about most on our planet, for the benefit of the people who we know personally, and those who we don't.

For Further Reading

Dawson, Bill. "Texas Tech Scientist Sees Intimidation Effort Behind Barrage of Hate Mail." *Texas Climate News*, 30 Jan. 2012, texasclimatenews.org/?p=4153.

Hayhoe, Katharine, and Andrew Farley. *A Climate for Change: Global Warming Facts for Faith-Based Decisions*. Faithwords, 2009.

"Katharine Hayhoe, Ph.D." *Texas Tech Department of Political Science*, n.d., www.depts.ttu.edu/polit icalscience/Faculty/Hayhoe_Katharine.php.

Nuccitelli, Dana. "Study: Katharine Hayhoe Is Successfully Convincing Doubtful Evangelicals about Climate Change." *The Guardian*, 28 Aug. 2017, www.theguardian.com/environment/cli mate-consensus-97-per-cent/2017/aug/28/study-katharine-hayhoe-is-successfully-convincing -doubtful-evangelicals-about-climate-change.

Sanders, Joshundra. "Expensive Denial: The Rising Cost of Ignoring Climate Change." *Bitch Media*, 5 Sept. 2017, www.bitchmedia.org/article/expensive-denial/rising-cost-ignoring-climate-change.

Schwartz, John. "Katharine Hayhoe, a Climate Explainer Who Stays above the Storm." *The New York Times*, 10 Oct. 2016, www.nytimes.com/2016/10/11/science/katharine-hayhoe-climate -change-science.html.

"Who I Am." *Katharine Hayhoe*, n.d., katharinehayhoe.com/wp2016/biography/.

Wagatwe Wanjuki

One in five US women experiences sexual assault on college campuses; 49.5 percent of multiracial women experience assault sometime in their lives; more than 90 percent of survivors do not report the crime ("Sexual Assault in the United States"). Wagatwe Wanjuki, assaulted while attending Tufts University, is one of the 10 percent who did report, and she is one of countless survivors who was failed by the system.

In her letter to Tufts, first published on the women-run (and now defunct) website the Establishment, Wanjuki uses the anguish of her assaults—which led to mental health issues, academic interference, and financial insecurity—to call out an educational system that abandoned her. Wanjuki filed her case with the Title IX office at Tufts in 2008, rather than with the police, assuming the process would be more humane. Initially, the office diligently pursued her case, but in the end dropped it without explanation (Flanagan and Tso). Wanjuki's perpetrator remained on campus until he graduated, while she suffered posttraumatic stress and the pain of feeling "surrounded by people who don't care about what happens to students" (Flanagan and Tso).

In the black feminist tradition—first named by Audre Lorde—of using anger toward action, or what Brittney Cooper calls "eloquent rage," Wanjuki and other survivors began to organize for clearer sexual assault policies at Tufts. In 2009 Wanjuki was instead expelled from the university due to "poor academic performance," which resulted from her trauma. In her letter, Wanjuki holds Tufts accountable for expelling, rather than supporting, her. She employs direct address to personify the university, refusing to let the administration hide behind policy or bureaucracy, insisting they see her humanity.

Shortly after Wanjuki was expelled, the national spotlight turned to campus sexual assault policy and Title IX, which protects students against gender discrimination, sexual assault, and violence. In 2011 the Obama administration issued a "Dear Colleague" letter articulating to universities their responsibility to respond promptly and fairly to sexual assault reports. The government promised strict reinforcement, and in 2014 Tufts was found in violation of Title IX by the US Department of Education's Office for Civil Rights. Tufts initially agreed to change its policies, only to quickly rescind, claiming the finding was unsubstantiated. This decision was met with campus protests and a warning from the federal government that it could withdraw funding from the university. Eventually, Tufts accepted the finding and committed to improved practices (Rinaldi).

While Tufts' efforts came too late to help Wanjuki, who graduated from Rutgers in 2014 with the help of a GoFundMe campaign, she is dedicated to ensuring her experience is not repeated. An award-winning activist and writer for several publications, including BuzzFeed, *Cosmopolitan*, and *Feministing*, Wanjuki co-founded the anti-rape organization Survivors Eradicating Rape Culture. Their first campaign, #JustSaySorry, garnered international media coverage. After the Trump administration dialed back Title IX protections, Wanjuki's message resonates more than ever: "Trust and believe survivors. Supporting us is a radical act against rape culture" (Wallace).

"Dear Tufts Administrators Who Expelled Me after My Sexual Assaults"

The Establishment, 2016

It's 5 a.m. I didn't take Ambien the night before since I'm running low and unsure when I'll get a refill. I don't love it as much as I used to, anyway; it still helps me fall asleep, but it no longer provides the nightmare-free slumber it first provided.

Motivated by suspicions of his infidelity, I find public forum posts my boyfriend made online. My heart drops when I read the series of posts he made to tell the other members about me and our dating life. My blood runs cold as I see the MRA-style quotation marks around "rape case" in one of his first posts about me. They joke about me lying and falsely accusing him of rape. He joins in. I cry myself to sleep; the man who says he loves me thinks I'm a liar, too.

I rush into the accountant's office, late for my morning appointment. Mornings have been a lot more difficult these past few months. The nightmares and depression have worsened since I was humiliatingly laid off in January and now I have the humiliating breakup to handle, too. When we start crunching the numbers, I realize that I don't have everything I need to file that day. If I hadn't had to hoard my ADD meds in the wake of losing my insurance, I know I would have had my shit together. Then, the appointment gets even worse: Thanks to my dad negotiating to settle my defaulted private student loans for less than was owed, I am going to owe

Uncle Sam about $10,000. I groan. I only am able to keep calm as the accountant tells me about tax payment plans by telling myself I will get my chance to cry alone in the car as I drive back home.

I muster the energy to leave my house for the first time in five days. *Desperate times call for desperate measures.* I've run out of Ambien and I have some speaking gigs coming up. I can't be a good speaker if I haven't slept. As I pull up to the drive-thru pharmacy window, I turn down the car radio that's playing my latest media interview talking about the portrayal of survivors. My prescriptions should be ready, but there is a problem with my health insurance—an increasingly frustrating, regular occurrence since the layoff. Medicaid doesn't cover Ambien so I sucked it up and bought a plan I can't afford through the Obamacare exchange. The pharmacist doesn't have the info for it. I hand her a printout, but she says that the insurance card I brought is incorrect. They won't be able to fill one of the prescriptions. "What can I do? I've been out for a while." I hope the pharmacist doesn't notice my voice cracking and the tears welling up in my eyes.

I wake up after getting only an hour of sleep to catch a flight—one of many flights that I take during the month of April to share my trauma with strangers around the country. I sleepily click through to an article giving an update about a survivor who was also betrayed by her school's administration. The similarities in our experiences were heartbreaking, but one stark difference hits me sharply in the heart; her life is moving forward. She's pursuing a career in medicine.

I try to hold down the bitterness rising within me as I struggle to lift myself up from bed. My childhood bed. In my parents' home. Because I cannot afford to live outside the home like a "real" adult. I feel a pang of jealousy as I think about my own stagnant life: unemployed, in debt, living at home with my parents, and possessing a college degree earned six years late from a different institution than I'd intended to graduate from. Not exactly the portrait of success. My own dreams of pursuing law were long destroyed since Tufts decided to kick me out. Now I financially scrape by through sharing my trauma on different stages year after year. I wish there was more to my abilities, but I take this privilege of being a paid public speaker and thank my stars for this one option.

The cab pulls into the airport; the sun hasn't even risen. I psych myself up for a potential (often racist) government-sponsored scalp massage at TSA. It's almost ironic how much personal invasion I have to endure to go to and from some of these speaking engagements addressing boundary violations.

Happy Sexual Assault Awareness Month to me.

Dear Tufts administrators present during my time on campus,

Do you ever think of me?

I often think of you. I wish it weren't this way, I promise. I feel like that ex-girl-friend who just won't admit to herself that "he's just not that into you." But as you can see from the scenarios above, even the most mundane life events—paying my taxes, reading an online article, going to the pharmacy—are seemingly forever tainted by your decision to force me off your campus almost seven years ago. I reported my sexual assaults to you and you did nothing. And then, instead of recognizing my floundering GPA as a cry for help, you chose to use it as an excuse to refuse to provide me academic accommodations and ban me from your school when I was a mere one year away from finishing my undergraduate degree.

I have to ask, how do you sleep at night? (I'm sure you do it much better than me.) How do you remain silent and go through your day-to-day knowing that you have failed numerous survivors who've lived on Tufts' campus?

How do you function knowing that students entrusted to your institution suffer from your ignorance and reluctance to do the right thing?

I don't know why you chose to be a part of Tufts' community. I chose it because as a high school senior, I was drawn to the school's supposed commitment to both academic excellence and being good citizens. Obviously it's been easier for you to talk the talk than to walk the walk. Seriously, how can you claim to want to create "informed, ethical, and engaged" citizens when you fail to properly engage with the problem of campus sexual assault or treat survivors ethically?

Your collective failure to assist me—a young, Black woman trying to recover after abuse—reaffirmed how I feared the rest of the world saw me: not valued. After having my body abused and my self-worth diminished by another student, your institutional refusal to do anything implied that you agreed with him.

Your message was clear: what happened to me didn't matter; I was not worth helping.

After being raped and in an abusive relationship, I felt like I had lost almost everything: my friends who ostracized me and then graduated on time, the confidence that I was intelligent and a good student, my dreams of studying abroad, and the hope of experiencing a healthy romantic college relationship. I had one last thing, though, that you took away from me: finally earning a degree from the college that I chose as a naïve 16-year-old high schooler.

It's amazing how much power the administrators occupying Dowling Hall have over the lives of thousands of students who pass through the Medford/Somerville campus. I now really get why civil rights laws like Title IX exist: your knowledge and apathy toward crises like the impact of gender-based violence prevent education from becoming anything close to "the great equalizer." That's why I am completely unsurprised that the Department of Education chose you as the first school officially declared in violation of Title IX for sexual violence—and you subsequently tried to back out of the voluntary resolution agreement with the government to improve your response to sexual misconduct.

While I didn't receive a degree from your *fine* institution, I did learn an invaluable lesson: that being a good person does not protect me from being unfairly harmed by others. And as your apathy toward my abuse and years of struggle afterward shows, being good doesn't guarantee that others will help when they serve as witness to my harm. I would tell you more about how much of my spirit you have broken, how every time I'm mistreated by someone I know and trust I think about the administrators who, frankly, ruined my life. But I know better than to expect that you'd actually listen to me almost seven years after you turned your back on me.

I now know better than to expect the best from people.

Happy Sexual Assault Awareness Month.

No love,
Wagatwe

FOR FURTHER READING

Brodsky, Alexandra. "How Much Does Sexual Assault Cost College Students Every Year?" *The Washington Post*, 18 Nov. 2014, www.washingtonpost.com/posteverything/wp/2014/11/18/how-much-does-sexual-assault-cost-college-students-every-year/.

Cooper, Brittney. *Eloquent Rage: A Black Feminist Discovers Her Superpower*. Picador, 2019.

Flanagan, Alexandra, and Phoenix Tso. "Inside the Student Activist Movement: Tufts and Sexual Violence." *Jezebel*, 19 Feb. 2014, jezebel.com/inside-the-student-activist-movement-tufts-university-1526094401.

Green, Erica L. "New U.S. Sexual Misconduct Rules Bolster Rights of Accused and Protect Colleges." *The New York Times*, 29 Aug. 2018, www.nytimes.com/2018/08/29/us/politics/devos-campus-sexual-assault.html.

Marcotte, Amanda. "Wagatwe Wanjuki Wants Justice for Sexual-Assault Survivors, but She Also Wants an Apology." *Salon*, 22 Aug. 2016, www.salon.com/2016/08/22/wagatwe-wanjuki-wants-justice-for-sexual-assault-survivors-but-she-also-wants-an-apology/.

Rinaldi, Jessica. "Tufts Accepts Finding It Violated Law in Sex Assaults." *Boston Globe*, 9 May 2014, www.bostonglobe.com/metro/2014/05/09/reversal-tufts-accepts-finding-that-violated-title-sexual-assault-cases/AljGY7mlMlgZRXmPIgsIxI/story.html.

"Sexual Assault in the United States." *National Sexual Violence Resource Center*, n.d., https://www.nsvrc.org/node/4737.

US Department of Education. "Dear Colleague Letter." *Office for Civil Rights*, 25 Sept. 2018, www2.ed.gov/about/offices/list/ocr/letters/colleague-201104.html.

Wagatwe Wanjuki. wagatwe.com/#intro.

Wallace, Aubrey. "Wagatwe Wanjuki: Campus Sexual Assault Activist." *Ravishly*, 8 Aug. 2014, ravishly.com/ladies-we-love/wagatwe-wanjuki-campus-sexual-assault-activist.

Kimberly Shappley

During and after the 2016 presidential election, strong political and cultural rifts in the United States stymied productive dialogue. Fueled by networks and news feeds preaching to their respective choirs, public discourse reflected an unwillingness to move past dichotomies. Kimberly Shappley, as the title of her piece suggests, represents a refreshing voice that demonstrates the ability to cross the aisle; further, she acknowledges the damage done in refusing to hear nuanced, complex views on topics often treated as black and white.

Shappley readily admits that she was the last person she expected to become an advocate for LGBTQ and transgender rights. A self-proclaimed Republican, Christian, and Texan, she found herself mother to a child with gender dysphoria. With pain and honesty, Shappley confesses to making choices that in hindsight she believes harmed her child. Through education, faith, and love for her child, she changed her views, and now she and her daughter Kai serve as activists for transgender rights, particularly in hopes of changing the minds of Christians. Shappley learned from other resources, like Jazz Jennings—a well-known YouTuber who went public as transgender at age six in a 2007 interview with Barbara Walters, and Debi Jackson—mother of a transgender youth and founder of Gender Inc, which provides services for transgender-inclusivity training. Kai and Kimberly Shappley's story was made into a documentary, *Trans in America: Texas Strong*, which won a 2019 Emmy Award for Outstanding Short Documentary.

The following piece concerns a controversial 2017 bathroom bill proposed in Texas that required people to use a bathroom aligned with the sex listed on their birth certificates (this particular bill died, but the issue has not). This was one of many bathroom bills proposed in state legislatures around the country designed to restrict bathroom usage for transgender people (see Kat Blaque's, Staceyann Chin's, and Julia Serano's contributions to this volume). Shappley draws on identification to persuade her audience, as her essay appears on the website TexasGOP-Vote, "A broad community of writers, activists, and legislators who believe that healthy debate will lead to a better Republican Party." Shappley acknowledges that before she had her experiential and researched evidence, she was intolerant of LGBTQ people. Her conversion experience revised her Christian context: "I was a hateful reflection of a loving God." Drawing upon maternal values to justify activism in spaces that some Christians reject, as well as love for innocent children, Shappley seeks to reclaim the unconditional love Christianity should provide—a lesson she admittedly learned nearly at the expense of her child.

"Texas Conservative Christian Mom Speaks out against SB6 'Bathroom Bill'"

TexasGOPVote, 2017

I am so proud to live in a country that cares so passionately about the safety of our children. This is a great starting point we can use toward common ground.

I am a registered Republican. I am a Christian. I have a degree in health science. I am the mother of a transgender child born Joseph Paul who we now call Kai.

From my earliest memories, I noticed the nature and temperament of this child was more similar to my daughter than to my sons. Around age two, a family member asked me if my child was gay because of her flamboyantly feminine mannerisms and love for all things girly. Not long after that, a friend who is a Christian psychologist who works predominantly with children asked me if I had noticed anything about my child that was different and went on to discuss some of the science behind gender dysphoria. In my ignorance, I immediately began to Google conversion therapy. Not the real science and risk behind it, but how to implement it.

I asked our daycare to put away all girly toys. When my child consistently and persistently insisted, "I am a girl," the adults in her life would get down on her level and look her in the eyes and firmly tell her, "No, you are a boy." My child went into depression. It is very difficult to witness depression in a formerly joyful toddler. Haircuts became a nightmare of horror movie screams of, "Stop. Stop. Please don't, Mommy. Please don't let them cut my hair." But I was adamant this child was going to have a flattop. This child would never get a single toy that she wanted, nor the birthday party theme she asked for.

One Monday afternoon I picked up my sobbing child from daycare. Her best friend had her fourth birthday party and we were not invited. The party had been the center of our conversations for weeks. Kai picked the perfect gift and gift bag and we waited for our invitation to get the details. I remember looking in the rearview mirror and seeing this sweet crying face as she said, "Her daddy said I couldn't go to the party because it's a girl party and I'm a freak."

My sweet child began praying for Joseph to go to Heaven and live with Jesus. Kai was begging the Lord to let her die. Moments like these helped me to realize transition was necessary. I didn't know how to do it. I just knew I needed to help my child.

I read research and studies from the American Academy of Pediatrics, American Psychological Association, and the University of Washington. If you don't understand why the transgender community is fighting so adamantly for our rights, try reading any of the reputable material available. I repeatedly watched the Jazz Jennings family interview, which had made me so righteously angry when it aired the first time, and I reached out to advocate moms of transgender children like Debi Jackson and was loved and supported by secret groups of loving, hurting, and prayerful Christian moms of LGBTQ children. Our own secret persecuted church. I've watched as our safe places to fellowship together, Freed Hearts and Serendipitydodah for moms, have grown to more than two thousand Christian members and growing.

Prior to our first outing with my child in a dress, I asked my adolescent son to talk to me about how he was feeling and would he be embarrassed to be seen with his brother in a dress. He said, "Mom. It's embarrassing that you make him wear boy clothes." My adult daughter commented, "Well, mom, we've always known." It is in these moments when I realized my child wasn't the one transitioning. I was.

At the beginning of this process, transgender wasn't really anything people were paying attention to. That was two years ago. When we "came out" last year to those who are closest to us, our country became a hostile environment for my family. Extended family, friends, and fellow Christians have disowned us and continue posting hurtful things about a subject they have not educated themselves about. Imagine seeing a post by someone you care for saying, "If I ever see a guy in a dress in the bathroom with my kid they will need a stretcher" and then realizing it is your child whom you love who is the guy in a dress they have just threatened. We have lost family. We have lost friends. I have had my fellow Christians tell me I'm going to hell and that I am turning my family over to Satan. I have grown so weary of "love the sinner, hate the sin." You are talking about a five-year-old who is committing no sin by being her authentic self. The Bible tells us some are born this way, some are made this way. My child is fearfully and wonderfully made for a time such as this.

We are private people. We are lifelong Republicans, we are Christian. We are a Houston-area family who only want to protect our daughter and live quietly. We did not want to speak out publicly, but the lieutenant governor has forced us out of our private lives and into the public arena to protect our daughter.

This is the face of a transgender child in Texas. I want Texans to look at my little girl's photo. Do we as a state really want to force her to go into the boy's bathroom? Why are we targeting innocent children for political games? SB6 puts my child's life in danger.

To those who love us and stand by us through this storm, I know this has challenged your beliefs. I know this has been hard for you. I thank you for loving us and praying for us and taking time to educate yourself.

To the church, come. Let us reason together. Let us be on the right side of history. Civil rights were not about water fountains in the sixties and they are not about bathrooms now. There is so much more at stake.

To the LGBTQ community, I'm sorry. I am so sorry for every time I plucked a Bible verse out of context and I hurt you with it. I was a hateful reflection of a loving God. Please forgive me.

My number one job in life is "a mom" and I am speaking out to protect my little girl. I urge Lieutenant Governor Patrick and other leaders to sit down with me and families like mine and educate themselves about transgender children.

For Further Reading

"About." *TexasGOPVote*, n.d., https://www.texasgopvote.com/about/our-mission.

Founder, Debi Jackson." *Gender Inc*, n.d., http://genderinc.com/about/founder-debi-jackson/.

Shappley, Kimberly, as told to Breanne Randall. "The Story of My Transgender Daughter Went Viral. Here's How Life Has Been for Us Since." *Good Housekeeping*, 20 July 2018.

Transkids Purple Rainbow Foundation. http://www.transkidspurplerainbow.org/.

Ananya Roy

After the 2008 economic recession, the worst in the United States since the Great Depression, California faced a $26 billion budget shortfall. The University of California, the nation's largest four-year public university system, fell $20 billion in debt and endured devastating cuts to its budget, faculty and staff furloughs, and a 32 percent tuition hike. Students and faculty did not meet these cuts quietly. In Berkeley they joined forces in sit-ins, walkouts, marches, and strikes, with Dr. Ananya Roy, then Distinguished Chair in Global Poverty and Practice, offering a strident voice in support of educational access.

Roy was born in Calcutta, India, to parents who taught her to "question every unsupported premise" (Friend). With training in urban planning, she is currently the Meyer and Renee Luskin Chair in Inequality and Democracy and professor of urban planning, social welfare, and geography at the UCLA Luskin School of Public Affairs. Roy is an award-winning teacher, who instructs students to be double agents, showing them how they can change the system from within. She teaches by example, using her voice from inside the educational system to seek educational transformation. At a panel discussion on "The Crisis of Education," Roy first offered the provocative declaration on which the piece that follows is based: "We Are All Students of Color Now." Her "we" is meant to include the newly precarious middle-class, white students whose family's income just surpasses the threshold to qualify for financial aid, and therefore encounter steep tuition increases without public aid. *Could solidarity form between old and new forms of exclusion?* she wonders.

In the following piece, Roy explains that her statement employs Gayatri Spivak's notion of "strategic essentialism." That is, she temporarily unifies people around a common or "essential" trait, in order to mobilize a collectivity. Roy shows how, in the current economy, white middle-class students share an educational vulnerability historically experienced by students of color. "We are all students of color" is meant to "insist on the recognition in the 1 percent nation that we are all outcast, abandoned, marginalized."

Roy describes the blowback of her rhetorical choice, which was delivered by both the Right, who accused her of "unwarranted racialization" of public education, and the Left (including her own students), who denounced her for ignoring the organizing history of people of color. Roy welcomed the questioning of her premise, writing, "The universalizing gesture that is inherent in strategic essentialisms *must be* subject to vigorous critique" (emphasis ours). In the feminist tradition, Roy's rhetoric is both provocative and invitational, creating a space here for a rich dialogue about the possibilities and limitations of collectives in a moment of acute economic inequality.

"We Are All Students of Color Now"

Representations, 2011

In their recent edited collection, "Against the Day: The Struggle for Public Education," Christopher Newfield and Colleen Lye (2011), outline the historical conjuncture of crisis and protest at the University of California.[1] Their analysis points to the dispersed and divergent mobilizations that constitute the struggle for public education in California—from student occupations to worker unions to faculty senates. It is at rare moments that these interests have coalesced as a movement with choreographed visibility and coordinated targets. And thus the struggle has been haunted by questions: What is this collectivity? On whose behalf is the public education movement waged? In whose name are buildings occupied and strikes called? Such questions speak to a fundamental question that is writ large in historical materialism: Who is the subject of history?

As Newfield and Lye note, one important moment in the struggle was March 4, 2010, a statewide Day of Action. Despite its multiple theaters of action—from rallies at the capitol in Sacramento to a freeway occupation in downtown Oakland—March 4 sought to connect "the campus crisis to the political crisis in California as a whole" (535). Inevitably, March 4 was also a performance. It required identifying and foregrounding testimonials by the embodied subjects of crisis. Student and faculty organizers valiantly worked to gather up such testimonials, and when they had been arrayed—in photos, YouTube videos, blogs, essays—it became clear that an important piece of this narrative was the crisis of the middle-class (read: white) student. Positioned just above the thresholds that mark the limits of financial aid eligibility, these students were vulnerable to sharply rising tuitions. Their lives were also entangled with a broader Californian, and indeed American, crisis: of declining middle-class fortunes, widespread home foreclosures, and unstable jobs. Performing protest meant foregrounding this crisis. It meant, as Chris Chen has noted, countering discourses of privilege through the making visible of precarity: "Public criticism of the movement continues to perceive the figure of the student primarily in terms of privilege rather than precarity and to interpret public education as fundamentally a vehicle for private advancement rather than a public good."[2]

Indeed, it was a generalized condition of precarity that I had hoped, in October 2009, to highlight through the statement "we are all students of color now." At a forum on the crisis of the public university, I had sought to foreground a supplemental crisis: that of collective politics. By asserting that "we are all students of color now," could a politics of solidarity be forged between old and new forms of exclusion, between the historically precarious subject marked by race and ethnicity and the emergent precarity of hitherto unmarked middle-class whiteness?

Following Gayatri Spivak, "students of color" can be understood as a strategic essentialism.[3] Making the case for anti-essentialist deconstruction, the constant critique of the categories that produce a sovereign subject, Spivak argues for the need to consider the "strategic use of a positivist essentialism in a scrupulously visible political interest" (3). Such an imperative arrives, she suggests, at moments of battle, for strategy itself is an "embattled concept-metaphor." Such moments present the "necessity to accept the risk of essence." "We are all students of color now" was offered in this spirit, as the "strategic use of essence as a mobilizing strategy," as an effort to define a "relation to collectivity."

This strategic essentialism was to travel, though in ways that I could not have anticipated. Right-wing critics saw the statement as an unwarranted racialization of the public education question. Writing in *Forbes* and then in the *Wall Street Journal*, Peter Robinson, a fellow at Stanford University's Hoover Institute and former speechwriter for President Reagan, resurrected the accusation of privilege: "We have all become students of color? A march on Sacramento that possesses the same moral dimension as the March on Washington? Let us remind ourselves just what the Berkeley protesters are demanding—not racial equality but money. For the poor and dispossessed? Scarcely. For themselves."[4]

Robinson's opinion pieces triggered angry emails that I received from conservative Californians. One email, with the subject line, "What year is it at Berkeley?" was especially illuminating, for it expressed deep anxiety about a revival of 1960s-style protest at Berkeley and then went on to ask why everything at Berkeley always had to be about race. The email revealed that implicated in the haunting question of collective politics was the politics of memory: of how the public education movement and its critics remember the 1960s. The Free Speech Movement, now safely enshrined in campus landmarks, from the Mario Savio steps to the Free Speech Movement Café, cannot be cordoned off from the incendiary battles over war, empire, capitalism, and race that also marked that historical moment, and that must be revived today.

Indeed, the strategic essentialism of "we are all students of color now" is meant to signal today's conjuncture of global neoliberalism and class inequality. America is after all the 1 percent nation, with the top 1 percent of American households holding a larger share of income than at any time since 1928. Such a pattern is no coincidence; it has been produced by federal and state bailouts, tax cuts, and subsidies for a wealthy minority, accompanied by systematic disinvestment in sectors that serve the majority of American households, including public education. To state that "we are all students of color now" is to reject the neoconservative discourse that increasingly positions public education as the new welfare dependent, with self-pleading students and faculty "eating at the taxpayer trough," a phrase I borrow from one of those anxious emails I received in the wake of Robinson's opinion pieces. It is to insist on the recognition in the 1 percent nation that we are all outcast, abandoned, marginalized.

But the universalizing gesture that is inherent in strategic essentialisms must be subject to vigorous critique. "We are all students of color now" was not a concept that could be reconciled with the complex politics of affinity and representation that Chris Chen presents in his analysis of the California student movement. My optimism about what Chen describes as the "radical instability of 'race' as a political signifier" was not widely shared (561). A year later, a student organizer of self-declared AB 540 status was to tell me how he had defied an unspoken ban and enrolled in my course on global poverty.[5] "Students of color organizers are very upset with your statement, Professor Roy. They think you have made their history of organizing irrelevant." If right-wing critics raged against a public education movement that they feared would revive "affirmative action" politics, then these young student-of-color organizers were eager to reject the twilight hour that they saw as "postracial politics." It was an uncanny convergence and it returned me to the haunting question of collectivity, collectivity as political imagination and historical agency.

We have perhaps reached the limits of strategic essentialism. The "embattled concept-metaphor" of "students of color" is unable to speak to the brutal differentiations that guard access to California's public universities. Each year, in one of the world's wealthiest economies, thousands of students are turned away from the community colleges and state universities. Where are students of color located in these structures of precarity? In the University of California, African American and Chicano/Latino students inch their way up in the proportion of admitted students. But in a white-minority state, their presence is more solidly marked at the campuses at the margins of the system: Merced and Riverside. At UC Berkeley, "underrepresented minorities" remain less than 20 percent of the student population.[6] How then are we all students of color now? How can precarity have political meaning in what is inevitably a bastion of elitism?

In closing, let me indicate one type of precarity that is worth considering as the grounds for strategic essentialism: debt. During several building occupations on the UC Berkeley campus, student protestors hung a banner, "College of Debtors." This was not a misrecognition by any means. While much of the national legislative scrutiny has focused on "for-profit" colleges and the heavy burden of debt that their students (many of them students of color) accumulate, it seems that indebtedness is a generalized condition of precarity for all college students. The Project on Student Debt notes that in 2008, at public universities in the United States, average debt was $20,200—not that much lower than the average debt burden of $33,500 for private for-profit universities and $27,650 for private nonprofit universities. Across all three categories, average debt had steadily risen since 2004. Who bears this burden of debt? Pell Grant recipients coming from families making less than $50,000 a year borrow heavily. But so must everyone else it seems. While at private for-profit universities, a staggering 96 percent of graduates had student loans; at private nonprofit universities and public universities the numbers too were high, 72 percent and 62 percent, respectively.[7] It is against this future of indebtedness that the case for public education must be made in California, and in America. In this struggle, we are all students of color.

NOTES

1. Christopher Newfield and Colleen Lye, "Introduction: The Struggle for Public Education in California," in "Against the Day: The Struggle for Public Education," special section of *Sovereignty, Indigeneity, and the Law,* special issue, *South Atlantic Quarterly* 110, no. 2 (Spring 2011): 529–38.

2. Chris Chen, "We Have All Become Students of Color Now: The California Student Movement and the Rhetoric of Privilege," in "Against the Day: The Struggle for Public Education," special section of *South Atlantic Quarterly* 110, no. 2 (Spring 2011): 559–64, 559.

3. Gayatri Spivak, *Outside in the Teaching Machine* (New York, 1993).

4. Peter Robinson, "Hell No, We Won't Pay! The Death of the Campus Protest Movement," *Forbes,* January 8, 2010, https://www.forbes.com/2010/01/07/berkeley-protest-california-opinions-columnists-peter-robinson.html#74ac5de82392.

5. AB 540 refers to California's Assembly Bill 540 that allows undocumented immigrants in California limited access to college education.

6. University of California data shows that between 2008 and 2010 admitted African American students increased from 3.8 percent to 4.2 percent, and admitted Chicano/Latino students increased from 20.7 percent to 23.3 percent. In the breakdown of the data by campus, underrepresented minorities made up 19.3 percent of freshmen admits at UC Berkeley in 2010 compared to 37.1 percent at UC Merced and 36.3 percent at UC Riverside; California Freshman Admissions for Fall 2010, University of California Office of the President, https://accountability.universityofcalifornia.edu/2016/chapters/chapter-7.html.

7. For a summary of this data, see Quick Facts about Student Debt, January 2010, The Project on Student Debt, http://projectonstudentdebt.org/files/File/Debt_Facts_and_Sources.pdf.

For Further Reading

"Ananya Roy." *UCLA Luskin School of Public Affairs*, n.d., https://luskin.ucla.edu/person/ananya-roy/.

DeRuy, Emily. "The Racial Disparity of the Student-Loan Crisis." *The Atlantic*, 24 Oct. 2016, www.theatlantic.com/education/archive/2016/10/why-debt-balloons-after-graduation-for-black-students/505058/.

Friend, Tad. "Protest Studies." *The New Yorker*, 6 July 2017, www.newyorker.com/magazine/2010/01/04/protest-studies.

Hacker, Andrew, and Claudia Dreifus. "The Debt Crisis at American Colleges." *The Atlantic*, 17 Aug. 2011, https://www.theatlantic.com/business/archive/2011/08/the-debt-crisis-at-american-colleges/243777/.

Roy, Ananya, and Abby VanMuijen. *Encountering Poverty: Thinking and Acting in an Unequal World*. U of California P, 2016.

Marjane Satrapi

Marjane Satrapi's comic memoir of growing up in Iran from the ages of ten through fourteen is an international bestseller, introducing audiences to the graphic novel as well as to a lived reality of the Islamic Revolution in 1979. Originally published as two volumes in French, *Persepolis* was translated into English and released in 2003; the third and fourth volumes in French became *Persepolis 2: The Story of a Return*. *Persepolis* received international acclaim and is credited with the increase in interest and sales in the graphic novel as a genre. Because of its cross-age appeal, *Persepolis* has been taught in secondary schools and colleges, but not without controversy—for instance, meeting with censorship in the Chicago Public Schools. In 2007 Satrapi wrote and directed an animated film version of *Persepolis* along with Vincent Paronnaud, which co-earned the Jury Prize at the Cannes Film Festival, garnered a French César, and was nominated for an Academy Award for Best Animated Feature.

Satrapi was born in 1969 to a clothing designer and an engineer; growing up in Tehran, her Westernized parents caught the notice of Iranian authorities after the revolution, and by 1984 they sent Satrapi to school in Austria, where she would have more freedom. After a brief return to Tehran, Satrapi completed art school in France and settled in Paris as an adult.

The broad appeal of *Persepolis*—it has been translated into twenty-four languages—may be in part due to the juxtaposition of an adolescent girl with typical interests in popular culture and music against the backdrop of a harrowing revolution in which her own family members are at risk and her Uncle Anoosh is executed. Her younger self, Marji, is precocious but also clings with youthful naiveté to the conviction that right should always prevail. She grapples mightily with her religious beliefs and the realities of the revolution. The minimalist black-and-white strip drawings depict a preteen living in an oppressive regime, inviting us to see both the inner workings of Marji's mind and daily life amid a revolution.

Satrapi's story and visuals conjoin for powerful rhetorical effect, especially during a historical moment when a Western lens often associates Iran with terrorism. As the *Time* reviewer Andrew D. Arnold writes, for US readers, "[Satrapi] pulls back the veil on a culture that utterly preoccupies us, but about which we know little. Its complicated personal portrait makes it impossible to think of Iran as the monolithic fundamentalist terror state of our fears."

In this excerpt, "The Veil," young Marji wrestles with new laws that require females to wear veils to school in the name of religion, pondering the purpose of religion. Marji is a girl full of confidence, never second-guessing that her thoughts should be relegated because she is young and female. We root for Marji as she imagines herself as a prophet, much to the consternation of her teacher and friends, wanting to demand a world that is just for all, where there is no pain, and where everyone can have a car. Through one child's eyes and imagery, Satrapi shares powerful messages of religion, power, and gender in ways ask readers to move beyond stereotypes of Iranian culture to more expansively view its humanity.

For Further Reading

Arnold, Andrew D. "An Iranian Girlhood." *TIME*, 16 May 2003, content.time.com/time/arts/arti cle/0,8599,452401,00.html.

Day, Jennifer. "*Persepolis*: A Class Act—Or Should Be." *Chicago Tribune*, 30 Mar. 2013, https://www .chicagotribune.com/entertainment/books/ct-xpm-2013-03-30-ct-prj-0331-persepolis-mar jane-satrapi-visual-dete-20130330-story.html.

"Emma Watson Interviews *Persepolis* Author Marjane Satrapi." *Vogue*, Aug. 2016, www.vogue.com/ article/emma-watson-interviews-marjane-satrapi.

Hattenstone, Simon. "Confessions of Miss Mischief." *The Guardian*, 28 Mar. 2008, www.theguard ian.com/film/2008/mar/29/biography.

Luebering, J. E. "Marjane Satrapi." *Encyclopaedia Britannica*, 20 Oct. 2014, www.britannica.com/ biography/Marjane-Satrapi.

Murphy, Bernadette. "With Poignancy, a Daughter of Iran Sets the Record Straight." *Los Angeles Times*, 17 June 2003, http://articles.latimes.com/2003/jun/17/entertainment/et-book17.

Satrapi, Marjane. *Persepolis: The Story of a Childhood*. Penguin Random House, 2003.

Satrapi, Marjane. *Persepolis 2: The Story of a Return*. Penguin Random House, 2003.

"The Veil": Excerpt from *Persepolis*

4

10–16. Marjane Satrapi's "The Veil," from *The Complete Persepolis* (New York: Pantheon, 2007). This excerpt from *Persepolis* features graphic novel panels with black-and-white drawings and text that show and tell Satrapi's experiences in Iran during the Islamic Resolution in 1980 when wearing a veil became obligatory. "The Veil" depicts the tension she felt between her family's modernity and her youthful hope of being a prophet in the Zarathustrian religion.

5

Jessica Valenti

Jessica Valenti has been called "one of the most successful and visible feminists of her generation" (Goldberg). In 2004, just two years out of college, she and her sister, Vanessa Valenti, co-founded the blog *Feministing*, which the *Nation* described as "a must-read for anyone concerned with the state of women's rights." The Valenti sisters began *Feministing* to promote the voices of and to provide information to young feminists. There clearly was an audience: in a 2009 interview, Jessica Valenti noted that the site had six hundred thousand monthly readers. Over a decade later, the site is still going strong, promoting change "online and off" while covering "a broad range of intersectional issues" by diverse feminists ("About Feministing"). While Jessica Valenti is no longer running the site, her feminist activism takes the form of books; articles in the *New York Times*, the *Washington Post*; and in columns for the *Guardian*.

Valenti is often situated with other women labeled as third-wave feminists (though she resists this label because of its generational boundaries) such as Jennifer Baumgardner and Amy Richards, who co-wrote *Manifesta*, and Rebecca Walker (Alice Walker's daughter), who coined the term *third wave*. Third-wave feminism focuses more on individuality and diversity than did earlier waves and responds to the false idea that we live in a postfeminist world. Helping younger women connect to feminism was a clear mission of *Feministing* and Valenti's first book, *Full Frontal Feminism: A Young Woman's Guide to Why Feminism Matters*, which is excerpted here.

The tone of *Full Frontal Feminism* is colloquial and open in its approach to feminism, covering topics such as wedding culture, shaming, and beauty. According to Valenti, her accessible rhetoric is "a political choice." Not surprisingly, *Full Frontal Feminism* received criticism, not just from conservatives but from some feminists. In her preface to the second edition, Valenti speaks to some critiques—notably the absence of trans issues and the cover of the first edition, which showed a white, flat-stomached woman's body.

The following excerpt from *Full Frontal Feminism* focuses on issues of sex and purity, forecasting themes in Valenti's well-known 2009 book, *The Purity Myth: How America's Obsession with Virginity is Hurting Young Women*. Valenti is candid about liking sex and insists there is no shame in pleasure, employing a directness that is often deemed improper or unfeminine. She makes no apologies for her position and forcefully asserts that other women shouldn't have to apologize, either. Valenti also speaks to the historical and cultural sexism that asserts control over women's bodies—and attitudes about their bodies—arguing that knowledge is power when it comes to sex, and that's what the patriarchy is afraid of. In so doing, she offers a different brand of sex education than most readers likely encountered in school or at home. With quips and some cursing, she teaches us that feminism and pleasure go hand-in-hand.

"Feminists Do It Better (And Other Sex Tips)": Excerpt from *Full Frontal Feminism*

2007

I'm better in bed than you are. And I have feminism to thank for it.

There's nothing more hackneyed than the notion that feminists hate sex (but I guess if you buy the ugly, man-hating stereotype, hating sex follows). Feminists do it better 'cause we know how to get past all the bullshit.

Women's sexuality is often treated like a commodity, a joke, or a sin. This is especially true for us younger women who end up getting totally screwed up by social influences telling us what "hot" or desirable behavior is. (Generally, it's flashing boobs or faux-lesbian make-out sessions. Never been a fan of either.)

When you're getting abstinence-only education during the day and *Girls Gone Wild* commercials at night, it's not exactly easy to develop a healthy sexuality. You're taught that sex before marriage is bad bad bad, but that if you want to be a spring-break hottie, you'd better start making out for the camera.

While these two messages are seemingly conflicting, they're actually promoting the same idea—that young women can't make their own decisions about sex. Whether it's a teacher telling you not to or a cameraman telling you how to, having sex that's about making yourself happy is a big no-no these days. Shit, you can't even buy vibrators in some states!

To get unscrewed, you really need to take a close look at all the insane things stacked up against women having a good old time in bed. And after marveling at the ridiculousness of things like the sexual double standard and the faux-sexy crap that's forced down your throat, you just learn to say fuck it.

Just (Don't) Do IT

Women are taught that we're only supposed to have sex under these bizarre arbitrary guidelines: only if you're married; only if it's for procreation; and only with another girl if guys can watch. So unless you're going to do it the way other people want, just don't.

You're a Dirty Lollipop

Nothing freaks me out/pisses me off more than abstinenceonly education. Basically, it's the most naïve form of sex education you can get: Sex is bad, don't have it until you're married, contraception doesn't work. Somehow educators think this will convince kids to not have sex. Compare that to comprehensive sex education that teaches abstinence but also makes sure that teens have medically correct information about contraception, STDs, and the like. It's reality-based sex ed that understands that no matter how many scare tactics you throw at people, they're still going to do what they want.

This isn't to say that I think holding off on sex is bad—abstain all you want, ladies. But if you're holding off, do it because you're waiting to have sex on your own terms. And don't *not* have sex because you think you're worthless if you do—which is exactly what these classes are saying.

As it stands now, the government is spending $178 million a year to tell young women they're big whores if they give it up,[1] and various other untruths. Most (80 frigging percent)[2] abstinence-only education programs give out false information about sex—all of it sexist, most of it bordering on the ridiculous.

The medical misinformation is not just untrue—it's straight-up dangerous. For example, these programs teach not only that condoms don't protect you from pregnancy or STDs and HIV, but that they could cause cancer.[3] (Condom cancer?) After kids are exposed to this bullshit, they are less likely to use contraception—'cause it doesn't work anyway, right? Because of abstinence-only education, we're going to have a generation of sexual dum-dums.

It seems unfathomable, but, somehow, teaching the truth about sex and contraception is just too scary for some folks. Conservatives and right-wing religious groups think that it's going to make us all slutty. I know proponents of the all-holy abstinence agenda bristle at the idea of girls being taught how to put a condom on a penis, even though studies show that real sex ed (you know—the kind that tells the truth) significantly reduces teenage girls' STD rates. Not to mention comprehensive sex ed actually delays teen sex and ensures kids are making informed decisions. Isn't that more important than being afraid that your kid isn't a virgin?

Apparently, not so much. Schools that get federal funding for abstinence-only sex ed *can't* teach safe-sex practices. You heard right. They can't even talk about it. Because god forbid your kids have safe sex. Much better that they resort to only-a-slut-would-use-a-condom sex. But what's just as disturbing as the bad science behind these programs is the unapologetic sexist crap they're spewing.

One program teaches that women need "financial support," while men need "admiration."[4] Another tells students: "Women gauge their happiness and judge their success."[5]

Another program tells a faux-fairytale that isn't so much about sex as about how women need to keep their mouths shut. One book used in abstinence curricula, *Choosing the Best*, tells the story of a knight who saves a princess from a dragon (original, I know). When the knight arrives to save her, the princess offers some ideas on how to kill the dragon. Her ideas work, but the knight feels emasculated, so he goes off and marries a village maiden, "only after making sure she knew nothing about nooses or poison."

The curriculum concludes with the moral of the story: "Occasional suggestions and assistance may be all right, but too much of them will lessen a man's confidence or even turn him away from his princess."[6] Hear that, gals? Shh . . . if you let on that you're smart, your prince on the white horse is likely to run scared!

Abstinence programs are also *huge* fans of making sex the ladies' responsibility. It's up to us to make sure it doesn't happen, because guys just can't help themselves. One program actually advises girls:

> Watch what you wear. If you don't aim to please, don't aim to tease. The liberation movement has produced some aggressive girls, and one of the tough challenges for guys who say no will be the questioning of their manliness. And because females generally become aroused less easily, they're in a good position to help young men learn balance in relationships by keeping intimacy in perspective.[7]

The logic is laughable. Seems that girls don't get horny, so it's up to us to make sure that The Sex doesn't happen. And if it does, well, you should have kept your legs closed, you big dummy. But really and truly, the following gem is my fave. It comes from an "educator" speaking at an abstinence conference last year: "Your body is a wrapped lollipop. When you have sex with a man, he unwraps your lollipop and sucks on it. It may feel great at the time, but unfortunately, when he's done with you, all you have left for your next partner is a poorly wrapped, saliva-fouled sucker."[8]

Holy. Shit. Is that clear enough for you? Without your precious "lollipop," you're a piece-of-shit, dirty-ass, already-sucked-on candy. Which is supposedly why you have to hold on to your most precious commodity—your virginity.

Our Hymens, Ourselves

I have never really understood what the big deal was about virginity. Really. Mine was lost without a great deal of fanfare to a high school boyfriend whom I dated for several years afterward. I expected to feel different—I didn't. The whole precious-flower-virginity thing always seemed silly to me. So imagine my surprise when I found out that I was just a used-up piece of trash (or candy) without it.

Remember how back in the day, your virginity was a valuable commodity and your "purity" was pretty much what your dad banked on to get a good price for when you got married? You think that's all in the past? Not even close.

One of the most disturbing stories I've ever heard was about Jessica Simpson and her dad, Joe. A gossip mag reported that during a ceremony when Jessica was twelve years old, Joe made her promise to stay a virgin until marriage. Wait, it gets worse. Jessica's dad, who is also her manager, gave her a promise ring and said, "I'm going to tell you how beautiful you are every day . . . and I'm going to be that person until the day you find a man to do that in my place."[9]

If you're like me, you're probably in the fetal position on the floor right now, trying to make that image go away. But this isn't unusual—there are virginity cards, rings, ceremonies, you name it. The one thing they all have in common is that girls' virginity and sexuality don't belong to them.

Not only are virginity pledges sooo creepy and wrong, they're not exactly effective. Recent studies have shown that teens who take virginity pledges are actually more likely to have oral and anal sex.

Their logic is that because it's not intercourse, it's not real sex. Somehow I don't think the folks who made up the whole pledge thing had sodomy in mind. (You would think the idea of good Christian girls taking it in the ass would motivate some change in the whole pledge system, but they're sticking to their guns.)

What kills me is that we're falling for this crap. Women feel so bad about losing their virginity that some of them are actually deluded by the idea that they can become "born again" virgins. Like a self-imposed dry spell. For fuck's sake, there are even women who are getting plastic surgery to get fake hymens put back in! Who the hell wants their hymen back?

And the people who are just shocked—shocked!—that younger women are looking to oversexualized pop culture to define themselves are the very same ones that are shoving virginity down our throats. (Not literally, of course. Ew.) For folks who are trying to tell us we shouldn't define ourselves by our sexuality, they certainly can't get past the whole dick-meets-vagina thing. And really, if you want to attach young women's worth to their virginity, you can't be surprised when they follow suit and attach all their worth to their sexuality. You can't have it both ways.
[. . .]

Just Do It (If You're So Inclined)

I was serious about feminism making me better in bed. You can't be good in that department unless you get past the antisex nonsense, and feminism allows you to do just that.

Feminism tells you it's okay to make decisions about your sexuality *for yourself.* Because when it comes down to it, what's more powerful and important than being able to do what you want with your body without fear of being shamed or punished?

Feminism teaches responsibility. You can't really enjoy yourself sexually if you don't have all the facts and aren't being safe. While conservative programs are doing their best to make sure that you stay in the dark about contraception, feminists are fighting to make sure that you have access to the information and resources you need to have safe sex.

And perhaps most important, feminism wants you to have fun. Sex isn't just about having babies after all, despite what young women are being taught.

"At Risk," My Ass

In itself, the act of having sex is considered irresponsible by some. These days, calling a teen "sexually active" is code for "troubled" or "at risk" (though if they're a product of abstinence-only education, I wouldn't disagree with the "at risk" part).

But really, what could be more responsible than taking control of your body by making informed decisions about your sexuality? What's really irresponsible is telling young women there's something wrong with having sex. Naturally, just calling yourself responsible doesn't quite cut it. I know it's annoying, but sometimes you have to get off your ass and do something.

Take Responsibility for Your Health

- Get thee to a gyno! Get regular checkups—no one wants a sick vagina, after all.
- If you've been subjected to abstinence-only education, get out there and find comprehensive information on sex (and pass it around to your friends!). Planned Parenthood is a great place to start; its website has a ton of information: www.plannedparenthood.com.
- Use protection. If you're having straight sex, use two forms of contraception if you don't want to get preggers. One of them must be condoms. Always. Every time.

Take Responsibility for Your Partners

• Love and attraction are curious things, and there aren't many women who don't have at least one partner they regret. But that doesn't mean we can't at least try to choose wisely. I never liked the word "promiscuity," because it's defined as having sex indiscriminately. So have sex with whoever you like, and as many people as you like, but I think we can all afford to be *a bit* discriminating.

• Don't have sex with someone who won't use protection.

• Don't have sex with someone who is anti-choice—they have no respect for your body or your ability to make decisions for yourself.

• Don't have sex with someone who doesn't respect your physical and emotional boundaries.

• Don't have sex with Republicans. (Okay, that one is just mine.)

Take Responsibility for Your Choices

• There'll be plenty on this later, but it's worth mentioning. As you probably know already, when it comes to the rights we have over our bodies, shit is going downhill. There are plenty of young women who don't have access to contraception and abortion. This is unacceptable. Fight the good fight in your schools, community, wherever, to make sure that you have as many choices as possible when it comes to your reproductive rights.

Take Responsibility for Other Women

• We're all in this together, ladies—so help your fellow woman out. Whether it's taking a friend to get birth control, helping someone come out, or even just not calling other girls nasty names—it makes a huge difference.

See—now no one can give you shit! On to the fun stuff.

NOTES

1. Sexuality Information and Education Council of the United States

2. Representative Henry Waxman, "The Content of Federally Funded Abstinence-Only Education Programs," US House of Representatives Committee on Government Reform, December 2004.

3. Gail Schontzler, "Abstinence Speaker Pushed Religion in School, Dad Charges," *The Daily Chronicle*, May 11, 2005.

4. Representative Henry Waxman

5. Ibid.

6. Ibid.

7. "In Their Own Words: What Abstinence-Only-Until-Marriage-Programs Say," Sexuality Information and Education Council of the United States, August 2005.

8. Quoted in Camille Hahn. "Virgin Territory," *Ms.* Magazine, Fall 2004.

9. "Jessica Simpson's Virgin Vow," Female First, December 30, 2004. Found online at www.femalefirst.co.uk/entertainment.

For Further Reading

"About Feministing." *Feministing*, n.d., feministing.com/about/.

Baumgardner, Jennifer, and Amy Richards. *Manifesta: Young Women, Feminism, and the Future*. Farrar, Straus and Giroux, 2000.

Bennet, Molly. "Jessica Valenti: Full Frontal Feminism." *The Nation*, 28 Sept. 2007, www.thenation.com/article/jessica-valenti-full-frontal-feminism.

Goldberg, Michelle. "Feminist Writers Are So Besieged by Online Abuse That Some Have Begun to Retire." *The Washington Post*, 20 Feb. 2015, www.washingtonpost.com/opinions/online-feminists-increasingly-ask-are-the-psychic-costs-too-much-to-bear/2015/02/19/3dc4ca6c-b7dd-11e4-a200-c008a01a6692_story.html?utm_term=.24c7ad08bb66.

Jessica Valenti. www.jessicavalenti.com/.

Solomon, Deborah. "Fourth-Wave Feminism." *The New York Times Magazine*, 13 Nov. 2009, www.nytimes.com/2009/11/15/magazine/15fob-q4-t.html.

Valenti, Jessica. *Full Frontal Feminism: A Young Woman's Guide to Why Feminism Matters*. Seal Press, 2007.

Valenti, Jessica. *He's a Stud, She's a Slut, and 49 Other Double Standards Every Woman Should Know*. Seal Press, 2008.

Valenti, Jessica. Introduction. *Full Frontal Feminism: A Young Woman's Guide to Why Feminism Matters*, 2nd ed., Seal Press, 2014, pp. 1–4.

Valenti, Jessica. *The Purity Myth: How America's Obsession with Virginity Is Hurting Young Women*. Seal Press, 2009.

V

Rhetorics of Work and Labor

The rhetors in this section address a range of complex issues women face as workers and laborers in the twenty-first century. They make bold and incisive arguments for workplaces that are more attuned to the needs and experiences of female workers and for cultural conversations that examine the relationship among gender, labor, poverty, and abuse. While studies on employment patterns consistently show that men outnumber women in the labor market, measurements of *only* paid work fail to account for the fact that in every area of the world, women work more unpaid hours than men—often on top of jobs outside the home (Gander). Women's participation in the (paid) labor force has grown at significant rates in the late twentieth and early twenty-first centuries; within the United States, women's employment doubled between 1950 and 2002 (Meece).

Women's increased participation in the labor market, though, is not without obstruction. For instance, women worldwide are more likely than men to work minimum wage jobs and to be classified as "working poor," employed full-time but not earning enough to move themselves and their families out of poverty (Meece). Linda Tirado speaks to this issue, providing an unflinching account of the labor involved in being poor—the work it takes, physically and emotionally, to survive.

While women make up about 60 percent of the global labor force, there remains significant gender segregation in the kinds of jobs women occupy, with the majority found in service-oriented careers. Women are also severely underrepresented in upper management and leadership roles. Sheryl Sandberg addresses this gap in her best-selling and controversial book *Lean In*, which offers advice on building a successful career, while balancing it with family life.

The rhetors in the section also point out the problems women face in male-dominated professions. Jennifer Pozner shows how a lack of gender representation in the media leads to coverage that fails to represent women's perspectives and therefore distorts the news. Captain Brenda Berkman, a firefighter who served on the front lines of Ground Zero after 9/11, is an example of the problem Pozner targets: she argues that women's labor in the 9/11 rescue and recovery effort was often erased in media coverage and insists that our historical records commemorate these contributions. Centering her experience as a military woman and Iraq War veteran, Senator Tammy Duckworth implores the US government to recognize the women and men who serve and the costs they bear for this labor. Addressing the rampant, but often hidden, problem of sexual harassment in the workplace, the former television host Gretchen Carlson offers legal and practical advice gleaned from her harassment suit against her then boss, former Fox News CEO Roger Ailes.

Of course, how one experiences the workplace, and labor practices, differs vastly depending on one's social location and geographic situation. Thanu Yakupitiyage draws attention to how natural disaster caused by climate change increases migration rates, as people emigrate to seek employment in other countries. Her editorial issues a rallying cry to join the People's Climate March and participate in International Workers' Day. The activist Ai-jen Poo highlights poverty and labor as transnational issues, showing how migration—often spurred by poverty and violence—makes women vulnerable to trafficking. The accompanying infographic by the National Domestic Workers Association (NDWA), which Poo directs, provides powerful graphics and statistics to raise awareness about the plight of domestic workers in and beyond the United States.

By making women's labor visible and insisting that the problems women face in the workplace are addressed, the rhetors in this section move us closer to a world where "women's work" is not a pejorative, but is labor valued on par with the work of men.

WORKS CITED

Gander, Kashmira. "Women Work More Unpaid Hours than Men in Every Region of the World." *Newsweek*, 24 May 2018, www.newsweek.com/women-work-more-unpaid-hours-men-every-region-world-942923.

Meece, Judith L. "Trends in Women's Employment in the Early 21st Century." *Educational Research and Evaluation*, vol. 12, no. 4, 2006, pp. 297–303.

Linda Tirado

In 2013 Linda Tirado first posted her piece about living as a poor person in the United States to a message board on the now-defunct blog *Gawker*. It went viral and was reprinted on the *Huffington Post*. Controversy over the piece—or, more accurately, its author—immediately followed suit. Some called it a hoax, due to Tirado's middle-class upbringing or the fact that she dropped out of college. But as Tirado explained in subsequent interviews, such scrutiny of her history deflected the discussion from issues of poverty and its psychological repercussions.

Tirado followed up with a book, *Hand to Mouth: Living in Bootstrap America*, dubbed by *Esquire* as one of the five most important books of 2014. In it, Tirado expands on the themes and experiences from the initial blog post, demonstrating how the crushing hopelessness of living in poverty can lead to coping mechanisms like smoking, relying on convenience food, and making short-term financial decisions. She shows that despair is deepened by dead-end minimum-wage work that is dehumanizing and humiliating. In his review of *Hand to Mouth*, David K. Shipler quotes a factory manager who asked employees to explain their high turnover. They confirm Tirado's point, insisting that "it wasn't the meager pay, the noise, the mind-numbing assembly lines, or the mist of plastic dust in the air." Instead, it was the indignity of not feeling "needed, necessary, or wanted" and of being treated like "just another body."

Hand to Mouth, called "part memoir, part polemic, and part howl of protest," describes someone moving in and out poverty, whose past includes working in fast food, sometimes receiving financial assistance from family, and sometimes receiving help from the government in the form of food stamps and Medicaid (Brockes). Tirado is married to an Iraq War veteran and has two children. She has worked on political campaigns and carved out time to write *Hand to Mouth* from funds raised via GoFundMe. An activist and active contributor on Twitter (@KillerMartinis), Tirado contributes to publications such as the *Guardian*, the *Daily Beast*, and *Elle*.

Tirado's original blog post, included here, features an immediacy, anger, and directness that conveys the import of her message. She makes no apologies for how she survives as a poor person; in fact, she explains that persistent hopelessness and lack of opportunities typically motivate seemingly bad decisions made by the poor. She also corrects many cultural narratives that misjudge poor people: that they are lazy or that they don't care, among others.

Shipler aptly captures once source of Tirado's rhetoric's effectiveness: "It's rare to hear directly from the poor. Usually their voices are filtered through journalists or activists. So Tirado's raw clarity is startling." Just as striking is the public reverberation of her post, initially sent as an informal comment on a blog only to incite national press. The public response highlights the limits of the national conversation on class and poverty: that poor people should be grateful for anything, should not speak up about their situations, and should have no pleasures or vices. Above all, the poor are scorned for not sufficiently striving for upward mobility—as if it is always achievable. Especially, Tirado reminds us, if the poor person is a woman.

"This Is Why Poor People's Bad Decisions Make Perfect Sense"

Huffington Post, 2014

There's no way to structure this coherently. They are random observations that might help explain the mental processes. But often, I think that we look at the academic problems of poverty and have no idea of the why. We know the what and the how, and we can see systemic problems, but it's rare to have a poor person actually explain it on their own behalf. So this is me doing that, sort of.

Rest is a luxury for the rich. I get up at 6:00 a.m., go to school (I have a full course load, but I only have to go to two in-person classes) then work, then I get the kids, then I pick up my husband, then I have half an hour to change and go to Job 2. I get home from that at around 12:30 a.m., then I have the rest of my classes and work to tend to. I'm in bed by 3. This isn't every day, I have two days off a week from each of my obligations. I use that time to clean the house and soothe Mr. Martini and see the kids for longer than an hour and catch up on schoolwork. Those nights I'm in bed by midnight, but if I go to bed too early I won't be able to stay up the other nights because I'll fuck my pattern up, and I drive an hour home from Job 2 so I can't afford to be sleepy. I never get a day off from work unless I am fairly sick. It doesn't leave you much room to think about what you are doing, only to attend to the next thing and the next. Planning isn't in the mix.

When I got pregnant the first time, I was living in a weekly motel. I had a mini fridge with no freezer and a microwave. I was on WIC. I ate peanut butter from the jar and frozen burritos because they were 12/$2. Had I had a stove, I couldn't have made beef burritos that cheaply. And I needed the meat, I was pregnant. I might not have had any prenatal care, but I am intelligent enough to eat protein and iron whilst knocked up.

I know how to cook. I had to take Home Ec. to graduate high school. Most people on my level didn't. Broccoli is intimidating. You have to have a working stove, and pots, and spices, and you'll have to do the dishes no matter how tired you are or they'll attract bugs. It is a huge new skill for a lot of people. That's not great, but it's true. And if you fuck it up, you could make your family sick. We have learned not to try too hard to be middle class. It never works out well and always makes you feel worse for having tried and failed yet again. Better not to try. It makes more sense to get food that you know will be palatable and cheap and that keeps well. Junk food is a pleasure that we are allowed to have; why would we give that up? We have very few of them.

The closest Planned Parenthood to me is three hours. That's a lot of money in gas. Lots of women can't afford that, and even if you live near one you probably don't want to be seen coming in and out in a lot of areas. We're aware that we are not "having kids," we're "breeding." We have kids for much the same reasons that I imagine rich people do. Urge to propagate and all. Nobody likes poor people procreating, but they judge abortion even harder.

Convenience food is just that. And we are not allowed many conveniences. Especially since the Patriot Act passed, it's hard to get a bank account. But without one, you spend a lot of time figuring out where to cash a check and get money orders to pay bills. Most motels now have a no-credit-card-no-room policy. I wandered around SF [San Francisco] for five hours in the rain once with nearly a thousand dollars on me and could not rent a room even if I gave them a $500 cash deposit and surrendered my cell phone to the desk to hold as surety.

Nobody gives enough thought to depression. You have to understand that we know that we will never not feel tired. We will never feel hopeful. We will never get a vacation. Ever. We know that the very act of being poor guarantees that we will never not be poor. It doesn't give us much reason to improve ourselves. We don't apply for jobs because we know we can't afford to look nice enough to hold them. I would make a super legal secretary, but I've been turned down more than once because I "don't fit the image of the firm," which is a nice way of saying, "GTFO, pov." I am good enough to cook the food, hidden away in the kitchen, but my boss won't make me a server because I don't "fit the corporate image." I am not beautiful. I have missing teeth and skin that looks like it will when you live on B12 and coffee and nicotine and no sleep. Beauty is a thing you get when you can afford it, and that's how you get the job that you need in order to be beautiful. There isn't much point trying.

Cooking attracts roaches. Nobody realizes that. I've spent a lot of hours impaling roach bodies and leaving them out on toothpick pikes to discourage others from entering. It doesn't work, but is amusing.

"Free" only exists for rich people. It's great that there's a bowl of condoms at my school, but most poor people will never set foot on a college campus. We don't belong there. There's a clinic? Great! There's still a copay. We're not going. Besides, all they'll tell you at the clinic is that you need to see a specialist, which seriously? Might as well be located on Mars for how accessible it is. "Low-cost" and "sliding scale" sounds like "money you have to spend" to me, and they can't actually help you anyway.

I smoke. It's expensive. It's also the best option. You see, I am always, always exhausted. It's a stimulant. When I am too tired to walk one more step, I can smoke and go for another hour. When I am enraged and beaten down and incapable of accomplishing one more thing, I can smoke and I feel a little better, just for a minute. It is the only relaxation I am allowed. It is not a good decision, but it is the only one that I have access to. It is the only thing I have found that keeps me from collapsing or exploding.

I make a lot of poor financial decisions. None of them matter, in the long term. I will never not be poor, so what does it matter if I don't pay a thing and a half this week instead of just one thing? It's not like the sacrifice will result in improved circumstances; the thing holding me back isn't that I blow five bucks at Wendy's. It's that now that I have proven that I am a poor person that is all that I am or ever will be. It is not worth it to me to live a bleak life devoid of small pleasures so that one day I can make a single large purchase. I will never have large pleasures to hold on to. There's a certain pull to live what bits of life you can while there's money in your pocket, because no matter how responsible you are you will be broke in three days anyway. When you never have enough money it ceases to have meaning. I imagine having a lot of it is the same thing.

Poverty is bleak and cuts off your long-term brain. It's why you see people with four different baby daddies instead of one. You grab a bit of connection wherever you can to survive. You have no idea how strong the pull to feel worthwhile is. It's more basic than food. You go to these people who make you feel lovely for an hour that one time, and that's all you get. You're probably not compatible with them for anything long-term, but right this minute they can make you feel powerful and valuable. It does not matter what will happen in a month. Whatever happens in a month is probably going to be just about as indifferent as whatever happened today or last week. None of it matters. We don't plan long-term because if we do we'll just get our hearts broken. It's best not to hope. You just take what you can get as you spot it.

I am not asking for sympathy. I am just trying to explain, on a human level, how it is that people make what look from the outside like awful decisions. This is what our lives are like, and here are our defense mechanisms, and here is why we think differently. It's certainly self-defeating, but it's safer. That's all. I hope it helps make sense of it.

FOR FURTHER READING

Brockes, Emma. "*Hand to Mouth* Review: Linda Tirado's Howl of Protest about the Plight of the Poor." *The Guardian*, 24 Sept. 2014, www.theguardian.com/books/2014/sep/24/hand-to -mouth-review-linda-tirado-poor-poverty.

Goldberg, Michelle. "Linda Tirado is Not a Hoax." *The Nation*, 11 Dec. 2013, www.thenation.com/ article/linda-tirado-not-hoax/.

"Poverty Facts." *Poverty USA*, n.d., povertyusa.org/facts.

Shipler, David K. "*Hand to Mouth* by Linda Tirado." *The New York Times*, 26 Dec. 2014, www.nytimes .com/2014/12/28/books/review/hand-to-mouth-by-linda-tirado.html.

Tirado, Linda. *Hand to Mouth: Living in Bootstrap America*. G. P. Putnam's Sons, 2014.

Tirado, Linda. "Meet the Woman Who Accidentally Explained Poverty to the Nation." *Huffington Post*, 24 Nov. 2013, www.huffingtonpost.com/linda-tirado/meet-the-woman-who-accide _b_4334428.html.

Sheryl Sandberg

Sheryl Sandberg's book *Lean In: Women, Work, and the Will to Lead* contends that professional women undersell themselves and can more ambitiously "lean in" to take a seat at the corporate table. Acknowledging that workplaces favor men, *Lean In* offers practical advice for women to reach their full potential. Sandberg has the corporate credibility to write such a book, as Facebook's chief operating officer, and before that, a vice president at Google, sharing that she was the only woman in the room for major workplace meetings and decisions.

Lean In was released in 2013—by 2018 it had sold over four million copies and become a cultural phenomenon, morphing into a website that invites women to join a Lean In Circle, support other women, and work on community awareness and global outreach. The website features stories by women of color, along with monthly newsletters and resources, to help women deal with issues like sexual harassment. The robust website is likely in part a response to the massive reach of the book and to the many critiques it received. Numerous feminist scholars pointed to the text's inattention to intersectionality, its adherence to neoliberalism, and its bias against single women and mothers.

The National Organization for Women argued that *Lean In* would not liberate women due to its non-intersectional feminism and requirement that women assimilate to the patriarchal workplace rather the workplace changing for women. Critics also target Sandberg's assumptions made based on her location as a privileged, white, able-bodied, married woman. (Sandberg has since written about these issues after her husband died unexpectedly in 2015.) The writer and cultural critic Roxane Gay admits that she appreciated *Lean In,* but she also cites its limitations, particularly in ceding that Sandberg valorizes bold leadership—traditionally male leadership—as the standard for success. Perhaps the most oft-cited critique came from the academic and public intellectual bell hooks, who explains that while she found attacks on Sandberg disheartening, particularly by those who didn't seem to have read *Lean In*, the book has clear oversights—namely, Sandberg's failure to address white supremacy or how globalization impacts corporate elites. Writes hooks, "Race is certainly an invisible category in Sandberg's corporate fantasy world."

Yet, hooks notes that it is Sandberg's personal narrative in *Lean In* that is perhaps "most seductive," sharing vulnerabilities and a modesty that suggests she is an everywoman figure. Such anecdotes are a central feature of *Lean In*'s introduction, such as when Sandberg describes (in a non-body-positive fashion) looking like a whale during her pregnancy. In the following excerpt, she also wisely anticipates potential critiques of the book in explaining its limitations and scope. Further, Sandberg combines logos via facts about gender inequality in the workplace with her own story as the often sole woman at the top. While some critics describe *Lean In* as "faux feminism," many credit Sandberg with reaching a more mainstream audience with feminist ideas they may not before have considered.

"Introduction: Internalizing the Revolution": Excerpt from *Lean In*

2013

I got pregnant with my first child in the summer of 2004. At the time, I was running the online sales and operations groups at Google. I had joined the company three and a half years earlier when it was an obscure start-up with a few hundred employees in a run-down office building. By my first trimester, Google had grown into a company of thousands and moved into a multi-building campus.

My pregnancy was not easy. The typical morning sickness that often accompanies the first trimester affected me every day for nine long months. I gained almost seventy pounds, and my feet swelled two entire shoe sizes, turning into odd-shaped lumps I could see only when they were propped up on a coffee table. A particularly sensitive Google engineer announced that "Project Whale" was named after me.

One day, after a rough morning spent staring at the bottom of the toilet, I had to rush to make an important client meeting. Google was growing so quickly that parking was an ongoing problem, and the only spot I could find was quite far away. I sprinted across the parking lot, which in reality meant lumbering a bit more quickly than my absurdly slow pregnancy crawl. This only made my nausea worse, and I arrived at the meeting praying that a sales pitch was the only thing that would come out of my mouth. That night, I recounted these troubles to my husband, Dave. He pointed out that Yahoo, where he worked at the time, had designated parking for expectant mothers at the front of each building.

The next day, I marched in—or more like waddled in—to see Google founders Larry Page and Sergey Brin in their office, which was really just a large room with toys and gadgets strewn all over the floor. I found Sergey in a yoga position in the corner and announced that we needed pregnancy parking, preferably sooner rather than later. He looked up at me and agreed immediately, noting that he had never thought about it before.

To this day, I'm embarrassed that I didn't realize that pregnant women needed reserved parking until I experienced my own aching feet. As one of Google's most senior women, didn't I have a special responsibility to think of this? But like Sergey, it had never occurred to me. The other pregnant women must have suffered in silence, not wanting to ask for special treatment. Or maybe they lacked the confidence or seniority to demand that the problem be fixed. Having one pregnant woman at the top—even one who looked like a whale—made the difference.

Today in the United States and the developed world, women are better off than ever. We stand on the shoulders of the women who came before us, women who had to fight for the rights that we now take for granted. In 1947, Anita Summers, the mother of my longtime mentor Larry Summers, was hired as an economist by the Standard Oil Company. When she accepted the job, her new boss said to her, "I am so glad to have you. I figure I am getting the same brains for less money." Her reaction to this was to feel flattered. It was a huge compliment to be told that she had the same brains as a man. It would have been unthinkable for her to ask for equal compensation.

We feel even more grateful when we compare our lives to those of other women around the world. There are still countries that deny women basic civil rights. Worldwide, about 4.4 million women and girls are trapped in the sex trade.[1] In places like Afghanistan and Sudan, girls receive little or no education, wives are treated as the property of their husbands, and women who are raped are routinely cast out of their homes for disgracing their families. Some rape victims are even sent to jail for committing a "moral crime."[2] We are centuries ahead of the unacceptable treatment of women in these countries.

But knowing that things could be worse should not stop us from trying to make them better. When the suffragettes marched in the streets, they envisioned a world where men and women would be truly equal. A century later, we are still squinting, trying to bring that vision into focus.

The blunt truth is that men still run the world. Of the 195 independent countries in the world, only 17 are led by women.[3] Women hold just 20 percent of seats in parliaments globally.[4] In the United States, where we pride ourselves on liberty and justice for all, the gender division of leadership roles is not much better. Women became 50 percent of the college graduates in the United States in the early 1980s.[5] Since then, women have slowly and steadily advanced, earning more and more of the college degrees, taking more of the entry-level jobs, and entering more fields previously dominated by men. Despite these gains, the percentage of women at the top of corporate America has barely budged over the past decade.[6]

A meager twenty-one of the Fortune 500 CEOs are women.[7] Women hold about 14 percent of executive officer positions, 17 percent of board seats, and constitute 18 percent of our elected congressional officials.[8] The gap is even worse for women of color, who hold just 4 percent of top corporate jobs, 3 percent of board seats, and 5 percent of congressional seats.[9] While women continue to outpace men in educational achievement, we have ceased making real progress at the top of any industry. This means that when it comes to making the decisions that most affect our world, women's voices are not heard equally.

Progress remains equally sluggish when it comes to compensation. In 1970, American women were paid 59 cents for every dollar their male counterparts made. By 2010, women had protested, fought, and worked their butts off to raise that compensation to 77 cents for every dollar men made.[10] As activist Marlo Thomas riley joked on Equal Pay Day 2011, "Forty years and eighteen cents. A dozen eggs have gone up ten times that amount."[11]

I have watched these disheartening events from a front row seat. I graduated from college in 1991 and from business school in 1995. In each entry-level job after graduation, my colleagues were a balanced mix of male and female. I saw that the senior leaders were almost entirely male, but I thought that was due to historical discrimination against women. The proverbial glass ceiling had been cracked in almost every industry, and I believed that it was just a matter of time until my generation took our fair share of the leadership roles. But with each passing year, fewer and fewer of my colleagues were women. More and more often, I was the only woman in the room.

Being the sole woman has resulted in some awkward yet revealing situations. Two years after I joined Facebook as chief operating officer, our chief financial officer departed suddenly, and I had to step in to complete a funding round. Since I had spent my career in operations, not finance, the process of raising capital was new and a bit scary. My team and I flew to New York for the initial pitch to private equity firms. Our first meeting was held in the kind of corporate office featured in movies, complete with a sprawling view of Manhattan. I offered an overview of our business and answered questions. So far so good. Then someone suggested that we break for a few minutes. I turned to the senior partner and asked where the women's restroom was. He stared at me blankly. My question had completely stumped him. I asked, "How long have you been in this office?" And he said, "One year." "Am I the only woman to have pitched a deal here in an entire year?" "I think so," he said, adding, "or maybe you're the only one who had to use the bathroom."

It has been more than two decades since I entered the workforce, and so much is still the same. It is time for us to face the fact that our revolution has stalled.[12] The promise of equality is not the same as true equality.

A truly equal world would be one where women ran half our countries and companies and men ran half our homes. I believe that this would be a better world. The laws of economics and many studies of diversity tell us that if we tapped the entire pool of human resources and talent, our collective performance would improve. Legendary investor Warren Buffett has stated generously that one of the reasons for his great success was that he was competing with only half of the population. The Warren Buffetts of my generation are still largely enjoying this advantage. When more people get in the race, more records will be broken. And the achievements will extend beyond those individuals to benefit us all.

The night before Leymah Gbowee won the 2011 Nobel Peace Prize for helping to lead the women's protests that toppled Liberia's dictator, she was at a book party in my home. We were celebrating the publication of her autobiography, *Mighty Be Our Powers*, but it was a somber night. A guest asked her how American women could help those who experienced the horrors and mass rapes of war in places like Liberia. Her response was four simple words: "More women in power." Leymah and I could not have come from more different backgrounds, and yet we have both arrived at the same conclusion. Conditions for all women will improve when there are more women in leadership roles giving strong and powerful voice to their needs and concerns.[13]

This brings us to the obvious question—how? How are we going to take down the barriers that prevent more women from getting to the top? Women face real obstacles in the professional world, including blatant and subtle sexism, discrimination, and sexual harassment. Too few workplaces offer the flexibility and access to childcare and parental leave that are necessary for pursuing a career while raising children. Men have an easier time finding the mentors and sponsors who are invaluable for career progression. Plus, women have to prove themselves to a far greater extent than men do. And this is not just in our heads. A 2011 McKinsey report noted that men are promoted based on potential, while women are promoted based on past accomplishments.[14]

In addition to the external barriers erected by society, women are hindered by barriers that exist within ourselves. We hold ourselves back in ways both big and small, by lacking self-confidence, by not raising our hands, and by pulling back when we should be leaning in. We internalize the negative messages we get throughout our lives—the messages that say it's wrong to be outspoken, aggressive, more powerful than men. We lower our own expectations of what we can achieve. We continue to do the majority of the housework and child care. We compromise our career goals to make room for partners and children who may not even exist yet. Compared to our male colleagues, fewer of us aspire to senior positions. This is not a list of things other women have done. I have made every mistake on this list. At times, I still do.

My argument is that getting rid of these internal barriers is critical to gaining power. Others have argued that women can get to the top only when the institutional barriers are gone. This is the ultimate chicken-and-egg situation. The chicken: Women will tear down the external barriers once we achieve leadership roles. We will march into our bosses' offices and demand what we need, including pregnancy parking. Or better yet, we'll become bosses and make sure all women have what they need. The egg: We need to eliminate the external barriers to get women into those roles in the first place. Both sides are right. So rather than engage in philosophical arguments over which comes first, let's agree to wage battles on both fronts. They are equally important. I am encouraging women to address the chicken, but I fully support those who are focusing on the egg.

Internal obstacles are rarely discussed and often underplayed. Throughout my life, I was told over and over about inequalities in the workplace and how hard it would be to have a career and a family. I rarely heard anything, however, about the ways I might hold myself back. These internal obstacles deserve a lot more attention, in part because they are under our own control. We can dismantle the hurdles in ourselves today. We can start this very moment.

I never thought I would write a book. I am not a scholar, a journalist, or a sociologist. But I decided to speak out after talking to hundreds of women, listening to their struggles, sharing my own, and realizing that the gains we have made are not enough and may even be slipping. The first chapter of this book lays out some of the complex challenges women face. Each subsequent chapter focuses on an adjustment or difference that we can make ourselves: increasing our self-confidence ("Sit at the Table"), getting our partners to do more at home ("Make Your Partner a Real Partner"), not holding ourselves to unattainable standards ("The Myth of Doing It All"). I do not pretend to have perfect solutions to these deep and complicated issues. I rely on hard data, academic research, my own observations, and lessons I have learned along the way.

This book is not a memoir, although I have included stories about my life. It is not a self-help book, although I truly hope it helps. It is not a book on career management, although I offer advice in that area. It is not a feminist manifesto—okay, it is sort of a feminist manifesto, but one that I hope inspires men as much as it inspires women.

Whatever this book is, I am writing it for any woman who wants to increase her chances of making it to the top of her field or pursue any goal vigorously. This includes women at all stages of their lives and careers, from those who are just starting out to those who are taking a break and may want to jump back in. I am also writing this for any man who wants to understand what a woman—a colleague, wife, mother, or daughter—is up against so that he can do his part to build an equal world.

This book makes the case for leaning in, for being ambitious in any pursuit. And while I believe that increasing the number of women in positions of power is a necessary element of true equality, I do not believe that there is one definition of success or happiness. Not all women want careers. Not all women want children. Not all women want both. I would never advocate that we should all have the same objectives. Many people are not interested in acquiring power, not because they lack ambition, but because they are living their lives as they desire. Some of the most important contributions to our world are made by caring for one person at a time. We each have to chart our own unique course and define which goals fit our lives, values, and dreams.

I am also acutely aware that the vast majority of women are struggling to make ends meet and take care of their families. Parts of this book will be most relevant to women fortunate enough to have choices about how much and when and where to work; other parts apply to situations that women face in every workplace, within every community, and in every home. If we can succeed in adding more female voices at the highest levels, we will expand opportunities and extend fairer treatment to all.

Some, especially other women in business, have cautioned me about speaking out publicly on these issues. When I have spoken out anyway, several of my comments have upset people of both genders. I know some believe that by focusing on what women can change themselves—pressing them to lean in—it seems like I am letting our institutions off the hook. Or even worse, they accuse me of blaming the victim. Far from blaming the victim, I believe that female leaders are key to the solution. Some critics will also point out that it is much easier for me to lean in, since my financial resources allow me to afford any help I need. My intention is to offer advice that would have been useful to me long before I had heard of Google or Facebook and that will resonate with women in a broad range of circumstances.

I have heard these criticisms in the past and I know that I will hear them—and others—in the future. My hope is that my message will be judged on its merits. We can't avoid this conversation. This issue transcends all of us. The time is long overdue to encourage more women to dream the possible dream and encourage more men to support women in the workforce and in the home.

We can reignite the revolution by internalizing the revolution. The shift to a more equal world will happen person by person. We move closer to the larger goal of true equality with each woman who leans in.

NOTES

1. International Labour Organization, *ILO Global Estimates of Forced Labour, Results and Methodology* (Geneva: ILO Publications, 2012), 13–14, https://www.ilo.org/global/topics/forced-labour/publications/WCMS_182004/lang--en/index.htm

2. Caroline Wyatt, "What Future for Afghan Woman Jailed for Being Raped?," BBC News, South Asia, January 14, 2012, https://www.bbc.com/news/world-south-asia-16543036.

3. According to the US State Department, there are 195 independent states in the world. See US Department of State, Independent States in the World, Fact Sheet (January 2012), www.state.gov/s/ inr/rls/4250.htm#note3. The calculation for the number of independent states led by women, defined as women serving as president or prime minister or other executive role, was derived from the most recent information released by the CIA prior to publication. See Central Intelligence Agency, Chiefs of State & Cabinet Members of Foreign Governments (December 2012), https://www.cia.gov/library/ publications/resources/world-leaders-1/

However, the calculation also includes two electoral changes not reflected in the CIA information—the election of Park Geun-hye, who will be the first female president of South Korea in 2013, and the end of Swiss president Eveline Widmer-Schlumpf's term in December 2012. It should be noted that Switzerland is led by a Federal Council comprised of seven members. Every year the Swiss Federal Assembly elects from among the seven Federal Council members a president and vice president. In 2013 the president of Switzerland will be Ueli Maurer. However, three of the seven Federal Council members are women (Eveline Widmer-Schlumpf, Simonetta Sommaruga, and Doris Leuthard). Elections vary from country to country in terms of when and how often they are held. Thus, the total number of women chiefs of state or heads of government will change as countries go through their next election cycle.

4. Inter-Parliamentary Union, *Women in National Parliaments* (2012), www.ipu.org/wmn-e/ world.htm.

5. Claudia Goldin, Lawrence F. Katz, and Ilyana Kuziemko, "The Homecoming of American College Women: The Reversal of the College Gender Gap," *Journal of Economic Perspectives* 20, no. 4 (2006): 133.

6. Catalyst, *Targeting Inequity: The Gender Gap in US Corporate Leadership* (September 2010), https://www.jec.senate.gov/public/_cache/files/90f0aade-d9f5-43e7-8501-46bbd1c69bb8/ lang-written-testimony-and-appendix.pdf.

7. Patricia Sellers, "Fortune 500 Women CEOs Hits a Milestone," CNNMoney, November 12, 2012, https://fortune.com/2012/11/12/fortune-500-women-ceos-hit-a-milestone/.

8. Catalyst, *2012 Catalyst Census: Fortune 500 Women Executive Officers and Top Earners* (December 2012), https://www.catalyst.org/research/2012-catalyst-census-fortune-500-women-exec utive-officers-and-top-earners/. Catalyst defines an "executive officer" as one who is "appointed and elected by the board directors," including the "CEO and up to two reporting levels below," and individuals who are "listed as executive officers in SEC filings"; see appendix 1, Methodology Section, 2009 Catalyst Census: Fortune 500, https://www.catalyst.org/wp-content/uploads/2019/02/2009_For tune_500_Census_Appendix_1_Methodology.pdf Catalyst, *2012 Catalyst Census: Fortune 500 Women Board Directors* (December 2012), www.catalyst.org/knowledge/2012-catalyst-census-for tune-500-women-board-directors; and Center for American Women and Politics, "Women Who Will Be Serving in 2013," https://cawp.rutgers.edu/history-women-us-congress.

9. US Equal Employment Opportunity Commission, 2011 Job Patterns for Minorities and Women in Private Industry, 2011 EEO-1National Aggregate Report (2011), www1.eeoc.gov/eeoc/ statistics/employment/jobpat-eeo1/index.cfm. The EEOC's definition of top corporate jobs includes executive- and senior-level officers as well as managers; Catalyst, *2012 Catalyst Census: Fortune 500 Women Board Directors*, and Center for American Women and Politics, *Record Number of Women Will Serve in Congress; New Hampshire Elects Women to All Top Posts*, Election Watch, November 7, 2012, https://www.cawp.rutgers.edu/sites/default/files/resources/pressrelease_11-07-12.pdf

See also Catalyst, *Women of Color Executives: Their Voices, Their Journeys* (June 2001), www.cata lyst.org/publication/54/women-of-color-executives-their-voices-their-journeys.

10. Ariane Hegewisch, Claudia Williams, and Anlan Zhang, *The Gender Wage Gap: 2011*, Fact Sheet (March 2012), https://iwpr.org/publications/the-gender-wage-gap-2011/;

Carmen DeNavas-Walt, Bernadette D. Proctor, and Jessica C. Smith, *Income, Poverty, and Health Insurance Coverage in the United States: 2010*, US Census Bureau, Current Population Reports, P60– 239 (Washington, DC: US Government Printing Office, 2011), 12, https://www.census.gov/prod/ 2011pubs/p60-239.pdf.

Statistics cited are drawn from calculations of the gender pay gap based on median annual earnings. According to Dr. Pamela Coukos, a senior program advisor at the Department of Labor's Office of Federal Contract Compliance Programs, the most commonly cited estimate of the gender pay gap is based upon the difference between men's and women's median annual earnings. Another widely used estimate of the gender pay gap is based upon the difference between men's and women's median weekly earnings. Some scholars believe weekly earnings are more accurate because they can better account for differences in the total number of hours worked, and since men often work more hours than women, this difference can account for some of the pay gap. Other scholars argue that the median annual earnings figure is preferable because it includes more types of compensation (such as bonuses, pensions, etc.). Importantly, both approaches find that women earn less than men. According to recent median annual earnings, women earn seventy-seven cents for every dollar men earn. According to recent median weekly earnings, women earn eighty-two cents for every dollar men earn.

11. Marlo Thomas, "Another Equal Pay Day? Really?" *Huffington Post*, April 12, 2011, https:// www.huffpost.com/entry/equal-pay-day_b_847021.

12. Sociologist Arlie Russell Hochschild coined the phrase "the stalled revolution" in her book *The Second Shift* (New York: Avon Books, 1989), 12.

13. It should be noted that not all female leaders are supportive of women's interests. See Nicholas D. Kristof, "Women Hurting Women," *New York Times*, September 29, 2012, https://www.nytimes .com/2012/09/30/opinion/sunday/kristof-women-hurting-women.html.

For research and discussion about how all women can benefit when more women are in positions of power, see chapter 11.

14. Joanna Barsh and Lareina Yee, *Special Report: Unlocking the Full Potential of Women in the U.S. Economy*, McKinsey & Company (April 2011), 6, https://www.mckinsey.com/~/media/McKinsey/ dotcom/client_service/Organization/PDFs/Exec_Summ_WSJ_Preview_Special_Report.ashx.

FOR FURTHER READING

Brooks, Rosa. "Recline, Don't 'Lean In' (Why I Hate Sheryl Sandberg)." *The Washington Post*, 25 Feb. 2014, https://www.washingtonpost.com/blogs/she-the-people/wp/2014/02/25/recline-dont -lean-in-why-i-hate-sheryl-sandberg/.

Gay, Roxane. "Women Shouldn't Have to Lead Like Men to Be Successful." *Fortune*, 12 Feb. 2015, fortune.com/2015/02/12/women-shouldnt-have-to-lead-like-men-to-be-successful/.

hooks, bell. "Dig Deep: Beyond *Lean In*." *The Feminist Wire*, 28 Oct. 2013, www.thefeministwire .com/2013/10/17973/

Lean In. LeanIn.org.

Luscombe, Belinda. "Life after Death." *TIME*, n.d., time.com/sheryl-sandberg-option-b/.

Newman, Judith. "Sheryl Sandberg's *Lean In*: 5 Years Later." *The Seattle Times*, 26 Mar. 2018, www
.seattletimes.com/explore/careers/lean-in-5-years-later/.

Pierce, Allison. "'Leaning in' Won't Liberate Us." *National Organization for Women*, 7 July 2015, now
.org/blog/leaning-in-wont-save-us/.

Rottenberg, Catherine. "How Neoliberalism Conquered Feminism, and What You Can Do about It."
The Conversation, 23 May 2018, theconversation.com/how-neoliberalism-colonised-feminism
-and-what-you-can-do-about-it-94856.

"Sheryl Sandberg." *Biography*, 16 Apr. 2019, www.biography.com/people/sheryl-sandberg.

Jennifer Pozner

In 2002, examining ongoing coverage that followed the September 11 attacks, Jennifer Pozner wrote a critique of the gender imbalance in US media coverage. As with many other voices in this anthology, her piece not only deftly analyzes her contemporary moment but serves as a prescient warning about the ramifications of not heeding her advice. Pozner is well qualified to level this critique as the founder of Women in Media & News, "A media analysis, education, and advocacy group [that] works to increase women's presence and power in the public debate." Additionally, Pozner is a writer and speaker on women in media and has been featured on numerous major networks and publications as well as on documentaries; notably, she was an advisor on *Miss Representation*. She authored *Reality Bites Back: The Troubling Truth about Guilty Pleasure TV*, which analyzes how reality television functions as backlash against gender and racial justice and exposed the inherent manipulations of the genre and its economic engine. Pozner's second book—*BREAKING (the) NEWS: Using Media Literacy to Decode What We Watch, Read, Hear, Play, Post, Buy, Believe, and Enjoy!*—is a graphic novel that brings her intersectional media analysis to the young adult audience.

Pozner's piece demonstrates how our media culture is gendered male. Using language that doesn't cloak her scorn—she describes one male commentator as "hissing" in his column and delights in sharing problematic quotes from big-name journalists—she shows how female perspectives are ignored, rendered invisible, or simply inaccurately reported. She cites poll after poll that suggests American women have complex views on military action in Afghanistan and Iraq post-9/11, examining how these polls were manipulated to indicate women's support for military action. When women in the media did critique the master narrative trumpeting war, they were typically disregarded. Throughout her piece, Pozner analyzes data and studies to demonstrate the large gender gap. At the same time, her tone employs both wit and disdain in laying out her evidence, leaving no doubt about her opinion as she forwards these facts.

Extending beyond how polls are rendered, Pozner posits that the extreme gender inequity in the media leads to distortion: just 11 percent of all experts on major news platforms were women before and after 9/11, and 92 percent of op-ed bylines in the month following were written by men. Pozner sees a range of solutions, including diversifying newsrooms to employ more women and people of color; covering the perspectives, ideas, and issues of women and people of color in a more nuanced and informed manner; and changing telecommunications policy to prioritize ethical journalism over the financial bottom line.

Since Pozner made this fervent call in 2002, much has changed with the Trump presidency and the #MeToo movement, causing a surge of attention to gender-related issues. And yet in 2017 men dominated Sunday news talk shows, men were featured two to one before women on National Public Radio, and of the one hundred highest rated talk shows, eighty-seven were hosted by men and only thirteen by women ("Status of Women"). Some promising movement has occurred with greater representation by journalists of color; also, men's bylines now account for "only" 52 percent of total bylines on reproductive issues in major newspapers. Clearly, much work remains to be done for better representation, so that, as Pozner expresses so pointedly, more accurate and democratic news and information can circulate.

"Missing in Action: Whatever Happened to the Gender Gap?"

AlterNet, 2002

Let's call it "The Case of the Missing Gender Gap." Ever since September 11, corporate media have denied that men and women have significant differences of opinion on terrorism and war, despite contradictory evidence in polls conducted before and after we dropped our first bomb on Afghanistan. To solve this mystery we have to start at the beginning of George W. Bush's new world order—when, in the president's words, anyone who did not support America's "war on terrorism" would be judged to be in cahoots with "the evildoers."

Following the devastating attacks, major news networks subjected a shocked nation to video clips of the Twin Towers being struck by planes, exploding in flames and collapsing, often accompanied by "Oh my God!" audio, on repetitive loop day and night. (Talk about a recipe for post-traumatic stress disorder.) These painful images sometimes appeared in split screen while anxious anchors interviewed current and former White House and Pentagon officials, security experts, and CIA spooks, who presented military retaliation and civil liberties rollbacks as necessary and inevitable. While such sources made up more than half the authorities appearing on NBC, ABC, and CBS in the week following the attacks, experts from the international law community who could advocate legal, nonmilitary responses to crimes against humanity were nowhere to be seen on these programs, according to a survey by the media watch group FAIR.

Feminists and progressives who dared give the question "Why do they hate us?" an answer more substantial than the ubiquitous "because we love freedom"— say, by noting that the Arab world has never forgotten Madeleine Albright's 1996 comment on CBS that half a million dead Iraqi children were "worth the price" of US sanctions—were quickly labeled traitors, or worse. When Susan Sontag sinned in the *New Yorker*'s first post–9/11 issue by noting that US foreign policy might have contributed to the vicious anti-American sentiment behind the attacks, *Newsweek*'s Jonathan Alter blasted her in a scathing column titled "Blame America at Your Peril." It was "ironic," Alter hissed, that "the same people always urging us to not blame the victim in rape cases are now saying Uncle Sam wore a short skirt and asked for it." And when a small but vocal peace movement called for the US to "prosecute the criminals" rather than bomb innocent Afghans, their dissent was either ignored or distorted by a derisive press—as when the *New York Times* reported a late September antiwar action in DC under the headline "Protesters in Washington Urge Peace with Terrorists."

Amid this "with us or against us" feeding frenzy, poll stories proliferated, with headlines like the *Washington Post*'s September 29 "Public Unyielding in War against Terror; 9 in 10 Back Robust Military Response." The numbers seemed overwhelming: the "9 in 10" figure measured Bush's approval rating, while upwards of four-fifths of the public generally supported some sort of military action. According to the *Post*, Americans were "unswerving" in their support for war and unified in their "demand for a full-scale response."

But were they, really? Buried at the end of the 1,395-word story was the striking information that women "were significantly less likely to support a long and costly war" then were men, and their hesitant support might develop into "hardened opposition" over time. In fact, though 44 percent of women said they'd favor a broad military effort, "48 percent said they want a limited strike or no military action at all."

The gender gap appeared again in an October 5 CNN/USA Today/Gallup poll, which found that 64 percent of men thought the US "should mount a long-term war" and just 24 percent favored limiting retaliation to punishing the specific groups responsible for the attacks—but that women were "evenly divided—with 42 percent favoring each option." Though 88 percent of women and 90 percent of men support some military action, women reconsider in greater numbers as soon as conditional questions are asked, Gallup's analysis showed. For example, only 55 percent of women said they would support military action if a thousand American troops would be killed, whereas 76 percent of men would still support a lengthy war under these circumstances; women were also much less likely than men to support war if it would continue for several years, bring about an economic recession, or provoke further terrorist attacks at home.

When presented with only two possible post–9/11 alternatives—"drop some bombs" or "do nothing"—it's not surprising that majorities of the public would choose the former. What's alarming is that politicians, pundits, and the press first roundly ignored the *Post* and Gallup data about women's more conditional approach to the "war on terrorism," then claimed the traditional gender gap familiar from the Persian Gulf and Kosovo crises had disintegrated with the Twin Towers.

Polls whose results seemed to confirm the media's image of a flag-waving, Rambo-embracing populace met with a much warmer reception. When an early November poll by the Council on Foreign Relations and the Pew Research Center for People & the Press found that women's support for increased military spending doubled from 24 to 47 percent after September 11, and that the same number of men and women (64 percent) now favor the creation of a missile-defense shield, a front-page *Christian Science Monitor* story reported that "Women's voices are resonating across the country and doing away—for the first time in recent history—with the gender gap on many military issues." The article was headlined "In This War, American Women Shed Role as 'Doves'"—even though separate Gallup data, also from November and referenced in the same article, showed that women were more than twice as likely as men to be "doves." The Pew research was featured in outlets from leading dailies to tabloids (e.g., the *Daily News*), debate shows (e.g., the McLaughlin Group) and the conservative press (e.g., *Insight on the News*). The *Washington Post* crowed, "When it comes to attitudes toward the military, men are from Mars, and so are women," while a *Washington Times* op-ed praised "Missile Defense's Feminine Mystique."

While polls were covered selectively, news content about women and war was often opportunistic. Outlets seized on the restrictive burqa forced on Afghan women as a symbol of the Taliban's cruelty and a reason why they should be vanquished, and ran triumphant visuals of women removing their coverings upon the Taliban's ouster—yet only rarely devoted serious attention to the history of extreme violence and sexual assault committed against Afghan women by the US-endorsed Northern Alliance, or asked whether they might oppress or violate women once installed in the Afghan government. On the domestic front, the Bush administration was portrayed as a bastion of women's empowerment. Andrea Mitchell began a late November MSNBC segment this way: "In the war on terrorism, American women are playing a major role at almost every level, especially the top. It's a striking contrast with the way women have been treated in Afghanistan." Republican bigwigs like Condoleezza Rice, Karen Hughes, and

Mary Matalin are "not only making the strategy; their gender is part of the strategy, a weapon to attack the Taliban's treatment of Afghan women," Mitchell said. As a result, a Republican official told the *Washington Post* in early January, George W. Bush "has not only erased any question about legitimacy, he has also erased the gender gap."

Perhaps the gradations in women's support for or opposition to the war didn't make the news because focusing on simple, surface-level "do you or don't you?" questions requires less research and investigation—always premium in our profit-driven, time-is-money media climate—and provided sexier numbers. Certainly women's differing degrees of dissent might have seemed inconsequential to some of the country's most powerful—and pro-war—journalists. *Time* magazine's defense correspondent Mark Thompson confessed to warm fuzzies for tight-lipped military leader Donald Rumsfeld, telling the *Chicago Tribune* that "although he has not told us very much, he has been like a father figure." With stars (and stripes) in his eyes, CBS' Dan Rather actually volunteered to suit up, telling *Entertainment Tonight* that if George Bush ever "needs me in uniform, tell me when and where— I'm there." ABC's Cokie Roberts unself-consciously admitted an almost blind faith in our boys at the Pentagon: "Look, I am, I will just confess to you, a total sucker for the guys who stand up with all the ribbons on and stuff," she told David Letterman. "And so, when they say stuff I tend to believe it." (This eager journalistic acceptance was surely music to the ears of the unnamed military official who told the *Washington Post*'s Howard Kurtz that lying would be an integral part of the Pentagon's press strategy.)

But to find the simplest reason why women's perspectives were missing or misrepresented by media, forget all this cerebral posturing. A college-style drinking game will do the trick. The rules are simple (and almost guaranteed not to get anyone drunk). Grab a few friends and the remote control, start flipping between network news broadcasts, pour a drink every time a female expert is interviewed about terrorism and war. I promise you, you'll end up parched—and peeved.

Take the Sunday morning talk shows on ABC, NBC, CBS, CNN, and Fox, for example. According to a study released in December by the White House Project, a nonpartisan women's leadership group, women were a measly 11 percent of all guests on five of these influential, agenda-setting programs from January 1, 2000 to June 30, 2001. As if this wasn't dismal enough, that number fell to just nine percent for six weeks after September 11. And women fared no better in print: in the month after the terrorist attacks, men wrote a whopping 92 percent of the 309 bylined op-eds published by the *New York Times*, the *Washington Post*, and *USA Today*, according to a survey I conducted for FAIR.

To Nancy Nathan, executive producer of NBC's *Meet the Press*, the underrepresentation of women on programs like hers is irrelevant. "I don't think the female viewpoint is different from the generic, overall viewpoint," Nathan told me. There's no conspiracy to suppress women's voices, she said, it's just that men hold most power positions in Washington, so they are the most sought-after guests. Women might have unique perspectives to add to health care or reproductive services discussions, she added, and with those sorts of stories the talk shows might be able to book people outside the male-dominated pool of officeholders. But programs like *Meet the Press* "are not having long discussions about issues that are not at the forefront of the agenda." The White House Project study's authors can "advocate more women on the air," Nathan said, "but the object here is to deliver the news, not to get women on the air."

Nathan's perspective perfectly echoes one of journalism's most entrenched conventions: news is what the powerful say and do, not what the public experiences. But Sunday morning talk shows move the public debate by framing certain topics as cutting edge and others as unimportant—if they were to address reproductive rights or health care regularly, those issues would be at the forefront. Not to mention that women are invested in all issues, not just abortion and breast cancer; women are ninety percent of the world's sweatshop workers, for example, and are doing groundbreaking work in feminist economics—meaning that journalism and those who rely on it suffer when women are overlooked as sources for stories on globalization, labor and world finance.

The news-follows-power principle not only eschews diversity, but its self-perpetuating cycle prevents change. Social and political issues will continue to be filtered through a primarily white, male, corporate lens, thereby reinforcing their authority and sidelining women, people of color, labor and all marginalized groups and issues.

The *Washington Post* columnist Judy Mann ended the year with this reflection:

> A society in which women are invisible in the media is one in which they are invisible, period . . . Women are a majority in the United States. By rights, in a democracy, we should occupy 50 percent of the slots on the op-ed pages of America's newspapers. We should occupy 50 percent of the top editorships in newspapers. We should be allowed to bring what interests us—as women and mothers and wives—to the table, and I don't mean token stories about childcare. I mean taking apart the federal budget and seeing if it is benefiting families or the munitions millionaires. I mean looking at the enormous amount of money we've squandered on the "war on drugs" and asking the obvious question: Why are we building more prisons instead of rebuilding broken lives? I mean challenging the miserly foreign-aid budget and raising hell because we are not doing our share to educate women and girls in emerging countries. The Taliban could never have taken root in a society that educated and empowered females.

This is the type of insight Mann has offered the *Post* for 23 years; the column, published on December 28, was her last. Mann—the first journalist to use the term "gender gap" in the press—is retiring right at a moment when women's voices are being thoroughly drowned out on the op-ed pages and the public stage.

Mann's final headline read, "A Farewell Wish: That Women Will Be Heard." For that wish to become reality, we need to force the issue. Write the *Post* and encourage them to replace Mann with an analytically and politically savvy feminist writer. Pressure the Sunday talk shows to interview female experts, and to recognize that women's concerns focus on cutting-edge issues, but will only be seen as such if they are subject to healthy debate in prominent forums. Contact local news outlets when women are ignored, distorted, or covered in opportunistic ways. Conduct studies calling attention to the gender breakdown of particular outlets' bylines and sources, then hold press conferences, release reports, and attempt to meet with editorial boards to discuss ways to improve. Organize around the concept that journalism has a responsibility to cover a variety of perspectives, not just those of people in power.

Media conglomerates are not magnanimous; they will not change their priorities without major incentives. In the 1930s, Eleanor Roosevelt would only speak to female reporters at her press conferences, forcing newspapers to employ women journalists. In the 1970s, newspapers and TV networks had to be sued before they'd stop discriminating against women in hiring and promotion; feminist columnist Anna Quindlen began her decade-long run on the *New York Times* op-ed page as a result of one of those class actions, and proceeded to write about gender, race, class, and sexuality issues as if they mattered.

It's time for us to reprioritize media as a top feminist issue. Today, Quindlen's spot at the *Times* is filled by Maureen Dowd, who's often as inclined to write about high-society balls as feminist concerns. Today, right-wing women like Ann Coulter, Kathleen Parker, Peggy Noonan, Mona Charen, Amy Holmes, and Laura Ingraham maintain a high profile in the mainstream media, while progressive feminist writers like media critic Laura Flanders or journalist Barbara Ehrenreich are most often heard in the Left press. And today, NBC darling Katie Couric's astronomical new salary notwithstanding, women still have little power inside the media industry: according to various studies (cited in "Power Shortage for Media Women," Extra!, August, 2001), they are only 13 and 14 percent of radio and TV general managers, 20 percent of news executives in Fortune 1000 news companies, and 12 percent of corporate board members in media/entertainment companies.

We need to ask ourselves: What are we going to do about this, today?

For Further Reading

"About the Author." *Reality Bites Back*, n.d., http://www.realitybitesbackbook.com/about-the-a uthor/

"About WIMN." *Women in Media & News*, n.d., http://www.wimnonline.org/.

Jones, Sarah. "The Great Remove: How Journalism Got so out of Touch with the People It Covers." *Columbia Journalism Review*, Spring/Summer 2018, https://www.cjr.org/special_report/jour nalism-class.php/.

Pozner, Jennifer. *BREAKING (the) NEWS: Using Media Literacy to Decode What We Watch, Read, Hear, Play, Post, Buy, Believe, and Enjoy!* First Second Books, forthcoming.

Pozner, Jennifer. *Reality Bites Back: The Troubling Truth about Guilty Pleasure TV.* Seal Press, 2010.

Reid, Calvin. "First Second to Launch World Citizen Comics." *Publishers Weekly*, 13 Mar. 2019, https://www.publishersweekly.com/pw/by-topic/industry-news/comics/article/79510-first -second-to-launch-world-citizen-comics.html.

"The Status of Women in the U.S. Media 2017." *Women's Media Center*, 2017, https://www.womens mediacenter.com/assets/site/reports/10c550d19ef9f3688f_mlbres2jd.pdf.

Brenda Berkman

September 11, 2001, marks the deadliest terrorist attack on US soil in the country's history, killing almost three thousand people. It also marks a day of incredible heroism, as rescuers, firefighters, and police officers ran into the burning buildings to save lives, tend to the wounded, and recover bodies. The firefighter Brenda Berkman was one of those heroes. She had the day off and was volunteering for a local political candidate. When she heard news of the attack, she immediately joined off-duty Brooklyn firefighters to help at the scene.

In a single day, the New York City Fire Department (FDNY) lost 343 of its members. In addition to bearing the trauma of the attack and grief over her lost colleagues, Berkman had to contend with sexist assumptions about the rescue efforts as an exclusively male undertaking. Whether through media depictions focused solely on men or funeral eulogies that celebrated a heroic "brotherhood," in the following speech Berkman highlights how the many women involved in the front lines of the 9/11 rescue efforts were simply erased from the public narrative.

Berkman then made it her mission to recover the stories and contributions of women, as she does in the speech included here, delivered at the 2001 National Women's Law Center awards dinner. In emphatic language, Berkman adds women's contributions to the history of 9/11, documenting their roles as firefighters, police officers, EMTs, doctors, nurses, chaplains, military, and Red Cross workers to show the reality of who was present at Ground Zero. Her work, Berkman argues, is to prevent historical amnesia that has plagued our country in the past.

This was not Berkman's first campaign to advocate on behalf of women. In 1977 Berkman was in her third year of law school when the FDNY opened its doors to women. They first had to pass two tests, however: written and physical fitness. Berkman passed the former and failed the latter, as did the eighty-nine other women who took the test. The test was clearly designed to keep women out, Berkman surmised, and she moved forward with a lawsuit. *Brenda Berkman et al. vs. the City of New York* became a highly publicized class-action lawsuit whose ruling required the FDNY to conduct a fairer test. That year, she and forty other women entered the service. Berkman served for twenty-five years, rising to the level of captain. During this time, she also founded the United Women Firefighters, received the Susan B. Anthony Award from the National Organization for Women, and was appointed by President Clinton as a White House Fellow, the first firefighter to be recognized this way (Reynolds). The PBS documentary *Taking the Heat: The First Women Firefighters in New York City* features Berkman's powerful story.

Now retired, Berkman continues to document history, both through her artwork, which includes a series of thirty-six stone lithograph images called *Thirty-Six Views of One World Trade Center* and by leading tours through the 9/11 Tribute Center. As she reminds us in her speech: "This struggle is not to preserve buildings—it is a struggle to preserve freedoms and diversity, including the rights of *women* to participate in *every* aspect of our civic duties."

"Remembering the 9/11 Women"

National Women's Law Center Award Dinner, Washington, DC, 2001

Who were these women? *Where* were the women rescue and recovery workers in the frenzy of media coverage of every little detail of Ground Zero that occurred after September 11? We have all seen the stories about the rescue dogs and the "brothers" who are riding bikes across the country in memory of the firefighters killed at the Trade Center. We had the *New York Times* opine about the return of the "manly man"—referring to male firefighters as the new cultural icons. We immediately had columns by right-wing pundits arguing that the lack of media coverage of women rescue workers was "proof" that women could not and should not *be* firefighters. Many of these stories were reported, written, or produced by women.

I am here to tell you that the reality is that women *were* at Ground Zero. They were there from the first minutes of the attack. Half of the women in the New York City Fire Department—and there are only 25 women out of 11,500 firefighters—put themselves in harm's way that first day and many days thereafter. Fortunately, none were killed.

There were also countless women EMTs, New York City police officers, Port Authority police officers, and other emergency workers who responded immediately. Three uniformed women lost their lives that day: Port Authority captain Kathy Mazza, NYPD officer Moira Smith and EMT Yamel Merino, who was working for a private ambulance service. Many more women were injured trying to save others—women who literally had to have pieces of the buildings removed from their bodies, women who suffered broken bones and other injuries requiring hospitalization.

Within hours of the first plane, Ground Zero was flooded with other women emergency workers and volunteers. Women by the dozens came from all over the country as part of search-and-rescue and other firefighter teams. Women nurses and doctors, women construction workers, women chaplains, military women, Red Cross women—women volunteering in every capacity, every minute of those first days and weeks. Women continued to work at Ground Zero. Women and men worked *together* as one, desperately searching for any sign of life.

The *reality* is that women contributed to the aftermath of the World Trade Center attack in every imaginable way. But the "face" that the media put on the rescue and recovery efforts in New York City is almost exclusively that of men. Where are the pictures or stories of Captain Kathy Mazza shooting out the glass in the lobby of one of the towers to allow hundreds of people to flee the building more quickly? Police officer Moira Smith helping people escape the towers and last seen going back in the building to help a trapped asthmatic person? EMT Yamel Merino tending to an injured person when she herself was struck by the falling building? The countless women who worked on the pile of debris to recover anyone that may have survived or the remains of the thousands of people who were in the building?

Women firefighters were made invisible at the hundreds of funerals for their fallen comrades—men we worked with for many years—our friends, *our* "brothers." At almost every funeral we attended, the mayor, the cardinal, the fire commissioner, and almost every eulogist—except of course when we ourselves were the eulogists—talked exclusively about the *men* and the *brothers* that our coworkers worked with. When I attended a funeral for one of my friends in St. Patrick's Cathedral, the cardinal asked the *men* who are the bravest to rise—totally ignoring the dozens of women firefighters and police officers in attendance from all over the country.

The word *fireman* totally eclipsed the gender-neutral and correct civil service term *firefighter*. Not quite as often but still all too frequently, the same happened as *policeman* returns to the exclusion of *police officer*.

Why did this happen? The *reality* is that women are on the front lines domestically and abroad in the war against terrorism and we need to do more to acknowledge that fact. After our past wars, the contributions of our mothers and grandmothers in the war efforts were ignored. During World War II, Japanese Americans were "disappeared" into camps. It was only recently that the historical amnesia about these events has been corrected. Those mistakes *should* have taught us that it is important to recognize the patriotism of *all* of our citizens.

The struggle against terrorism and to preserve our way of life will be a long one. We will need to show our children and the world just exactly *what* it is that we are fighting for.

This struggle is not to preserve buildings—it is a struggle to preserve freedoms and diversity, including the rights of *women* to participate in *every* aspect of our civic duties.

We *all* must make it our fight to raise the profile of women in this struggle—not just to give credit where credit is due—but also ensure that American women are not made invisible like the women of Afghanistan have been forced to be invisible by the Taliban. The *United* States as a society is better than that. I would ask all of you to do everything you can to show our children that:

Women ARE firefighters

Women ARE patriotic

Women ARE heroes.

We should do no less for the women who put themselves on the line not just on 9/11 but every day—especially those who gave their lives to protect our freedoms.

FOR FURTHER READING

Hagen, Susan, and Mary Carouba. *Women at Ground Zero: Stories of Courage and Compassion.* Storybook Press, 2008.

Reynolds, Eileen. "On 9/11, Women Were Heroes Too." *NYU,* 9 Sept. 2016, www.nyu.edu/about/news-publications/news/2016/september/fdny-captain-brenda-berkman-on-9-11.html.

Roy, Ban, director. *Taking the Heat: The First Women Firefighters in New York City.* PBS, 2006.

Tammy Duckworth

In 2018 Illinois senator Tammy Duckworth made news for being the first sitting US senator to give birth while in office. She was also the first disabled female veteran elected to the US House of Representatives and the Senate and only the second female Asian American senator. Duckworth, raised in Southeast Asia and Hawaii, is the daughter of a Thai mother and an American father who served in the Vietnam War and stayed in the region to assist refugees. Born to a family who has served in the military since the Revolutionary War, Duckworth joined the ROTC and trained as a Blackhawk helicopter pilot. She was at work on a PhD in political science when her National Guard troop was deployed to Iraq. While piloting a helicopter during a mission, Duckworth's plane was shot down by Iraqi insurgents, ultimately taking her legs and the use of her right arm. Her crew did not leave her, and Duckworth credits them with saving her life.

During her recovery, Duckworth was promoted to major and awarded the prestigious Purple Heart, bestowed to military members wounded or killed in the line of duty. She became an advocate for veterans' care and was nominated by President Obama to be the assistant secretary for public and intergovernmental affairs in the US Department of Veterans Affairs.

Duckworth chronicles her military story in the piece included here, published in *Politico* while she was still a congresswoman. Her column frames larger lessons about service both in the military and outside: nobody should be left behind and everyone deserves a second chance. Duckworth draws these values from her time in military service to account for the commitments she brings to government service. Her narrative conjoins a rhetoric of patriotism with an ethic of care and service. She deftly intertwines a theme of unshakeable faith in country, traditionally deemed masculine and conservative, with a communal message about lifting up others for the collective good of the country. During a time when less than .5 percent of Americans serve in the military, compared to 12 percent during World War II, and with just 20 percent of Congress having served in the military compared to 70 percent in 1975, Duckworth uses her ethos as a veteran to educate civilians (Eikenberry and Kennedy). She argues that the ethics and service promoted by the military should drive how we function as a nation, especially as we face the human and economic consequences of war.

"What I Learned at War"

Politico, 2015

The US military has been a part of me since long before I signed up myself. I saw war up close early. I was born in Bangkok in 1968 and grew up in Southeast Asia with my Thai mom and my American father, who first came to the region to fight in Vietnam and stayed to work assisting refugees. I remember my mother taking me as a very little kid to the roof of our home in Phnom Penh, Cambodia, to look at the bombs exploding in the distance. She didn't want us to be scared by the booms and the strange flashes of light. It was her way of helping us to understand what was happening.

Southeast Asia was home for much of my childhood, but I moved to Hawaii when I was in high school. My first direct encounter with the military was when I joined ROTC as a graduate student, although my father, who served in the US Marine Corps, can trace the military service in our family all the way back to the Revolutionary War. I was interested in becoming a foreign service officer; I figured I should know the difference between a battalion and a platoon if I were going to represent my country overseas someday. What I didn't expect was to fall in love with the camaraderie and sense of purpose that the military instills in you and even with the misery of training. The thing is, when we were exhausted and miserable, my fellow cadets and I were exhausted and miserable together. When the instructor yelled, he wasn't singling anyone out, but yelling at all of us, together. It took all of us working as a team to succeed.

And thank God for that. I am alive today—a proud member of Congress and an even prouder wife and new mother—because my buddies learned the same lessons. I had been pursuing a PhD in political science when my National Guard unit was sent to Iraq. Eight months into our deployment, in November 2004, a rocket-propelled grenade fired by Iraqi insurgents tore through the pilot's side of the Blackhawk helicopter I was flying. My right leg was vaporized; my left leg was crushed and shredded against the instrument panel. My pilot in command miraculously brought down the helicopter safely. I went from being the most senior member on board to the weakest. I could easily have died that day, but my crew wouldn't give up on me. They pulled me from the disabled aircraft and, when help arrived, insisted I be attended to first even though some of them were also seriously injured.

That day, and so many others when I served, illustrated the two most important lessons the military taught me: Never leave anyone behind—not on the battlefield and not in our country. And never put a service member in harm's way without understanding the cost—the very real and very human cost—of war. That's why I committed my time at the Illinois Department of Veterans' Affairs and at the federal VA, as well as my time in Congress, to making sure that veterans have the opportunity to achieve that American dream that they defended for the rest of us.

That day, I lost both of my legs, but I was given a second chance at life. It's a feeling that has helped to drive me in my second chance at service—no one should be left behind, and every American deserves another chance. These two lessons inform everything I do in Congress—every minute of every day, whether discussing how best to defeat the Islamic State or debating the merits of a trade deal, or trying to figure out how to provide traveling moms with a clean, safe place at airports to breastfeed their babies.

You don't have to suffer war injuries to understand how tough life can be. The military has a great support network—hundreds of people helped save me, heal me and move me on with my life. Not everyone can count on help like that when tragedy strikes their families, their health or their careers; the recent recession has been devastating for many families. The least I can do as an elected official is to try to make sure working families are not left behind and to offer them help through benefits like education and a higher minimum wage.

As for war, families like mine, with fathers and brothers and sisters and mothers in the service, are always the first to bleed. We will serve and serve proudly. We will go wherever the country needs us. I am not a dove. I believe strongly that if the country's national security interests dictate that we put boots on the ground, then let's do it and be aware of the true costs, both economic and human. I'm also not a reckless hawk, with scant appreciation for what the men and women in uniform—and their families—sacrifice every single day to keep the rest of us safe.

Our efforts in Iraq cost our economy more than a trillion dollars, and we will be caring for our Iraq and Afghanistan veterans for at least the next 50 years. The next time we go to war, we should truly understand the sacrifices that our service members and the American people will have to make. Which is why, when my colleagues start beating the drums of war, I want to be there, standing on my artificial legs under the great Capitol dome, to remind them what the true costs of war are.

FOR FURTHER READING

Eikenberry, Karl, and David M. Kennedy. "Americans and Their Military, Drifting Apart." The New York Times, 26 May 2013, www.nytimes.com/2013/05/27/opinion/americans-and-their-military-drifting-apart.html.

Nelson, Rebecca. "The Dark Humor of Tammy Duckworth, Iraq War Hero and Gun Control Advocate." GQ, 29 Sept. 2016, www.gq.com/story/tammy-duckworth-iraq-war-hero-and-gun-control-advocate-interview.

Stack, Liam. "Tammy Duckworth Becomes First U.S. Senator to Give Birth While in Office." *The New York Times*, 9 Apr. 2018, www.nytimes.com/2018/04/09/us/politics/tammy-duckworth-birth .html.

"Tammy Duckworth." *Biography*, 6 Feb. 2018, www.biography.com/people/tammy-duckworth -21129571.

"Tammy Duckworth: The Mother Making History in the US Senate." *BBC*, 27 Jan. 2018, www.bbc .com/news/world-us-canada-42803733.

Gretchen Carlson

Gretchen Carlson may seem a surprising figure in the fight against sexual harassment. After all, she is best known as the former chipper host of *Fox & Friends* on Fox News, a show and network hardly associated with championing women's rights. Yet the first classes Carlson signed up for at Stanford University in 1989, after being crowned Miss America the previous year, were in feminist studies, where she wrote about her conflicted feelings over pageant participation. Though Carlson's classmates expressed surprise at her presence in feminist courses, she writes, "That's who I've always been at my core. People have underestimated and misrepresented me" (Setoodeh).

In July 2016 Carlson sued Roger Ailes, conservative media and political powerhouse and founder of Fox News, for sexual harassment. Within fifteen days, he was ousted from the network, and while other women sued Ailes, some credited Carlson with stimulating the #MeToo and #TimesUp movements, which led to numerous lawsuits against high-powered male moguls, journalists, and actors. While Carlson's high-profile case triggered a domino effect, the response to these movements often privileged famous white women's experiences and overlooked victims of color (Butler). (See Tarana Burke's contribution to this volume.)

After her departure from Fox News, Carlson was named one of *TIME*'s 100 Most Influential People and turned her focus to sexual harassment in the workplace. She began with her book, *Be Fierce: Stop Harassment and Take Your Power Back*, which highlights Carlson's experiences of workplace harassment, details the barrage of responses she received from women across the globe, and provides legal and logistical information from experts about handling sexual harassment. All of this culminates in a text that is part memoir, part validation of women's experiences, and part pragmatic advice on changing workplace sexual harassment laws.

Carlson began her career as a local journalist, working for CBS before Fox News, where she hosted her own show until her contract was not renewed. Her return to television as a host for A&E and Lifetime Network documentaries signals, Carlson's website notes, that one can continue a career after being blacklisted. Carlson is also the first Miss America to serve as chair of the Miss America Organization, and under her leadership the organization ended the swimsuit competition in order to place less emphasis on women's physical appearance. For this and other reasons, she received some backlash from within the organization.

In the following *Variety* column, Carlson seizes the *kairotic* moment, spurred by the wave of public lawsuits that followed her own, to emphasize that we must harness the energy now to change laws. Her urgent temporal markers—"it's time"; "coming to an end"; "make changes now"; "first steps"—and declarative phrasing attest to the significance and timeliness of the issue. Carlson reminds us that one in three women are harassed at work and 71 percent of the cases aren't reported. It's time, she insists, for greater employer accountability and for legal changes that both make it easier for women to come forward and that prevent harassment from happening in the first place.

"Sexual Harassment Reckoning Has Been a Long Time Coming"

Variety, 2017

As 2017 comes to a close, the landscape of sexual harassment claims and the manner in which companies are handling them are changing at breakneck speed.

Over the past 17 months, we've seen more and more women all across the country mustering the courage to speak out en masse, and amazingly, they're no longer being instantly called liars and having their stories pushed aside.

One of the most positive developments is how quickly companies are holding harassers publicly accountable and taking action to right egregious wrongs.

This is a welcome and long overdue change. When my story broke in July 2016, I felt incredibly isolated. In recent times, nobody had taken on such a powerful titan for harassment and won. But in short order, could it be we're actually seeing the end of a cover-up culture and the demise of a system that in many cases was rigged against the victims?

Companies are rushing to catch up. Whether the "bad behaviors" were known on the inside is a question being asked at NBC, NPR, the *Atlantic*, and many other companies facing harassment scandals. Whether executives knew, suspected or just "heard things" doesn't matter. Many of the outed predators held their jobs for decades, secure in the knowledge that accusers would be intimidated, maligned or otherwise silenced.

Too often in offices all across America, leadership focuses on damage control—settling with victims and surrounding harassers with assistants, lawyers, and PR teams to mitigate the fallout. But as I discovered in researching my book "Be Fierce," until recently, perpetrators rarely lost their jobs. Instead, many companies normalized harassment—and thus enabled it to continue.

But when my complaint went public, droves of women contacted me. They sent letters and emails, messaged me on Twitter and even stopped me on the street. Maybe it was because of my harasser's stature, or because I was a familiar (daily) face on TV, but these women thought I would listen. They were right. And it set off a tidal wave of victims with newfound voices.

Just two months ago, their stories might have shocked you: female executives called "cum-dumpsters" by their peers on a daily basis; women given lists of sexual favors to perform for simple perks like an office with a window; army lieutenants tossing dollar bills at female soldiers and yelling, "Dance for me!" And on and on. Every profession. Every walk of life. Every woman. Now we're regaled daily with public accounts of powerful men exposing themselves, assaulting colleagues, and intimidating anyone who gets in their way.

America is now at a tipping point; real change is finally possible, and there can be no turning back. The rise of the public apology is a good sign. I got a rare public apology from my boss's parent company, which, to me, was more important than anything else. In contrast, harassers are now apologizing in the first news cycle. This acknowledges something important: Sexual harassment isn't "bad behavior"—it's illegal behavior. Whether it's gender discrimination or crosses the line into sexual abuse, assault, or rape, executives must treat it like any other workplace crime.

Reports say that at least one in three women is sexually harassed at work. But since 71% of harassment is never reported, the real number is much higher. And in the past when women found the courage to complain, it often made things worse for them. Almost every woman who reached out to me was re-victimized after coming forward—by being slandered, blacklisted, demoted, or, in many cases, fired. The vast majority never worked in their chosen careers again. That's not only wrong, it's outrageous.

NBC's Matt Lauer was fired because of a formal complaint but also, as has been reported, because multiple news outlets were getting ready to break their stories. The takeaway is that companies must stop waiting for tenacious journalists to do what responsible corporate executives should be doing. Make changes now, before a sexual harassment problem spirals out of control and becomes a crisis.

Bottom line: It's time to unrig the system. The culture of concealment and denial is coming to an end.

Ending nondisclosure agreements for discrimination and harassment claims is crucial. Of course, business and trade secrets must be protected, but NDAs weren't created to hide dirty laundry. NDAs that protect harassers and keep other victims from coming forward have no place in 2017 corporate culture.

Changing how victims come forward is vitally important. "We've never received any complaints" means there's a serious problem with the process. Organizations can address this by creating a separate, independent track for harassment investigations—a process that's separate from the top brass and human resources departments. I've heard from a lot of good people in HR, but let's face it: If the harasser is the same person who signs your paycheck, there's an inherent conflict of interest. Appointing an independent ombudsman, or authorizing more than just one group of individuals across an organization to hear complaints, would be a good first step.

Companies can also identify and reach out to victims who were pushed out and offer them their jobs back. It's reprehensible that thousands of victims have had their American dream stripped away. Let's stop talking about what "great guys" these predators were, and start hiring back the women who courageously came forward.

These are important changes companies can make today. They shouldn't require an act of Congress (though I'm working on that). For the past year, I've been meeting with senators and representatives on Capitol Hill to craft a bipartisan bill to end forced arbitration in employee contracts. Forced arbitration protects harassers and takes away all employees' constitutional right to a jury trial. Companies who want to get ahead of the next harassment bombshell should pick up the phone, call Congress, and voice support. As we approach the New Year, wouldn't it be great for something constructive to get done for women?

These are just first steps. Companies can do much more to promote equality and safe workplaces. They can put more women in top positions and pay women the same as their male counterparts. They can also give more women a seat in the boardroom. They need to be accountable and transparent. Good for PR? Yes. Good for business?

For sure.

Across every industry, leaders are asking, "Who's next?" And while more startling revelations are anticipated, that's not the point. It's not about who's next, it's about what's next.

FOR FURTHER READING

"About Gretchen Carlson." *Gretchen Carlson*, n.d., www.gretchencarlson.com/about/.
Butler, Bethonie. "Gabrielle Union on #MeToo: 'The Floodgates Have Opened for White Women.'"
   The Washington Post, 8 Dec. 2017, www.washingtonpost.com/news/arts-and-entertainment/
   wp/2017/12/08/gabrielle-union-on-metoo-the-floodgates-have-opened-for-white-women
   /?utm_term=.c0d26f3c0236.
Carlson, Gretchen. *Be Fierce: Stop Harassment and Take Your Power Back*. Center Street, 2017.
Carlson, Gretchen. *Getting Real*. Viking, 2015.

Galanes, Philip. "Catharine MacKinnon and Gretchen Carlson Have a Few Things to Say." *The New York Times*, 17 Mar. 2018, www.nytimes.com/2018/03/17/business/catharine-mackinnon-gretchen-carlson.html.

Kipnis, Laura. "Kick Against the Pricks." *The New York Review of Books*, 21 Dec. 2017, www.nybooks.com/articles/2017/12/21/kick-against-the-pricks/#fn-*.

Setoodeh, Ramin. "Gretchen Carlson Gets Fierce." *Stanford Magazine*, 1 Mar. 2018, medium.com/stanford-magazine/gretchen-carlson-gets-fierce-74df8bc07708.

Sherman, Gabriel. "The Revenge of Roger's Angels." *New York Magazine*, 21 Sept. 2016, nymag.com/daily/intelligencer/2016/09/how-fox-news-women-took-down-roger-ailes.html.

Thanu Yakupitiyage

While the following piece is a call to action for the People's Climate March and International Workers' Day in 2017, Thanu Yakupitiyage's message reverberates far beyond these events in its explanation of the link between climate change and migration. The article's particular exigence follows two decisions made by the Trump administration: (1) to pull out of the Paris Agreement, a commitment among over two hundred countries to keep global warming below two degrees Celsius and to aid countries in combating climate change ("Paris Agreement"); and (2) to displace immigrant communities through the Muslim ban, which prevents nationals from seven Muslim-majority countries from entering the United States, increases deportations from the United States, and limits the number of refugees who can enter the country. Yakupitiyage demonstrates that climate change and migration, both consequences of globalization, are deeply intertwined and will only intensify if the United States and other countries fail to act.

Born in Sri Lanka and raised there and in Thailand, Yakupitiyage moved to the United States for college at age eighteen. After graduating with her master's in communication, she worked at the New York Immigration Coalition, a refugee and immigration advocacy organization, and then for 350.org, a global grassroots climate movement. As her website notes, Yakupitiyage also serves as an advocate through "DJing and electronic music production as a medium to create sound narratives that weave in stories about migration, queer communities, communities of color, and the sounds of the immigrant metropolis."

Throughout her editorial, published in *Huffington Post*, Yakupitiyage employs statistics to show the impact of climate change on displaced populations. It is anticipated that by 2050, two hundred million people will be forced to relocate as a result of climate change (Lanktree). Building a solid, research-supported argument, Yakupitiyage focuses on numerical data and sources, such as the Pentagon and the United Nations, who have stated that conflicts and wars are exacerbated by climate issues. Yakupitiyage ends, as do many in this collection, with finding hope amid despair and bleak statistics, drawing on examples of powerful activism already underway. She also calls readers to action, insisting that the more we coalesce around interconnected issues, the more voices will be amplified, and the closer we can come to halting the speed of climate change and its disastrous results.

"Why I March: Climate Change and Migration Have Everything to Do with Each Other"

Huffington Post, **2017**

It's pretty ironic that among Donald Trump's first policies on his agenda were a crackdown on immigrant communities, followed by the dismantling of climate and environmental protections. By rolling back the little progress the US has made on climate change—as well as slashing the budget of the Environmental Protection Agency and lifting a moratorium on federal coal leases—Trump's administration is sending a global message: the US (a country that considers itself a leader) will not meet any commitment to bring down greenhouse gas emissions or invest in clean energy jobs. Meanwhile, the world is warming at an alarming rate, with each year hotter than the last. And while the planet warms and more climate-related disasters take place—droughts get longer, rain patterns shift, land becomes infertile, food and water become scarce, and sea levels rise—more and more people are migrating due to climate change impacts. These are often the world's poorest people, from regions that have done the least to contribute to the severity of the climate crisis.

By disregarding the necessity for bold action on climate change, the Trump administration and climate deniers everywhere (the United States, China, India, and Russia have the highest emission rates) are ensuring that communities across the globe continue to be displaced and have no choice but to migrate for their own survival.

While Trump and many in his administration throw brown and black immigrants under the bus using hateful and racist isolationist tactics, calling for "Muslim bans" and empowering Immigration and Customs Enforcement (ICE) to deport millions with little to no due process, his administration's short-sighted and deliberate decisions to invest in the fossil fuel industry means that he is effectively aiding the process of creating more migrants.

It is estimated that by 2050, there will be 200 million people displaced by climate change-related impacts. According to the International Displacement Monitoring Centre, since 2008, an average of 26.4 million people per year have been displaced from their homes by disasters brought on by natural hazards. Climate change causes migration, and people migrate to flee the impacts of climate change on their homelands.

Make no mistake: people should have the right to migrate no matter what. However, the majority of migration happens because people need access to a better life. If there is no way for them to live in their homelands ravaged by climate change and other socioeconomic impacts, they are left with no choice but to move.

We see this all over the world. In the United States, people in the Gulf are already being internally displaced due to rising sea levels. Isle de Jean Charles in Louisiana, home to the Biloxi-Chitimacha-Choctaw tribe, has lost 98% of its land and most of its population to coastal erosion and rising sea levels since 1955. The population of the island is now down to less than 85 residents from the previous hundreds. In January 2016 the federal Department of Housing and Urban Development (HUD) funded the Isle de Jean Charles Resettlement Project, the first allocation of federal dollars to move 400 tribe members struggling with the impacts of climate change to inland locations. (This year, the Trump administration is proposing to slash the HUD budget by $6 billion.)

In Mexico, farmers have been dealing with severe drought for decades, leading to a loss of agricultural productivity. The outcome? More rural Mexicans are migrating to the United States for better futures. One study found climate change-driven changes to agricultural livelihoods have impacted the rate of emigration to the United States, estimating that by 2080, climate-change-induced migration from Mexico could be up to 6.7 million people. Another study argues that undocumented migration to the US from rural Mexico very much has to do with climate change and the declining livelihoods of farmers facing droughts and lack of rainfall.

And while many factors have led to the conflict in Syria, some argue that severe drought that started in 2006, worsened by a warming climate, drove Syrian farmers to abandon their crops and flock to cities, helping trigger the civil war. It is widely acknowledged, including by the Pentagon, that climate change acts as a threat multiplier, intensifying conflict and war. The United Nations estimates that there are over five million Syrian refugees now. Within his first 100 days in office, Donald Trump made two attempts to ban refugee resettlement to the US from Syria as part of his "Muslim ban."

The climate crisis has been decades in the making, but it's worsening each day that politicians and their fossil fuel ilk sow doubt about its existence. Meanwhile, many Western nations are seeing a rise in xenophobia and anti-immigrant sentiment at the same time as the displacement of people hits a record high. The road ahead requires that we collectively do what's right—we must stand up for the rights of migrants everywhere who deserve dignity and respect as they seek better lives for themselves and their families, as we build bold and just solutions to the climate crisis.

That's why these major actions in the upcoming days are so important. On April 29th, I'll join tens of thousands in the People's Climate March in Washington, DC. There are over 314 sister marches across the United States and around the world. On the 100th day under the Trump administration, we will surround the White House and put forward our vision to build bold solutions for climate, jobs, and justice. Together with a broad spectrum of communities, including Indigenous peoples, workers, immigrants, and communities of all backgrounds, we understand that mitigating the climate crisis is a matter of social, economic, racial, gender, and immigrant justice.

Then on May 1st, workers and immigrants everywhere will participate in the annual International Workers' Day. In light of the assaults on immigrant communities in the United States, this May Day is of particular importance. . . . We will harness the energy of the climate march back into our communities to build local solutions and to stand in solidarity with immigrants. We will resoundingly say, "No Ban, No Wall, No Raids," and push back against a white supremacist and anti-immigrant agenda that aims to divide people, disrespecting the very workers that help uplift America.

There is hope. We've seen people fearlessly stand up for justice and it's imperative that we keep up the momentum. Communities around the world are advocating for more clean energy solutions such as solar paneling and wind power, as well expanding green jobs. We saw the power of inspirational Indigenous-led movements like #NoDAPL that called on thousands to push back against destructive pipeline projects. And thousands rose to the occasion to protect and defend immigrants impacted by Donald Trump's Muslim ban, as well as to continue to push back against unjust deportations through creating sanctuary spaces.

The clock is ticking for our planet and our communities. Only by seeing these issues as inherently connected can we rise up to demand a fair and just world.

FOR FURTHER READING

"About." *350.org*, n.d., https://350.org/about.

"About." *Thanushka DJ Ushka*, n.d., https://thanushka.com/about.

"About Us." *New York Immigration Coalition*, n.d., https://www.nyic.org/about-us.

Das, Kavita. "Thanu Yakupitiyage Is Amplifying Sounds, Immigrant Voices." *NBC News*, 16 July 2019, https://www.nbcnews.com/news/asian-america/thanu-yakupitiyage-amplifying-sounds-immigrant-voices-n600761.

Davenport, Coral. "Major Climate Report Describes a Strong Risk of Crisis as Early as 2040." *The New York Times*, 7 Oct. 2018, https://www.nytimes.com/2018/10/07/climate/ipcc-climate-report-2040.html.

Feng, Shuaizhang, Alan B. Krueger, and Michael Oppenheimer. "Linkages among Climate Change, Crop Yields and Mexico-US Cross-Border Migration. *Proceedings of the National Academy of Sci-*

ences of the United States of America, 10 Aug. 2010, https://www.pnas.org/content/107/32/14257 .long.

"Global Estimates 2015: People Displaced by Disasters." *Internal Displacement Monitoring Center,* July 2015, http://www.internal-displacement.org/publications/global-estimates-2015-people -displaced-by-disasters.

Lanktree, Graham. "Surge of 200 Million Climate Change Refugees Will Reverse Global Healthcare Progress." *International Business Times,* 23 June 2015, https://www.ibtimes.co.uk/surge-200 -million-climate-change-refugees-will-reverse-global-healthcare-progress-1507548.

"The Paris Agreement." *United Nations Climate Change,* n.d., https://unfccc.int/process-and-meet ings/the-paris-agreement/the-paris-agreement.

Zanolli, Lauren. "Louisiana's Vanishing Island: The Climate 'Refugees' Resettling for $52M." *The Guardian,* 15 Mar. 2016, https://www.theguardian.com/environment/2016/mar/15/louisiana -isle-de-jean-charles-island-sea-level-resettlement.

Ai-jen Poo

In the June 2017 issue of the *Atlantic*, the Pulitzer Prize–winning author Alex Tizon published the harrowing story of Eudocia "Lola" Tomas Pulido, the domestic worker who raised him. As he came of age, he also came to realize that Lola was not a paid employee; she was enslaved by his parents. Tizon writes:

> She was 18 years old when my grandfather gave her to my mother as a gift, and when my family moved to the United States, we brought her with us. No other word but *slave* encompassed the life she lived. Her days began before everyone else woke and ended after we went to bed. She prepared three meals a day, cleaned the house, waited on my parents, and took care of my four siblings and me. My parents never paid her, and they scolded her constantly. She wasn't kept in leg irons, but she might as well have been. (Tizon)

Ai-jen Poo's piece was part of a series of responses to Tizon's article. Poo, the director of the National Domestic Worker Alliance (NDWA), uses this opportunity to highlight that Lola's story, while shocking, is not an anomaly. Poo explains that Lola is one of many women trafficked into slavery in the United States, but most are never named, their stories never told.

The daughter of Taiwanese immigrants and a graduate of Columbia University, Poo has dedicated her life to shining light on women who provide domestic care, many of whom are immigrants of color. Employing first-person narrative to describe her encounters with survivors of slavery and trafficking, Poo explains that these women have two commonalities: invisibility and vulnerability. Often, they are fleeing violence or poverty, or they are falsely promised education or wages by their employer; when these promises are reneged, escape is impossible due to sexual, physical, or emotional abuse or threats to report their immigration status. To Lola's story, Poo adds the tales of Lilly and Karmo, two women lured into slavery in the United States. By naming them, she invites readers to connect with them as women as humans, using story to build a pathway to awareness and to spur action.

Poo's leadership takes the shape of numerous campaigns, trainings, and legislative efforts to advocate for both domestic worker rights and for families and caregivers involved with eldercare. In 2000 she joined forces with Filipina and South Asian domestic workers' organizations to found Domestic Workers United, which was pivotal in the passage of the Domestic Workers' Bill of Rights in 2010, legislation that provides basic labor protections to New York State domestic workers (NDWA). In 2012 Poo's name appeared on both *TIME*'s list of the 100 Most Influential People in the World and *Newsweek*'s list of 150 Fearless Women. In 2014, in recognition of her activism, Poo was named a MacArthur Genius Fellow. Poo's writing has been published in the *New York Times, Glamour,* and on CNN.com. In 2016 she published *The Age of Dignity: Preparing for the Elder Boom in a Changing America.*

While Poo's activism spans two decades, most Americans likely first encountered her as Meryl Streep's guest to the 2018 Golden Globe Awards, a year when many celebrities walked the red carpet with activists in order to raise awareness about women's issues around the globe. True to character, Poo used the moment to spotlight women who are forgotten and unseen, and to encourage others to aid the movement. As she suggests in this column, if Tizon had known about an organization like NDWA, Lola's story might have had a very different ending.

"Lola Wasn't Alone"

The *Atlantic,* 2017

There are few subjects more painful than slavery. The word itself conjures images of the most shameful and ugly parts of humanity and our past, histories most would prefer to distance themselves from. This may in part be why, in just two short days, the *Atlantic*'s article "My Family's Slave," by the journalist Alex Tizon about his family's enslavement of a woman named Eudocia "Lola" Tomas Pulido, has caught the attention of and moved thousands of readers. The title itself is shocking in its admission of slavery tucked right into a modern American home.

The story of Pulido is extraordinary in many ways, especially in terms of the length of her enslavement. But what should be more shocking is that her story is not as rare as one would hope. While slavery today doesn't include the chains and horrors typically associated with it, it is unmistakably slavery, existing in modern America. In an ordinary American community. In a residential neighborhood. Where neighbors met her.

She was enslaved. She lived among us, hidden in plain sight. And there are many more women like her.

How does this happen in America today? Some of this story's readers have blamed immigrants, claiming that such a practice is un-American. Some have pointed the finger at Tizon's Asian family, claiming that Filipino culture is at the root of this case of slavery.

But I can tell you, having worked with domestic workers since the mid-1990s, that extraordinary acts of cruelty are unfortunately not limited to people of any one culture. To the contrary, completely ordinary people can be incredibly cruel when they have a decided power advantage and no checks on their power. There is a known pattern of abuse with foreign diplomats and professionals who import "help" from their home countries, but Americans enslave people too. There is a deep history of these arrangements among families at the US-Mexico border where US citizens regularly exploit the insecure citizenship status of workers by forcing them to clean, cook, and take care of children and elders. And across the country, community organizers have encountered enslaved and exploited domestic workers in city after city.

How can such a thing still happen? The pervasiveness of the problem is in a sense an answer to that question: When there is an extreme power imbalance, people—particularly women—are vulnerable to slavery. In every story I've heard from women who have survived these atrocities, there are two commonalities: invisibility and vulnerability.

There are many other examples of stories like Lola's, stories sensitive enough that the last names of the women who told them have been withheld here. For example, there was Lilly, who was brought to Texas at the age 15 by a couple of American executives at a technology company. They promised her an American education and a path out of poverty for her family in Jamaica, in exchange for working as a live-in nanny for their three children. Instead, as soon as they arrived, they cut off her communication with her family and the outside world. For 15 years, her mobility was restricted. She was not allowed to leave the house unaccompanied or talk to any of the neighbors. And she was never paid.

And there was Karmo, who came from Nepal to a Virginia suburb, also escaping extreme poverty, to work for an Indian diplomat. Upon arrival, she was forced to work from early morning until late at night, isolated and prohibited from talking to other people. Karmo's passport was confiscated by her employer and she was told she could be picked up by the police if she complained. For both Lilly and Karmo, the extreme economic hardships of their families left them vulnerable to false promises of a better life; once in America, force, fear, and lack of other jobs and options made it hard for them to leave.

Slavery doesn't just happen in a vacuum, as some perversion from the bigger economic context that people live in. Deep poverty and few options for economic mobility make a person vulnerable to slavery. Language and cultural barriers, and being a woman make a person vulnerable to slavery. Being dependent on an employer for visa access makes a person vulnerable to slavery. Immigration laws that trap a person in the shadows for fear of deportation keep them vulnerable.

The organization I lead, the National Domestic Workers Alliance, and our affiliates have found that for women who have survived slavery or trafficking, the single most important factor for enabling women to escape from slavery is knowing that they are not alone and that they will be supported when they do.

If Tizon had known there was an organization of women who shared Lola's experience and helped her connect to them—and if Lola had known she was not alone, met other women like her, and seen that it was possible to rebuild and live a different life—would her story have ended differently?

The National Domestic Workers Alliance started a campaign with this question in mind. It's called "Beyond Survival," and its goal is to support women who have survived extreme abuse by giving them a chance to heal, connect with others like them, and, for those who choose to do so, share their experiences publicly so that others may be encouraged to escape enslavement. Through this campaign and an organization called Adhikaar, Karmo not only found the courage and support to escape, but she now organizes and assists others like her in New York City. Additionally, programs like these can help policy-makers learn how to best address the needs of survivors.

Their stories and Lola's story remind us that we must take courageous action to end trafficking and slavery. Their resilience brings us face to face with the most painful aspects of humanity, so that we may collectively become more humane.

FOR FURTHER READING

"Ai-jen Poo." *MacArthur Foundation*, 2014, www.macfound.org/fellows/924/.

National Domestic Workers Alliance. www.domesticworkers.org/.

Poo, Ai-jen, and Ariane Conrad. *The Age of Dignity: Preparing for the Elder Boom in a Changing America*. New Press, 2016.

Tizon, Alex. "My Family's Slave." *The Atlantic*, 26 June 2018, www.theatlantic.com/magazine/archive/2017/06/lolas-story/524490/.

National Domestic Workers Alliance Infographic

The National Domestic Workers Association (NDWA) was founded in 2007 to lend voice and visibility to the fifty-three million domestic workers around the world. These workers, the majority of whom are women, are vulnerable to exploitation and abuse and are largely unprotected by labor laws. By training domestic workers with organizing and leadership skills, sponsoring legislative campaigns, and raising awareness, this worker-led movement advocates for the respect and recognition of an often overlooked group (NDWA).

In the following infographic, the NDWA takes advantage of a medium that melds story, data, and visuals to raise awareness about the trafficking of domestic workers. Use of the infographic has boomed in the twenty-first century, thanks to the form's rhetorical effectiveness in a digital world. As the *Forbes* contributor Cheryl Conner explains, infographics strongly appeal to twenty-first-century audiences with progressively shorter attention spans. They also leverage viewers' ability to absorb information faster through graphics and appeal to their emotions through images. Their easy shareability on social media allows for the increased circulation of a message.

The NDWA's infographic deftly employs the medium's affordances to increase viewers' awareness of domestic workers' plight, to explain their vulnerability to abuse, and to call the audience to action, with clear directions for becoming involved. Using an eye-catching, large font, the infographic pulls readers' attention to the word *trafficking*, an abuse often associated with sex workers, not domestic workers. In fact, as the text explains, of those forced into labor, sex exploitation constitutes 22 percent and labor exploitation 68 percent. Employing typography and color to attract the eye to central ideas, the infographic balances blank space, graphics, and text to lead the reader vertically through the text, finally landing on the NDWA website, where readers can seek more information and join the NDWA's efforts. As NDWA director Ai-jen Poo illuminates in "Lola Wasn't Alone," the trafficking of domestic workers is modern-day slavery; this infographic spotlights the exploitation of female workers that too often hides in plain sight.

National Domestic Workers Alliance, Human Trafficking and Domestic Workers Infographic

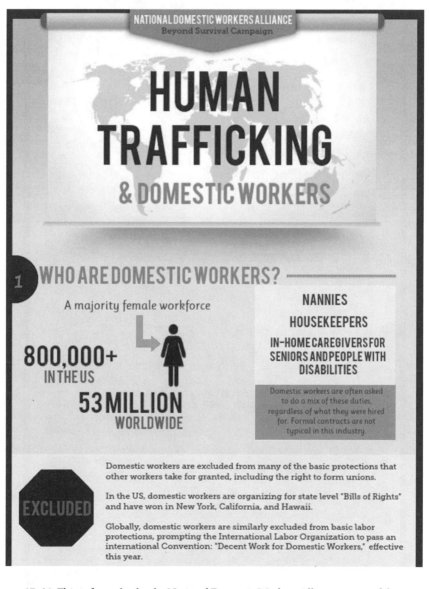

17–21. This infographic by the National Domestic Workers Alliance is part of the organization's Beyond Survival Campaign. It provides facts and disrupts myths about human trafficking.

HOW ARE DOMESTIC WORKERS TRAFFICKED?

2

VULNERABLE

Some come to the US on official work visas that are tied to the diplomats or international officials who abused them

Some are undocumented workers whose employers threaten that the police will arrest or deport them if they try to complain or escape

Common Elements

- Passport and visa withheld/stolen
- False contracts, switched contracts
- Lack of pay or severely low pay
- Excessive working hours
- Change of promised job duties
- Physical or sexual abuse
- Being kept in house, unable to leave
- Phone calls, letters, visits monitored
- Threats to family at home
- Immigration-related threats
- Verbal and emotional abuse
- Culturally-specific coercion

As Domestic Workers
Lack of labor rights & recognition, working behind closed doors in private households

As Women
Gender inequality, discrimination, and violence

As Immigrants
Fear of deportation/family separation

Then, as trafficked persons: overlooked by law enforcement, policy makers, media, and even anti-trafficking activists

Law enforcement does not prioritize these cases because there are few witnesses and usually only one victim. Prosecutors rarely take up these cases because they are difficult to win. This makes awareness and community organizing even more important.

MYTHS AND FACTS ABOUT HUMAN TRAFFICKING

3

In fact, when it comes to the 20.9 million people in forced labor in the world, the International Labor Organization (ILO) estimates that the breakdown between sex exploitation and traditional labor is about 22% to 68%, respectively.

Myth: Human trafficking is a problem faced only by women and girls in the sex trade

FACT: People of ANY age, gender, ethnicity, education level, immigration status can be trafficked into ANY kind of work- including agriculture, domestic work, construction, restaurants, and prostitution

Myth: Human trafficking usually involves kidnapping and physical violence

FACT: Physical harm is not required to prove that someone is a victim. Fraud, emotional abuse, threats to family members, and immigration-based threats are often used by traffickers to control victims. Most are not kidnapped, and some survivors entered work arrangements willingly, only to be trafficked later in the course of their employment

Myth: The solution to ending human trafficking is more laws and stricter penalties

FACT: We don't have a solution yet. These approaches are only addressing one side of the problem. In order to find sustainable, rights-based ideas, we should be listening to survivors, and organizing around labor, gender, and immigration rights to prevent trafficking in the first place

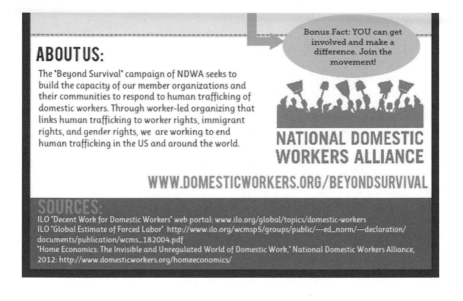

ABOUTUS:

The "Beyond Survival" campaign of NDWA seeks to build the capacity of our member organizations and their communities to respond to human trafficking of domestic workers. Through worker-led organizing that links human trafficking to worker rights, immigrant rights, and gender rights, we are working to end human trafficking in the US and around the world.

Bonus Fact: YOU can get involved and make a difference. Join the movement!

NATIONAL DOMESTIC WORKERS ALLIANCE

WWW.DOMESTICWORKERS.ORG/BEYONDSURVIVAL

SOURCES:
ILO "Decent Work for Domestic Workers" web portal: www.ilo.org/global/topics/domestic-workers
ILO "Global Estimate of Forced Labor" http://www.ilo.org/wcmsp5/groups/public/---ed_norm/---declaration/documents/publication/wcms_182004.pdf
"Home Economics: The Invisible and Unregulated World of Domestic Work," National Domestic Workers Alliance, 2012: http://www.domesticworkers.org/homeeconomics/

FOR FURTHER READING

"About Us." *National Domestic Workers Alliance*, n.d., https://www.domesticworkers.org/about-us.

Conner, Cheryl. "The Data Is In: Infographics Are Growing and Thriving in 2017 (And Beyond)." *Forbes*, 19 Oct. 2017, www.forbes.com/sites/cherylsnappconner/2017/10/19/the-data-is-in-infographics-are-growing-and-thriving-in-2017-and-beyond/#6a02c4ee137c.

Covert, Bryce. "The New Federal Domestic Workers Bill of Rights Would Remedy Decades of Injustice." *The Nation*, 30 Nov. 2018, www.thenation.com/article/federal-domestic-workers-bill-of-rights-harris-jayapal-labor/.

Ricard-Guay, Alexandra, and Thanos Maroukis. "Human Trafficking in Domestic Work in the EU: A Special Case or a Learning Ground for the Anti-Trafficking Field?" *Journal of Immigrant & Refugee Studies*, vol. 15, no. 2, 2017, pp. 109–21.

VI

Rhetorics of Identities
and the Body

Perhaps nowhere has women's rhetorical work been more clearly recognized—and warranted—than through appeals connected to identities and bodies. We can trace the historical devaluing of women's bodies at least to Aristotle, who deemed women mutilated males, forwarding both biological and political sexism. In response, women across centuries, from Margery Kempe to Sojourner Truth to Gloria Anzaldúa, have intervened with what we now call *rhetoric of the body* or *writing the body*, in which they reclaim the material body as inseparable from subjecthood and identity. Of course, ownership, objectification, and surveillance of women's bodies endures, as is evident in issues ranging from human trafficking to reproductive rights to sexual and domestic abuse. In the face of these injustices, women in the twenty-first century continue to (re)write the body, challenging cultural inscriptions and offering new possibilities for living and being. They articulate malleable possibilities for identities of womanhood, advocate for equity among genders, and celebrate the expansive ways gender is embodied. In so doing, they push audiences toward greater empathy, knowledge, and action.

Opening the section, Melissa Harris-Perry addresses the cultural misrecognition of black women as evidenced in the public response to Hurricane Katrina. As she shares survivor stories from black women and highlights the racial gap between how black and white audiences perceived media coverage of the hurricane, she conveys a cornerstone of rhetorical work—that identity and ideology are integral to how we experience, interpret, and convey the world around us—as well as to who is seen and valued and who is ignored or misrecognized.

Often, women's embodied experiences are hidden from view due to cultural shaming; consequently, we lose opportunities to build community and connection. Jennifer Baumgardner, Tarana Burke, and Eve Ensler seek to correct this, as they describe how listening to the experiences of other women shaped their own stories and deepened their empathy for others. All three have spearheaded projects that recognize and value women's embodied experiences. For Baumgardner, this involves gathering stories from women who have had an abortion, which disrupts the "mass secrecy" that often shrouds the procedure. For Burke, founder of the Me Too movement, hearing the stories of a young girl's assault prompted her to share her own experience—and ultimately to create an organization that allows girls and women to share assault stories without shame. Eve Ensler, known for penning *The Vagina Monologues* and establishing One Billion Rising, compares the arbitrariness of her uterine cancer, and her exemplary medical care in the West, with the deliberate femicide and sexual assault of women she works with in the Congo, whose lives and pain too often remain invisible and unaddressed.

Makers featured in this section—Kat Blaque, Hana Shafi, Jessamyn Stanley, and Christina Yahya—employ media like YouTube, Instagram images, and art to offer more expansive possibilities for identity and female embodiment. Their renderings of and from the human body—using the bathroom of one's choice, eating without shame, practicing yoga, menstruating—show what is possible when women's bodies are embraced. Their body-positive work intervenes in a culture that bombards us with unattainable standards of beauty and narrow definitions of gender normativity. In a spoken-word performance, the trans activist Julia Serano further disrupts normative assumptions, challenging the assumed linkage between genitalia and gender identity by narrating her life as a woman with a penis.

Gabrielle Blair and Karen Hitselberger directly connect issues of identity and the body through purposeful use of new forms: Twitter threads and selfies. Blair engages the staccato microform of a Twitter thread to argue that men are responsible for unwanted pregnancies, something most often assigned solely to women's bodies. Through images featuring her disabled body and an accompanying essay, Hitselberger reclaims the selfie to display the complex, and often joyful, reality of living in a disabled body.

The remaining rhetors in this section demonstrate that it is not only impossible to parse identities into distinct categories but to do so betrays the wholeness of intersectionality. Michelle Denise Jackson writes a haunting piece on the ramifications of having a black, female body, invoking Sandra Bland's death. Staceyann Chin draws from her identity as a "black lesbian immigrant artist from Jamaica" to argue that that one's body is a "valuable tool of a necessary revolution"; her poetic prose celebrates fluidity and upends strictures that force bodies and identities into rigid, binary categories. Christina Cauterucci interrogates the labels *lesbian* and *queer* as identity markers, and while she argues that labels necessarily reduce identity and exclude, she also acknowledges their potential to foster shared identity and belonging. Closing this section, Joanna Hedva illuminates the power of multiplicity in a compelling lyrical essay that intersects issues of physical and mental health, disability, race, gender, and sexuality. Hedva reappropriates the identity of the "sick woman" to honor all those in our culture who are vulnerable, invisible, and uncared for. For Hedva, as for all the rhetors in this section, writing from the body, and centering marginalized identities, provides a powerful means to reclaim agency, forge connection, and spur action.

Melissa V. Harris-Perry

"A state that shames its citizens," Melissa Harris-Perry writes, "violates the foundational social contract of liberal democracies: government's commitment to respect individual dignity" (108). And yet, as Harris-Perry shows brilliantly in *Sister Citizen: Shame, Stereotypes, and Black Women in America*, African American women are shamed repeatedly. They are misrecognized by society and, in turn, learn to misrecognize themselves. Harris-Perry likens this repetition of shaming to living in a crooked room and being told to stand up straight—the structures of inequity become invisible, while the individuals who struggle to gain footing are blamed.

Writer, professor, and television commentator and editor, Harris-Perry has dedicated her career to correcting those acts of misrecognition, particularly as they apply to African Americans. She writes for a wide audience, melding personal narrative, empirical research, and literary analysis. In the following excerpt from *Sister Citizen*, "Disaster," Harris-Perry highlights the experience of Phyllis Montana-LeBlanc, an African American woman displaced from her New Orleans home in the wake of Hurricane Katrina. After the hurricane struck the Gulf Coast in August 2005, broken levees caused massive flooding, leaving millions of people homeless. Local, state, and federal governments faced strong public criticism for insufficient response to the devastation. Writing in 2015, the *Slate* political columnist Jemelle Bouie observes that Katrina has become a "synonym for dysfunction and disaster, a prime example of when government fails in the worst way possible … And the disaster still haunts black political consciousness in ways that most white Americans have never been able to acknowledge."

Harris-Perry forwards this overlooked perspective by detailing Montana-LeBlanc's attempts to seek help after the storm. At every turn, she feels shamed and misrecognized, treated as less than human. Alongside Montana-LeBlanc's story, Harris-Perry places empirical research that shows a deep divide along racial lines over how the public understood the aftermath of Katrina. For white people, Katrina was largely understood as a natural disaster followed by government and bureaucratic failure; for black Americans, it was experienced as a "racial disaster" (138). In the following excerpt, Harris-Perry underscores the emotional and political consequences of misrecognizing the human beings, and the systemic problems, at the eye of the storm.

Harris-Perry has had to challenge misrecognition in her professional life as well. A graduate of Wake Forest (BA) and Duke University (PhD), Harris hosted the MSNBC show *Melissa Harris-Perry* from 2012 to 2016, which covered political, cultural, and community issues. She lovingly described the show as "nerdland," where she, a tenured professor, sought to bring intellectual issues to a public audience. In a culture where, as Harris-Perry contends, black women are often categorized as hypersexual jezebels, caretaking Mammies, or stoic matriarchs, she sought public recognition as a black, female public intellectual. Unfortunately, Harris-Perry's stint at MSNBC ended in a battle with the network and her eventual resignation after they preempted her show "without comment or discussion or notice" and shut her out of election coverage. Rather than sign a non-disparagement clause, which she described as a "gag order," Harris-Perry exited without a severance package. In exchange, she preserved her freedom to speak.

"Disaster": Excerpt from *Sister Citizen: Shame, Stereotypes, and Black Women in America*

2011

I was herded like cattle like everybody else regardless of my ability to pay for services. Nobody cared. I was just as low on that totem pole as that lady who was on welfare with five kids.

Denise Roubion-Johnson, Hurricane Katrina survivor

To commemorate the first anniversary of Hurricane Katrina in August 2006, HBO premiered a documentary film directed by the African American filmmaker Spike Lee. *When The Levees Broke: A Requiem in Four Acts* uses the enduring images of human suffering in New Orleans and the compelling narratives of hurricane victims to capture the tragedy of the disaster.[1] Although the film is political in its thesis and conclusions, it is fundamentally an emotional tale about the heart of the experience of Katrina for the people of New Orleans.

The most compelling citizen survivor to share her story in Lee's movie is Phyllis Montana-Leblanc. Her personal testimony and stinging analysis are the captivating thread holding the film together. Irrepressible, honest, insightful, and frequently profane, Leblanc is the impassioned voice of New Orleanians who were abandoned in the aftermath of the storm. Without a hint of irony she moves seamlessly between cursing the "fuckers" in local, state, and federal government who left her and her neighbors to die and praising the "Lord God Almighty" who delivered them from the flood. She describes being hungry, hot, exhausted, and frightened. She recounts being herded like an animal, treated like a slave, and shunted from place to place, all in an accent and idiom that belong fully and exclusively to the people of New Orleans. Though it is her personal story, to listen to Leblanc is to hear the city itself speaking. In 2008 she expanded on her role in Lee's documentary by publishing a memoir titled *Not Just the Levees Broke*.[2] The text, one of the most powerful first-person accounts by an African American woman to emerge from the storm, has a raw, urgent immediacy; it reads more like spoken language than written text. Having begun this book with a view of Hurricane Katrina framed by Zora Neale Hurston's fictional account in *Their Eyes Were Watching God*, let us now return to Katrina, this time guided by the true story of Phyllis Montana-Leblanc.

Recognition and Visual Disaster

Like all New Orleans natives, Leblanc is both cautious and confident about storms. She does not evacuate for every bad forecast but instead tries to discern how serious the storm is likely to be. In the days leading up to Katrina she finds the news reports confusing and is unsure about evacuating. "Every time they tell us there's a hurricane, people begin running for their lives and nothing happens." Ultimately Leblanc and her sister choose to stay in the city because their elderly mother "says her legs are hurting . . . and we both know we aren't leaving our mama." So, like many New Orleanians connected by deep social networks, Leblanc stays in the path of the storm because it is impossible to imagine leaving part of her family behind. As a result, she and her husband, along with her mother, sister, and nephew, are trapped when her apartment complex is first battered by Katrina's winds then flooded by the levee breach. As days pass without electricity, gas, or running water, Leblanc desperately tries to call for help. Finally she gets through to an operator but is frustrated to learn that the operator cannot connect her to 911 or help her in any substantive way. Through her fear and agony she questions the operator, saying, "I am a person, a living breathing person with a heart beating inside of a body, and you can't help me?"[3]

Leblanc's demand that the operator acknowledge her as a "living breathing person" is a request for recognition. She is asking to be seen and to be recognized as a human who was in need and deserving of help. Throughout her memoir, Leblanc repeats this craving for recognition. She and her family have dire material needs— for safety, food, water, shelter, clothing, medicine, and rest—but they also need to feel that someone acknowledges their humanity. Repeatedly she recounts instanc-

es of misrecognition and the shame it brings. Over and over she resists these shaming moments by reasserting her humanity. Her story makes recognition a critical
part of the struggle for survival.

Phyllis Montana-Leblanc reminds us that in addition to being a physical disaster, Hurricane Katrina was a catastrophe of misrecognition. When the levees
failed in New Orleans—trapping thousands of Americans and destroying a major
city—it became one of the few televised American tragedies.[4] Until the events in
New Orleans, only the destruction of the World Trade Center in 2001 had allowed
Americans to share their fellow citizens' trauma in real time. Unlike September
11, a single, terrible moment replayed by the media, the horror of New Orleans increased daily, produced new images of agony and death, and generated increasingly awful narratives of suffering. Americans throughout the nation witnessed hours
of grisly footage and the destruction of one of America's most distinctive cities.
The nation was able to watch the faces of their fellow citizens as they were unable
to feed their children, comfort their parents, or find their partners.

And we did watch. A Pew Foundation survey conducted within days of the
disaster showed that Americans were glued to their televisions.[5] Seventy percent
of Americans reported that they paid very close attention to news of the hurricane—nearly twice as many as said they paid close attention to the war in Iraq. In
addition, nearly 90 percent of Americans received most of their information about
the disaster from television. About half of these viewers reported that the cable
news channels CNN, MSNBC, and CNBC were their primary source of information. These sources offered blanket coverage of the disaster, beaming thousands
of images of destruction and suffering into American homes. Because it was so
highly visible, Hurricane Katrina offered many opportunities for recognition and
misrecognition. Issues of race, gender, and politics were literally framed by what
Americans saw.

If most Americans were watching the same unfolding tragedy from the same
news sources, it is reasonable to expect that they formed a general consensus about
the disaster and its meaning. No such consensus existed. Data collected in the
weeks and months following the levee breach show that black and white Americans had vastly different opinions about the storm despite having seen very similar
images. This reinforces the lesson that recognition is always a matter of interpreting and giving meaning to the images we encounter. For example, one academic
study offered evidence that the coverage of Katrina differed markedly between the
black press and mainstream newspapers. Black papers were far more likely to refer
to race and poverty and far less likely to attribute the situation of those left in New
Orleans to their individual responsibility.[6] Another study showed that media coverage actually made the residents of local communities that hosted Katrina evacu-
ees less supportive of the poor and of African Americans.[7]

Hurricane Katrina was not color-blind in its effects, and Americans were not color-blind in their interpretations of the disaster. There was a vast racial disparity between how black and white Americans understood the lessons of the storm. Nearly all respondents to this early Pew survey were discontent with the government's response to the emergency, but white and black Americans viewed the disaster across a wide perceptual gulf. While 71 percent of blacks believed that the Katrina disaster showed that racial inequality remains a major problem in the country, a majority of whites (56 percent) felt that racial inequality was not a particularly important lesson of the disaster. Seventy-seven percent of African Americans believed the federal government response was fair or poor, and although a majority of whites agreed, the percent was much smaller (55 percent). In a stunning racial disjuncture, 66 percent of African American respondents believed that if most of the victims had been white, the response would have been faster. Seventy-seven percent of whites believed that race made no difference.

In short, while most white Americans saw the hurricane's aftermath as tragic, they understood it primarily as a natural disaster followed by technical and bureaucratic failures. Most black Americans saw it as a racial disaster. For black Americans, the catastrophe was not just a matter of slow government response; the lack of coordinated response was itself an indication that black people did not matter to the government. This racial gap suggests that many African Americans believed that their white counterparts misperceived the realities of the storm. By this interpretation, white Americans were not recognizing the role played by racial inequality and bias, and because they could not or would not recognize it, they would surely fail to address it.

The connection between recognition and potential political action was important. Survey data make clear that the vicarious experience of the disaster had immediate and dramatic political consequences. The Pew study reported that 67 percent of Americans believed that President George W. Bush could have done more in his handling of the relief effort, and nearly 60 percent rated the federal government's response as fair or poor.[8] The disaster also caused many Americans to reconsider the nation's security, with 42 percent reporting that the events surrounding Hurricane Katrina made them feel less confident that the government could handle a major terrorist attack. In the aftermath of the hurricane, President Bush's job approval ratings plummeted and never fully rebounded.[9] The Democratic Party won a majority in the House of Representatives and the Senate and won the White House in 2008. Many observers point to the Katrina disaster as both a national tragedy and a political turning point.[10] The failure of the Bush administration to respond to the crisis in New Orleans mattered politically.

Although the partisan effects of recognition became obvious in the years following Katrina, the racial terms of recognition mattered as well. Throughout her nightmare Leblanc is convinced that the refusal to acknowledge her humanity is related to her race. After a five-day ordeal, she and her husband finally reach Louis Armstrong Airport, where they await evacuation. The airport has become a place of squalor, filth, and death. Feeling trapped and frightened, she becomes increasingly distraught and worries they may never escape to a safe location. A core feature of her anguish is her sense that the officials in charge of the rescue are cruel and unwilling to acknowledge her. This uncaring attitude is embodied in the expressionless, armed guards in the airport. Leblanc becomes irate watching their robotic responses to such enormous distress. "My emotions are starting to crumble. My mind is falling apart and I don't care anymore. This is wrong and it is driving me crazy. I can't hold it together anymore . . . 'This is inhuman! We are human beings! Look at us, look at us!' They never budge. They never even look at me and I know they can hear me because I am standing right under them at the bottom of the escalators." For Leblanc this refusal to recognize her is not incidental but racial. Her experience of surviving Katrina repeatedly draws forth an analogy to slavery. When she finally makes it to an evacuation center in Houston and takes her first shower in nearly a week, she begins to weep as she reflects on her experience.

"I burst into tears, but soft tears so nobody can hear me. My heart is so broken. My government, in my country, does not care about me, us: the Chocolate People. The tears fall down my face soft and quick, but fall hard on the wooden plank underneath my feet. And then I feel like a slave again. I mean, I know that I could never insult the history of my ancestors by comparing what I am going through with what they endured. But this has the 'air of enslavement.' That is how I feel. So I decide to try to wash that feeling away with that little tiny piece of soap."

Leblanc's tears are not just personal; they are political. Her suffering is not solely about the loss of home, the agony of hunger, or the separation from family; Leblanc weeps the tears of an abandoned citizen. She recognizes herself as linked to a tradition of black suffering. For her, Katrina is a form of temporary enslavement. She is haunted by nightmares for months afterward. One recurring dream combines her sense of racial and political betrayal. "Sometimes in my dreams I see the mayor of New Orleans, the governor of Louisiana, and the president of the United States watching me die and they are laughing and they are all saying that I'm just one less nigger in the world."[11]

In chapter 3 I argued that shame is an emotional response to misrecognition. This is true at both the individual and the collective level. Phyllis Montana-Leblanc uses the word *shame* throughout her memoir. She repeatedly experiences shame during the evacuation when she is ignored or misrecognized by others, especially those in positions of authority. While waiting to board a flight at Louis Armstrong Airport, she waits in a very long line to retrieve a bagged meal. As she stands in line, she notices that black people in the line are being treated differently from their white counterparts. White storm victims are encouraged or allowed to request specific items in their bag, but African Americans are told that they must accept whatever is given.

The people who are giving out the food bags are mostly white and the people making requests for a particular type of cookie or chips are being satisfied and when the black people ask for the same they are told that they can only get what is left over, but then another white person requests their choice and gets it. I saw this with my own two weary eyes. I just take what is given to me and walk away, feeling somewhat shameful and honestly like a nigger, an animal.

Her sister experiences shame for needing to rely on charity. She says, "I feel so ashamed of myself. I mean people are feeding us! And cheaply, I might add. It might seem like I don't appreciate what they're doing, but I do. I'm rather taking a shot at how our government has left us in a position to have to make people feed us like a pack of animals."[12]

When Leblanc first sees images of the flooded city, at the Houston evacuation center, her anger returns as she thinks of how many people have died in the flood. But as she watches the devastation wrought on her home and remembers the long delay in government response, she again wants to hang her head. "I can't believe my eyes. The water from the levees has practically covered our entire city! They don't show bodies but they are saying that tens of thousands are 'feared dead, drowned.' 'Feared'? What in the fuck do they mean, 'feared'? Had they come when we got hit, there would be no 'feared.' I just put my head down in shame and walk back to where Ron is sitting."[13]

Leblanc's memoir encourages us to consider the political effects of the misrecognition that accompanied Hurricane Katrina. Leblanc is not the only African American survivor to speak of shaming and humiliation as core aspects of the experience. D'Ann Penner and Keith Ferdinand collected dozens of oral histories from displaced black New Orleanians in their book *Overcoming Katrina: African American Voices from the Crescent City and Beyond*. Many of their narrators tell of being shamed by military and government personnel who misperceive them as dangerous, poor, and criminal.[14] One of the narrators, Denise Roubion-Johnson, is a middle-class black nurse who was trapped in New Orleans because her husband, a stroke survivor, was too ill to evacuate. During the storm she finds a room at University Hospital for her husband and son and offers her nursing assistance in exchange. She is trapped along with patients and other medical staff for more than five days without necessary equipment or supplies. The first rescuers who appear are local people in small boats. When military personnel finally arrive, on the sixth day after the levee breach, they treat the survivors roughly rather than with compassion. Roubion-Johnson attributes this behavior to racial discrimination.

"We were labeled as 'poor black people,' and we looked the part. We were smelly, so it didn't matter that I live in this Eastover house that I built, and l drive a Lexus RX 350, and I make a substantial income. None of that was relevant. Katrina was the great equalizer. I got frisked just like the woman next to me from the housing project. I had to stand in line in the hot sun, just like everybody else. I had to go to the bathroom, just like everybody else. I got yelled at to shut up, just like everybody else."[15]

Rubion-Johnson's description shows how collective humiliation arises from the stereotypes of the crooked room. She is adamant that no person, black or white, rich or poor, deserved to be treated badly in these difficult circumstances. She is also clear that the rough treatment she gets is related to the negative race and class stereotypes that influence how black Americans are perceived.

NOTES

1. *When the Levees Broke: A Requiem in Four Acts* premiered at the New Orleans Arena on August 16, 2006. The television premiere aired in two parts on August 21 and 22, 2006, on HBO. The film was shown in its entirety on August 29, 2006, the one-year anniversary of Katrina's landfall. The film had wide-reaching consequences for American understandings of the disaster through its curriculum component "Teaching the Levees." "Teaching the Levees" is an official curriculum that includes supporting materials and web-based resources. The curriculum, funded by the Rockefeller Foundation and created by educators from Teachers College, Columbia University, takes the film as the basis for a pedagogical intervention for discussions of race and national politics in schools, colleges, and community organizations.

2. Phillis Montana-Leblanc, *Not Just the Levees Broke: My Story During and After Hurricane Katrina* (New York: Atria, 2008).

3. Ibid., 5, 46.

4. Portions of this chapter come from my article "Do You Know What It Means . . . : Mapping Emotion in the Aftermath of Katrina," *Souls* 9, no. 1 (2007): 28–44.

5. The Hurricane Katrina Survey, sponsored by the Pew Research Center for the People and the Press, obtained telephone interviews with a nationally representative sample of one thousand adults living in continental US telephone households. The survey was conducted by Princeton Survey Research International. Interviews were done in English by Princeton Data Source, LLC, September 7–8, 2005. Statistical results are weighted to correct known demographic discrepancies. The margin of sampling error for the complete set of weighted data is ±3.5 percent.

The oversample of African Americans is designed to allow a sufficient number of interviews for reporting results from this demographic group. The national sample of telephone households was supplemented with an additional 103 interviews with African Americans whose households had been recently contacted for past Pew Research Center national surveys. Demographic weighting was used to ensure that the survey results reflect the correct racial and ethnic composition of national adults, based on US Census information.

6. Kimberly Gross and Marcie Kohenak, "Race, Poverty, and Causal Attributions: Media Framing of the Aftermath of Hurricane Katrina" (Unpublished ms, presented at Midwest Political Science Association, April 2007).

7. Daniel Hopkins, "Flooded Communities: Explaining Local Reactions to the Post-Katrina Migrants" (Unpublished ms, presented at American Political Science Association, 2009).

8. News sources mattered for the conclusions that Americans drew about the efficiency of presidential response. Seventy-three percent of CNN watchers reported that the president could have done more, but only 50 percent of Fox News viewers agreed. Forty-six percent of those whose primary source of Katrina coverage was Fox News believed that the president had done all he could.

9. This Pew survey reports a 50 percent approval rating for President Bush in January 2005 and a 40 percent approval rating immediately following Katrina.

10. Jonathan Weisman and Michael Abramowitz, "Many See Storm as President's Undoing," *Washington Post*, August 26, 2006.

11. Montana-Leblanc, *Not Just the Levees Broke*, 90–91, 101, 171.

12. Ibid., 81, 111.

13. Ibid., 102.

14. One such story comes from Harold Toussaint and is recorded in Penner and Ferdinand, *Overcoming Katrina*. He reports, "All these federal police saw was that I was black, and blacks are criminal. That's what I got from them when we needed them most. It was discouraging to be treated as an enemy combatant rather than someone who needed to be rescued" (53). Toussaint goes on to describe this misrecognition as shaming experience: "The military people that came from the outside treated us like we were diseased or contaminated" (54). Psychologists describe shame as the feeling of being a malignant self. This sense of contamination is a description of shame.

15. Ibid., 74.

FOR FURTHER READING

Bouie, Jamelle. "Where Black Lives Matter Began." *Slate*, 23 Aug. 2015, www.slate.com/articles/news_and_politics/politics/2015/08/hurricane_katrina_10th_anniversary_how_the_black_lives_matter_movement_was.html.

Harris-Perry, Melissa V. *Sister Citizen: Shame, Stereotypes, and Black Women in America*. Yale UP, 2013.

Lee, Spike, director. *When the Levees Broke: A Requiem In Four Acts*. HBO, 2006.

Jennifer Baumgardner

Jennifer Baumgardner is perhaps best known for her co-authored book with Amy Richards, *Manifesta*, published at the turn of the twenty-first century to explain and complicate third-wave feminism and to invite young women to the movement. *Manifesta* is hip in tone, created "to fill a gap in the lives of young women . . . who yearn for a connection to feminism" (xxvii). It became a go-to text for many younger feminists, though it was also critiqued for its focus on white, middle-class feminism; when Richards and Baumgardner issued a new edition in 2010, they addressed this criticism in the preface, demonstrating that feminism requires ongoing self-reflection (Martin).

Though readers may have discovered Baumgardner through the popularity of *Manifesta*, her feminist activism spans nearly three decades. She served as the youngest editor of *Ms.* magazine, editor in chief of *Women's Review of Books*, and executive director at the Feminist Press. To further circulate a feminist message, Baumgardner co-founded the speakers' bureau Soapbox, Inc., and co-created Feminist Camp, "a front-row seat to feminist work, activism, and action beyond classroom theories" ("WTF"). For Baumgardner, feminism and activism go hand in hand, an ethic promoted throughout her work. *I Had an Abortion*, Baumgardner's film produced with and directed by Gillian Aldrich, challenges the secrecy and shame connected to abortion. While nearly 1.3 million women in the United States have abortions each year, almost no women speak about them amid the divisive abortion debate. The film, the T-shirts she created ("I Had an Abortion"), and her book *Abortion & Life* help to share stories from women across a demographic spectrum of age, race, class, and religion. As Baumgardner explains of the T-shirt, the point is not to "be glib" about abortion, but to indicate "how incredibly common it is and how isolated women are from other women who have had [abortions]. Part of the paralyzing stigma of abortion is reinforced by silence" (Eagle). *Abortion & Life* is part written essays by Baumgardner, part photo essays by the photographer Tara Todras-Whitehill, and part testimonials by women who have had abortions.

In the introduction to *Abortion & Life*, Baumgardner traces her evolving beliefs as a pro-choice advocate. Through personal narrative, she maps key events through the lens of her touchstones and experiences: growing up in North Dakota in the 1970s with liberal parents, visiting abortion clinics around the country to hear women's myriad reasons for seeking abortions, giving birth to her own child, and not personally having an abortion. Through her narrative, Baumgardner argues for storytelling as critical to the pro-choice movement. In listening to others' stories, she contends, we will understand the abortion debate with deeper nuance. Baumgardner writes, "Our personal stories will tell us where the political movement needs to go."

"Introduction": Excerpt from *Abortion & Life*

2008

I don't remember when I first heard the word *abortion*. What I do recall is this: By age four I knew, generally, how babies were made because my mother became pregnant with my sister Jessica and insisted on explaining to us, in the most clinical and explicit terms possible, about vaginas, sperm, eggs, and intercourse. My parents weren't hippies—far from it, in fact, having been raised in small-town North Dakota during the 1950s. I too was raised in North Dakota, but I was a child of the 1970s and my youth was colored by the cultural movements of the time, including feminism.

The second wave of feminism ushered in consciousness and discussion about birth and bodies, as well as a woman's right to control both of these things herself. My mother recalls showing my Grandma Gladys the photos of childbirth in *Our Bodies, Ourselves* and Grandma— who had given birth to eight children, three when she was still a teenager—saying that she had never glimpsed a baby's head crowning out of a vagina. She was fascinated. We had *Ms.* magazine in the house, with its frequent headlines about reproductive freedom, and I think I absorbed what ending an unwanted pregnancy was before anyone ever talked to me about it.

The first real conversation I had about abortion occurred when I was ten and my family was visiting friends in Iowa City. The mother in that family, Laurel Bar, was a strong feminist, intense and intimidating to me at that age. Laurel had two identical pins the size of half dollars on her kitchen bulletin board, both depicting the pro-choice symbol of that generation—a wire hanger with a red bar struck through it. I was intrigued and asked if I could have one. She held a pin out and looked me right in the eye. "I'll give this to you," she said sternly, "but only if you wear it and understand what it means." Her intensity made me momentarily nervous, but at the same time, I was flattered that she was taking me seriously. I took the button from her, and I took its message to heart. The point of that button was, of course, the assertion that a woman should never be forced to thrust a hanger through her cervix and into her uterus because she is pregnant and has no access to a legal abortion.

For Laurel's generation, for Laurel herself, this hanger meant something literal. Laurel was the sole confidante (with the exception of the girl's mother) to a friend who'd had an illegal abortion in 1964. The girl's mother, who insisted that the father could never find out, had found the abortionist and taken her terrified daughter to an actual back alley to meet her fate. After the abortion, the girl bled copiously. Six years later, Laurel flew with another pregnant friend to New York City, this time for a legal abortion. "The difference was staggering," Laurel now recalls. "The second friend just walked out of the clinic, came back to the hotel, and was completely fine. No secrets; no hemorrhaging."

For my generation in the United States, though, the hanger doesn't evoke memories of barriers that women faced. The image is abstract, not quite relevant—a marker of another time and, despite claims to the contrary, not likely to be part of our future, even if *Roe v. Wade*, the 1973 Supreme Court decision that made abortion legal in all fifty states, were to be overturned.

A current symbol of reproductive freedom—what would that be? A gun with a strike through it to represent the clinic violence that marked the 1980s to mid-'90s, killing three doctors and four other clinic workers? The fleshy pink faces of Senator Jesse Helms and Representative Henry Hyde, both of whom signed into law restrictions that mean poor women have very limited access to early abortion and birth control information? Angels' wings, to indicate the thousands of women who have abortions and yet believe that a fetus has a soul and is watching over them? Or an open mouth, to illustrate the growing movement of women who are speaking out about their abortion experiences, from the after-abortion counseling groups like Backline and Exhale to the zine *Our Truths/Nuestras Verdades* to the films *Silent Choices* and *The Abortion Diaries*? These are some of the images that have animated the last few decades and that speak to the experience of my peers— younger women and men raised in the wake of legal abortion.

After years of thinking and writing about abortion, I have learned many things that bolster my belief that supporting abortion rights (without restrictions) is the most ethical position one can take. I have seen ample evidence that abortion is the result, not the cause, of social problems. Dilemmas such as inadequate access to health care, female poverty, and sexual violence remain pernicious, and there is no doubt that if we addressed those issues, we'd reduce the need for abortion. Seventeen percent of those who terminate unplanned pregnancies are teenagers, many of whom have shrinking access to sex education or birth control since most states accept federal money that mandates abstinence-only education. Meanwhile, women on Medicaid often receive less effective generic forms of the birth control pill that contain only eighty percent of the hormones in brand-name pills. When I hosted poor women who had traveled to New York for abortions, every single one said she got pregnant while on the pill, leading me to believe that generic birth control is a problem that must be addressed.

For those people horrified about abortion—and I am more sympathetic to this perspective than I once was—it is crucial to confront social injustices that precede the embryo, fetus, or baby; and to accept that it might not be possible to ever truly abolish abortion. In fact, countries in which abortion is legal and those in which it is a crime have similar abortion rates, according to a 2007 report by the Guttmacher Institute (generally considered to be the best, most accurate source for reproductive health research) and the World Health Organization; and the abortion rate is dropping more quickly in countries that provide aboveground procedures. But as I explore later in this book, it may nonetheless be possible to be authentically, actively, radically pro-life; learning how to do so *ethically* is the real challenge for people who believe the fetus has a soul.

While I'm absolutely opposed to compulsory pregnancy, I have also evolved my position over the years. I began my pro-choice activism as a gung-ho young feminist who bought into received wisdom and bumper sticker slogans (*Get Your Laws Off My Body!*) more than I trusted my own ability to understand the issue. I had an instinct that abortion rights were intrinsically tied to women's human rights, but I mainly absorbed what others—women I respected—had to say about the issue and its complexities. Since then, I've visited abortion clinics around the country and observed what happens to the remains of eight-week, twelve-week, and fourteen-week aborted fetuses. I have hosted half a dozen women in my tiny apartment, sad ladies who traveled long distances to get twenty-four-week abortions that take three days to accomplish. Since 1995, I have helped raise thousands of dollars to pay for low-income women's abortions, coproduced a documentary of women's abortion stories, sat on the board of an abortion fund, and I've written on the subject for at least ten magazines, from the *Nation* to *Glamour* to *Jane*.

I haven't had an abortion to date, but I did become accidentally pregnant in 2004. That unplanned event resulted in my son Skuli and deepened my gratitude for how things have changed because of the feminist movement of the '60s and '70s. Would I have been so encouraged to have a child out of wedlock without that movement? Would I have thrived if I didn't have access to a good job and the sense that a woman shouldn't be dependent on a man any more than a fish be dependent on a bicycle? My pregnancy actually increased my interest in abortion. I embarked on a campaign called the "I Had an Abortion" project in late 2003, and by the time the film of the same name was nearly complete in late 2004, my appreciation for the profundity of the issue was growing, like my body, every day.

The more I began to talk to people about their abortion experiences, the more questions I had. Really basic queries that I had simply never asked myself, such as: *How do women experience abortion? How do men experience it?* That led to: *Why aren't there more after abortion resources? Why aren't more women allowed to invite their partners into the procedure room (or anywhere besides the waiting room) if it has been established that they want the support?* And: *If you admit you are sad about your abortion, does that mean abortion is wrong? Can you be a feminist and pro-life? What happens to birth mothers dealing with adoption? If you aren't at all sad about getting rid of your pregnancy, can you admit that publicly without being called a monster?*

After years of interviewing women about their abortion experiences, I still see myself in the ten-year-old girl who solemnly accepted a no-more-coat-hangers pin to wear. I honor the women who lived through that time. Even so, my role as an advocate for abortion rights has moved from winning support for pro-choice legislation to examining how this generation's experience of abortion is shifting. I want to thereby shed light on the ethics and laws that dictate women's human rights, and I believe our personal stories will tell us where the political movement needs to go.

Can storytelling—mere talking—truly protect our rights? Our personal stories give the movement its authenticity. Our personal stories actually strengthen our political position. And fortunately I'm not alone in this belief. During the fall of 2007, Dr. Susan Wicklund called for more openness about the stories behind abortion in her book *This Common Secret: My Journey as an Abortion Provider.* Former Planned Parenthood president Gloria Feldt looked to personal experiences for her 2003 book *Behind Every Choice Is a Story.* Likewise, the independent providers who make up the Abortion Conversation Project have been creating connective tissue between the issue and the women they serve for more than a decade. (A recent initiative, called "Mom, Dad, I'm Pregnant," generates resources to help girls communicate with their parents about their pregnancy, as it is a time when most girls really need the support of their parents or other trusted adults.) In 2004, the Feminist Women's Health Center, based in Washington State, produced a report entitled, "Listening to the Women We Serve: Young Women's Attitudes about Abortion and Choice." The report found that most of the women coming to clinics for abortions rarely thought about the subject, believed most people were opposed to the procedure, didn't know that one-third of women in the US would have at least one abortion in their lives, and nearly half did not vote *nor identify* as pro-choice. However, explains Portland-based activist Grayson Dempsey in a speech in which she discussed the report, "When put in focus groups with other women where they could talk openly about their experiences," women suddenly connected to the issue. Those same "apathetic" women became outraged at the restrictions on abortion that were being introduced and passed at the state and federal levels. Ultimately, Dempsey noted, some of these women got mobilized and became activists and pro-choice voters. It began with a personal conversation, a chance to talk with other women about what had happened to them. Speaking out about their own stories led to a political awakening and was a catalyst for becoming activists.

People often question whether or not this is a good time to speak openly and truthfully about the more controversial issues surrounding abortion. Given the many enemies this legal procedure has, aren't we just handing anti-abortion foes fodder if we talk about the fact that some women feel like the clinic was a factory experience, or if we encourage women to discuss their ambivalent feelings about the fetus? Why examine the gory aspects of laterterm procedures? There are many reasons, to my mind, that space for honesty is crucial right now. The first is to iden-tify places where the actual provision of terminations—and abortions are first and foremost an issue of public health—can be improved for the patient. We want a clinic experience that is medically sound and patient-sensitive. Since abortion is so rarely treated as a medical issue, though, another critical reason that open conver-sation should be encouraged is to provide entry points *within the pro-choice move-ment* for the person who is ambivalent. "The extreme pro-choice side is clear and confirmed," says feminist author Amy Richards, "and the extreme pro-life com-munity is concrete and resolved too. But those two sides taken together represent a tiny minority." She is right. The vast majority of Americans don't want abortion to be recriminalized but are uncomfortable talking about and even facing the real-ities of the procedure.

Few women who have unplanned pregnancies today have personal experiences of a time when aborting was illegal or when being a single mother meant social doom. The days when a woman or girl had to be willing to pay any sum and en-dure any danger or humiliation in order to get an abortion are for the most part over, and we are grateful for that. Meanwhile, the generation that has lived with the rights that our mothers' generation fought so hard for has the opportunity to move the abortion issue forward; it has been hopelessly gridlocked for most of my life as a battle between the life of a woman and the life of a fetus. It's not a step back into pre-feminist times to feel differently about the fetus, procedures, and unplanned pregnancy than our mothers' contemporaries did and often still do.

The battle for abortion rights unfolds in a generational way because women who get pregnant today do so in a time where we simply know more about fetuses than other generations did: We see sonograms, experience sophisticated prenatal testing, and read dramatic stories about babies born at twenty-three weeks gesta-tion managing to survive. Science has discovered much about fetal development in the years since 1973. Delicate, lifesaving or spine-repairing surgery can now be performed on a fetus that is only five months old and while in the womb, as has been documented by photos of the Nashville surgeon Dr. Joseph Bruner operat-ing on the twenty-one-week-old fetus Samuel Armas. A preemie born as young as twenty-two weeks (going to full term is thirty-seven to forty weeks of gestation) and weighing just ten ounces can now live if medical care is provided until he or she is around five pounds.

Women who get pregnant today know that it is no longer a social death sentence for being a single mother or having a child out of wedlock; in fact, in 2005, thirty-seven percent of children were born outside of marriage in the US, a rate which has been increasing since 1970. Meanwhile, the teen pregnancy rate is decreasing (now at the lowest level in sixty-five years, according to the CDC's National Center for Health Statistics), and the rate of women in their thirties and even forties having children is on the rise, many of them unmarried. As mentioned, I have a child, whom I quite contentedly raise—from separate homes—with his father, Gordon, and we were never married. Abstinence-only education is passing for sexuality education, but most young people have access to online information about sex, diseases, and birth control that was exponentially harder to find even in the '80s, at the height of comprehensive sex ed.

Most significantly, the map of the states where abortion procedures are available has changed irrevocably. If *Roe* were overturned, I would be horrified and sad, but not because it would return us to the bloody, repressive past. In 1967, abortion was illegal in all fifty states; in 1973, before the *Roe* decision, it was legal in just four. If we lost the protection of *Roe* today, there would be a good twenty states in which abortion would still be legal. Those would be the states where it is currently the least difficult to access abortion. In other words, if you are worried about what would happen if *Roe* were overturned, you are already seeing it. The women who would be most affected are the exact ones (young and/or poor women) who already lack access.

Recalibrating our views on abortion can represent real progress, as a woman can now afford to acknowledge that she may be emotionally conflicted about the life growing inside her. She can be openly sad about what ending a pregnancy might mean to her: a break with her religion, a conflict with her sense of self, perhaps even recognition that the relationship she is in can't support this development.

Women and men who are involved with abortions today have complex experiences and stories. More than a few of us young feminists have a growing belief that a fetus is something more than just a blob of tissue. This understanding is buoyed by the incredible view that modern technology gives us of the inside of a womb. Today's abortion rights movement has to come to terms with the truth of graphic anti-abortion images, which is that fetuses *have* fingers and toes as early as nine weeks.

And like our second-wave counterparts, women who have abortions today are in good company—one in three women will have an abortion by the age of forty-five. And yet these same women often feel very alone in their experiences. There is still mass secrecy surrounding this particular pregnancy event. My hope for this book (and the inspiration for the "I Had an Abortion" project) is to undermine that big shameful *secret*. First, by reviewing the history of abortion and abortion laws; next, by telling women's stories and putting faces, literally, on the issue; and finally, by looking at what the future of reproductive justice might entail. I have also included a resource guide in the back of this volume with just a fraction of the innovative activist groups, films, and books that delve into the issue of abortion rights; and I offer some suggestions about how to strengthen a woman's right to control her body and her life in today's changing political landscape.

Some of what I write might be seen as turning away from the radical history of abortion rights in search of a compromised "middle ground." I would argue, however, that the cornerstones of a new feminist theory of abortion rights will be created by those whom unplanned pregnancy most urgently affects—women born post-*Roe*. Still, as in the past, abortion is a part of life—just as sex and death are. Abortion is not new: The ancient Egyptians had recipes for abortion-inducing medicines, and some female slaves in the antebellum US practiced abortion rather than creating more slaves upon whom their masters could build their fortunes. As these enslaved women demonstrated, abortion is intricately connected to being a parent—the vast majority of women who get abortions will also become mothers or are already mothers. "Women have the power to give life," as health and human rights activist Loretta Ross says (echoed by many women throughout this book), "and we have the power to not give life."

For Further Reading

"About." *Jennifer Baumgardner*, n.d., www.jenniferbaumgardner.net/about/.

Adams, Elliot C. *American Feminist Manifestos and the Rhetoric of Whiteness*. 2006. Bowling Green State U, PhD dissertation.

Baumgardner, Jennifer. *Abortion & Life*. Akashic Books, 2008.

Baumgardner, Jennifer, and Amy Richards. *Manifesta: Young Women, Feminism, and the Future*. Farrar, Straus and Giroux, 2010.

Eagle, Amy. "'I Had an Abortion' T-Shirts Stir up Controversy." *Chicago Tribune*, 4 Aug. 2004, https://www.chicagotribune.com/news/ct-xpm-2004-08-04-0408040194-story.html.

Jensen, Michelle. "Riding the Third Wave." *The Nation*, 27 Nov. 2000, www.thenation.com/article/riding-third-wave/.

Martin, Courtney. "A Manifesta Revisited." *The American Prospect*, 22 Mar. 2010, prospect.org/article/manifesta-revisited-0.

McFadden, Caroline R. *Critical White Feminism: Interrogating Privilege, Whiteness, and Antiracism in Feminist Theory*. 2011. U of Central Florida, Master's thesis.

"WTF is Feminist Camp?" *Feminist Camp*, n.d., www.feministcamp.com/home.

Tarana Burke

In 2017 a moment meant to showcase the ubiquity of sexual assault served as a reminder of how white privilege results in continued disparities. The actress and activist Alyssa Milano shared the hashtag #MeToo in response to the mounting sexual assault allegations against the movie producer Harvey Weinstein. The stunning response on social media culminated in over twelve million shares and reactions on Facebook within twenty-four hours (Garcia). The moment was also one where Tarana Burke, the true originator of a "me too" movement, "felt a sense of dread, because something that was part of my life's work was going to be co-opted and taken from me and used for a purpose that I hadn't originally intended" (Garcia). Milano worked to correct the situation, making clear in public venues that Burke had begun the movement, and that its purpose should not be lost: to center the survivors of sexual assault. The momentum that followed resulted in *Time* magazine naming Burke, Milano, and other whistleblowers the 2017 Person of the Year: The Silence Breakers.

This widespread reckoning that unfolded over social media was forced to expand its focus to the movement Burke began in 2006 and to highlight the erasure of women of color within feminist movements. Burke—an activist, organizer, and survivor—founded the nonprofit group Just Be Inc. and served as senior director at Girls for Gender Equity, both focused on supporting young women of color. While the "me too" movement seeks to support all survivors of sexual violence, Burke's commitment to girls of color serves as a reminder that sexual violence is both prevalent and pervasive in black and brown communities; harrowing statistics show that "almost half (49.5%) of multiracial women and over 45% of American Indian/Alaska Native women are subjected to some form of sexual violence in their lifetime" (Smith et al).

The pain and poignancy in the birth of the movement is crystallized in "The Inception," posted on Just Be Inc.'s website. Here, Burke recalls the moment that began "me too": a girl named Heaven confessed her story of abuse to Burke, and Burke remained silent about her own history of abuse. Burke carried heavy remorse for not sharing her story, for not saying "me too." Told in an intimate way, Burke conveys the shame and trauma that kept her—and keeps so many victims—from revealing the truth. In keeping silent in that moment, Burke was motivated to begin what is now a movement of millions to break the silence, to invite victims to find peace and solidarity in sharing the stories behind the statistics of sexual assault and violence.

"The Inception"

Just Be Inc.

The me too Movement™ started in the deepest, darkest place in my soul.

As a youth worker, dealing predominately with children of color, I had seen and heard my share of heartbreaking stories from broken homes to abusive or neglectful parents when I met Heaven. During an all-girl bonding session at our youth camp, several of the girls in the room shared intimate stories about their lives. Some were the tales of normal teenage angst and others were quite painful. Just as I had done so many times before, I sat and listened to the stories, and comforted the girls as needed. When it was over the adults advised the young women to reach out to us in the event that they needed to talk some more or needed something else—and then we went our separate ways.

The next day Heaven, who had been in the previous night's session, asked to speak to me privately. Heaven was a sweet-faced little girl who kind of clung to me throughout the camp. However, her hyperactive and often anger-filled behavior betrayed both her name and light, high-pitched voice and I was frequently pulling her out of some type of situation. As she attempted to talk to me that day though the look in her eyes sent me in the other direction. She had a deep sadness and a yearning for confession that I read immediately and wanted no part of. Finally, later in the day she caught up with me and almost begged me to listen . . . and I reluctantly conceded. For the next several minutes this child, Heaven, struggled to tell me about her "stepdaddy," or rather her mother's boyfriend, who was doing all sorts of monstrous things to her developing body . . . I was horrified by her words, the emotions welling inside of me ran the gamut, and I listened until I literally could not take it anymore . . . which turned out to be less than 5 minutes. Then, right in the middle of her sharing her pain with me, I cut her off and immediately directed her to another female counselor who could "help her better."

I will never forget the look on her face.

I will never forget the look because I think about her all of the time. The shock of being rejected, the pain of opening a wound only to have it abruptly forced closed again—it was all on her face. And as much as I love children, as much as I cared about that child, I could not find the courage that she had found. I could not muster the energy to tell her that I understood, that I connected, that I could feel her pain. I couldn't help her release her shame, or impress upon her that nothing that happened to her was her fault. I could not find the strength to say out loud the words that were ringing in my head over and over again as she tried to tell me what she had endured . . . I watched her walk away from me as she tried to recapture her secrets and tuck them back into their hiding place. I watched her put her mask back on and go back into the world like she was all alone and I couldn't even bring myself to whisper . . . **me too**.

For Further Reading

Garcia, Sandra E. "The Woman Who Created #MeToo Long Before Hashtags." *The New York Times*, 20 Oct. 2017, https://www.nytimes.com/2017/10/20/us/me-too-movement-tarana-burke.html.
"Get Statistics." *National Sexual Violence Resource Center*, n.d., https://www.nsvrc.org/node/4737.
Girls for Gender Equality. https://www.ggenyc.org/.
"Purpose." *Just Be Inc.*, n.d., http://justbeinc.wixsite.com/justbeinc/purpose-mission-and-vision.
Smith, Sharon G., et al. *The National Intimate Partner and Sexual Violence Survey (NISVS): 2010–2012 State Report.* 2017. National Center for Injury Prevention and Control, Centers for Disease Control and Prevention, Atlanta, GA.

Eve Ensler

A Tony Award–winning playwright, performer, and activist, Eve Ensler is best known for *The Vagina Monologues*, written in 1996, in which women across age, ethnic, and racial lines directly address the audience with stories about their vaginas. Praised for its unique amalgamation of humor, wisdom, and candor, *The Vagina Monologues* unabashedly highlights the shame and stigma that accompany sexual violence.

Ensler knows trauma firsthand. In her 2008 book *Insecure at Last*, she describes her history of being raped and beaten by her father between the ages of five and ten. Writing became Ensler's means of escape and route for activism; it also became a vehicle for her to forge connections with other women. Following the success of *The Vagina Monologues*, Ensler and a group of friends created V-Day to support local activists in raising global awareness about sexual violence, including rape, genital mutilation, and incest. On February 14, *The Vagina Monologues* is staged royalty-free around the world to educate and raise proceeds for violence prevention groups; in twenty years, the movement has raised over $100 million.

As Ensler describes in the following article, a trip to the Democratic Republic of the Congo, where she talked with survivors hospitalized as a result of gang rape and torture, served as a catalyst for Stop Raping Our Greatest Resource: Power to the Women of the DRC. Ensler juxtaposes her experience and treatment of uterine cancer, which is "painful but arbitrary," with the atrocities experienced by the women and children of the Congo, which are "systematic, strategic and intentional." Around her—a white woman in the West—is a team of doctors, advanced medical technology, friends and advocates and, above all, people who see her as human. Meanwhile, for the people of the Congo, "The international power elite appear to be doing nothing."

Ensler has continued to expand her activism to the global sphere, most recently through the One Billion Rising Campaign, named for the staggering statistic that one billion women of the world's seven billion people will be raped or beaten during their lives. During the event's launch on February 14, 2013, groups of women joined forces in cities around the world to "express their outrage, strike, dance, and RISE in defiance of the injustices women suffer, demanding an end at last to violence against women" (One Billion Rising). However, the inaugural event was not without controversy. Ensler did not take into account that February 14 is a momentous day for Indigenous women in Canada, when they participate in their own event, Women's Memorial March, to honor missing and murdered Indigenous women. Following a publicized conflict between Ensler and Lauren Chief Elk, One Billion Rising eventually changed the date of its event and Ensler publicly apologized.

Ensler has also been accused of a white savior complex—imposing her Western feminist view of liberation on women whose lives are deeply different from her own. The Canadian professor Gada Mahrouse further contends that One Billion Rising seems to "pay little attention to the transnational and intersectional systems of power (including gender, race, class, sexuality, and dis/ability, imperialism, colonialism, war and occupation) that make women *differently* vulnerable to violence" (Gonzalez-Berg). Indeed, Ensler's use of dance as activism—particularly in others' countries—has also raised the ire of critics. Ensler explains the choice this way: "When you are raped, you are forced to leave your body because it is a landscape of terror and pain. It feels contaminated and polluted. Just the act of releasing your trauma when you dance can make you feel part of a community" (Khaleeli). Yet critics insist that a white woman's invitation to raise up and dance, issued to women of color in developing countries, is patronizing and misguided. Asks an Iranian woman, "Who is someone else to come to my country and claim to 'help' me by telling me to 'rise' above the experiences I have had?" (Gyte).

The heated conflicts over One Billion Rising, ironically, point to the issue Ensler raises in the following piece: our experiences as women depend greatly on our racial histories, our geographic location, and our relation to privilege. The criticisms of her work raise important issues about global feminist projects, problematizing the role of white, Western feminists in speaking for women of color and highlighting the danger of collapsing differences among women, even in movements that strive for solidarity.

"My Cancer is Arbitrary: Congo's Atrocities Are Very Deliberate"

The *Guardian*, 2010

Some people may think that being diagnosed with uterine cancer, followed by an extensive surgery that led to a month of debilitating infections, rounded off by months of chemotherapy, might get a girl down. But, in truth, this has not been my poison. This has not been what pulses through me late at night and keeps me pacing and awake. This has not been what throws me into moments of unbearable darkness and depression.

Cancer is scary, of course, and painful. It tends to interrupt one's entire life, throw everything into question and push one up against that ultimate dimension and possibility of dying. One can rail at the gods and goddesses: "Why? Why now? Why me?" But, in the end, we know those questions ring absurd and empty. Cancer is an epidemic. It has been here forever. It isn't personal. Its choice of the vulnerable host is often arbitrary. It's life.

For months, doctors and nurses have cut me, stitched me, jabbed me, drained me, cat-scanned me, X-rayed me, IV-ed me, flushed me, and hydrated me, trying to identify the source of my anxiety and alleviate my pain. While they have been able to remove the cancer from my body, treat an abscess here, a fever there, they have not been able to even come close to the core of my malady.

Three years ago, the Democratic Republic of Congo seized my being. V-Day, a movement to stop violence against women and girls, was invited to see firsthand the experience of women survivors of sexual violence there. After three weeks at Panzi hospital in Bukavu, where there were more than 200 women patients, many of whom shared their stories of being gang-raped and tortured with me, I was shattered. They told me about the resulting loss of their reproductive organs and the fistulae they got—the hole between their vagina and anus or vagina and bladder that no longer allowed them to hold their urine or faeces. I heard about nine-month-old babies, eight-year-old girls, 80-year-old women who had been humiliated and publicly raped.

In response, taking the lead from women on the ground, we created a massive campaign—Stop Raping Our Greatest Resource: Power to Women and Girls of DRC—which has broken taboos, organised speak-outs and marches, educated and trained activists and religious leaders, and spurred performances of *The Vagina Monologues* across the country, culminating this month with a performance in the Congolese parliament. V-Day activists have spread the campaign across the planet, raising money and consciousness. In several months, with the women of Congo, we will be opening the City of Joy, a community for survivors where women will be healed in order to turn their pain to power. We have also sat and pleaded our case at Downing Street, the White House, and the office of the UN secretary general. We have shouted (loudly) at the Canadian parliament, the US Senate, and the UN Security Council. Tears were shed; promises were made with great enthusiasm.

As I have lain in my hospital bed or attempted to rest at home over these months, it is the phone calls and the reports that come in daily from the DRC that make me ill. The stories of continued rapes, machete killings, grotesque mutilations, outright murdering of human rights activists—these images and events create nausea and weakness much worse than chemo or antibiotics or pain meds ever could. But even harder to deal with, in the weakened state that I have been in, is knowing that despite the ongoing horrific atrocities that have taken the lives of more than 6 million people and left more than 500,000 women and girls raped and tortured, the international power elite appear to be doing nothing. They have essentially written off the DRC and its people, even after continued visits and promises.

The day is late. It is almost 13 years into this war. The Obama administration, as in most situations these days, refuses to take a real stand. Several months ago I visited the White House to meet a high official to engage the First Lady in our efforts to end sexual violence in Congo, believing that her solidarity would galvanise attention and action. I was told, essentially, that femicide was not her "brand." Mrs. Obama, I was told, was focusing on childhood obesity. It surprised me that a woman with her capabilities lacked ambidextrous skills (or was it simply interest and will that was absent?). Then we have Secretary Clinton, who at least after much pressure visited the DRC almost a year ago, and made promises that actually meant a huge deal to the people. They were excited that the US government might finally prioritise building the political will in the Great Lakes region to end the war there. But, of course, they are still waiting. And then there is the UN. The anaemic and glacial pace and the death-like bureaucracy continue to allow and, in the case of Monuc and the security council, even help facilitate a deathly regional war.

Two weeks ago, in Kinshasa, one of Congo's great human rights activists, Floribert Chebeya Bahizire, was brutally murdered. In the same week, at Panzi Hospital, the family of a staff member were executed. A 10-year-old boy and 12-year-old girl were gunned down in their car on their way home. Murdering and raping of the women in the villages continues. The war rages on. Who is demanding the protection of the people of Congo? Who is protecting the activists who are speaking truth to power? At a memorial service last week in Bukavu, a pastor cried out: "They are killing our mammas. Now they are killing our children. What have we done to deserve this? *Where is the world?*"

The atrocities committed against the people of Congo are not arbitrary, like my cancer. They are systematic, strategic, and intentional. At the root is a madly greedy world economy, desperate for more minerals robbed from the indigenous Congolese. Sourcing this insatiable hunger are multinational corporations who benefit from these minerals and are willing to turn their backs on the players committing femicide and genocide, as long as their financial needs are met.

I am lucky. I have been blessed with a positive prognosis that has made me hyperaware of what keeps a person alive. How does one survive cancer? Of course— good doctors, good insurance, good luck. But the real healing comes from not being forgotten. From attention, from care, from love, from being surrounded by a community of those who demand information on your behalf, who advocate and stand up for you when you are in a weakened state, who sleep by your side, who refuse to let you give up, who bring you meals, who see you not as a patient or victim but as a precious human being, who create metaphors where you can imagine your survival. This is my medicine, and nothing less will suffice for the people, for the women, for the children of Congo.

For Further Reading

Chief Elk-Young Bear, Lauren. "There Is No 'We': V-Day, Indigenous Women and the Myth of Shared Gender Oppression." *Model View Culture*, 3 Feb. 2014, https://modelviewculture.com/pieces/there-is-no-we-v-day-indigenous-women-and-the-myth-of-shared-gender-oppression.

Ensler, Eve. "Eve Ensler Statement in Response to the Open Letter by Lauren Chief Elk." *One Billion Rising Revolution*, 30 May 2013, https://www.onebillionrising.org/18315/eve-ensler-statement-response-open-letter-lauren-chief-elk/.

Ensler, Eve. *Insecure at Last: a Political Memoir*. Villard, 2008.

Ensler, Eve. *In the Body of the World: A Memoir*. Picador, 2014.

Ensler, Eve. *The Vagina Monologues*. Villard, 2007.

One Billion Rising. www.onebillionrising.org/.

Gonzalez-Berg, Justine. "The Emerging Legacy of One Billion Rising." *Hampshire Political Writing Workshop*, 26 Feb. 2013, popdevprogram.wordpress.com/2013/02/26/one-billion-rising/.

Gyte, Natalie. "Why I Won't Support One Billion Rising." *HuffPost UK*, 16 Feb. 2014, www.huffingtonpost.co.uk/natalie-gyte/one-billion-rising-why-i-wont-support_b_2684595.html.

Khaleeli, Homa. "One Billion Rising: How Can Public Dancing End Violence against Women?" *The Guardian*, 13 Feb. 2015, www.theguardian.com/lifeandstyle/womens-blog/2015/feb/13/one-billion-rising-public-dancing-violence-women-eve-ensler.

R. D. "'The Vagina Monologues,' 20 Years On." *The Economist*, 9 Jan. 2018, www.economist.com/blogs/prospero/2018/01/greater-sum-its-parts.

Kat Blaque

When it comes to transgender issues, bathrooms are a battleground. While most public bathrooms are marked with clear binary gender delineations, transgender people are not. The controversy, then, stems over disagreement about whether transgender people have a right to use the bathroom that aligns with their chosen identity. In 2016 the Obama administration declared that Title IX, a federal law that prohibits sex discrimination in educational settings, protects the right of transgender students to choose their appropriate bathroom; in 2017 the Trump administration rescinded those protections.

Kat Blaque, a transgender YouTuber, weighs in on the issue in a piece for the *Huffington Post*. With characteristic frankness, she describes both the pain of feeling unsafe in a boys' locker room as an adolescent and the privilege of now passing as a cisgender woman, which allows her to use the women's room without question. This demonstration of how identity is complexly experienced is illustrative of Blaque's platform as an intersectional transgender activist and educator.

Here and in her vlog, Blaque—who identifies as a black, trans, plus-sized woman—uses the power of story to help marginalized people feel seen and to extend the range of identities, and issues, recognized by those whose stories differ from her own. "I make a point of showing myself in my most raw and vulnerable moments because seeing that in other people has helped me so much" (Tonic). She also encourages questions and dialogue. Each week, for instance, Blaque provides candid answers to viewers' questions, while she sips from her "True Tea" mug. Her honest approach resonates with her vlog's subscribers, who number over one hundred thousand, and her Facebook followers, where she averages between five and six million views per week (Tonic). Blaque also speaks to college students on campuses around the country.

In the following piece, Blaque directly addresses the fear-based rationale for denying transgender people the right to use the bathroom that corresponds with their gender identity, which is "the idea that trans women are predatory sexual deviants by nature." Bathroom laws, in this formulation, are designed to protect cisgender girls and women from transgender predators. Blaque forcefully shuts this down, arguing that the focus of concern should shift to the more common cisgender male predators. Indeed, research shows that states with anti-discrimination laws have not seen increased incidents of sexual assaults in bathrooms, and in fact, that it is far more common that transgender people are assaulted in bathrooms than the other way around (Grinberg and Stewart). Drawing from her embodied knowledge, Blaque shares that as survivor of sexual assault, she finds this line of thinking offensive.

Never mincing words or ducking controversial issues, Blaque makes the most of her ability to reach audiences through multiple media, always directed toward a more inclusive, intersectional future.

"Defecating While Trans"

Huffington Post, 2016

Using the bathroom as a trans person can be a very complicated task. While cis people (cis meaning non-trans) just naturally look at one of two of their options and walk into a bathroom without a second thought, for trans people, choosing a restroom is like deciding if you want to risk the chance of being harassed or physically assaulted. It's an imposition most trans people find themselves in eventually and it can make the natural task of defecating and urinating a far more challenging task than it needs to be.

I was always an androgynous kid that people didn't quite know how to place. It didn't help that in my teen years, I started developing breasts for reasons still unknown to me. When I'd try to change in the boy's locker room, before and after PE, I'd arouse stares from confused teenage boys who didn't understand why I had breasts. Heck, I hardly understood myself. I'll never forget changing once, as I did, hunched over in a corner with my chest facing my locker. I was about to do the same old T-shirt trick that I used to do where I switched my shirt as quickly as possible by grabbing a shirt as I take one off. Then out of nowhere, I felt a pair of clammy hands grope my breasts before completing the second phase of the switcheroo. These weren't the hands of a bully who wanted to joke about my "man tits," they were the hands of someone who was curious and confused because what I had were unmistakably breasts. I pushed him away from me and looked back at him only to see a blank and inquisitive stare. He wasn't doing this with the attention of his peers that would laugh at his joke. He wanted to feel my breasts for his own gratification and this confused and terrified me. That was the last time that I used the boy's locker room. I'd been groped before by other students, but this was the line for me. I started changing for PE by leaving class early and changing in deserted restrooms and avoiding the locker room altogether. I made it my goal in school to do everything I could to get out of taking physical education and having to be forced to fit into a category that I clearly didn't belong to.

I didn't accept that I was a trans woman until college, but before then I identified as genderqueer, which for me meant that my gender wasn't binary. I was happier with myself and my growing understanding of my own body, but bathrooms became more complicated because unless someone knew me, seeing me in the men's room was confusing and I wasn't totally comfortable with using the women's room. So using the restroom became a complicated game where I'd try to use the restroom when I knew very few people would be using it. I felt like a spy, rushing into that horrid restroom with that broad linear stick figure, making sure that no one saw me enter and no one saw me leave. Sometimes, I'd sit in a stall, just waiting for the bathroom to clear before I felt comfortable leaving. Looking back, this was a bit silly, but it felt necessary to me at the time. I went to CalArts, and at CalArts there were two single-person bathrooms behind a single door. This was ideal for me because regardless of gender, everyone walked through the same door and used relatively similar facilities. It felt like the safest bathroom for me to use and since I was an animator and my school was close to it, I'd often opt for it. This was the only bathroom I used in the entire school and this wasn't an issue most of the time. However, when I started having labs and classes in the basement, things became complicated. If I had to go, I'd have to travel from two extreme ends of the campus in order to do my business. So I had to . . . compromise. Without being too explicit, I started a system where I'd use alternative methods of relieving myself. These methods felt dehumanizing and to be honest—disgusting, but even at an art school, I feared the repercussions of me using a bathroom of a gender binary that I didn't fit into. At least not yet.

As I came to understand my gender, I recognized that I was dealing with a lot of denial and internalized transphobia. I realized that I was binary trans and after that realization things became a lot easier for me and I suddenly found myself fitting in seamlessly with society. I "pass," which means that people just assume that I'm cis in my day-to-day. So using the women's restroom was natural for me. For almost a decade I've been using the women's restroom and I can confidently say that I've never had an issue. I travel across the country for work so I've used the ladies' room in the North, South, East, and West and have never once had an issue. When I hear about these bathroom debates, I frankly find them laughable because without knowing it, you've likely used the restroom with a trans person and it was completely uncontroversial.

The ease in which I use the women's room is a privilege. I have the benefit of being able to look cis and never have my gender questioned. I'll never forget accidentally walking into the men's room years ago and having a guy laugh and tell me I was in the wrong restroom. Passing is survival and the ability to pass is a privilege that not all trans people have or want. Many trans people are flaunting their ability to pass by turning to social media in order to protest bathroom legislation across the country. While I understand the point, I can't ignore the queer kid that I was that didn't feel comfortable in either restroom. These are the people that are often forgotten in this conversation and I honestly struggle to come up with a solution. What makes me feel comfortable now didn't make me feel comfortable back then. I can only speak for myself and the way in which I've relieved myself my entire adult life, and for me the bathroom is a nonissue. I'd stick out like a sore thumb in the men's room and attention is the last thing I want when I'm trying to empty my bowel.

The fearmongering around trans bathroom usage is upsetting to me as a survivor of both rape and sexual assault. Often the threat of rape is dangled in front of cis people as a real issue, but frankly I find that to be silly. This may sound harsh, but if a man wants to rape a woman in the women's room, he isn't going to put on a dress before doing so and upon capture argue that he's transgender and therefore belonged in the women's restroom. That isn't real and in that equation, the person committing the offense is not trans, but cis. We act like there is this magical line drawn between restrooms and I'd hate to shatter fantasies, but there isn't. The harsh reality is that a little white figure in a dress isn't going to stop a sexual predator from entering the restroom. They'll do it anyways. The division gives you a false sense of safety and overlooks the true nature of sexual assault, including that women can sexually assault and rape other women. Furthermore, I find it laughable that colleges and high schools are expressing concern for women on their campuses because we've seen time and time again that schools are more invested in maintaining their image than properly addressing sexual assault on campus. Married to these fearmongering tactics is this idea that trans women are predatory sexual deviants by nature, but if cis men are dressing as women to harass women in the restroom, how does that reflect poorly on trans women? Mike Huckabee fondly stated that he'd love the chance to spy on teen girls showering as a teenager and wishes he could have claimed to be trans to be able to do so now. What's being overlooked are the depraved and sick desires of some cis men to abuse these laws. They should be punished, not trans women.

Plenty of cis people will read this and say things like "I respect trans people, but they should have their own bathrooms" and I'll be honest and say that regardless of the law and regardless of unsolicited opinions, I'm going to use the women's room as I have been, because in reality, no one cares. When you're in a public restroom, how often do you think of the genitalia of the person in the stall next to you? I never have. When I'm in a public restroom, I want to do my shameful business and leave without making eye contact with anyone and pretend that it never happened. It's unsettling to hear the various sexual fantasies cis people have about what trans people do in public restrooms. The reality is that trans people are more likely to see violence and to be assaulted in restrooms than vice versa. We just want to pee and shouldn't have to make every BM and pee a political statement.

At the end of the day, we all defecate and urinate. It's natural and it helps our bodies stay healthy and clean. Unfortunately, for trans people, the natural task of relieving themselves is political and honestly, it shouldn't be. YouTube Space LA has a bathroom that is unisex with wall-to-wall stalls. It cuts down on building cost and allows everyone to use the restroom regardless of their gender, but if that makes you feel uncomfortable, there's a separate personal restroom. Is it weird at first? Sure, but I think it's the future. A future that will take adjusting, but one that is more inclusive and less erasing.

FOR FURTHER READING

Grinberg, Emanuella, and Dani Stewart. "3 Myths That Shape the Transgender Bathroom Debate." *CNN*, 7 Mar. 2017, www.cnn.com/2017/03/07/health/transgender-bathroom-law-facts-myths/index.html.

Guerrero, Desiree. "After Being Outed, Kat Blaque Became a Role Model for Trans Youth." *ADVOCATE*, 1 May 2017, www.advocate.com/advocate50/2017/5/01/blaque-out.

Hersher, Rebecca, and Carrie Johnson. "Trump Administration Rescinds Obama Rule on Transgender Students' Bathroom Use." *NPR*, 23 Feb. 2017, www.npr.org/sections/thetwo-way/2017/02/22/516664633/trump-administration-rescinds-obama-rule-on-transgender-students-bathroom-use.

"Kat Blaque." *YouTube*, n.d., www.youtube.com/user/TransDIYer.

Tonic, Gina. "This Woman Was the Most Body Positive Vlogger of 2015." *Bustle*, 12 Jan. 2016, www.bustle.com/articles/134110-this-woman-was-the-most-body-positive-vlogger-of-2015.

Body-Positive Images

For many women, social media is a "toxic mirror" (Simmons). It inundates us with (often altered) images of idealized bodies, links worthiness with "likes," and prompts harsh self-scrutiny. Psychological research bears this out, showing that across cultures, there is a strong association between social media use and negative body image, extreme dieting, body surveillance, and self-objectification in adolescents (Holland and Tiggeman).

Enter the body-positive movement, which aims to improve girls' and women's relationships to their bodies and depict a more expansive and inclusive range of human forms. To do so, it celebrates bodies that are marginalized, hidden, or degraded in our culture. The three images included here depict body-positive images rendered through photography and drawings, each circulated heavily on Instagram. In addition to making visual arguments for embracing one's body, their very presence in a medium known for curating perfection functions as what Nedra Reynolds calls a "feminist interruption," a rhetorical strategy that allows the rhetor to change the direction of the conversation.

Hana Shafi's image, *The Scales*, contests the way women learn to use a number on a scale to measure how they feels about themselves. Shafi is a Canadian freelance journalist and artist, who illustrates under the name Frizz Kid and identifies as an Indo-Persian feminist. Her recent book, *It Begins with the Body: Poems and Illustrations*, shares the challenges and joys, experienced through the body, of coming of age as a young girl of color. The drawing included here is one of the weekly "affirmation images" she posts on Instagram, Tumblr, and Twitter. These affirmations—which address mental health, sexual assault, body image, and emotional wellness—interrupt the barrage of cultural messages women receive that transmit narrow conceptions of beauty and perfection. Here, a woman with unshaved legs stands on a scale, refusing to equate weight with worthiness, inviting other women to embrace the same affirmative message. As Shafi explains in an interview with Mashable, "Often when we're struggling, we feel like our story is constantly getting invalidated, stigmatized and shamed. I want people to see my work and feel valid, feel safe or feel whatever they need to feel to cope with the difficulties in their life" (Dupere).

The photograph of Jessamyn Stanley practicing yoga adorns the cover of her book *Every Body Yoga* and was widely disseminated on social media sites. The beau-

tiful image of a full-bodied African American woman in a mermaid pose interrupts the deluge of thinness and whiteness often associated with Western yoga.
The photo exemplifies Stanley's greater project to make yoga—and conceptions of
wellness and beauty—more expansive and inclusive. Stanley's Instagram account
has garnered hundreds of thousands of followers, demonstrating the appeal of
both her body-positive message and her use of yoga as a wellness practice. As a self-
described "large-bodied" African American woman, Stanley often found herself in
yoga studios surrounded by thin white people (Brennan). So she began a practice
at home and posted photographs of her poses on Instagram, where she asked fellow practitioners for feedback. This required her to face her body—both through
her practice and in the photographs she took—which she had always been "deeply
afraid of" (Brennan). As Stanley said in an interview with CNN, "The whole interaction between my ego and the camera is, I believe, a huge part of how I was able to
start to have a different conversation with myself about my body." Stanley stresses,
however, that recovering from a negative body image is like recovering from any
addiction. She is in a "permanent state of recovery," and yoga is the best tool she's
found for healing (Brennan).

The third image included here, *Natural Stains*, features the menstrual blood
women are taught to hide at all costs. It interrupts cultural practices of marking
women's bodies, and bodily functions, as shameful, moving them out in the open
to normalize and affirm women's embodied lives. Revealing the hidden is the focus of the Australian artist Christine Yaha's Instagram account and website called
Pink Bits. Here, she celebrates women of all colors and body sizes—her images
depict women nursing babies, masturbating, and menstruating. Yaha is an eating
disorder survivor, and she describes illustrating women as part of her healing process. The reviewer Sara Cartelli aptly describes the power of Yaha's art: "In a social
world dominated by filters and the obsession of appearing impeccable, for once,
someone reminds us that normality is extraordinarily imperfect and above all, that
there would be nothing to be ashamed of."

FOR FURTHER READING

Brennan, Allison. "How She Fights Being 'Deeply Afraid of' Her Body." *CNN*, 12 Apr. 2017, www
    .cnn.com/2017/04/12/health/jessamyn-stanley-yoga-profile/index.html.
Cartelli, Sara. "The Truth about Being a Woman: The Illustrations of Pink Bits." *The Eat Culture*, 18
    Apr. 2018, www.theeatculture.com/en/truth-about-being-woman-illustrations-pink-bits/.
Dupere, Katie. "These Illustrated Affirmations Will Brighten Any of Your Bad Days." *Mashable*, 26
    Oct. 2016, mashable.com/2016/10/26/self-care-illustrations/.
Holland, Grace, and Marika Tiggemann. "A Systematic Review of the Impact of the Use of Social
    Networking Sites on Body Image and Disordered Eating Outcomes." *Body Image*, vol. 17, 2016,
    pp. 100–110.

Reynolds, Nedra. "Interrupting Our Way to Agency: Feminist Cultural Studies and Composition." *Feminism and Composition Studies: In Other Words*, edited by Susan Carole Funderburgh, Susan Jarratt, and Lynn Worsham, Modern Language Association of America, 1998, pp. 58–73.

Scott, Ellen. "Meet the Eating Disorder Survivor Whose Illustrations Are Inspiring Women to Love Their Bodies." *Metro*, 19 Sept. 2017, metro.co.uk/2017/09/19/meet-the-eating-disorder-survivor-whose-illustrations-are-inspiring-women-to-love-their-bodies-6939741/.

Shafi, Hana. *It Begins with the Body*. Small Press Distribution, 2018.

Simmons, Rachel. "How Social Media Is a Toxic Mirror." *Time*, 19 Aug. 2016, time.com/4459153/social-media-body-image/.

Stanley, Jessamyn. *Every Body Yoga: Let Go of Fear. Get on the Mat. Love Your Body*. Workman, 2017.

Hana Shafi, *The Scales*

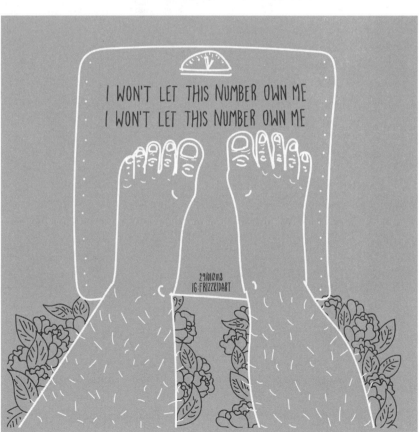

22. Hana Shafi's drawing "The Scales" depicts the unshaved legs and feet of a woman weighing herself and proclaiming, "I won't let this number own me."

Jessamyn Stanley, *Every Body Yoga*

23. This photo of Jessymn Stanley in a mermaid yoga bind circulated on Instagram and is featured on the cover of her book *Every Body Yoga*. Stanley wears a black sports bra and briefs, celebrating yoga for women of all sizes. Photo credit: Hannah Khymych.

Christine Yahya, *Natural Stains*

24. Christine Yaha's drawing, "Natural Stains," portrays the back of a woman lying on her side with menstrual blood soaking through her white underwear.

Julia Serano

In an interview with the *New York Times*, Julia Serano offers the following guidance to young trans people: "The only thing you can do is try not to let other people's expectations dictate what you do or what you become" (Carstensen). As a trans woman, slam poet, biologist, author, activist, and performer, Serano lives her own advice. Through multiple rhetorical and poetic forms, she delivers messages that challenge gender binaries and combat transphobia and misogyny. In her book *Whipping Girl: A Transsexual Woman on the Scapegoating of Femininity*, now in its second edition, Serano forwards a groundbreaking "Trans Woman Manifesto" that boldly demands "the end of the scapegoating, deriding, and dehumanizing of trans women everywhere," for no "sexual minority is more maligned or misunderstood than trans women" (11). An end to this insidious treatment of transwomen, Serano argues, requires the dismantling of gender identity based on biology and the privileging of masculinity over femininity.

"96 Percent" was first delivered as part of a 2007 spoken-word event called "The 'Penis' Issue: Trans and Intersex Women Speak Their Minds," in which Serano both performed and organized. Describing the exigency for the panel, Serano writes, "For too long, women with 'penises' have only existed in the public consciousness as the occasional punchlines of jokes, as movie plot twists, or as an underground niche in the sex industry . . . Here we speak for ourselves, about our lives, and on our own terms."

For Serano, speaking on her own terms means sharing that coming out as transgender, as a woman with a penis, feels dangerous, like an impending explosion that she must defuse. This pressure to defuse the situation led her to rely upon the rhetorical tactic of making a penis joke—getting the audience to laugh at her own expense. The problem, Serano explains, is that this strategy backfired: it reified that a woman with a penis is funny. So now, rather than strive to put her audience at ease, she implores them—and all of us—to consider why we place so much emphasis on genitals to determine a person's identity.

Serano's title, in fact, is based on the finding of a study that shows the deep association between the penis and maleness. When shown a drawing of a human with a mix of gender attributes (long or short hair, waist size, genitalia), 96 percent of the time participants determined that the presence of a penis made the figure a male. Serano aims to challenge this deep-seated assumption, and in doing so, insists that we must "dephallocize the penis—to extricate the concepts of male privilege and power from the flesh and blood of our bodies." That is, she disrupts a metonymic relationship between the two—where "penis" has come to stand in for "masculinity." Through a melding of testimony, gender analysis, and cultural critique, Serano argues that we can only dismantle genital-based assumptions about gender if we operate from the understanding that masculinity is a social and cultural construct, and the penis is a part of the human body—sometimes a woman's, and sometimes a man's.

"96 Percent"

JuliaSerano.com, 2007

It's 2004, and once again I'm on stage in another bar doing another spoken-word set. I introduce my next piece: "Here's another poem about my penis!" The audience laughs, a couple people hoot and holler.

I've been performing spoken word for a couple of years now. Half of the shows that I do are queer-themed events, the other half poetry slams where the majority of the audience is straight. Often these audiences will react very differently to specific poems or passages, a sign of their different perspectives and sensibilities. But both queer and straight audiences always enthusiastically laugh at my penis one-liner—apparently amusement over my bodily incongruity appeals to some kind of lowest common denominator. Many people view sexuality as a continuum, with straight folks on one end and queer folks on the other, but that's not how things look to me.

I exist at a bizarre nexus of the universe where both ends of that spectrum come around to meet. After all, the only thing that your average twentysomething frat boy has in common with your average middle-aged lesbian feminist is a mutual fear of falling for someone like me: a woman who just so happens to have a penis.

Part of the reason why people laugh when I say, "Here's another poem about my penis," is the seemingly non-self-conscious, almost flippant, way that I say it, as if to give the impression: "Whatever, no big deal." But that's not how I feel on the inside. In my mind, whenever I deliver that line, I feel like I'm diffusing a bomb. I conjure up images of a movie or TV protagonist, with wire cutters in hand, fumbling with the red and the green wires, unsure of which one to cut. Just as it looks like they are going to slice the red wire, they make an impulsive decision with only a few seconds left to cut the green wire instead and suddenly everything is quiet.

Nothing explodes. It's a triumph of intuition over conscious thinking; gut feelings over endless mind wringing.

When I make quips about my penis in public, that's usually what it is—a gut feeling—instinctual, reflexive. It's most certainly not the smartest or safest thing for me to say, but I'm not trying to be smart. My intention is simply to diffuse an explosive situation.

Whenever I perform spoken word, or any time I come out to someone as transsexual, the "penis issue" is always present. For a while, I thought that perhaps I was imagining it, that it was simply a product of my own paranoia or insecurity. But that hypothesis flew completely out the window when I began to do Transgender 101 workshops for college and high school students. As soon as I would finish my opening spiel and announce that I'd be happy to answer any of their questions, I would immediately be barraged by genitalia-themed inquiries: Have you had surgery? Do you plan to have it someday? Why would you ever want to get rid of your penis? If you're attracted to women, wouldn't it make more sense to keep it? Does your penis still get erect? Can you still get a girl pregnant? How can you possibly call yourself a woman if you still have a penis?

The "penis issue" is also in play (only slightly less blatantly) in the way people tend to attach the adjectives *pre-op* or *post-op* to descriptions of transwomen, even in contexts where one's genitals are irrelevant. Whenever I catch someone doing this, I'll often nonchalantly begin to refer to all men as either circumcised or uncircumcised, and to all women as either pre- or post-menopausal, just to make a point of how demeaning and objectifying unnecessary information can be sometimes.

The "penis issue" is the elephant that awaits me in nearly every room I enter; I can either pretend to ignore it or acknowledge its existence. That's probably why I came up with the here's-another-poem-about-my-penis one-liner in the first place. Initially, it felt freeing and empowering to take on that taboo, to break that silence, until I realized that that approach was probably backfiring. After all, I was simply inviting people to laugh at the fact that I was a woman with a penis without bringing into question their assumptions and prejudices. Much like the fat stand-up comic who makes self-deprecating jokes about their own eating habits without ever challenging societal-wide anti-fat sentiment, I was merely reaffirming the belief shared by most in the audience: That the very notion of a woman with a penis is inherently ludicrous.

I realized then that gender-variant women will continue to have to deal with other people's "penis issues" until we turn the tables and ask the world this question: Why do so many people—even those who are otherwise well-meaning, open-minded, progressive, pro-trans, and anti-sexist—continue to get so hung up over the status of our genitals?

In the 1970s, sociologists Suzanne Kessler and Wendy McKenna carried out an experiment to determine how we see gender.[1] They showed participants a series of drawings of people who had a mix of typically male and female attributes: short or long hair, flat chest or breasts, narrow or wide hips, body hair or not, and of course, either male or female genitals. They found that male cues always tended to trump female cues—in other words, figures with a mix of masculine and feminine attributes tended to be read as men rather than women. This disparity was particularly acute for genitals. If the figure with mixed gender attributes had a vagina, people only saw it as female 64 percent of the time—in other words, 36 percent of the time other male cues trumped the presence of a vagina. The reverse was not true: If the figure had a penis, it was read as male 96 percent of the time, often even when all of the other gender attributes were feminine.

So while I relate to my trans male friends who have transitioned in the other direction, I would suggest that the deck is somewhat stacked in their favor. Trans men tend to "pass" better and to freak people out less because of the way we've all been trained to see gender.

And while I empathize with my non-trans sisters when they say they are often accused of not being "real" women because they aren't stereotypically feminine or because they are bisexual or lesbian, I don't think that it's quite accurate to say that we are in the exact same boat. As a trans woman, my issue is not merely that people see me as being inadequately or insufficiently female, it's that as soon as they discover that I have a penis, there is a 96 percent chance that they will see me as a man.

That statistic—96 percent—leaves a deep imprint on the lives of many gender-variant women. A couple of years ago, I was invited to participate in a panel on MTF [male-to-female] transitioning at a transgender-themed conference. Each panelist was asked to give the moderator a handful of potential questions that we felt might be useful for the audience. One of the questions I offered was, "How does one manage the difficulties associated with navigating one's way through the world as a woman with a penis?" At the panel, when the moderator raised my question, the other three trans female panelists, who had been quite chatty up until that point, suddenly went silent. Their bodies sat eerily still as if all of the body language had been leeched from them. This had nothing to do with being embarrassed about being transsexual—after all, they were all enthusiastically taking part in this panel. The reason why they kept silent was because they knew better than to answer that question. They knew that the mere mention of having had a penis, past or present tense, would lead 96 percent of those in attendance to lump them in the "man" category.

As someone who is regularly presumed to be a non-transsexual woman, and whose body these days appears female in pretty much every way except one, I find it bizarre that 96 percent of the population will throw all of that evidence out the window—dismissing my female identity, body, and lived experiences—and consider me a "man" solely based on my genitals. (And they try to convince me that I'm the one who is mentally disordered?)

Look, this has nothing to do with logic, nothing to do with biology. The problem here is symbolism. In this male-centered world, nothing symbolizes male and masculine power more that the penis. And unfortunately, many of the folks who are most vocal about challenging male domination—feminists and lesbians—often hypocritically buy into this very same phallocentrism when they describe the penis as a tool of rape and oppression.

In the trans community, people often talk about the male/female gender binary as though it were the cause of all of our marginalization. But frankly, as a trans woman, sometimes I struggle more with a different (and often unarticulated) binary, one in which the penis is either glorified or demonized, nothing in between. One can see this dichotomy at work in popular depictions of transsexual women: the psychiatric stereotype of the trans woman who absolutely despises her "penis" on one extreme, and the "she-male" porn image of a trans woman grasping her engorged cock on the other.

Some might find this surprising, but I've found that the people who are least attached to such symbolism tend to be trans and intersex women. We know our own bodies to be mere flesh and blood, and therefore rightly recognize this glorifying and demonizing imagery as something that is projected onto us, a framework that enables other people to objectify us, either as abominations or as androgyne fuck fantasies. Many of us develop far more complex, nuanced, and varied views about our own genitals, recognizing them as a part of our physical bodies and a source of sexual pleasure, albeit one that is often at odds with our own mental self-image and/or societal assumptions regarding gender.

If I had to pick one word that best describes how I feel about my own penis, it would be *ambivalence*. This is not to be confused with apathy—after all, I have lots of really intense memories and emotions regarding my penis, it's just that they often exist in contradiction to one another:

As a child, wishing desperately that I could make my penis disappear. As a young adult, recoiling from the word transsexual, in part, because I couldn't imagine parting with it.

In my late teens, being in absolute awe of penetration sex, of how amazing it was to feel my genitals inside my girlfriend's genitals.

In my early thirties, a few months after being on female hormones, for the first time sporting a strap-on dildo and entering my wife in that manner, blown away by how it all made so much more sense to me than any other penetration experience in my life.

As a crossdresser in my late twenties, as the man I was with non-consensually tried to force himself on me. I'm eventually able to get away, but to this day, I still sometimes deal with the psychological aftermath of that traumatic event. Then, as a trans dyke at Camp Trans seven years later, a woman from the Michigan Womyn's Music Festival arrogantly lectures me about how I shouldn't be allowed inside women's spaces because my penis might trigger sexual abuse survivors.

Let me say this: I can't think of any act that is more insulting, more condescending, more entitled, or more triggering to me than having a non-trans woman, oblivious of her own non-trans privilege, lump me into the same category as the guy who tried to date rape me.

I don't have the luxury of seeing my penis in black-and-white, cut-and-dry terms. For me, the penis does not represent power or privilege, because I am regularly marginalized for having one. It is both my center of sexual pleasure and a signifier of something that I don't identify with. It is a constant source of cognitive dissonance, something that has always felt somewhat alien to me, yet nevertheless it is a part of my body. Sometimes I'll successfully forget that it's even there, and then other times, I am excruciatingly aware of its existence. As a performer, I regularly take the stage and proudly recite unflinching spoken word pieces about being a woman with a penis, then the next day, I'll be paranoid over whether there's a visible bulge underneath my jeans or dress. Like I said, my penis provokes feelings of ambivalence.

A few years back, an anthology was published called *Dick for a Day*, featuring women writers—many of them feminist—answering the question: "What would you do if, by some mysterious means, you had a penis for one day?"[2] Not surprisingly, more than half the women imagined that this also automatically involved them becoming fully male as well (undoubtedly another sign of how our culture views women with penises as inherently oxymoronic and nonsensical). Those writers who did imagine themselves as women with penises invariably took the glorifying route, indulging in adventures like writing their names in the snow, masturbating, receiving blow jobs, and penetrating beautiful women. Some even imagined that their penis gave them more confidence, that it led to promotions at work, and so forth.

What I found most telling was that not a single person imagined what it would *really* be like to be a woman with a penis. No one explored whether or not they would have to hide it, how they might manage that information on dates, or the potential animosity they might face if random strangers discovered its presence. No one raised the issue of what it might be like to be watching a movie or TV show and be blindsided by one of those crass and belittling "she-male" jokes and to know that it is you who is being ridiculed. No one wondered what it would be like to be shut out of certain women's spaces, to be turned away from a rape crisis center or a battered women's shelter because of the size and shape of their genitals. And no one addressed the issue of male homophobic/transphobic hysteria and the violence that is regularly inflicted on women with penises. In fact, one writer even bragged about how she would whip it out if some obnoxious guy tried to make the moves on her, just to see the look of horror on his face. What a fucking farce. As someone who regularly finds herself in that very same situation, I choose not to "whip it out," and do you want to know why? It's because I'd rather not fucking die.

The most offensive thing about that book is the fact that almost every writer presumed that if she were a woman with a penis that she would somehow be more privileged than she currently is without it. Bullshit! By buying into the male-centric belief that the penis is synonymous with power and privilege, these writers invisibilized the very real struggles faced by gender-variant women. They appropriated our situation while leaving behind our very real life circumstances.

The world will not begin to be safe for gender-variant women such as myself until at least three things happen:

First, people have to get it in their heads that genital assumption—the common belief that all men have penises and all women do not—is merely an incorrect presumption on their part. Just as it's arrogant to automatically assume that every person you meet is straight, it is similarly entitled to presume that every person is non-trans and has the genitals that you expect them to have.

Second, we need to recognize that being a woman and having a penis are not necessarily in contradiction with one another. And I'm not merely talking about sex toys here—if I had a dollar for every dyke I've met who gets off on girls wearing strap-on cocks, but who would hypocritically balk at the idea of being with a trans woman, I'd be a very rich lady. No, what I'm saying is that we need to move beyond the 96 percent mentality, where male traits always trump female ones, where a woman's female identity, personality, life experiences, and the rest of her body can be brought into question or outright dismissed because of the mere presence of a penis.

Third, we need get over our compulsion to either glorify or demonize the penis. In other words, we need to dephallocize the penis—to extricate the concepts of male privilege and power from the flesh and blood of our bodies. I'm not saying that we need to completely obliterate all symbolism and view the penis as an amorphous blob of flesh. All I'm asking is that we allow for other possibilities, that we create a little room for ambivalence.

In order for all of this to happen, gender-variant women cannot merely sit on the sidelines and allow others to appropriate and caricature our real life experiences. If we truly wish to move beyond the "penis issue," then we must begin to honestly put forward our own varied and nuanced personal perspectives as women who do not conform to other people's genital assumptions. We must speak openly about the countless ways in which we are marginalized because of our genitals, as well as the ways in which we are sometimes empowered by them. We must allow ourselves to say that it's okay to get rid of it if we want, but it is also okay to find it beautiful.

For me, one of the few things scarier than standing up in front of the audience and talking about my penis for fifteen minutes, is the fact that I have invited five other amazing and powerful women writers and performers to do the same. We are each different people and we each have had different life experiences, so no doubt we will each discuss and deal with the "penis issue" differently. What I hope that you, the audience, will come away with is this sense of diversity and difference, and perhaps even a sense of ambivalence.

NOTES

1. Suzanne J. Kessler and Wendy McKenna, *Gender: An Ethnomethodological Approach* (Chicago: University of Chicago Press, 1978), 142–55.

2. Fiona Giles, *Dick for a Day: What Would You Do If You Had One?* (New York: Villard, 1997).

FOR FURTHER READING

"About Julia." *Julia Serano*, n.d., www.juliaserano.com/about.html.

Carstensen, Jeanne. "Julia Serano, Transfeminist Thinker, Talks Trans-Misogyny." *The New York Times*, 22 June 2017, https://www.nytimes.com/2017/06/22/us/lgbt-julia-serano-transfemi nist-trans-misogyny.html.

Serano, Julia. *Outspoken: A Decade of Transgender Activism and Trans Feminism.* Switch Hitter Press, 2016.

Serano, Julia. *Whipping Girl: A Transsexual Woman on Sexism and the Scapegoating of Femininity.* Seal Press, 2016.

Talusan, Meredith. "The Lasting Transgender Legacy of Julia Serano's 'Whipping Girl.'" *BuzzFeed*, 6 Mar. 2016, www.buzzfeed.com/meredithtalusan/the-lasting-transgender-legacy-of-whipping -girl.

Gabrielle Blair

In 2017 *Politico* dubbed the Twitter thread—tweets by one user strung together in a connected series—"the literary genre of our epoch" (Heffernan). When Twitter launched in 2006, tweets were limited to 140 characters; in 2017 they were expanded to 280. This, coupled with Twitter threads, has given Twitter what Virginia Heffernan describes as a "call to something that Twitter culture, in its far-off playful days, used to condemn implicitly: earnest commitment to a train of thought." Heffernan also notes that unlike op-eds and cable news "debates," the genre of threads are "funny and likable, and the tone is refreshingly pushy, urgent." Some have called Twitter threads a version of mansplaining or "manthreading," while others have likened the form to a poem (Bohn).

Gabrielle Blair demonstrates the rhetorical possibilities of the thread in a series of tweets that describe men's responsibility in unwanted pregnancies. Blair, who positions herself as "mother of six, and a Mormon," holds a BFA in graphic design and founded her blog, *Design Mom*, in 2006 with posts on motherhood and home design. She is the author of the best-selling book *Design Mom: How to Live with Kids*. Blair posted the sixty-three-tweet thread in the fall of 2018 amid Brett Kavanaugh's Supreme Court confirmation process, which was fraught with allegations of sexual assault in his past, as well as the perception that he may someday vote to overturn *Roe v. Wade*.

Blair argues, point by point, that men are responsible for unwanted pregnancies. Here, she challenges the deeply held assumptions in American culture that men can focus on pleasure while women bear the responsibility for birth control. Instead, she argues that men can easily take action to stop causing unwanted pregnancies. She uses the thread to break down her argument, each point a distilled punch on topics ranging from birth control for women to condoms and vasectomies, linking to studies that support her claims. Intertwined with logos, Blair also offers satirical examples, such as castration for men who cause unwanted pregnancies, to highlight the disproportionate demands placed upon women with regard to reproductive health.

The post went viral—it was retweeted over 65,000 times and received over 165,000 "likes" within two days, garnering coverage on sites in Canada, Australia, and elsewhere. The thread may have struck a chord due to the *kairotic* moment:

Blair notes on her blog that she had written the post months before but was compelled to publish it during the Kavanaugh scandal. Or perhaps the popularity stemmed from her ethos as a religious mom of multiple children with a feminist position on reproductive rights. Either way, its form and argument were a fit for twenty-first-century audiences, during a time when reproductive rights were (and still are) under threat and women wielded social media to resist government control of their bodies.

Twitter Thread on Abortion

2018

25–47. A reproduction of a thread of tweets by Gabrielle Blair (@designmom) about abortion and reproductive rights from September 13, 2018.

Gabrielle Blair @designmom · 13 Sep 2018   ⌄
If you want to stop abortion, you need to prevent unwanted pregnancies. And
men are 100% responsible for unwanted pregnancies. No for real, they are.
Perhaps you are thinking: IT TAKES TWO! And yes, it does take two for
intentional pregnancies.

　♡ 549　　↻ 5.1K　　♡ 32K

Gabrielle Blair @designmom · 13 Sep 2018   ⌄
But ALL unwanted pregnancies are caused by the irresponsible ejaculations of
men. Period. Don't believe me? Let me walk you through it. Let's start with this:
women can only get pregnant about 2 days each month. And that's for a limited
number of years.

　♡ 423　　↻ 3.9K　　♡ 27K

Gabrielle Blair @designmom · 13 Sep 2018   ⌄
That makes 24 days a year a women might get pregnant. But men can _cause_
pregnancy 365 days a year. In fact, if you're a man who ejaculates multiple
times a day, you could cause multiple pregnancies daily. In theory a man could
cause 1000+ unwanted pregnancies in just one year.

　♡ 150　　↻ 3.2K　　♡ 24K

Gabrielle Blair @designmom · 13 Sep 2018   ⌄
And though their sperm gets crappier as they age, men can cause unwanted
pregnancies from puberty till death. So just starting with basic biology + the
calendar it's easy to see men are the issue here.

　♡ 81　　↻ 2.4K　　♡ 21K

Gabrielle Blair @designmom · 13 Sep 2018   ⌄
But what about birth control? If a woman doesn't want to risk an unwanted
pregnancy, why wouldn't she just use birth control? If a women can manage to
figure out how to get an abortion, surely she can get birth control, right? Great
questions.

　♡ 51　　↻ 1.9K　　♡ 17K

Gabrielle Blair @designmom · 13 Sep 2018   ⌄
Modern birth control is possibly the greatest invention of the last century, and I
am very grateful for it. It's also brutal. The side effects for many women are
ridiculously harmful. So ridiculous, that when an oral contraception for men was
created, it wasn't approved…

　♡ 128　　↻ 6.3K　　♡ 36K

Gabrielle Blair @designmom · 13 Sep 2018

... because of the side effects. And the list of side effects was about 1/3 as long as the known side effects for women's oral contraception.

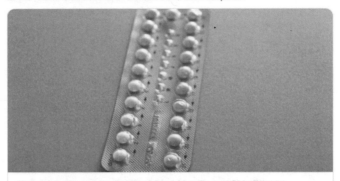

Male Birth Control Study Killed After Men Report Side Effects
Science has failed yet again to come up with hormonal birth control for men. The most recent study was stopped because the men reported pr...
npr.org

○ 158   ↻ 6.4K   ♡ 34K

 Gabrielle Blair @designmom · 13 Sep 2018

There's a lot to be unpacked just in that story, but I'll simply point out (in case you didn't know) that as a society, we really don't mind if women suffer, physically or mentally, as long as it makes things easier for men.

○ 154   ↻ 11K   ♡ 59K

Gabrielle Blair @designmom · 13 Sep 2018

But good news, Men: Even with the horrible side effects, women are still very willing to use birth control. Unfortunately it's harder to get than it should be. Birth control options for women require a doctor's appointment and a prescription. It's not free, and often not cheap.

○ 101   ↻ 3.0K   ♡ 27K

Gabrielle Blair @designmom · 13 Sep 2018

In fact there are many people trying to make it more expensive by fighting to make sure insurance companies refuse to cover it. Oral contraceptives for women can't be acquired easily, or at the last minute. And they don't work instantly.

○ 55   ↻ 2.3K   ♡ 22K

Gabrielle Blair @designmom · 13 Sep 2018

If we're talking about the pill, it requires consistent daily use and doesn't leave much room for mistakes, forgetfulness, or unexpected disruptions to daily schedules. And again, the side effects can be brutal. I'M STILL GRATEFUL FOR IT PLEASE DON'T TAKE IT AWAY.

○ 64   ↻ 2.2K   ♡ 25K

 **Gabrielle Blair** @designmom · 13 Sep 2018

I'm just saying women's birth control isn't simple or easy. In contrast, let's look at birth control for men, meaning condoms. Condoms are readily available at all hours, inexpensive, convenient, and don't require a prescription. They're effective, and work on demand, instantly.

◯ 88   ⇄ 3.1K   ♡ 25K

Gabrielle Blair @designmom · 13 Sep 2018

Men can keep them stocked up just in case, so they're always prepared. Amazing! They are so much easier than birth control options for women. As a bonus, in general, women love when men use condoms. They keep us from getting STDs, they don't lessen our pleasure during sex...

◯ 87   ⇄ 2.2K   ♡ 21K

Gabrielle Blair @designmom · 13 Sep 2018

... or prevent us from climaxing. And the best part? Clean up is so much easier — no waddling to the toilet as your jizz drips down our legs. So why in the world are there ever unwanted pregnancies? Why don't men just use condoms every time they have sex? Seems so simple, right?

◯ 81   ⇄ 2.3K   ♡ 25K

 Gabrielle Blair @designmom · 13 Sep 2018

Oh. I remember. Men _don't_ love condoms. In fact, men frequently pressure women to have sex without a condom. And it's not unheard of for men to remove the condom during sex, without the women's permission or knowledge. (Pro-tip: That's assault.)

'Stealthing' Is A Scary New Sex Trend Trying To Make Assault OK
Everyone needs to know about this.
huffingtonpost.ca

◯ 179   ⇄ 5.0K   ♡ 34K

 Gabrielle Blair @designmom · 13 Sep 2018

Why would men want to have sex without a condom? Good question. Apparently it's because for the minutes they are penetrating their partner, having no condom on gives the experience more pleasure.

◯ 67   ⇄ 2.1K   ♡ 17K

Gabrielle Blair @designmom · 13 Sep 2018   ⌄

So... there are men willing to risk getting a woman pregnant — which means literally risking her life, her health, her social status, her relationships, and her career, so that they can experience a few minutes of _slightly_ more pleasure? Is that for real? Yes. Yes it is.

　　🗨 116　　⟲ 9.0K　　♡ 53K

Gabrielle Blair @designmom · 13 Sep 2018   ⌄

What are we talking about here pleasure-wise? If there's a pleasure scale, with pain beginning at zero and going down into the negatives, a back-scratch falling at 5, and an orgasm without a condom being a 10, where would sex _with_ a condom fall? Like a 7 or 8?

　　🗨 86　　⟲ 1.5K　　♡ 16K

Gabrielle Blair @designmom · 13 Sep 2018   ⌄

So it's not like sex with a condom is _not_ pleasurable, it's just not _as_ pleasurable. An 8 instead of a 10. Let me emphasize that again: Men regularly choose to put women at massive risk by having non-condom sex, in order to experience a few minutes of slightly more pleasure.

　　🗨 103　　⟲ 3.5K　　♡ 27K

Gabrielle Blair @designmom · 13 Sep 2018   ⌄

Now keep in mind, for the truly condom-averse, men also have a non-condom, always-ready birth control built right in, called the pull out. It's not perfect, and it's a favorite joke, but it is also 96% effective.

> **What is the Effectiveness of the Pull Out Method?**
> If you do it correctly, pulling out is a pretty effective way of preventing pregnancy. But it can be hard to do it the right way every time.
> plannedparenthood.org

　　🗨 110　　⟲ 1.7K　　♡ 16K

Gabrielle Blair @designmom · 13 Sep 2018   ⌄

So surely, we can expect men who aren't wearing a condom to at least pull out every time they have sex, right?

Nope.

And why not?

　　🗨 35　　⟲ 1.6K　　♡ 16K

Gabrielle Blair @designmom · 13 Sep 2018   ⌄

Well, again, apparently it's _slightly_ more pleasurable to climax inside a vagina than, say, on their partner's stomach. So men are willing to risk the life, health and well-being of women, in order to experience a tiny bit more pleasure for like 5 seconds during orgasm.

　　🗨 74　　⟲ 2.4K　　♡ 22K

Gabrielle Blair @designmom · 13 Sep 2018

It's mind-boggling and disturbing when you realize that's the choice men are making. And honestly, I'm not as mad as I should be about this, because we've trained men from birth that their pleasure is of utmost importance in the world. (And to dis-associate sex and pregnancy.)

💬 68   ⇄ 3.2K   ♡ 28K

Gabrielle Blair @designmom · 13 Sep 2018

While we're here, let's talk a bit more about pleasure and biology. Did you know that a man CAN'T get a woman pregnant without having an orgasm? Which means that we can conclude getting a woman pregnant is a pleasurable act for men.

💬 313   ⇄ 2.2K   ♡ 19K

Gabrielle Blair @designmom · 13 Sep 2018

But did you further know that men CAN get a woman pregnant without HER feeling any pleasure at all? In fact, it's totally possible for a man to impregnate a woman even while causing her excruciating pain, trauma or horror.

💬 26   ⇄ 2.5K   ♡ 22K

Gabrielle Blair @designmom · 13 Sep 2018

In contrast, a woman can have non-stop orgasms with or without a partner and never once get herself pregnant. A woman's orgasm has literally nothing to do with pregnancy or fertility — her clitoris exists not for creating new babies, but simply for pleasure.

💬 53   ⇄ 2.5K   ♡ 23K

Gabrielle Blair @designmom · 13 Sep 2018

No matter how many orgasms she has, they won't make her pregnant. Pregnancies can only happen when men have an orgasm. Unwanted pregnancies can only happen when men orgasm irresponsibly.

💬 73   ⇄ 3.8K   ♡ 26K

Gabrielle Blair @designmom · 13 Sep 2018

What this means is a women can be the sluttliest slut in the entire world who loves having orgasms all day long and all night long and she will never find herself with an unwanted pregnancy unless a man shows up and ejaculates irresponsibly.

💬 136   ⇄ 4.4K   ♡ 32K

Gabrielle Blair @designmom · 13 Sep 2018

Women enjoying sex does not equal unwanted pregnancy and abortion. Men enjoying sex and having irresponsible ejaculations is what causes unwanted pregnancies and abortion.

💬 106   ⇄ 6.9K   ♡ 39K

Gabrielle Blair @designmom · 13 Sep 2018

Let's talk more about responsibility. Men often don't know, and don't ask, and don't think to ask, if they've caused a pregnancy. They may never think of it, or associate sex with making babies at all. Why? Because there are 0 consequences for men who cause unwanted pregnancies.

◯ 411   ⟲ 4.1K   ♡ 30K

Gabrielle Blair @designmom · 13 Sep 2018

If the woman decides to have an abortion, the man may never know he caused an unwanted pregnancy with his irresponsible ejaculation.

◯ 24   ⟲ 1.0K   ♡ 11K

Gabrielle Blair @designmom · 13 Sep 2018

If the woman decides to have the baby, or put the baby up for adoption, the man may never know he caused an unwanted pregnancy with his irresponsible ejaculation, or that there's now a child walking around with 50% of his DNA.

◯ 22   ⟲ 963   ♡ 11K

Gabrielle Blair @designmom · 13 Sep 2018

If the woman does tell him that he caused an unwanted pregnancy and that she's having the baby, the closest thing to a consequence for him, is that he may need to pay child support. But our current child support system is well-known to be a joke.

◯ 38   ⟲ 1.3K   ♡ 13K

Gabrielle Blair @designmom · 13 Sep 2018

61% of men (or women) who are legally required to pay it, simply don't. With little or no repercussions. Their credit isn't even affected. So, many men keep going as is, causing unwanted pregnancies with irresponsible ejaculations and never giving it thought.

◯ 57   ⟲ 1.4K   ♡ 13K

Gabrielle Blair @designmom · 13 Sep 2018

When the topic of abortion comes up, men might think: Abortion is horrible; women should not have abortions. And never once consider the man who CAUSED the unwanted pregnancy. If you're not holding men responsible for unwanted pregnancies, then you are wasting your time.

◯ 63   ⟲ 4.2K   ♡ 23K

Gabrielle Blair @designmom · 13 Sep 2018

Stop protesting at clinics. Stop shaming women. Stop trying to overturn abortion laws. If you actually care about reducing or eliminating the number of abortions in our country, simply HOLD MEN RESPONSIBLE FOR THEIR ACTIONS.

◯ 120   ⟲ 7.6K   ♡ 36K

Gabrielle Blair @designmom · 13 Sep 2018

What would that look like? What if there was a real and immediate consequence for men who cause an unwanted pregnancy? What kind of consequence would make sense? Should it be as harsh, painful, nauseating, scarring, expensive, risky, and life-altering…

💬 26 ⇄ 1.5K ♡ 14K

Gabrielle Blair @designmom · 13 Sep 2018

… as forcing a woman to go through a 9-month unwanted pregnancy?

💬 21 ⇄ 1.3K ♡ 14K

Gabrielle Blair @designmom · 13 Sep 2018

In my experience, men really like their testicles. If irresponsible ejaculations were putting their balls at risk, they would stop being irresponsible. Does castration seem like a cruel and unusual punishment? Definitely.

💬 36 ⇄ 1.4K ♡ 13K

Gabrielle Blair @designmom · 13 Sep 2018

But is it worse than forcing 500,000 women a year to puke daily for months, gain 40 pounds, and then rip their bodies apart in childbirth? Is a handful of castrations worse than women dying during forced pregnancy & childbirth?

💬 52 ⇄ 1.5K ♡ 15K

Gabrielle Blair @designmom · 13 Sep 2018

Put a castration law on the books, implement the law, let the media tell the story, and in 3 months or less, tada! abortions will have virtually disappeared. Can you picture it? No more abortions in less than 3 months, without ever trying to outlaw them. Amazing.

💬 78 ⇄ 1.7K ♡ 15K

Gabrielle Blair @designmom · 13 Sep 2018

For those of you who consider abortion to be murder, wouldn't you be on board with having a handful of men castrated, if it prevented 500,000 murders each year?

💬 89 ⇄ 3.0K ♡ 21K

Gabrielle Blair @designmom · 13 Sep 2018

And if not, is that because you actually care more about policing women's bodies, morality, and sexuality, than you do about reducing or eliminating abortions? (That's a rhetorical question.)

💬 21 ⇄ 2.4K ♡ 25K

Gabrielle Blair @designmom · 13 Sep 2018

Hey, you can even have the men who will be castrated bank their sperm before it happens — just in case they want to responsibly have kids some day.

💬 15 ⇄ 1.1K ♡ 12K

Gabrielle Blair @designmom · 13 Sep 2018

Can't wrap your head around a physical punishment for men? Even though you seem to be more than fine with physical punishments for women? Okay. Then how about this prevention idea: At the onset of puberty, all males in the U.S. could be required by law to get a vasectomy.

◯ 133   ⟲ 2.0K   ♡ 17K

Gabrielle Blair @designmom · 13 Sep 2018

Vasectomies are very safe, totally reversible, and about as invasive as an doctor's exam for a woman getting a birth control prescription. There is some soreness afterwards for about 24 hours, but that's pretty much it for side effects.

◯ 147   ⟲ 1.6K   ♡ 14K

Gabrielle Blair @designmom · 13 Sep 2018

(So much better than The Pill, which is taken by millions of women in our country, the side effects of which are well known and can be brutal.)

◯ 25   ⟲ 942   ♡ 11K

Gabrielle Blair @designmom · 13 Sep 2018

If/when the male becomes a responsible adult, and perhaps finds a mate, if they want to have a baby, the vasectomy can be reversed, and then redone once the childbearing stage is over. And each male can bank their sperm before the vasectomy, just in case.

◯ 52   ⟲ 1.3K   ♡ 13K

Gabrielle Blair @designmom · 13 Sep 2018

It's not that wild of an idea. 80% of males in the U.S. are circumcised, most as babies. And that's not reversible.

◯ 40   ⟲ 997   ♡ 12K

Gabrielle Blair @designmom · 13 Sep 2018

Don't like my ideas? That's fine. I'm sure there are better ones. Go ahead and suggest your own ideas. My point is that it's nonsense to focus on women if you're trying to get rid of abortions. Abortion is the "cure" for an unwanted pregnancy.

◯ 53   ⟲ 1.4K   ♡ 16K

Gabrielle Blair @designmom · 13 Sep 2018

If you want to stop abortions, you need to prevent the "disease" - meaning, unwanted pregnancies. And the only way to do that, is by focusing on men, because: MEN CAUSE 100% OF UNWANTED PREGNANCIES. Or. IRRESPONSIBLE EJACULATIONS BY MEN CAUSE 100% OF UNWANTED PREGNANCIES.

◯ 127   ⟲ 4.0K   ♡ 24K

Gabrielle Blair @designmom · 13 Sep 2018

If you're a man, what would the consequence need to be for you to never again ejaculate irresponsibly? Would it be money related? Maybe a loss of rights or freedoms? Physical pain?

💬 55   ⟲ 1.1K   ♡ 11K

Gabrielle Blair @designmom · 13 Sep 2018

Ask yourselves: What would it take for you to value the life of your sexual partner more than your own temporary pleasure or convenience?

💬 32   ⟲ 2.1K   ♡ 18K

Gabrielle Blair @designmom · 13 Sep 2018

Are you someone who learns better with analogies? Let's try this one: Think of another great pleasure in life, let's say food. Think of your favorite meal, dessert, or drink.

💬 6   ⟲ 718   ♡ 8.6K

Gabrielle Blair @designmom · 13 Sep 2018

What if you found out that every time you indulge in that favorite food you risked causing great physical and mental pain for someone you know intimately. You might not cause any pain, but it's a real risk.

💬 17   ⟲ 746   ♡ 9.0K

Gabrielle Blair @designmom · 13 Sep 2018

Well, you'd probably be sad, but never indulge in that food again, right? Not worth the risk!

💬 10   ⟲ 657   ♡ 8.3K

Gabrielle Blair @designmom · 13 Sep 2018

And then, what if you further found out, there was a simple thing you could do before you ate that favorite food, and it would eliminate the risk of causing pain to someone else. Which is great news!

💬 7   ⟲ 673   ♡ 8.8K

Gabrielle Blair @designmom · 13 Sep 2018

BUT the simple thing you need to do makes the experience of eating the food slightly less pleasurable. To be clear, it would still be VERY pleasurable, but slightly less so. Like maybe you have to eat the food with a fork or spoon that you don't particularly like.

💬 16   ⟲ 692   ♡ 9.3K

Gabrielle Blair @designmom · 13 Sep 2018

Would you be willing to do that simple thing, and eliminate the risk of causing pain to someone you know intimately, every single time you ate your favorite food?

OF COURSE YOU WOULD.

💬 21   ⟲ 701   ♡ 9.9K

Gabrielle Blair @designmom · 13 Sep 2018
Condoms (or even pulling out) is that simple thing. Don't put women at risk.
Don't choose to maximize your own pleasure if it risks causing women pain.

  ⃝ 330   ⇄ 1.6K   ♡ 17K

Gabrielle Blair @designmom · 13 Sep 2018
Men mostly run our government. Men mostly make the laws. And men could
eliminate abortions in 3 months or less without ever touching an abortion law or
evening mentioning women.

  ⃝ 33   ⇄ 958   ♡ 8.0K

Gabrielle Blair @designmom · 13 Sep 2018
In summary: STOP TRYING TO CONTROL WOMEN'S BODIES AND
SEXUALITY. UNWANTED PREGNANCIES ARE CAUSED BY MEN.

The end.

  ⃝ 1.2K   ⇄ 3.7K   ♡ 23K

For Further Reading

Blair, Gabrielle. *Design Mom: How to Live with Kids.* Artisan, 2015.

Blair, Gabrielle. "My Twitter Thread on Abortion." *Design Mom,* 13 Sept. 2018, https://www.design
    mom.com/twitter-thread-abortion/.

Bohn, Dieter. "A Small Defense of the Twitter Thread." *The Verge,* 3 Aug. 2017, https://www.theverge
    .com/2017/8/3/16086132/twitter-thread-poem-defense-appreciation.

Heffernan, Virginia. "The Rise of the Twitter Thread." *Politico,* Sept./Oct. 2017, https://www.politico
    .com/magazine/story/2017/09/05/twitter-thread-social-media-trend-215539.

Pattee, Jyl. "Viral Abortion Twitter Thread Teaches Marketers 8 Must-Implement Strategies." *For-
    ward Influence,* 16 Sept. 2018, https://forwardinfluence.com/abortion-twitter-thread/.

Karin Hitselberger

In her 2014 TEDx talk, "I'm Not Your Inspiration, Thank You Very Much," the late Stella Young popularized the term *inspiration porn*, challenging the societal tendency to bring disabled people into view only as inspirational objects for able-bodied people. For example, inspiration porn might feature people with disabilities overcoming challenges or maintaining a "good attitude," despite living with hardship. As Young explains, inspiration porn makes able-bodied people feel better about their own lives by objectifying those with disabilities. Even more, it reinforces a societal lie about disability: "We've been sold the lie that disability is a Bad Thing, capital B, capital T. It's a bad thing, and to live with a disability makes you exceptional. It's not a bad thing, and it doesn't make you exceptional" (Young).

In the following blog entry and images, Karin Hitselberger, a graduate student and blogger for *Claiming Crip*, argues—and shows—that the culturally ubiquitous selfie can provide a counternarrative to disabled people as inspiration porn. A counternarrative allows a marginalized group to author their own experiences or, in Hitselberger's words, "flip the script," in order to challenge the master stories told about them. By flipping the lens of her cell phone's camera, Hitselberger shows how disabled people can represent themselves as subjects of their everyday lives. "We are everything," she writes, "ranging from parents and children to bookworms and party girls."

Selfies became mainstream in 2013, a trend popularized by celebrities using these phone-captured self-portraits to interact with fans. They are now pervasive in image-based social media platforms like Instagram, whose users are predominately female. More often than not, however, the selfie is an altered image, where the photographer applies filters and editing tools to "beautify" their natural appearance: blemishes are covered, wrinkles are erased, lips are plumped, and eyes are brightened. Unsurprisingly, research shows that heavy photo–based social media use is linked to self-objectification, body dissatisfaction, and pursuit of thinness. The accompanying culture of "likes" and commenting can further exacerbate pressure to equate self-worth with others' "approval" of one's appearance (Makwana et al.).

Hitselberger, however, uses selfies as her ultimate "rebellion." Her selfies are not designed to conform to societal standards, but to upend them. She reminds us that there is rhetorical power in using a dominant form in a new way, by sharing images that tell a different story about disabled people, women, fulfillment, and beauty. When Hitselberger upends norms to center the disabled body, she helps all of us see more generous possibilities for the selfie and, more importantly, the self.

"Cheeky, Not Tragic: Defining Anti-Inspiration Porn"

Claiming Crip, 2017

I love selfies.

I am an unapologetic selfie queen, and I'm always ready to defend the value of this modern medium. As a plus-sized disabled woman selfies are much more than a fun way to show off my style. They are my ultimate rebellion and my way of building what I call anti-inspiration porn.

As opposed to *inspiration porn*, a term coined by late activist, Stella Young, which portrays disabled people as tragic figures, or superheroes who exist only to enrich nondisabled people, selfies flip the lens and allow disabled people to tell our stories our own terms.

Anti-inspiration porn is images of what it means to be disabled in real life.

Half-drunk selfies taken in dark clubs while spending time with friends.

Sexy selfies taken to showcase the beauty of our bodies, medical devices, scars, and all.

Hospital glam selfies that show being disabled or sick doesn't stop us from having our own style or wanting to express ourselves. Proof that learning to pass as nondisabled is not the key to living a beautiful, valuable, and amazing disabled life. Being disabled is not something we need to apologize for, dance around, or hide.

These are the photos that depict us genuinely enjoying and loving life, not in spite of who we are but because of it. A declaration that we are beautiful and worthwhile just as we are, selfies show that disabled living is a completely valid way of living, never a consolation prize. Selfies are complex depictions of disability as both a blessing and a curse. They are the images that show that who we are is not problematic, but are also the images that may make you uncomfortable.

Pictures that make no attempt to hide wheelchairs, prosthetics, or scars, and in fact present them proudly. Moments of owning your identity, and your body. Waiting for therapists or doctor's appointments, declaring that disability and illness are simply a part of our lives. Shattering the myth that disabled people always take everything in stride, selfies can show us in pain and struggling. They are not poised photos taken by others to exploit, objective, and dehumanize the disabled experience. They are a firsthand reclamation of our awesomeness as disabled people.

Through selfies, we can showcase the complex relationship many disabled people have with the bodies we've been given. Instead of providing an outsider perspective on the everyday lives of disabled people, selfies show the intimate realities of our real lives. Instead of painting our bodies and identities as shackles to be cast off and problems to be overcome. Instead of portraying us as lesser versions of our nondisabled counterparts, selfies depict the rich diversity and value of our lives.

By flipping the lens, selfies have allowed us to flip the script. Placing the individual as photographer and subject offers people who exist outside of the institutionalized structures of beauty and normalcy to display ourselves in traditionally off-limits roles. They have the power to disrupt the status quo, and call into question the current narrative of what it means, and looks like, to be disabled in today's world.

Selfies are the ultimate anti-inspiration porn by saying we do not exist to remind nondisabled people that life could always be worse. Disability is not a fate worse than death—in fact, far from it. With disability, we can still be friends, lovers, students, and coworkers. We are everything, ranging from parents and children to bookworms and party girls. They display our bodies, not as something to be overcome, but rather as things to accept, live in, love in, and even celebrate. They are the antidote to the carefully posed feel-good images of disabled people that perpetuate the idea that the only good disability is one that can be overcome. Our selfies are declarations that we are beautiful and worthwhile just as we are.

Anti-inspiration porn shows disabled lives and bodies are not worthy of pity. It demonstrates the complexity of a community, culture, and identity. Most of all, it rejects the notion that a disabled body is a bad body. Anti-inspiration porn, particularly selfies, showcases the power of learning to live with your body, the good and the bad, instead of destroying it.

They say being disabled is not a bad thing, just another way of living.

They declare a refusal to be disgusted by your own existence.

When you're disabled, refusing to hate your body is the most radical thing you can do.

48. Karin Hitselberger is pictured in a wheelchair alongside her friend, enjoying time at a bookstore.

49. In this selfie, Karin Hitselberger makes a "duck face" for the camera.

FOR FURTHER READING

Davis, Zachary. "The Long, Empowering History of Selfies." *The Boston Globe*, 10 Nov. 2017, www
    .bostonglobe.com/ideas/2017/11/10/the-long-empowering-history-selfies/cH2iOfdEO
    hoR14xCcfLjxJ/story.html.
Makwana, Bindal, et al. "Selfie-Esteem: The Relationship between Body Dissatisfaction and Social
    Media in Adolescent and Young Women." *The Inquisitive Mind*, vol. 1, no. 35, 2018, www.in
    -mind.org/article/selfie-esteem-the-relationship-between-body-dissatisfaction-and-social-me
    dia-in-adolescent.
Young, Stella. "I'm Not Your Inspiration, Thank You Very Much." *TED*, Apr. 2014, www.ted.com/
    talks/stella_young_i_m_not_your_inspiration_thank_you_very_much.

Michelle Denise Jackson

The body is a source of knowledge, a location from which to speak and claim authority. But too often for women and others who are marginalized, the body is also a bearer of pain, inscribed by histories of oppression, violence, and denigration. Across centuries, and today, women rhetors write their bodies to give voice to experiences written on their flesh. Michelle Denise Jackson's piece, first published on the black feminist digital platform *For Harriet,* is an embodied testimony, illuminating how the story of her body is intertwined with those of other black women: in this case, that of Sandra Bland.

Sandra Bland, twenty-eight, was an African American woman who was pulled over in July 2015 by Brian Encinia for not signaling her turn. The arrest occurred one mile from Bland's alma mater, Prairie View A&M University in Texas, where she had just been hired as an outreach coordinator. The routine arrest escalated into a shouting match when the trooper ordered Bland to exit the car without saying why. Encinia is captured on police dashcam video and, as of 2019, unearthed video from Bland's cell phone, pulling a stun gun and yelling, "I will light you up. Get out. Now. Get out of the car" (Queally). Out of the camera's view, a brawl ensued, with Bland screaming, "You are about to break my wrist" and proclaiming that she could not hear, as Encinia slammed her head to the ground (Lai et al.). In the arrest affidavit, Encinia recorded that Bland kicked him. She was charged with assaulting a public servant—a felony—and was jailed in lieu of $5,000 bail. Three days later, Bland was found dead in the jail cell, hanging from a metal shaped hook, a trash liner turned into a noose around her neck. Images of Bland, healthy and vibrant before the incident and despondent in the mug shot, along with video of the arrest, saturated the media.

This is how Michelle Denise Jackson—an activist, television writer, and storyteller—came to know Bland, to feel the pain of Bland's trauma in her own physical being. In her essay, Jackson artfully uses rhetorical identification to draw parallels between her life and Bland's and to implicitly invite the reader to do the same. Jackson repeats Sandra Bland's full name as her mantra, a reference to the #SayHerName movement, which documents the often overlooked black women brutalized by the police (see Kimberlé Crenshaw's contribution to this volume). Jackson narrates her painful realization that no matter what she does, no matter how hard she tries to be "the right kind of black," dominant culture will view her black body as a threat, as a rationale to justify excessive and needless violence. This imprints trauma on all of those living in black bodies. By writing the anguish she bears in the wake of Bland's death, Jackson calls us to remember, to feel, Sandra Bland's embodied wholeness, as a path to restore the dignity of black lives and black bodies.

"Reflections on Sandra Bland: My Black Body Was Not Meant to Bear All This Trauma"

For Harriet, **2015**

Today, I do not feel like smiling. I only wish to buttress myself within the confines of my bed. I wish to keep the world at bay.

I never know when this will happen. I wake up each morning, intent on being productive. I have plans. I have to-do lists. And then, I cannot move. I am emotionally and mentally paralyzed, and so my body follows suit.

Oh, what a strange friend my body and I have become. My body is the gateway. My body is vessel, a vehicle. And so many times within the last year, I have stalled it out. I have burdened it with too much, made it heavy.

Today, my body is heavy.

It has been over a week since I learned a new name: Sandra Bland. It has been over a week since this new name became a mantra, a meditation that I and so many other Black people repeat to ourselves throughout our days. I know her face now better than I know the faces of some of my relatives.

I have seen her smiling Facebook photos. I have watched her "Sandy Speaks" videos. In all of these, she is bold and vibrant and complicated. She is Black and alive. She is so full of life. She is still here.

I have seen dashcam footage of her arrest. Of the fifty-plus-minute video, I watched half of it. I couldn't hold the rage. I couldn't keep the cells of my body from vibrating with a fury that so many Black people in America are familiar with. How the cells of her body must've been vibrating with fury when Officer Brian Encinia pulled her over. How the cells of her body must've been vibrating with fury when he told her she was under arrest, but could not tell her what for. When he opened her car door and told her he would drag her out. When he pointed his Taser at her and told her he would "light her up!" When he put her in handcuffs and threw her Black body—now vibrating with fear, I am so sure—on the ground.

I have seen her mugshot, in which she looks defeated and hurt. In which she looks so hurt, she almost looks lifeless—and this has caused many to speculate whether her mugshot was taken after her death.

Today, I have repeated Sandra Bland's name as a mantra. Her name is a prayer I wish I did not know, along with so many other names. Along with so many other Black women, men, and children's names we learn for the wrong reasons. We learn their names not to celebrate and lift them up while they're still alive; but instead, to honor and mourn them after they are taken from us.

My mouth wishes it didn't know how to say her name. And yet, #SayHerName is the call of action that follows her name in almost every Facebook status, tweet, and online article I read.

And so I say her name. I write her name. I think her name. As we all do.

Today, my body is heavy, as I reckon with the fact that Sandra Bland is—or was—not so much different than I am.

She was a college-educated Black woman in her twenties. I am a college-educated Black woman in her twenties. She was beginning a new chapter of her life by taking a job at Prairie View A&M University. I am beginning a new chapter of mine by starting grad school. She was pulled over for a "routine traffic violation." I, too, have been pulled over by police officers, and questioned whether it was the broken taillight or my black skin that was the criminal offense. She "mouthed off" at a police officer by expressing her annoyance. I, too, have been frank about my irritation with a police officer who pulled me over.

And in this reckoning, my body becomes familiar with a new trauma. I have already accepted that I, as a Black woman, will move in this world and be marked as "other," as "dangerous," as "problem," as "deserving of less than my full humanity." I learned this trauma early.

But this new trauma is one I was unprepared for. It's the realization that everything I thought could protect me will not. I was brought up to believe that if I did the "right" things, if I was the "right kind of Black," I would be okay. I could survive a routine traffic violation. Any officer who pulled me over would see the indications of my "good Black upbringing," and would know that I am not a threat.

But my Black body is always a threat. Our Black bodies, so full of life, are always a threat. Sandra Bland is gone because she was a threat. She is dead now because Officer Brian Encinia saw her as a threat. Her honesty, her boldness, her questioning, her insistence on knowing her rights were threatening. We may never know exactly what happened at the Waller County Jail, but we do know that Sandra Bland is dead because an officer saw her and her Black body as threatening.

And the trauma of knowing that at any moment, I can be removed from this world because someone with the law and a gun by his side could deem me threatening, is one that I cannot bear.

FOR FURTHER READING

Crenshaw, Kimberlé. *Say Her Name: Resisting Police Brutality against Black Women*. African American Policy Forum, Center for Intersectionality and Social Policy Studies, Columbia Law School, 2015.

Davis, Kate and David Heilbroner, directors. *Say Her Name: The Life and Death of Sandra Bland*. HBO, 2018.

Lai, K. K. Rebecca, et al. "Assessing the Legality of Sandra Bland's Arrest." *The New York Times*, 20 July 2015, https://www.nytimes.com/interactive/2015/07/20/us/sandra-bland-arrest-death-videos-maps.html.

Queally, James. "What Happened to Sandra Bland before She Died in a Texas Jail?" *Los Angeles Times*, 28 July 2015, www.latimes.com/nation/nationnow/la-na-nn-sandra-bland-20150728-htmlstory.html.

Staceyann Chin

Staceyann Chin is an artist, writer, and activist, whose contribution to the 2006 anthology *We Don't Need Another Wave* challenges feminism's depiction in mainstream media. Her piece marks and anticipates continued difficulties for those who identify as nonbinary. For instance, Chin invokes the issue of gender-neutral bathrooms in advance of the bathroom bill wars that proliferated in the next decade (see Kat Blaque's and Kimberly Shappley's contributions to this volume). As the historian Neil J. Young explains, the United States has a long history of weaponizing public bathrooms to discriminate based on gender, race, and sexuality, most notably by separating bathrooms by race during the Jim Crow era. More broadly, Chin's essay is a lyrical rumination on how gender fluidity is navigated in real lives and relationships. Chin blends the details of daily life with emotional, sexual, and intellectual desires to illuminate the limitations of labels and definitions, particularly as white patriarchal culture sets and regulates them.

Chin's essay emerges from her lived experiences; as Felicia R. Lee describes in a profile in the *New York Times*, "A part-black, part-Chinese lesbian immigrant from Jamaica, Staceyann Chin finds poetry in belonging everywhere and no place in particular." Chin's 2009 memoir, *The Other Side of Paradise*, garnered positive reviews; it offers a warm but unflinching narrative of growing up parentless in Jamaica. Chin has also excelled as a performer, a standout in the Tony Award–nominated show *Russell Simmons Def Poetry Jam*. Chin gave birth in 2012, and she also writes about being a single lesbian mother.

In "On Rooms to Fight and Fuck and Crow," Chin's form refuses linearity, unspooling in ways that mirror its argument against categorization. Along the way, she shows the limitations of the terms we use to name ourselves and others, calling for more expansive ways to announce, "I am here." Her narrative is driven by urgency, including incendiary language and insistence that passivity and silence make one complicit. Indeed, Chin seems to predict the fervor over gender identity that would play publicly out in the years ahead. Or perhaps her piece simply reminds readers that such struggles have long been deeply ingrained in our cultural fabric.

"On Rooms to Fight and Fuck and Crow"

We Don't Need Another Wave, 2006

Twenty-seven and counting, she fixes the smooth cuffs of a white dress shirt. The long sleeves hang neatly creased from her arms. Her collar rises crisp at the neck. A matching undershirt absorbs the sweat from her skin. Her cleavage teases the coral blue of a cotton Fruit of the Loom brassiere.

The shirttails flap insolent against her thighs. High on her hips, printed panties peek out indecent, like her full mouth. She quickly adds lipstick and expertly spikes her short hair. Only then does she step back from the mirror to check her size eleven shoes.

In 1960, this getup might have seemed questionable. In 2001, the breathtaking boneblack of leather and lace and tailored pants is stunning. A modem enigma of balance and symmetry, she is the familiar, arranged just slightly askew.

In Jamaica, a woman could get killed for being that ambiguous. Androgynous, sexy, and politically aware, she strides across the room, reckless and smelling of mermaids and musk. She always moves me from the inside—often incites in me a desire to write about the places I have never been; at night we tell each other stories of Rwanda, Mwanza, and the bullfights in Madrid.

Beneath both our breasts beats a yen for the mundane: a house, a yard, free education, universal health care. We dare to dream of a world where boys can wear high heel shoes and still be considered men. We think every girl should know how to choose a good moisturizer, strap on a dildo, and spot a misogynist on sight.

I love that she is neither butch nor femme. I love that she *loves* being a woman.

With her I can talk about the parts of me I am still struggling to understand. In the quiet of her red-and-orange bed, I am able to admit that I do not understand much of what informs the discourse on being transgender. Between the defensive arguments and the sterile mechanisms of misunderstanding, segments of the gay, lesbian, bisexual, and transgender community gape angry and insensitive to the needs we each carry, hurtful and unattended, under our skins.

Mouth over mine, she reminds me to walk gentle on these questions protruding knifelike from my pen. We miss seeing masculine women who still identify as women. We miss attitude and the parts erased, in name and body and hearts.

I don't want to feel abandoned, but I do. I wonder how you could leave a self you sat so sensual in. I wonder if you miss the curved parts of the selves you once were. I wonder if it is wrong of me to ask.

But in these times of apathy and self-indulgence, silence is the enemy of resistance. So I invite conversation. With so few voices at our disposal, each body is a valuable tool of a necessary revolution. And we stand on the border of a landscape shifting decisive to black and white as if its borders were never gray.

These unanswered questions and contradictions rub awkward against the loud postfeminist generation squawking easy toward assimilation. I resist that narrative because everyone is not equal yet. Everyone does not yet have the right to be whom she fancies, to love whom he chooses, to re-create an image of a truer self.

Perhaps it is envy that pushes me green against the tide, but I believe we need to interrogate the veins of we who are most difficult to define. Only then can we better understand how we love, or why we hate each other, why we systematically hate ourselves.

I do not want to be a part of any binary dynamic that kills desire and instinct. No part of me nurses the fragile, indecipherable desire to fit in. Skin, pussy, and original sin render me the madwoman in the proverbial attic. All day, I navigate a war of terror perpetuated on the bodies of women, on bodies of color, on poor people whose crime is that they do not earn enough.

The issues we are currently facing are myriad and daunting.

Parts of the whole are simple enough. Transgender men and women need to use the restroom. And everyone should have the freedom to enter a bathroom without having to explain whether a cock or a cunt lies under a dress or a suit.

But the history of gender and abuse cannot be ignored. The power dynamics between men and women do not automatically shift with surgery and/or a change of outfit and hairstyle. Women, both transwomen and biowomen, do not yet feel safe in the company of men they do not know.

I think we just need more bathrooms. From which everyone is free to choose: all-gender bathrooms; trans bathrooms; bio-men and -women bathrooms. That we have not come thus far is fact. Until women and men are equally safe, I take great care in deciding where I unbutton my cargo pants. If we are to consider the needs and histories of all concerned, progressive politics and practicality must meet in conversation.

And while we hammer out the details, we need to invent new ways to talk, to see each other, to begin the process of unlearning the hate and misogyny and brutality of our patriarchal world.

I believe we are so much more than the crass invention of a form. I am more than this pussy, these breasts, and what the least evolved of bigoted men have expected of me. My body parts are only *parts* of a complicated whole. No currency of superimposed gender, whether borrowed or sold in the market of marginalized identities, marks me as man or woman.

Many of us question who we could be if we weren't so terrified of looking square at our flawed selves. These wounds we acquire from arguing mean we have not talked enough.

This business of being modern and progressive and activist and woman extends complex from my current vantage point. I mourn this world rushing uncommunicative and unnuanced toward a crude language not large enough to discourse the definition of our bodies as more than constructed. We cannot even agree on a list of pronouns, let alone philosophical commandments on how to be after we are done dueling. In this neofeminist dialogue, *lesbian* has become a dirty word, synonymous with cowardly or incomplete. The word *woman* is now the framework upon which is hung the weak-breasted, dim-witted creatures turning ugly under the unkind gaze of progress. We march like sheep along a patriarchal gender line. Each of us forced to choose one of the two ways of saying *I am here*, flailing in the twilight of none of us knowing where to stand, where to sit, or where to use the toilet.

Taking a piss shouldn't be so complicated.

And if we were being honest about the powers that be, we would admit that this is not about urinals, or genders, or even upside-down letters painted on a restroom door. This age-old argument is about the shortage of spaces, exclusive to bodies that cannot be collapsed into recognizable definitions of an archaic social order.

There are simply not enough rooms for androgynous dykes, or black faggots, or straight niggers, or political kikes, or articulate coconuts, or bisexual gooks. In the construct that holds us in our places, there is no room for the nonstereotype. Fuck you if you cannot be labeled as blue or red.

All this is distraction in the debate about why black high schools still have fewer computers than white high schools in any state of the union, why LGBT teens are still under siege in every public school in this liberated country, why blade dykes with multiple degrees still cannot afford their own apartments, why every sexuality expert on CNN is always male and/or white.

This conundrum of inclusion and exclusion of identities is not about whether this community likes or dislikes trannies. This is about the shortage of resources set aside for voices not recognizable to a white supremacist mainstream.

We need to stop picking on each other and start throwing punches at the wealthy white men, both gay and straight, who refuse to make space for all the *other* bodies paying taxes and constructing cars and building satellites and writing poems and voting and making music for them to sing.

We need to make space for every lesbian, every tranny, every bisexual teenager, every girl who says she needs a room of her own. In every home, everybody needs to know there is one door they can close behind them. Everyone needs a place where they can shut the world out.

The complicated lists of letters are irrelevant, the pills are a matter of choice, but for the world in which we live, funding is what is necessary to dearly mark territories out for individual or group safety. When every single body, regardless of sex, sexuality, or race, has food and education and the freedom to see an unfettered self, then and only then will we be able to look honestly at what or who we are and how we may agree or disagree.

Until then, calling me Mohammed does not make me an American Arab. Announcing that I am also Chinese does not make me any less of a nigger in North America.

Today, I am a black lesbian immigrant artist from Jamaica. That statement does not tell you that I love to eat copious amounts of Dominican food. But it does tell you that if I am not careful, I could be brutally killed when my lover and I visit the beautiful country of my birth. It also tells you that if I raise a son in the United States, the police will pull him over more than once in his North American life. It tells you I am not likely to have health care.

Statements about who we are point out the privileges we derive or don't derive from how fucked-up the world is to people who are poor and/or of color. We cannot ignore those social groupings of identities until what they mean has been examined and confronted and effectively reformed.

Call me a woman until I earn as much as any man. Call me a nigger until my rights are the same as a white person's.

Until everyone is equal, I am invoking my right to enter a safe room where I can speak out loud, and fight with fury, and fuck and eat and crow.

Until then, help me to fight for your right to at least one room into which only you are allowed to go.

For Further Reading

Berger, Melody, Ed. *We Don't Need Another Wave: Dispatches from the Next Generation of Feminists.* Seal Press, 2006.

Chin, Staceyann. *The Other Side of Paradise.* Simon & Schuster, 2009.

Drum, Kevin. "A Very Brief Timeline of the Bathroom Wars." *Mother Jones*, 14 May 2016, https://www.motherjones.com/kevin-drum/2016/05/timeline-bathroom-wars/.

Lee, Felicia R. "A Def Poetry Jam of Her Very Own." *The New York Times*, 17 July 2005, https://www.nytimes.com/2005/07/17/theater/newsandfeatures/a-def-poetry-jam-of-her-very-own.html.

Young, Neil J. "How the Bathroom Wars Shaped America." *Politico*, 18 May 2016, https://www.politico.com/magazine/story/2016/05/2016-bathroom-bills-politics-north-carolina-lgbt-transgender-history-restrooms-era-civil-rights-213902.

Christina Cauterucci

"The LGBTQ initialism is not just a random collection of letters that represent identities; rather, these letters are history embodied," writes the scholar and activist Jeffry J. Iovannone. Names are interlinked with identity and visibility, and subjects who have been relegated to society's margins have not historically had power to name and define themselves. For this reason, Christina Cauterucci grapples with the cultural implications of exchanging the identifier *lesbian* for *queer*, a common choice among millennial women. The following piece was part of *Slate's* series "Outward," designed to expand perspectives on LGBTQ issues.

Literally meaning "odd" or "strange," *queer* was long deployed as a pejorative term for people with same-sex attractions and, especially, "effeminate" men. Beginning in the 1980s, amid the AIDS crisis, the gay community began to reclaim the term, with the activist group Queer Nation famously proclaiming, "We're Here, We're Queer, Get Used to It!" In 2016 the Gay and Lesbian Alliance Against Defamation (GLAAD) added the Q to LGBT in its style guide, and *queer* is now regularly employed in mainstream media as an umbrella term for any identity that isn't straight or cisgender (Steinmetz).

But Cauterucci, a graduate of Georgetown University and former DC editor of the queer women's blog *Where the Girls Go*, explains that *queer* is as rhetorically powerful for what it refuses to define as for what (and whom) it does. *Queer* is a fluctuating term, one that rejects neat categories of sexualities and genders and even refuses to be categorized as a single part of speech. *Queer* is a noun, but it's also an adjective and a verb. *Queering* means to resist "regimes of normal" (Warner), to see beyond binaries, categories, and boundaries in favor of more limitless possibilities for living and being.

Melding personal narrative with cultural and historical analysis, Cauterucci explains that while she embraces *queer*, she also worries about the limitations of a term so expansive and amorphous. Detailing her efforts to organize a queer tea/dance party, Cauterucci traces the evolution of the party's name to include women and all queer and trans people who aren't cisgender men. While describing the party as for "non-cismen" is functional, Cauterucci explains, it is not without problems—it defines who they are against, who they are not. It sets in relief the losses of leaving the term *lesbian* behind—namely, the specificity of a label that clearly signifies women loving, and being sexually attracted to, women. *Queer*, Cauterucci argues, in a male-dominated culture, can easily default to men; and use of the term *queer* has not sidelined gay male culture as it has for women.

In the end, Cauterucci isn't able to—or strategically avoids—reaching a solid conclusion. As she explains, "Queer women have long committed themselves to never-ending cycles of self-examination and reorientation to radical politics," ever attentive to who is being left out. In fact, the process of examining and unsettling the labels that Cauterucci both argues for and enacts might well constitute a queer rhetorical act: one that calls for a reality that both recognizes the possibility of community and doesn't result in transgender, or any kind, of exclusion.

"For Many Young Queer Women, *Lesbian* Offers a Fraught Inheritance"

Slate, 2016

Some years ago, a close friend and I developed a not-so-subtle code for queer women too basic for our tastes: We'd make an "L" with our thumbs and forefingers against our foreheads, like the loser sign that was popular when we were in middle school. In this case, the "L" stood for *lesbian*.

We, too, were lesbians—generally speaking. But the women my friend and I mocked (and trust, I am duly shamed by this memory) were what we'd call "capital-L lesbians." We were urban-dwelling and queer-identified and in our 20s; the other women came from the suburbs, skewed older, and were, we presumed, unversed in queer politics. We traveled in circles of dapper butches and subversive femmes; the other women either easily passed as straight or dressed generically sporty in cargo shorts and flip-flips. A woman in this category was *clearly* down with the assimilationist, trans-exclusive politics of the likes of the Human Rights Campaign. She was the kind of dyke for whom the laughably niche *Cosmopolitan* lesbian-sex tip "tug on her ponytail" might actually apply.

In other words, we shared a common sexual orientation, but little, if any, cultural affiliation. In the space between "lesbian" and "queer," my friend and I located a world of difference in politics, gender presentation, and cosmopolitanism. Some of our resistance to the term *lesbian* arose, no doubt, from internalized homophobic notions of lesbians as unfashionable, uncultured homebodies. We were convinced that our cool clothes and enlightened, radical paradigm made us something other than lesbians, a label chosen by progenitors who lived in a simpler time with stricter gender boundaries. But with a time-honored label comes history and meaning; by leaving *lesbian* behind, we were rejecting, in part, a strong identity and legacy that we might have claimed as our own. While all identities are a product of their respective historical moments, starting from scratch is a daunting prospect. And so we're left in a gray area of nomenclature, searching for threads of unity in our pluralism, wondering what, if any, role *lesbian* can play in a future that's looking queerer by the day.

Cultural connotations aside, the main reason my friend and I felt (and still feel) more comfortable with *queer* than *lesbian* was practical: The word *lesbian*, insofar as it means a woman who is primarily attracted to women, does not correctly describe our reality. My personal queer community comprises cisgender and transgender women; transgender men and transmasculine people; and people who identify as non-binary or genderqueer. One friend told me *queer* works better for her and her female spouse because *lesbian* implies a kind of sameness she doesn't see in her relationship or those of her peers. In her circles, as in mine, most romantic partnerships lean butch-femme or involve at least one trans or genderqueer person. Many of us have had or are currently enmeshed in sexual or romantic relationships with people who aren't women. Using *lesbian* to refer to my queer sphere (e.g., "She's hosting a lesbian potluck!") excludes many people I consider my peers. In most young, urban queer communities, at least, *lesbian*, in its implication of a cisgender woman to cisgender woman arrangement, is both inaccurate and gauche.

But then, it's hard to organize around a community without a name. I co-host monthly queer tea-dance parties in the warmer months, and my partners and I have struggled to promote our event to our desired audience. We called it a "ladies' tea dance" for the first few years; one of my fellow co-hosts was a well-known trans guy in the community, and we thought his leadership would be enough to make it clear that anyone with social connections to queer women would be welcome, too. When some transgender attendees told us that the "ladies" terminology felt exclusive, we agreed, and started using the word *queer* on its own. But in DC, as in most places, queer parties that get labeled without a gender often default to gay men, who crowd the rest of us off the dance floor. And while we'd never turn away cis gay men (one of our favorite guest DJs is one), I believe it's important to carve out spaces that explicitly focus on women, especially as lesbian bars and publications shutter en masse. Basically, we wanted to promote our party to women—plus all queer or trans people who aren't cisgender men.

Unfortunately, there's no word for that. So my peers and I have found ourselves using the phrase *not cis men* to describe the makeup of our friend groups, political identity groups, and the people we want to come to our dance parties. It's functional, but a bit hollow: There's a feeling of being uprooted from time, place, and meaning that comes with defining ourselves by what we are not. *Lesbian* has a rich political and social history; *not cis men* establishes our identities quite literally on someone else's terms. It gives cis men power and presence, assets they already disproportionately control, in conversations that have nothing to do with them. And it reaffirms cis male identity as the norm from which all others deviate. *Not cis men* is the *nonwhite people* to *people of color.*

That said, nonspecificity is part of the appeal. *Not cis men* and *queer* are broad enough to include not only transgender and genderqueer people (and those who date them) but bi- and pansexual women who are often sidelined in lesbian society. Still, an increasing number of young people who are more or less straight are identifying as queer as a statement of political world view rather than sexual orientation. *Lesbian* leaves no doubt that a woman's sexual and romantic affinities run toward other women. In a world that preferences heterosexual pairings, lesbians face a very different reality than queers-in-name-only, giving the term the power of a blunt, plainspoken, unapologetic declaration. *Sex and the City,* funnily enough, neatly captured this debate way back in 1999. In one episode, a few art-world lesbians reject Charlotte's attempts to insert herself into their cabal, telling her, "If you're not going to eat pussy, you're not a dyke."

That seductively simple definition of *dyke* or *lesbian* would never fly in most circles of queer women today, attuned as we are to multiplicities of gender and genitals. But the male variation—"if you're not going to suck cock, you're not a faggot"—is less likely to raise hackles in the average clique of gay men. Where spaces that cater to lesbians and queer women are very likely to accommodate transgender and nonbinary people, too, social gatherings of gay men are typically far less diverse, gender-wise. And our femininity-devaluing society leaves far more room for women than men to claim a fluid sexual orientation, meaning queer women are more likely to have current or former partners who aren't women. That's why it's both easy and usually accurate to label circles of gay men as "gay men"—and why gay men are relatively free from the perpetual infighting over labels and politics that seems common among segments of queer women.

Of course, gay men are no more monolithic than queer women are. But generalizations are often instructive, especially when they ring true. Communities of queer women have long committed themselves to never-ending cycles of self-examination and reorientation to radical politics, prioritizing inclusion and calling each other out, for better or for worse, when an assumption of shared experience leaves someone out. Communities of gay men, on the other hand, have largely hewed to a coherent, unifying cultural through-line. They have rich lexicon of campy icons and references; new bars popping up like crabgrass in DC; quite a few contemporary films and TV shows just or mostly about them; a vibrant party culture that's survived decades of gentrification and a deadly public health crisis; and enough hookup apps to cover desired mates from twink to daddy. Queer women have an atrophying network of physical and digital spaces; a largely unrecorded history most of us know very little about; precious few authentic pop culture representations; and no hookup apps with a critical mass of users. If there's a "lesbian" culture today, what is it? In 10 years, will it still be around? Can we still claim even a modicum of connection to the history of our forebears if we look back at them with chagrin or consider ourselves a different species altogether?

Without a label that's at once inclusive, accurate, and specific, it's hard to imagine how *not cis men* might ever create the kind of tangible, identifiable touchstones that make gay male culture so rich and durable. (Granted, that durability is one upshot of a culture that doesn't engage as readily with more inclusive notions of gender and sexuality.) Losing *lesbian* means losing a well-defined commonality around which to socialize and mobilize. Perhaps that commonality was never as common as it seemed; at any rate, it's clear that *lesbian* doesn't properly explain our collective identity any more. But as queer women and our comrades mourn the losses of lesbian bars and media outlets the nation over, it's worth wondering how we might expect a dance party or magazine to cater to us when our identities and politics appear to prevent us from sharing a name.

There's something very queer about rejecting all labels and insisting on making home in the gaps between. As a practical matter, though, it is no easy feat to organize or serve a community that's defined by its fragmentation. Well-intentioned attempts at inclusive language should be applauded, though many will inevitably fall short; and we are not vampires who must be explicitly invited by name to cross the threshold of a nightclub. If lesbians and queer women can acknowledge that our collective identity defies conventional labels, we must accept that, until we come up with a new vocabulary to describe our world, no one label will ever feel quite right. The lightning-fast evolution of queer terminology shows no signs of slowing, and no amount of internecine bickering will ever result in a name that pleases everyone. Instead, the endless calling-out of inadequate verbiage that counts as queer discourse these days threatens to undermine any hope of preserving the good stuff, the connective tissue of lesbian culture that doesn't depend on transgender exclusion.

Maybe, instead of depending so hard on labels to give us identity and meaning, queer-not-cis-men should focus our energies on bringing our own identities and meanings to what spaces we have left, whether they invite us by our preferred terms or something adjacent. Queer people have generations of experience reclaiming words and cultural traditions that weren't explicitly meant for us. The tea dance is a brilliant example of our capacity for reinvention and asserting belonging from within. If queers can transform a formal social gathering for biscuit-nibbling heterosexuals into a mainstay of the gay party circuit, imagine what we could do with *lesbian*.

FOR FURTHER READING

Butler, Judith. *Gender Trouble*. Routledge, 2006.

Iovannone, Jeffry J. "A Brief History of the LGBTQ Initialism." *Medium*, 9 June 2018, https://medium.com/queer-history-for-the-people/a-brief-history-of-the-lgbtq-initialism-e89db1cf06e3.

Steinmetz, Katy. "Why 'LGBTQ' Will Replace 'LGBT.'" *Time*, 26 Oct. 2016, time.com/4544704/why-lgbtq-will-replace-lgbt/.

Warner, Michael. *The Trouble with Normal: Sex, Politics, and the Ethics of Queer Life*. Harvard UP, 2003.

Johanna Hedva

"What is so destructive about conceiving of wellness as the default, as the standard mode of existence, is that it invents illness as temporary. When being sick is an abhorrence to the norm, it allows us to conceive of care and support in the same way," explains Johanna Hedva in the following piece. Hedva is described on their website biography as a Korean American "writer, artist, musician, and performer . . . raised in Los Angeles by a family of witches." They have published in myriad venues, including *Triple Canopy, Black Warrior Review, Mask Magazine, Asian American Literary Review*, and GenderFail. Hedva's art has been shown at Performance Space New York, the Getty's 2013 Pacific Standard Time, the Los Angeles Architecture and Design Museum, and the Museum of Contemporary Art on the Moon, among other venues.

"Sick Woman Theory" has been translated into multiple languages, indicating the resonance of the piece. Deftly weaving narrative and theory through a voice both sharp and soulful, Hedva depicts chronic illness through lenses of race, class, neoliberalism, labor, politics, and social justice. While the ambition of so many ideas collected in one space can feel overwhelming—rhetorically mirroring chronic illness—readers are included through compelling use of narrative. Hedva openly bares their personal experience with chronic illness as a way to honor the sicknesses that have come to them: endometriosis, bipolar disorder, PTSD, depersonalization/derealization disorder, and autoimmune disease. In this rendering, they link individual struggles to social and cultural regimes of oppression. For example, Hedva underscores how individuals are treated differently by the medical industry depending on gender, race, and socioeconomic status. They also invoke frustration at being unable to participate in Black Lives Matter protests due to health restrictions, teaching readers that being *able*, a term Hedva use expansively, to protest in the normative sense of marching in the streets is, in fact, a privilege.

Hedva's troubling of stable notions of gender adds further complexity to the piece. Though Hedva identifies as gender nonbinary, they explain that the title "Sick Woman Theory" uses the term *woman* as a deliberate rhetorical choice. Though the term can exclude, they reclaim it for their gender-fluid friend, for whom it mattered greatly to call herself a woman. For Hedva, *woman* is also meant to signify anyone outside of normative identity or pushed to society's margins. In a rhythmic pattern with both aural and visual impact, they repeat, "The Sick Woman is ..." naming those often forgotten or disregarded. This repetition underscores the myriad people unseen and uncared for within a capitalist economy that establishes illness as only temporary. Sick Woman Theory reveals how gender and disability are co-constructed: to be sick or disabled or to require care is to be feminized, rendered weak, needy, fragile, and devalued by society.

Conversely, since care is associated with the feminine, a politics of care, which is a politics undervalued in patriarchal culture, is foregrounded in Hedva's essay. Care for the self and other is a radical form of protest; Hedva argues it nurtures community, supports interdependency over independence, and challenges capitalism (see Sara Ahmed's contribution to this volume). In a demonstration of care and support for others, Hedva closes the piece with recommended texts that highlight the writing of women, queer people, trans subjects, disabled writers, and authors of color. As Sara Ahmed argues, the traditional politics of citation, or who gets named or credited for their ideas, is a "screening technique," a practice that establishes traditional (white, male, cis-) scholars as the nexus and other sources as orbiting additives. By centering those usually marginalized, both in this reading list and throughout their piece, Hedva teaches us how to see each other, to stretch our empathy, and to build a radical kinship.

"Sick Woman Theory"

A version of this essay was originally published by *Mask Magazine* in January 2016, edited by Hanna Hurr and Isabelle Natasia, 2017

1.

In late 2014, I was sick with a chronic condition that, about every 12 to 18 months, gets bad enough to render me, for about five months each time, unable to walk, drive, do my job, sometimes speak or understand language, take a bath without assistance, and leave the bed. This particular flare coincided with the Black Lives Matter protests, which I would have attended unremittingly, had I been able to. I live one block away from MacArthur Park in Los Angeles, a predominantly Latino neighborhood and one colloquially understood to be the place where many immigrants begin their American lives. The park, then, is not surprisingly one of the most active places of protest in the city.

I listened to the sounds of the marches as they drifted up to my window. Attached to the bed, I rose up my sick woman fist, in solidarity.

I started to think about what modes of protest are afforded to sick people—
it seemed to me that many for whom Black Lives Matter is especially in service,
might not be able to be present for the marches because they were imprisoned by.
a job, the threat of being fired from their job if they marched, or literal incarceration, and of course the threat of violence and police brutality—but also because
of illness or disability, or because they were caring for someone with an illness or
disability.

I thought of all the other invisible bodies, with their fists up, tucked away and
out of sight.

If we take Hannah Arendt's definition of the political—which is still one of the
most dominant in mainstream discourse—as being any action that is performed
in public, we must contend with the implications of what that excludes. If being
present in public is what is required to be political, then whole swathes of the population can be deemed *a*-political—simply because they are not physically able to
get their bodies into the street.

In my graduate program, Arendt was a kind of god, and so I was trained to
think that her definition of the political was radically liberating. Of course, I can
see that it was, in its own way, in its time (the late 1950s): in one fell swoop she
got rid of the need for infrastructures of law, the democratic process of voting, the
reliance on individuals who've accumulated the power to affect policy—she got
rid of the need for policy at all. All of these had been required for an action to be
considered political and visible as such. No, Arendt said, just get your body into the
street, and bam: political.

There are two failures here, though. The first is her reliance on a "public"—
which requires a private, a binary between visible and invisible space. This meant
that whatever takes place in private is not political. So, you can beat your wife in
private and it doesn't matter, for instance. You can send private emails containing
racial slurs, but since they weren't "meant for the public," you are somehow not racist. Arendt was worried that if everything can be considered political, then nothing
will be, which is why she divided the space into one that is political and one that is
not. But for the sake of this anxiety, she chose to sacrifice whole groups of people,
to continue to banish them to invisibility and political irrelevance. She chose to
keep them out of the public sphere. I'm not the first to take Arendt to task for this.
The failure of Arendt's political was immediately exposed in the civil rights activism and feminism of the 1960s and '70s. "The personal is political" can also be read
as saying "the private is political." Because of course, everything you do in private
is political: who you have sex with, how long your showers are, if you have access to
clean water for a shower at all, and so on.

There is another problem too. As Judith Butler put it in her 2015 lecture, "Vulnerability and Resistance," Arendt failed to account for who is allowed in to the public space, of who's in charge of the public. Or, more specifically, who's in charge of who gets in. Butler says that there is always one thing true about a public demonstration: the police are already there, or they are coming. This resonates with frightening force when considering the context of Black Lives Matter. The inevitability of violence at a demonstration—especially a demonstration that emerged to insist upon the importance of bodies who've been violently *un*-cared for—ensures that a certain amount of people won't, because they can't, show up. Couple this with physical and mental illnesses and disabilities that keep people in bed and at home, and we must contend with the fact that many whom these protests are for, are not able to participate in them—which means they are not able to be visible as political activists.

There was a Tumblr post that came across my dash during these weeks of protest, that said something to the effect of: "Shout out to all the disabled people, sick people, people with PTSD, anxiety, etc., who can't protest in the streets with us tonight. Your voices are heard and valued, and with us." Heart. Reblog.

2.

I have chronic illness. For those who don't know what chronic illness means, let me help: the word "chronic" comes from the Greek "khronos," Latinized to "chronos," which means "of time" (think of "chronology"), and it specifically means "a lifetime." So, a chronic illness is an illness that lasts a lifetime. In other words, it does not get better. There is no cure.

And think about the weight of time: yes, that means you feel it every day. On very rare occasions, I get caught in a moment, as if something's plucked me out of the world, where I realize that I haven't thought about my illnesses for a few minutes, maybe a few precious hours. These blissful moments of oblivion are the closest thing to a miracle that I know. When you have chronic illness, life is reduced to a relentless rationing of energy. It costs you to do anything: to get out of bed, to cook for yourself, to get dressed, to answer an email. For those without chronic illness, you can spend and spend without consequence: the cost is not a problem. For those of us with limited funds, we have to ration, we have a limited supply: we often run out before lunch.

I've come to think about chronic illness in other ways.

Ann Cvetkovich writes: "What if depression, in the Americas, at least, could be traced to histories of colonialism, genocide, slavery, legal exclusion, and everyday segregation and isolation that haunt all of our lives, rather than to be biochemical imbalances?" I'd like to change the word "depression" here to be all mental illnesses. Cvetkovich continues: "Most medical literature tends to presume a white and middle-class subject for whom feeling bad is frequently a mystery because it doesn't fit a life in which privilege and comfort make things seem fine on the surface." In other words, wellness as it is talked about in America today, is a white and wealthy idea.

Let me quote Starhawk, in the preface to the new edition of her 1982 book *Dreaming the Dark*: "Psychologists have constructed a myth—that somewhere there exists some state of health which is the norm, meaning that most people presumably are in that state, and those who are anxious, depressed, neurotic, distressed, or generally unhappy are deviant." I'd here supplant the word "psychologists" with "white supremacy," "doctors," "your boss," "neoliberalism," "heteronormativity," and "America."

There has been a slew of writing in recent years about how "female" pain is treated—or rather, not treated as seriously as men's in emergency rooms and clinics, by doctors, specialists, insurance companies, families, husbands, friends, the culture at large. In a recent article in the *Atlantic*, called "How Doctors Take Women's Pain Less Seriously," a husband writes about the experience of his wife Rachel's long wait in the ER before receiving the medical attention her condition warranted (which was an ovarian torsion, where an ovarian cyst grows so large it falls, twisting the fallopian tube). "Nationwide, men wait an average of 49 minutes before receiving an analgesic for acute abdominal pain. Women wait an average of 65 minutes for the same thing. Rachel waited somewhere between 90 minutes and two hours," he writes. At the end of the ordeal, Rachel had waited nearly fifteen hours before going into the surgery she should have received upon arrival. The article concludes with her physical scars healing, but that "she's still grappling with the psychic toll—what she calls 'the trauma of not being seen.'"

What the article does not mention is race—which leads me to believe that the writer and his wife are white. Whiteness is what allows for such oblivious neutrality: it is the premise of blankness, the presumption of the universal. (Studies have shown that white people will listen to other white people when talking about race, far more openly than they will to a person of color. As someone who is white-passing, let me address white people directly: look at my white face and listen up.)

The trauma of not being seen. Again—who is allowed in to the public sphere? Who is allowed to be visible? I don't mean to diminish Rachel's horrible experience—I myself once had to wait ten hours in an ER to be diagnosed with a burst ovarian cyst—I only wish to point out the presumptions upon which her horror relies: that our vulnerability should be seen and honored, and that we should all receive care, quickly and in a way that "respects the autonomy of the patient," as the Four Principles of Biomedical Ethics puts it. Of course, these presumptions are what we all should have. But we must ask the question of who is allowed to have them. In whom does society substantiate such beliefs? And in whom does society enforce the opposite?

Compare Rachel's experience at the hands of the medical establishment with that of Kam Brock's. In September 2014, Brock, a 32-year-old black woman, born in Jamaica and living in New York City, was driving a BMW when she was pulled over by the police. They accused her of driving under the influence of marijuana, and though her behavior and their search of her car yielded nothing to support this, they nevertheless impounded her car. According to a lawsuit brought against the City of New York and Harlem Hospital by Brock, when Brock appeared the next day to retrieve her car she was arrested by the police for behaving in a way that she calls "emotional," and involuntarily hospitalized in the Harlem Hospital psych ward. (As someone who has also been involuntarily hospitalized for behaving "too" emotionally, this story feels like a rip of recognition through my brain.) The doctors thought she was "delusional" and suffering from bipolar disorder, because she claimed that Obama followed her on Twitter—which was true, but which the medical staff failed to confirm. She was then held for eight days, forcibly injected with sedatives, made to ingest psychiatric medication, attend group therapy, and stripped. The medical records of the hospital—obtained by her lawyers—bear this out: the "master treatment plan" for Brock's stay reads, "Objective: Patient will verbalize the importance of education for employment and will state that Obama is not following her on Twitter." It notes her "inability to test reality." Upon her release, she was given a bill for $13,637.10.

The question of why the hospital's doctors thought Brock "delusional" because of her Obama-follow claim is easily answered: Because, according to this society, a young black woman can't possibly be that important—and for her to insist that she is must mean she's "sick."

So, as I lay there, unable to march, hold up a sign, shout a slogan that would be heard, or be visible in any traditional capacity as a political being, the central question of Sick Woman Theory formed: How do you throw a brick through the window of a bank if you can't get out of bed?

3.

Before I can speak of the "sick woman" in all of her many guises, I must first speak as an individual, and address you from my particular location.

I am antagonistic to the notion that the Western medical-insurance industrial complex understands me in my entirety, though they seem to think they do. They have attached many words to me over the years, and though some of these have provided articulation that was useful—after all, no matter how much we are working to change the world, we must still find ways of coping with the reality at hand— first I want to suggest some other ways of understanding my "illness."

Perhaps it can all be explained by the fact that my moon's in Cancer in the 8th House, the House of Death, or that my Mars, Saturn, and Pluto—in astrology, the three "malefics," or evil forces—are in the 12th House, the House of Illness, Secrets, Sorrow, and Self-Undoing. Or, that my father's mother escaped from North Korea in her childhood and hid this fact from the family until a few years ago, when she accidentally let it slip out, and then swiftly, revealingly, denied it. Or, that my mother suffers from undiagnosed mental illness that was actively denied by her family, and was then exasperated by a 40-year-long drug and alcohol addiction, sexual trauma, and hepatitis from a dirty needle, and to this day remains untreated, as she makes her way in and out of jails, squats, and homelessness. Or, that I was physically and emotionally abused as a child, raised in an environment of poverty, addiction, and violence, and have been estranged from my parents for 14 years. Perhaps it's because I'm poor—according to the IRS, in 2014, my adjusted gross income was $5,730 (a result of not being well enough to work full-time)—which means that my health insurance is provided by the state of California (Medi-Cal), that my "primary care doctor" is a group of physician's assistants and nurses in a clinic on the second floor of a strip mall, and that I rely on food stamps to eat. Perhaps it's because I'm queer and gender nonbinary, first coming out to my parents at age 14; finally leaving home at age 16 with the last black eye I was willing to receive from my mother's hand. Perhaps it can be encapsulated in the word "trauma." Perhaps I've just got thin skin, and have had some bad luck.

It's important that I also share the Western medical terminology that's been attached to me—whether I like it or not, it can provide a common vocabulary: "This is the oppressor's language," Adrienne Rich wrote in 1971, "yet I need it to talk to you." But let me offer another language, too. In the Native American Cree language, the possessive noun and verb of a sentence are structured differently than in English. In Cree, one does not say, "I am sick." Instead, one says, "The sickness has come to me." I love that and want to honor it.

So, here is what has come to me:

Endometriosis, which is a disease of the uterus where the uterine lining grows where it shouldn't—in the pelvic area mostly, but also anywhere, the legs, abdomen, even the head. It causes chronic pain; gastrointestinal chaos; epic, monstrous bleeding; in some cases, cancer; and means that I have miscarried, can't have children, and have several surgeries to look forward to. When I explained the disease to a friend who didn't know about it, she exclaimed: "So your whole body is a uterus!" That's one way of looking at it, yes. (Imagine what the ancient Greek doctors—the fathers of the theory of the "wandering womb"—would say about that.) It means that every month, those rogue uterine cells that have implant-ed themselves throughout my body, "obey their nature and bleed," to quote fellow endo warrior Hilary Mantel. This causes cysts, which eventually burst, leaving be-hind bundles of dead tissue like the debris of little bombs.

Bipolar disorder, complex PTSD, panic disorder, and depersonalization/dereal-ization disorder have also come to me. This can mean that I live between this world and another one, one created by my own brain that has ceased to be contained by a discrete concept of "self." Because of these "disorders," I have access to incredi-bly vivid emotions, flights of thought, and dreamscapes, to the feeling that my mind has been obliterated into stars, to the sensation that I have become nothingness, as well as to intense ecstasies, raptures, sorrows, and nightmarish hallucinations. I have been hospitalized, voluntarily and involuntarily, because of it, and one of the medi-cations I was prescribed once nearly killed me—it produces a rare side effect where one's skin falls off. Another cost $800 a month—I only took it because my doctor slipped me free samples. If I want to be able to hold a job—which this world has decided I ought to be able to do—I must take an antipsychotic medication daily that causes short-term memory loss and drooling, among other sexy side effects. These visitors have also brought their friends: nervous breakdowns, mental collapses, or whatever you want to call them, three times in my life. I'm certain they will be guests in my house again. They have motivated attempts at suicide (most of them while dis-sociated) more than a dozen times, the first one when I was nine years old.

Finally, an autoimmune disease (or several?) that continues to baffle all the doctors I've seen, has come to me and refuses still to be named. On the same day this essay was originally published in *Mask Magazine*, a neurologist diagnosed me with "100% fibromyalgia," as a "place to start." More than one year before this, my "primary care" doctor had referred me to see a neurologist, rheumatologist, and immunologist, so I could begin testing for MS and other autoimmune diseases that some of my symptoms pointed to. My insurance has yet to approve these referrals, or to find a specialist within 150 miles who is covered by my plan; the neurologist who diagnosed my fibro agreed to see me out-of-network, cash-only, as a favor to a friend. I don't have enough space here—will I ever?—to describe what living with an autoimmune disease is like. I can say it brings unimaginable fatigue, pain all over all the time, susceptibility to illnesses, a body that performs its "normal" functions monstrously abnormally or not at all.

4.

With all of these visitors, I started writing Sick Woman Theory as a way to survive in a reality that I find unbearable, and as a way to bear witness to a self that does not feel like it can possibly be "mine."

The early instigation for the project of a "Sick Woman Theory," and how it in-herited its name, came from a few sources. The primary one was a way to think how illness, disability, and vulnerability *feminize*—e.g., render "weaker" and "more fragile"—any person who requires care. One was in response to Audrey Wollen's "Sad Girl Theory," which proposes a way of redefining historically feminized pa-thologies into modes of political protest for girls: Critical of Sad Girl Theory's centering of whiteness, beauty, heteronormativity, and middle-class resources, I started to think through the question of what happens to the sad girl who is poor, queer, and/or not white, when, *if*, she grows up. Another was incited by reading Kate Zambreno's *Heroines*, and feeling an itch to fuck with the concept of "hero-ism" at all, and so I wanted to propose a figure with traditionally antiheroic quali-ties—namely, illness, idleness, and inaction—as capable of being the symbol of a grand theory. One of the most resounding influences was from the 1973 feminist book *Complaints and Disorders*, which differentiates between the "sick woman" of the white upper class, and the "sickening women" of the nonwhite working class. And if Sick Woman Theory has a guardian godmother, it would be Audre Lorde.

Sick Woman Theory is for those who are faced with their vulnerability and un-bearable fragility, every day, and so have to fight for their experience to be not only honored, but first made visible. For those who, in Audre Lorde's words, were never meant to survive: because this world was built against their survival. It's for my fellow spoonies, my fellow sick and crip crew. You know who you are, even if you've not been attached to a diagnosis: one of the aims of Sick Woman Theory is to resist the notion that one needs to be legitimated by an institution, so that they can try to fix you according to their terms. You don't need to be fixed, my queens—it's the world that needs the fixing.

I offer this as a call to arms and a testimony of recognition. I hope that my thoughts can provide articulation and resonance, as well as tools of survival and resilience.

And for those of you who are not chronically ill or disabled, Sick Woman Theo-ry asks you to stretch your empathy this way. To face us, to listen, to see.

5.

Sick Woman Theory is an insistence that most modes of political protest are inter-nalized, lived, embodied, suffering, and no doubt invisible. Sick Woman Theory redefines existence in a body as something that is primarily and always vulnerable, following from Judith Butler's recent work on precarity and resistance. Because Butler's premise insists that a body is defined by its vulnerability, not temporarily affected by it, the implication is that it is continuously reliant on infrastructures of support in order to endure, and so we need to reshape the world around this fact.

Sick Woman Theory maintains that the body and mind are sensitive and reactive to regimes of oppression—particularly our current regime of neoliberal, white supremacist, imperial-capitalist, cis-hetero patriarchy. It is that all of our bodies and minds carry the historical trauma of this, that it is the world itself that is making and keeping us sick.

To take the term "woman" as the subject position of this work is a strategic, all-encompassing embrace and dedication to the particular, rather than the universal. Though the identity of "woman" has erased and excluded many (especially women of color and trans/nonbinary/genderfluid people), I choose to use it because it still represents the uncared-for, the secondary, the oppressed, the non, the un, the less than. The problematics of this term will always require critique, and I hope that Sick Woman Theory can help undo those in its own way. But more than anything, I'm inspired to use the word "woman" because I saw this year how it can still be radical to be a woman in the 21st century. I use it to honor a dear friend of mine who came out as genderfluid last year. For her, what mattered the most was to be able to call herself a "woman," to use the pronouns "she/her." She didn't want surgery or hormones; she loved her body and her big dick and didn't want to change it—she only wanted the word. That the word itself can be an empowerment is the spirit in which Sick Woman Theory is named.

The Sick Woman is an identity and body that can belong to anyone denied the privileged existence—or the cruelly optimistic promise of such an existence—of the white, straight, healthy, neurotypical, upper- and middle-class, cis- and able-bodied man who makes his home in a wealthy country, has never not had health insurance, and whose importance to society is everywhere recognized and made explicit by that society; whose importance and care dominates that society, at the expense of everyone else.

The Sick Woman is anyone who does not have this guarantee of care.

The Sick Woman is told that, to this society, her care, even her survival, does not matter.

The Sick Woman is all of the "dysfunctional," "dangerous," and "in danger," "badly behaved," "crazy," "incurable," "traumatized," "disordered," "diseased," "chronic," "uninsurable," "wretched," "undesirable," and altogether "dysfunctional" bodies belonging to women, people of color, poor, ill, neuro-atypical, differently abled, queer, trans, and genderfluid people, who have been historically pathologized, hospitalized, institutionalized, brutalized, rendered "unmanageable," and therefore made culturally illegitimate and politically invisible.

The Sick Woman is a black trans woman having panic attacks while using a public restroom, in fear of the violence awaiting her.

The Sick Woman is the child of parents whose Indigenous histories have been erased, who suffers from the trauma of generations of colonization and violence.

The Sick Woman is a homeless person, especially one with any kind of disease and no access to treatment, and whose only access to mental health care is a 72-hour hold in the county hospital.

The Sick Woman is a mentally ill black woman whose family called the police for help because she was suffering an episode, and who was murdered in police custody, and whose story was denied by everyone operating under white supremacy. Her name is Tanesha Anderson.

The Sick Woman is a 50-year-old gay man who was raped as a teenager and has remained silent and shamed, believing that men can't be raped.

The Sick Woman is a disabled person who couldn't go to the lecture on disability rights because it was held in a venue without accessibility.

The Sick Woman is a white woman with chronic illness rooted in sexual trauma who must take painkillers in order to get out of bed.

The Sick Woman is a straight man with depression who's been medicated (managed) since early adolescence and now struggles to work the 60 hours per week that his job demands.

The Sick Woman is someone diagnosed with a chronic illness, whose family and friends continually tell them they should exercise more.

The Sick Woman is a queer woman of color whose activism, intellect, rage, and depression are seen by white society as unlikeable attributes of her personality.

The Sick Woman is a black man killed in police custody, and officially said to have severed his own spine. His name is Freddie Gray.

The Sick Woman is a veteran suffering from PTSD on the months-long waiting list to see a doctor at the VA.

The Sick Woman is a single mother, illegally emigrated to the "land of the free," shuffling between three jobs in order to feed her family, and finding it harder and harder to breathe.

The Sick Woman is the refugee.

The Sick Woman is the abused child.

The Sick Woman is the person with autism whom the world is trying to "cure."

The Sick Woman is the starving.

The Sick Woman is the dying.

And, crucially: The Sick Woman is who capitalism needs to perpetuate itself. Why?

Because to stay alive, capitalism cannot be responsible for our care—its logic of exploitation requires that some of us die.

"Sickness" as we speak of it today is a capitalist construct, as is its perceived binary opposite, "wellness." The "well" person is the person well enough to go to work. The "sick" person is the one who can't. What is so destructive about conceiving of wellness as the default, as the standard mode of existence, is that it *invents illness as temporary.* When being sick is an abhorrence to the norm, *it allows us to conceive of care and support in the same way.*

Care, in this configuration, is only required sometimes. When sickness is temporary, care is not normal.

Here's an exercise: go to the mirror, look yourself in the face, and say out loud: "To take care of you is not normal. I can only do it temporarily."

Saying this to yourself will merely be an echo of what the world repeats all the time.

6.

I used to think that the most anti-capitalist gestures left had to do with love, particularly love poetry: to write a love poem and give it to the one you desired, seemed to me a radical resistance. But now I see I was wrong.

The most anti-capitalist protest is to care for another and to care for yourself. To take on the historically feminized and therefore invisible practice of nursing, nurturing, caring. To take seriously each other's vulnerability and fragility and precarity, and to support it, honor it, empower it. To protect each other, to enact and practice community. A radical kinship, an interdependent sociality, a politics of care.

Because, once we are all ill and confined to the bed, sharing our stories of therapies and comforts, forming support groups, bearing witness to each other's tales of trauma, prioritizing the care and love of our sick, pained, expensive, sensitive, fantastic bodies, and there is no one left to go to work, perhaps then, finally, capitalism will screech to its much-needed, long-overdue, and motherfucking glorious halt.

An earlier version of the essay was first published in *Mask Magazine* in January 2016, edited by Hanna Hurr and Isabelle Natasia. This text is adapted from the lecture, "My Body Is a Prison of Pain so I Want to Leave It like a Mystic but I Also Love It & Want It to Matter Politically," delivered at Human Resources, sponsored by the Women's Center for Creative Work, October 7, 2015, Los Angeles, California.

Recommended Texts

Arendt, Hannah. *The Human Condition.* Chicago: University of Chicago Press, 1958.

Berkowitz, Amy. *Tender Points.* Oakland, CA: Timeless, Infinite Light, 2015.

Berlant, Lauren Gail. *Cruel Optimism.* Durham, NC: Duke University Press, 2011.

Brown, Stephen Rex. "Woman Held in Psych Ward over Obama Twitter Claim." *NY Daily News,* March 23, 2015.

Butler, Judith. "Vulnerability and Resistance." REDCAT, December 19, 2014.

Cvetkovich, Ann. *Depression: A Public Feeling.* Durham, NC: Duke University Press, 2012.

Ehrenreich, Barbara, and Deirdre English. *Complaints and Disorders; the Sexual Politics of Sickness.* Old Westbury, NY: Feminist Press, 1973.

Fassler, Joe. "How Doctors Take Women's Pain Less Seriously." *Atlantic,* October 15, 2015.

Federici, Silvia. *Caliban and the Witch: Women, the Body and Primitive Accumulation.* New York: Autonomedia, 2003.

Halberstam, Jack. "Zombie Humanism at the End of the World." Lecture, Weak Resistance: Everyday Struggles and the Politics of Failure, ICI Berlin, May 27, 2015.

Harney, Stefano, and Fred Moten. *The Undercommons: Fugitive Planning & Black Study.* New York: Minor Compositions, 2013.

Hedva, Johanna. "My Body Is a Prison of Pain so I Want to Leave It like a Mystic but I Also Love It & Want It to Matter Politically." Lecture, Human Resources, Los Angeles, October 7, 2015.

Kafer, Alison. *Feminist, Queer, Crip.* Bloomington: Indiana University Press, 2013.

Lazard, Carolyn. "How to Be a Person in the Age of Autoimmunity." *Cluster Mag,* January 16, 2013.

Lorde, Audre. *A Burst of Light: Essays.* Ithaca, NY: Firebrand Books, 1988.

Lorde, Audre. *The Cancer Journals.* Special ed. San Francisco: Aunt Lute Books, 1997.

Mantel, Hilary. "Every Part of My Body Hurt." *Guardian,* June 7, 2004.

Mingus, Mia. *Leaving Evidence.* http://leavingevidence.wordpress.com/

Miserandino, Christine. "The Spoon Theory Written by Christine Miserandino." *But You Don't Look Sick: Support for Those with Invisible Illness or Chronic Illness,* April 25, 2013.

Rich, Adrienne. "The Burning of Paper Instead of Children." In Adrienne Rich's *Poetry and Prose: Poems, Prose, Reviews, and Criticism,* edited by Barbara Charlesworth Gelpi. New York: W. W. Norton, 1993.

Salek, Yasi. "Audrey Wollen on Sad Girl Theory." *CULTIST ZINE,* June 19, 2014.

Starhawk. *Dreaming the Dark: Magic, Sex, & Politics.* 2nd ed. Boston: Beacon Press, 1988.

Thurman, Judith. "A Loss for Words: Can a Dying Language Be Saved?" *New Yorker,* March 30, 2015.

Vankin, Jonathan. "Kam Brock: The Reason They Threw Her In A Mental Ward Was Crazy—What Happened Next Was Even Crazier." *Inquisitr News,* March 24, 2015.

Zambreno, Kate. *Heroines.* Semiotext(e) / Active Agents, 2012.

FOR FURTHER READING:

"About." *Johanna Hedva,* n.d., https://johannahedva.com/about.html.

Ahmed, Sara. "Making Feminist Points." *feminstkilljoys,* 9 Nov. 2013, https://feministkilljoys .com/2013/09/11/making-feminist-points/.

Permission Credits

Chimamanda Ngozi Adichie: Copyright © 2015 by Chimamanda Adichie, used by permission of the Wylie Agency, LLC.

Amy Alexander: original source, NPR Code Switch Project.

Sara Ahmed: "A Killjoy Survival Kit," in *Living a Feminist Life*, Sara Ahmed, pp. 235–49. Copyright © 2017 Duke University Press. All rights reserved. Republished by permission of the copyright holder. www.dukeupress.edu.

Jennifer Baumgardner: From *Abortion & Life*, published by Akashic Books, www .akashicbooks.com.

Christina Cauterucci: From *Slate*, December 20, 2016. Copyright © The Slate Group. All rights reserved. Used by permission and protected by the Copyright Laws of the United States. The printing, copying, redistribution, or retransmission of this content without express written permission is prohibited.

Mike Coppola/Women's March on Washington/Getty Images.

"We Must Not Forget Detained Migrant Children," Edwidge Danticat, the *New Yorker*, © Conde Nast.

Alicia Garza: First publication rights with the Feminist Wire.

Emma Gonzalez: "A Young Activist's Advice: Vote, Shave Your Head and Cry Whenever You Need To" adapted from "The Rally: February 17" by Emma Gonzalez; from *Glimmer Of Hope: How Tragedy Sparked A Movement* by the March for Our Lives Founders. Copyright © 2018 by March for Our Lives Action Fund. Used by permission of Razorbill, an imprint of Penguin Young Readers Group, a division of Penguin Random House, LLC. All rights reserved.

Index

abortions, 145–50, 176; bans on, 45–47; illegal, 389–90; men and, 423, 429–31; rates of, 388, 391, 394; sharing stories of, 388–95
Adams, Gina, 219–20
Adichie, Chimamanda Ngozi, 134–40
affirmative action, 53–57
Affordable Care Act, 48–52
Afghanistan, 191, 194, 196
African Americans, police and, 19–20, 55–57, 85–88, 459
agency, 4, 123; assumed lack of, 119, 121; rape victim reclaiming, 235–49
agriculture, 363
Ahmadinejad, Mahmoud, 38, 41
Ahmed, Sara, 154–64
Ailes, Roger, 356–59
Alexander, Amy, 125–28
Ardalan, Parvin, 40–42
Arendt, Hannah, 456–57
Arnold, Andrew D., 305
Available Means (Ritchie and Ronald), 5

Bacchetta, Paola, 195–200
Baghdad Burning: Girl Blog from Iraq, 188–92
Bailey, Jennifer, 71–74
bathroom bills, 295–98, 404–8, 443, 445–46
Baumgardner, Jennifer, 388–95

Berkman, Brenda, 348–51
Beyoncé, 8, 134, 141–44
bin Laden, Osama, 194
birth control, men's responsibility for, 422–33
Black Futures Lab, 169
Black Lives Matter, 14, 54, 128, 165–66, 169–74, 455–57
Blair, Gabrielle, 422–33
Bland, Bob, 175
Bland, Sandra, 439–41
Blaque, Kat, 404–8
blogging, 188–92, 255, 276, 314, 325, 422–23, 434–37
bodies, women's, 462; disabilities and, 434–37; identity and, 375–77; seen as threat, 439–41; trauma inflicted on, 439–40
body image, 102, 409–10, 412, 434–37
Bolz-Weber, Nadia, 93–96
Bordo, Susan, 25–26
Boylorn, Robyn, 113–15
Brock, Kam, 459
Brous, Sharon, 80–84
Brown, Michael, 85–88, 170
Burke, Kenneth, 165
Burke, Tarana, 396–98
Bush, George W., 196; Hurricane Katrina and, 383, 387n8; response to policies of, 195–200

Campt, Tina, 195–200
cancer, 400–403
capitalism, and sickness, 463–65
care, politics of, 455, 463–65
Carlson, Gretchen, 356–59
Cartelli, Sara, 410
Castile, Philando, 85–87
Cauterucci, Christina, 448–52
Chen, Chris, 302
child care, *vs.* abortions, 145–50
child separation, 59–61, 202–6
Chin, Staceyann, 443–47
Christianity: House of All Sinners
    and Saints in, 93–96; transgender
    rights and, 295–98
civil disobedience, Newsome's,
    232–33
civility, demands for, 58–61
civil rights, 54–57, 180. *See also* hu-
    man rights
climate change: migration and, 324,
    361–64; skeptics of, 287–89
Clinton, Hillary, 23; Michelle Obama
    speaking for, 62–70; as presiden-
    tial nominee, 18, 25–36
Coes, Jemelleh, 260–63
collaboration, 26, 176–77
collectives, 15; feminist, 194–200;
    Muslim women's, 38–39; women
    working as, 141–42
colonialism/imperialism, 120–21, 123
Costolo, Dick, 105
counterpublics, 12
craftivism, 151–52, 219–20
Crenshaw, Kimberlé, 6, 107–12
criminal justice system, 178–79
Crunk Feminist Collective, 113–15
Cruset, Jennine Capó, 268–75
Cullors, Patrisse, 169–70
Cvetkovich, Ann, 457–58

Dakota Access Pipeline (DAPL),
    216–18, 219
Danticat, Edwidge, 202–6
Day of Action, March 4, 300
"Day Without Immigrants," 127
"Day Without Women," 126–27
DeGraffenreid, Emma, 110
de la Cruz, Cathy, 90
democracy, 213–15
Democratic National Convention,
    26–36
Democratic Republic of the Congo,
    399, 401–3
Dempsy, Grayson, 392–93
disability, 455; activism and, 176, 181,
    434–37
discrimination: against black women,
    12, 109–12; effects of, 136; medi-
    cal, 50–52; overlap of gender and
    race, 110; privilege and, 111–12;
    racial, 128, 385; sex, 443; against
    women, 38, 41–44, 131–32, 148,
    179–80, 333–34, 346
Doe, Emily (anonymous), 235–49
domestic workers, 324; abuse of,
    366–69; National Domestic
    Worker Alliance of, 369–73; rights
    for, 123, 169
Dopico, Ana María, 75–76
Downey, Shannon, 151–52
DREAM Act, 264–67
Duckworth, Tammy, 352–54

Earth Democracy, 208–15
Ebadi, Shirin, 3, 38–44
economy: Clinton's proposals for, 32–
    33; Earth Democracy *vs.*, 208–15;
    inequalities in, 301–2; women's
    advancements in, 331–32; in
    Women's March values, 179–80

education: of black girls, 258–63; college funding, 299–303; experience of immigrant students in, 264–75; experience of Islamic girls in, 307–13; as human right, 251, 258–59; impediments to, 251–52, 255; minorities in universities, 276–80, 303n6; sexual assaults on college campuses, 290–94; student activism, 299–303; Taliban's opposition to, 255, 257–58

El Salvador, abortion ban in, 45–47

employment, 323; lack of women in media, 340–45

Encinia, Brian, 439–41

Ensler, Eve, 399–403

environment, 181, 217. *See also* climate change

equal pay, 180

Equal Rights Amendment, 181

erasure: of Black queer women, 170, 172–73. *See also* recognition/misrecognition

essentialism: biological, 132–33; strategic, 301–2

experience, as evidence, 165–66

Faith Matters Network, 71–74

feminism, 8, 113–14, 145; books in, 155–56; crunk, 113; divisions within, 126–27, 141, 176; inclusive, 107–8, 130, 138; media depictions of, 443–47; recognition of, 285–86; rhetorical, 11; second-wave, 389; self-care in, 154–64; third-wave, 314, 388; transgender people and, 130–31; transnational, 9–10, 119–24; white, 116–18; women's pleasure from sex and, 315, 317, 319

Gamergate, 229–30

gaming culture, 227–30

Garza, Alicia, 169–74

Gay, Roxane, 134, 330

Gbowee, Leymah, 334

gender, 113, 417, 455; bathroom bills and, 404–8; challenging norms of, 129, 446; fluidity of, 443–47, 451, 454; sex *vs.*, 130–33

gender differences, 323, 331, 458; in abortions, 148; economic, 125–26, 331–33, 338n10; in media coverage, 340–47; in opinions on war and terrorism, 341–46; in STEM, 252, 283–85

gender dysmorphia, 295–98

gender identity, 132, 414–21, 454

gender injustice, 135–36, 330–33

gender justice, 178–79

gender relations: around violence against women, 222–26; Michelle Obama on, 65–66, 68; subjugation in, 95–96

gender roles, 95–96, 261

Ghitis, Frida, 26

Glenn, Cheryl, 11

globalization, 9; corporate, 209–11, 213

GMOs, 208

González, Emma, 75–79

Gray, Freddie, 71

guns, 35, 75–79

Haiti, 202–6

Harris-Perry V., 379–86

Hayhoe, Katharine, 287–89

health care, 30, 32, 48–52

Hedva, Johanna, 454–65

Heffernan, Virginia, 422

heteropatriarchy, 171, 174

Hitselberger, Karin, 434–37
homicide, of women, 47
hooks, bell, 141–44, 330–31
House of All Sinners and Saints, 93–96
Houska, Tara, 216–18
human rights, 174, 178, 179, 251, 257
humor, 16
Hurricane Katrina, 379–87

identification, 166, 287, 439
identity, 404, 454; bodies and, 375–77; forming, 271, 273, 275, 283; intersectionality and, 6–7; labels and, 443–47; in Sick Woman Theory, 448–52
identity politics, 110, 128
IKAR, 80–84
illness, 454–65
immigrants, 123; experience of, 264–75; trafficking and abuse of, 366, 369; undocumented, 264–67; in Women's March values, 175–76, 181
immigration policies, 59–61, 202–6, 361, 362
Inderpal, Grewal, 195–200
indigenous people, 180; broken treaties with, 219–20; fight against Dakota Access Pipeline, 216–18
individualism, 23
inspiration porn, 434–37
International Day of the Girl, 64
International Women's Day, 62
International Workers' Day, 361, 364
internet, 3, 99–101, 103–5
intersectionality, 16, 75, 376; in Black Lives Matter, 169, 172–73; Blaque's, 404–8; identity and,

6–7; importance of, 107–12, 128; labels and, 446–47; Women's March and, 125–28, 175
intersex people, 131–32
Iran, 38–41, 44; experience of girls in, 305–13
Iraq, 354; life under occupation, 188–92
ISIS, 34
Islam, 258; experience of girls in, 306–13
Israel, 34, 80

Jackson, Michelle Denise, 439–41

Kaplan, Caren, 195–200
Karmo, 368–69
Kasky, Cameron, 77
Keene, Adrienne, 276–80
Kessler, Suzanne, 417
Khorasani, Noushin Ahmadi, 38, 40–44
Koyama, Emi, 129–33

Lauer, Matt, 358
LeBlanc, Phyllis Montana-, 379–82, 384–85
Lee, Spike, 380
Leibovich, Mark, 25
Let Girls Learn Initiative, 62, 64
LGBTQIA movement: transgender rights, 295–98; trying for inclusiveness, 449–52
liberation, 122, 175, 177; race and, 172, 400
Lilly, 368
Lorde, Audre, 157, 162, 462
Lye, Colleen, 300
lynchings, 71–74

Madden, Caroline, 91
making, rhetorical, 6
Mann, Judy, 345–46
mansplaining, 89–92
March for Our Lives, 77
Marjorie Stoneman Douglas school, 75–79
Martin, Trayvon, 4, 169, 171
McKenna, Wendy, 417
McLerran, Jennifer, 219
McSpadden, Lezley, 85–88
media: coverage of Hurricane Katrina aftermath, 382, 387n8; coverage of women in, 323–24, 348; depictions of feminism in, 443–47
memoir, 10
#MeToo movement, 4, 356, 396
Mexico, climate change in, 363
middle class: economic pressure on, 299–300
Middle East, peace efforts in, 80–84
migration, causes of, 324, 361–64
Milano, Alyssa, 396
military, 122; women in, 352–54
Miller, Chanel, 235–49
miscarriages, 45–47
misogyny, 103; in gaming culture, 227–30; reports of experiences of, 222–26; Trump's, 24, 35, 64–65
Mitchell, Andrea, 343–44
Moallem, Minoo, 195–200
Mock, Janet, 141, 143
Mohanty, Chandra Talpade, 119
Moore, Darnell L., 170
motherhood, 48–49, 86–87, 145; choosing, 147, 391, 394–95; difficulties of, 147
Muslims, 195; experience of girls, 306–13; Trump's ban on, 206, 363–64

Nathan, Nancy, 344–45
National Domestic Worker Alliance (NDWA), 366, 369–73
national security, 34, 43–44
National Women's History Week, 116–18
Native Americans: broken treaties with, 219–20; as college students, 276–80; fight against Dakota Access Pipeline, 216–18; rights of, 208–9
Newfield, Christopher, 300
Newsome, Bree, 3, 232–33
nonviolence, 257

Obama, Barack, 25, 62, 68
Obama, Michelle, 62–70
occupation, US, of Iraq, 188–92
One Billion Rising, 399–400
One Million Signatures Campaign, 38, 40–43
Osinski, Keegan, 92

Palestine, 80
parenting, immigrants', 202–6
Parvin, Ahmadi Khorasni, 38, 40–44
patriarchy, 93–94, 255, 315
Pelosi, Nancy, 23–24, 48–52, 58–59
People's Climate March, 364
Persepolis (Satrapi), 305–13
podcasts, 98
polarization, Middle East, 81–83
police: brutality by, 128, 169, 178, 439–41; treatment of African Americans by, 19–20, 55–57, 85–88, 459

political, *vs.* the personal, 80–84, 456
politics, representations of women in,
     25–26
Poo, Ai-jen, 366–69
postfeminist era, 107
poverty, 323–29
Pozner, Jennifer, 340–47
pregnancy, men's responsibility for,
     422–33
privilege, 112, 176, 396; cis men as
     default and, 450–52; of masculini-
     ty, 414, 419–20
pro-life movement, 145–50, 392–93
protests: new and old methods of,
     166–67; sick people and, 455–59;
     suppression of, 39–40
public sphere, women's representation
     in, 24–25
Pulido, Eusia "Lola" Thomas, 367, 369

race, 113, 396. *See also* intersection-
     ality
race relations, 71–74
racial differences, 126, 148, 458; in
     criminal justice system, 178–79;
     Hurricane Katrina and, 379–87
racial justice, 169, 178
racism, 83; anti-Black, 87–88, 172–74;
     Clinton on, 32–35; women ac-
     cused of, 58–59
rapes: of Emily Doe, 235–49; men on,
     99–100
recognition/misrecognition, 379–86,
     387n14, 457–58, 463
religion, 23; climate change and,
     287–89. *See also* Christianity;
     Islam
reproductive rights, 45–47, 315–17,
     320, 392–93, 422–33; in Women's
     March values, 179, 184

resilience, 19–20
rhetoric, women's, 166, 314; definitions
     of, 3; embodied, 155, 166, 375;
     feminism *vs.*, 15, 18; protest, 189,
     219; public *vs.* private, 23
rhetorical feminism, 11
rhetorical sway, 14–16, 166–67
Ritchie, Joy, 5, 10
Rivera, Angy, 264–67
Riverbend, 188–92
Robinson, Peter, 301
Rodger, Elliot, 224
Ronald, Kate, 5, 10
Roy, Ananya, 299–303
Rubion-Johnson, Denise, 385–86

Samin, Suzanne, 227–30
sanctions, against Iraq, 191–92
Sandberg, Sheryl, 330–36
Sanders, Bernie, 25–26
Satrapi, Marjane, 305–13
#SayHerName movement, 439–40
school shootings, 75–79
Schumer, Chuck, 58–59
Schwartz, John, 287
science, faith *vs.*, 287–89
Seattle, Chief, 208–10
selfies, 434–37
September 11, 190–92; media coverage
     of, 341–42; responses to, 196, 342;
     women first responders to, 348–51
Serano, Julia, 414–21
sex: gender *vs.*, 130–33; responsibility
     in, 319–20; women's pleasure from,
     315–20
sex education, 252, 315–20, 390, 394
sexual assaults: bathroom bills and,
     404–5, 407–8; on college campus-
     es, 290–94; in educational institu-
     tions, 252; privilege and, 396

sexual harassment/misconduct: in educational institutions, 252; power and, 95; treatment of victims of, 357–59; Trump's, 24, 64–65; of undocumented women, 264; workplace, 324, 356–59

sexuality: exploitation, 122–23; liberation, 122

Shafi, Hana, 409, 411

shaming/stigma, 410; about abortion, 149, 388, 394–95; about sexual assault, 396–98; about sexual pleasure, 314–15; of African American women, 379–87; misrecognition and, 382, 384, 387n14

Shappley, Kimberly, 295–98

Shipler, David K., 325–26

Shiva, Vandana, 208–15

Shook, Theresa, 175

Sick Woman Theory, 459, 462–63

silencing, 3, 96; about sexual assault, 396–97; challenges to, 3, 19, 222–26; of women in gaming, 227–30

slavery, 366–69

social media, 184, 396, 409–10; effects of, 3, 5–6, 165, 167

Solnit, Rebecca, 89

Songoyele, KaDeja, 10

Sostaita, Barbara, 116–18

Sotomayor, Sonia, 53–57

Spivak, Gayatri, 299–300

Standing Rock protest, 216–18

Stanley, Jessamyn, 409–10, 412

state violence, 172–73. See also police, brutality of

STEM (Science, Technology, Engineering, and Math), 252, 281–86

Sterling, Alton, 85–87

storytelling, 399; flipping script of,

434, 436; importance of, 389, 392–93, 396–97

students, activism after school shootings, 75–79

Summers, Larry, 331

Supreme Court, Sotomayor on, 53–57

Swinarksi, Claire, 145–50

Syria, 363

Taliban, 194; opposition to education, 257–58; treatment of women, 255, 343–44

temporary protected status, 206

terrorism: opinions on, 341–46. See also war on terror, US

Terry, Jennifer, 195–200

testimony/testimonial agency, 11–13, 24, 439

Thurman, Erica, 141–44

#TimesUp movement, 356

Tirado, Linda, 325–29

Title IX protections, 290, 293–94

Tizon, Alex, 366–67

Tometi, Opal, 169–70

trafficking and abuse, of domestic workers, 366, 369–73

transfeminism, 129–33

transgender people, 130, 445, 446; advice to, 414–21; rights of, 295–98

Trump, Donald: Clinton on, 29, 32–36; environment and, 216, 362; immigration policies of, 59–61, 202–6, 361, 362; protests of, 125, 175, 186; treatment of women, 24, 58, 64–65

Tsai, Janet, 281–86

Tufts University, handling of sexual assaults, 290–94

Turner, Brock, 235–49

Twitter, 89, 105, 422–23

United Nations, 80, 255–56
United States, 80, 342, 362–63; response to September 11, 190–92, 196
Until We Are Free (Ebadi), 38
Urquilla, Jeannette, 23, 45–47

Valdes, Jennifer Anzardo, 205–6
Valenti, Jessica, 314–20
Valoy, Patricia, 119–24
violence, against women, 178, 222–26, 232, 257, 399, 401–2
vlogging, Blaque's, 404–8
voting, 68–69

Walker, Alice, 113
Wanjuki, Wagatwe, 290–94
war, 181; Clinton on, 34–35; gender differences in opinions on, 341–46; lessons from, 352–54; transnational feminist theories on, 195–200
war on terror, US, 195, 350–51
Waters, Maxine, 58–61
Weiss, Penny, 129
Weiss, Sasha, 222–26
West, Lindy, 98–106

When the Levees Broke (Lee), 380, 386n1
#WhyWeCan'tWait campaign, 110, 112
Williams, Serena, 143
woman, 463; concept of, 7–8, 463
womanism, feminism *vs.*, 113
women, portrayals of, 194, 227, 229
Women's March, 125–28, 165–66, 176; organizers, 175–82; signs at, 184–86
work, 180
workplace: lack of women in leadership, 332–34, 336, 337n3; obstacles to women in, 334–35; sexual harassment, 324, 356–59; women reaching potential in, 330–36

Yaha, Christine, 410, 413
Yakupitiyage, Thanu, 361–64
#YesAllWomen, 222–26
Young, Stella, 434–35
Yousafzai, Malala, 255–59
Youth Leadership Council, New York State, 265–66

Zimmerman, George, 169